The Bloomsbury Companion to New Religious Movements

Bloomsbury Companions

Bloomsbury Companions is a major series of single volume companions to key research fields in the humanities aimed at postgraduate students, scholars and libraries. Each companion offers a comprehensive reference resource giving an overview of key topics, research areas, new directions and a manageable guide to beginning or developing research in the field. A distinctive feature of the series is that each companion provides practical guidance on advanced study and research in the field, including research methods and subject-specific resources.

Other volumes in the series of Bloomsbury Companions include:

Hindu Studies, edited by Jessica Frazier, foreword by Gavin Flood
Islamic Studies, edited by Clinton Bennett
Jewish Studies, edited by Dean Phillip Bell
Religion and Film, edited by William L. Blizek

The Bloomsbury Companion to New Religious Movements

Edited by

George D. Chryssides and
Benjamin E. Zeller

Bloomsbury Academic
An imprint of Bloomsbury Publishing Plc

BLOOMSBURY
LONDON · OXFORD · NEW YORK · NEW DELHI · SYDNEY

Bloomsbury Academic
An imprint of Bloomsbury Publishing Plc

50 Bedford Square	1385 Broadway
London	New York
WC1B 3DP	NY 10018
UK	USA

www.bloomsbury.com

BLOOMSBURY and the Diana logo are trademarks of Bloomsbury Publishing Plc

Hardback edition published 2014
This paperback edition published 2016

© George D. Chryssides and Benjamin E. Zeller, 2014, 2016

George D. Chryssides Benjamin E. Zeller have asserted their right under the Copyright, Designs and Patents Act, 1988, to be identified as Authors of this work.

All rights reserved. No part of this publication may be reproduced or transmitted in any form or by any means, electronic or mechanical, including photocopying, recording, or any information storage or retrieval system, without prior permission in writing from the publishers.

No responsibility for loss caused to any individual or organization acting on or refraining from action as a result of the material in this publication can be accepted by Bloomsbury or the author.

British Library Cataloguing-in-Publication Data
A catalogue record for this book is available from the British Library.

ISBN: HB: 978-1-4411-9005-5
PB: 978-1-4742-5644-5
ePDF: 978-1-4411-9829-7
ePub: 978-1-4411-7449-9

Library of Congress Cataloging-in-Publication Data
A catalog record for this book is available from the Library of Congress.

Series: Bloomsbury Companions

Typeset by Newgen Knowledge Works (P) Ltd., Chennai, India
Printed and bound in Great Britain

*To Eileen Barker
on the occasion of the 25th anniversary of INFORM,
which she founded and directed.
June 2013*

Contents

Notes on Contributors — x
Foreword by Massimo Introvigne — xvii
Acknowledgements — xx
Table of Acronyms — xxi
How to Use This Book — xxiii

Introduction — 1

Part I Research Methods and Problems — 23

1. Fieldwork — 25
   Stephen E. Gregg

2. The Insider/Outsider Problem — 29
   George D. Chryssides

3. Material Culture — 33
   Alex Norman

4. Pagan Studies — 37
   Graham Harvey

5. New Age — 41
   Steven J. Sutcliffe

6. Mormon Studies — 47
   Douglas J. Davies

7. Japanese NRMs — 53
   Birgit Staemmler

8. Sexuality Studies — 57
   Megan Goodwin

9. Media Studies — 61
   Stephen Jacobs

Contents

| 10. | Ritual Studies
Lee Gilmore | 67 |

Part II Current Research and Issues — 71

11.	Jonestown and the Study of NRMs Rebecca Moore	73
12.	Conversion and Brainwashing James T. Richardson	89
13.	Charisma and Leadership David G. Bromley	103
14.	Prophecy Jon R. Stone	119
15.	Millennialism Catherine Wessinger	133
16.	Violence James R. Lewis	149
17.	Opposition to NRMs George D. Chryssides and Benjamin E. Zeller	163
18.	Legal Issues Anthony Bradney	179
19.	Gender Megan Goodwin	195
20.	UFO Religions Christopher Partridge	207
21.	Researching Esoteric Groups Kennet Granholm	221
22.	African New Religious Movements Afe Adogame	235
23.	Vernacular/Lived Religion Marion Bowman	253

Part III New Directions in the Study of New Religious Movements — 271

| 24. | Globalization
Liselotte Frisk | 273 |
| 25. | Science
Benjamin E. Zeller | 279 |

26.	The Role of the Internet Jean-François Mayer	285
27.	Invented Religions Carole M. Cusack	291
28.	Race and Ethnicity Marie W. Dallam	295
29.	Children and Generational Issues E. Burke Rochford, Jr.	301
30.	Healing Holly Folk	307
31.	Travel and New Religious Movements Alex Norman	313

Part IV   Resources: A–Z   319

Part V   Resources   353

Chronology   355
Academic Resources for the Study of New Religious Movements   365
Bibliography   371
Index   415

Notes on Contributors

Afe Adogame received his PhD (History of Religions) in 1998 from the University of Bayreuth, Germany and he is currently Senior Lecturer in Religious Studies and World Christianity at the University of Edinburgh, UK. His fields of research/teaching expertise include: African Religions and Religions of the new African Diaspora; African New Religious Movements; Migration and Globalization; Sociology of Religion; and Methods and Theory in the Study of Religion. His latest book publication is *The African Christian Diaspora: New Currents and Emerging Trends in World Christianity* (Bloomsbury Academic 2013).

Marion Bowman is Senior Lecturer in Religious Studies, the Open University (UK). A past President of both the British Association for the Study of Religions and The Folklore Society, and an executive board member of Working Group on Ethnology of Religion, SIEF (Societe Internationale d'Ethnologie et de Folklore), she works at the interstices of religious studies and folklore/ethnology. Her research interests include vernacular religion, pilgrimage, material culture, spiritual economy, and a long-term study of Glastonbury, England, on which she has published extensively. Her latest book is *Vernacular Religion in Everyday Life: Expressions of Belief*, co-edited with Ülo Valk (Equinox 2012).

Anthony Bradney is Professor of Law at Keele University (UK). His publications on law and religion include *Law and Faith in a Sceptical Age* (Routledge-Cavendish 2009) and *Living Without Law: An Ethnography of Dispute Avoidance and Resolution in the Religious Society of Friends*, with Fiona Cownie (Ashgate 2000).

David G. Bromley is Professor of Religious Studies in the School of World Studies and Professor of Sociology in the L. Douglas Wilder School of Government and Public Affairs at Virginia Commonwealth University. He has written or edited over a dozen books on religious movements. Books published since 2000 include *Cults and New Religions*, with Douglas Cowan (Blackwell/Wiley 2008); *Teaching New Religious Movements* (Oxford University

Press 2007); *Defining Religion: Critical Approaches to Drawing Boundaries Between Sacred and Secular*, with Arthur Greil (Elsevier Science/JAI Press 2003); *Cults, Religion and Violence*, with J. Gordon Melton (Cambridge University Press 2001); and *Toward Reflexive Ethnography: Participating, Observing, Narrating*, with Lewis Carter (Elsevier Science/JAI Press 2001). Dr Bromley is former president of the Association for the Study of Religion; founding editor of the ASR's annual series, *Religion and the Social Order*; and former editor of the *Journal for the Scientific Study of Religion*, published by the Society for the Scientific Study of Religion. He is currently Project Director of the World Religions and Spirituality Project at Virginia Commonwealth University.

George D. Chryssides studied at the universities of Glasgow and Oxford, and has taught at various British universities. He was Head of Religious Studies at the University of Wolverhampton, UK, from 2001 to 2008, and is now Research Fellow at York St John University. He has published extensively, principally on new religious movements, and his books include *Historical Dictionary of Jehovah's Witnesses* (Scarecrow Press 2008), *Heaven's Gate: Postmodernity and Popular Culture in a Suicide Group* (Ashgate 2011) *Christians in the Twenty-First Century* (with Margaret Z. Wilkins Equinox 201) and *Historical Dictionary of New Religious Movements* (Scarecrow Press 2012).

Carole M. Cusack is Professor of Religious Studies at the University of Sydney (Australia). Her research concerns 'alternative' religion(s) in the West from the Middle Ages to the present, focusing on: 1) Christian marginalization of alternative religion(s); 2) inverse processes of medieval Christianization and de-Paganization, and contemporary de-Christianization and re-Paganization; and 3) the challenge alternative religion(s) pose to definitions of 'religion' and the discipline of 'religious studies'. She is author of *Invented Religions: Imagination, Fiction and Faith* (Ashgate 2010), co-editor of *Handbook of New Religions and Cultural Production* (Brill 2012) and co-editor of *Journal of Religious History* (Wiley).

Marie W. Dallam is Assistant Professor of American Religion and Culture at the University of Oklahoma Honors College. She is the author of *Daddy Grace: A Celebrity Preacher and His House of Prayer* (New York University Press 2007), and co-editor of *Religion, Food, and Eating in North America* (Columbia University Press 2014). She has published in journals including *Nova Religio*, *Religion Compass*, and *Studies in Popular Culture*.

Douglas J. Davies, Professor in the Study of Religion at Durham University (UK), trained in anthropology and theology. His books cover issues in religious studies, the ritual and belief of death, the Church of England, and Mormonism for example *Joseph Smith, Jesus, and Satanic Opposition: Atonement, Evil and the Mormon Vision* (Ashgate 2010), *Introduction to Mormonism* (Cambridge 2003),

The Mormon Culture of Salvation (Ashgate 2000). He holds a higher Doctorate of Letters (Oxford), an Honorary Doctorate (Uppsala University Sweden), and is an Academician of the UK Academy of Social Science and Fellow of the Learned Society of Wales.

Holly Folk is Associate Professor in the Liberal Studies Department at Western Washington University in Bellingham, Washington. Her research focuses on social protest and alternative healing, and her current book project examines early chiropractic and its ties to nineteenth-century irregular medicine. Folk serves on the board of the Communal Studies Association and the Steering Committee of the New Religious Movements Group of the American Academy of Religion.

Liselotte Frisk is Professor of Religious Studies at Dalarna University, Falun, Sweden. Her dissertation (1993) dealt with six new religious movements and their relationship with society. After that she has conducted one research project about changes in new religious movements over time and two projects considering the New Age, spirituality and popular religion. Her current research project deals with children in minority religions. Liselotte Frisk is the chair of Nordic Network for Research on New Religiosity and has been chair of the International Society for the Study of New Religions from 2009–13. She is also co-editor of the *International Journal for the Study of New Religions* and *Aura*, the Journal for the Nordic Network for Research on New Religiosity.

Lee Gilmore specializes in the study of ritual, new religious movements, and religion and nature. The author of *Theater in a Crowded Fire: Ritual and Spirituality at Burning Man* (University of California Press 2010), she was the co-editor of *AfterBurn: Reflections on Burning Man* (University of New Mexico Press 2005). She currently teaches online for San José State University and previously taught at California State University, Northridge. Her PhD in Cultural & Historical Studies of Religions was completed at the Graduate Theological Union in 2005.

Megan Goodwin is Visiting Assistant Professor of Religious Studies at Elon University (USA). Her research focuses on gender, sexuality and minority religions in the contemporary United States. Her publications explore the relevance of gender theory to the study of North American religions, rhetorics of sexual intolerance among North American new religious movements, and religious language in graphic novels; her article on gendered magical practices among medieval Scandinavian and contemporary American Norse religious communities is forthcoming in *Magic and the Modern* (University of Pennsylvania Press).

Notes on Contributors

Kennet Granholm is Assistant Professor in History of Religions at Stockholm University (Sweden) and Docent in Comparative Religion at Åbo Akademi University (Finland). His main research interest lies in contemporary esotericism, particularly in relation to mass media and popular culture. He is the author of the forthcoming *Dark Enlightenment: The Historical, Sociological, and Discursive Contexts of Contemporary Esoteric Magic* (Brill) and editor (with Egil Asprem) of *Contemporary Esotericism* (Equinox Publishing 2013) and has published numerous articles on contemporary esotericism, popular culture and new religions (for a full list see http://kennetgranholm.com). He is the co-founder of the Contemporary Esotericism Research Network (ContERN, http://contern.org) and the Scandinavian Network for the Academic Study of Western Esotericism (SNASWE, http://snaswe.blogspot.se).

Stephen E. Gregg studied at the University of Wales, where he later taught. He currently teaches within the Department of Theology, Philosophy and Religious Studies at Liverpool Hope University. His research focuses on 'alternative' religious narrative and ritual in relation to 'mainstream' worldviews. His publications include *Jesus Beyond Christianity* (Oxford University Press 2010) and *Engaging with Living Religion* (Routledge, forthcoming) and he has guest-edited a special issue of the *International Journal for the Study of New Religions* (2012) on the theme of 'New Religions and Dialogue'. His pedagogic research focuses on student participation in fieldwork, and he has led student fieldwork tours in Europe, Asia, North America and across the UK.

Graham Harvey is Head of Department of Religious Studies at the Open University (UK). He researches among Pagans and indigenous peoples (especially Anishinaabeg and Maori). He is particularly interested in the vitality of 'animistic' ways and knowledges, and in the democratizing or liberating potential of ritual and performance cultures. His most recent book, *Food, Sex and Strangers: Understanding Religion as Everyday Life* (Acumen 2013) experiments with redefining 'religion' in relation to material, performance and vernacular religion among Pagans, indigenous peoples and others in the real (participative) world.

Massimo Introvigne teaches Sociology of Religious Movements at the Pontifical Salesian University in Torino, Italy, and is the managing director of CESNUR, the Center for Studies on New Religions. The author of some 60 books, he also serves as chairperson of the Observatory of Religious Liberty created by the Italian Ministry of Foreign Affairs.

Stephen Jacobs is Senior Lecturer in Media, Religion and Culture at the University of Wolverhampton (UK). He is author of *Hinduism Today* (Continuum 2010). He has published on religion and the media. He is currently engaged in ethnographic research on the Art of Living, a global meditation movement.

Notes on Contributors

James R. Lewis is an extensively published scholar in the field of new religious movements and Professor of Religious Studies at the University of Tromsø (Norway). He currently co-edits three book series and is the general editor for the *Alternative Spirituality and Religion Review* and for the *Journal of Religion and Violence*. Recent publications include (co-authored with Nicolas Levine) *The Children of Jesus and Mary* (Oxford University Press 2010), *Violence and New Religious Movements* (Oxford University Press 2011) (co-edited with Olav Hammer) *Religion and the Authority of Science* (Brill 2011), and *Cults: A Reference and Guide* (Equinox 2012).

Jean-François Mayer is Director of the Religioscope Institute in Fribourg (Switzerland) and editor of the Religioscope website (www.religion.info). An historian by training, he focuses on contemporary religious movements and related developments, including topics such as religion and the internet, and religion and politics. He is the author of ten books in French, some translated into other languages, and numerous articles (list of publications available at: http://mayer.info). In 2013, he was elected president of the International Society for the Study of New Religions (ISSNR).

Rebecca Moore is distinguished Professor of religious studies at San Diego State University, with a PhD in religious studies from Marquette University (1996). Dr Moore specializes in American religions, focusing on new religious movements. Her most recent book is *Understanding Jonestown and Peoples Temple* (Praeger 2009). She co-manages the website Alternative Considerations of Jonestown and Peoples Temple (http://jonestown.sdsu.edu), a digital archive of relevant primary source documents. She also directs San Diego State University's Metropolitan Area Pluralism Study (MAPS), which locates, charts and digitally publishes a visual and descriptive guide to the religious diversity that exists in the San Diego-Tijuana border region (http://geoinfo.sdsu.edu/MAPS/).

Alex Norman is a Lecturer at the Department of Studies in Religion, University of Sydney. His book, *Spiritual Tourism* (Continuum 2011), examines the intersection of travel and secular spiritual practice by contemporary Westerners. With Carole M. Cusack he is co-editor of the *Handbook of New Religions and Cultural Production* (Brill 2012). He is managing editor of the *Journal of Sociology*, and co-editor of the *International Journal for the Study of New Religion*. His research interests include tourism and religion, new religious movements, food, photography and the practice of secular spirituality in the everyday. He hopes to make tourism a more thoroughly examined subject in the study of religion.

Christopher Partridge is Professor of Religious Studies in the Department of Politics, Philosophy and Religion at Lancaster University (UK). His research and writing focuses on alternative spiritual currents, countercultures and popular music. He is the author of *The Re-Enchantment of the West: Alternative*

Spiritualities, Sacralization, Popular Culture and Occulture, 2 vols (Bloomsbury 2004, 2005), *Dub in Babylon: Understanding the Evolution and Significance of Dub Reggae in Jamaica and Britain from King Tubby to Post-punk* (Equinox 2010), *The Lyre of Orpheus: Popular Music, the Sacred, and the Profane* (Oxford University Press 2013), the editor of several books, including *UFO Religions* (Routledge 2003) and *Encyclopaedia of New Religions* (Oxford University Press 2004), and co-editor of *Religions in the Modern World: Traditions and Transformations* (Routledge 2009), *The Lure of the Dark Side: Satan and Western Demonology in Popular Culture* (Equinox 2009), and *Holy Terror: Understanding Religion and Violence in Popular Culture* (Equinox 2010). He is also co-editor of the series 'Studies in Popular Music' (Equinox) and 'Studies in Religion and Popular Music' (Bloomsbury).

James T. Richardson, JD. is Professor of Sociology and Judicial Studies at the University of Nevada, Reno, where he directs the Judicial Studies graduate degree programme for trial judges and also teaches in Sociology and Social Psychology. He has done research on new religious movements for decades, focusing most recently on the interaction of law and religion and how legal systems are used to exert social control over minority religions. His most recent books are *Regulating Religion: Case Studies from Around the Globe* (Kluwer 2004) and *Saints under Siege: The Texas Raid on the Fundamentalist Latter Day Saints* (with Stuart Wright, New York University Press 2011).

E. Burke Rochford, Jr. is Professor of Religion at Middlebury College in Vermont. He has researched the Hare Krishna movement since 1975 and has written numerous articles as well as two books on the movement, *Hare Krishna in America* (Rutgers University Press 1985) and *Hare Krishna Transformed* (New York University Press 2007).

Birgit Staemmler is researcher at the Department of Japanese Studies, University of Tübingen (Germany) and currently funded by the Horst- und Käthe-Eliseit-Stiftung. Her research foci are new religions, spirit possession and shamanism in Japan and Japanese religions and the internet. She is author of *Chinkon kishin: Mediated Spirit Possession in Japanese New Religions* (Lit Verlag 2009) and co-editor of *Japanese Religions on the Internet: Innovation, Representation and Authority* (Routledge 2011 with Erica Baffelli and Ian Reader) and *Establishing the Revolutionary: An Introduction to New Religions in Japan* (Lit Verlag 2011 with Ulrich Dehn).

Jon R. Stone is Professor of Religious Studies and affiliate faculty in American Studies at California State University, Long Beach. He is the author of *A Guide to the End of the World: Popular Eschatology in America* (Garland Science 1993), *On the Boundaries of American Evangelicalism: The Postwar Evangelical Coalition* (Palgrave Macmillan 1997), *Prime-Time Religion: An Encyclopedia of Religious Broadcasting* (Greenwood 1997, with J. Gordon Melton and Phillip Charles Lucas), and

Notes on Contributors

editor of *Expecting Armageddon: Essential Readings in Failed Prophecy* (Routledge 2000) and *Readings in American Religious Diversity* (Kendall Hunt 2012, with Carlos R. Piar, 4 vols), among others. His article, 'Prophecy and Dissonance: A Reassessment of Research Testing the Festinger Theory' (*Nova Religio*, May 2009), received the 7th Annual Thomas Robbins Award for Excellence in the Study of New Religions.

Steven J. Sutcliffe is Senior Lecturer in the Study of Religion in the School of Divinity, University of Edinburgh. His chief interests lie in the modern history of alternative spiritualities and in interdisciplinary theorizing about 'religion'. He is the author of *Children of the New Age: A History of Spiritual Practices* (Routledge 2003), editor of *Religion: Empirical Studies* (Ashgate 2004) and co-editor of *New Age Spirituality: Rethinking Religion* (Acumen 2013).

Catherine Wessinger is the Rev. H. James Yamauchi, S. J. Professor of the History of Religions at Loyola University, New Orleans. She is the author of *How the Millennium Comes Violently: From Jonestown to Heaven's Gate* (Seven Bridges Press 2000); editor of *Millennialism, Persecution, and Violence: Historical Cases* (Syracuse University Press 2000); editor of *The Oxford Handbook of Millennialism* (Oxford University Press 2011); editor of three Branch Davidian autobiographies (2007, 2009, 2012); and editor of two books on women's religious leadership (1993, 1996). She is co-general editor of *Nova Religio: The Journal of Alternative and Emergent Religions*.

Benjamin E. Zeller is Assistant Professor of Religion at Lake Forest College (USA). He researches religious currents that are new or alternative, including new religions, the religious engagement with science and the quasi-religious relationship people have with food. He is author of *Prophets and Protons: New Religious Movements and Science in Late Twentieth-Century America* (New York University Press 2010), co-editor of *Religion, Food, and Eating in North America* (Columbia University Press 2014) and co-general editor of *Nova Religio: The Journal of Alternative and Emergent Religions*.

Foreword

Massimo Introvigne

This *Companion* represents a significant cultural event. Ideally, it closes an era, characterized by bitter controversies about 'cults', sums up what that era was all about, and introduces us into the new climate of the second decade of the twenty-first century, where cooler tempers may prevail and the model of the moral panic may be gradually dismantled. When I and some colleagues – Eileen Barker, J. Gordon Melton, Jean-François Mayer – founded CESNUR, the Center for Studies on New Religions, in 1988 the moral panic model was largely prevailing.

As described by Cohen (1972), and later by Jenkins (1992) and by Goode and Ben-Yehuda (1994), moral panics start with a basis in reality, but escalate through exaggeration and folk statistics when comments appropriate for one or more particular incidents are generalized. This happened, with respect to the 'cults', in the United States after the suicides and homicides in Jonestown, Guyana (1978), and in Europe after the killings associated with the Order of the Solar Temple in Switzerland, France and Quebec (1994, 1995 and 1997). It is in escalating – not in creating – the moral panic that moral entrepreneurs with vested interests enter the picture.

Even some of the European parliamentary and other official reports generated after the Solar Temple incidents – although not all of them – followed a typical moral panic model, in four stages (see Richardson and Introvigne 2001).

First, the model claims that some minorities are not really 'religions' but something else: 'cults' or 'sects' (something different from genuine religions), criminal associations or agents of foreign imperialism. This is not a particularly new argument, and was used against the Mormons since the nineteenth century. In civilizations where religious liberty is recognized as a value and constitutionally protected, the only way to discriminate against a religious minority is to argue that it is not religious at all, by manipulating the genuine difficulties in defining 'religion' within a pluralistic scenario discussed by this *Companion*.

Second, the model posits that what distinguishes genuine religions from groups falsely claiming their right to the religious label is something called brainwashing, mental manipulation or mind control. Since religion is, by rhetorical definition, an exercise of free will, a non-religion may only be joined under some sort of coercion. A paradigm – introduced when critics accused early Mormons of hypnosis – resurfaced, after the Cold War conveniently supplied the metaphor of brainwashing, in the 1970s cult wars in the United States and elsewhere. By the end of the 1980s the first 'crude' theories of brainwashing had been largely debunked in the English-speaking debate, but a second generation of brainwashing theories emerged. They did not claim to explain why people *join* certain movements; rather, they would explain why groups may make more difficult for members to *leave* by maximizing their exit costs. However, crude first-generation brainwashing theories are still used in simplistic comments about 'cults' by the media and certain politicians.

Third, since brainwashing theories are the object of considerable scholarly criticism, the model requires as a third step discrimination among sources and narratives. The French and Belgian parliamentary reports explicitly stated that they were aware of scholarly objections against the mind control model, but they made the ethical choice of preferring over and against these objections the accounts of 'victims'. By 'victims' these documents meant those normally defined by social scientists as 'apostates'. These are the former members converted into active opponents of the group they have left. Although many such ex-members resent being called 'apostates' the term is technical, not derogatory, and has been used by social scientists for decades (see Bromley 1998). Some sort of term is in fact necessary in order to distinguish between 'apostates' and other ex-members who do not turn against their former group. Empirical evidence on the prevalence of apostates among former members is available only for a limited number of new religious movements, but uniformly suggests that they are a minority. Most former members have mixed feelings about their former affiliations, and are not interested in joining crusades against the group they left. 'Apostates' are an interesting minority. The model, however, regards them as if they were the only representatives of the whole larger category of former members.

Objections that 'apostates' are not necessarily representative are met by the fourth stage of the model. 'Cults' or 'sects' are not religions. They are not because they use brainwashing, while religions are by definition joined out of free will. We know that they use brainwashing because we rely on the testimony of 'victims' (i.e. 'apostates'). We know that 'apostates' are representative of the groups' membership, or at least former membership, because they are screened and selected by private, reliable watchdog organizations. These are the moral entrepreneurs: the anti-cult organizations which, the model assumed, are more reliable than academics because the former, unlike the latter, have a 'practical' experience and work with 'victims'.

Moral panics are not created by a single hidden hand. Nor do they normally die when a hidden hand is exposed. They disappear when either the general public loses interest in the issue, or is reached by more balanced assessments and statistics. Calmer assessments by academics were available since at least the late 1980s, but they were not easily socialized. Counter-movements against academics accused of being 'cult apologists' were not surprising. They are part and parcel of every self-respecting moral panic. Ultimately, however, societies do come – perhaps after a long and painful trial and error process – to identify and assess in a more realistic way the objective conditions at the roots of the moral panic. Thus, real evils are confronted from what they are, and lunatic fringes exposing imaginary evils are marginalized. Finally, we now seem to be close to this happy end, although not everywhere in Europe and the world. This *Companion* is an important step in this process. But messengers of balanced, if not necessarily good, news should continue their work, even if shooting the messenger may remain, in this controversial field, a popular game.

Acknowledgements

In authoring or editing any book innumerable debts are engendered. The editors wish to first thank our contributors who cheerfully responded to our queries, suggestions, and occasional proddings and have each produced extremely strong final products. We also want to thank our editor at Bloomsbury Lalle Pursglove who has supported this project from its inception. We thank our respective spouses, Emily Mace (Benjamin Zeller) and Margaret Wilkins (George Chryssides) for their encouragement. Benjamin Zeller thanks his colleagues and administration at Lake Forest College (USA) for their support as well and both editors are indebted to colleagues worldwide who have met at various CESNUR gatherings and enabled us to try out ideas on these topics. We also thank W. Michael Ashcraft for sharing with us his research on the history of the field of the study of new religious movements. Our thanks also go to Margaret Wilkins for compiling the index to the volume.

The editors are indebted to the increasing number of scholars who have gained recognition in NRM studies – a field that is fraught with controversy and sometimes misunderstanding. Among colleagues whose contribution has been particularly outstanding is Eileen Barker, Emeritus Professor of the London School of Economics, founder of INFORM, the United Kingdom's leading informational resource on new religions, and one of the founders and forerunners of the field of the study of new religious movements. She has guided countless others, worked tirelessly to further the academic study of religion and been a friend and mentor to nearly everyone who studies new religious movements. On this twenty-fifth anniversary of the founding of INFORM, it is with pleasure that the editors and contributors dedicate this book to her.

Table of Acronyms

3HO:	Healthy, Happy, Holy
AAR:	American Academy of Religion
ACM:	anti-cult movement
AFF:	American Family Foundation
AGP:	Advanced Growth Process
AIC:	African initiated/indigenous/independent churches
ANRM:	African new religious movement
ATF:	United States Bureau of Alcohol, Tobacco, Firearms
BBC:	British Broadcasting Corporation
BCE:	Before Common Era
CAN:	Cult Awareness Network
CAUSA:	Confederation of the Associations for the Unification of the Societies of the Americas
CAW:	Church of All Worlds
CCM:	Christian Countercult Movement
CE:	Common Era
CENERM:	Centre for New Religious Movements
CESNUR:	Centro studi sulle nuove religioni (Center for Studies on New Religions)
CFF:	Citizens Freedom Foundation
CIA:	Central Intelligence Agency
CND:	Campaign for Nuclear Disarmament
COG:	Children of God
COSG:	Church of the SubGenius
ELF:	Erisian Liberation Front
EWCA:	England and Wales Court of Appeal
FAIR:	Family Action Information and Rescue/Resource
FBI:	Federal Bureau of Investigation
FLDS:	Fundamentalist Church of Jesus Christ of Latter Day Saints

Table of Acronyms

FRA:	European Agency for Fundamental Rights
FREECOG:	Free the Children of God
GTU:	Graduate Theological Union
HIM:	Human Individual Metamorphosis
ICSA:	International Cultic Studies Association
INFORM:	Information Network on Religious Movements
ISAR:	Institute for the Study of American Religions
ISKCON:	International Society for Krishna Consciousness
JSCPR:	Japan Society for Cults Prevention and Recovery
LDS:	Latter-day Saints
MEP:	Member of the European Parliament
MILS:	*Mission interministérielle de lutte contre les sectes* (Interministerial Mission in the Fight Against Cults)
MIVILUDES:	*Mission interministérielle de vigilance et de lutte contre les dérives sectaires* (Interministerial Mission for Monitoring and Combatting Cultic Deviances)
MRTCG:	Movement for the Restoration of the Ten Commandments of God
NGO:	Non-Governmental Organisation
NRM:	New Religious Movement
OTS:	Ordre du Temple Solaire (Order of the Solar Temple)
PEN:	Personal Experience Narrative
POEE:	Paratheo-Anametamystikhood of Eris Esoteric
PRINERM:	Primal New Religious Movement
RIRC:	Religious Information Research Center
RLDS:	Reorganized Church of Jesus Christ of Latter Day Saints
SDA:	Seventh-day Adventist
SYDA:	Siddha Yoga Dham Association
TM:	Transcendental Meditation
UC:	Unification Church
UFO:	Unidentified Flying Object
UNADFI:	Union Nationale des Associations de Défence des Familles (National Union of Associations for the Defence of Families)
WEA:	Workers' Educational Association
YWCA:	Young Women's Christian Association

How to Use This Book

The *Bloomsbury Companion* series offers researchers and students single-volume companions to key research fields in the humanities. To paraphrase from the series overview, *Companions* offer an overview of key topics, research areas, new directions and a manageable guide to beginning or developing research in the field.

The editors envision this book as a guide to the major areas of research in the study of new religious movements (NRMs), a field within the study of religion that has achieved some level of prominence and institutionalization. This *Companion* provides authoritative considerations of various topics that we study within the field that will prove useful to introductory students and advanced researchers alike. The text is also a map of where the scholarship has been and where we hope to see the field go. The editors and authors have highlighted what we consider the most salient of themes and issues relating to the study of NRMs, focusing on topics currently generating scholarly debate and written by leading scholars.

The five sections of the book each have different focuses. Contributing experts have authored the chapters within the first three sections of the book: research methods and problems, current research areas and new directions in the study of NRMs. Each of the chapters in these three sections considers a key concept that either has been central to the study of new religions, is currently a major topic of debate, or our authors argue should become such topics of study. The authors include founding scholars and established researchers within the field of the study of NRMs as well as new voices of rising scholars.

The fourth section, an A-Z reference to major topics in the study of new religious movements authored by the editors, serves as a reference to central features of new religions and their scholarship. The editors have self-consciously avoided repetition where possible, so major themes considered in later sections receive less attention in this section.

The final section of the book contains resources for the study of new religious movements, including a chronology, list of website and encyclopaedic

How to Use This Book

resources, bibliography, and works cited. The bibliography is not merely a replication of the works cited for the *Companion*, as it focuses only on key texts in the study of NRMs.

Finally, a few words on what this book is not. The *Companion* is not a dictionary or encyclopaedia. Some relevant topics have been excluded, either because of space or because of a dearth of interest from the current generation of scholars. Each chapter offers an individual author's academic perspective on the topic considered therein, and they are meant as scholarly contributions in their own sense and not mere reference texts. Nor is the *Companion* a guide to different NRMs. While many such groups receive treatment in these pages, contributors have focused on themes in the study of NRMs rather than the new religions themselves. The chapters mentioning particular religious movements by name, such as those on Mormon Studies, Pagan Studies, or the impact of Jonestown on the study of NRMs, are not about these religions themselves but about how we as researchers study them.

The editors hope that *The Bloomsbury Companion to New Religious Movements* serves as a key text for the study of NRMs for years to come.

Introduction

Chapter Outline	
Transitions in the 1960s and 1970s	2
The Impact of Jonestown	6
Definitional Issues	12
Sociology and the Study of NRMs	15
Beyond Sociology	18
Recent Developments and Current Trends	19

Although new religious movements (NRMs) have emerged throughout the centuries, the study of them is very recent. When Christianity began as a first-century NRM, and published its own texts, the initial response was persecution by Jewish and the Roman authorities rather than systematic appraisal, although there were debates from time to time between Jewish scholars and Christian protagonists. As Christianity emerged as a world religion, different Christian theologies were championed, and the early Church thought it necessary to distinguish between orthodox belief and heresy. Accordingly Church Fathers like Tertullian, Athanasius, and later Augustine authored a number of polemical writings. This is to say that as a new religious movement, Christianity encountered the same types of resistance that recent NRMs have experienced. As it transformed from new religion to established religion – in both the colloquial and official sense of a 'religious establishment' – it became the source of resistance rather than the target.

Christianity's rise to become the world's largest religion, coupled with its preoccupation with sound doctrine and the elimination of heretical thinking tended to ensure that its places of learning generally focused on systematic theology and biblical interpretation, with little room for the teaching of other faiths, let alone NRMs. In the United Kingdom in the mid-1960s there were only 16 university lecturers who taught the study of the world religions. In the

United States the field of religious studies was still just emerging as its own field distinct from biblical studies or anthropology. The idea of teaching NRMs was unthinkable. If theology aimed at discovering the truth about God, organizations like the Church of Jesus Christ of Latter-day Saints (Mormons) and Jehovah's Witnesses appeared to offer error rather than truth. Comparatively speaking, they were numerically small, and these New Christian movements used the Bible, the true interpretation of which was already being taught in theological seminaries. There were a few early attempts to offer critiques of these 'modern heresies'. In R. A. Torrey's edited collection of tracts, written between 1901 and 1915, entitled *The Fundamentals – A Testimony to the Truth* (and giving the name 'fundamentalism' to the movement that followed), a few contributors offered critiques of Mormonism, the Millennial Dawn movement (now Jehovah's Witnesses), Spiritualism and Christian Science. In 1913 the Rev. Lewis B. Radford delivered the Moorhouse Lectures in St Paul's Cathedral, Melbourne, which set out to criticize Seventh-day Adventism, Theosophy, Christian Science, and the eastern doctrines of karma and reincarnation, subsequently published as *Ancient Heresies in Modern Dress*. Other early studies included William C. Irvine's *Timely Warnings* (1917 – later re-titled *Heresies Exposed*) and Gaius Glenn Atkins' *Modern Cults and Religious Movements* (1923), and the Society for the Propagation of Christian Knowledge (SPCK) published a series of pamphlets on specific organizations. Such attacks on new religions continued into the 1960s: of the later examples the best known is probably Anthony A. Hoekema's *The Four Major Cults* (1963): Hoekema was a professor of systematic theology and his book is a detailed exposition and critique of Christian Science, Jehovah's Witnesses, Mormonism and Seventh-day Adventism. Other writers treated the NRMs as curiosities or exoticisms, namely Elmer T. Clark's *The Small Sects in America* (1949) and Marcus Bach's *Strange Sects and Curious Cults* (1961). Yet most of the material published on NRMs before the late 1960s was produced from specific Christian denominational perspectives, and like the writings of the early Church Fathers, polemical in nature.

Transitions in the 1960s and 1970s

A number of factors in the late 1960s and early 1970s changed the character of the NRM scene and the way in which they were studied. Advances in global communication and travel made available a new range of new religions to seekers. Previously, proponents of new teachings were prepared to travel the world to proclaim their ideas: for example, the Mormon Church sent missionaries to England and Wales in the 1840s; Vivekananda toured the United States and Europe in 1899; Helena P. Blavatsky and Henry Steel Olcott 'discovered' Krishnamurti in India in 1908; Pir Harzat Inayat Khan brought Sufism to the

United States in 1910; and Charles Taze Russell and other Watch Tower 'pilgrims' travelled from the United States to Europe and beyond – to cite a few examples. However, travel was by boat, and was slow and difficult, although these missions were by no means ineffective.

By the 1960s air travel had become commonplace, and increased standards of wealth made it possible for many people to travel around the world. The idea of taking a 'gap year' before going to university enabled many younger people to travel abroad and, in many cases, to have the opportunity of direct acquaintance with eastern religion. In the United States, the emergence of the counterculture led many youth to drop out of college altogether and pursue spiritual seekerhood rather than formal education. Reciprocally, Hindu, Buddhist, Sufi and other teachers from overseas found it possible to come to the West. Television, which was now a social necessity rather than a luxury, gave a high visibility to several of the new religions that were traversing the globe. The Vietnam War provoked a backlash in the counterculture that asserted itself in the Hippie movement, and the fact that ministers of religion and seminary students were exempt from the draft resulted in increasing numbers of younger people studying religion. Added to all this, the universities were expanding, both in the United States and the United Kingdom, and their interest in religion was beginning to move beyond the study of Christianity.

Improved global communication brought about a new wave of NRMs. Although some of the newer ones were indigenously Christian, such as the Jesus People Movement, others were unrelated to Christianity – for example the Hare Krishna Movement, Guru Maharaji's Divine Light Mission, Transcendental Meditation, Soka Gakkai and Westernized Zen Buddhism – and could not be viewed as 'Christian deviations' like the majority (although not all) of the previous generation of NRMs. One important exception to this pattern was the Unification Church (UC), popularly known as 'the Moonies', whose founder-leader Sun Myung Moon settled in the United States in 1972, coming from Korea, and whose organization claimed a Christian identity. The 'Jesus People' or 'Jesus Freak' movement offered another counterexample of a Christian new religious wave, particularly in its institutional form of the Children of God, a Christian NRM that combined elements of the counterculture with an apocalyptically oriented form of Christianity. This new religious landscape, however, did not deter the Christian countercult movement from proliferating its critiques of these forms of spirituality. The best known of these is undoubtedly Water Martin's *The Kingdom of the Cults*, first published in 1965, but expanded in 1985 to encompass the non-Christian movements. Bob Larson's radio countercult ministries helped to disseminate the evangelical Protestant critique of NRMs.

A number of factors effected a change in the literature on new religions. Part of the process of secularization in the United Kingdom and the United States was increasing ignorance of the Christian faith and, with it, a decreasing concern for matters of orthodoxy and heresy. Some of the hostility to foreign NRMs was fuelled by racism, which still prevails on both sides of the Atlantic, but criticism turned away from matters of theology to issues concerning the human harm that these newer religions allegedly caused. While the countercult movement was predominantly Christian, offering evangelical Protestantism as an alternative to cultism, opposition to 'the cults' gave rise to a secular anti-cult movement (ACM), which ostensibly sanctioned freedom of belief, but which sought to oppose the phenomena that popularly became associated with NRMs, such as brainwashing, splitting up families, extortionate charges, interrupting one's education, exploiting their members by making them spend long hours fundraising and subjecting them to poor living conditions while leaders allegedly enjoyed lives of luxury. The ACM's focus was not on what NRMs taught, but what they did.

A further factor influencing the birth of the study of NRMs in the Anglophone world was also at work. Outside of the Western context, a growing number of Japanese scholars had turned their attention to the emergence of NRMs in post-war Japan. Including such groups as Soka Gakkai, Shinnyo-en, and Aum Shinrikyō, these Japanese NRMs (*shinshūkyō*) gained tremendous attention in the wake of the end of the Japanese state religious establishment after the Second World War. English language studies such as H. Neill McFarland's *The Rush Hour of the Gods: A Study of New Religious Movements in Japan* (1967) introduced many Western scholars to the topic. McFarland also provided an example of rooting his rigorous objective study of NRMs in sociological and historical methodologies rather than theology or biblical studies. The text became a model that scholars working outside of Japan looked to when engaging in their own studies of NRMs.

The inception of the academic study of NRMs is synchronous with the rise of several sociological concerns. Sociology had become an established and growing subject at universities. Classical sociologists such as Max Weber had paved the way for empirical study with his Church/sect typology, which highlighted the distinction between a society's dominant form of religion, to which the majority are deemed to belong by default and which tends to legitimate the *status quo*, and the 'sect', membership of which is more likely to be by conscious decision, which tends to make greater demands on its members, and which often opposes the dominant culture's values. Weber's Church/sect distinction, although influential, is somewhat blunt, and it was further refined by Ernst Troeltsch, Howard Becker and others.

We shall return to the question of typologies later. In the meantime, a number of observations are appropriate. First, although the word 'Church' might have been appropriate enough to characterize the dominant religion of Weber's early twentieth-century Bavaria, it is inappropriate to other cultures, particularly

Asian ones. NRMs are not exclusively Western, but are now acknowledged to be a global phenomenon. Second, it seems useful to distinguish between organizations that have split away from a parent religion, for example Mormons and Jehovah's Witnesses, who separated themselves from mainstream Protestant Christianity, and organizations that either have no obvious parent religion (such as Scientology) or come from outside Christianity, such as Buddhist or Indian guru-led societies. Becker referred to the former as 'sects' and the latter as 'cults'. However – third – the word 'cult', despite its widespread popular currency, has the disadvantage of being pejorative. To use Steven Sutcliffe's phrase, it 'lacks predictive content': in other words, it is difficult to know whether, and on what grounds, we should attach the label 'cult' to a spiritual organization. It is possible that in studying NRMs academics are continuing to follow the rather nebulous cluster of groups that are so-called by the media and the ACM. It was Harold W. Turner who devised the term 'new religious movement' as an alternative to cult, since it was a term that proved acceptable both to the proponents of NRMs and to those who studied them (Berner 2000, 267).

The later sociological studies of NRMs essentially belonged to the sociology of deviance. Leon Festinger's famous piece of covert research, *When Prophecy Fails* (1956), focused on a small UFO group, whose name and members are pseudonymized in the interests of confidentiality, but which is now known to be Sananda, led by Dorothy Martin. Martin (aka Mrs Keetch) had predicted the arrival of space visitors who would collect the group at a predetermined date and time, which failed to materialize. The group's behaviour in the wake of unfulfilled prophecy confirmed Festinger's hypothesis that the faith-maintenance of those who remained in the group after the failed prophecy was strengthened rather than diminished. John Lofland's later study, *Doomsday Cult* (1969), was also a covert pseudonymized study, of followers of the 'Divine Precepts' – now known to be an account of the early days of the Unification Church in California's Bay Area, led by its Korean pioneer Young Oon Kim (1915–89). Significantly, Lofland's introduction recounts that his decision to investigate the Unification Church was only made when a flying saucer convention was cancelled, and he was left with a free day to research some other organization. Lofland's study, like Festinger's, is mainly a narrative, recounting the behaviour of the various members of the group, and its progress.

A further piece of sociological research is worth mentioning in this context: Robert W. Balch and David Taylor's research in the 1970s on Human Individual Metamorphosis (HIM), later known by the more familiar name of Heaven's Gate, whose 39 remaining members committed collective suicide on 22–24 March 1997. In common with Festinger and Lofland, Balch and Taylor's research was covert, and consisted in 'going native' or 'living in', travelling with the group. (Contrary to rumour, they did this when the leaders were travelling on their own, and never actually met Bonnie L. Nettles and Marshall Herff Applewhite.)

Balch and Taylor aimed to study conversion, commitment, and disengagement within the group, in the course of which they provide important first-hand testimony of this organization's progress during the late 1970s.

It is sometimes asked why scholars sometimes devote so much time and energy studying minority groups that appear to have little significance. One answer is that a small group like Heaven's Gate can suddenly mushroom into public prominence, and academics can be called upon to answer obvious key questions like, 'What was the group like?' and 'Why did it happen?' This of course is not the only reason for studying NRMs. Collectively the study of each helps to form an overall picture of the world's religious landscape; they have features in common with other groups (such as Sanandan's and Heaven's Gate's preoccupation with UFOs); they interact with other features of society; and they often provide evidence concerning issues that they have in common, such as how they react to unfulfilled prophecy, what brings about conversion and apostasy, how do they react to external threats and to mainstream society and religion.

The Impact of Jonestown

The mass deaths in Jim Jones' Peoples Temple at Jonestown, Guyana in 1978, profoundly shook society and had an untold impact on public attitudes to new religions, as well as to the academic study of them. A mass suicide on such a scale had only been surpassed when 960 Sicarii Jews died collectively at Masada in 73 CE rather than surrender to the Romans. The death toll at Jonestown was not far short of the Masada Jews, totalling 918 in all. Many of them apparently took their own lives by collective drinking poison, although their voluntariness has been called into question – the alternative was being shot by armed guards, and at least 200 children were murdered (Moore 2011a, 98). To the vast majority of people it was incomprehensible that suicide could be enacted on such a large scale, and the event inevitably caused speculation about what might lead seemingly ordinary people from normal living to such abnormal dying. Since people in normal circumstances are not amenable to rational persuasion to commit suicide, the 'brainwashing' theory provided an obvious answer: there must be something malevolently distinctive about the leader and the environment in which his followers are placed that makes them amenable to such irrational persuasion.

Although largely rejected by scholars, the brainwashing theory has an academic pedigree, traceable to the work of Robert Jay Lifton, who worked as psychiatrist in the US Air Force during the Korean War of 1951–3. Lifton was particularly interested in post-traumatic stress disorder, and studied the effects of the environment to which the Korean military authorities subjected American prisoners of war. He concluded that there were altogether eight components of 'thought reform': milieu control; 'mystical manipulation', a demand for purity; 'sacred science' (promotion of the group's ideology as the unsurpassable truth); 'loading the language' (special 'insider' vocabulary); 'doctrine over person'; 'dispensing of existence' (the absolute right to claim who does or does not belong); and 'thought-terminating cliché' (the use of buzzwords or platitudes that appear substantive, but lack truly significant meaning). Lifton's ideas have found their way into the ACM, who typically itemize 'marks of a cult', drawing on these ideas, and Lifton has particularly influenced the writings of anti-cult authors Margaret Singer and Steven Hassan, both of whom have championed the brainwashing hypothesis. The brainwashing hypothesis met with two decisive blows, one academic, and the other legal. Thomas Robbins and Dick Anthony were the first to challenge the theory, in an article entitled 'The Limits of "Coercive Persuasion" as an Explanation for Conversion to Authoritarian Sects', published in 1980. Other studies followed. Marc Galanter, a professor of psychiatry, argued against the dangers of 'medicalizing' NRM membership by conceiving of it in pathological terms. Perhaps better known is Eileen Barker's *The Making of a Moonie: Brainwashing or Choice?* (1984) which resulted from studying the Unification Church over a period of two years, attending its notorious camps at Boonville and Camp K for extended periods, and extensively interviewing its members. Barker had studied the process, not merely the alleged result. Barker found that, of 1,017 attendees at workshop seminars around London in 1979, only 15 per cent completed the 21-day workshop (the third in a series of classes), 10 per cent signed up either to full-time or part-time membership for more than a week, 4 per cent remained affiliated in January 1983 and a mere 3.5 per cent remained as full-time members at the beginning of the same year. Out of those who visit a Unification centre for the first time, no more than 0.005 per cent will have any association with the Unification Church two years further on. As Barker points out, such statistics do not suggest irresistible coercion rather than freedom to choose whether or not to belong. In fact, any university with such a phenomenal drop-out rate would not be allowed to remain in existence! Barker was not alone in attacking the brainwashing theory. Other academics – in particular Dick Anthony, Thomas Robbins, James T. Richardson and James Beckford – attacked the popularly held theory that the so-called cults exercised mental manipulation.

Meanwhile, Singer's presumed expertise was being challenged in the courts. Singer had acted as an expert witness in around 40 such cases. However, her opinions were challenged by numerous scholars, mainly sociologists and psychologists, who filed *amicus curiae* briefs in a number of significant legal cases. In one such case (*U.S. vs. Fishman* 1990) ex-Scientologist Robert Fishman claimed diminished responsibility, having been charged with mail fraud. Singer's evidence was successfully challenged by Anthony, causing the judge to conclude:

Although Dr. Singer and Dr. Ofshe [a colleague of Singer's] are respected members of their fields, their theories regarding the coercive persuasion practiced by religious cults are not sufficiently established to be admitted as evidence in federal law courts. (Melton 1999). Despite the overwhelming lack of support for brainwashing theory in academic circles, the ACM remains unconvinced by scholarly research, and their continued allegiance to Singer and a small handful of American psychiatrists, such as R. J. Lifton, Eli Shapiro, and L. Jolyon West signalled a divide between academic approaches to NRMs and the ACM's general antipathy to academic research. Increasingly isolated from mainstream scientific researchers of new religious movements, the ACM brands Barker and other academics who base their findings on empirical evidence and consider alternative hypotheses as 'cult apologists', misleadingly suggesting that they are speaking in favour of 'cults'.

During the 1970s the ACM became organized and, as part of the process, produced its own literature. The Christian Countercult Movement (CCM) had already made its own mark on the NRM scene by producing books and pamphlets commending evangelical Christianity as a superior alternative to 'cultism'. The 1970s saw the rise of more secular groups such as Citizens Freedom Foundation (CFF), founded by Ted Patrick, renamed the Cult Awareness Network (CAN) in 1984. Among CAN's leaders were Galen Kelly, Cynthia Kisser, and Rick Ross, who later attracted public attention for his public statements and his attempts to advise the ATF and FBI during the Waco siege in 1993. In the United Kingdom, FAIR (Family Action Information and Rescue, later renamed Family Action Information and Resource) was set up by a Member of Parliament in 1976, and in Europe a number of cult-monitoring organizations took their rise. CAN drew substantially on the work of Lifton, Singer and others, and, although most of its literature is not academic, it provides useful primary source material for those researching the ACM. (Ironically, CAN became bankrupt in 1996, following a law suit brought against them by the Church of Scientology, which subsequently bought up the organization.) The American Family Foundation, founded by psychiatrist John Clarke in 1987, had greater aspirations to academic credibility, publishing a journal entitled *Cultic Studies Review*. Some of its critics were somewhat scathing about its contents, claiming that the material was second-rate. In 2004 it gained higher prestige by its new name, the International Cultic Studies Association, under Michael D. Langone's directorship, and published the *International Journal of Cultic Studies*, to which a number of well-known academics contributed, including Eileen Barker and James R. Lewis.

In Europe, the Lutheran World Federation held an international consultation on new religious movements in 1977. One significant outcome was the decision to set up a service to disseminate information about NRMs, which led to the launch of the journal *Update* by the Dialog Center International, a Christian countercult organization founded some four years previously by Johannes Aagaard (1928–2007). Aagaard was a missiologist who had travelled in Asia, where his encounters with Westerners who had converted to eastern faiths caused him to assert his own evangelical Christianity against these alternatives. *Update*, renamed *Areopagus* in 1987, attracted articles mainly from NRM critics, although the names of a number of independent scholars, such as Roy Wallis, James A. Beverley, Irving Hexham and Susan Palmer, appear occasionally in the contents lists.

Missiology is an important, yet often overlooked, component in the study of NRMs. Harold W. Turner (1911–2002) was a Presbyterian minister and academic who took up a post in Fourah Bay College, Sierra Leone. By chance he came into contact in the mid-1950s with the Church of the Lord Aladura and met its founder-leader Adeleke Adejobi. This fired his enthusiasm to study the African Independent Churches (AICs), which hitherto had received little scholarly attention. Turner's career took him to Nigeria, and then to Britain, where he held posts at the Universities of Leicester and Aberdeen. During his career Turner amassed a large collection of scholarly articles and primary source material on new religions – some 26,000 items in all – which he donated to Selly Oak Colleges in Birmingham, UK, when he became the founder and director of its Centre for New Religious Movements (CENERM) in 1981. This collection is now part of the special collections in the Cadbury Research Library at the University of Birmingham.

Turner's principal interest was the way in which new religions arose from the interaction of Christian mission with primal societies. Missionaries, being keen to maximize their converts and distribute parts of the Bible as widely as possible, at times failed to ensure the authenticity of the transmission of the Christian message. Communities were sometimes left to devise their own interpretations of a gospel that a colporteur had left them, and at times new converts in their newly found zeal would preach what they took to be Christian teaching, but which they had not thoroughly assimilated, without appropriate supervision from more mature Christians. This frequently led to syncretism between Christianity and indigenous religious, of which the AICs are one example. Having been born in New Zealand, to which he returned periodically, Turner also studied the ways in which Aboriginals assimilated Christianity, as well as a number of cargo cults. Although Turner did not study the Unification Church extensively, it was one well-known example of Korean NRMs that arose from the interaction between Korean folk shamanism and Christianity. In order to provide an umbrella term designate these new religions, Turner used the term PRINERM, meaning 'primal new religious movement', and gave the name NERMs to the wider phenomenon of 'cults' or 'sects', as they have been popularly labelled.

Shortly after the founding of CENERM, Peter B. Clarke (1940–2011) founded the Centre for New Religions at King's College, London. Clarke had formerly been Professor of African History at the University of Ibadan, Nigeria, and his main research interests were in African and Brazilian NRMs. Clarke inaugurated a series of academic seminars at King's, later to be superseded by Eileen Barker's INFORM seminars, when the Information Network on Religious Movements was set up in 1988. One important outcome of the King's College conferences was the founding of the journal *Religion Today*, first published in 1985, and becoming the much more scholarly *Journal of Contemporary Religion* in 1995.

Until the late 1980s the main sources of public information were the anti-cult and countercult organizations. They had achieved some success in advising European politicians in their attempts to control the activities of NRMs. In 1983 Alain Vivien had written a report, 'The Cults in France: Expression of Moral Liberty or Carriers of Manipulations?; and the following year Euro-MP Richard Cottrell presented a report to the European Parliament entitled 'Report on the Activity of Certain New Religious Movements within the European Community'. These publications, as well as the ACM's newsletters and information pamphlets remain useful primary source material for those wishing to research the phenomenon of anti-cultism, but of course are less valuable for accurate understanding of the NRMs themselves. INFORM was therefore founded as an attempt to provide objective information on NRMs, in contrast to the often misinformed and scaremongering campaigning of the ACM, which presupposed stereotypical beliefs about 'cults', such as brainwashing, authoritarian leadership, financial exploitation and so on. In the same year as INFORM was founded, another organization was set up in Torino, Italy: a number of scholars, mainly from the history and sociology of religion, got together and established CESNUR (Center for the Study of New Religions) under the directorship of Massimo Introvigne. CESNUR produces a wide variety of publications on NRMs, and hosts an extensive website, largely containing past conference proceedings. Its annual conference is attended mainly by academics from numerous countries, and also – to a somewhat lesser extent – by NRM members themselves. Introvigne's personal library, consisting of some 50,000 volumes, is available for consultation at CESNUR's headquarters.

In North America several independent groups also began to coalesce around the study of new religions, most notably a group of sociologists of religion who adopted empirical and more objective approaches to studying the topic. In the mid-1970s, Jacob Needleman, J. Stillson Judah, and Charles Glock convened one of the first academic groups to study NRMs, at the Graduate Theological Union (GTU, a consortium of seminaries and schools of religion) in Berkeley, California. With funding from the United States' National Endowment for the Humanities and several other foundations, this group organized conferences

Introduction

and an archival collection of materials related to NRMs, allowing North American scholars to more easily study the topic. The scholars associated with the GTU research group published some of the first American studies of NRMs, most notably Glock and Robert N. Bellah's edited collection *The New Religious Consciousness* (1976). Contributors to this anthology offered some of the very first studies of groups such as ISKCON, Healthy-Happy-Holy, Divine Light Mission, Synanon, Christian World Liberation Front, the Church of Satan, and a few other meta-movements such as Jewish Identity, Catholic Charismatics, the religious aspects of the New Left, and the Human Potential Movement. This research group also led to John Lofland and Rodney Stark's groundbreaking study of religious conversion, 'Becoming a World-Saver: A Theory of Conversion to a Deviant Perspective', based on their studies of the Unification Church (1965). The work of the GTU research group provided the groundwork for an entire generation of subsequent researchers.

Simultaneously, J. Gordon Melton was founding the Institute for the Study of American Religions, which focused much of its energy on NRMs and documenting the religious diversity that they represented. Melton founded the organization in the Chicago metropolitan area in 1969, moving it to Santa Barbara, California in 1985. Under Melton's leadership the ISAR focused on obtaining and archiving materials related to the new religious movement of the United States. By the time of the move to Santa Barbara the ISAR held more than 40,000 individual archival materials. Melton and the ISAR later donated these materials to the Special Collections department of the library of the University of California, Santa Barbara where they formed the locus of the American Religions Collection. This collection, along with another like it assembled by Judah at the GTU in the San Francisco Bay Area, serve as the two main archival repositories for the study of new religious movements in the United States.

Around the same time, some of the NRMs themselves were attempting to gain academic credibility. The Church of Jesus Christ of Latter-day Saints has for several decades had its own academic establishments, the best known of which is Brigham Young University, and Mormon Studies has been an academically credible field of study, with many Mormon scholars contributing to the history and theology of the church. During the 1970s and 1980s the Unification Church sponsored large numbers of academic conferences. While a number of these were introductions to *Divine Principle* for clergy and academics, and discussions of themes in Unification thought, UC teachings constituted only a small proportion of conference themes, which spanned the social sciences, the environmental and physical sciences, and wider theological and religious topics, with a particular focus on Christian ecumenism and interfaith studies. These last two themes related to the UC's quest to 'unite' the world's religions (although the exact meaning of this aspiration is not altogether clear). The Unification Church set up its own theological seminary in Barrytown, New York, primarily for the training of its own leaders, but whose staff included members of a variety of religious backgrounds, and not merely Unificationists. Allied to the seminary and the conferences were a number of in-house publishing organizations: in addition to the seminary's own publications, New Era Books, the Pergamon Press, and the Rose of Sharon Press, among others, brought out numerous volumes, principally on religious themes. Although the Bhaktivedanta Book Trust, owned by International Society for Krishna Consciousness (ISKCON), primarily produced copies of its own religious texts and popular material promoting Krishna Consciousness, the *ISKCON Communications Journal* solicited academic contributions from a number of well-known academics. Several ISKCON members entered doctoral programmes in Indology and related fields, and have published on Vaishnavism and related religious phenomenon in peer-reviewed academic presses, most notably Bryant and Eksrand's *The Hare Krishna Movement*, published by Columbia University Press.

Mention has been made above of the Christian countercult movement, but it should not be thought that all Christians actively endeavour to evangelize members of NRMs. A number of Christian denominations have given more organized responses regarding the phenomenon. In 1986 the Catholic Truth Society published a report by its bishops, entitled 'Sects: The Pastoral Challenge'. In the same year the Lutheran World Federation and the World Council of Churches collaboratively organized a further consultation on NRMs at Free University, Amsterdam, attended by a number of well-known academics and commentators specializing in NRMs, including Harold Turner, Eileen Barker, Johannes Aagaard and Jean-François Mayer.

Eventually the study of NRMs became institutionalized within the academy. The American Academy of Religion created a programme unit to study the topic in 1984, and several journals were founded, including *Nova Religio: The Journal of Alternative and Emergent Religions* (1997). More recent years have seen the establishment of a second journal, the *International Journal for the Study of New Religions* published by the European-based International Association for the Study of New Religions (2010). Certainly the field of the study of NRMs has achieved maturity.

Definitional Issues

At the same time, several very important issues remain unresolved in the study of NRMs. Most crucially, scholars working within the field do not have a commonly accepted definition of the terms 'new religious movements', 'new religions' or even 'alternative religion'. The study of religion more broadly has similar problems, with a fundamental disagreement on the definition of the term 'religion'. Like religious studies more widely, scholars of NRMs have debated the definition of the foundational term, and continue to do so.

The definitional issue, as always, remains a central one. Yet the flowering of the academic study of religion despite a lack of agreement on the nature of religion itself indicates that there is little reason for pessimism within the field of NRM studies. That scholars of new religions cannot agree on a definition of the term 'NRM' may in the long run be a signal of strength, as it has been for the study of religion more broadly. Certainly researchers bring their own definitions to their research agendas, as thus far the field has been able to function despite a shared definition of the central term. The distinction between a religion and a religious movement offers one avenue for considering the various perspectives on the nature of the object of study of NRM scholars. The choice by Turner and others to use the phrase 'religious movements' rather than 'religions' tied the field to the study of social movements, a broader subfield within the field of sociology and political science. Social movements can be diffuse, centralized, limited in scope, totalistic, parochial or international, and as such the idea serves as a useful foundation for defining the concept of NRM, since NRMs also possess such different characteristics. Early scholars of social movements attempted to explain their origin and operation using a variety of social theories, most notably social deprivation theory – the idea that these movements provide avenues for the deprived to exert influence or seek solace – and resource mobilization theory, which envisions social movements as rational actions by individuals to gain control over crucial social resources. These theoretical approaches were inherited by the initial researchers into NRMs, most notably the early work on conversion to NRMs by John Lofland and Rodney Stark, which utilized deprivation theory, and the later sociological work by Stark and William Sims Bainbridge, developing out of resource mobilization theory (Lofland and Stark 1965; Stark and Bainbridge 1979).

While scholars of NRMs occasionally disagree on whether a movement merits consideration as a 'religious movement', there is general consensus that the category is quite wide. Most scholars would agree that explicitly supernaturalistic groups are clearly religious movements, but researchers generally include new religions with less overtly supernatural-oriented ideologies, such as Jediism or Raelianism, that seem to look like other religious groups. Since definitions of 'supernatural' and 'natural' also vary, this distinction is sometimes far from clear. Generally scholars have taken two approaches to defining the 'religion' part of 'NRM'. First, if a group refers to itself as a religion or religious movement, researchers tend to at least initially consider it as such. The case of Jediism, a NRM predicated on the fictional worldview of the samurai-like order from the *Star Wars* series, provides one example of this. Few Jediists claim any sort of supernatural ability or even reference to supernatural elements. Yet in positioning itself as a religious movement – most famously in Australia and then in other parts of the Commonwealth – Jediism falls within the scope of the study of new religious movements. Second, researchers of NRMs have tended to accept as NRMs those groups that 'look like' other religious movements. This includes movements with similar organizational structures, belief systems, functions or practices to other religions. For much of its history, the leaders and members of the UFO movement known as Heaven's Gate did not refer to the group as a religion. Yet the movement's various qualities included religious beliefs and practices, and Heaven's Gate clearly functioned as a religion in the lives of its adherents. Scholars therefore have treated it as one.

Finally, the academic study of NRMs faces the question of what constitutes 'new'. Initially, researchers took a rather basic and intuitive approach. If a group was new to the people around it, it was an NRM. Scientology, ISKCON, the Children of God, and the Unification Church – to name the most notable of the NRMs during the formative stage of the field – were all new in this way of thinking. Yet as the groups matured and time marched on, the notion of what counts as 'new' became more acute. Should scholars in the second decade of the twenty-first century talk about Scientology as new, given that the group emerged in the 1950s? All the NRMs that had formed as the field of NRM studies emerged are now equally mature. Eileen Barker has proposed that scholars consider any religion founded after the Second World War as 'new' for the purposes of the study of new religious movements (Barker 1990, 145). Since global culture fundamentally transformed in the aftermath of the Second World War, especially in terms of interconnectivity and social developments, Barker's suggestion certainly has merit. Many scholars have followed her approach, though others have not, notably those working on Japanese NRMs who tend to include groups founded in the nineteenth century as new religious movements.

Yet Barker's suggestion of defining NRMs as groups formed after the Second World War precludes from our consideration some of the groups that scholars of new religious movements have generally studied. The Nation of Islam, Father Divine's Peace Mission Movement and nearly all of the American 'Black Messiahs' all emerged before the war. The Jehovah's Witnesses similarly originated long before that time. Even some of the NRMs that did not formally incorporate until after the Second World War, for example ISKCON, can trace their organizational and ideological lineage back to before the Second World War. Such an approach would also mean that the historical NRMs such as the Shakers, Adventists, or Mormons, would no longer merit consideration as new religious movements.

Complicating this discussion is the concept of 'new new religions', as championed by J. Gordon Melton. Again, the field owes its terminological background to scholars of Japanese NRMs, who coined the term *shin-shinshūkyō*, which literally translates as 'new new religions' to refer to the NRMs founded after 1970. Melton has argued that Anglophone scholars would do well to adopt this terminology as well, but he applies it to movements founded since the 1990s. Melton envisions these new new religions as different from the new religions that preceded them, but still part of an on-going and natural process of religious change within free societies. He offers the concept of new new religions as a useful one for scholars since it helps us differentiate between the groups we study, and calls us to re-examine the way we study them (Melton 2007).

We will not solve the problem of definition in this introduction, nor even in this *Companion*. Suffice it to say, different scholars assume different definitions of NRMs based on their academic, personal and methodological preferences. Researchers trained in sociology are more apt to consider only recently founded movements as NRMs. Historians by contrast tend to use a much broader definition and include older groups. Those with anthropological backgrounds tend to follow a third trajectory, defining NRMs based on how new they are to the cultures in which they are present. All of these approaches are valid, broadening the scope of the field and encouraging interdisciplinary conversation.

Sociology and the Study of NRMs

As should already be clear, the study of new religious movements is indelibly tied to developments in the sociological study of religion. Weber and Troeltsch's Church/sect typology laid the groundwork for much of the study of new religions that followed. As this Introduction has noted, Weber's distinction between church (strong culturally dominant institutions) and sects (smaller alternative groups making greater demands on their members) is not unproblematic. Nevertheless it became one of the assumed typologies in the study of NRMs. Much of the early sociological study of new religious movements focused on extending and critiquing this and other typologies of NRMs. Some of these typologies eschewed sociological approaches altogether, instead grouping NRMs as parts of families of other religions, and considering 'cult' 'sect' or 'new religious movement' as mere subcategories of the overall category of 'religion'. Robert S. Ellwood Jr.'s *Religious and Spiritual Groups in Modern America* (1973) exemplifies this approach. He used broad family categories to encompass the new religious movements he studied, namely those of Theosophical traditions; Spiritualism; initiatory groups (what many scholars today would call esotericism); Neopaganism; Hindu movements; and other Asian movements. J. Gordon Melton's encyclopaedias and other reference books follow similar trajectories, sorting NRMs according to the religious families to which Melton ascribes them, rather than envisioning sociologically oriented categories within a typology. This has the advantage of blurring the sometimes-artificial distinction between NRM and other religions, and demonstrating their connections to the traditions from which they emerged. It does not however encourage sustained comparisons between NRMs or the development of theoretical understandings of NRMs as a phenomenon.

Building on the work of Weber and Troeltsch, Roy Wallis provided one of the earliest attempts to extend the cult/sect typology to the contemporary Western world. Wallis extended the distinction – which Weber and Troeltsch originally based on how the group related to broader society – to focus primarily on the nature of authority. According to this typology, a 'cult' rooted authority in what Wallis called 'epistemological individualism', wherein individuals possessed the primary religious authority. Sects on the other hand demonstrated 'epistemological authoritarianism', wherein the organization or group possessed primary authority. Cults tend to be more fragile and because of their support for individualism are ultimately less stable social movements, whereas sects tend towards more authoritarian ideologies and therefore demonstrate more cohesion and stability (Wallis 1974). While Wallis' cult/sect typology did not have lasting input, it did serve as a bridge between the study of NRMs in the early days of the sociology of religion to more contemporary approaches. More recently, J. Gordon Melton and David G. Bromley have challenged the Weber-Troeltsch-Wallis lineage with their own typology of NRMs predicated on the relation of a new religion to broader society and social categories, meaning that NRMs fall within categories of dominant, sectarian, alternative or emergent (Bromley and Melton 2012).

One of the most influential sociological typologies of NRMs emerged from the work of Rodney Stark and William Sims Bainbridge, whose work on new religious movements was part of their broader attempt to develop a new sociological theory of religion. Stark and Bainbridge define sects as schismatic groups that have deviated from an existing religious movement, whereas cults are innovative or imported groups or religious traditions new to their environment. Within the category of cult they differentiate three subtypes: audience cults, which offer vague or weak supernatural promises (which they call 'compensators') to be consumed by a vague or loosely delineated audience; client cults, in which an organized religious provider 'sells' 'valued but relatively specific' compensators to affluent consumers; and cult movements, full fledged mini-religions offering general compensators (Stark and Bainbridge 1979, 126–7). The two sociologists as well as their later collaborators applied their typology to a range of times and places, ranging from America in the Roaring Twenties to mid-nineteenth-century Wales (Stark, Bainbridge, and Kent 1981; Stark, Finke, and Iannaccone 1995).

Stark, Bainbridge and their collaborators eventually published several books elaborating on their typology of NRMs and envisioning what they called 'cult formation' as a fundamental part of the religious ecosystem. They developed what came to be called the rational choice model of the sociology of religion, which posits religious adherents as rational actors who 'consume' religion(s) from a religious marketplace. Using the language of macroeconomics, proponents of rational choice envision NRMs as new religious suppliers that appear to sell their products in niche markets to a relatively constant demand for religious satisfaction and membership. NRMs that position themselves successfully and are able to sell themselves well grow into more established religions (in both the legal and informal sense of the word). They champion an idea of a 'religious economy' that encompasses both old and new religious movements, but wherein NRMs thrive only in open religious economies, namely nation states without established churches or legal impediments to the emergence of new 'religious firms' (Stark and Bainbridge 1985; Stark and Bainbridge 1987; Finke and Stark 1992).

The rational choice approach clearly creates room for the study of new religious movements within the field of the sociology of religion, since it envisions NRMs as a natural part of the religious landscape. In fact, it makes the study of NRMs central to the scientific study of religion, since the emergence of new groups functions as one of the fundamental forces in the religious marketplace, according to this theory. It also positions individual NRMs as examples capable of being studied in order to elucidate broader forces and trends in the religious marketplace. As Bainbridge himself argued, 'New Religious Movements are like the fruit flies and bacteria studied by geneticists. By being small and fast-changing, and possessing distinctive characteristics, they give scientists clear vision into the processes that creates and sustain new culture.. . . Cult is culture writ small' (Bainbridge 2002, 43). Yet the theory is not without its critics among scholars within the field of NRM studies. One reason for this is that the rational choice approach contradicts another major theory within the sociology of new religious movements, that of secularization theory.

Secularization is one of the fundamental theories within the sociology of religion, though its influence has waxed and waned over the decades. It owes its origin to Peter L. Berger, one of the foremost Austrian-American sociologists in the post-war period. Berger defined secularization as 'the process by which sectors of society and culture are removed from the domination of religious institutions and symbols' (Berger 1967, 107). For Berger, secularization was the by-product of religious diversity and the decline of monoreligious cultures wherein a single religion was taken for granted as the ultimate and only truth, the 'Church' in Weber's terminology. Secularization was therefore a natural part of the evolution of religion in human culture, since it followed from globalization and exchange. Later theorists, such as Steve Bruce, trace secularization to the rise of science and technology that followed in the wake of the renaissance, industrial revolution and post-war boom (Bruce 2002). The development of other social actors such as government or medicine has effectively made religion irrelevant in most peoples' daily lives, argue the proponents of secularization theory. On a social level, religious actors and groups no longer possess the influence they once did and cannot dominate society. On an individual level, while people might still declare themselves as members of one religion or another, they no longer look to religion to satisfy their most important needs. Religion continues to exist, but with less importance than it once did.

Secularization theory helps explain the decline of religious influence and adherents in the West, particularly in Western and Northern Europe and Canada. Within the approach of secularization theory, sociologists have identified NRMs as either the dying breaths of religion, or religious responses to secularization that either challenge some aspects of it or attempt to create new space for religious life. Hence, as James Davison Hunter explains, new religions represent a 'protest against modernity' and an attempt to engage in 'demodernization' within the scope of alternative social movements (Hunter 1981). Within NRMs, individuals still accept religions as offering the sort of dominion and control that they used to in premodern societies. The social world of an NRM instructs its members what to wear, how to eat, whom to marry and what job to work at. Its social world generally offers religious answers to questions of how to structure society and how individuals ought to relate to each other within those societies. Hence NRMs represent 'blips' within the overall scheme of secularization.

As should be clear, secularization and rational choice envision two completely different views of the sociology of religion, and position NRMs differently within each of those perspectives. Much ink has been spilled over which approach is more accurate, and sociologists continue to debate this matter. Since secularization theory works so well to explain changes in the United Kingdom, Northern Europe, and Western Europe, its most vocal supporters have generally studied these regions. Rational choice models by contrast assume an American-style free religious market as the default mode of religious operation, and since the model helps explain developments in the United States, most proponents of rational choice are American sociologists. What is important for scholars of NRMs is that both models envision new religious movements as important parts of the religious ecosphere – or 'marketplace', to use rational choice's wording – though each understand new religions differently.

Beyond Sociology

The field of NRM studies owes much of its early development and vibrancy to sociology, but in recent decades many other approaches to studying new religious movements have taken root. Many of these approaches are covered in the essays included in this volume, namely those focusing on material culture, media studies and ritual studies. These new approaches serve to highlight the multifaceted nature of NRMs, as well as their cultural influences and implications.

Another model for studying NRMs is that of history. The vast majority of new religious movements that have spawned over the centuries are defunct, though some – such as Christianity, Islam and Bahá'í have become major world religions. Historians of NRMs look to more recent new religious innovators and movements using their own methodological tools. While it makes little sense to refer to groups such as the Shakers (originating in the eighteenth century) or Adventists (nineteenth century) as 'new', they certainly were within the context of their times. The essay on Mormon Studies within this Companion makes the case that, from a historical perspective, the inception of Mormonism mirrors the way in which Christianity took its rise, and Douglas Davies highlights some of the problems in distinguishing between authentic history, as seen by the outsider, and the insider's interpretation, viewed with the eyes of faith.

The proliferation of approaches to studying NRMs reveals how the areas of research interest for today's scholars have evolved from the earlier research questions. The first generation of scholars who investigated NRMs were almost all sociologists, and therefore primarily interested in sociological questions such as recruitment and conversion, belief maintenance, defection and the institutionalization of charisma. While none of those matters are entirely settled, the first generation of research laid the groundwork for subsequent studies. Today there are many sociologists still working on NRMs, but specialists in history, ritual studies, media studies and many other fields have joined them. New research questions relate to issues such as how sacred space and sacred rites can contribute to our understanding of a religious community, how a religion's message is produced and received through relatively new media such as radio, television, and most recently the internet, how the law of the land can restrict or liberate religious organizations and how they respond to legislation.

Recent Developments and Current Trends

Two key themes in the study of NRMs have emerged in recent times. The first is violence. The violent end to the Branch Davidian community at Waco in 1993 reinforced the popular belief that new religions were dangerous and that their members could come to a cataclysmic end. The ensuing catastrophes of the Order of the Solar Temple in 1994 and 1995, Aum Shinrikyō's sarin gas attack on the Tokyo underground, followed by Heaven's Gate in 1997, and the Movement for the Restoration of the Ten Commandments of God in Uganda in 2000, added further fuel to popular and anti-cult apprehension. The attack on the World Trade Center by Al Qaeda terrorists on 11 September 2001 enabled the public to make further connections between religion and violence, and caused both the media and the academic world to give new attention to groups connected with Islam.

Some of these incidents were related to apocalyptic beliefs, since the years 1993, 1997 and 2000 could be construed as the completion of a period of two millennia (depending on one's calculations) after Jesus' birth. Apocalypticism in fact is inexorably linked to both NRMs themselves and the study of NRMs. Many of the most important new religious movements embrace or embraced apocalypticism, most notably groups in the Adventist tradition (such as the Branch Davidians), Jehovah's Witnesses, the Children of God, Christian Identity and other Christian millennial groups. Catherine Wessinger has developed several theoretical models for understanding varieties of apocalypticism and reasons why some apocalyptic groups tend towards violence sectarianism and other do not. She distinguishes between 'progressive millennialism' wherein the apocalypse is dependent on human involvement and usually quite graduate and positive, and 'catastrophic millennialism', in which the apocalypse is sudden, violent and externally imposed. Wessinger notes that both types of millennialism can lead to a full range of behaviours, from violence to utopianism (Wessinger 2000a). Wessinger's approach has become quite influential in the study of new religious movements, and is explained in her contribution to this *Companion*.

A second theme that emerged was the advent of the internet. The World Wide Web was in its infancy in the mid-1990s. Several of the members of Heaven's Gate had helped to generate income for the group by offering their services to the public as web designers, and their own website had helped to disseminate co-founder/leader Marshall Herff Applewhite's teachings. The public, not fully understanding the potential of the World Wide Web, feared that the group had used the internet as a powerful recruiting tool, and fears arose about how other groups might lure unwary web surfers into joining exploitative or dangerous 'cults'. In the decade and a half since the Heaven's Gate suicides, both the Web and our understanding of it have advanced considerably. Now that the vast majority of religious organizations in the developed world have a web presence, the web offers the opportunity for NRMs to present their views publicly, unfiltered by prejudice and lack of understanding from the media and the ACM. The Web has also presented the possibility of creating new expressions of religion or indeed completely new religions ('cyber-religions') that operate exclusively online. In academia too, the Web has transformed research methods in the study of religion in general – not just NRMs – by the wealth of source material that is instantly available from one's desktop, and by the proliferation of electronic journals, some of which exist exclusively online such as *Diskus*, *The International Journal of Mormon Studies* and *Alternative Spirituality and Religion Review*.

In addition to the definitional problems already discussed, another pertinent issue lurking behind the term 'NRM' is whether our study of new religious movements perpetuates an unnatural distinction between 'new religions movements' and other forms of religion. Critics might assail NRM studies as reifying the boundary between centre and periphery, or mainstream and alternative. Some scholars of NRMs have in fact used just such language, referring to new religious movements as 'alternative' religions or as outside of the mainstream. According to this critique, by positioning our subject matter as something other than 'mainstream religion', we actually do rhetorical violence to our subjects. Certainly this criticism has some merit. To continue to define groups such as the Jehovah's Witnesses or Latter-day Saints as 'alternative religions' limits their ability to define themselves as the uniquely authentic versions of religious truth, from which other forms have deviated.

Yet this criticism fails to account for two important facts: that NRMs do in fact differ in significant ways from other religions, and that the voices of scholars of NRMs are not in fact the most influential ones when it comes to which religions are considered mainstream or alternative. To continue the examples of the Jehovah's Witnesses or Mormons, both groups continue to engage in religious practices and hold religious beliefs that mark them as quite dissimilar from the various traditions that are generally considered 'mainstream'. Jehovah's Witnesses do not celebrate the major Christian holidays, which is one of the fundamental markers in many contemporary societies of what marks a person as 'Christian'. Mormons possess their own religious scriptures, most notably the Book of Mormon, which they believe possesses equivalent revelatory authenticity and legitimacy to the Jewish-Christian scriptures. For most other Christians, whether they be Orthodox, Catholic or Protestant, this marks Mormons as distinctly other. By recognizing these two groups as 'alternative', scholars of NRMs are not so much reifying an artificial distinction between centre and periphery as they are recognizing a distinction that already exists within religious culture.

Numerous other new themes have attracted the attention of the most recent generation of scholars studying NRMs, themes explored in this volume. While researchers of the present and past are loathe to predict the future, it is fair to say that global society will continue to produce new religious movements, and scholars will continue to press on in studying these groups.

Part I
Research Methods and Problems

1 Fieldwork

Stephen E. Gregg

It has been previously noted that the post-1970s Study of New Religions entails an interdisciplinary methodological approach which has been 'created primarily on the basis of the cumulation of fieldwork research projects' (Bromley 2007a, 67). In the introduction to this volume, the editors have skilfully charted the development of this distinct discipline with regard to the wider Study of Religion and the Sociology of Religion and in this short chapter I wish to address the multi-methodological heritage of fieldwork research to explore its centrality to the study of new religions. It should be noted at the outset, however, that NRMs present a particularly challenging focus of study for fieldwork – often due to political or ethical issues that will be addressed below – but also simply for the fact that this relatively newly emergent academic discipline borrows from a diversity of methodologies which at the same time both enriches and 'complicates the task of assembling a coherent corpus of knowledge' (Bromley 2007a, 66). Perhaps unsurprisingly, therefore, the history of NRM scholarship is a history of diverse fieldwork methodologies complicated by both the evolving nature of the discipline within the Academy and also influenced by perceptions and understandings of NRMs within wider society. Central to many of these research projects, however, is the concept of *verstehen* (Barker 1984, 20), the Weberian terminology for *understanding* a belief or action within the social context relevant to the worldview of the individual or community in question. This has often been a challenging issue for NRM scholars due to the huge diversity of traditions bracketed within NRM studies, and also due to the sometimes countercultural or controversial nature of the customs and beliefs of the groups which are studied. But, as Whitehead (1987) has argued, detailed fieldwork is particularly central to the study of NRMs as 'if unfamiliar cultural systems are not substantially portrayed, they are easily reduced to silly stereotypes' (Whitehead 1987, 10).

Eileen Barker describes the ethical and political aspects of research as the ways in which 'we evaluate our own and others' construction of reality' (Barker 1995c, 7) and in so doing she highlights the problems of studying groups perceived to be controversial or problematic to 'mainstream' society. Key questions for NRM scholars in this respect are – what groups should be studied? (Bromley 2007a, 67), how should findings be written up? (Barker 1995c, 22) and how does one balance methodological agnosticism with participant observation? (Palmer 2010, xviii). Elisabeth Arweck (2006) has noted that the outcomes of research on NRMs often involve negotiation between subject and researcher, citing Wallis' *The Road to Total Freedom* (1976)[1] – a publication which was edited in negotiation with the Church of Scientology – as a prime example, where she argues that it is 'less easy to distinguish between primary [insider] and secondary [outsider] constructions' of reality (Arweck 2006, 64). Of course, this raises ethical as well as methodological issues, particularly with regard to the projection of a religious worldview by (or about) a group which may appear to be at odds to its documented actions or 'public' profile. This concern highlights Wallis' and Barker's understanding of the 'construction' of NRMs into 'externalist' and 'internalist' observations (Arweck 2006, 65) – a particular understanding of the insider/outsider issue within the study of religion which is specifically related to NRM studies by Chryssides in the relevant chapter of this volume.

Of course, 'Fieldwork' is rather a blunt instrument with which to describe a wide variety of research methodologies, and a deep discussion of wider methodological meanings is beyond the scope of this chapter. However, by 'Fieldwork' I encompass a range of methodologies from simple quantitative interviewing to deep qualitative 'full blown' ethnography. Below, I shall outline interesting case studies that utilize covert, overt and what I shall label qualified-externalist approaches. I shall end by suggesting some questions pertinent to the future development of fieldwork in NRM studies.

In an early example of fieldwork, first published in 1956 and based on research undertaken in 1954, Leon Festinger's *When Prophecy Fails* (Festinger et al. 2008 [1956]) utilized a covert form of surveillance to undertake a now (in)famous study of the Sananda movement in Chicago – a methodology which would make most modern University ethics committees run screaming to the hills. It should be remembered, though, that Festinger was not a specialist in Religion, but a scholar of Psychology who was using a religious group as a case study, more interested in confirming his own theory of 'cognitive dissonance' subsequent to a traumatic event in the life of the community than in understanding the worldview, ritual and actions of the group in normal religious life and practice. It should also be noted that the book was criticized for the ethical problems that arise from covert research at the time of the original publication (Festinger et al. ix). In the 1960s, John Lofland and Rodney Stark undertook covert research in 1962–3 to explore the process of conversion within the Unification Church in the Pacific Northwest of the United States (Lofland and Stark 1965). Like Festinger before them, they employed direct covert participant observation with the group, but also extended this to include interviews with etic voices – often friends and family members of converts. Similarly, in 1975, Balch and Taylor (Balch and Taylor 1977) 'joined' a movement in Oregon, USA to undertake covert research on a small UFO group – a group which would later come to world-prominence in religious movements as Heaven's Gate, whose members would commit mass suicide in 1997. In many ways, Balch and Taylor's research provokes the most interesting questions concerning the ethics and efficacy of covert research. Indeed, while acknowledging the ethical objections to their fieldwork, they note that, borrowing Goffman's term (Goffman 1959), they were able to gain access to the 'backstage region' of the movement and thus 'ask the right questions' of members and ex-members. Such a research method unquestionably opened up areas of knowledge that would be denied to overt researchers and, it may be argued, meant that the researchers were more effectively able to engage with the 'lived religion'[2] of the movement – akin to Malinowski's 'actions' of a social group (Parsons 2002) – rather than the 'represented religion' – akin to Malinowski's 'norms' of a social group – which was the normative projected 'party line' of the movement.

Subsequent to the early covert studies of NRMs, the field matured with what is rightly considered a classic of the genre – Eileen Barker's *The Making of a Moonie: Brainwashing or Choice?* (1984). An overt piece of research which centred upon in-depth interviews, participant observation and questionnaires (Barker 1984, 17), the work provides a pro-forma for any scholar starting out in their engagement with NRMs. Subsequent to Barker (although based on earlier research) Whitehead published *Renunciation and Reformulation: A Study of Conversion in an American Sect* (1987) which is an important study as it utilized contemporary anthropological methods – borrowing particularly from Levi-Strauss and Geertz – highlighting the dependence on much later NRM fieldwork on anthropological method and practice. Whitehead also stands apart for the simple fact that she provides one of the very few early academic explanations (as opposed to apostate polemic) of Scientology – it remains an invaluable source. Moving to more recent texts, Susan Palmer's overt research with the Nuwaubian Nation (Palmer 2010) is an interesting example of the methodological problems of a white woman researching a patriarchal black supremacist movement. Indeed, during her fieldwork, Palmer was 'accepted' by the community elders as a 'white angel' – a relational change which shifted her on the scale of 'externalist' and 'internalist' mode of research in the eyes of the movement. A final recent example of an interesting field study is Healy's *Yearning to Belong* (2010) which examines Guru-Disciple Yogic Traditions from the view of an ex-member. Such work lays important foundations for what may be described as a qualified-externalist approach in the understanding of movements without recourse to apostate polemic or disengaged externalism.

To conclude, I wish to raise one issue which I think will transform our understanding of what it means to 'perform' fieldwork in the study of NRMs – the issue of virtual religions. As the editors have outlined in their introduction, the internet has transformed academic engagement with NRMs over the last 20 years, but in the last few years a subtle shift has occurred. No longer is it simply the case that religions having a presence on the Web as a method and form of communication within their communities and to external communities, but it is now clear that religions are existing as web-based communities (Gelfgren 2010) – for example religions within Second Life (Barrett 2010), the teachings and communities of some Jedi Churches and the very New New Religion of Kopimism – a file-sharing anti-copyright movement recently recognized as a religion by the Swedish government (BBC 2012) – exist almost entirely online – a phenomenon linked to Campbell's conception of 'networked religion' (Campbell 2011b). If, therefore, a researcher reads postings in chatrooms or web fora is it meaningful to understand this as a form of covert research? How does one perform fieldwork when there is no physical 'field'? Even if you 'out' your Second Life avatar as a researcher there is a spacial and experiential distance created which radically alters how a generation of scholars brought up on physical engagement, embodied learning and participant observation relate to (and with) their subjects. The methodological development, study and 'performance' of fieldwork relating to new religious movements since 1945 has reflected the evolving approaches to NRMs, from both within the Academy and within wider society, and also the evolving nature of NRMs themselves. We've come a long way since Festinger. It's clear we've still got a long way to go.

Notes

1 It should be noted that this work was primarily a sociological survey of publically available material, rather than a close ethnographic study.
2 For more information on these terms, see Gregg and Scholefield, *Engaging with Living Religion* (London: Routledge, forthcoming 2014).

2 The Insider/Outsider Problem in the Study of NRMs

George D. Chryssides

The expression 'making the strange familiar and the familiar strange' possibly originates from the German poet Novalis (1772–1801), but it is better known among ethnographers. Prevalent media descriptions of so-called cults as 'bizarre' and 'wacky' highlight my challenging task as an NRM scholar of making sense of their worldviews. The idea that NRMs have an inside and an outside harks back to an early controversy in the study of religion, when writers such as Emile Durkheim, Rudolf Otto and Mircea Eliade defined religion in terms of 'the supernatural', 'the holy' and 'the sacred', indicating that its nature was *sui generis* and could not be grasped by those who had failed to experience it. The debate among anthropologists and philosophers as to how – or indeed whether – another culture, worldview or religion can be understood from outside continues.

Like most, but not all, researchers, I have investigated NRMs as an outsider. While some researchers distance themselves from the group under investigation, for example simply confining themselves to interviewing informants, my own preference has been to gain acquaintance with NRMs as lived religions, undertaking participant-observation or occasionally 'living in'. Such attempts to build a 'bridge of understanding' between researcher and NRM raise a variety of important issues. The first and most obvious one is evaluating my informants. Insiders are not homogeneous, and differ in terms of their time spent within the movement, their degree of acquaintance with their group's beliefs and practices, their stage on their spiritual path and their status within the organization. Such differences are interrelated, but not necessarily in proportion to each other. In Scientology, for example, where one's spiritual status is formally rated (pre-clear, clear, Operating Thetan), the leaders are not necessarily those with high Operating Thetan rankings.

The diversity and complexity of NRMs create serious ambiguities about 'inside' and 'outside'. As Helen Waterhouse points out, being an 'insider' to Buddhism does not necessarily promote one's understanding of the Soka Gakkai: on the contrary, Buddhists in Theravada tradition have a distinct lack of empathy for this organization, even going so far as to deny its claim to a Buddhist identity. Waterhouse also draws attention to ambiguities about what being an insider actually means: is a Soka Gakkai 'member' someone who attends meetings, someone who has formally applied for membership, someone who practises chanting or someone who owns a *gohonzon* (the principal ritual object)? Not all NRMs define membership in the same way; some are not membership organizations, and others have degrees of initiation, or different categories of membership – for example the Unification Church recognizes full-time membership, 'home church' membership and associate membership. Commitment is not an all-or-nothing matter, and most NRMs have seekers, acolytes, signed-up members and lapsed members. All of this serves to blur the insider/outsider distinction.

The participant-observer's presence can readily alter the phenomenon to be studied. I cannot readily ascertain how a group functions without my presence, and the anti-cult movement (ACM) frequently alleges that NRMs are adept at public relations exercises, particularly for visiting academics. Conversely, my own participation has an effect on the group; on various occasions I have been asked to contribute to discussions, say a prayer, and even give my testimony, all of which no doubt differ from typical insider contributions. The phenomenon contributes to 'cognitive contamination' – an expression devised by Peter Berger, and which Arweck develops further in the study of NRMs.

One strategy for reducing the disparity between researcher and subjects is covert research, in which the researcher assumes insider status as a piece of temporary role-play. Understandably the subjects of such research tend to resent it when it is discovered, and university ethics committees do not view it very favourably. Nonetheless, some important covert studies of NRMs have been carried out, such as Leon Festinger's *When Prophecy Fails*, John Lofland's *Doomsday Cult* and Robert W. Balch and David Taylor's 1975 research on the Heaven's Gate group. Such research does not eliminate the problem, however; as Festinger wrote, 'our influence on the group [was] somewhat greater than we would like' (1956, 253).

Participation inevitably raises the question of how much of my identity I am prepared to give up in participation, and how much of the NRMs' identity I allow to impinge on my personal life. In researching a religious group adherents may ask me details about myself, or my role as researcher may require participation in activities that run counter to my own convictions. Some researchers, such as David Gordon (1987), recommend maintaining a distance, even presenting arguments against what they hear. Others, such as Anthony Robbins (1973) prefer to avoid such discussion, believing that this distracts from the activity of data collection. Friendships may arise naturally from prolonged contact with informants, and in my own studies of Jehovah's Witnesses this has proved invaluable in creating trust and opening doors. However, it might be suspected that this compromises the researcher's role, making one more prone to portray the organization in more favourable light, since negative representation could be construed as betrayal and close the door to further cooperation. There can be no uniform answer to the question of imposing limits to participant-observation. In studying New York's Vodou community, Karen McCarthy Brown was prepared to undergo Vodou initiations, including a ritual marriage to the spirits Ogou and Danbala – a remedy her informant Mama Lola recommended to her for coping with personal difficulties in her life.

A further issue relates to the distinction between 'experience-near' and 'experience-distant', first made by psychoanalyst Heinz Kohut (1971) and now well-known in ethnography. The former concepts are those that are familiar to the group being studied (sometimes called 'emic' concepts), the latter are those used by the specialist researchers ('etic' vocabulary). The question of the relationship between these two sets of concepts can sometimes be problematic. In line with the Unification Church's preferences I am prepared to describe them as 'New Christian' rather than 'semi-Christian' or 'pseudo-Christian'. However, I am less sympathetic to ISKCON's insistence that it should not be described as an NRM. Organizationally, it is undoubtedly new, having been founded by Prabhupada in 1965, and no scholar can uncritically accept its claim to have ancient history going back to the third millennium BCE. Etic concepts belong to the scholar, not to the NRM.

My discussion so far presupposes that the scholar is the 'outsider', but this is not always the case, and a fair number of scholars are themselves aligned to NRMs. Their activity is 'reflexive ethnography': their community is not a strange world that needs to be made familiar to themselves, but rather a familiar world that needs also to be made familiar to others who perceive it as strange. The question of whether the believer or the unbeliever understands a religion better has no clear answer. The believer may have a more accurate understanding of his or her religion, greater empathy, and better access to information and relevant 'gatekeepers', while outsiders may contend that they have more objectivity, less uncritical acceptance of claims made by the religious group under study and the ability to entertain critical questions about an NRM.

I have commented on varieties of insider. However, there is also a multiplicity of outsider stakeholders. Arweck identifies several: the media, the ACM, ex-members, public authorities, the churches, lawyers, counsellors and of course academics. Arweck describes these as a 'chorus of voices', although perhaps 'cacophony' would be a more appropriate description, since they have different perspectives and agendas. Each of these sources has its own spectrum too: while some parts of the Christian Church align with the countercult movement, other factions are more open to dialogue. One particular category of outsider merits comment: the ex-member. Ex-members' testimony is given privileged status by the anti-cult and countercult movements. Those who gain prominence tend to be vocal, and they are frequently presented as heroes: victims, survivors, sometimes escapees, or people who have been 'rescued' from a 'destructive cult'. At times they claim a superior vantage point: they have allegedly seen both sides of the 'cult', being erstwhile insiders who have had the scales removed from their eyes. (Of course, members could equally claim to have seen both sides: they have once been blind to the truth, but now can see.) Beckford, however, places a different interpretation on the ex-member: whatever the cause of apostasy, the ex-member is frequently embarrassed at having joined the NRM in the first place, and devises a scenario to account for his or her initial involvement, often involving 'brainwashing' allegations (Beckford 1985, 197).

More research needs to be carried out on ex-members. Although disaffected members have louder 'voices', others have left without necessarily becoming disenchanted. Former members whom I have met have had quite mundane reasons for lapsed allegiance: one did not like going out in the dark to attend meetings; another thought her Dianetics course was 'quite good' but saw no reason to take a subsequent one. Further research is needed to ascertain fuller reasons for disengagement and provide more detailed profiling of ex-members. Ex-members too may have left the organization, but continue with its practices – as has been known to happen with some ISKCON devotees, blurring even further the insider/outsider distinction.

My discussion has indicated that insiders and outsiders – in both old and new religions – are not simply two sets of voices, but sound a complexity of often discordant notes. Amidst the cacophony, the researcher's role is perhaps like the conductor of this inharmonious choir, bringing in the different voices where their contributions are needed. There may never be a melodious outcome, but at least we can endeavour to resolve some of the more strident discords.

3 Material Culture

Alex Norman

Chapter Outline

What is 'Material Culture'?	34
Material Culture and NRM Studies	34

While much of the early study of religions focused on belief and texts, the study of material culture and religions is relatively new. Indeed, the study of material religion itself is a recent development in the fields of archaeology and anthropology. The focus of such study includes folklife, cultural geography, architecture, landscape, decorative arts, and archaeological findings, though it should be noted that archaeology has, by definition, only limited contributions to make to the study of NRMs new religious movements (NRMs) as they are 'new'. For the study of this presents a valuable contribution to scholarly knowledge, for above all what material culture looks for is the intrusion of the human on the environment. Examples such as the temple architecture of the Bahá'í, the candles and incense of new age practitioners or reappropriated sites such as Stonehenge come easily to mind. However, the study of material culture and NRMs ought to seek more than such high visibility markers. The fashioning, shaping, and arranging of the world that arises from an assumed distinction between nature and culture results in worldview being inscribed constantly and everywhere (Glassie 1999). Accordingly, the study of NRMs and material culture involves seeking objects that people have used in their lives broadly, not just in explicitly religious ceremonies or rituals, as they bear traces of the everyday articulation of worldview by religious practitioners.

What is 'Material Culture'?

Lest confusion arise, however, it should be clear that the study of material culture and NRMs does not involve looking for objects alone. E. B. Tylor's famous pronouncement that culture is 'that complex whole which includes knowledge, belief, art, law, morals, custom, and any other capabilities and habits acquired by man as a member of society' (1903, 1), serves to remind us that culture is more than simply things. The date, provenance, and style of an object are of importance, but only initially. What is of more interest, especially to the scholar of religion is the use, particularly in terms of the role of the object in the world and the worldview of the practitioner. Consequently, we must also search for evidence of the circulation, use, mediation and common meanings understood for objects. Material things, their symbolic value, and their use are central in attempting to conceptually organize accounts of human cultures through time and space (Hicks 2010). To organize accounts of NRMs we then need to look for such things as clothing (for example), its use, the norms and mores associated with it, how it is implemented in religious practice and in secular life and how it is disposed of once its function or value has ceased. This means that central to the study of the material culture of NRMs are bodies and how they put things to work together in order to produce outcomes in relation to worldview. What is clear in attempting to draw up a list of examples of the material cultures of NRMs, is how familiar one must be with a religious tradition in order to have a sense of its materiality. In order to achieve this, scholars must engage not simply in the study of surface features of groups, but in rich description and careful analysis of the contents, functions and symbolic interactions of religions. Methodologically this requires time and an interdisciplinary commitment from the researcher, and speaks to the value of material culture in the study of NRMs, as it suggests that our principal means of accessing them is their very materiality.

Material Culture and NRM Studies

Taking a cue from the editors of the journal *Material Religion* (Meyer et al. 2010), the focus for scholars interested in NRMs and their material culture should be placed on bodies, things, places and practices. In many respects there can be 'no such thing as immaterial religion' (Meyer et al. 2010, 201); certainly not as far as the academic study of it is concerned. The central question for the present chapter must therefore be concerned with how NRMs occur, materially. This is distinct from the question of how religion is expressed. The assumption is that the study of material culture and religion should look not for things that are mixed in with religion, but for things that are inextricable from it. Indeed, materializing the study of religion helps steer discussions away from understandings that identify certain figures or beliefs as the irreducible core of 'religion'. Belief, common as a definitional component of religion, has little relevance in the study of material culture beyond speculation and inference. That is, belief is fundamentally immaterial; it is, however, materialized in the practice of religions and especially in its inscription onto bodies, things and places. The study of material culture therefore accounts for belief by commenting on what is actually done by practitioners. This, of course, is problematic; belief can be inferred from objects, but it can also be faked, or mistaken by the observer. The study of material culture and religions thus places greatest emphasis on practice, going against the dominant course of the academic study of religions that emphasized texts and beliefs (following the hegemonic Protestant Christian model). Importantly, belief can be understood materially in the way that it configures the material world. For the believer there is an expectation about bodies, about things, and about practices, all of which help to shape the world they live in. Indeed, a wholly immaterial religion is hard to conceive.

The study of material culture and religion thus moves away from the metaphysical-textual hegemony that was born from the Western European study of religions. Anthropology, in particular, has offered a methodological counterpoint to this in the form of ethnography. Studies emerging from this tradition have yielded fascinating insights to the variety of ways belief and worldview can be materialized by practitioners of NRMs. Zeller's (2012) analysis of food practices in the Hare Krishna movement provides a useful example. The growing, preparation, and eating of food is, of course, thoroughly material, but so too are the seemingly theologically unimportant cookbooks that are found in many Hare Krishna households. These not only advise on culinary method, but on theological rationale, offering practical avenues for believers to manifest their devotion to Krishna. As Zeller argues, the cookbooks 'encapsulate ISKCON food practices and create a foodway, or food culture, a system of relating to food that encompasses rules, traditions, recipes, and mores' (Zeller 2012, 692). This materialization of the NRM provides a crucial access point and agency not only for believers to express their beliefs, but for scholars too, who are provided substantial, empirical evidence of lived religiosity.

Similar examples of material culture access for NRM studies can be found in Pagan traditions. Rountree (2010, 47) notes of Maltese Pagans that 'the Pagan identity of most . . . was outwardly unreadable most of the time, unless you happened to recognize the dainty tattooed anklet of Pagan runes or the *ankh* pendant they wore.' In a social context within which Pagan beliefs and practices are seen as heretical and breaking social norms, many individual Pagans choose to materialize their religion carefully, often privately. Aspects of material culture here, in particular their use and mediation, explicate not only the worldview of practitioners, but the prevailing social norms and mores against which they are contrasted. That we can understand the symbolic aspect of the object for the believer is, clearly, important, but so too is the way in which it is hidden from public scrutiny. The material dimension here tells us also about the social context in which a tradition is operating.

New Age religions have had no shortage of cultural criticism for their putative materialistic bent. Certainly Antoine Faivre's (1994) typology of New Age beliefs identifies mediation through symbolic images, sacred objects or mandalas as a core typological component. The use and circulation of Tarot cards, healing crystals and amulets have become synonymous with New Age religiosity. Further, the Mind Body Spirit Festival phenomenon, that can be found around the world, reminds us that the material cultures of NRMs can find their way into the lives of believers as well as the merely curious (Hamilton 2000). The use of these objects is characterized as variegated in intent and method between individuals, paralleling the general theoretical consensus that views New Age spirituality as eclectic (Sutcliffe 2003a). We can also find the New Age inscribed on the landscape itself with locations such as Glastonbury and Findhorn now functioning much like pilgrimage sites (Bowman 2008; Sutcliffe 2003a). These multifarious NRM material cultures provide scholars with valuable empirical data on economics, politics, folkways, foodways, indeed the full range of a NRM's social milieu is opened up through the study of its material culture.

As these examples illustrate, rather than focusing on the style or form of objects alone, scholarship in material culture and NRMs looks to intention and use to illustrate the lived dimension of religions. Understanding material culture is at the heart of religious studies. Religions cannot operate immaterially, nor can they do away with practices concerned with mediation, use and circulation of the material. Indeed, often the only points of access scholars of NRMs have with them are through points of mediation or use of their materiality. We must be sure to include the embodiment of belief in our study of NRMs. Further, if our approach to the study of humanity is to be empirical we must emphasize that the contents of the belief systems we encounter are shaped by the social and physical world around them.

4 Pagan Studies

Graham Harvey

Paganism is a new religion that is evolving within the modernist West, drawing on older influences to engage with contemporary concerns. These basic facts generate much of the programme of Pagan Studies. The gift of being able to observe a new religion in the making, and as it diversifies, engages with wider movements and contributes to the larger world, has proved exciting for scholars in many disciplines (e.g. Religious Studies, History, Sociology, Anthropology, Cultural Studies, Gender Studies and Folklore). Attention seems to be deliberately drawn to the newness of Paganism by the North American preference for the term 'Neopaganism' (or 'neo-Paganism'). However, wider reference to 'Paganism' without the addition of 'neo' should not be taken as an emphasis on older inheritances, but perhaps as disinterest in making an issue of origins.

Briefly stated, the influences that have shaped Paganism include a heady brew of classicism, romanticism, celticism, naturalism, naturism, anti-clericalism, ritualism, bardism, esotericism, individualism, communitarianism, evolutionism, feminism, anarchism, rationalism, different kinds of activism (from anti-war, pro-festivals, anti-globalization, and pro-justice movements to climate change and occupy movements) and some folk and rural traditions. Quite evidently, some of these conflict with each other and their mixtures do not always result in experiences or systems that seem coherent to insiders let alone to outsiders. Indeed, it is often the experimental and fluid nature of Paganism, resulting from such fusions and entanglements, that suggests topics for research, teaching and discussion.

Academic interest in Paganism was initially represented in entries in encyclopedias surveying contemporary religions or new religious movements (such as Gordon Melton's *Encyclopedia of American Religions*, 1978). A carefully researched book by the journalist Margo Adler, *Drawing Down the Moon* (1979), provided a foundational overview – and later editions remain important. In the 1980s, Paganism was included in courses concerned with 'new religions' or 'NRMs'. Only in Continuing Education or Adult Education centres (e.g. at London's WEA centres) were there any short courses about Paganism, but these did not result in academic qualifications or credits. Mostly they introduced popular elements of Paganism such as magic, witchcraft and/or esotericism. Research by anthropologists (such as Tanya Luhrmann) and historians (such as

Ronald Hutton) began to result in doctoral theses and publications in the 1980s and 1990s. Growing interest in Goddess Spirituality among feminist scholars resulted in theological works such as Carol Christ's *Laughter of Aphrodite* (1987). A series of international conferences at Bath Spa, Newcastle upon Tyne, Lancaster and Winchester in the 1990s brought researchers and practitioners together to debate interdisciplinary approaches and understandings.

The establishment in 1996 by Chas Clifton (Colorado State University) of the Nature Religions Scholars Network email discussion list signalled interest in Paganism among scholars debating 'religion and ecology' or 'religion and nature'. By 2005 members of that group had formed a separate unit within the American Academy of Religion (AAR) identified as 'Contemporary Pagan Studies'. While still offering papers to new religions, religion and ecology, and other units in the AAR's annual conference, the existence of a dedicated group indicates the maturing of Pagan Studies in its own right. The establishment of an international, peer-reviewed journal, *The Pomegranate*, not only provides a venue for disseminating and debating research about Paganism but also further distinguishes such work from that regarding other religions.

Paganism is rarely if ever the sole subject of a taught course or module. Sometimes it is considered alongside either 'esotericism' (from which it inherited ritual patterns and magical theories) or 'New Age' (which is also a 'democratised esotericism' in Hanegraaff's terms but has not so radically embraced nature or embodiment). Paganism is most likely to be included as one religion among many in modules devoted to new or contemporary religions. Approaches to it depend on specific disciplinary interests and methods, but generally it is the practice or performance of Paganism that is the focus of attention rather than any textual or elite tradition. Questions about nature, ritual and gender predominate among the critical themes interrogated through attention to Pagan practice and rhetoric. But there is also interest in social dynamics, relations with other traditions including Christianity (Pearson 2007), indigenous religions (Welch 2007), and secularization, especially arising from contestations of modernist disenchantment (Partridge 2004, 2005).

Much of the research about Paganism has been qualitative but quantitative surveys occasionally address the question of how many Pagans there are. It is generally agreed that no precise answer can be given because of the nature of Pagan affiliation and self-identification. That is, Pagans do not all belong to groups, even in their immediate locality or nation state, and many identify with more than one organization or subscribe to several publications. The frequent assertion that 'Paganism is a fast growing religion' is usually based on unsystematic observations of increasing numbers of participants in Pagan festivals, public rituals or pub 'moots', or in increasing subscriptions to Pagan magazines. The most comprehensive quantitative survey of Pagan affiliations and attitudes was conducted in the United States in the 1990s (Berger, Leach and

Shaffer 2004) and is currently being updated. Some national censuses (e.g. those in the United Kingdom) and attitude surveys (e.g. the European Values Survey) have also provided useful data about age and gender profiles and about the complex interplay of individualism and communal values among Pagans (Lassander 2009).

Among the demographic changes that have become evident in both qualitative and quantitative research is an increase of young people identifying as Pagans either within Pagan families or as newcomers. The latter have given rise to the label 'teen-witches', but are evident among other kinds of Paganism. They are one result of the complex interaction between this religion and popular culture, especially in the form of TV and films aimed at younger audiences (e.g. *Charmed* and *Buffy*). This is not to dismiss the phenomenon as a fad but to value it as, among other possibilities, further evidence of the need to clarify contemporary processes and discourses of enchantment along with dis- and re-enchantment.

Paganism was first popularized by self-identified Witches or Wiccans in the United Kingdom (people like Gerald Gardner and Alex and Maxine Saunders) and then globally – but predominantly in Europe and its (ex-)colonies. Its diversification has included the rapid growth of different kinds of Paganism: initially Druidry, Heathenry and Goddess Feminism but more recently many kinds of 'ethnic' Paganism derived from particular cultures, for example the Slavic 'Native Faith' movements. Pagan debates about ethnicity and other forms of heritage continue to attract scholarly attention (e.g. Strmiska 2005). Similarly, questions about Pagan relations with indigenous peoples and their religious ceremonies (e.g. the Lakota style 'sweat lodge') are debated by Pagans, indigenous peoples and the scholars interested in both (broad) communities.

In addition, Paganism attracts academic attention for its potential for testing emerging critical issues. The Pagan choice of ritual rather than text-use or creed as a defining centre challenged the trajectory of Protestant Christian and Enlightenment anti-ritualism and, therefore, serves as a laboratory in which to test theories about disenchantment, communitas and the value of cognitive or performative approaches. Following a 'performative turn' in religious studies, a more recent 'material turn' has also found a focus for study in Pagan material culture, for example the veneration of statues, the use of amulets, the construction of altars and 'magical' jewellery. The frequent identification of Paganism as a 'nature religion' contributes significantly here. Although 'nature' is a polyvalent term (embracing everything from romanticism and ruralism to localism and animism) it intersects with current interdisciplinary interests in embodiment, emplacement and performance.

Tensions within Paganism arising from the blending of originally distinct influences (as noted above) impact on emerging debates among Pagans about activism and ethics. One of the more fertile tensions is that between esotericism (efforts to improve an individual's true / inner self) and animism (treating the world as a multi-species relational community). Again, this invites engagement by scholars testing theories about personhood, relationality, individualism, community-building and a range of themes. It also illustrates a way in which Pagan ideas and practices sometimes evolve following encounters with academic publications or speakers. Pagans are voracious readers of many genres (from botanical books to fantasy novels) and seem determined to read and respond to everything academics write or say about them.

It is noteworthy, in this context especially, that many but not all of the scholars who research among or teach about Paganism are themselves Pagans (myself included). This is hardly unique to Paganism but, as elsewhere, causes consternation among those who promote what they imagine to be 'scientific' or 'objective' approaches. It is true that Pagan Studies can be conducted with the benefit of the Pagan community in mind. It can also generate largely descriptive representations (e.g. merely applying an existing analysis to a differently located group). While these rarely get through peer-review into publication, they may aid students to appreciate an issue when they see it as having local impact. Generally, scholars of Paganism (whether they identify as Pagans or as not-Pagans) reflect on their positions and approaches in relation to those they research or teach about. It could be said that they are testing more relational than objectivist scholarly practices. Certainly, however, Pagan Studies does not take place in a Pagan enclave but is thoroughly in touch with wider disciplinary and interdisciplinary matters.

5 New Age

Steven J. Sutcliffe

'New age' is among the most disputed of categories in the study of new religions in terms of finding agreement on the specific content, structure, boundaries and impact of the phenomenon. Since such disputes reproduce in miniature a much wider debate about the cross-cultural stability of content and clarity of boundaries of the category 'religion', the study of New Age tantalisingly reproduces issues central to the study of religion in the modern world. This gives added theoretical value to the revitalized 'big picture' approach to the study of New Age for which I argue below.

Given the apparent profusion of New Age beliefs and practices, a useful preliminary distinction can be made between New Age in a strict and limited sense – *sensu stricto* – and New Age in a more broad and diffuse sense – *sensu lato*, following Hanegraaff's model (1996). In terms of the earliest sense – New Age *sensu stricto* – a fine-grained modern social history can be reconstructed of practitioners' uses of the term 'new age' as a millennialistic signifier for an imminent new era or collective moment of awakening, which believers expected (and in some cases, still expect) to dawn in the wake of a global catastrophe of economic, military or ecological dimensions (Sutcliffe 2003a). This usage of 'New Age' is typical of the period between the 1920s/1930s and the mid-to-late 1960s and is characterized by an ascetical, supernatural and 'other-worldly' orientation ascribed to 'the coming new age', understood as an objective event heralded by transcendent beings. Since the 1970s, however, New Age has typically been used as an umbrella label for a more 'this-worldly', corporeal and even sensual cluster of beliefs and practices promoting an expanded sense of spirituality, practical healing and enhanced insight and knowledge, set within a re-enchanted cosmos populated by a variety of deities and powers, but with the 'spiritual growth' of human beings placed firmly at its centre. This more broad and diffuse worldview – New Age *sensu lato* – is strongly immanentist and retains only traces of the original millennialistic goal in the form of the transformative expectations which are attached to its typical components, such as the many body practices for cultivating insight, healing and well-being, divinatory and mediumistic techniques, or the popular discourse on a revivified 'spirituality' adapted to post-industrial societies. These more diffuse *sensu lato* expressions are marked locally by both popular and countercultural (culture-critical) influences, and in many cases travel under new names such as 'holistic' or 'mind body and spirit', or revived rubrics such as 'occult' or 'esoteric', use of which stretches back to the late nineteenth century. These *sensu lato* expressions tend to blur boundaries between expressions of 'religion' and 'culture', they dilute *sensu stricto* expressions of millennialistic change into a vaguer interest in 'transformation' and they lack the strong structures and authorities of prototypical religious organizations. In these and related respects they challenge researchers working with more formative models of new religious movements or with traditional models of 'religion'. As a result New Age beliefs and practices have remained analytically elusive despite their increased visibility in many societies.

If we accept that beneath the surface of changing names and fluid structures there exists a more-or-less coherent yet dispersed field of beliefs and practices, an immediate problem is what to call it. A combination of tension between other-worldly (*sensu stricto*) and this-worldly (*sensu lato*) frames of reference, plus the hyper-inclusivity of content in respect of *sensu lato* forms, has encouraged a proliferation of descriptors at both popular and academic levels. This is seen most obviously in the multiplicity of surrogate names in use, often in one and the same event or publication, such as 'holistic', 'esoteric' and plain 'spiritual'. Hybrid forms such as 'Jew Age' (Ruah-Midbar and Klin-Oron 2010) and analog terms such as 'Next Age' (Introvigne 2001) have further relaxed border 'check points' and fostered migration of key *sensu lato* themes and practices into neighbouring formations.

This organic growth in terminologies is reflected in the rather haphazard accumulation of academic descriptions of New Age rather than the more unified theoretical model developed through critique and debate that one might hope for. For example, representations of New Age in North America have tended to include new Pagan identities and practices whereas in Europe the two groups have been more sharply separated out; this *laissez-faire* outcome should be probed further by examining the role of practitioners themselves in shaping categorical outcomes for particular tactical ends. Another example of the 'defocusing' impact of methodological toleration in New Age studies is the coexistence of significant historiographical differences between on the one hand genealogies of New Age within 'western esotericism' (Hanegraaff 1996) and on the other hand within a social and cultural history of popular practices and dispositions (Sutcliffe 2003a); while the two are not mutually exclusive, there are significant differences between methodologies and outcomes in these and related approaches which deserve closer engagement. The overall picture is one of aggregation rather than argument in which 'New Age' has come to signify different things among different academic constituencies, tending to theoretical fissiparity rather than focus.

As with definitions of 'religion', this dissensus about a common object of study has generated some rich and lively exchanges. But more than 25 years since the first peer-reviewed academic article (Sebald 1984), the subfield of 'New Age Studies' has not produced a clear set of cumulative and synergistic research questions. The main question has remained the problem of demarcating 'New Age' phenomena within wider cultural formations (Chryssides 2007; Hess 1993; Klippenstein 2005). Certainly this issue remains pertinent, not least within an unsympathetic wider taxonomy of 'world religions' which residualizes the raw and liquid phenomena of New Age. But if the question of demarcation is not incorporated within a more ambitious research programme, it will atrophy. Sutcliffe (2003b) argues that scholarly interests have in fact devolved from the 'first wave' of macro-level analyses of the content and boundaries of the so-called New Age Movement (Heelas 1996; York 1995) towards what he identifies as a 'second wave' of more localized, variegated and contextualized studies. This second wave has produced rich micro-level ethnographies and histories: for example, Bender (2007) on American reincarnation narratives, Macpherson (2008) on reiki in Scotland and Gilhus (2012) on angels in Norway. It has also fostered mid-range or meso-level analyses of local and regional dynamics: for example, Possamai (2006) on detraditionalized spiritual 'seekers' in Melbourne, Australia; Wood (2007) on the social class dynamics of small groups in the English East Midlands; and Mulholland (2011) on the psychologically 'compensatory' function of New Age in post-'Celtic Tiger' Ireland.

The second wave is devolved and centrifugal in method, taking its lead from the empirical data and unpacking them within specific contexts in an increasingly globalized geography (Frisk 2007b; Rothstein 2001). As a result we now know much more about the interaction between particular beliefs and practices and the dominant culture in specific locations and circumstances. These lines of enquiry are likely to blossom further as more scholars turn their attention to practices and beliefs which until recently have been considered aesthetically and intellectually marginal or subaltern from the perspective of more conservative academic methodologies. Such practices are now being reclaimed within burgeoning studies of the popular, especially within cultural studies broadly conceived where they are often an object of personal interest for the scholar herself: for example, Ross (1991) on the subjective attractions of 'softer' New Age science and technology, and Barcan (2011) on the allure of 'complementary' healthcare in secular modernity.

The risk with the 'second wave' of studies, however, is that, as with assumptions about the self-evident status of the larger category 'religion', the form, content and structure of the core beliefs and practices are taken for granted as the scholar becomes absorbed in questions of context, interpretation and reception. Because this kind of work is increasingly being pursued out with religious studies departments, scholars may in any case be less well versed in wider theories of religion. In order therefore to complement the rich mosaic yielded by the 'centrifugalists', I would like to sketch four avenues of interlinked 'centripetal' enquiry which seek to focus the theoretical and comparative potential of new age within the systematic study of religion.

First, there is room for new macro-theoretical approaches in which New Age is tackled not in relation to 'new religious movements', as in the first wave, but in relation to specified general theories of 'religion' (Sutcliffe and Gilhus 2013). For example, there is room to develop cognitive studies of the mechanisms behind the spread and appeal of New Age ideas and practices; to further analyse New Age practices within a comparative study of folk and popular religion; and not least to theorize New Age data as Durkheimian 'elementary forms' of religion – no longer collected on far-flung colonial frontiers but in the streets, homes and businesses of modern Western societies.

Second, the field requires more nuanced histories of the modern networks and enclaves of 'alternative spirituality' from which New Age beliefs and practices emerged, especially in the first half of the twentieth century. A fuller set of social and cultural histories will also help to differentiate the historiography of religion in modernity, especially in the European and American heartlands of New Age. This requires in the first instance a detailed mapping of the modern historical and spatial distension of the 'cultic milieu' (Campbell 1972) which has served as a matrix both for the production of new expressions of 'spirituality', and as a resource for the growth of specific new religions.

Third, the relationship between New Age in the 1970s and 1980s and the multilateral contemporary discourse on 'spirituality' in various spaces and disciplines – Christian, healthcare, psychotherapy, social work – merits sustained discourse analysis. The popular language of 'spirituality' emerged as a *lingua franca* around the time of decline in usage of New Age *sensu stricto* but we know surprisingly little about its subtle conditions of emergence despite its near-ubiquitous uptake across a range of domains. An examination of themes and tropes entering the discourse on popular spirituality from New Age circles would be illuminating and timely.

Fourth, more nuanced attention is required to the cultural capital provided by New Age beliefs and practices for certain social groups – especially middle and lower middle classes – within modern risk societies. The economic and ideological commitments of New Age and holistic formations require to be teased out with sensitivity: for example, the analyses of 'New Age capitalism' and 'capitalist spirituality' respectively by Lau (2000) and Carrette and King (2005) raise pertinent issues but suffer from rather polarized arguments as Heelas (2008) has shown. A more sensitive and integrated approach could involve analysing core values of New Age *sensu lato* – especially subjectivity, self-reliance and voluntarism – as ingredients in the creation of 'spiritual capital' (Verter 2003). This new form of symbolic capital could assist in negotiating detraditionalized identities and statuses among the middle and lower middle classes, and for articulating the interests of emerging middle classes, especially within marketized economies. A spiritual capital analysis could also help to understand the parallel development of a more critical, countercultural strain of the same core values, but now developed in the service of vitalistic, sustainable and ecological lifestyles.

These four fresh avenues of enquiry, some already in progress, contain diverse emphases but share a commitment to producing a theoretical big picture of New Age in the context of general models of religion. Taking up the challenges of a 'third wave' of New Age studies focused on macro-level analysis will repay the investment of second wave scholars and reward the foresight of the first wave pioneers who put New Age on the scholarly radar. It will help to move the study of New Age phenomena from the margins and towards the centre of the modern study of religion.

6 Mormon Studies

Douglas J. Davies

Chapter Outline	
Self-identity, Reflexivity: Sensitivity and Desire	47
History, Faithful and Critical	48
Insider/Outsider	50

Research Methods and Problems in Mormon Studies reflect the study of Christianity in microcosm. As with Christianity's emergence from Judaism, even the question of whether this group should be classified as 'new' is beset with difficulties. Further issues of identity, authenticity, and group conflicts surround the very name 'Mormonism', one often disliked by members as a disparagement by critical outsiders. If we add to this the role of research by members, their engagement with critics and potential friends, then Mormonism's microcosm of Christianity's macrocosm becomes clearer still.

Self-identity, Reflexivity: Sensitivity and Desire

How, then, should researchers name this group that was formally inaugurated in the United States in 1830 as The Church of Christ? Earliest members, clustering around the founding prophet Joseph Smith, were loosely described as the Church of the Latter-day Saints until a formal revelation of 1838 (*Doctrine and Covenants* 115: 3, 4) announced the name – The Church of Jesus Christ of Latter-day Saints, often abbreviated to LDS. Much name giving and calling depends upon intention: in 1995, for example, leaders adjusted visual presentations by increasing the font size of 'Jesus Christ' and reducing that of 'The Church of . . . of Latter-day Saints' while, in 2001, leaders expressed a preference for 'the Church of Jesus Christ' while affirming the full, revelation-given, earlier title.

Following Joseph Smith's murder in 1844 the larger group of members migrated, becoming established in Utah as the Mormonism best known to outsiders. Others did not migrate, but gathered around other leaders as with the Reorganized Church of Jesus Christ of Latter Day Saints (RLDS – now called the Community of Christ) who developed a sizeable following in Missouri with Independence as their headquarters and, until 1996, were led by lineal descendants of Joseph Smith. The subtle distinction between the nominal format 'Latter-day' (LDS) and 'Latter Day' (RLDS) Saints has demarcated these groups for years. In 1972 the RLDS renamed themselves 'the Saints Church' and, in 2001 the 'Community of Christ', reflecting their theology as more Protestant mainstream: they did not follow the temple-ritual-exaltation developments of the LDS. Yet others followed James Strang in his strongly sabbatarian and Israel-like island community in Lake Michigan (Davies 2010, 21–56). One other contemporary stream, often called Mormon Fundamentalist churches, lie outside the Utah church that they regard as having abandoned the exaltation-doctrine of plural marriage in the 1880–1920s period. Theoretically speaking, it is notable that Mormon 'Fundamentalism' focuses on the practice of polygyny and not as with, for example, Protestant 'Fundamentalism' and its stress on biblical literalism.

All these variants reflect aspects of 'the restored gospel' and offer researchers comparative materials for understanding what all devotees emphasize as the 'restoration' of truth and church order by God. None would self-identify as a 'new' religious movement, a terminological issue also of relevance for researchers as is the issue of whether Mormonism should be regarded as a new world religion. American sociologist Rodney Stark (1984) offered statistical projections depicting Mormon growth that might mirror that of Islam, suggesting that by 2050 there would be between 29 and 79 million Mormons in the world. In 2012 there are some 14 million on the books, though the dedicatedly active are more difficult to ascertain. While both 'new' and 'world religion' terminology carries an appeal of success for church leaders they often also wish to retain a strong 'Christian' identity, one that several major Christian traditions dispute. Here, again, formal descriptions encapsulate values and aspirations of identity valuable to researchers.

History, Faithful and Critical

Within its strong self-identity and divergence from established Christian groups, the LDS tradition has long advocated learning and knowledge. Joseph Smith's School of the Prophets (1833–6) helped core leaders engage with biblical language and thought while, today, Brigham Young University at Provo, Utah, stands as a flagship of learning across all disciplines: local churches run

'Seminary' at early morning doctrinal study-centres. Institutional reflexivity is also evident in the remarkable fact that earliest Mormonism, though an essentially millenarian group, established a Church Historian to keep formal records that complemented Joseph Smith's narrative of his own life-experience and reception of revelations and which continue in personal and family journals, in extensive genealogical research underpinning temple rites for the dead, and in recorded patriarchal blessings formally given to individuals.

Mormonism is history-rich which poses major challenges of engagement with historical material almost irrespective of the major focus of research. History can, however, be problematic as well as succoring, especially when, as for much of the later twentieth century, commentators pinpointed 'history' as the way in which Mormons conducted their 'theology'. Indeed, it was sometimes said that history replaced theology which made sense of the Restoration of divine truth and church organization as recorded, sequential phenomena. In scholarly terms, however, it becomes problematic as to how such phenomena should be appropriately identified. When is a narrative of personal experience a clear and verifiable account of 'actual' events, and when is it a description of personal emotions and reconstructed scenarios? Did Joseph Smith's First Vision, formally committed to writing in 1832, take place in 1820 or 1823; had a single divine Father or both the Father and his Son appeared in it? And what of angelic visitations and revelations to Joseph Smith allied with his finding the hidden plates depicting ancient cultural life in America of groups that had migrated from Israel? Such issues were and are open to historical, theological, and confessional consideration as are many religious phenomena including appearances of the Virgin Mary, the reception of stigmata in Catholic cultures or the resurrection and miracles in Christianity at large. The issue of faith in interpreting these remains paramount, posing appropriate research approaches for LDS and non-LDS alike. Because Mormonism is, sociologically speaking, a 'new religious movement', emerging in recent times when newspapers, books, pamphlets, and legal records were all extensive, the capacity for critical analysis and disagreement is enormous. The further capacity of archaeology and even of genetics to subject LDS claims of ancient migrations from Israel to Meso-America opens up realms with significant consequences for both church members, anti-church groups and for strictly academic researchers. The very phrase 'faithful history' typified some of these issues, marking the interface of faith and of historical analysis. Some interesting dimensions of more recent LDS self-reflection have included technical study of early Christianity, biblical languages, with Patristic theologies also considered to see what authentic teaching was lost or retained in the sub-apostolic Christian period and now fully restored through Joseph from the 1830s.

Just how church leaders, who may often have no expertise in these academic fields but who ultimately control access to some key church archive material, deal with diverse interpretations poses its own issue for researching Mormons. Further issues emerge from formal excommunication of some whose interpretations pass beyond bounds of acceptability, and the existence of individuals and groups holding divergent and diverse ideas, as well as numerous anti-Mormon individuals and groups, all raise issues for LDS scholars and, certainly, for non-LDS researchers in Mormonism.

Insider/Outsider

These themes of orthodoxy, heterodoxy, heresy, and varied opinion raise in distinctive ways this insider/outsider issue, a concept of considerable yet complex status in the study of religion. In Mormon Studies the fact that non-members are not allowed inside LDS temples where some of the most crucial rituals of salvation, or exaltation in LDS terms, are conducted makes the point. Moreover, members are honour bound not to disclose their temple knowledge. Non-members do, occasionally, have opportunity to enter a temple prior to its consecration after building or refurbishment: they see ritual space but no ritual. All may, by contrast, participate in local church buildings and rites. While some faithful Saints do feel able to discuss some appropriate aspects of their temple experience, numerous dissident Mormons have advertised their knowledge and the internet has ensured that practically nothing remains secret. Still, both LDS and non-LDS researchers are limited in what they can say publicly. In technical terms such issues led to my own non-LDS researcher's analysis of what I called 'sacred-secrecy' (Davies 2000, 80–2).

This kind of issue highlights ethical aspects of research in terms of what to say about what one knows, what knowledge is appropriately public, and how writing influences one's relationships with members. Once it was easy for anthropologists to study distant preliterate groups and rehearse their findings 'back home' to highly literate readership, but times have changed. The LDS are a highly literate people and one often studies them amidst one's own broad culture. However, it is not simply, or not even, the fact that what one writes will be read by LDS that matters, for prime ethical issues concern the dignity of the 'subject' as the researcher has engaged and continues to engage with him or her. Moreover, to invoke gender is to note that the LDS emphasize a male–female division of ritual and domestic labour in terms of ultimate salvation in eternal family groups with significant consequences for the topics of single people, feminism, divorce and homosexuality. The task of understanding and reporting these domains carries its own gravity of emphasis, potential personal bias, and the ongoing venture of maintaining and developing relationships with the overall LDS world and its sub-sets.

These issues demonstrate the need for methodological care both in the study of the complex sense of changing identity of religious groups and of researchers. They highlight the importance of the historical frame of reference underlying changes in identity, and the awareness that some new religious groups grow older as do some researchers whose ethical sense of their work carries importance for their ongoing engagement with group members.

7 Japanese NRMs

Birgit Staemmler

As in any other country, too, Japanese new religions were highly influenced by their founders' religious backgrounds and the general cultural, social and legal setting. Contrary to European or North American countries, Japan has never been dominated by one religious tradition to the exclusion of all others. Neither have these religions been predominantly monotheistic. Japanese religious pluralism includes: (mainly Mahayana) Buddhism, Shinto – which may very briefly be defined as an institutionalized form of folk beliefs and which came to play an important if unfortunate role as State Shinto between the late 1800s and 1945 – Confucianism, Shugendō (an indigenous form of mountain asceticism), some Christianity (prohibited until 1973 yet an important factor in Japan's process of modernization since the late 1800s) and a large variety of folk religious beliefs and practices. All of these co-existed more or less peacefully, fulfilling different religious tasks and thus providing a fertile nurturing ground for the development of new religious movements – maybe 400 in total (*Shinshūkyō Jiten*, RIRC). These are usually said to have developed in four distinct phases, although some scholars merge phases two and three: 1) the second half of the eighteenth century when Japan's feudal system had become marode and Western nations forced it to open its borders; 2) the 1920s and 30s when growing political awareness in Japan coincided with the economic crisis, the awakening and repression of socialist ideas and the rise of ultra-nationalism; 3) the immediate post-war period when freedom of religion was officially granted for the first time and religious organizations became exempt from taxation and, thus, many religious movements were founded or emerged from hiding and became officially registered; and 4) the decade or so after the oil-shock of the 1970s when the drawbacks of Japan's rapid economic growth – such as the limits of natural resources and environmental damages, a rigid educational system followed by a seemingly meaningless working life – began to show. The new religions of the fourth phase are generally referred to as 'new new religions' (*shin-shinshūkyō*) because they mark a generational change within new religions (Shimazono 2001, 13) in their shift of focus – salvation in the beyond rather than this-worldly happiness – and in changed membership patterns as described by, for instance Nishiyama and Ōmura (1988), Wieczorek (2002, 88–93) and particularly Shimazono (2001 and 2004) and Okuyama (2002).

Before 1945 new religions in Japan had been referred to as 'quasi religions' (*ruiji shūkyō*) or as 'newly arisen religions' (*shinkō shūkyō*) until, in the 1970s, the neutral term 'new religion' became common (Shimazono 1992, 31–7 = *Shinshūkyō Jiten*, 2a–5a). In recent years, however, the term 'cult' (*karuto* in Japanese) has become widely used in Japan including all the negative implications associated with it in the Anglo-American world. Many attempts have been made to classify the numerous and diverse Japanese new religions. Most common classifications are their periods of origin and the religious tradition most influential for their doctrines (Buddhism, Shinto, Christianity and 'others'). Others distinguish between new religions' foci on magico-religious elements and on belief (Nishiyama and Ōmura 1988, 169–77), or distinguish between foci on local folk belief and practices, on complex doctrinal systems and on ethics and moral values (Shimazono 1992, 62–80). Classification by size would lead to approximately a dozen large new religions claiming more than half a million members, up to 50 medium-sized new religions of between 100,000 and 500,000 members, and finally a few hundred small new religions with often less than 10,000 members (Earhart 1989, 10; N. Inoue 1992, 19; Shimazono 1992, 106).

Research on Japanese new religions has been published in Japanese as well as in Western languages. It developed in three stages beginning with comprehensive introductory research, followed by studies on specific new religions or, alternatively, on specific aspects of one or more new religions, which continue until today although the Aum affair of 1995 significantly reduced their number and changed their topics.

Comprehensive studies on new religions began with works by, for example, Hiroo Takagi (1958), Clark B. Offner and Henry van Straelen (1963), Harry Thomsen (1963), Neill McFarland (1967) and Klaus-Peter Köpping (1974). They all described the phenomenon of new religions and introduced several individual organizations thereby generally acknowledging the existence of new religions as subject for academic study and preparing the way for research about individual aspects thereof. Later comprehensive publications increasingly included the results of detailed studies, such as Shigeyoshi Murakami (1980), Ken'ya Numata (1988), Shigeru Nishiyama and Eishō Ōmura (1988), Susumu Shimazono (1992) and Nobutaka Inoue (1992). After 1995 followed Hiroshi Kozawa (1997), Hiromi Shimada (2007), Masako Watanabe (2007), an introduction recently edited by Ulrich Dehn and myself (Staemmler and Dehn 2011), and the *Handbook of East Asian New Religious Movements* to be edited by Franz Winter and Lukas Pokorny (expected for 2013/14).

Research on specific new religions initially seemed to continue pre-existing approaches to the study of religions and, hence, frequently concentrated on the founders and their doctrines (e.g. Laube 1978; Shūkyō Shakaigaku Kenkyūkai 1987; Bernegger 1987; Wöhr 1989; Stalker 2008). Focus is still either on problematic or conspicuous or, alternatively, on easily accessible new religions – the latter often as topic for master or doctoral research. The former include, for instance, Daniel Métraux (1988, 1992 and 2001) and Levi McLaughlin (2003 and 2009) on Sōka Gakkai, Brian McVeigh (1991 and 1997) and Winston Davis (1980) on Sūkyō Mahikari, Iris Wieczorek on Kofuku no Kagaku, Shinnyo-en and GLA (2002), and Benjamin Dorman on Pana Wave (2003 and 2005a) on the one hand, and on the other hand H. Byron Earhart on Gedatsukai (1989), Helen Hardacre on Reiyūkai (1984) and Kurozumikyō (1986), a collection of papers on Shūyōdan Hōseikai edited by Susumu Shimazono (1992), Stewart Guthrie on Risshō Kōsei-kai (1988), Ulrich Lins (1976), Jean-Pierre Berthon (1985), Nancy Stalker (2008) and Birgit Staemmler (2009) on Ōmoto, Inken Prohl on World Mate (2006), and Monika Schrimpf on Shinnyo-en and PL Kyōdan (expected for 2013).

Major works about specific aspects of new religions concentrate on issues relevant in either the current academic discourse or up-to-date social developments. Examples are discussions of women's roles in new religions (e.g. Wöhr 1989 and S. Inoue 1995), Kenji Ishii and Susumu Shimazono on consumer society, media and religion (1996), the activities of Japanese new religions abroad (Clarke and Somers 1994; Clarke 2000 and 2006 and a special issue of the *Japanese Journal of Religious Studies* in 1991), and distinctions between new religions and new new religions on the one and the Japanese equivalent of the New Age Movement on the other hand (see especially Shimazono's work, but also Watanabe 2007). In 1990 the first edition of the *Shinshūkyō Jiten*, the invaluable Japanese encyclopaedia of new religions, was published which sorted and summarized many of these research results and combined them with data about most major new religions active in Japan.

On 20 March 1995, however, the situation of and research about new religions in Japan changed as five members of the new religion Aum Shinrikyō killed 12 people and injured several hundreds with poisonous gas in the Tokyo subway during the morning rush hours. Aum Shinrikyō has since been disbanded and several of its members, including its founder Shōkō Asahara (born 1955) tried and convicted. The 'Aum affair' however, has had far-reaching consequences not only for the direct and indirect victims of the poisonous gas but also for the position of all other religious organizations in Japan, for the study of these organizations and for the Japanese society as a whole. In the wake of the 1995 Aum affair the mass media published a vast amount of, often sensationalist, articles on Aum, whereas most Japanese scholars seemed at a loss for words. Many, often non-Japanese scholars analysed the development of Aum Shinrikyō, such as Ian Reader (1996 and 2000), Susumu Shimazono (1997), Martin Repp (1997, 2005, 2011a and b), Stefano Bonino (2010) and, only recently, Erica Baffelli and Ian Reader (2012) with a special issue of the *Japanese Journal of Religious Studies* evaluating the implications of the Aum affair.

Research on new religions by Japanese scholars declined sharply after 1995 while the Japanese anti-cult movement gained significant momentum. Apart from the 'evil cult' versus 'good religion' issue, novel topics that emerged after the Aum affair are new religions – especially Sōka Gakkai and, more recently, Kōfuku no Kagaku – and politics (e.g. Ehrhardt 2009; Höhe 2011; Kisala 1999 and 2005; Klein 2011; Marshall 1981; and McLaughlin 2009), publications about new religions and Japanese nationalism (Shimazono 2001 and Iida, Nakano and Yamanaka 1997) and financial aspects of new religions (e.g. Shimada 2008 and Sakurai 2009). Simultaneously however, Japan, too, experienced the rise of the internet era and scholars began examining the relationship between (new) religions and (new) media as, for example, Benjamin Dorman (2003, 2005b, 2011 and especially 2012), Takanori Tamura with Akira Kawabata (2007) and with Daiyū Tamura (2011), Erica Baffelli (2005, 2007 and 2011), Petra Kienle and myself (2003) and a special issue of *Nova Religio* (2007).

It is to be expected that, with the end of the immediate post-Aum era (Baffelli and Reader 2012, 23–4), the devastating catastrophe that shook Japan in March 2011, and ongoing social change – aging population, rise of unemployment, environmental issues and so on – research on new religions in Japan will turn to new topics in the foreseeable future.

8

Sexuality Studies

Megan Goodwin

The field of sexuality studies offers critical insight into the study of new religious movements. The codification of sexual behaviours is a defining characteristic of many NRMs. And certainly the public sphere has made much of 'cults' and 'sex scandals'. It is surprising, then, that so few scholars of new religious movements attend to concerns of sexuality.

Thinking critically about sexuality means challenging cultural assumptions about what is 'normal' to do with (to, on, in) one's body, as well as thinking hard about where our ideas of normalcy came from. NRM scholars who engage sexuality must address not only heteronormativity (the primacy and normalization of heterosexuality), but also sexuality as an identity, sexual object choice as a practice, gender presentation and transgressive sexual behaviours. Critical theories of sexuality consider how, where, why, and which embodied practices, identities, and presentations garner cultural privilege or exclusion and silencing. As such, closer and more consistent attention to concerns of sexuality could facilitate a more theoretically rigorous scholarship of new religious movements.

Several key premises about sexuality should inform scholarly engagement with NRMs. Foremost among these must be the terms' universal importance: cultural assumptions about 'normal' gendered behaviours and sexual practices shape us all. Thus a theoretically rigorous approach to sexuality in new religious movements must attend to the ways groups are shaped by their relationships to hetero- as well as homosexuality; such an inquiry should also interrogate how, when and why certain groups institute transgressive sexual practices (e.g. non-monogamy, cross-generational relationships, celibacy). Consideration of sexuality is especially pertinent to NRM studies because, as Lorne Dawson notes, such movements are 'so often accused of sexual deviance' (2006, 126–41).

Second, the study of sexuality is neither interchangeable with nor reducible to the study of gender. Rather, each term informs the other. Queer theorist Judith Butler suggests that heteronormativity – the cultural assumption that heterosexuality is both exclusively natural and universal – *creates* gender by requiring binary roles. Butler calls this the 'heterosexual matrix,' which 'assumes that for bodies to make sense there must be a stable sex expressed through a stable gender (masculine expresses male, feminine expresses female) that is oppositionally and hierarchically defined through the compulsory practice of heterosexuality' (1990, 151). That is, heteronormativity makes sense of sexual bodies in hierarchical, binary, reproductive terms – and thus compels certain gendered behaviours.

Third, Western cultures value some sexual acts and gendered behaviours more than others: those acts and behaviours usually correspond to a hierarchical, binary, reproductive understanding of human embodiment. Those who engage in 'normal' sexual acts and gendered behaviours are considered sane, respectable, law-abiding, worthy of social mobility, institutional support and marital benefits (Rubin 1984, 12). Unrepentant sexual transgressors and 'gender outlaws' (see Bornstein) may be accused of mental illness, disrespectability, and criminality, as well as restricted social and physical mobility, loss of institutional support and economic sanctions (Rubin 1984, 12). Mainstream cultures often interpret unconventional religious beliefs or practices as evidence of sexual transgression, and engagement in sexual transgression often invites mainstream suspicion towards NRM theologies and praxes.

Accepting these premises – the universal importance, imbricated construction, and hierarchical cultural valuation of sexual behaviours – allows insight into the function and significance of gender and sexuality studies for NRM scholarship. NRMs often deploy transgressive sexual practices to distance themselves from and correct mainstream culture. However, these transgressions render NRMs hypervisible and sometimes provoke suspicious, invasive or even violent responses from mainstream. The insights provided by sexuality studies allow scholars to interrogate the ways NRMs use sexuality to create space for difference or secure access to privilege, while often being denied privilege on the grounds of sexual transgression.

New religious movements create space for unconventional modes of sexual practice. A number of NRMs have incorporated transgressive sexual practices in order to correct or distance themselves from mainstream culture: consider the Shakers' apocalyptic celibacy; the Oneidan practices of complex marriage, male continence, and stirpiculture; David Koresh's strategy of 'winning in the bedroom'; and the Children of God's 'flirty fishing' technique. Often, religiously defined gender roles require such transgressive sexual practices – the patriarchal theology of Mormon fundamentalisms stipulates plural marriage as a condition for salvation, while the Unification Church's doctrine compels both periods of celibacy and marriages arranged by Sun Myung Moon. In these ways, NRMs facilitate sexual difference.

However, mainstream religions and governments often assume that participation in groups with restrictive gender roles or sexual practices must be involuntary or irrational. Eileen Barker (1984), David Chidester (2003) and J. Z. Smith (1988) have all convincingly demonstrated that NRM members' unconventional beliefs and practices are neither necessarily coerced nor illogical. Critics of

NRMs nevertheless presume that charismatic leaders or cultural programming coerce or dupe their devotees into transgressive sexual behaviours or seemingly oppressive gender roles. NRM critics and anti-cult activists – as well as mainstream media and politics – often portray adult male members as sexually predatory and oppressively patriarchal, and female, adolescent, and child NRM members as in need of rescue (Gibson 2010). As I noted above, Dawson has observed the frequency with which NRMs are accused of sexual deviance; I have argued elsewhere that mainstream religions and professedly secular institutions target minority religions as sexually deviant in an attempt to abject sexual abuse, coercion and exploitation from the public sphere (Goodwin 2013).

Professed concern for women and children has proved an extremely effective rhetorical strategy to marginalize NRMs (Duffy 2012). The 2008 raid on the Fundamentalist Church of Jesus Christ of Latter Day Saints (FLDS) Yearning for Zion Ranch in Eldorado, Texas serves as a poignant example. In response to largely unsubstantiated allegations of institutionalized religious coercion and child sexual abuse, the polygamous FLDS community in Eldorado experienced the 'largest state custodial detention of children in U.S. history' (Wright and Richardson 2011).[1] The Yearning for Zion raid was not an isolated incident: concern for women and children incited the disastrous 1993 raid on the Branch Davidian compound in Waco, Texas and has incited the removal of more than 500 minors from Family International households between 1989 and 1993 (Shepherd and Shepherd 2011). Popular depictions of the women and children of NRMs as victims and dupes of sexual coercion or gendered exploitation have incited widespread anxiety regarding and even violence towards marginal religions.

Some NRMs also deploy anti-gay rhetoric and practices, either during attempts to 'mainstream' or to distance themselves from 'fallen', presumably secular sexualities (Warner 2004). Late nineteenth-century Latter-day Saints and Seventh-day Adventists had widely disparate views on sex; but by the mid-twentieth century, Adventists and Mormons increasingly championed 'dyadic gender roles' and actively condemned homosexuality (Vance 2008). Sexually transgressive NRMs – such as the Children of God, the Unification Church, and the Rajneesh movement – often rhetorically distance themselves from homosexuality; such rhetoric can be read as an attempt to access cultural privilege by invoking heteronormative status (Goodwin 2009). Thus these NRMs volley for social approbation among abjected countercultures, rather than challenging the premises of cultural disapproval: rather than reject anti-cult criticisms based on sexual normalcy, these groups insist they're not as 'weird' or 'bad' as other marginalized groups (McCloud 2004).

Scholarly engagement with sexuality provides insight into NRMs' use of homophobic rhetoric to gain access to privilege, anti-cult panics about the coercion of NRM women and children, the complex agency of NRM members and the ways NRMs provide space for embodied difference. In these ways, sexuality studies might facilitate a more theoretically rigorous scholarship of new religious movements.

Note

1 Contrary to many apologetic scholarly accounts, however, evidence gathered during the raid allowed the state of Texas to classify nearly 125 FLDS adults as 'designated perpetrators' of sexual abuse and neglect (though allegations of neglect far outnumbered those of sexual abuse). Twelve FLDS men were indicted and several were recently convicted on charges related to underage marriage (Duffy 2012).

9 Media Studies

Stephen Jacobs

Chapter Outline	
Production	61
Texts	62
Reception	63
Conclusion	65

NRMs and the media intersect in a variety of complex ways. For example many NRMs are themselves prolific and sophisticated media producers, and NRMs often appear in both factual and fictional mainstream media productions. Consequently, in the media saturated context of the contemporary world, media studies has the potential to make a major contribution to the study of NRMs.

Media studies draws on a wide range of theories and methodological approaches and is concerned with the diverse range of media forms including: print, radio, film, television and new media. Despite the extent and diversity of media studies as an academic field of interest, it is possible to suggest that there are three main focal points in the study of the media: production, text, and reception.

Production

Although oral communication is an important aspect of the communicative process both within groups and to the outside world, most NRMs also produce an abundance of printed material, pamphlets, magazines and books intended for distribution both within the group and to outsiders. While NRMs, because of production costs and media regulations, have tended not to be involved in any substantial way with the broadcast media of radio and television, most NRMs have made significant use of new media. Almost all NRMs have some online presence, use social networks sites and may upload videos to sites such as *YouTube*. Hugh Urban in his essay on Heaven's Gate, argues that many 'alternative spiritual forms . . . seem not only compatible with, but ideally suited to the ever-changing and endlessly transformable world of mass communications' (2011, 111).

Mainstream media outlets often produce news-reports, documentaries and fictional representations of NRMs. These representations of NRMs frequently antagonize the NRM themselves. For example, the *Southpark* episode '*Out of the Closet*',[1] first aired in 2005, in which Stan is identified as the reincarnation of L. Ron Hubbard, and John Sweeney's exposé on *Panorama*[2] in 2007 incensed many Scientologists. NRMs only make the news when they are perceived as a problem. For example the Branch Davidians did not merit any national or international coverage until ATF agents laid siege to their community in Waco in 1993. This of course is in large part because of the nature of the news itself (see Cowan and Hadden 2004). However, as Stuart Hoover has argued (1998, 2–4) the reporting of this tragic event was woefully inadequate because of the presuppositions of journalists and editors about religion in general and NRMs in particular.

Media production is hierarchically structured. The individual media producer is embedded within a particular organization, which is located within a particular media industry, which in turn is situated within a specific society (see McQuail 2000, 248). A key question when considering production asks, who is influential in influencing the ways that NRMs are framed in the media? James Richardson (1995, 159–62) argues that the anti-cult lobby has been very successful in influencing media producers in representing NRMs as deviant and threatening. Consequently the dominant media discourse in both fictional and 'factual' representations of NRMs is in terms of cults.

Texts

The key question of any textual analysis is how a particular individual or group is represented. Stuart Hall (1997) indicates that representation is a signifying practice; it is how one thing can stand for another. Most media studies scholars adopt a constructionist approach to representations, which holds that representations are not neutral indicators of some objective reality, but are actively implicated in the construction of meaning. If the predominant representations of NRMs are in terms of cults led by a psychologically manipulative leadership who prey on vulnerable individuals, this does not necessarily reflect a reality but has the potential to shape public perceptions about non-mainstream religions.

Terminology is of course absolutely critical in any textual analysis of media representations of NRMs. In particular the term 'cult' is widely utilized in the media to refer to non-mainstream religions. The term 'cult' has been so frequently articulated with ideas about coercion and exploitation, that it is taken for granted that any group identified as a cult is automatically regarded as inherently deviant. Sean McCloud cogently argues that journalistic representations have been complicit in 'identifying false or inauthentic religion and thus symbolically establishing boundaries between a mainstream religious center and a suspect periphery' (2004, 4).

While there have been a number of studies of how NRMs are represented in the news, particularly in relation to the events at Waco (Jones and Baker 1994; Richardson 1995), there are almost no studies on fictional representations of NRMs, yet vulnerable individuals drawn into mysterious cults led by a Svengali character makes for good drama.[3] NRMs are also satirized in various shows such as *The Simpsons* 1998 episode 'The Joy of Sect' in which Homer joins the Movementarians, and is brainwashed. Lynn Neal (2011) points out that these fictional representations perpetuate various stereotypical tropes, which construct a perception of NRMs as deviant and dangerous.

NRMs themselves are prolific media producers, and this material provides a tremendous resource for the study of NRMs. Many NRMs produce their own official publications, such as *The Watchtower*, the magazine of the Jehovah's Witnesses Originally entitled *Zion's Watchtower*, which has been in continuous production since 1879, is produced in 195 different languages and has a print run of over 42 million (*The Watchtower*, 21 July 2012). Many members of NRMs also produce autobiographical texts, indicating how joining a NRM has transformed their lives.[4] One must also not forget texts that are produced by the anti-cult lobby and disaffected ex-members. While the use of close textual analysis of mediated representations, using methods such as critical discourse analysis, can reveal the ideological presuppositions of the media producers, it cannot reveal anything about how these texts are understood by audiences, readers and internet users. For this we must turn to a discussion of how such texts are received by audiences.

Reception

While I have indicated that media representations may shape public perceptions about NRMs, most media scholars reject the notion of the passive audience. Stuart Hall (2000) has argued that the meaning of media texts is not fixed, but texts are open to a variety of interpretations (or decodings to use

Hall's terminology) which are contingent on a number of contextual factors. Hall argues that if there are demographic differences between the producer and the receiver of media texts, there is likely to be a divergence between the intended meaning of the encoder and the meaning derived from that text by the decoder. This is pertinent, as how members of NRMs decode media texts will be influenced by their beliefs and sense of identity. Hall suggests that there are three possible decoding positions: *preferred,* where encoding and decoding are relatively consistent; *negotiated,* where there is some discord; and *oppositional,* where there is dissent between encoding and decoded meanings.[5] It is not unreasonable to suggest that highly committed members of some NRMs, particularly those that have a world-rejecting ethos, will adopt an oppositional position stance in relation to mainstream and commercial media texts. The oppositional stance entails that the receiver 'detotalises the message in the preferred code in order to retotalise the message within some alternative frame of reference' (Hall 2000, 517). In other words membership of an NRM will often entail that the primary frame of reference for decoding media texts will be the belief system of the group.

Many NRMs are cautious, if not hostile to mainstream media, suggesting that the values of commercial media are antithetical to the values of their religious beliefs. However, no NRM is homogenous (despite many media representations suggesting that joining a 'cult' inevitably undermines individual autonomy), and many other demographic factors such as class, education and so on will also have an impact on how individual members of NRMs will respond to both media in general and particular media texts.

Daniel Stout and David Scott (2003), in their study of Mormons and media literacy, observe that some Mormons would not watch Steven Spielberg's film *Schindler's List* because it is 'R-rated' and accepted the church's leadership assessment that this rating inevitably entailed that the film must be 'degrading and damaging to the spirit' (Stout and Scott 2003, 151). However, other members of the Mormon Church, basing their media choices on other criteria such as artistic merit or personal judgement, did decide to view *Schindler's List*. This suggests that just as viewers' positioning in relationship to interpreting media texts can be preferred, negotiated or oppositional, so too can members' attitudes to particular aspects of a NRM's values.

Many media representations tend to portray NRMs in terms of cults and we only hear about these minority religious groups if there is a problem, for example the siege at Waco, or if there is an event that is perceived as being particularly abnormal, such as the mass weddings organized by the Unification Church.[6] While individuals can interpret these (mis)representations from different positions, these dominant media tropes tend to cultivate an evaluation of NRMs as marginal, inauthentic, dangerous and deviant.

Conclusion

Overall there is a lack of research into the complex relations between media and NRMs. Further research into NRMs as media producers is required. The media texts produced by NRMs provide an invaluable resource for academics. Various forms of textual analysis, such as content analysis or critical discourse analysis, can be utilized in a more rigorous way than so far has been the case in the study of NRMs' media output. Further research is also required into the ways that the mores of particular NRMs might influence members' choice of what media texts they engage with, and the ways in which they decode these texts.

While there have been some studies into the ways that NRMs have been represented in the media, the majority of these have been focused on what Anson Shupe and Jeffrey Hadden (1995, 82) term 'crisis events'. While in many ways this is determined by the nature of the news, there is scope for further research on media representations of more routine aspects of NRMs. In particular there is a dearth of research into fictional representations of NRMs in film, television dramas and other programmes. There is also a critical need for empirical audience research to identify in what ways audiences' perceptions of NRMs have been shaped by the dominant media representations of NRMs as dangerous cults.

Notes

1. There is some anecdotal evidence that Isaac Hayes who is a Scientologist, and was the voice of Chef, quit the show because of this episode. There are also some claims that the Scientologists pressurized Hayes to quit. However Hayes has consistently denied both these allegations.
2. Scientologists made a response to the BBC *Panorama* programme entitled *BBC Exposed* in which they claim that the BBC 'Has sold its soul, compromised its integrity and can no longer be trusted'. This riposte can be viewed on *YouTube* http://youtube.com/watch?v=V7iFj1L5HnQ
3. See for example *CSI* Season 4, Episode 6 (2005) *Shooting Stars* in which members of a UFO cult commit suicide. Lynn Neal (2011) provides a useful list of dramas that have narratives about cults.
4. Followers of Indian-derived transnational guru movements tend to be very prolific producers of autobiographies. See for example Michael Fischman's *Stumbling Into Infinity*, which tells about how his life was transformed by meeting Sri Sri Ravi Shankar and becoming an active members of Art of Living.
5. Hall emphasizes that there must be 'some degree of reciprocity between encoding and decoding moments' for communication to take place (2000, 515).
6. See for example *Married to the Moonies* – Channel Four, first shown on 31 May 2012.

10 Ritual Studies
Lee Gilmore

The study of ritual poses questions about performance, action and lived religious experience that are often underutilized strategies for examining new religious movements. Contemplating the relationships between ritual and religion, whether new or ancient, raises perennial questions as to what can and what cannot be considered religion, what can and cannot be considered ritual, as well as the degree to which ritual may or may not be seen as a key aspect of a given religious tradition. For example, the Transcendental Meditation movement does not call itself a *religion*, yet makes central use of meditation techniques that are indisputably grounded in Hindu religious practices and ritual traditions. On the other hand, Scientologists do not typically describe their practices – that is auditing, assists, and group process, among others – as *ritual*, and while they have developed a basic liturgy and other ceremonial elements, such as rites of passage, in general these activities are of relatively minimal importance. Nevertheless, they vigorously defend their claim to constitute a religion (see Cowan and Bromley 2007). And as a counterpoint to both of these perspectives, eclectic and esoteric ritualizing tends to be central to Contemporary Paganism, and Pagans often define their religious orientations more by the *doing* (or being) of Paganism, rather than by the believing (see Harvey 2012; Magliocco 2004). These examples illustrate the obvious extent to which attention to the problem of ritual is needed for NRM studies.

Numerous disciplines engage with the study of ritual, including anthropology, psychology, performance studies and liturgics among others. Ritual studies attempts to explain *why* people perform such actions, and to interpret their sometimes multiple meanings and contexts. Ritual action is often understood as constructing social identities and communities, while also revealing tensions within those groups and constructs, and there is an increasing focus on the extents to which ritual fields are dynamic, contested and transcultural (Hüsken 2007; Michaels et al. 2010) Furthermore, ritual theorists also seek to discern whether or not those are even the right questions to ask, as well as to understand the extent to which 'ritual' itself is a Western scholarly construct that distorts as much as it illuminates about 'other' cultural traditions. In the mutual interest in emergent religious expressions, there is a good deal of potential synergy between ritual studies and the study of new religious movements.

This very brief introduction highlights a few key ideas of particular relevance and utility for NRM studies by discussing just a handful of foundational scholars for ritual studies.

Among the most influential, and now most critiqued, ritual theorists was the anthropologist Victor Turner, who significantly expanded upon Arnold van Gennep's ideas about *rites of passage* (Turner 1969; 1974; 1982; Turner and Turner 1978; Van Gennep 1960). Turner focused on the phenomenon of *liminality* as a social and ritual status set apart from the mundane world and perceived as being 'betwixt and between', alongside an experience he called *communitas*, marked by temporary disruptions of normative social orders and feelings of collective unity. The periodic *anti-structure* of liminality and communitas was seen to ultimately reinforce social structures and hierarchies, and Turner understood ritual chiefly as a mechanism for personal and social transformation. He combed the globe in search of cultural symbols that could be shown to illustrate these supposedly universal social processes, leading towards a certain theoretical circularity – that is 'these phenomena illustrate my theory of communitas because they exhibit features of communitas'. Furthermore, much of his most influential work was written amid the turbulent 1960s and 1970s, and many of the sentiments that he took to be hallmarks of rites of passage – social rejuvenation, status reversals, communitarian values, altered states of consciousness and ecstatic experience – were also key discourses for some of the NRMs and other 'countercultural' movements that emerged in that era. Despite their limitations, Turner's frameworks continue to have descriptive utility and can also be viewed to some extent as *prescriptive* strategies for some contemporary 'alternative' religious movements, where liminality and communitas are taken to be hallmarks of authentic ritual experience (Gilmore 2010; St John, ed. 2008).

Ronald Grimes (who was once a student of Turner's) has been central to the development of ritual studies as a distinctive sub-discipline. His development of 'ritual criticism' is especially helpful for thinking about ritual creativity and change within new and other emergent religious developments, and entails assessing both the meaning and efficacy of a given rite or ritual system, from both emic and etic perspectives. According to Grimes, ritual should be understood not as a fixed or universal category but rather should be 'employed as a hermeneutical principle, [such that] the idea of ritual becomes a metaphor, a tool to "think by."' (Grimes 1990, 21). Grimes often formulates typologies as tools for analysis and comparison, for example outlining six 'modes of ritual sensibility' (Grimes 1995, 40). He also separates ritual from the requirements of belief, expanding his analytical scope to include activities not traditionally considered as ritual, such as watching television, medical procedures, or housework, and noting how rituals can migrate across cultures and acquire new or modified meanings (Grimes 2000). More recently, Grimes turned his attention to representations of ritual in film and television, posing questions about media frames and perspectives that are pertinent for a variety of ethnographic and scholarly depictions of ritual contexts (Grimes 2006). For example, he critiques commercial video documentaries on ritual that distance, distort, and eroticize, identifying these media production strategies as a type of ritualized behaviour. He also thinks through the ways in which, 'shooting rites' –that is the process of capturing and editing both moving and still images of ritual – 'documents, reveals, validates, publicizes, mystifies, constructs, dramatizes, violates, (dis) embodies, and complicates' (Grimes 2006, 38). Most generally, Grimes' special focus on ritual creativity, invention and adaptability – as well as his broad view on ritualizing in cultural contexts not normatively understood as *religious* – can be particularly helpful for analysing new and emergent ritual traditions and communities.

Numerous other scholars have made important contributions to the study of ritual, but I have space to note just a few more influential perspectives here. Catherine Bell was the author of two well-known books on the subject of ritual. The first of these demonstrated the ways in which the major theory on ritual in the Western scholarly tradition has rested on a fundamental privileging of thought over action and emphasized the extent to which rituals are continuously contested and negotiated fields of meanings (Bell 1992). Her slightly more recent work contained an extensive critical survey of the history of modern, Western thought on ritual and ultimately argued that ritual is a 'reified' concept that has been constructed by Western scholars who 'assume that there is a substantive phenomenon at stake, not simply an abstract analytical category' (Bell 1997, 253). Roy Rappaport on the other hand argued that ritual is a universal, or near universal, category of action that has had a central and indispensable role in defining human evolution and thus human nature. Defining ritual as 'the performance of more or less invariant sequences of formal acts and utterances not entirely encoded by the performers', he argued that ritual communicates concepts that cannot be adequately expressed through language alone (Rappaport 1999, 24). Lastly, Caroline Humphrey and James Laidlaw developed an innovative and comprehensive theory of ritual performance, based on a close study of Jain puja. Beginning with the premise that ritual can be 'deeply ambiguous', they question whether scholars' persistent search for ritual's hidden *meanings* were in fact always the best questions to pose. Instead, they saw the key dynamic as ritual's 'intrinsic directedness', thus attempting to account for the extent to which ritual actors can bring a variety of both personal and cultural meanings, intentions and feelings (including their absence) to ritual actions (Humphrey and Laidlaw 1994).

This short survey only scratches the surface. The search for methodological traction between NRM studies and Ritual Studies raises a number of questions, particularly considering the problems of authenticity that often challenge new religious movements. The issue of whether ritual is a universal human phenomenon or a reified scholarly construct invites questions basic to the study of religion generally. In some respects, both Ritual Studies and NRM studies include within their scope a jumble of activities that may be related to one another only by the cultural and scholarly perspectives and associations that lead us to group and study them thus. When labelling diverse modern religious movements as NRMs, it is important to remember to neither overgeneralize nor to collectively 'other' these traditions, by positioning them as somehow disconnected from less marginalized religions. Additionally, questions about ritual efficacy and interpretive frames also have considerable potential utility for embarking on fieldwork with NRMs, and the extent to which ritual theories may themselves influence contemporary and emergent ritual practices may also be a fruitful direction to explore. Furthermore, the search for the intrinsic 'meanings' of rituals leads to insights about the extent to which ritual traditions and ritual performances may often have multiple, dynamic, and contested interpretations, both internally and externally, as well as collectively and individually. Finally, the relatively recent turn in ritual theory towards examining ritual dynamics, ritual change, and ritual reinvention in shifting transcultural contexts, may be particularly pertinent to scholars of religious movements that are emerging precisely from those rapidly changing global circumstances.

Part II
Current Research and Issues

11 Jonestown and the Study of NRMs: How Survivors and Artists are Reshaping the Narrative of Jonestown

Rebecca Moore

Chapter Outline	
How Scholarship Has Changed	75
The Voices of Survivors	76
The Voices of Artists	82
The Lessons of Jonestown for NRM Studies	87

The mass deaths that occurred in Jonestown on 18 November 1978 came at a time of great public anxiety about cults. The repeal of the Asian Exclusion Act by the US Congress in 1965 had altered the American religious landscape by allowing the immigration of yogis, rishis and gurus from the East. The 1960s counterculture had created a welcoming environment for new religions. Young, white, college students destroyed the hopes of their parents by dropping out of the larger society and joining the Moonies, the Children of God, the Hare Krishnas and other unconventional religions. An anti-cult movement arose to rescue these children, who were believed to have been brainwashed and held against their will. Family members did not believe that normal young adults would voluntarily sell flowers on street corners or live monastically– or communally – unless they had been coerced by a mesmeric guru to repeat mantras until their conscious will had snapped.

Thus, the news that more than 900 men, women and children had died in a mass murder-suicide ritual in a remote jungle commune confirmed popular stereotypes about cults and cultists. Media accounts of the deaths emphasized the difficulties of life in Jonestown and dehumanized the victims by repeatedly displaying images of corpses. Reporters spoke primarily with Peoples Temple apostates – the only accessible individuals with first-hand knowledge of the group – in order to understand the organization. A spate of lurid books by journalists, former members, and pop psychologists emerged within the first two years, and reinforced the narrative framed by the media in the week after the tragedy: a deranged leader named Jim Jones ordered the assassination of a US congressman and then led his brainwashed followers to their deaths in a jungle encampment.

Despite this inauspicious beginning, scholarship concerning new religious movements underwent a remarkable transformation following the events in Jonestown. As academics examined the history of Peoples Temple more closely, they observed that it did not support the conclusions about NRMs reached by prior research: the majority of members were neither young nor white; the group was multiracial, multigenerational and crossed class lines; aspirations were for a this-worldly political utopia rather than an other-worldly spiritual paradise; the group interacted extensively with outsiders until its members moved to Guyana, in South America, where they then lived in a highly encapsulated community. In addition, researchers began to study the opponents of NRMs, the anti-cultists, as carefully as they studied the cults themselves. They assessed the accounts of ex-members as well as the narratives of surviving members. They challenged the media frame by which new religions were discussed, represented and reported. This might have happened eventually without Jonestown, but the tragic and complicated history of the event accelerated the process by subverting long-held beliefs about cultists, about cults and about what we think of new religions.

This chapter reflects upon the ways in which scholarship about new religious movements has changed as a result of Jonestown. Yet more importantly, it examines how the story of Jonestown is being shaped today by Peoples Temple survivors with firsthand knowledge and memory of the group; and by artists using various media with no direct knowledge or experience of the group. I use the word 'story' rather than 'history' because I believe that these narratives and interpretations are the building blocks of later histories. Borrowing Mikhail Bakhtin's language, I show how research, debate and interpretation continuously act against the centripetal forces that seek to centralize and unify all discourse about Jonestown. The event itself, and the accounts that explain, define, and refine it, seem to defy closure by academics, survivors or artists.

There are numerous accounts about Peoples Temple and Jonestown: more than a hundred scholarly and popular books and articles have attempted to assess the group and its ending. Rather than rehearse Peoples Temple's history in this brief chapter, I direct the reader to three books and one website. Hall's *Gone From the Promised Land* (1987) is the most complete and analytical of all scholarly works. Moore's *Understanding Jonestown and Peoples Temple* (2009b) is more accessible and aimed at a lay audience. *Dear People: Remembering Jonestown* (2005), edited by Denice Stephenson, is a lively collection of primary source documents that trace the history of the group from its earliest days, through the end and beyond. Finally, the website *Alternative Considerations of Jonestown and Peoples Temple* (http://jonestown.sdsu.edu) provides a comprehensive digital history representing a variety of viewpoints.

How Scholarship Has Changed

Peoples Temple and the events in Jonestown radically reshaped the study of new religious movements. We can outline a field 'before' as distinct from a field 'after'. Before Jonestown, scholars were interested in conversion careers (Richardson 1978) and the 'new religious consciousness' (Needleman and Baker 1978), while popular books focused on brainwashing (Conway and Siegelman 1978; Stoner and Parke 1977). After Jonestown, a well-organized anti-cult movement used the deaths to corroborate their claims that new religions were inevitably toxic (Shupe and Bromley 1982). 'Every cult, sect, and occult group became a potential Jonestown' (Streiker 1984, 13).

Within a few years, though, articles and books began to appear that undermined the dominant anti-cult viewpoint. Smith (1982) chastised the academic profession for failing to consider the larger story of Peoples Temple, and pointed out that the press featured only the 'pornography of Jonestown'. Levi (1982) edited a collection of essays that approached Jonestown from scholarly, as opposed to popular, perspectives. Hall (1987) located Peoples Temple within the context of American cultural history. Chidester (1988) identified rituals of exclusion that had served to alienate the public from those who died. He also developed a theology of Jim Jones based upon hundreds of audiotapes made by Peoples Temple and recovered by the FBI following the mass deaths.

Simplistic notions of cult essentialism – the belief that new religions operate within a vacuum, impervious to external influences or events – gave way to more complex explanations of the interactions that new religions experience with their environments. The tragic showdown at Waco, Texas between the Branch Davidians and the FBI in 1993 brought about a re-evaluation of theories of cult violence, the role that outsiders play in these incidents and renewed interest in how Peoples Temple differed from other NRMs. Robbins and Anthony identified the ways that exogenous (external) and endogenous (internal) factors interacted within Peoples Temple in contrast to the Branch Davidians (1995). Hall had already noted the role of cultural opponents in his study of Jonestown, but developed this theory of interactionism further as a result of his analysis of the Branch Davidians and the Solar Temple. He described a 'tendency that governmental authorities share with the anti-cult movement, a tendency to see the dynamics of "cults" as internal to such groups, rather than examine external social interaction in conflict between a sectarian group and opponents and authorities themselves' (Hall 1995, 230). Wessinger (2000a) created a typology of millennial violence in which she distinguished between Jonestown (a fragile millennial group), Mount Carmel (an assaulted millennial group) and the Montana Freemen (a revolutionary millennial group). Wessinger's examples of religious violence all demonstrated the role that outsiders played in the final outcome. Bromley and Melton (2002) further analysed the elements that led to 'dramatic denouements' in incidents of violence after Jonestown.

The horrifying spectacle of hundreds of bodies decaying in the jungle was replaced in 2001 by a new image of religious violence: the burning twin towers of New York City. The anti-cult movement attempted to make links between terrorists and cults (Wright 2009), and news writers made comparisons between Jim Jones and Osama bin Laden. In many respects, however, 9/11 bumped Jonestown off the map, as academics turned to investigate the rise of other forms of religious extremism. A new wave of literature exploring the nexus between religion, terror and martyrdom emerged. Nevertheless, interest in Peoples Temple remains high, three decades after its supposed demise.

The Voices of Survivors

Surviving members are providing a unique window onto life in Peoples Temple. This group of remarkable people is rare in the history of alternative religions because they are not united by either hatred or love of the group, but by their shared losses in Jonestown. Moreover, many of them did not abandon the group; rather, the group left them. It is thus important to define what is meant by the term 'survivor' in this context. I am using the word rather broadly to include those who left the group as defectors (in Temple language) before the deaths; those who escaped from Jonestown on the day of the deaths; those who survived by being elsewhere in Guyana, especially in Georgetown, the capital city, rather than Jonestown that day; and those living in San Francisco and Los Angeles at the time of the deaths. Some today call these people the 'Peoples Temple community', but others reject this identification, preferring either to be called a survivor, a former member or even a defector (as a badge of honour).

Research about people surviving cults abounds in the domain of psychology and recovery, where clinical professionals counsel those whose damaging experiences in NRMs have disrupted ordinary life. There is a large body of literature that explores the level of neuroticism, depression and other mental disorders occurring in ex-cultists. While Jonestown looms large in these sources, only a single study focuses directly on Jonestown survivors (Hatcher 1989), though Streiker (1984) describes the reaction of former members of Peoples Temple who were involved in a recovery centre they established in Berkeley prior to the deaths.

San Francisco Mayor Dianne Feinstein appointed Dr Chris Hatcher, a clinical psychiatrist at the University of California, San Francisco Medical Center, to coordinate public safety resources, job and welfare assistance, and mental health counselling in the city following the deaths in Jonestown and the assassinations ten days later of her predecessor George Moscone and Supervisor Harvey Milk. What Hatcher found were Temple survivors who 'wanted a chance at a job, any job', and whose primary goal 'was to establish stability in their day-to-day lives' (Hatcher 1989, 135). Working with a team of city and county professionals, Hatcher helped the survivors to find work, or, when this was impossible, to apply for welfare support. 'Some welfare workers, when confronted with Peoples Temple members in person, simply refused to assist them,' he reports, 'and their supervisors were reluctant to take action to deal with this issue' (Hatcher 1989, 135).

Hatcher identifies a half dozen factors relating to psychological adjustment of the survivors with whom he worked. He notes that they tended to believe the world inside the Temple was better than the external world, and this feeling 'competed strongly with the grief over the loss of others at Jonestown' (Hatcher 1989, 136). Survivors had a difficult time explaining to others why they had been part of Peoples Temple. Moreover, subgroups remained a strong force for a long time, with loyalist survivors describing the positive elements of Jonestown, and critical defectors emphasizing the destructive side. Fear of former members who had participated in punishments was high. Thus, no uniform pattern of coping existed among those who survived Peoples Temple.

In addition, Hatcher distinguishes a range of landmarks in the adjustment pattern of survivors. The first stage was one of shock, disbelief, and immobilization, closely followed by affiliation with a known Temple subgroup; in other words, with Temple members with whom one felt comfortable. The year following the deaths comprised the search for structure in daily life, exchanging information with other survivors, feeling frustrated with the external world, and having conflicting and alternating images about Jonestown and the Temple. At some point in the process, the majority of survivors began to vent anger at Jim Jones and Temple leadership, and this was followed first by anger at oneself for participating and then accepting responsibility for one's actions. During the decade after Jonestown, the survivors constructed new lives, even while maintaining primary contact with those in their Temple subgroup. Hatcher characterizes the final stage as one encompassing these new lives. 'The low rate of subsequent criminal involvement or psychiatric hospitalization for Guyana survivors is quite remarkable,' he comments (Hatcher 1989, 146).

Hatcher's anecdotal observations were compiled after the first ten years of his work with survivors. Without a quantitative study, it is impossible to draw any conclusions about the mental health and stability of these former members. Some have been treated for clinical depression, some have struggled with alcohol and drug addiction, and some have lived on the margins of society. Others have become productive members of society: school teachers, librarians, writers, carpenters, salespersons and social workers.

An informal profile of survivors is being constructed, however, through the publication of personal reflections and observations on the website *Alternative Considerations of Jonestown and Peoples Temple*. Begun in 1998, the site has developed far beyond the imagination of its founders, my husband Fielding McGehee and myself. It has become a memorial site for those who died; a repository of primary source documents generated by Peoples Temple; a collection of reflections and observations made by former members, both defectors and loyalists alike; a compendium of scholarly analyses, student papers, articles by members of the general public; and a venue for online debates about issues of controversy. *Alternative Considerations* lets survivors continue the processes Hatcher noted in the early years of their recovery: namely, deconstructing their experiences in the Temple, sharing information they had not known in the hierarchical structure of the group, arguing with one another on contested issues – Was the Temple a religious organization? Did Jim Jones have paranormal abilities? – and simply maintaining contact with those with whom they had experienced some of the best and the worst moments of their lives. Many grieved, and continue to grieve, the loss of feelings of closeness, community, commitment and purpose that they had felt as members of Peoples Temple.

The psychology and recovery literature seems to neglect the issue of survivor grief, although some therapists do note a sense of grief over lost opportunities due to cult involvement, and grief over the loss of purpose and direction (Hamburg and Hoffman 1989; Langone 1993; Schwartz and Kaslow 2001). Feelings of depression, confusion, suicide, guilt, shame and betrayal are frequently noted (e.g. Jacobs 1989), though a case study of former members of the Unification Church reported positive social adjustments, and strong 'affiliative feelings' with those still part of the church (Galanter 1999, 165). An analysis of former members of a Jesus People movement, called Shiloh, found that they underwent feelings of grief and loss (Goldman 1995). A search of the database PsycARTICLES on grief resulted in 325 entries; adding the word 'cult' produced no articles. A search of PsycINFO on grief resulted in 12,543 entries; adding the word 'cult' produced six articles, only one of which was truly relevant. Mapel (2007) – relying in part upon Rice (1990), who describes the feelings of ex-Catholic priests – analyses the grief that ex-Buddhist monks experienced upon leaving their life in the monastery.

In short, the psychological studies generally do not address the grief that attends leaving a new religious movement. This is a serious omission, especially when considering the survivors of Jonestown who suffered the loss of their community, as well as feelings of disenfranchised grief that resulted from the stigmatized deaths of family members. 'The horrifying deaths, and the sensationalistic responses they elicited, created a climate that disenfranchised those who wanted to mourn the loss of their relatives in Jonestown' (Moore 2011b, 46).

The deaths in Jonestown – with parents killing their children, and conflicting reports emerging concerning the level of coercion that occurred – clearly were stigmatized. Survivors returning to the United States were called 'baby killers'; some lost their jobs when their connection to Peoples Temple was discovered. Family members, especially those in the African American community, felt shame and an inability to mourn in public. The popularity of the phrase 'drinking the Kool-Aid' further alienated survivors and relatives by trivializing what had happened. Public sympathy reserved for victims of tragedy, like those who died in the World Trade Center attack, simply did not exist on a widespread public level for the victims of Jonestown. Over time, however, this situation has changed for a number of reasons.

First, the Jonestown Institute (which essentially is Fielding and myself) serves as a clearinghouse that has allowed survivors and family members to identify each other and to connect in virtual reality and in real life. In addition to publishing primary sources, research and *the jonestown report* – an online journal that contains news about research projects, artistic works and current events relating to the Temple – the Jonestown Institute created the only comprehensive listing of those who died on 18 November 1978. This list has attracted many family members who are searching for relatives to the website. The process continues as they make contact with former members, attend survivor gatherings and gain opportunities to learn more about their relatives from those who knew them directly.

Second, annual memorial services helped to change the relationship between defector and loyalist survivors. Beginning with the first anniversary in 1979, the Rev. Jynona Norwood, an African-American pastor whose mother, aunt, and cousins died in Jonestown, organized annual memorial services at Evergreen Cemetery in Oakland, where more than 400 bodies are buried. In the early years, no more than a handful of Jonestown survivors attended. More and more began to come once 10 years had passed; after 20 years had elapsed a group of 30 gathered in a nearby restaurant following the service to talk with each other. Survivors continued to assemble at Evergreen Cemetery each year until the twenty-fifth anniversary in 2003, at which time they held a second, private ceremony exclusively for former Temple members. Many defectors and loyalists saw each other for the first time in decades. One former member described the experience at the graveside in this way:

> I felt gratitude that despite the myriad ways we each took action in those final years, oftentimes casting each other as the adversary, we were able to come and be together, remembering not only the ones who died and were killed, but also to remember ourselves in that earlier time and to perhaps close the circle in some profound and inexplicable way after all these years. (Anonymous 2004)

Paradoxically, the deaths in Jonestown offered the means for reconciliation. Survivors could share in the loss of loved ones and the loss of their community. Even outspoken critics of Jim Jones and the Temple felt connected to those with whom they had suffered much. The installation of four large granite plaques at Evergreen Cemetery in 2011, amidst some controversy – they included the names of everyone who died on 18 November 1978, including that of Jim Jones – has also enfranchised the formerly suppressed and hidden grief, since there is now a physical location (as opposed to an internet site) where relatives can find their loved ones by name.

Third, personal, face-to-face discussions among survivors brought a hidden history to light. Because the Temple had a highly compartmentalized structure of social organization, few individuals had a complete picture of its operation. Beginning with the private service in 2003, and at each one that has followed, survivors told stories that few others knew. They shared experiences of pain, terror, laughter and happiness. They argued about whether or not they were brainwashed; they disputed Jim Jones' mental health; they compared conflicting memories of the same events. They also wrote their stories, observations, and reflections in *the jonestown report*, thereby enlarging the body of knowledge of life in Peoples Temple and in Jonestown by providing firsthand testimony.

Several other factors also helped to create a type of survivor community (as distinct from a new church). The California Historical Society, the repository of thousands of pages of documents and hundreds of photographs from Peoples Temple, welcomed survivors into its research library. There the survivors pored over photographs, year after year, to identify those whom historical researchers were unable to name. It was a unique turnabout: the subjects themselves working in the research library to help future historians understand who they were.

Another factor that connected former members was the research and production of a documentary-style play from the writers of *The Laramie Project*. In 2002 a group of defectors, loyalists, and even a woman who escaped Jonestown on foot on 18 November, gathered in San Francisco to discuss plans for the drama with Leigh Fondakowski, the lead writer. Fondakowski and three other writers spent the next three years interviewing almost 50 former members, relatives and others. When *The People's* [sic] *Temple* premiered in Berkeley in April 2005, one reviewer noted that the audience were active participants in the drama. 'The play has also been a catalyst for others to come together and re-explore their personal history with the Temple,' wrote Bellefountaine (2005). 'It is helping them to share their stories with others, thus preserving them for history and future interpretations.' The play brought together still more former members who had remained closeted or apart for various reasons. Although few believed that *The People's Temple* adequately captured their personal experience, they nevertheless felt it was the best attempt to communicate the ambiguity and complexity that they had ever seen.

The success and reach of *The People's Temple*, along with the passage of time, prompted a number of survivors to self-publish autobiographical accounts and poetry describing their experiences. One of the earliest self-published works was Hyacinth Thrash's as-told-to book *The Onliest One Alive* (Thrash 1995). Since then Leslie Wagner Wilson published *Slavery of Faith* (2009) and Laura Kohl published *Jonestown Survivor* (2010), two books which offer divergent, yet fascinating, accounts of life in Peoples Temple. What is unique about all of these volumes is that they detail life before, during and after Jonestown. Most previous first-person popular accounts, whether self-published or commercially published, end with the deaths in Jonestown.

Garrett Lambrev, who defected in 1973, and Teri Buford O'Shea, who defected in October 1978, three weeks before the deaths, have published volumes of poetry. Some, though not all, of the poems in Lambrev's *Dogstar and Poems from Other Planets* (2007) discuss Jonestown, while the majority of O'Shea's work in *Jonestown Lullaby* (2011) concerns her experiences in, and reflections about, Peoples Temple. O'Shea's poem 'Forgiveness' captures the journey the survivors have travelled.

> You
> > Familiar with
> > > Original pain
> > Squeezed my hand
> > > In one brave act
> > > > Of forgiveness
> > So please
> > > Hold me gently
> > > > In your soul

Teach me
> The lost art
>> Of living
>>> After death
> Has ruled
>> So long

O'Shea's poem expresses the feelings many survivors have had, and articulates the reconciliation that has occurred among formerly competing factions.

The survivors of Jonestown defy easy classification as former cult members. It would seem that Peoples Temple attracted those who were more politically active and socially aware than members of other groups. This awareness seemed to give them personal strength to overcome many obstacles. It also undoubtedly served to give them a collective sense of identity that other ex-cult organizations lack. There is a general feeling that because they have been through hell, they can survive anything. Although the experience of a number of survivors belies this generalization, the very fact that there is an informal group of survivors indicates how different Peoples Temple is from other new religions. The discussions they have today, coupled with their written observations, make the process of writing history both vibrant and vigorous.

The Voices of Artists

In 2000 I asked 'is the canon on Jonestown closed?' and rather gloomily conjectured that it was (Moore 2000). Although I outlined the contours of three categories of literature in that essay – popular, scholarly and conspiratorial – I privileged scholarly work because I believed it provided a more complex look at Peoples Temple that accounted for questions of race, gender, cultural opponents and ideology. What I failed to foresee was the tremendous impact of Jonestown on the artistic imagination. Creative representations of events have served to keep Jonestown and Peoples Temple at the forefront of cultural considerations in ways that were inconceivable in 2000.

Bakhtin's essay 'Discourse in the Novel' (1981) helps to explain the amazing fecundity of Jonestown. In that essay the Russian literary theorist identifies 'centripetal forces' that tend to centralize and unify overarching discourses, canonizing ideological systems into a single 'unitary language' (Bakhtin 1981, 271). Yet this centralizing drive operates against the centrifugal pull of diversity and dialogue. 'This dialogic orientation . . . creates new and significant artistic potential in discourse' (Bakhtin 1981, 275). Although he was discussing the novel, Bakhtin's theory of heteroglossia – in which any given utterance must be

Jonestown and the Study of NRMs

understood against 'a background made up of contradictory opinions, points of view, and value judgments' (Bakhtin 1981, 281) – works well when applied to descriptions of Jonestown. No single statement about it will suffice, given the babble of rival claims and depictions.

Bakhtin describes the 'generic stratification of language' (Bakhtin 1981, 289), giving as examples the language of the lawyer, the doctor, the teacher and so on. Using the idea of canons on Jonestown we might call them the language of the public, the scholars and the conspiracy-minded. To this list I suggest adding the language of the artistic interpreter. Bakhtin notes, 'that these languages differ from each other not only in their vocabularies; they involve specific forms for manifesting intentions, forms for making conceptualization and evaluation concrete' (Bakhtin 1981, 289). At any given moment, then, representations of Jonestown, and in regard to art, the *idea* of Jonestown, contend with each other in competing languages of heteroglossia (Bakhtin 1981, 291). This requires the consumer of information about Peoples Temple and Jonestown to participate in the dialogue, since understanding is active rather than passive, with both the artist and the recipient dynamically engaged.

It is easy to encounter the heteroglossia of Jonestown. Literary works such as novels and books of poetry; artistic works such as paintings and sculpture; musical works such as individual songs and complete operas; and dramatic works such as plays and films, have broadened public understanding of this unique religious movement far beyond the confines of historical or sociological studies. At the Jonestown Institute we have come to call Jonestown studies and projects 'The Vortex', a place into which individuals are drawn for personal and professional reasons. Some survive and even flourish in the Vortex; some escape after a brief time of being hurled about; and some are chewed up and damaged by their encounter. We never know who will be a casualty. Yet the immensity of the catastrophe continues to draw individuals into itself.

One explanation for this is that the subject of Peoples Temple is attracting a generation of interpreters who grew up after Jonestown. Andrew Brandou's series of Jonestown paintings, called 'As a man thinketh, so he is', features cute furry animals engaged in murderous acts. In one painting, Jim Jones is portrayed as a friendly lion rescuing a rabbit from real and imaginary threats. The artist was 10 years old when the deaths occurred, and since he was attending Catholic school at the time, he heard daily sermons on the tragedy. His siblings, who were considerably older, described the events in ways that did not correspond to what authority figures were saying. As an adult, Brandou says he

> became driven to understand exactly 'what' had taken place, not only to the victims of circumstance who became 'a nation's tragedy' but to myself, as a frightened child suddenly forced to question authority. [T]hese are the forces

which have always driven me for my series regarding [P]eoples [T]emple. (Brandou 2007)

As a result of this self-reflexive child-adult perspective, the artist painted the history of Peoples Temple in a picture-book style, though one that was not immediately indicative of the original story. Brandou explains that he did not want to mock anyone or glorify the tragedy, and it is true that the connection with Peoples Temple and Jonestown is not immediately clear from the paintings. He adopted this perspective, 'because [I] am coming from a youthful perspective, as an outside observer trying to reverse engineer an "unsolvable" situation' (Brandou 2007). Brandou's outsider status is one that a number of younger interpreters can claim. The events in Jonestown have not been overdetermined for them as they have been for those whose historical memories of the events tend to be fixed and hardened.

Other artists use Jonestown as the point of departure for explorations that extend beyond the events themselves. Laura Baird's *Jonestown Carpet* is an interpretation of the famous aerial photograph taken by David Hume Kennerly of the brightly coloured bodies spread out upon the grounds of Jonestown. Baird explains that the impetus for the work, which was ten years in the making and remains deliberately unfinished, was the death of her sister in 1980 (Baird 2004). She describes 'a highly memorable moment' occurring in 1983, when:

> A faint wisp of green stuff in Kennerly's photo quite suddenly and emphatically became a banana leaf. Abstract shards of color soon began to emerge as distinct figures, some with limbs, some with limbs conjoined, apparently expressing terminal gestures of affection and consolation. In this way the subject I chose in 1981, the aerial photograph, seemed to transcend itself and became something else. Perhaps, as others have said, it became hyperreal. I don't know of any terms that fit the picture precisely as I see it. (Baird 2004)

The *Jonestown Carpet* realizes Baird's intention of presenting appearances and encouraging perception. Her subject was not Jonestown, but rather the representation of Jonestown; and now her representation adds another level of interpretation.

Bakhtin's critique of stylistics (the branch of linguistics that studies literary styles) can also be applied to novels and poetry about Jonestown. He argues that traditional stylistics is deaf to dialogue, and that it conceives of literary works as though they were hermetically sealed and self-sufficient, constituting 'a closed system presuming nothing beyond themselves' (Bakhtin 1981, 273). He asserts that various works, and their styles, act as rejoinders to other rejoinders participating in the same dialogue. This dialogical engagement is quite apparent in works about Jonestown that come from a Guyanese novelest, a British-Guyanese poet and an African-American poet.

Wilson Harris' *Jonestown* (1996) is a dreamlike novel that uses the story of Jonestown as a way to examine the effects of colonialism and postcolonialism in Guyana. Harris is interested in history and memory, especially the erasure of the precolonial memory due to the extermination of indigenous peoples. He justifies his obtuse literary style, saying 'The lives and limbs of those who have perished need to be weighed as incredible matter-of-fact that defies the limits of realistic discourse' (Harris 1996, 82). Moreover, as Harris says elsewhere, the novels written by and about all-white characters in the eighteenth and nineteenth centuries, who ignored all other peoples, were the product of imperialism (Harris 2002). Thus *Jonestown*, the ostensible account of Francisco Bone – the fictional sole survivor of the Jonestown holocaust – describes the state of the colonized. When Bone encounters his skeleton-twin in some sort of nether world, his twin says:

> You danced into GRAVE LAND on primordial feet. But in fact *you are alive, you survived the holocaust*, you possess – it is true – all the appearances of having died. But you belong to the living extremities of the WASTE LAND. You are almost in a post-wasteland grave. Almost in. Almost there. Not quite.... (Harris 1996, 147, italics in original)

The Waste Land, aside from referring to T. S. Eliot's famous poem, serves as the metaphor for contemporary Guyana and the plight of all colonized peoples. Harris' novel, therefore, exemplifies Bakhtin's decentralizing tendency in the literature about Jonestown because he assesses Jonestown from within a Caribbean context and from outside a North American context.

Fred D'Aguiar also examines Jonestown as an insider of British-Guyanese descent, and as an outsider to the United States (though he currently teaches at Virginia Tech University) in the book of poems titled *Bill of Rights* (D'Aguiar 1998). Like Harris, D'Aguiar uses the story of Jonestown to examine the contemporary life of the dispossessed, from Brixton to Glasgow to Tiger Bay. He 'puts Jonestown within the context of the surge and flow of immigrants across continents, always demonstrating an awareness of the legacy of domination' (Moore 2009, 76). The deaths in Jonestown are larger than a single place, and *Bill of Rights* is a song of protest against oppression in Jonestown, in Guyana and around the world.

Finally, Carmen Gillespie writes from a dual vantage point: as an African American she is a member of a minority and a cultural outsider in the United States; but regarding Jonestown, where 70 per cent of the residents were black, she is an insider cognizant of African-American culture. Gillespie's poetry collection *Jonestown: A Vexation* (2011) uses dictionary definitions of 'vexation' to structure the poems in the volume. She presents 'found' poems that emerge from a number of texts: things Jones said; newspaper headlines; a mélange of a dictionary definition, a CDC description and an encyclopedia entry; and a series of 918 X's titled *Schemata: A Requiem*. Gillespie's poems communicate outrage at the terrible loss, but also convey a sense of commitment and high purpose that the community felt at some points in its existence. Several poems suggest that Jonestown was not a prison camp: 'There, there were flowers'; 'There, there was loving'; 'There, there was color'; 'There, there was laughter.' Here Bakhtin's 'dialogic imagination' exists within the covers of a single volume.

A closing example of Bakhtin's heteroglossia comes from musical works, which rely upon 'acts of recognition' (Bakhtin 1981, 278) to make their statement. Jonestown has its own history of symbols, languages, and meaning, upon which songwriters and musical groups capitalize. While only a single musical work can yet be called symphonic – Frank Zappa's *Jonestown* – there are countless popular interpretations, ranging from thrash rock to rap to electronica, that incorporate Jonestown's 'contradictory multiplicity' (in Bakhtin's words, p. 278). Electronica, in particular, mixes sound from Peoples Temple audiotapes into digital mashes that often transmit a message of terror or warning, though rarely of sympathy. Sometimes mere shock value is the point, as in the name of the rock group the Brian Jonestown Massacre. Musicians from the group Cults inserted themselves into home movies from Peoples Temple in a music video for some shock value as well. An earlier, high concept video treats their song 'Go Outside' in an entirely different way. Isaiah Seret, producer of the second video, explains that he 'couldn't help but notice their [Jonestown residents'] similarity to my current community of friends that is, smart, tolerant, with spiritual inclinations and a yearning for shared community' (Seret 2011). The producer describes reactions to the video, including those from a former Temple member, and concludes:

> While it's easy in hindsight for us to dismiss Jim Jones and the tragedy as some kind of anomaly in history, through making this video, I learned that at the beginning these followers were promised two things we all want: a meaningful life (closer to God); and financial security. These are two things that are very hard to pass up. (Seret 2011)

Seret acknowledges the layers of meaning already surrounding Jonestown, yet produces his own 'rejoinder' to the ongoing dialogue over Peoples Temple.

The Lessons of Jonestown for NRM Studies

Hatcher's work with Peoples Temple survivors reveals that former members of all opinions shared the belief that 'society has learned little from the mass suicides and murders at Jonestown' (Hatcher 1989, 146). There is something about moralizing certitudes that undermines the magnitude of the event; and, conversely, the enormity of what happened subverts any and all attempts to 'explain'. Academic analyses seem to miss the dialogical nature of representations of Jonestown, including those of scholars themselves. Little, if any, consensus exists in the scholarly literature, especially when we pit psychologists and psychiatrists against sociologists and historians.

The voices of survivors and artists serve as a salutary counterbalance to scholarly assessments of Peoples Temple and Jonestown. They act centrifugally against efforts to unify discourse about Jonestown. Moreover, artists and survivors seem to take heteroglossia for granted.

The internet has played a significant role in these developments. First, it has allowed survivors to continue to be in dialogue and reflection. Unlike the polarizing animosity ex-members have for some groups today (e.g. Scientology or The Family International), a sort of fellowship of common loss exists that enables survivors of all opinions to meet, talk and ponder their experiences in Peoples Temple. 'Whenever participants in an historic event gather to reminisce, it is a continuation of that history' (Bellefountaine 2005). A panel of Temple survivors spoke at the 2011 meeting of the American Academy of Religion meeting in San Francisco. The audience got to see firsthand the debates that continue, as panel members argued with each other about White Nights and suicide rehearsals. These ongoing discussions, both online and off, continue to be revelatory.

A second reason the internet has shaped discourse about Peoples Temple is that it has introduced the group to a new generation of people for whom the cult wars of the 1970s and 1980s are irrelevant. This generation finds Jonestown a powerful subject for works of art, literature, and music, that attempt to meditate upon life's deepest mysteries: good and evil; life and death; humanity and inhumanity. They consider Peoples Temple outside the confines of religion, or cults, and place it within the larger frame of existential meaning.

In Scott Blackwood's award-winning novel *We Agreed to Meet Just Here*, one of the characters is a Jonestown survivor. According to this narrative, Odie Dodd, a Guyanese doctor, was the one who shot Jones after everyone else had died. In his old age, Odie wanders off from the Texas town where he now lives, and where he continues to have conversations with Jim Jones. They exchange stories, and when Jones tries to redirect the one Odie is telling, the physician asserts, 'The story doesn't end where you say' (Blackwood 2009, 237).

The story of Jonestown is still being written – by scholars, by survivors and by artists. The earlier cult wars drew deep divisions between those who focused on the welfare of individuals and those who considered groups as a whole within a larger social or historical context. Those living outside the world of scholarship, however, are not bound by any of these constraints. As long as they find Jonestown the stimulus for continued reflection, the story doesn't end where we say.

12 Conversion and Brainwashing: Controversies and Contrasts

James T. Richardson

Chapter Outline	
Meanings of Conversion	90
Processes of Conversion	92
Agents of Conversion	95
Consequences of Conversion	96
'Brainwashing'	98
Conclusions	100

Controversy and contrast have been part and parcel of conversion research associated with religious groups, especially newer ones, for decades (Beckford 1985; Bromley and Richardson 1983; Hackett 2008). Similar comments can be made about closely related theories and research associated with recruitment to social movements of other types. There has been significant scholarly discussion and even controversy over the meaning of conversion/recruitment and the processes, agents and consequences thereof (Machalek and Snow 1993; Malony and Southard 1992; Marty and Greenspan 1988; Rambo 1993). Each of these intertwined issues will be addressed in turn, starting with the many contrasting meanings attributed to conversion to religious groups as well as other types of movements. The contrasting term of 'deconversion' also will be examined, noting that this term is a necessary complement to any review of conversion itself, since most people who join religious or other social movements eventually terminate their participation, moving on to other roles and affiliations.

After discussing each of these four aspects of conversion/deconversion the popular and quite negatively connoted, pseudo-scientific term 'brainwashing' will be examining in light of the theoretical and empirical analysis presented herein. This term has become virtually hegemonic as a popular explanation of why intelligent and well-educated youth would participate in so-called new religious movements (NRMs), sometimes referred to by the pejorative term 'cult' or 'sect' (Dillon and Richardson 1994; Richardson 1993). A number of scholars have discussed how the concept has been involved in a number of legislative and legal actions involving NRMs, as societal leaders and others have sought ways to exert social control over NRMs. 'Brainwashing' has been a handy 'social weapon' to use against these sometimes quite unpopular groups, and its use deserves attention from any scholars or others interested in conversion.

Meanings of Conversion

Conversion for many, especially in the general public, typically means a total and near instantaneous change of beliefs, behaviours and even personality of an individual. The model or paradigm for this view of conversion is what allegedly occurred with Saul of Tarsus, whose conversion experience on the road to Damascus is thought to have been rapid and totally life changing (Richardson 1985a). A sharply contrasting focus on a conversion assumes that it can be much more gradual and less thorough-going in terms of it effects of the convert. This latter approach assumes that conversion can contribute to changes in lifestyle or behaviour, but that conversion does not change one's basic personality (Paloutzian, Rambo and Richardson 1999). The former more radical interpretation of conversion is more often associated with those who join unusual or new and different religious groups, referred to in recent decades as NRMs. However, a more gradual or partial change occurring in a convert may be the best way to describe what is happening with most people who affiliate with an NRM. This less dramatic and pervasive view of conversion is also illustrated by what is referred to as 'denominational switching', in which people move from one denomination to another for social reasons, but with few major changes in lifestyle or beliefs (Marty 2012; Roof and Hadaway 1979). NRM participants often seem to be involved in 'conversion careers' that are somewhat analogous to denominational switching, as they move from one NRM to another, or to some other type of experience (Richardson 1978, 1980).

Whether the more rapid and radical view of conversion is in fact a useful way to characterize such affiliation decisions remains to be seen, however, as the interpretation may say more about the views and values of those observing the apparent radical change than it does about what is actually taking place with the alleged convert. This more constructionist perspective of the meaning of conversion for scholars and non-scholars alike is discussed in Richardson's (1985a) positing of reasons for a more activist orientation towards conversion[1] and in Beckford's (1978a) discussion of how members of the Jehovah's Witnesses define and view their conversion.

Other differences of opinion have occurred on whether conversion to religious or other social movements is mainly a cognitive process (Brown and Caetano 1992), or if it is behavioural and experiential in origin and effects. Do people change their minds as a key and immediate precursor to conversion, with behavioural and other changes following as a consequence? Or do they engage in behaviours and social interactions within a social network that in turn contributes to a subsequent change of cognitions? Most research supports the latter contention, attributing changes of belief and behaviour to the social context in which a person is involved (Snow, Zurcher, Ekland-Olson 1980). Social ties are most important, leading to the conclusion that 'conversion usually is deciding to agree with your best friend'. The social network perspective explains much of what has happened concerning participation in NRMs as well as other changes in religious affiliation (Rochford 1980; Stark and Bainbridge 1980). And participation in other social movements also often depends on social ties, and flows along social networks.

Yet another difference in meaning concerns the 'why' of conversion, a topic that overlaps the consideration of agency below. Popular theories of conversion that have predominated for decades focused on strains and frustrations that might encourage individuals to seek alternative lifestyles and belief systems. These theories were developed decades ago from research on more unusual religious groups and movements such as snake handling groups in Appalachia or 'holy roller' religious groups. This perspective seemed to be based on an assumption that something was wrong with anyone who converted to one of those odd groups. The 'psychopathological' approach to conversion was in vogue from some time, according to Rod Stark (Stark 1965; also see Bainbridge 1984), but, although still persisting in some accounts applying such terms as deprivation to religious conversion, was generally replaced more recently by many scholars focusing on new religious movements (NRMs) or other social movements. I and other researchers found that an agency-oriented approach emphasizing volition of the convert more useful and with more explanatory power (Dawson 1992, 2006; Heirich 1977; Lofland 1979; Richardson 1985a; Straus 1976, 1979). Research on NRM members found that most were choosing to do something different than traditional career and life course expectations would dictate, but for what on close examination could, from their perspective, be viewed as quite understandable reasons. Similar conclusions were reached by a number of researchers such as Jerome Skolnick on political social movements of the past few decades (Skolnick 1969).

All of the above considerations on meaning of conversion also should be applied to consideration of deconversion. Scholars have noted that one of the best kept secrets of NRMs and their critics is the very high attrition rates of the groups, and the fact that most NRMs are actually quite small (Bird and Reimer 1982; Richardson, van der Lans and Derks 1986; Skonovd 1983; Wright 1987). Religious or other social movement groups do not want to advertise how small they actually are, and neither do those in the so-called anti-cult movement (ACM) who seek to promote efforts at social control of the groups. However, it is clear that the relatively small membership in most NRMs and many other social movement groups makes deconversion as important a phenomenon of study as is conversion and recruitment.

It should be obvious that most who participate in NRMs or other social movements do so only temporarily, and that they eventually 'return home' or decide to try some other group or movement as they seek meaning and purpose in their lives. As noted above, the term 'conversion careers' (Richardson 1978, 1980) has been applied to the pattern discerned in studies of NRMs participants flowing in and out of various movements, some of them quite different in orientation, beliefs and values. Participation is often viewed as temporary, and the level of personal commitment may be low, as potential converts keep their options open, and make 'side bets' (Becker 1960) or other commitments that will allow them options if they decide to stop participating. As negotiations take place about whether to be a part of a given group, problems may arise that cause an individual to move on sooner instead of later. And even later, the individual may reassess based on experiences they have had in the group that have disillusioned them (Wright 1987). Beckford's (1978b) careful analysis of how and why people leave the Unification Church is quite useful for understanding this oft-ignored process of leaving.

Processes of Conversion

Arguments have arisen concerning how people go about converting, or being converted. Is conversion a singular process, occurring rapidly, as supposedly occurred with Saul of Tarsus? Or is the conversion process more gradual, less thorough-going, and with multiple logically related steps? Which view is more typical and therefore generalizable across settings and groups? Also, it is important to understand that each instance of conversion actually involves a negotiation between the potential convert and the group to which they are considering affiliating. The positing of some magical and all-powerful techniques that can overcome the will of potential converts is not a very useful perspective to bring to conversion research (see discussion below of so-called brainwashing). Such a perspective belies the agency (see below) of the potential convert, and that they can, and often do, simply 'vote with their feet' and walk away from a group in which they were considering participating or a group that they had in fact joined for a time. This may occur, for example, when a participant recognizes that the potential costs of participation outweigh the perceived benefits of being or remaining involved. The analysis underlying a decision to move on and leave a group may be provoked by an emotional response to some action, such as a leader doing some that offends the morals of the participant, but there seems little reason to deny that participants in NRMs and other movement groups possess human agency and have the capacity to make decisions (see Beckford 1978b).

Multi-step processes of joining an NRM have been described in scholarly writings about several of the more controversial NRMs. Included are Burke Rochford's work on the Hare Krishna (1985), Eileen Barker's research on the Unification Church (1984), psychiatrist Marc Galanter research on several NRMs (Galanter 1980), my own work (with colleagues) on different Jesus Movement groups (Richardson, Stewart, and Simmonds 1979; Richardson and Stewart 1979), and my own summary of recruitment processes in several NRMs (Richardson 1992), among others. All these processes involve an initial contact, invitations to participate in certain activities of the group (a meal or perhaps a study of sacred documents), followed by entreaties (for those who pass initial muster) to participate in a more lengthy and intensive recruitment process, often at a different and more secluded site. This multi-step process has the effect of exposing the potential convert to the culture of the group, while also allowing group leaders to assess the 'fit' of the potential convert to the group.

The process is also the time when negotiations take place between the possible new member and the group, clearly demonstrating the agency of the individual, a topic which we discuss below. Whether or not a person decides to convert and become a participant depends on the outcome of those negotiations, which can be quite openly entered into by both parties. The negotiations sometimes involve a power and resource differential between the candidate and the group, for the group might be able to offer material goods such as food, shelter and friendship to individuals with few resources or alternatives. However, at other times the candidate might have resources (such as an advanced degree or special training) that the group needs for its own welfare, changing the dynamic of the negotiations dramatically (see last section of Richardson 1993c and Beckford 1978b for more on such negotiations).

One of the most used process models for conversion was produced in the 1960s by John Lofland and Rodney Stark (1965), developed as a part of Lofland's dissertation study of the early beginnings of the Unification Church in America. That so-called world-saver model combined features of the historical 'psychopathological' approach to conversion with the newer 'agency oriented' approach being developed from studies of social movements and NRMs.

Included were elements that focused on long-term tensions, strains, and frustrations supposedly felt by potential converts, coupled with the possession of a 'religious rhetoric' or problem-solving perspective (the latter contrasted to political and psychiatric perspectives). Also included was a factor focusing on reaching a 'turning point' when the person felt a need to change the direction of their life. These elements reference the traditional and more deterministic view that if someone converted they were being forced to do so by psychological forces beyond their control. These elements, although appealing logically and historically, have received little support in subsequent research attempting to test the model (Greil and Rudy 1984; Snow and Phillips 1980), or the step model has been extended and refocused to better fit recruitment to NRMs (Richardson and Stewart 1979). That research revealed that many people were suffering frustrations and strains of various types, but few of them joined NRMs or any other movement. And the notion of a turning point has come to be viewed as an after-the-fact 'reconstruction of biography' by those who decide to participate.

Instead the contemporary focus has been on the elements of the Lofland/Stark model that were more agency oriented and reflected a growing recognition that social networks, emotional ties, and context were much more important, while de-emphasizing cognitive aspects of conversion as well. The model incorporated the idea that a potential convert would self-define themselves as a 'seeker' wanting something different in their lives, which is a clear recognition of agency operating in such situations. The Lofland/Stark model then includes several 'situational factors' that are wholly contextual and non-cognitive, and are more dependent on the development of emotional ties between potential converts and the group's representatives. The model's authors include the development of affective ties between the potential convert and the group and the diminishing of such ties with outsiders such as family members or friends. The last element of the model is the development of intensive interaction, best accomplished through communal living situations, leading to the new convert becoming a 'deployable agent'. That intense interaction supposedly would build up more emotional ties between the potential convert and the other members of the group (see Richardson 1979, chapter 9, and Richardson and Stewart 1979).

This popular model contained something for everyone, be they traditionalist or more cognizant of newer research-based findings about why people were joining religious or other social movements. The model served as a bridge between the old and the new, which explains its immense appeal in studies of conversion and recruitment.

In the late 1970s Lofland developed a newer version of his model that completely dropped out the predisposing characteristics and elaborated on the process whereby more emotional aspects of the process were emphasized (Lofland 1979). His 'Becoming a world-saver revisited', includes elements in the conversion/recruitment process such as 'picking up' which refers to the methods developed by the UC and other groups to establish initial contact with a potential convert. This is followed by 'hooking', which describes ways to entice the person to remain with the group long enough to establish some emotional connection, and 'encapsulating', which is a detailed elaboration of how intensive interaction from the earlier model actually operated in UC recruitment efforts.

The later elements of the new Lofland model are 'loving', which is a reference to the core element of the process, 'love bombing', that UC recruiters used to convince potential recruits, and 'commitment', which is when new recruits are tested by being assigned duties that will demonstrate their commitment to the group. Lofland closes presentation of his new model with an important point that NRM researchers should start studying how potential recruits go about converting themselves, using the groups as a vehicle. He says that his earlier model assumed a passive actor, whereas research has shown that this is not the case, and that potential converts are active agents, making their own decision about what is best for them. And to this idea we now turn.

Agents of Conversion

The Lofland/Stark model and particularly its later refinement by Lofland raised the crucial question of who is in charge of a conversion or a decision to participate in a religious or other type of group? Is it the person experiencing the conversion? Or is it some external agent attempting to bring about a conversion of a 'target individual' or even perhaps some internal pressure over which the individual has little control? Is the individual powerless to overcome these various pressures that could lead them to convert? If both internal and external forces seem to be working, perhaps even in concert, how does human agency fit into the picture?

These types of questions are both empirical and philosophical in nature, and incorporate the issue of what it means to be a human being (see Kilbourne and Richardson 1989a). Can a human being be influenced to the extent that they give up their personhood and do whatever an external agent tells them to do, and do they always succumb to internal needs or external pressures over which they have little control? Or is it possible that a volitional person can and does use a religious group as a vehicle to accomplish something they are choosing to do, and that conversion may fit the 'game plan' of an individual to effect change in their life? This latter view has come to the forefront in studies of participation in NRMS for both males and females, as I and other scholars have shown.

There have been claims that NRMs were particularly exploitive of females, given their predominately male-dominated hierarchies of authority (Jacobs

1984). However, scholars such as Susan Palmer (1994) have claimed that many young women in NRMs were using those NRMs to accomplish their own goals, which might include escape from a traditional female role in the dominant society. Roger Straus, a student of John Lofland, after doing considerable research inside Scientology and also relying on research on other NRMs, concluded that many young people were using NRMs as vehicle whereby they could attempt to accomplish personal change and achieve personal goals (Straus 1976, 1979). Indeed, other research by scholars such as Eileen Barker (1984), Ted Nordquist (1978), and Brock Kilbourne (1986) has demonstrated that quite often NRMs participants were acting out their ideals, and that they were actually more compassionate and interested in helping others than counterparts in traditional religious groups or other 'normal' people.

This line of NRM research has contributed to the abandonment of the traditional deterministic and psychopathological perspective of conversion to religious groups, and helped replace with what this author and others have referred to as a new more 'active' research paradigm that assumes agency on the part of participants (Dawson 1992; Richardson 1985a). The more agency-oriented perspective also helps understanding of the deconversion phenomenon, as well, as participants may, and often do, decide to leave one group and join another, or return to a more traditional lifestyle. James Beckford, in an early study of the Unification Church described the group as a kind of 'flow through' organization that understood the fact that many recruits would not remain in the group for very long, thus raising the issue of how best to make use of fresh recruits (Beckford 1978b). Making use of new recruits on fundraising teams was apparently a calculated decision on how best to help the overall organization with the new recruits, who early on were joining the UC in relatively large numbers.

Consequences of Conversion

What are the effects of conversion and what changes when one converts to a religious group? There is considerable scholarly literature indicating that participation in 'ordinary' religious groups usually is a healthy choice, both physically and mentally (Koenig, King and Carson 2012). Religion can and does help many people integrate into a normal kind of life in their communities, and it can furnish meaning and purpose to a person's life (Frankl 2006). However, huge controversies have raged about participation in NRMs, with some claiming that participation ruins lives by breaking ties with families and disrupting career plans for young people who convert (Langone 1993; Singer 1979). Clearly such consequences did occur, and were very upsetting to some parents, some of whom were well-placed enough within the structure of society to force attention to the 'cult problem' by politicians, the media and others.

However, as discussed above in section on agency, others saw NRMs as vehicles whereby converts could take charge of their lives and strike out in different directions to act out new goals and implement their youthful idealism. Also, participation in NRMs has been credited by some scholars with playing an important role in changing lifestyles in a more positive and healthy direction, particularly in terms of stopping the use of drugs and other problematic behaviours that have been a part of the youth culture of the past several decades and helping participants move towards more integration with normal society (Muffler, Langrod, Richardson, Joseph and Ruiz 1997; Robbins and Anthony 1978, 1982; Robbins, Anthony and Curtis 1975). Some of that literature will be summarized herein, reminding readers of the milieu that was present in the 1960s and 70s for many youth in Western societies.

Participation in most Jesus Movement organizations (on which I have done much research) resulted in dramatic changes of behaviour for many that involved cessation of smoking tobacco, drinking alcohol, use of hard drugs and dropping out of a subculture that encouraged casual sex (Richardson, Stewart, and Simmonds 1979).[2] Participants in Jesus Movement groups and other NRMS also often were trained to accomplish jobs that taught them a work ethic and gave them useful skills for a career, even if it was not the one that the person's parents might have preferred. These changes in behaviour also occurred in other NRMs, as well documented by a number of researchers examining the clinical and personality effects of participation in NRMs (Richardson 1985b, 1995). Sociologists Tom Robbins and Dick Anthony, as well as I and one of my students, likened these positive effects to reintegrative and healing functions of NRMs, and referred to NRMs as serving an important 'halfway house' and healing function for many participants in NRMs (Kilbourne 1986; Kilbourne and Richardson 1984; Robbins and Anthony 1982).

Psychiatrist Marc Galanter did a number of studies of various NRMs, including some of the more notorious ones such as the Unification Church (for one example see Galanter 1980), and ended up writing a very interesting article in the *American Journal of Psychiatry* on the 'relief effect' that occurred when young people leading somewhat troubled lives joined an NRM (Galanter 1978; also see Galanter and Diamond 1981). He suggested that the discipline of psychotherapy could learn much from examining what it was about NRM participation that led to the ameliorative effects that he found in his research on several NRM groups.

The controversy over the consequences of converting, even temporarily, to an NRM seemed to derive in part from disciplinary differences in the meaning of participation in NRMs. Brock Kilbourne and I published an article in the *American Journal of Psychology* focusing on this issue and summarizing much of the literature supporting positive effects of NRM participation (Kilbourne and Richardson 1984). Most sociologists and psychologists of religion were finding generally positive effects from participation, whereas some scholars and researchers with a more clinical focus were defining NRM participation as a mental health problem, and seeking ways to encourage deconversion and movement back into a more traditional lifestyle (Clark 1979; Singer 1979). The latter interests were readily accepted by many in our society, particularly parents concerned about their son or daughter apparently giving up on long-planned career goals to participate in a strange and new religious group. This concern leads directly to the closing section, a discussion of so-called brainwashing.

'Brainwashing'

'Brainwashing' is a metaphor, but has become a powerful social weapon to use against unpopular groups or other entities which are attempting to recruit participants. It is impossible to wash someone's brain, of course, but the term has come to refer to any form of disfavoured persuasion. The concept is the antithesis of agency and volition, and assumes that individuals can be tricked or persuaded by some magical psychological techniques to literally change their minds if not their basic personality. The brainwashing perspective also assumes that individuals are passive objects which can be taken advantage of easily by modern gurus with almost any sort of message. The concept is quite deterministic in its underlying philosophy (see Anthony 1990, 1999; Richardson 1993c; Richardson and Kilbourne 1983).

This 'Manchurian Candidate' type of concept has become embedded in everyday parlance in the English language, and variants of it have developed in other languages as well. The term appears in television programmes, film, legislative reports and court cases around the world. What is amazing about this rapid spread and popular acceptance of the concept is that we can actually find the first time the term was used in the English language. This occurred in the 1950s with writings from Edward Hunter, who was retained by the American CIA to describe what was happening in the Communist takeover of China. His propagandistic treatments of this significant historical development have coloured perceptions of China since then (Hunter 1951).

After Hunter's writings invented the term it was then used to describe what took place with American prisoners of war in Korea in the 1950s, when a handful of those prisoners decided to remain in North Korea instead of be repatriated after the war ended (Richardson and Kilbourne 1983; Schein 1961; Schein, Schneier and Becker 1959; Solomon 1983). That application of the term gave the concept more impetus and helped add it to the lexicon in America. Then the concept became the term of choice to refer to the recruitment of many well-educated young people to the controversial new religions, sometimes called 'cults', that arose in public consciousness in the 1960s and 70s. As Joel Fort (1985) and others have indicated, the implicit linking of 'cults' to the communist menace was a stroke of genius, and had the result of making this relatively new concept an everyday part of the English language. The anti-cult movement adopted the term and promoted its usage in many different ways, particularly with the mass media organizations, which found the concept quite useful in promoting their own interests (Delgado 1977; Shupe and Bromley 1980; Singer 1979; Richardson 1993b,c; Richardson and Stewart 2004).

The pseudo-scientific brainwashing concept also was useful for a time in legal actions against some NRMs that were filed by former members or others (usually parents) over participation of young people in the groups. The claim that the groups had 'brainwashed' people into joining was a popular part of the societal outcry of concern about the NRMs, and judges and juries responded, acting in normative ways to assist in social control attempts of the new and controversial groups and movements (Anthony 1990; Anthony and Robbins 1992; Richardson 1991, 1993b). Some large judgements were rendered against a few NRMs such as Scientology in the 1970s and early 1980s, even though some of these were overturned on appeal.

It took years before the court systems in America finally concluded that brainwashing-based testimony did not meet usual standards of admissibility for supposedly scientific testimony (Anthony and Robbins 1992; Ginsburg and Richardson 1998). I and others, including especially Dick Anthony, played a role in these efforts, assisting some professional organizations in filing 'amicus' ('friend of the court') briefs in key cases, and also consulting with some NRMs as they tried to defend themselves against claims that they brainwashed their members.[3]

The key cases that led to the eventual demise of the use of 'brainwashing' in legal actions occurred in federal courts in California and Washington, DC. In *U.S. v. Fishman* (743 F. Supp., N.D. Cal., 1990) a former participant in Scientology who was charged with embezzlement attempted to use a diminished capacity and insanity defense in his criminal trial based on claims that he had been brainwashed by the Scientologists, causing him to be susceptible to actions over which he had little control. The Judge rejected his argument, based mainly on submissions by Dick Anthony, who consulted on the case for the prosecution (Anthony and Robbins 1992). This judgement made it clear that using such a defense in a criminal case was not going to pass muster using usual admissibility criteria.

Given that the burden of proof is much higher in criminal cases, it was unclear whether brainwashing-based arguments would carry the day in civil actions for damages. However, this was resolved at about the same time, at least as far as federal courts were concerned by *Green and Ryan v. Maharishi Mahesh*

Yogi et al. (US District Court, Washington, DC, 13 March 1991, Case #87–0015 OG). In this case the testimony of the major proponent of brainwashing theories in legal actions, clinical psychologist Margaret Singer, was disallowed at the trial court level and that decision was affirmed by the Federal Court of Appeals for the District of Columbia. There were similar decisions rendered subsequent to these key precedents in cases involving NRMs (see Anthony and Robbins 1992) and also the decision influenced what happened with such cases in state courts. Thus the brainwashing concept lost much of its utility in legal actions as the courts finally starting assessing the concept from a scientific perspective, and recognizing that it was being used to undercut freedom of religion for participants and NRMs (Richardson 1991).

However, the brainwashing term became a cultural product that was disseminated overseas, and it became quite useful to politicians, mass media, and those private and governmental groups fighting against NRMs and other minority faiths in other countries, particularly Western Europe. The term, or some of its variants (i.e. 'mental manipulation' in France and some other countries[4]) was used to construct a negatively connoted meaning for NRMs in governmental reports, media discussions, legislation, and even major court cases in Western Europe, as shown by writings of myself and others (Anthony 1999; Richardson 1996a; Richardson and Introvigne 2001). Indeed, the term, in a quite dramatic and ironic twist, came to be used for a time in China by Chinese authorities attempting to exert control over the Falun Gong. It was obvious that Chinese authorities found the term useful in its references to the Falun Gong, and it made use of it until after 9/11, at which time the term 'terrorist' was found to be more useful (Edelman and Richardson 2005).

Conclusions

This overview has traced the evolution of the meaning of the term conversion over recent decades that were highlighted by considerable attention shown to the recruitment to controversial new religious movements. These unexpected phenomena sparked great interest in why otherwise bright, well-educated, and relatively affluent young people would choose to abandon their pre-planned life course and career path to join some new and strange religious group. First efforts to do research were informed by traditional approaches that were more psychological, negative and deterministic in orientation. However, researchers who actually went into the groups to do field work quickly learned that such approaches were not fruitful, and that they did not assist in explaining what was taking place with NRMs' conversion efforts. Following the lead of research finding similar things in studies of other social and political movements, most NRM researchers adopted a more agency-oriented perspective that also took into account the social nature of decisions to participate in NRMs. Theories that focused on social networks and emotional ties came to the fore, and were accepted by most doing research on NRMs. Such theories are controversial, as shown by the conflict between those attempting to do and present research findings derived from actual research on NRMs and those whose interest were better served by defining NRM participation in negative terms, with claims that such movements and groups needed to be controlled. The brainwashing metaphor became a staple in the social control efforts of governments and others to exert control over the new religious phenomena that were developing around the Western world. This pseudo-scientific concept still is powerful, and has become hegemonic with the general public and officials in a number of Western nations, even as it has lost some credibility within the legal systems of those societies.

Notes

1 This article was written partially in response to the Lofland and Skonovd (1981) article on 'conversion motif' that was not focused on the exercise of agency by participants.
2 One prominent Jesus Movement organization, the Children of God, did practise more open sexual expression within the group in its early history, and even engaged for a time in 'flirty fishing', using sex as a recruitment tool (Richardson and Davis 1983). However, all other Jesus Movement groups known to me were quite strict and regulated sexual contact, only allowing it between married couples. See Richardson, Harder, and Simmonds (1979) for a full description on one other such group that regulated sexual activity quite rigorously.
3 After these efforts to limit brainwashing-based testimony being proffered by some major proponents of such theories two of the proponents sued this author and others involved in that effort. Several of those involved, plus the American Sociological Association and the American Psychological Association, were sued in federal court in New York for violating racketeering statutes. After that suit was finally dismissed, the two plaintiffs filed another suit for libel in California State Court, and also lost there. Such suits, though not successful, caused considerable difficulty for those involved as plaintiffs, who had to defend themselves, sometimes at considerable expense. Richardson (1996b, 1998) describes these legal actions and subsequent events in considerable detail.
4 France has been very active over the years promoting its quite secular social control approach to minority religions in other countries. See http://www.cesnur.org/2001/jan30.htm for an example of the actions of French representatives in China. There is evidence that such efforts were also made in a number of other countries, including Poland and Estonia. The use of the term 'mental manipulation', which is the French version of 'brainwashing', in the discussions in other countries usually means that the French have been there.

13 Charisma and Leadership: Charisma and Charismatic Authority in New Religious Movements (NRMs)

David G. Bromley

Chapter Outline	
Conceptualizing Charisma	104
Social Environment and the Establishment of Charismatic Authority	106
The Origination of Charismatic Authority	107
The Development of Charismatic Authority	110
Maintenance of Charismatic Authority	112
Charismatic Leadership Transition	114
Conclusions	116

It is virtually axiomatic in social science theory on religion that religion is socially constructed. The work of major theorists, Karl Marx, Max Weber, Sigmund Freud and Peter Berger, all proceed from the premise that humans create the gods rather than the reverse, although the theories founded on this common premise move in dramatically different directions. For purposes of this essay religion is understood to involve constructions of a transcendent, sacred power source (variously conceptualized as gods, powers, forces, realms, planes, worlds) that operates to create meaning, order and control in social groups. Religious organizations and their leaders are those that mediate access to the transcendent, sacred power source. The core elements of actual religious organizations, both new and established groups, include myth, ritual, authority and organization. The focus here is on authority, and particularly charismatic authority, as it has been constituted in contemporary NRMs.

In the social science literature, Max Weber's work is most often taken as the starting point in analyses of leadership. Weber (1964) identifies three ideal types of authority: traditional authority, rational-legal authority and charismatic authority. While all three types of authority are found in a broad range of social organizations, charismatic leadership is particularly central to the study of NRMs. Scholars studying NRMs generally agree that during the developmental first generation of these movements charismatic leadership is usually the predominant form of leadership. In this formative period it is often the case that the charismatic leader symbolizes and virtually embodies the group's identity.

The key elements of charismatic authority as an ideal type identified by Weber are that such leaders are *perceived* to possess exceptional abilities, their perceived abilities are understood to have a supernatural source, and the leader-follower relationship is characterized by high emotional intensity and follower trust in the leader. What the study of contemporary NRMs offers to the social science theory of religion is the opportunity to observe these elements of charismatic authority as they are being developed; that is, to study the social construction of this pivotal element of religion as it is occurring. I shall address several issues concerning charismatic authority in NRMs: how charisma is conceptualized, social environments conducive to the emergence of charismatic authority, how charismatic authority originates and then develops and the process of leadership transition in charismatically led groups.

Conceptualizing Charisma

In his influential formulation of charismatic authority, Max Weber has defined charisma as a 'certain quality of an individual's personality by virtue of which he is set apart from ordinary men and treated as endowed with supernatural, superhuman, or at least specifically exceptional powers or qualities. These are such as are not accessible to the ordinary person, but are regarded as of divine origin or as exemplary, and on the basis of them the individual concerned is treated as a leader' (1964, 358). Charisma is found and cultivated in a variety of institutional arenas – governmental, corporate, therapeutic, military and religious – because of its capacity to mobilize and unify organizations. In all organizational contexts the common quality that distinguishes charismatic authority is endowment with an extraordinary quality that is unavailable to others. Charismatic authority therefore involves both a claim of exceptional abilities by the putative charismatic individual and acceptance of those claims by followers, who may also advance those claims on behalf of the leader. The relationship is therefore one of strong emotional intensity. In religious organizations, the exceptional ability is attributed to a connection with a transcendent, sacred power source. In both secular and religious contexts charismatic authority creates a relationship of moral authority by the leader and moral obligation on the part of followers once they accept and recognize the exemplary qualities of the leader (Katz 1972, 1975).

Katz points out that charismatic authority rests on the imputation of an inherent state of being (essence) since all that individuals can actually observe is behaviour. At the most general level, the imputation is one of moral superiority on some dimension that legitimates both authority and submission. One important factor in the solidity of charismatic authority, then, is that the qualities imputed to the leader are understood to be inherent states of being and not simply extraordinary behaviours. Further, the attribution of charisma involves a re-balancing of rights and responsibilities through which followers grant a superordinate status to the charismatic leader and assume a subordinate status, creating a social reality that is continuously enacted by leaders and followers. In some cases, leaders construct a charismatic persona and followers assume new personal identities that ground their core social identities in a superordinate-subordinate relationship.

In religious organizations two broad types of charismatic authority may be identified, priestly and prophetic, although as Chryssides (2001) notes, charisma may be expressed in a variety of forms. Priestly figures lead religious organizations that are an integral component of the established social order and thus assume an accommodative stance with other established institutions while prophetic leaders are antinomian and create religious movements that challenge the established order. As founders of challenging religious movements, NRM leaders tend towards the prophetic, which means that they typically claim and are accorded a higher level of moral status while their adherents accept lower moral status and hence a greater degree of obligation and commitment. Given the moral imbalance in a strong prophetic relationship, the reliance of charismatic leaders on continuing demonstrations of their charismatic abilities, and the importance of followers acceding to charisma claims, there is an ongoing, stringent testing of loyalty and commitment for both leaders and followers.

The extent of charismatic authority claimed by prophetic figures varies considerably. It is one thing to claim to be a channel or a voice box for a transcendent entity, as JZ Knight (Ramtha) and channellers and apparitionists do, and quite another to claim to be a prophet or a god, as Ammachi and Sai Baba have. The level of charisma claims is a significant matter as the higher the claim level the greater the moral authority of leaders over followers, and this is one factor in how tightly ordered internally a movement is initially. In general, groups in which charismatic leaders claim god-like status are more tightly ordered while channelling and apparitional groups are more loosely organized networks.

Social Environment and the Establishment of Charismatic Authority

NRMs are by definition social movements that challenge the established social order through the creation of groups with new leadership, organization and membership. They typically begin with a charismatic founder/leader and a small coterie of followers. Charismatic leaders are often regarded as the source of NRMs and of movement development, but it can be equally well argued that NRM leaders' success in establishing themselves is contingent on the existence of a pool of potential recruits. As Hall and Schuyler (2000, 118) note, to achieve even modest success, 'a countercultural religious movement must offer a formula of salvation that resonates with the existential needs, interests, and anxieties of its audiences'. Fledgling leaders may enunciate a new message, but the creation of an organizational context for that message and for a charismatic leadership career depends in substantial measure on the availability of potential recruits with whom the message resonates. The emergence and development of NRMs, including both potential leaders and recruits, occur in response to some perceived type of crisis moment in the established social order. Emerging charismatic leaders of NRMs may interpret the crisis and shape the response to it, but, at the outset at least, they are also the product of the moment.

Crisis moments occur when existing cultural narratives no longer offer plausible interpretations of lived realities and/or social arrangements do not allow attainment of culturally defined values and goals. During crisis moments there is a search for alternative symbolic and social pathways. Both the future charismatic leader and potential recruits respond to the crisis, and so there is a symbiotic relationship between those who nominate a solution to the crisis and those who resonate with the proposed solution. The connection between crisis, available pools of recruits and the emergence of NRMs was clearly evident in the last half of the twentieth century.

For example, in the wake of Japan's humiliating defeat in the Second World War and South Korea's devastation as a result of both Japanese occupation and the Korean War, each society experienced a proliferation of charismatic leaders establishing NRMs following the cessation of armed combat. A similar surge of religious innovation occurred during the 1960s and 1970s in the United States and Western Europe, with a major catalyst being the divisive Vietnam War.

One indication of the importance of a responsive pool is that new movements may remain quiescent until a pool of potential recruits appears. For example, Unificationism arrived in the United States in 1959 but languished in obscurity until the early 1970s when Sun Myung Moon arrived to assume personal leadership of the movement and a large pool of countercultural protesters were available to be recruited. In some cases where potential recruit pools are large and long term, they can create a membership base and stature for a charismatic leader very quickly. For example, traditionalist Catholic and Protestant pools have provided immediate membership bases for Marian apparition and revival movements, respectively, with movements sometimes gaining thousands of followers within a period of weeks (Bromley and Bobbitt 2011).

The actual impact of potential recruit pools over time is complex, however. While such pools can provide the impetus for movement formation and enhance the stature of a charismatic leader, they also entail risks for both leader and movement. As a crisis subsides, the supply of potential recruits diminishes, while high membership turnover rates often continue. This occurred with three of the most visible and controversial NRMs of the 1970s – Unificationism, the Children of God/The Family International (hereafter, The Family International), and the International Society for Krishna Consciousness (hereafter, ISKCON). Each movement flourished during the period of countercultural protest, but membership declined rapidly thereafter. Many NRMs in the West functioned as transitional affiliations between adolescence and adulthood for members during the crisis period of the 1960s–1970s, and youthful interest waned thereafter. Similarly, Sai Baba's worldwide movement has served as a means of connecting religious traditionalism and secular modernity for a contemporary generation of upwardly mobile and diasporic Hindus. In order to remain successful, NRMs often must identify alternative recruit pools, as ISKCON did by substituting diasporic populations from former Soviet bloc countries for countercultural dropouts, or by relying on procreation rather than conversion for a membership base as The Family International has.

The Origination of Charismatic Authority

NRMs usually originate in one or a series of transformative moments in the lives of individuals who go on to become charismatic founder/leaders. The details of these reported transformative moments are likely to bear a strong resemblance to what are termed 'paranormal' or 'anomalous' experiences (precognition, apparitions, visions, out-of body, past lives) that are commonplace across a range of cultures and may be interpreted as either secular or religious. However, the transformative moments that lead to NRM formation are pivotal as they divide the charismatic individual's life into 'before and after' and become the legitimation base for subsequent public charisma claims. What distinguishes ordinary subjective experiences from the putatively extraordinary experiences that launch NRMs is a conviction that the experience constitutes a connection with a transcendent sacred power source and a claim that the experience creates a unique spiritual status for the individual. Several patterns in the originating experiences in NRM formation have been observed that are helpful in understanding how the process of charisma creation occurs.

The charismatic leaders of NRMs tend to emerge from the margins of the social order where institutionalized patterns are not as effective and where changes in those patterns have greater negative impact. These individuals directly experience the associated tensions and contradictions, and their lives reflect their personal marginality. For example, John Paul Rosenberg, the founder of Erhard Seminar Training, left his family and moved across the country to start life over as Werner Erhard. He had been an encyclopedia salesman. Moses David Berg, founder of The Family International, had been an itinerant evangelist who was unsuccessful in his religious career and was over 50 years old when he began to lead the group of Jesus Freaks who became the early membership base of the movement. The leader of the Branch Davidians, David Koresh, was the product of a dysfunctional family, a high school dropout, and held a series of menial jobs before joining the Branch Davidians as a handyman. The transformative moments they subsequently report emanate from often extended periods of personal turbulence during which they struggle with a conventional way of life.

Individuals who evolve into charismatic leaders of NRMs typically report an 'in the moment' transformative encounter, revelation or enlightenment. For example, the channeller JZ Knight reported that she was sitting in her kitchen when the 35,000-year-old warrior, Ramtha, suddenly appeared as a purple pillar of light. Raël, founder of the Raelians, was unexpectedly confronted by a UFO visitation and a meeting with a representative of the Elohim while walking in an area of inactive volcanoes to which he felt drawn. While these kinds of events are conveyed as unconnected to prior life experiences, the evidence suggests that they likely have been in the making for an extended period of time. The life histories of charismatic leaders often reveal an extended period of self-described spiritual exploration and struggle that at some point is followed by a moment during which that struggle is resolved and clarity is achieved. Since individuals who become charismatic leaders of NRMs are in the process of offering solutions outside of those available through the established social order, this type of two-step, problem-solving process appears to be the path through which transformative moments occur. From this perspective, the spiritual discoveries are not unlike creative moments experienced by other types of culture workers (poets, artists, novelists). However, charismatic leaders' narratives of transformative moments are presented as a connection with a transcendent sacred power source and are a first step in establishing their extraordinary qualities.

Following the transformative moment, there is a period of time during which future charismatic leaders try to make internal sense of what has transpired.

Four observations are pertinent here. First, this period may be brief or lengthy, Sun Myung Moon, for example, reports having struggled for several years with what he experienced as a godly assigned mission to complete Jesus' mission. Second, when the moment does occur, future charismatic leaders most often report that it was unanticipated and occurred at the initiative of the transcendent power source, which serves to legitimate the claim. There is also, of course, a caveat that they were selected for certain propitious qualities. The representation of transcendent power approached them unexpectedly, as it did for Raël, JZ Knight and Sun Myung Moon. Third, as Stark (1987, 1996) has pointed out, individuals confronted with extraordinary experiences are most likely to interpret them in terms of their existing stock of knowledge. It is no accident, for example, that Catholics are likely to experience visions of the Virgin Mary, while Protestants rarely do, and that Protestants are more likely to attribute a revelatory experience to a visitation of the Holy Spirit. Fourth, when they do decide to disclose their experiences to others, they are most likely to approach personal intimates such as friends and relatives. This step is crucial as it transforms what had been a subjective reality into a social reality.

The transfer of the transformative moment narrative to the public sphere has two major consequences. One is that for the experience to have charismatic career and movement mobilization potential the narrative must be fashioned in such as way as to be relevant to the tensions being experienced by potential recruits. Initially, for example, the founder of the Metropolitan Community Church, Troy Perry, had a dream in which he was told that God loved him. He later concluded that this must mean that God loved all gay people, and this insight led him to establish a church for the gay population. The other consequence is that public revelation leads to the formation of alliances as supporters and opponents respond to the emerging narrative. The contemporary hugging saint from India, Ammachi, for example, encountered immediate, strong rejection from her family when she initiated charismatic claims of becoming one with Krishna. The experience of apparitionist Mary Ann van Hoof confirms both of the latter points. She initially interpreted the Virgin's appearance as assistance with her personal troubles and inability to perform her domestic duties. However, this was soon translated into a more broadly relevant issue of morality when her husband offered support and suggested that Mary's appearance might have been a response to wickedness in the world. It is this linking of what C. Wright Mills (Mills 1967, 395–6) termed 'private troubles' and 'public issues' that produces resonance between the emerging charismatic leader and the potential pool of recruits.

The new mythic narrative being constructed arguably fares best if it simultaneously incorporates sufficiently prophetic elements to distinguish it from already established religious dogma and yet maintains some connection to existing traditions. Stark (1987, 1996) observes that one factor in the success of

Mormonism is that it has incorporated enough elements of Christian mythology to render conversion to Mormonism plausible for Christians. NRM founder/leaders have developed a variety of ways of simultaneously connecting to and distancing from established religious traditions. Common techniques for accomplishing this include accepting the basic myth but claiming new revelations that clarify or extend existing doctrine. Such 'progressive revelation' was an ongoing occurrence in The Family International and in all of the channelling and apparition movements. A related technique is accepting the sacred text but discovering secrets contained within the text that legitimate a new movement. Sun Myung Moon referred to the Bible as a 'cryptogram' and created a major reinterpretation of the text that included a redefinition of the source and nature of original sin (Bromley and Shupe 1979, 45). Branch Davidian leader David Koresh was in the process of unlocking the secrets contained in the Book of Revelation's Seven Seals at the time of the final assault on the community by federal agents. Yet another technique is to accept the legitimacy of the established mythic tradition but claim that existing religious groups no longer live the tradition. The leader then gathers a 'faithful remnant' that will unswervingly adhere to the tradition and be divinely rewarded for its fidelity. The Twelve Tribes designed exactly this role for itself and began pursuing the objective of constructing twelve tribes that will set the stage for the endtimes. In addition to connecting private troubles and public issues, then, connecting to established religious traditions while at the same time creating a new and distinctive message is integral to charismatic career development.

The Development of Charismatic Authority

Evidence from NRM research indicates that once claims to charismatic authority have been made the claim is solidified and stabilized. Two related processes through which this is accomplished are the construction of a new persona that distinguishes the leader's former, more mundane identity from the new, more elevated status and the development of a hagiography (spiritual biography). The charismatic persona is not static, however, as leaders may either increase or decrease their claims over time.

Typical means of creating a new persona are changing one's name and changing one's appearance. Taking on a new name is a way of symbolically creating a new individual. For example, Werner Erhard, founder of est, was born John Paul Rosenberg; Branch Davidian Leader David Koresh was born Vernon Howell; and Raelian leader Raël was born Claude Vorilhon. Charismatic leaders also may change their appearance in various ways, at least during the period when they are acting out their charismatic personas. When she displays her Ramtha persona, JZ Knight dons loose-fitting clothing, adopts a more masculine appearance and alters her voice. Lonnie Frisbee, legendary evangelist who was instrumental in building the Calvary Chapel with Chuck Smith, wore biblical-era robes and adopted a hair and beard style that resembled popular depictions of Jesus. A second means of constructing a new persona involves the fashioning of hagiographies. The themes, events, heroic deeds contained in hagiographies support the charismatic authority claims of NRM leaders, and their extraordinary abilities typically emerged at an early age. The activities of Scientology's founder, L. Ron Hubbard, have been woven into an elaborate tapestry that depicts him as an extraordinary individual from youth. He was reputed to be a searcher for truth in a variety of ways, as a world traveller, navigator, sailor, and pilot, for example. More importantly, he discovered the principles through which all humankind can develop its true, infinite potential. Similarly, Anton LaVey, founder of the Church of Satan, created a life history in which, prior to his leadership in the church, he had been a circus lion tamer, stage hypnotist, nightclub organist, police department photographer and instrumentalist in the San Francisco Ballet Orchestra. He also claimed romantic liaisons with Marilyn Monroe and Jayne Mansfield. Followers also participate in the process by creating and spreading stories of experiencing the divine qualities of the leader, being healed of infirmities and witnessing miraculous performances by the leader.

Charismatic authority claims do not necessarily remain static. Once an NRM has formed it is commonplace for the charismatic leader to alter charisma claims. There are occasional cases in which charismatic leaders renounce their claims. For example prior to David Koresh's assumption of leadership in the Branch Davidans, his predecessor, Lois Roden, issued a prophecy that failed and then attempted to renounce her charismatic authority and disband the movement in the wake of her failure. Similarly, after three failed predictions of the endtime date, Family Radio's Harold Camping apologized for his failures and disavowed any future predictions. It is much more common for leaders to heighten their status claims over time. Moses David Berg began his religious career as Uncle Dave, preaching to members of the counterculture in a coffee house, but within a short time had taken the name Moses and then claimed the status of God's endtime Prophet. Vernon Howell entered the Branch Davidian community as a handyman, assumed movement leadership, and within a short time had announced himself to be a messianic figure, David Koresh. Rajneesh/Osho initially adopted the title Acharya (enlightened teacher) and later became Bhagwan (Self-Realized One, the pure essence of the divine). Heightened charisma claims can have a major impact on the movement. While new claims are sometimes met with resistance and defections, the longer-term outcome may be a more tightly knit group. Those who remain in the movement accept a greater degree of moral obligation to the leader, and new recruits begin membership with the expectation of greater obligation.

Maintenance of Charismatic Authority

Since charismatic authority is socially constructed through claims of charismatic leader and acceptance by followers, leaders have at stake both in protecting their status and monitoring acceptance by followers. Charismatic leaders of NRMs therefore have developed a number of strategies for preserving their status. These include maintaining distance from followers; providing periodic evidence of their extraordinary abilities; preventing their movements from adopting settled, institutionalized patterns of living; creating constantly changing conditions within the movement; increasing demands for commitment both to the movement and to the leader; and controlling potential competitors.

Two related problems that new leaders face are becoming too familiar and ordinary by virtue of continuous interaction with members and providing followers the opportunity to observe them outside of their charismatic roles. Numerous groups, such as the Twelve Tribes, Calvary Chapel, and The Family International, began by the leader intensely interacting with converts, sometimes even taking them into their own homes. The ordinariness problem is more acute for charismatic leaders claiming god-like qualities as it is difficult to maintain such lofty status if their mundane, human qualities become too apparent. By contrast, this problem is diminished for leaders making weaker claims. Channellers and apparitionists, for example, are expected to exhibit extraordinary traits only during the moments when they are connected to transcendent power, and the charismatic persona is reserved for such occasions. Going into trance, as JZ Knight and Nancy Fowler do, provides boundary markers that protect them from more general expectations of charismatic performance. It is not surprising, therefore, that leaders making strong charisma claims often separate themselves at some point from followers and limit interactions to ritualized encounters. The Family International constitutes an extreme case. Moses David Berg left the United States a short time after forming the movement, and he was never seen again by members outside of his small inner circle. Even if a group remains communal, the leader is likely to establish a separate residence and maintain separation except for ritualized meetings. Osho/Rajneesh and Love, the leader of the Love Israel movement, both adopted that solution.

By virtue of their claims to high moral status, charismatic leaders are expected to demonstrate their extraordinary qualities periodically. Katz (1975, 1382) notes that, 'As security for their risky investments in granting extraordinary powers to the charismatic individual, in releasing themselves from proscriptions to heed the call, and in obtaining relief from obligations to mundane others, [followers] demand the right to make frequent audits of the status of charisma.' Charismatic leaders respond to this expectation by performances that confirm their extraordinary abilities. Sai Baba materializes a variety of objects at the behest of devotees; Marian apparitionists, such as Nancy Fowler at Conyers,

Georgia, maintain regular scheduled visitations by the Virgin at which there are new revelations; and the Solar Temple produced carefully choreographed holographic events at which the ascended masters were made to appear.

Another set of problems that confront the charismatic leader involves a settling of the movement over time. During NRMs' early histories they are populated entirely by new converts with high commitment levels and willingness to sacrifice their personal lives in order to achieve movement goals. However, as members grow older and begin to form families and careers, there is a tendency to seek more settled lives. This kind of settling diminishes the leaders' capacity to maintain the same high level of control over followers despite their charismatic authority. Leaders draw on a predictable set of tactics for resisting movement settling. Producing continuous change within the movement undermines stability and predictability for followers and leaves the charismatic leader as the only source of order. The Family International is a quintessential example of such constant change. Moses David Berg constantly changed movement missions, leadership structure, community size and physical location through the movement's early history as he sought to have sole control over its direction. Similarly, Sun Myung Moon organized Unificationism in the United States as a series of projects that were constantly changing and replaced leaders in the limited movement bureaucracy every few years to prevent individuals from becoming functionaries. A related tactic for preventing settling is periodically relocating the group. During the early history of Heaven's Gate, for example, Marshall Applewhite and Bonnie Nettles created a highly transient lifestyle for the group, with locations changing every few months. Jim Jones moved the Peoples Temple from Indiana across the country to California and then later to an isolated community in Guyana.

In order to provide assurance of their own authority and of followers' loyalty, charismatic leaders may increase the personal demands on followers. One way in which this has been accomplished is by altering familial organization and sexual practices of members. For example, David Koresh tested the loyalty of his male followers by demanding sexual access to their wives and daughters as part of his messianic mission to create a new spiritual lineage. Sun Myung Moon required sexual celibacy of his followers for several years until he approved a 'blessing' (marriage) under his spiritual authority. Osho/Rajneesh moved in the opposite direction, urging his followers to pursue open sexual relationships with a succession of partners rather than marriage. Both celibacy and free love had the same effect as strong intermediate relationships between leader and followers were prevented. A more extreme example of loyalty testing was Jim Jones' use of periodic, ritualized 'suicide rehearsals' at Peoples Temple. Community members were required to consume what they were told was 'poison' as a test of their trust in Jones.

Finally, charismatic leaders of NRMs always face the possibility of direct challenges to their charismatic status or, more generally, to their movement leadership. These challenges can come from various sources; although charismatic leaders most often survive challenges, this is not always the case. In the Osho/Rajneesh movement, Ma Anand Sheela quickly rose to a leadership position after Rajneesh withdrew into a period of silence. She began to assume Rajneesh's spiritual authority, unilaterally adopting the title of Boddhisattva. However, her heavy-handed tactics led Rajneesh to reassert his authority and denounce her when he re-emerged from his silence; she was ultimately both stripped of her authority within the movement and later prosecuted for criminal activities she had orchestrated. The outcome was quite different in the Church of Satan. Anton LaVey, founder of the Church of Satan, initially supported the leadership development of Michael Aquino, who quickly became his second-in-command. However, when the two began to disagree theologically, Aquino challenged LaVey by invoking the presence of Satan. Aquino reports being given a mandate for a new church, the Temple of Set; on that basis he and a number of LaVey's followers formed a new, schismatic group. Challenges are not restricted to the leadership ranks. In the Love Family, the movement leader, Love, became financially irresponsible, detached from followers and drug dependent. When confrontations with Love proved ineffective in altering his behaviour, members simply began defecting. As Balch (1988b, 214) chronicles that process, 'as the full extent of Love's corruption became known, the pace of defection accelerated. By the end of 1983 almost 85 percent of Love's followers had left the community.'

Charismatic Leadership Transition

Most charismatic leaders of NRMs appear to maintain their leadership positions through their lifetimes, but this is not always the case. Crises within the movement that make their continuation problematic, the development of organizational complexity, and the combination of aging and ongoing pressures seem to lead to adjustments in charismatic authority that are not the direct result of charismatic challenges. The final challenge, of course, comes with the death of the founder, which presents the charismatic leader and the movement with a major leadership transition.

In some cases, charismatic leaders decide to renounce or diminish their charismatic status. As already noted, both the Branch Davidian leader, Lois Roden, and the Family Radio's Harold Camping renounced their charismatic authority following crises triggered by failed prophecies. The Divine Light Mission and its teenage guru, Maharaji, arrived in the United States from India in 1971 and grew rapidly. However, in the 1980s the movement experienced a major schism when Maharaji rejected his mother's control over the movement and wedded an American follower. Maharaji subsequently disbanded the movement, abandoning his role as 'lord of the universe' and assuming the role of 'humanitarian leader'. Rajneesh/Osho arrived in the United States from India in 1981 and established a ranch, Rajneeshpuram, in Oregon. The movement subsequently became embroiled in a number of conflicts; Rajneesh was ultimately charged with several crimes and deported. In the wake of these events he returned to India, renounced his guru status, assumed the name Osho and reassumed his earlier teachings with a correspondingly reduced charismatic status. Steve Hill, the charismatic evangelist who led the Brownsville Revival during its period of explosive growth, simply left the revival after it had peaked and assumed the pastorship of a local church where he assumed a more conventional ministerial role.

It is more common for charismatic leaders of groups that grow and stabilize to routinize or relinquish their administrative duties while preserving their charismatic status. For example, Sun Myung Moon resisted settling tendencies within Unificationism for a number of years but later maintained his charismatic status as Lord of the Second Advent while turning over administrative responsibility of his extensive network of religious and corporate organizations to his children. A number of years after building the Raelian movement, Raël, followed a similar path. After establishing Clonaid, an organization offering a variety of cloning services, he appointed a top female Raelian bishop, Dr Brigitte Boisselier, as a primary administrative official within the movement. L. Ron Hubbard founded the movement that began as Dianetics and then evolved into Scientology. He established the first Church of Scientology in 1954 and actively led the movement's development for over a decade. Hubbard began resigning his organizational positions in 1966 in order to devote himself to further research and writing. He retained the title of 'Founder', however, and remained the dominant influence in the movement until his death in 1986. Troy Perry, a leading voice in the gay rights movement, founded the Metropolitan Community Church in 1968. He retired as Moderator of the church in 2005 but remained its spiritual inspiration.

The precariousness of charisma, as described by Weber, becomes evident at the death of the charismatic leader. There is reason to expect that the death of a founder/leader, who often personally embodies a movement, could lead to a movement unravelling. However, research on the developmental histories of NRMs indicates that most movements survive the transition of leadership attending the death of the founder/leader. Numerous movements that emerged during the 1960s and 1970s are now in their second generation of leadership. These would include, for example, the Church of Scientology, ISKCON, Osho/Rajneesh, The Way International, Transcendental Meditation and Integral Yoga. In virtually all cases the second generation of leadership exercises bureaucratic rather than charismatic authority. Leadership transition is not necessarily a tranquil process, however. Melton (1991, 9–10) notes that leadership succession process proceeds most smoothly when a group has achieved internal stability prior to the leader's passing. The transition process in ISKCON demonstrates this point. Although Swami Prabhupada appointed a Governing Body Commission, individual gurus possess considerable independent charismatic authority. As a result, disputes over leadership legitimacy in ISKCON persisted more than three decades after Prabhupada's death in 1977.

Conclusions

All contemporary religions were new religions at some time, and NRMs are significant with respect to religion because they offer insight into how new forms of religion emerge and develop. The vast majority of scholarship on religion centres on religious traditions that originated centuries or millennia ago, making it problematic to ascertain how these traditions survived and developed during their early histories, before they successfully became integral parts of their respective social orders. Contemporary NRMs offer the opportunity to observe the social construction of religion as it is occurring.

Based on research conducted on charisma and charismatic authority in NRMs, I have argued that such authority involves a claim to heightened moral authority vis à vis followers; in NRMs charismatic authority moves in a prophetic direction. Charismatic leadership in NRMs typically emerges in an environment characterized by some degree of social dislocation that produces both nominations of solutions to perceived crisis by future leaders and resonance with those nominations by future followers. Charismatic authority begins with a transformative moment during which the future leader putatively connects with a transcendent, sacred power source, legitimating subsequent authority claims.

Leaders then create a new persona that distinguishes their ordinary and charismatic identities, which legitimates their moral authority claims and sacrifices by their followers. Once developed, charismatic authority is not stable, however. Leaders therefore develop a variety of measures to sustain followers' commitment. These involve demonstrations of extraordinary abilities, preventing movement settling, and controlling challenges to their power base. While most charismatic leaders are able to sustain their positions, they are compelled by inevitable realities to address the emergence of a rising second generation of membership and leadership. It is commonplace for long-time leaders to relinquish some measure of organizational control as movements grow in size and complexity and to plan for an eventual leadership transition. Movements that do plan leadership transitions tend to display greater stability.

What a thorough examination of charismatic leadership in NRMs reveals, then, is the complexity and precariousness of charisma as a leadership form. This finding, of course, corroborates Max Weber's seminal formulation. The study of charisma in NRMs adds to Weber's theorizing a close, empirical analysis of the dynamics of charisma development. In this way, the analysis of charismatic leadership in NRMs contributes some foundational insights into how religion as a human enterprise is socially constructed.

14 Prophecy

Jon R. Stone

Chapter Outline

Prophecy and Prophets	122
Festinger and Failed Prophecy	123
Festinger-Inspired Research on Failed Prophecy	126
Prophecy and Prophets in NRMs	129

Modern episodes of endtime prophecies abound. Few attract public attention; fewer still gain large followings. Indeed, were it not for field research by social scientists, most world-ending predictions would pass virtually unnoticed by the society at large, entering 'the historical record only at those points where outsiders stumble upon them or where they reach a level of high public visibility' (Barkun 1974, 43). But from time to time the Western media and the wider public's interest *is* drawn to one or another prediction of a coming doom. Such an event occurred in May 2011 – the event ominously referred to as 'Judgement Day'.

Briefly recounted: some months prior to the year 2011, long-time religious broadcaster Harold Camping (b. 1921) revealed to his Family Radio listeners in Oakland, California, that the Judgement Day foretold in the Book of Revelation would take place at exactly six o'clock in the evening of 21 May; the end of time itself would arrive later that year on 21 October. From roughly August 2010 to May 2011, Camping and his supporters stepped up their proselytizing efforts, warning the world through various forms of mass media that only those who repented would be spared God's wrath. But, when neither his predicted earthquake nor the expected rapture of believers to heaven occurred, Camping, now ridiculed by press and public alike, retreated to the seclusion of his home to reflect upon his seeming error. Many of his closest followers were benumbed by shock and confusion; most others fell away in shame. When Camping reappeared days later, he announced to the world that Judgement Day had in fact occurred but it had been *spiritual* – that is, an 'earthquake' that shook humanity to the core – not *literal* lest all human life perish before God's appointed time (see *Daily Mail* 2011; Family Radio 2011; and Phan 2011).

In the aftermath of 'Apocalypse Not', as many in the press mockingly called it, social scientists and historians of religion were quick to point out comparisons between Camping and William Miller (1782–1849), the nineteenth-century Baptist farmer whose own calculations from passages in the Bible had led him to predict that rapture and doom would befall the world sometime between March 1843 and March 1844 – later extended to October 1844 (see Miller 1844). As with Camping and his Family Radio listeners, Miller and his followers actively publicized the prediction and then prepared themselves for the day of their salvation. But when that day passed into night, and their long night passed into yet another day, Miller and his expectant followers were overcome by grave disappointment.[1]

Although media fascination with Camping's Judgement Day prediction quickly faded, it was replaced by the public's growing interest in the approaching end of the ancient Mayan long-count calendar, an event that was expected to occur on 21 December 2012 (see Sitler 2006 and 2012). Prompted by the work of José Argüelles (1939–2011), the spiritual guru behind the 1987 worldwide harmonic convergence gatherings, some new age leaders had come to believe that the close of the thirteenth, or last, *pik* cycle of the Mayan calendar would usher in an era of universal peace and harmony. However, a greater number of proponents of the Mayan prophecy were less optimistic, fearing instead that the termination of the last *pik* cycle would signal the end of time itself. For them, the predicted Mayan consummation of time would bring with it 'the eruption of severe solar outbursts, a geo-magnetic pole inversion, a collision with a rogue planet, [or] even an invasion of space aliens' – the scenario varying from one writer to the next (Sitler 2012, 62). As is now known, the thirteenth *pik* cycle ended with neither peace nor perdition but pity mixed with scorn.

In the popular mind, *prophecy* and *prophets* have generally been associated with doomsday predictions, the assumption being that such predictive activities are what essentially define prophecy. Even among sociologists and historians there has likewise been a tendency to associate prophecy with prediction and the prophet with catastrophic visions of the end of time (see, for instance, Barkun 1974; Cohn 1970; Robbins et al. 1997; and Wessinger 2000a). As a result, nearly all of the social science literature on prophecy and on prophetic movements reflects an almost singular scholarly focus on endtime predictions and on the consequences of prophetic failure for the individuals and movements that had believed in and prepared themselves for those predictions.

By contrast, anthropologists who study prophecy and prophets have tended to define and apply these terms much more freely, albeit inconsistently – the words *prophecy* and *prophet* effectively becoming umbrella terms under which a wider variety of religious activities have been subsumed. For example, in their collection of case studies on prophets in Eastern Africa, David Anderson and Douglas Johnson point out the lack of definitional clarity that typifies most anthropological studies on prophecy. Among ethnographers, they lament, 'the term prophet has more often been applied rhetorically than precisely; in fact its very lack of precision has encouraged its wide application' (1995, 1). Effectively, they conclude, '[t]his indiscriminate use of terms has created a number of obstacles in the way of any comparative study of prophets; for we find that in many cases the only common element uniting a variety of persons or offices is the title "prophet" imposed upon them in different ethnographies or histories' (Anderson and Johnson 1995, 2). Thus, under the headings 'prophecy' and 'prophet', one commonly finds reported in field work among African tribes such diverse religious phenomena as prognostication, oracular utterances, spirit possession, divination, channelling and spiritual mediumship, ritual incantations, magic, shamanistic trances, physical and spiritual healing, fortune-telling, numerology, clairvoyance, the interpretation of signs and omens, as well as close attention to dreams and visionary experiences – 'a host of functionaries with apparently overlapping or related roles' (Anderson and Johnson 1995, 2).[2] Given the breadth of activities that fall under the rubric of prophecy, classifying prophets is itself fraught with numerous challenges (cf. Lewis 1989).[3]

One immediate challenge for sociologists and historians who study new religious movements (NRMs) has not been in crafting more precise definitions as much as it has been in how to conceive of prophecy and its role in NRMs *apart* from predicting world-ending events, and yet, still allowing for a variety of predictive activities to be included in their descriptions and analyses. As it currently stands, the narrowly conscribed focus by social scientists on prophecy as endtime predictive activities has yielded two main lines of inquiry. The first, following the seminal work of psychologist Leon Festinger (1956 and 1957), has been on the social and psychological consequences of failed prophecy. The second, largely following the work of the religious historian Catherine Wessinger, has been to identify and trace the development of religious movements that are or have been organized around one of two types of prophetic predictions – namely world-ending or world-transforming events – and then examine one of three responses to such a prediction, whether through catastrophic, progressive or avertive means (see Wessinger 1997, 2000a and 2011, chapters 1–4).

Because the second of these lines has more to do with millennial expectation than with prophecy or prophetic activities proper, it will not concern us in this overview of research in prophecy and prophets in NRMs. In this essay, then, the aim will be first to examine prophecy in NRMs through the narrower lens of research focused on prediction and failure (the so-called Festinger theory) and then, second, to widen the lens and view the phenomenon of prophecy as not merely one type of religious activity – prediction, typically doomsday prediction – but as a much broader religious phenomenon that manifests itself in a variety of ways. As among those ways, prophecy can provide divine or other-worldly guidance to an individual or a religious community as well as offer divinely inspired answers or solutions to any number of physical needs or spiritual concerns. But because the literature on failed prophecy is extensive, most of this essay will concern itself with research on prophetic failure as opposed to the phenomenon of prophecy more generally, on which research has been noticeably sparse. But first, for the purposes of the broader discussion, it will be necessary to define both prophecy and prophets.

Prophecy and Prophets

More properly defined, prophecy is divinely inspired speech, with prophets being those individuals who claim or are thought by their followers to speak on behalf of or through the power of a divine or supernatural being. Prophets are individuals who, as Max Weber had observed, feel within themselves a 'consciousness of power'. They represent 'a purely individual bearer of charisma'. Though, as Weber had noted, '[t]he prophet's claim is based on personal revelation and charisma', some prophets may augment their charismatic authority by practising 'divination as well as magical healing or counseling' (1963, 46–7).[4] What is more, the distinction that scholars might draw between those prophets who receive sacred knowledge through direct means (e.g. spirit possession or a heavenly vision) or through indirect means (e.g. rigorous textual study to find keys to interpreting prophetic signs or to pinpointing specific historical events that portend their fulfilment), rarely, if ever, comes into consideration.

Not all inspired messages are predictive; fewer still concern universally transformative events or experiences.[5] The picture then should not simply be one of a religious group or movement preparing for an earth-shattering event. Rather, it should be the broader image of a religious community closely following the guidance provided by a prophet-leader, one who claims or is thought to speak with divine inspiration or who transmits sacred knowledge to those eager to know the will of a god or other transcendent being. Bestowed with divine authority and discernment, prophets step into 'a particular moment in human history' (Heschel 1969, xiv) to offer a new perspective or understanding, a solution or liberating 'breakthrough' to a socially debilitating dilemma, or a way out of a spiritual desert or spiritually dark age in history (Weber 1963, xxix).

Thus, prophecy can be viewed first and perhaps foremost as a divinely inspired dialogue between a prophet and a people. The 'word of the Lord' that is received 'in season and out' and offered to followers is not necessarily one of impending doom. Often, very often, the message that the prophet brings is one of comfort, guidance, encouragement, admonition or instruction (see Aune 1983; Heschel 1969; Lindblom 1962; Wilson 1980). Whether, in the Weberian sense, the prophet as a 'purely individual bearer of charisma . . . proclaims a religious doctrine or divine commandment' of an *ethical* or *exemplary* character (1963, 46), the prophet functions primarily as a medium – an open channel – who stands between a people and the sacred will or divine favour after which they seek, between the known and a myriad of unknown worlds.

Festinger and Failed Prophecy

When, in the 1950s, Leon Festinger, Henry Riecken and Stanley Schachter published their landmark case study, *When Prophecy Fails* (1956), the words *prophet* and *prophecy* tended to be used by social scientists as shorthand for a charismatic leader and for the religious movement that his or her visionary experiences inspired (as a more recent example, see Miller 2001). Weber himself had spoken of prophets (and saviors) as using various means, including 'the possession of a magical charisma' to secure both recognition for their message and a following for their sacred mission in the world – whether that message and mission be cast in ethical or exemplary terms. 'For the substance of the prophecy', to quote Weber, '. . . is to direct a way of life to the pursuit of a sacred value', that is, 'to systematize and rationalize the way of life, either in particular points or totally' (Gerth et al. 1958, 327; on ethical and exemplary prophets, see 1958, 284–5 and Weber 1963, xxxv–xxxvi and 55–6). Weber did not concern himself with the *predictive* activities often associated with Hebrew prophets – their messianic and chiliastic visions – favouring instead the broader role that prophets (and saviors) came to play in founding or renewing a religion. Indeed, Weber had argued that during an extraordinary moment in time – such as 'moments of psychic, physical, economic, ethical, religious, or political distress' (Barkun 1974, 88) – the prophetic mantle comes to rest upon an individual who is recognized as possessing exceptional gifts equal to that moment and offering either a restoration of tradition or a transformation of it (see Weber 1963, xix and 46; cf. Anderson et al. 1995, 11–12).

While many historians continued to examine connections between historical periods of crisis and the emergence of prophets who addressed themselves to those crises, Festinger and his colleagues would lay out a path – a research trajectory – that would be adopted, in one form or another, by sociologists and social psychologists. The Festinger theory of cognitive dissonance – that individuals seek to reduce the perceived inconsistencies between the beliefs they have and the reality they experience (1957, 9–11) – was a marked departure from earlier crisis theories and even earlier deprivation theories, both of which had been offered to explain the origins and persistence of millennial and other endtime movements, if not of religion itself. By contrast, Festinger et al. did not focus on prophecy as a religious response to social upheavals or cultural crises ('macro' issues) but on the social and psychological consequences of prophetic disconfirmation or failed predictions for individuals and religious movements ('micro' concerns). Without exaggeration, Festinger's unexpected answer to the simple question, 'What happens when a prophecy fails?', has generated scores of studies and perhaps hundreds of scholarly and non-scholarly applications, many not at all related to religion (see Stone 2000; Tumminia et al. 2011).

In its basic formulation, the Festinger theory states that an unequivocal disconfirmation of a prophesied event creates a crisis of belief, especially if an individual or group is committed wholeheartedly to the prediction and has taken 'irrevocable actions because of it' (1956, 3). The dissonance created by the false cognition results in psychological discomfort, even distress. In turn, the discomfort gives rise to countervailing pressures to relieve the discomfort. Attempts by believers to reduce their dissonance, note Festinger et al., 'represent the observable manifestations that dissonance exists' (1956, 26). Though one would expect a person simply to abandon his or her belief in what appears to be a false or inaccurate prediction, Festinger and his colleagues argued instead that not only will the believer recover his or her faith in the prediction, but will try to convince others that the prediction and their beliefs are in fact true, even hoping to convert them.

The case that Festinger et al. presented in support of their thesis was that of the 'Seekers', the pseudonym of a UFO spirit-contact movement led by a 'Mrs Marian Keech' (her real name was Dorothy Martin) who had received through auto-writing a message from Sananda (Jesus), one of the heavenly Guardians, who warned her of a coming cataclysmic flood across North America. This terrific event would take place on 21 December 1954. But, just before this disaster would strike, Sananda promised to rescue Mrs Keech and her small band of followers (about 12 in all) by sending spaceships that would transport them to safety. For their part, the Seekers were commanded to bear witness and thus bring as much heavenly light into a dark world as possible. In preparation for this event, the Seekers expended all their energies and every available resource at their command, to the point of quitting their jobs and greatly straining relationships with friends and family members.

In their book, Festinger and his colleagues recount in great detail the frantic last hours in which the Seekers anxiously awaited the arrival of the spaceships, their disappointment when the spaceships failed to appear and their overall response to the failed prediction. After a brief period of doubt and confusion, early the next morning Mrs Keech received a spirit-message congratulating her and her group for their faithfulness: '"Not since the beginning of time upon this Earth has there been such a force of Good and light as now floods this room and that which has been loosed within this room now floods the entire Earth"' (1956, 169). That is, because of their faith, the cataclysmic flood had been called off. Their disappointment gave way to enthusiastic triumph. The Seekers had saved the world (for examples of similar UFO groups, see Wojcik 2003).

Unexpectedly, the Seekers' next action was to proselytize: they shared their message of triumph with whomever would listen, including the press. Such a response struck Festinger as logically inconsistent with what they observed as the patent fact of prophetic disconfirmation. One would expect most people to abandon a disproven belief (cognition) in favour of a proven one. Instead, Mrs Keech and her followers experienced a 'recovery of conviction' by both reaffirming their faith in the prediction and then by actively seeking ways to convince others that their faith had saved the world. This, then, is the heart of the Festinger thesis as derived from the case of Mrs Keech and the Seekers: in the face of undeniable evidence that a person's belief is wrong, a person 'will frequently emerge, not only unshaken, but even more convinced of the truth of his beliefs than ever before. Indeed, he may even show a new fervor about convincing and converting other people to his view' (p. 3). Denying or rationalizing a disconfirmed belief cannot eliminate dissonance, for, according to Festinger, disconfirmation of one belief calls into questions other related beliefs. To shore up weakened religious beliefs requires social support. To assuage doubt and recover conviction, believers must therefore surround themselves with others who are likewise convinced that their beliefs are true, hence the proselytizing efforts (p. 28).

Still, although Festinger et al. placed emphasis on a heightening of evangelistic activities as the primary means by which shaken believers relieve dissonance, successful conversion of non-believers does not appear to be a necessary component of dissonance reduction. Rather, it is the proselytizing activity itself – the proclamation of their beliefs to outsiders – that serves to reduce dissonance and helps reconfirm faith. While Festinger reported that evangelistic activities among the Seekers 'increased meteorically following disconfirmation' (p. 212), no actual conversions by outsiders took place. In fact, 'the group failed to win a single new convert' – a failure that Festinger attributed to the Seeker's lack of proselytizing skill (p. 232).

At the same time, Festinger and his colleagues did not hold that *all* experiences of failed prophecy would spark evangelistic fervour. Accordingly, they offered five conditions under which, in the wake of 'unequivocal disconfirmation of a belief', one might expect to see an increase in proselytizing activity (pp. 3–4). As outlined, Festinger's five conditions were as follows: 1) There must be conviction; 2) There must be commitment to this conviction; 3) The conviction must be amenable to unequivocal disconfirmation; 4) Such unequivocal disconfirmation must occur; 5) Social support must be available subsequent to the disconfirmation (p. 216; cf. Festinger 1957, 247–8).

Festinger-Inspired Research on Failed Prophecy

Though at its publication *When Prophecy Fails* piqued interest among social psychologists and other social scientists, most reviews of Festinger et al. were unfavourable, some calling it a work of fiction, others pointing to flaws in Festinger's assumptions and still others pointing to even deeper flaws in their method of gathering data (see Johnson 2011). Despite these initial criticisms, in the decades since the time of its publication, the Festinger thesis readily found interdisciplinary application outside social psychology. For instance, scholars in fields as diverse as history, anthropology, literary theory, biblical studies, theology, rhetoric, and those as unlikely as architecture and business management, sought to adapt Festinger et al.'s findings to their own work (see, as only a handful of examples, Carroll 1979; Gager 1975; Lee 1996; Murphy 2003; O'Leary 1994).

But soon enough, a number of social scientists began to compare Festinger's test case with the experiences of similar predictive prophecy groups to see if Festinger's conditions and responses would replicate. In the first such published case, that of an American Pentecostal Christian sect leader who had predicted a nuclear attack, Jane Hardyck and Marcia Braden (1962) noted that the group responded to the failed prophecy differently from Mrs Keech's Seekers. In fact, Mrs Shepard's True Word movement, some 103 in number who had lived 42 days in bomb shelters, emerged without the least sign of dissonance and with little inclination to proselytize. The prediction, they came to believe, had been merely a test of faith. Indeed, many True Word members testified that the stay in the shelters had actually strengthened their faith (p. 138). To account for this striking difference, Hardyck and Braden offered two additional conditions to the five provided by Festinger et al.: 'The two suggestions we have made for further conditions are that the group provide only minimal social support for its members and that the group receive ridicule from the outside world' (p. 141). Unlike Mrs Keech and the Seekers, Mrs Shepard and her followers were more tightly knit and had not been ridiculed before or after the failed prediction occurred. Instead, the True Word group was publicly praised for raising awareness of the need to prepare for a nuclear disaster.

Festinger-inspired studies published subsequent to Hardyck et al. have tended to move the conversation in one of two directions: 1) field research examining real-time and near real-time responses to a failed prophecy, noting the specific conditions under which a movement survives prophetic disconfirmation;

2) comparative and historical research interested in discerning, theoretically, the typical responses to failed predictions as well as the adaptive strategies employed by leaders and members to reduce or in some way manage the cognitive dissonance experienced in the face of disconfirmed beliefs (see Dawson 1999; Stone 2011; Tumminia et al. 2011).

Generally speaking, field researchers have noted that how group members experience a failed prediction can account for the success or failure of a group. Success, as such, is most likely if the beliefs and goals of the movement are seen to transcend the predicted event (Balch et al. 1983; Balch et al. 1997; Dein 2001; Shaffir 1995), or if the experience – the prophetic moment – is transformed into a ritualized event (Dein 2010; Palmer et al. 1992; Sanada et al. 1975; Tumminia 1998). To the latter, Susan Palmer and Natalie Finn (1992) examined the 'rite of apocalypse', a collective experience of a prophetic fulfilment as a *rite of passage* for members. As they explained, 'waiting for world's end is a *symbolic* act ... and it requires the presence of ritual actors and the organization of sacred time and sacred space' (p. 409, emphasis added). This rite or ritual involves a gathering of members at a specified time and place to witness the predicted event. The symbolism employed in the rite transfers symbolic meaning to the expected event. The prophet-leader becomes essential to the transmutation of the prophesied moment and of those who experience the event with him or her. In fact, Palmer et al. placed great stress on the leader's 'skill and flexibility in facilitating groups, reinterpreting doctrines, and "orchestrating" ritual' as 'essential for bringing about a "successful" apocalypse – an event which might well be considered the magnum opus in a charismatic cult leader's career' (p. 399). A successful 'rite of apocalypse' thus depends upon the creative ritual-making skills of the prophet-leader, essential skills that Festinger's Mrs Keech did not appear to possess.

By contrast, researchers and theorists approaching the issue historically and comparatively have tended to question the very assertion that a predictive prophecy fails – for the believer. As early as the 1970s, Neil Weiser (1974) bluntly asserted that '[p]rophecies cannot and do not fail for the committed' (p. 20). The reason: after a disconfirmation, a group member's immediate behaviour is aimed largely at reaffirming such beliefs, either through 'the conscious and/or subconscious rationalization of the event' (p. 20). In addition, while organizational resources, such as rationalizations, come to the fore whenever members of a religious movement experience dissonance, according to Joseph Zygmunt (1972), rationalizations are only one of three main responses to a failed prophecy, what he interchangeably termed 'adaptive patterns of response' and 'modes of adaptation' (pp. 259–60; Prus [1976] speaks of the 'management of dissonance', with reaffirming faith being the most common management pattern, pp. 132–3).

Zygmunt held that dissonance reduction largely depended upon the adaptive strategies that religious groups and their leaders employed. Through adaptation, expected events that fail to take place are not viewed as *dis*-confirmations of belief but *non*-confirmations of predictions that are believed to be in the process of confirmation. According to Zygmunt, this supposed *sleight-of-mind* is possible because, '[e]lements of ambiguity or uncertainty concerning the exact nature of expected events and especially the manner in which they will be brought about are also quite common, making empirical invalidation more difficult to perceive and creating a context favorable to "prophecy-validating" selective interpretations' (p. 247). There exists sufficient ambiguity in language and in events as to allow empirically framed predictions to be open to non-empirically-framed (re-)interpretations (cf. Stone 2000, 13–14; Zygmunt 1970, 934). Briefly summarized, Zygmunt's three responses to failed prophecy and their respective 'modes of adaptation' to dissonance are as follows: 1) acknowledge error and restructure the group along more modified lines of expectation; 2) assign blame, either internally or externally, and redirect organizational resources toward either purifying or reviving the group, toward greater evangelistic activities, or toward critique of the non-believing social order; 3) refuse to accept the failure of a prophecy but reinterpret the group's beliefs along more symbolic and, hence, more unfalsifiable lines (see pp. 259–65; Stone 2011, 52).

A decade later, J. Gordon Melton (1985), following the lead of Weiser, Zygmunt and Prus, also challenged the assumption that predictive prophecies fail for the committed believer and argued that the denial of failure is, in fact, the most common response (p. 21). Melton also criticized Festinger et al. for assuming that predictive prophecy is what defined messianic and millennial movements – an assumption incorrectly attributed to the two main movements referenced by Festinger et al. for support of their thesis: Sabbatai Zevi and the Sabbataians (1666) and William Miller and the Millerites (1844). As Melton observed, 'though one or more prophecies may be important to a group, they will be set within a complex set of beliefs and interpersonal relationships. They may serve as one of several important sources determining group activity, but the prediction is only one support device for the group, not the essential rafter' (p. 19). Additionally, Melton argued that while disconfirming evidence might present cognitive challenges to members, those challenges serve paradoxically to strengthen beliefs and membership ties to the movement. This happens because leaders and members reflect upon the 'failed' event, recast the prophecy in spiritual terms, and then reinterpret its meaning in ways that help reintegrate members into the group (see Prus 1976; cf. the discussion in Dein et al. 2008). When a prophecy 'fails', spiritualization of the prediction and reaffirmation of commitment to the group are, for Melton, the most common of Zygmunt's three responses and modes of adaptation as well as the most effective means of managing dissonance.

Before concluding, one obvious question needs to be answered: What has nearly 60 years of research into failed prophecy yielded? That is, what do we now know about predictive prophecy movements that we did not know before all the research spurred by Festinger et al.? At the risk of being accused of being overly simplistic, I would offer the following observation and conclusion. The observation: Most studies on failed prophecy point to one obvious flaw in Festinger et al.: he and his colleagues placed too much emphasis on outward-directed activities – specifically proselytizing – as the main way by which believers assuage the dissonance they might experience in the wake of prophetic failure. The conclusion: Believers tend to respond to 'failed' prophecy in ways that reaffirm their faith. Few truly committed individuals will abandon their beliefs.

Prophecy and Prophets in NRMs

Though much of the research on prophecy has focused on answering the question of what happens when predictions *fail*, a broader examination of the non-predictive role of prophecy and prophetic inspiration in new and alternative religions has been left noticeably neglected and underdeveloped. Interestingly, while Festinger et al. (1956) had opened a window into the interplay between prophets and their followers, few scholars have thought to peer through that window (see Stone 2011, 57–64). Festinger et al.'s prophet, Mrs Keech, had been exposed to a number of New Age ideas that had been emerging at the time. In fact, from their narrative, one learns that prior to her experience as a channel between seen and unseen worlds, Mrs Keech had attended theosophy lectures, had read *Oahspe* as well as works by Guy Ballard ('I AM') and had joined a local dianetics group, becoming 'cleared' by the auditor (1956, 33–4). It had been only after the initial spirit-contact encounter that Mrs Keech began to gravitate towards UFO contactee groups. What is more, many in Mrs Keech's inner-Seeker-circle had travelled a similar spiritual path. The extraterrestrial messages that Mrs Keech, Bertha Blatsky and Ella Lowell received, though at times contradictory, were all thought by them and their followers to be from divine or supernatural beings (see pp. 92–3, 103–4, 115–17).

The story presented by Festinger et al. was by no means unique, as one finds similarities in the media and messages of numerous NRMs past and present. A number of other 'prophets' have likewise been possessed directly by some or another spirit or by extraterrestrial beings thought to be gods. For instance, the experience of Mrs Keech, who was prompted to write spirit-inspired communications, and her colleagues, who spoke on behalf of a divine or exalted being, bears analogy to that of Theosophy founder Madame Blavatsky (1831–91), who described her own spirit-contact experiences as if another person were dwelling within her – at times standing beside her, at other times taking control and directing messages through her hand or tongue (Ellwood 1979, 114). Blavatsky is no less a prophetic figure as, say, the prophet Ezekiel, though few scholars if any have examined her prophetic gift in comparison to biblical exemplars. The same is the case with Mark Prophet and Elizabeth Clare Prophet who founded Summit Lighthouse in 1958, later renamed The Church Universal and Triumphant. Both believed themselves to be channels of the ascended masters. However, unlike the biblical prophets, in *their* messages Mrs Keech, Madam Blavatsky, and Mark and Elizabeth Prophet spoke of light from above coming into the world in the form of deeper knowledge, a light that would enlighten the benighted and thus bring greater spiritual and deeper mental potential for all humankind.

Additionally, many prophets in NRMs have received their messages through dreams or heavenly visions (such as Shaker founder Mother Ann Lee, Ghost Dance prophet Wovoka, Ellen G. White, prophet of Seventh-day Adventism, and Aimee Semple McPherson, founder of the Church of the Foursquare Gospel), or been visited by angels (Joseph Smith, Jr.), or by aliens (Claude Vorilhon, renamed Raël). A few have been given the gift of interpretive insight, the ability to discern heavenly signs, the skill to heal the physically and spiritually sick or to travel throughout the astral plane. Examples of these types of prophets include Emanuel Swedenborg, Andrew Jackson Davis, Phineas Quimby and Mary Baker Eddy. And while a few others have undergone severe physical or spiritual ordeals, a handful of these 'prophets' have come to believe that they had died and been resurrected. Of these, Jemima Wilkinson, the Publick Universal Friend, and Katsuichi Motoki of the Ichigen-no-Miya movement come to mind. There have also been those who believed – or were believed to be – human embodiments of God or of some divine or extraterrestrial being come to earth. Among these, one could name Robert Matthias and his 'Kingdom', Father Divine, Nation of Islam founder W. D. Fard, Unification Church founder Sung Myung Moon, as well as Aum Shinrikyō's Shōkō Asahara, Ernest and Ruth Norman of Unarius, and 'The Two' of Heaven's Gate. Regrettably, even given these prominent examples, scholarship has yet to penetrate the phenomenon of prophecy and its central role in many NRMs beyond mere passing mention.

Indeed, it has only been within the past decade that social scientists have begun to concentrate attention on the dynamic of prophecy within NRMs. For example, two recent studies that examine non-predictive instances of prophecy are those authored by William Bainbridge (2002) and edited by Gordon Shepherd and Gary Shepherd (2010), both of which focus on The Family International (Children of God). In the former, the topic of prophecy is found scattered throughout parts of the book (see pp. 3–20, 60–8, and 79–87). In the latter, essentially an arrangement of transcribed interviews, the central role of prophecy in The Family is brought to light through the lengthy comments by members and leaders of the movement. Sadly, the volume by Shepherd et al. does not offer analysis beyond the observation that, contra Weber and Rodney

Prophecy

Stark, prophecy does not always end but it can remain a persistent dynamic within a NRM, serving both to preserve a vital link to the divine as well as maintain group cohesion across generations (see pp. 4–6).

Thus, to conclude, while much of the preliminary work on prophecy in NRMs has been largely descriptive, if not discursive, much more empirical, historical and comparative research in non-predictive forms of prophecy has yet to be undertaken. Indeed, the types of prophets and the means through which these prophets receive their messages provide researchers a much more fertile field of investigation in NRMs than has been heretofore cultivated.

Notes

1 Though denounced as *false* prophets by their detractors, neither Miller nor Camping claimed divine inspiration. Rather, both men simply regarded themselves as dedicated students of Scripture who had found the key to unlocking the eschatological secrets of the Bible, secrets available to any devout person committed to sincere and intensive scriptural study (cf. Camping 2010; Himes 1842, 40; Rupp 1844, 668–91).

2 Elsewhere (Stone 2011, citing Anderson et al. 1995, 6), the elaborate variety of prophets in Eastern Africa has already been pointed out: 'some prophets inherit their status while others are seized by spirits; some gain knowledge through inspiration, while others receive spirit instruction; some earn a living by divination, others do not; some declaim against magic, while others use sorcery; some prophets live within a community, while others wander from place to place; some are revolutionaries, while others are keepers of tradition; some emerge during times of crisis, while others are "destroyed" by crisis; and some prophets bring war, while others bring peace' (p. 61, footnote 10).

3 To the 'two central problems' identified in the literature on prophets and prophecy ('haphazard and indiscriminate use of terms' and 'the significant emphasis to the study of prophets in the context of political crisis or radical social action' [p. 13]), Anderson and Johnson offer researchers a 'new understanding' (i.e. definition) of the prophet as one who 'makes declarations through inspired speech', declarations that 'concern public, and not just private matters'. Moreover, they continue, 'the manner of inspiration and form of pronouncement will vary according to the idioms available to the prophet or which the prophet refines or creates, and according to the tradition (expectation) within which a prophet operates' (p. 14). Despite this more focused working definition of prophet, Anderson and Johnson admit that '[o]ur contributors do not all adopt this terminology' (p. 14).

4 Accordingly, Weber defined a prophet as 'a purely individual bearer of charisma, who by virtue of his mission proclaims a religious doctrine or divine commandment. No radical distinction will be drawn between a "renewer of religion" who preaches an older revelation, actual or supposititious, and a "founder of religion" who claims to bring completely new deliverances. The two types merge into one another' (Weber 1963, 46). It is fairly evident from this definition that Weber, as noted by Anderson et al., 'was, in fact, less interested in the analysis of specific charismatic leaders than in the study of charismatic movements in general' (1995, 12). Prophets inspire people; people form movements based on the prophet's message; and, over time, these new movements become recognized as religions.

5 As terms, 'prophecy' and 'prophet' have been adapted by social scientists from the fields of Classics and biblical studies, where the Greek word *prophetes* (fem., *prophetis*) is used to describe the ancient Greek oracle as well as the Hebrew and Israelite prophets (*nevi'im*) in the Bible. The Hebrew terms given to describe a number of functionaries in the Bible include the general term *mantis*, which refers to a variety of prophetic activities, *nabi* (one called to speak or one who predicts; a proclaimer), *hozeh* or *ro'eh* (seer, usually of things lost or hidden), *qozem* (diviner or soothsayer), and *mal'ak yhwh* (messenger of the Lord). For a fuller discussion of these terms, see Anderson et al. 1995, 7–10; Sawyer 1993, 1–22; Westermann 1967, 99–100. In the New Testament, prophecy takes on a predictive cast, the coming of Jesus being specifically understood as the fulfilment of Israel's messianic yearnings as voiced by the prophets in the Hebrew Bible (see Aune 1983, 153–69, and Barton 2007, 5–7, 13–15; cf. Anderson et al. 1995, 2–10). As Anderson et al. observe, '[t]he Christian identification of prophets . . . emphasized prophets as predictors, looking forward to, and therefore justifying the Messiah. The authority of the ancient prophets rested not just on their antiquity, nor on their bearing witness to God's will, but on the fulfillment of their predictions in the person of Jesus Christ' (1995, 9). The shift from Greek and Jewish understandings of prophets as delivering a divinely inspired message – whether predictive, instructive or admonitive – to the ancient Christian view of prophets as foretelling the coming of Jesus as the Messiah (see Eusebius' *Ecclesiastical History*, Book I, Ch. 2, 23–27), or seeing ahead to the end of the present evil age, helps us reckon with how predictive types of prophecy came to define prophetic activity almost to the exclusion of all other types.

15 Millennialism

Catherine Wessinger

Chapter Outline

Types of Millennialism	134
Relevance of Pioneering Millennialism Studies to Contemporary Studies	136
Revolutionary Millennial Movements	139
The Interactionist Perspective	140
Psychology of Apocalyptic Violence	145
Millennialism and Dates and Continued Research	146
Conclusion	148

An imminent transition to a collective salvation is often preached by founders and apostles of new religious movements (NRMs), and the belief may motivate people to change their lives to convert and join. Millennialism studies is, therefore, an important sub-area of new religions studies. Scholars of new religions have studied millennial expectations and creativity in a wide range of new and alternative groups and movements. New religions scholarship has built on earlier studies of millennialism, and through case studies illuminated patterns, dynamics and trajectories of millennial movements.

New religious movements that become involved in violence are usually millennial movements, therefore, new religions scholars have produced intensive case studies to discern causal factors of the violence. In response to the Jonestown, Guyana deaths of 918 people in 1978, and the deaths of 86 people in the Branch Davidian-federal agent conflict in 1993, as well as deaths involving other NRMs through the 1990s, new religions scholars have explored connections between millennialism and violence, producing what has been termed the *interactionist perspective* (Richardson 2001). The interactionist perspective emphasizes that the *quality of interactions* between outsiders and believers contributes to the potential for a violent outcome, or what David G. Bromley terms a *dramatic dénouement*: 'a juncture at which one or both [parties] conclude that the requisite conditions for maintaining their core identity and collective existence are being subverted and that such circumstances are intolerable' (in Bromley and Melton 2002, 11). New religions scholars are often sociologists and historians of religions, but psychologists, psychoanalysts and psychiatrists have also been studying millennialism and violence, and their conclusions are compatible with those of new religions scholars.

The study of millennialism in new religions studies will remain important since the human religious imagination continues to produce expectations of overcoming finitude and achieving permanent well-being (salvation) for collectivities of people.

Types of Millennialism

Millennialism and *millenarianism* are terms used by scholars to refer to 'belief in an imminent transition to a collective salvation, in which the faithful will experience well-being and the unpleasant limitations of the human condition will be eliminated' ('Millennial Glossary' in Wessinger 2011, 720). Religion is often understood as having an 'ultimate concern', which is the goal that is the most important thing to believers (Baird 1971).[1] While most religions express belief in a spiritual world that impinges on life in the material world, there are also belief systems with ultimate concerns that reject belief in a spiritual world and therefore have a secular orientation. In both spiritual and secular religions the ultimate concern is part of a worldview consisting of understandings of reality and human nature, and there will be methods utilized to achieve the goal delineated in the thought system. Secular movements sometimes called 'political religions' (Voegelin 2000, 19–74) typically include movements that fit the definition of 'millennialism' delineated here. Millennial movements, whether or not they believe in a spiritual realm, have an ultimate concern of achieving a salvation for a group of people, which can be called 'the millennial kingdom'.

The terms *millennialism* and *millenarianism* were taken by historians of religions from the mention in the New Testament book of Revelation of the kingdom of God on Earth lasting 1,000 years (a millennium, see Rev. 20.1–4). However, the scholarly study of religious movements finds that expectations of a *Millennium* (the anticipated collective salvation) does not necessarily mean that the collective salvation is limited to a 1,000-year period. Movements in various cultures conform to millennial patterns even in cases where Judaism, Christianity and Islam – the three traditions most closely associated with millennialism – are not influences. Therefore, *millennialism* as a category constructed by scholars to promote understanding of particular phenomena has been applied to traditionally religious (concerned with spiritual realms) and also secular movements in a variety of contexts.

Although the seminal work by Norman Cohn (1970 [1957], Introduction, unnumbered first page) stipulates that millenarianism is concerned with a terrestrial salvation, the study of NRMs indicates that the expected salvation may be earthly, heavenly or both. Secular millennial movements, of course, will be concerned with an earthly salvation. Cohn's definition stresses that the Millennium is believed to be accomplished by or with the help of supernatural agencies. Study of NRMs in the twentieth and twenty-first centuries indicates that the agent or agency may be considered superhuman, but not necessarily supernatural. For example, History or Progress (in the case of secular movements), or extraterrestrials may be considered to be directing superhuman agents (Wessinger in Wessinger 2011, 4–5). Cohn's definition indicates that the Millennium is believed to arrive imminently. A sense of imminence is important in a millennial movement, but is difficult to sustain over time. As an NRM matures and becomes more accommodated to mainstream culture, millennial expectations may become 'managed' by institutional leadership (Jacqueline Stone in Wessinger 2000b, 277–9).

To facilitate further cross-cultural study, the terms *catastrophic millennialism* and *progressive millennialism* have been offered as substitutes for *premillennialism* and *postmillennialism*, which are bound to Christian beliefs about whether Jesus Christ will return *before* or *after* the Millennium. Catastrophic millennialism and progressive millennialism may have *prophets* (individuals believed to receive communications from unseen sources of authority), *messiahs* (persons believed to be empowered by the divine or superhuman agent to create the collective salvation) or not (Wessinger in Robbins and Palmer 1997, 47–59, 2000a, 2000b; in Wessinger 2011, 3).

Catastrophic millennialism is belief in 'an imminent and catastrophic transition' to the collective salvation ('Millennial Glossary' in Wessinger 2011, 718). Society is seen as being so corrupt that it has to be destroyed, and humans will be judged as to whether or not they are worthy to be included in the millennial kingdom. This perspective is also called *apocalypticism* after Apocalypse (Revelation), the last book in the New Testament. It involves a *radical dualism* (Wessinger 2000a), a rigid perspective of 'good versus evil', 'us versus them'.

Progressive millennialism is 'belief that the imminent transition to the collective salvation will occur through improvement in society'. It is optimistic about the possibility of society to improve. 'The belief is that humans working in harmony with a divine or superhuman plan' will create the collective salvation ('Millennial Glossary' in Wessinger 2011, 721). A sense of the *imminence* of the transition is also important in the progressive millennial pattern. Progressive millennialism may emphasize divine or superhuman intervention, peaceful efforts at personal and social transformation, or violence to achieve the collective salvation. According to Robert Ellwood, progressive millennialists resorting to violence desire to speed progress up to an apocalyptic rate (in Wessinger 2000b, 242). Both violent progressive millennialists and catastrophic millennialists possess a radical dualistic outlook that demonizes opponents within and outside the movement, and therefore rationalizes their elimination.

Catastrophic millennialism and progressive millennialism are not mutually exclusive. Groups or movements may emphasize either catastrophic or progressive themes in response to changing circumstances. For a close study of this phenomenon see Phillip Charles Lucas on the Holy Order of MANS (Lucas 1995; Strozier and Flynn 1997, 121–32).

The study of NRMs has illuminated hitherto overlooked millennial patterns. *Avertive apocalypticism* stresses that expected imminent catastrophe can be averted if humans take steps to return to a correct relationship to the divine or superhuman agent. These steps involve correct faith and ritual activities. Some secular avertive apocalyptic movements address problems believed to endanger either humanity as a whole or an elect group. *Avertive millennialism* combines avertive apocalyptic ideas with progressive millennialism. It is believed that if the imminent destruction can be averted, a collective salvation will be achieved. Daniel Wojcik has described cases of avertive apocalypticism in Our Lady of Roses (Marian apparition movement in Bayside, New York), and avertive millennialism in twentieth-century Native American restoration movements, and examples of environmental millennialism (in Wessinger 2011, 66–88; Wojcik 1997). David Redles has demonstrated that the violence of German National Socialism was aimed at averting imagined imminent destruction of Germans by 'the Bolshevik Jew' and to establish a collective salvation for Germans in the Third Reich (Redles in Strozier et. al. 2010, 156–74; in Wessinger 2011, 529–48; 2005).

An ancient pattern of millennialism was termed *nativist millennialism* (Lanternari 1963) when it was discerned in nineteenth- and twentieth-century movements among people who regarded themselves as oppressed by foreign colonizing powers that were destroying their traditional religions and ways of life, and removing them from their sacred lands. Nativist millennialism may have catastrophic or progressive themes, and may be peaceful or violent (Rosenfeld in Wessinger 2011, 89–109).

Relevance of Pioneering Millennialism Studies to Contemporary Studies

Cohn's *Pursuit of the Millennium* (1970) first published in 1957, and Yonina Talmon (1966) offered similar definitions of millennialism that have been refined in light of new religions studies. Cohn's book studies numerous medieval apocalyptic expectations, movements and peasant revolts that today would be identified as NRMs.

Robert Linton (1943), Vittorio Lanternari (1963), Anthony F. C. Wallace (1956) and Peter Worsley (1968) studied 'culture clash' (Lanternari 1963) or 'revitalization' (Wallace 1956) movements, identified here as nativist millennial movements, which have relevance for understanding religious responses to colonialism on the part of Native Americans, Africans, Indians, Maori and peoples of Oceania. Garry Trompf (in Wessinger 2011, 435–53; 1990) points out that only those 'cargo cults' on Pacific islands aimed at collective salvation in a completely transformed world are genuine millenarian movements; participants in other movements aspired to take possession of foreign cargo by magical means.

The category of nativist millennialism is relevant to the study of participants in the contemporary Euro-American nativist millennial movement (Wessinger 2000a, 158–217), which includes Freemen, Sovereign Citizens, Identity Christians, militia members, and 'lone wolf' actors such as Timothy McVeigh, who carried out the bombing of a federal office building in Oklahoma City, Oklahoma, on 19 April 1995, which killed 168 people, including 19 young children. These subgroupings within the broad Euro-American nativist millennial movement have received in-depth study by Michael Barkun (1997), Jeffrey Kaplan (1997) and Stuart A. Wright (2007).

Another revolutionary nativist millennial movement is the contemporary international Jihadist, or radical Islamist, movement, which is a new phenomenon of a transnational and multiethnic nativist millennial movement. The radical Islamist view is that 'true' Muslims constitute an *umma* (nation). Radical Islamists resort to violence to resist Western capitalism and values, as well as attack perceived 'hypocritical' Muslims and Muslim governments seen as aligned with Western governments. This movement has the goal of creating a 'true' Islamic state, the *khilafa*, in which Islamic law, *sharia*, will be strictly enforced (Jeffrey T. Kenney in Wessinger 2011, 688–713; Wessinger 2006, 184–92).

Michael Barkun in *Disaster and the Millennium* (1974) argues that apocalypticism emerges in response to repeated disasters, which can range from famines, invasions and consequent loss of land, way of life, and economic survival, to social change or natural disasters. Repeated disasters can often be discerned in contexts that produce nativist millennial movements, such as the Ghost Dance movement among Plains Indians in North America (Michelene E. Pesantubbee in Wessinger 2000b, 62–81, in Wessinger 2011, 463–6), the Xhosa Cattle-Killing movement in South Africa (Christine Steyn in Wessinger 2000b, 185–93; Landes 2011, 91–122) and the Pai Marire movements among the Maori of New Zealand (Jean E. Rosenfeld in Wessinger 2011, 98–100; 1999).

But disasters do not necessarily produce millennial movements, and religious responses to disasters do not necessarily involve millennialism. After apocalyptic texts become part of scriptures, as is the case with the Hebrew Bible, the New Testament, and the Qur'an, they become resources for future millennialist interpretations as believers seek meaning in the face of finitude.

Paul Boyer's *When Time Shall Be No More* (1992) traces the origins of apocalyptic belief from the Hebrew Bible to the New Testament, through early Christianity, medieval Europe, the Protestant Reformation, and prophetic speculations in the American colonies, to discern premillennial movements in nineteenth- and twentieth-century America expecting the Second Coming of Christ. Boyer discusses the rise of Christian Dispensationalism in Great Britain, especially as preached by John Nelson Darby (1800–82), to influence British and American premillennialists, notably the American Cyrus Scofield (1843–1921), who produced the influential *Scofield Reference Bible*. Christian Dispensationalists believe that God deals with humanity in 'periods' or 'dispensations', and that the end of the present age is close. They believe that faithful Christians will be lifted up to join Christ in the air in a 'Rapture' (based on 1 Thess. 4.17), after which there will be terrible violence and plagues during a tribulation, in which those 'left behind' will have the option of becoming Christians. Jesus Christ will return at the end of the tribulation period, destroy the Antichrist's army in the battle of Armageddon, throw the Antichrist, the False Prophet, and Satan into the lake of fire, judge humanity, and establish God's kingdom on Earth. Boyer discusses how the dropping of atomic bombs on Hiroshima and Nagasaki, Japan, in August 1945 by the United States, and the founding of the state of Israel in 1948, prompted the incorporation of nuclear war and Israel into Christian Dispensationalist apocalyptic scenarios, notably by Hal Lindsey's *The Late Great Planet Earth* (1970), which has sold more than 28 million copies. Christian Dispensationalists have exercised political clout on the Republican Party and Republican Presidents since the 1980s.

In the last decade of the twentieth century and into the following temporal millennium, the thirteen-volume *Left Behind* series by Tim LaHaye and Jerry Jenkins, three prequels, forty books in *Left Behind: The Kids* series, three movies, and three video games spread Christian Dispensationalist ideas to millions of children, adolescents, and adults, Catholics as well as Protestants. James W. Jones stresses that Christian Dispensationalism's radical dualism is as dichotomizing as the rigid outlook of terrorists he has interviewed (in Strozier et. al. 2010, 102–3).

In 1959 Carl Gustav Jung observed in his booklet, *Flying Saucers: A Modern Myth of Things Seen in the Sky*, that extraterrestrials function as 'technological angels' in many contemporary movements. In UFO millennial movements the earthly 'masters' of Helena P. Blavatsky, the founding philosopher of the Theosophical Society, and the 'ascended masters' of other groups within the broader Theosophical movement, are transformed into extraterrestrials. Studies of UFO millennial movements are found in the in-depth case studies of the Unarius Academy of Science by Diana Tumminia (2005) and the Raelians by Susan Palmer (2004a); edited books and chapters have been published by James R. Lewis (1995, 2003), and Christopher Partridge (2003); and chapters by Mikael Rothstein, Andreas Grünschloss, John A. Saliba, Benjamin E. Zeller and Ted Peters. Robert Pearson Flaherty (in Wessinger 2011, 587–610) and Daniel Wojcik (in Partridge 2003, 274–99) provide surveys of UFO millennial groups. A special issue of *Nova Religio* (14, no. 2 [2010]) guest-edited by Paul Brian Thomas is dedicated to examining 'ET-inspired religions', many of which are millennial.

Revolutionary Millennial Movements

Revolutionary millennial movements are a distinctive type of NRM that can cause immense destruction and deaths. The ultimate concern of participants is the creation of a collective salvation for a designated group.

Through the centuries China has produced numerous revolutionary millennial movements. In the nineteenth century the Taiping Revolution, which blended Christian and Chinese apocalypticism, caused the deaths of an estimated 20 million people. The twentieth-century Chinese Communist revolution that established in 1950 the People's Republic of China led by Mao Zedong (1945–76) likewise killed millions. Mao's 'radical social restructuring' and his 'permanent revolution' in the PRC, during the Great Leap Forward agricultural and industrial experiment 1958–61 and the Cultural Revolution 1966–76, caused the deaths from starvation, overwork and executions of many more millions than the Taiping Revolution (Scott Lowe in Wessinger 2000b, 221). The Bolshevik Revolution of workers and peasants in Russia 1917–22 (Landes 2011, 318–52) led to the creation of the USSR led by Vladimir Lenin 1922–4; death estimates from war and famine range from 7 to 10 million. Joseph Stalin's rule of the USSR 1941–6, resulted in millions of people sent to labour camps and exile in remote areas, caused the Soviet famine of 1932–3, followed by the Great Purge of 1937–9 in which hundreds of thousands were executed. These and other Marxist revolutions and forced restructurings of societies, such as the Khmer Rouge rule in Cambodia 1975–9 that killed 1 to 2 million people by execution and starvation (Richard C. Salter in Wessinger 2011b, 281–98), were revolutionary progressive millennial movements aiming to speed progress up by killing those deemed to impede it.

German Nazism was a revolutionary avertive millennial movement with obvious nativist characteristics. The goal was to save the German *volk* from imagined imminent destruction by Jews and thereby establish the Third Reich as a collective salvation for ethnic Germans. The radical dualism promoted by Hitler and other Nazi leaders demonized Jews and urged their eradication to avert what they believed was imminent apocalyptic destruction of Germans by 'the Bolshevik Jew'. Violence to accomplish this was considered to be carrying out God's will. Nazism arose in an interactive context in post-World War I Germany as Germans were confronted with the humiliation of defeat, threats to their traditional culture by the changed morality in the Weimar Republic, and despair caused by rapid inflation that threatened economic survival (David Redles in Strozier et. al. 2010, 156–74; in Wessinger 2011, 529–48l; 2005).

German National Socialism demonstrates that when millennialist movements become involved in violence there may be *apocalyptic victims* who do not share responsibility for the violence that destroyed them. In the case of the Nazi movement, these victims include the approximately 6 million Jews, and the thousands and millions of Roma, handicapped, prisoners of war, Poles, Russians, Ukrainians, Belarusians, Serbs, homosexuals, Catholic priests and Jehovah's Witnesses who were killed in the Holocaust.

Analysis of German National Socialism as a millennial movement was anticipated by Cohn (1970 [1957]), and received sustained study by James M. Rhodes (1980), Nicholas Goodrick-Clarke (1993), David Redles (2005), Karla Poewe (2006) and Robert Ellwood (in Wessinger 2000b, 241–60). Jacqueline Stone has contributed a seminal study of the roles played by Japanese Buddhist millennialism based on the Lotus Sutra before, during, and after World War II (in Wessinger 2000b, 261–80), but thorough studies of millennial aspirations associated with Japanese imperialism remain to be done.

Specialists in Islam and new religions scholars have analysed the contemporary international Jihadist movement as a revolutionary millennial movement whose participants resort to terrorism because it is not a socially dominant movement, and the complex interactionist contexts that produce Jihadist terrorists have been noted (Cook 2005; Jeffrey T. Kenney in Wessinger 2011, 688–713; Hall 2009; Rosenfeld in Wessinger 2011, 100–4; Wessinger 2006, 184–92; Al-Rasheed and Shterin 2009).

The Interactionist Perspective

The interactionist perspective on millennialism (and new religious movements) and violence had its beginnings in the scholarly studies of the assassination of 5 members of the party of Congressman Leo Ryan (1925–78), including Ryan himself, and wounding others on 18 November 1978 by residents of Jonestown, Guyana, who then returned to Jonestown and participated in the murders and suicides of 909 people of all ages by injection or ingesting a mixture of cyanide and sedatives. The members of Peoples Temple living in Jonestown had hoped they were creating a new society free of racism, sexism, classism and ageism.

In contrast to the *cult essentialist* perspective (Hall 2000, 16) promoted by the anti-cult movement and the media, which places all blame for the Jonestown deaths on a 'cult' leader, Jim Jones (1931–78), and his allegedly 'brainwashed' followers, the early books by Rebecca Moore (e.g. 1985), the study by John R. Hall (1987), Mary McCormick Maaga's book (1998), and Moore's recent book (2009b) emphasize *interactions* between members of Peoples Temple and Jonestown with outside opponents that created a context in which mass murder and suicides were carried out to preserve the ultimate concern of maintaining the cohesiveness of the community. Individuals with Concerned Relatives were aggressive in filing lawsuits against Jim Jones and Peoples Temple and prompting negative media coverage as well as investigations and punitive actions by federal agencies that threatened the existence of Jonestown, which was already failing due to financial strains and the erratic behaviour of an over-medicated Jim Jones. The departure of Ryan's party with defectors, whom Jones feared would reveal the abuses within Jonestown, was the precipitating factor for the murders and suicides. Thus Jonestown became what Wessinger (2000a; in 2000b, 25–33) terms a *fragile millennial group*, which resorts to violence to preserve its ultimate concern threatened with failure by a combination of internal weaknesses and external pressures.

In the 1990s several violent incidents involving millennial groups tragically provided additional material for case studies. The first was the conflict in 1993 between Branch Davidians and federal law enforcement agents at Mount Carmel Center outside Waco, Texas. In contradiction to the cult essentialist perspective promoted by the government and media, new religions scholars found that a full consideration of the case had to take into account the unnecessary paramilitary raid carried out by Bureau of Alcohol, Tobacco, and Firearms agents on 28 February in which four ATF agents and six Branch Davidians died, the fifty-one-day siege conducted by Federal Bureau of Investigation agents who surrounded the residence with tanks and subjected the Branch Davidians to 'stress escalation' techniques of bright spotlights and high-decibel sounds through the nights, and a tank and CS-gas assault carried out by FBI agents on 19 April, which culminated in a fire that killed seventy-six Branch Davidians of all ages, including two fetuses. Nine people escaped the fire. The Branch Davidian case represents the largest loss of life in law enforcement actions on American soil.

The Branch Davidians believed in an apocalyptic theology of martyrdom based on the interpretations of the Bible's prophecies by David Koresh (1959–93), but it took the actions of the federal agents to activate that theology. The first scholarly studies were by James D. Tabor and Eugene V. Gallagher (1995) and the volume edited by Stuart A. Wright (1995).

The release of sarin gas on the Tokyo subway in 1995 by members of Aum Shinrikyō, an apocalyptic sect led by Shōkō Asahara (b. 1955), brought to light the group's earlier murders, confinement and mistreatment of dissidents, and release of sarin gas in Matsumoto, Japan in 1994. Ian Reader (2000) has provided the definitive study of Aum Shinrikyō, in addition to the volume edited by Robert J. Kisala and Mark R. Mullins (2001). In 2012 Erica Baffelli and Ian Reader guest-edited a special issue of *Japanese Journal of Religious Studies* (39, no. 1) on 'The Impact and Ramifications of the Aum Affair'. Articles by Japan specialists examine the founding of Hikari no Wa ('Circle of Light') by Joyu Fumihiro, the former spokesperson for Aum Shinrikyō, the impact of the Aum controversy on Soka Gakkai, religious organizations and politics after the Aum affair, the Neo-Nationalist response to the Aum crisis, and depictions of 'horrific cults' in *manga* after Aum. Benjamin Dorman compares scholarly reactions to the Branch Davidian and Aum Shinrikyō incidents. Ian Reader discusses how Aum's use of chemical and biological weapons has raised concern globally among counterterrorism analysts about extremist religious groups possessing and utilizing weapons of mass destruction. Although Aum Shinrikyō was acquiring weapons of mass destruction with the revolutionary intention of overthrowing the Japanese government in a national Armageddon, Wessinger (2000a, 120–57) has argued that at the points in time that members used these weapons and committed other acts of violence, Aum Shinrikyō was a fragile millennial group seeking to preserve the threatened charisma of their guru, Shōkō Asahara, on which the accomplishment of the millennial kingdom was believed to depend.

A variety of millennial movements in tension with mainstream society, or involved in violent conflicts, are examined in the book edited by Thomas Robbins and Susan J. Palmer (1997).

In 2000 John R. Hall, with Philip D. Schuyler and Sylvaine Trinh published *Apocalypse Observed*, and Catherine Wessinger published *How the Millennium Comes Violently*, each providing comparative case studies of Jonestown (1978), the Branch Davidians (1993), Solar Temple (1994), Aum Shinrikyō (1995) and Heaven's Gate (1997). The Wessinger volume also includes chapters on the Montana Freemen (1996) and Chen Tao (1998) as examples of potentially volatile apocalyptic groups that were handled carefully by law enforcement agents. Hall analyses these cases in terms of categories of the *warring sect* and groups espousing a *mystical apocalypse of deathly transcendence*. Wessinger offers the categories of *assaulted millennial group, fragile millennial group* and *revolutionary millennial movements*, stressing that a group or movement may possess characteristics of multiple categories simultaneously, or may shift from one to another in response to events. Also in 2000 Wessinger published an edited volume, *Millennialism, Persecution, and Violence*, with chapters that contribute to the interactionist perspective.

To an examination of Peoples Temple and Jonestown, Branch Davidians, Solar Temple, Heaven's Gate, and Aum Shinrikyō, John Walliss in *Apocalyptic Trajectories* (2004) adds consideration of the Movement for the Restoration of the Ten Commandments of God (MRTCG) in Uganda, an apocalyptic Catholic Marian apparition group, which in 2000 was discovered to have caused the deaths of at least 778 people – hundreds in a church that was set on fire, and hundreds more killed and then buried at locations owned by the group. Walliss assesses the roles played by challenges of *cultural opponents* (Hall in Wright 1995, 205–35) to the leaders' authority and charisma and to the groups' millennial goals. He points out that the suicides of 39 Heaven's Gate members and the murders and possible suicides of MRTCG members were the result of largely internal weaknesses and pressures. He concludes that a fragile millennial group does not necessarily have to experience a great deal of external opposition. In consonance with conclusions drawn by Ian Reader (2000; in Wessinger 2000b, 158–82) concerning Aum Shinrikyō, Walliss argues that violence involving a fragile millennial group 'can result from imagined opposition and perceived persecution' (2004, 245) as well as confrontational opposition.

Cults, Religion, and Violence edited by Bromley and Melton (2002) contains thoughtful chapters by sociologists and historians of religions in the interactionist school who examine sources of volatility in NRMs, crises of charismatic legitimacy, roles played by public agencies, the different types of 'cult-watching' groups and specific cases involved in violent incidents.

A notable exception to the interactionist perspective is Kenneth G. C. Newport's *Branch Davidians of Waco* (2006), which takes a cult essentialist perspective towards events in 1993, while providing a fine history of the Davidians of Victor Houteff (1885–1955), and the Branch Davidians of Ben Roden (1902–78), Lois Roden (1905–86) and Vernon Howell / David Koresh based on archival sources. Newport argues that the Branch Davidians were 'theologically primed' to die in a fire, and that once the conflict was initiated by the ATF assault, the deaths of the Branch Davidians were inevitable. He repeats the government's defense arguments in the wrongful death civil trial in 2000, and the report of the investigation by special counsel John C. Danforth (2000), to the effect that federal agents' actions did not contribute to the deaths of Branch Davidians. (For a hermeneutical examination and critique of the Danforth Report see Rosenfeld 2001.)

Wright and Wessinger express disagreement with Newport's view on the 1993 conflict at Mount Carmel, to which Newport responds, in a special issue of *Nova Religio* (13, no. 2 [November 2009]). Wright argues that evidence that the Branch Davidians committed mass suicide is not 'unassailable' (as claimed by Newport based on government sources), and points to numerous instances of federal agents lying, and mishandling, losing, and concealing evidence, and the federal judge's rulings that prevented presentation of key evidence in the civil trial. Wright discusses the technicalities of the tank and CS-gas assault on 19 April 1993, including the nature of CS particles as poisonous and flammable. Although CS is a riot control agent intended for outdoor use, its vapours are lethal in enclosed spaces. The gas in which CS particles were suspended on 19 April 1993 was toxic and flammable methylene chloride.

Wessinger argues that examination of Branch Davidians' conversations picked up by surveillance devices in conjunction with Branch Davidians' statements to FBI negotiators indicates that FBI decision-makers had ample information that Branch Davidians expected to die in a fire if they were attacked a second time. She argues that the FBI tank and CS assault on 19 April, despite a breakthrough in negotiations on 14 April in which Koresh offered his exit plan, raises the question of whether FBI decision-makers intended for Branch Davidians to come out alive. Although a surviving Branch Davidian, Graeme Craddock, testified that an order to light fires was called out inside the building on 19 April about 12:00 noon, this did not occur until after the Branch Davidians had been gassed continually since 6:00 a.m., tanks were driving through and demolishing the building and small children and their mothers huddled inside a concrete vault with an open doorway were gassed by a tank from 11:31 to 11:55 a.m. In 1999 Col. Rodney L. Rawlings, who was the head military liaison in Waco in 1993, told Lee Hancock with the *Dallas Morning News* that he and FBI agents were listening to audio captured by surveillance devices in real time during the assault, and that the children and mothers inside the vault could be heard crying and praying.

In his response, Newport disputes the claim that FBI agents contributed to the deaths of the Branch Davidians. He does not believe that there could have been a massive cover-up of wrongdoing on the part of federal agents. He accepts the conclusions in the Danforth Report. He argues that the Branch Davidians set fire to themselves to achieve their ultimate concern of rebirth into a new life in an anticipated millennial kingdom.

A recently published collection of articles in the interactionist school is *Violence and New Religious Movements* edited by James R. Lewis (2011). Its chapters include reprinted articles, including James T. Richardson's *Terrorism and Political Violence* article summarizing the interactionist perspective, general treatments and case studies of 'the big five' plus MRTCG, treatments of violence and other NRMs, many of which were millennial, deprogramming violence, and an updated version of the *Nova Religio* article by Richardson and Bryan Edelman on state-sponsored violence against Falun Gong practitioners in the People's Republic of China from 1999 to the present. Their article demonstrates how a government may label a group a 'cult' prior to taking concerted actions to eradicate it by harming its members.

Falun Gong, a *qigong* movement led by Li Hongzhi (b. 1951) said to have millions of practitioners, attracted the ire of Chinese Communist leaders on

25 April 1999, when about 10,000 practitioners surrounded the headquarters of the Chinese Communist Party in Beijing in a quiet, daylong protest against negative depictions of Falun Gong in state-controlled media. As Falun Gong practitioners were arrested, imprisoned, tortured and killed, Li's online rhetoric became more apocalyptic and encouraged practitioners in China to step forward in peaceful demonstrations to 'validate the Fa' (Dharma) and thereby defeat the demon politicians ruling the PRC. He said that practitioners who failed to do so were breaking away from 'humanness' and lost their opportunity to achieve 'Consummation'. By 2001 Li's statements on the Falun Gong website shifted from encouraging practitioners to put themselves in harm's way to waging 'spiritual warfare' against Communist officials by sending forth 'righteous thoughts' (Rahn 2002, 55, 57–9; Wessinger 2006, 173–6). Nevertheless Falun Gong continues to be an assaulted millennial movement whose practitioners are imprisoned and abused, with perhaps as many as 3,000 deaths since 1999.

China specialists plus new religions scholars conducting participant-observation in the Falun Gong diaspora community, plus Richardson and Edelman on the legal aspects in the PRC, contributed articles to a special issue of *Nova Religio* on Falun Gong (6, no. 2 [April 2003]). David Ownby (2010) has provided the definitive religious studies treatment of Falun Gong and the controversy.

Psychology of Apocalyptic Violence

Psychologists, psychoanalysts, and psychiatrists have been interested in the psychology of apocalypticism and millennialism, especially of leaders and followers whose groups commit or become involved in violence. In 1994 psychoanalyst Charles B. Strozier published *Apocalypse* on the psychology of apocalyptic fundamentalism. In 1999 psychiatrist Marc Galanter published a revised and updated edition of his 1989 book, *Cults: Faith, Healing and Coercion*, studying the characteristics of *charismatic groups*. Also in 1999 psychiatrist Robert Jay Lifton, following up on his earlier work, especially on Nazis, published a book analysing Aum Shinrikyō based on interviews conducted in Japan.

The edited book, *The Fundamentalist Mindset* (Strozier et. al. 2010), explores the potential and actualized violence of catastrophic millennial and progressive millennial movements with pronounced radical dualistic outlooks. The psychologists, psychoanalysts, and historians contributing to this volume agree with historians of religions and sociologists in new religions studies that a rigid sense of us versus them and demonization of perceived opponents contributes to conflict and violence.

These points are brought out in James W. Jones (2008), which examines Jihadism, Aum Shinrikyō, and the violent imagery and latent violence in

American Christian Dispensationalism and the *Left Behind* series. Jones suggests that revolutionary and terrorist millennial violence are motivated by rage in reaction to humiliation by a cultural and religious 'other', and are encouraged in contexts that emphasize submission to an authoritarian God or leader. These movements are characterized by a dichotomized outlook of good versus evil that requires a strong boundary between the group and outside society, elimination of those designated as evil, 'a drive for purity' to protect the group from contamination, and 'the inability to tolerate ambivalence and ambiguity . . .' (Jones 2008, 135–6).

This analysis seems applicable to revolutionary millennial movements and terrorists, whereas with assaulted millennial groups and fragile millennial groups each case must be examined on its own merits. Jones' insights will apply to some, but certainly not to all, cases of millennialism and violence. Opponents to a millennial group may possess a more rigid dualistic perspective than millennialists, especially if the millennialists persist in seeing opponents as 'souls to be saved'. This seems to have been the case with the Branch Davidians (Doyle 2012, 135).

Millennialism and Dates and Continued Research

Millennialism is not necessarily tied to specific dates, but certain dates often excite millennial imaginations as well as concerns of authorities to maintain public order. This was the case in the 1990s in relation to the anticipated new temporal millennium, purportedly 2,000 years after the birth of Jesus Christ, which saw fears of a projected Y2K bug that would affect computer systems and the violent episodes that have been discussed (Cowan 2003b).

In 1999 in anticipation of possible apocalyptic violence on New Year's Eve 1999–1 January 2000, the FBI published a report titled 'Project Megiddo', Canadian Security Intelligence Service published 'Doomsday Religious Movements', and scholars Ehud Sprinzak, Yaakov Ariel, Uri Ne'eman and Amnon Ramon submitted a report to Israeli intelligence services, 'Events at the End of the Millennium: Possible Implications for the Public Order in Jerusalem'. These documents were published in the *Terrorism and Political Violence* 14, no. 1 (2002) special issue, guest-edited by Jeffrey Kaplan, and reprinted in *Millennialism Violence: Past, Present and Future* (Kaplan 2002), with articles by Michael Barkun, Eugene Gallagher and Benjamin Beit-Hallahmi analysing the three reports respectively. Additional articles discuss Aum Shinrikyō (Ian Reader), lack of apocalyptic concern in Finland (Leena Malkki), 'Cult and Anticult Totalism', (Dick Anthony, Thomas Robbins and Steven Barrie-Anthony) and medieval millennialism (Richard Landes and E. Randolph Daniel).

The 1990s saw an increase in the scholarly study of millennialism that has continued into the twenty-first century. *The Year 2000: Essays on the End* edited by Strozier and Flynn (1997) contains essays on a variety of millennial topics by psychoanalysts and historians of religions, including one of Richard Landes' articles on millennial expectations focused on the years 1000 and 1033. Landes' Center for Millennial Studies at Boston University promoted scholarship on millennialism published online and in Landes' *Encyclopedia of Millennialism and Millennial Movements* (2000).

The American Academy of Religion included the Millennialism Studies Group as a programme unit 1997–2003. Britain and Ireland have centres promoting on-going study of millennialism and holding conferences. John Walliss is director of the Centre for Millennialism Studies at Liverpool Hope College, and Crawford Gribben directs the Millennialism Project at Trinity College Dublin.

Other encyclopedias, edited volumes and handbooks were published in the new temporal millennium focusing on the range of cultural creativity in millennial movements. The Millennialism and Society series with Equinox, edited by Brenda E. Brasher, published three volumes: *War in Heaven/Heaven on Earth: Theories of the Apocalyptic* (O'Leary and McGhee 2005); *The End That Does: Art, Science, and Accomplishment* (Gutierrez and Schwartz 2006); and *Gender and Apocalyptic Desire* (Brasher and Quinby 2006). *Expecting the End* (Newport and Gribben 2006) contains chapters on diverse movements. *Historical Dictionary of Jehovah's Witnesses* (Chryssides 2008) presents scholarly information on the international apocalyptic movement that originated with a Bible study group led by Charles Taze Russell (1852–1916) in the 1870s, and was given its present name by its second leader, Joseph Franklin Rutherford (1869–1942). *End of Days* (Kinane and Ryan 2009) contains chapters ranging from origins of apocalypticism in Judaism and Christianity, to apocalypticism in the New World, to the First World War, Nazi millennialism, to millennial expressions in America, to 'Zombie Apocalypse' in popular culture. John Walliss edited the Apocalypse and Popular Culture series with Sheffield Phoenix Press with six volumes addressing millennialism in film (Walliss and Quinby 2010), the internet (Howard 2011), the *Left Behind* series (Gribben and Sweetnam 2011), music (Partridge 2012), comic books and graphic novels (Clanton 2012) and television (Aston and Walliss 2013).

In 2011 Landes published *Heaven on Earth*, his master analysis of millennial expressions through the ages and in various cultures, in which he presents his categories of millennialism, his 'roosters' and 'owls' (apocalyptic prophets, and anti-apocalyptic clerics) theory of attitudes towards apocalypse, to which he adds 'bats' (historians working with texts produced by owls), and 'turkeys' (historians of millennial phenomena). Landes describes nativist millennial movements, Pharaoh Akhenaten's promotion of *imperial millennialism* – millennialism from the top down, the Taiping Revolution as an example of *demotic millennialism* – millennialism that arises from the grassroots, and the French Revolution. Landes provides a needed analysis of the millennial aspects of Marxism in its various forms, focusing on the Bolshevik Revolution. He also discusses Nazism, UFO groups and the global Jihadist movement.

In 2011 Wessinger published *The Oxford Handbook of Millennialism*, which contains 35 chapters by specialists to examine millennialism in cross-cultural perspective. In 2012 Newport and Joshua Searle published an edited volume, *Beyond the End: The Future of Millennial Studies*, with chapters contemplating millennialism studies past and present, and the human concerns and needs addressed in millennial phenomena.

Conclusion

Scholars in new religions studies, and more broadly in millennialism studies, have contributed numerous case studies of fascinating, sometimes benign, sometimes fun, and sometimes violent and tragic, millennial groups and movements. New religions studies has offered the interactionist perspective on religion and violence that is relevant to understanding factors in *oppositional milieus* (Hall 2009) that produce terrorists. Understanding the dynamics and factors in trajectories leading to violence is necessary to avoid or prevent violence involving millennial groups.

Millennial aspirations will continue into the future. Environmental millennialism will become more prominent as people respond to increasing climate and environmental changes (Robin Globus and Bron Taylor in Wessinger 2011, 628–46). Millennial and apocalyptic themes will continue to be expressed in popular media and the internet (Douglas E. Cowan in Wessinger 2011, 611–27).

The 21 December 2012 date, allegedly marking the end of the Mayan calendar, boosted new age millennialism, similar to how the 'Harmonic Convergence' on 16–17 August 1987 promoted the 2012 date (Sitler 2012). Christian Dispensationalism, the Jihadist movement and millennial and apocalyptic expectations focused on Israel will continue in the future.

As shown in Hall (2009) the millennial stakes are higher than ever due to weapons of mass destruction and environmental degradation. Until the end of the world as we know it, there will be plenty for new religions students to study.

Note

1. The definition of 'ultimate concern' utilized here differs from the usage of Christian theologian Paul Tillich, who coined the term.

16 Violence

James R. Lewis

Chapter Outline	
The Big Five (Six)	150
Interpreting NRM Violence	156
Suicide Cults	158

Since at least the 1970s, there has been widespread public concern about the potential for violence within religious groups referred to variously as 'sects', 'cults', 'new religions' or 'new religious movements' (NRMs). This is in large part the result of violent incidents involving NRMs that have made international headlines, particularly the Jonestown murder-suicides (1978), the ATF/FBI raid on the Mount Carmel community (1993), the Solar Temple murder-suicides (1994, 1995 and 1997), the Tokyo subway poison gas attack (1995) and the Heaven's Gate suicides (1997). However, far and away the great majority of NRMs are not violent and show little or no propensity to become violent, especially in contrast to the much greater violence sometimes associated with 'mainstream' religions.

There now exists a reasonably substantial body of academic literature devoted to this issue. This literature tends to be dominated by sociological approaches that consist primarily of retrospective analyses of the most prominent groups involved in violent incidents. More recently, the tendency has been to construct general models that take external as well as internal factors into account. This multi-factor view is the underlying orientation of David G. Bromley and J. Gordon Melton's important anthology, *Cults, Religion, and Violence* (2002). Despite subsequent publications, the Bromley-Melton volume remains the field's state-of-the-art theoretical statement on NRMs and violence.

A complicating factor in understanding NRM-related violence is that alternative religions have been highly controversial. Not only have NRMs been the subject of sensationalized media coverage, but they have also provoked the emergence of advocacy groups devoted to the destruction of NRMs. These opposition groups are often collectively referred to in academic treatments of new religions as the 'anti-cult movement' (usually abbreviated 'ACM'). The participation of ACM spokespersons in the debate over the potential dangers of NRMs has clouded the issue by promoting a generalized negative stereotype of 'sects' or 'cults' which assumes that the extreme actions committed by members of a handful of alternative religions characterize all NRMs. This is especially the case with a 'hot-button' topic like violence. As a consequence, any comprehensive attempt to come to grips with this issue must also analyse the appeal of such stereotypes, and must carefully distinguish empirical concerns from pseudo-concerns.

After the most extreme incidents took place in the mid-1990s, a number of survey treatments were published, including: Catherine Wessinger's *How the Millennium Comes Violently* (2000a), John R. Hall et al.'s *Apocalypse Observed* (2000), and John Walliss' *Apocalyptic Trajectories* (2004). What all of these books share is a focus on five or six groups involved in the most extreme acts of violence. There have also been a number of academic monographs and anthologies published on one or the other of this handful of groups, from David Chidester's *Salvation and Suicide* (1988) to James R. Lewis, (ed.) *The Order of the Solar Temple* (2006) to Kenneth Newport's *The Branch Davidians of Waco* (2006). None of these volumes substantially add to the analyses found in Bromley and Melton's *Cults, Religion, and Violence*. A recent collection, Madawi Al-Rasheed and Marat Shterin, (eds.) *Dying for Faith* (2009), brings together chapters on NRM violence with chapters on other forms of religious violence, particularly Jihadist violence, but none of the contributors make any attempt at cross-fertilization between these research areas, and the chapters on NRM-related violence say nothing substantially new.

The most recent contribution to this literature is Lewis' new edited volume, *Violence and New Religious Movements* (2011). Individual contributors to that collection took the further step of examining instances where religious leaders have initiated the murder of members (Knutby Filadelfia) and ex-members (New Vrindaban). Contributors also analysed groups that have *almost* been involved in major incidents of violence (Rajneeshpuran) and NRMs that seem to have all of the characteristics of violent groups, but which *never* exploded into violence (e.g. 3HO and Sikh Dharma Brotherhood). The volume also examined violence *against* new religions (e.g. Falun Gong).

The Big Five (Six)

Though different analysts include different sets of the NRMs involved in violence, for the most part they all examine the groups that we might refer to as the 'Big Five' – the Peoples Temple, the Branch Davidians, the Order of the Solar Temple, Aum Shinrikyō and Heaven's Gate. While violence involving the latter four took place in a narrow span of the five years between 1992 and 1997, the Peoples Temple mass murder-suicide event took place over a dozen years prior. There was also a religious group in Uganda involved in a mass murder – that some observers insist was a mass suicide – which took place in 2000.

The Peoples Temple: Jim (James Warren) Jones originally founded an independent congregation called Community Unity. There he put into place his vision of a Pentecostal-style worship and a social service activism across racial boundaries. By the late 1950s the congregation was renamed the Peoples Temple and began to emulate many of the features of Father Divine's Peace Mission. Jones saw Father Divine (1879–1965) as a role model, though Jones was white and most of his followers were black. In 1960 the Peoples Temple affiliated with the Christian Church (Disciples of Christ) and the following year Jones received a Bachelor of Science degree from Butler University in Indianapolis.

In 1964, after returning from a two-year travel sabbatical to diffuse community controversy about the congregation's activities, he was ordained as a Disciples of Christ minister. Believing that Indianapolis was a dangerous area for a future nuclear war, he moved the congregation to Ukiah, California. The success of his ministry there made him wealthy and influential, and he added a congregation in Los Angeles. His social work earned him community awards and praise in church journals.

There were areas of concern, however. He began claiming he could raise people from the dead. It was rumoured he held dictatorial control over the personal lives of followers and abused some children. In 1977, facing media exposure, he moved to a colony in Guyana, South America, he had founded in 1973, and it soon swelled to more than 900 inhabitants as 'Jonestown'. The group still faced court charges, and Jones began to speak of the possibility of group suicide. In November 1978 Congressman Leo Ryan and others visited Jonestown to investigate. Ryan and most of his group were shot to death and almost all the residents of Jonestown also died via poison or gunshot. The name 'Jonestown' has since served for many to stand for and sum up the dangers of religious 'cults'.

Branch Davidians: Vernon Howell was brought up in a Seventh-day Adventist Church in Tyler, Texas, that his mother attended. He later joined the Branch Davidians – a small group descended from another group, the Shepherd's Rod, that had splintered from the SDA in the 1930s – and became a favourite of the leader, Lois Roden, who eventually named him as her successor. In 1990 Vernon Howell legally adopted the name David Koresh. By 1992, Koresh had concluded that the apocalypse would occur in America rather than Israel, and the group began adopting a survivalist outlook, stockpiling large amounts of food, weapons, ammunition and fuel. Koresh renamed the Mount Carmel community 'Ranch Apocalypse'.

Accusations of misbehaviour on the part of Koresh and some other residents of the Branch Davidian headquarters began to circulate among anti-cultists and others. The accusations were those frequently used against many unconventional religions by their opponents. The most frequent accusations alleged child abuse and possession of firearms. Local authorities investigated the child abuse allegations and found them groundless. The federal Bureau of Alcohol, Tobacco and Firearms (ATF) of the Department of the Treasury obtained search and arrest warrants on the weapons charges.

On 28 February 1993, a force of 76 agents of the ATF raided the Branch Davidian community. The raid turned into a shoot-out between federal agents and Branch Davidians who chose to defend themselves. The resulting standoff turned into a 51-day siege that ended on 19 April when the FBI launched a new attack on the Davidian complex. Agents of the federal government used military equipment to batter holes in buildings through which they injected noxious gas in an attempt to force the Davidians outside. A fire ignited in the buildings and over 80 members died.

Order of the Solar Temple: Joseph Di Mambro, the founder of the Order of the Solar Temple (Ordre du Temple Solaire, or OTS), had been fascinated with esotericism from a young age. Like a number of other esoteric groups in France, the OTS claimed a lineage going back to the Knights Templar, a medieval order of knights declared to be heretics by King Philip IV of France and disbanded. Recognizing his intelligence and charisma, Di Mambro brought Luc Jouret in to become the public face of his organization.

The Temple's teachings stressed occult-apocalyptic themes, bringing together three traditions on the end of the world: a) the idea found in some (but by no means all) new age groups of an impending ecological catastrophe; b) some neo-templar movements' theory of a cosmic 'renovatio' revealed by the ascended masters of the Grand Lodge of Agartha; c) the political ideas of a final international bagarre propagated by survivalist groups both on the extreme right and on the extreme left of the political spectrum.

On 8 March 1993, a crucial episode in the history of the Solar Temple occurred in Canada. Two Temple members, Jean Pierre Vinet, engineer and project-manager for Hydro-Quebéc and Herman Delorme, an insurance broker, were arrested as they were attempting to buy three semiautomatic guns with silencers, illegal weapons in Canada. Daniel Tougas, a police officer of Cowansville and a Temple member, was temporarily suspended from office on charges of having helped the two. On 9 March, judge François Doyon of Montreal committed them to trial, freeing them on parole. Luc Jouret – who according to police reports asked the two to buy the weapons – was also committed to trial, and an arrest warrant was issued against him. (The Temple leader could not be found, as he was in Europe at the time.) The event drew the attention of the Canadian press on what newspapers called 'the cult of the end of the world'.

On 4 October, a fire destroyed Joseph Di Mambro's villa in Morin Heights, Canada. Among the ruins, the police found five charred bodies, one of which was a child's. At least three of these people seemed to have been stabbed to death before the fire. On 5 October, at 1:00 a.m., a fire started in one of the centres of the Solar Temple in Switzerland, the Ferme des Rochettes, near Cheiry, in the Canton of Fribourg. The police found 23 bodies, one of which was a child's, in a room converted into a temple. Some of the victims were killed by gunshots, while many others were found with their heads inside plastic bags. The same day, at 3:00 a.m., three chalets, inhabited by members of the Solar Temple, caught fire almost simultaneously at Les Granges sur Salvan, in the Valais Canton. In the charred remains were found 25 bodies, along with remainders of devices programmed to start the fires, and the pistol which shot the 52 bullets destined for the people found dead in Cheiry.

Aum Shinrikyō: On 20 March 1995, a poison gas attack occurred in a Tokyo subway that killed 12 people and injured many others. Within a few days of the attack, Aum Shinrikyō, a controversial Japanese religious group, was fingered as the most likely suspect. Aum Shinrikyō was founded by Master Shōkō Asahara in Tokyo in 1987. A form of Tantric Buddhism, Aum Shinrikyō's teachings emphasized yoga practices and spiritual experiences. By the time of the subway incident, Aum Shinrikyō had acquired a large communal facility near Mount Fuji and a following of approximately 10,000 members in Japan.

In addition to the usual teachings that go hand in hand with mainline Buddhism, Master Asahara was also fascinated with the future. Like many other Japanese spiritualists, he was fascinated by Western biblical prophecies as well as by the prophecies of Nostradamus. Perhaps influenced by the apocalyptic flavour of these predictions, Asahara himself began preaching an apocalyptic message to his followers. In particular, he prophesied a confrontation between Japan and the United States before the end of the century that would in all likelihood decimate his home country.

Asahara was, in fact, so certain about an impending conflict between Japan and the United States that he actually began preparing to wage war. Unable to match the conventional military might of the United States, Aum scientists investigated unconventional weapons, from biological agents to poison gas. The subway attack was motivated by increased police scrutiny of the Aum Shinrikyō, with the idea of distracting police attention away from the movement. There had also been smaller-scale acts of violence carried out against the enemies of the group – in one case poison gas was released near their Mount Fuji Center in an attack on local critics. It was this latter assault that led the police to begin investigating Aum Shinrikyō in the first place.

In the end, it was Asahara's own pronouncements that drew police attention to Aum Shinrikyō. In particular, Master Asahara had predicted that gas attacks by terrorists would occur in the not-too-distant future. This made him an obvious target of suspicion. Hence the subway attack, far from diverting attention away from Aum Shinrikyō, actually had the opposite effect.

Heaven's Gate: Marshall Herff Applewhite (aka 'Bo'; 'Do') and Bonnie Lu Nettles ('Peep'; 'Ti') founded one of the most unusual flying saucer religions ever to emerge out of the occult-metaphysical subculture. 'The Two', as they were sometimes called, met in 1972. In 1973, they had an experience which convinced them that they were the two witnesses mentioned in Revelation 11. Preaching an unusual synthesis of occult spirituality and UFO soteriology, they began recruiting in New Age circles in the spring of 1975. Followers were required to abandon friends and family, detach themselves completely from human emotions as well as material possessions, and focus exclusively on perfecting themselves in preparation for a physical transition (i.e. beaming up) to the next kingdom (in the form of a flying saucer) – a metamorphosis that would be facilitated by ufonauts.

For their followers, the focus of day-to-day existence was to follow a disciplined regime referred to as the overcoming process or, simply, the process. The goal of this process was to overcome human weaknesses – a goal not dissimilar to the goal of certain spiritual practices followed by more mainstream monastic communities. For Applewhite, however, it appears that stamping out one's sexuality was the core issue.

Details about how the group came to attach apocalyptic significance to the Hale-Bopp Comet are tantalizingly scanty. In 1997, someone outside the group had come to the conclusion that a giant UFO was coming to earth, 'hidden' in the wake of Hale-Bopp. This individual then placed his opinion on the internet. When Heaven's Gate retrieved this information, Applewhite took it as an indication that the long awaited pick-up of his group by aliens was finally about to take place. The decision that the time had come to make their final exit could not have been made more than a few weeks before the mass suicide.

The idea that the group might depart via suicide had emerged in Applewhite's thinking only within the last few years. The earlier idea – an idea that had set Heaven's Gate apart from everyone else – was that group of individuals selected to move to the next level would bodily ascend to the saucers in a kind of 'technological rapture'. Applewhite may have begun to rethink his theology after his beloved partner died because, in order to be reunited with Nettles, her spirit would have to acquire a new body aboard the spacecraft. While the death of Nettles may or may not have been the decisive influence, he later adopted the view that Heaven's Gate would ascend together spiritually rather than physically.

The Movement for the Restoration of the Ten Commandments of God: The Movement for the Restoration of the Ten Commandments of God (MRTCG) was a doomsday religious group in Uganda that made headlines in the wake of what was initially thought to be a mass suicide on 17 March 2000. About 530 died in a fire that gutted their church in Kanungu, Uganda, on Friday, 17 March 2000. In the days following the tragedy, police discovered innumerable other bodies at different sites. These others had been murdered prior to the group holocaust.

The movement was founded by excommunicated Roman Catholic priests, nuns and a former prostitute. The group taught that the Catholic Church was badly in need of reform. Their own rules were said to be channelled from the Virgin Mary. Leaders taught that the Ten Commandments needed to be restored to their original importance. Mary, it was said, stated that the world would come to an end unless humans started to follow the Ten Commandments closely. The group initially believed that the end of the world would take place on 31 December 1999. During 1999, members sold their possessions in preparation for the end times when they would be transported to heaven. They slaughtered cattle and had a week-long feast. When the end did not come, the date was changed to 31 December 2000. Later, it was taught that the Virgin Mary would appear on 17 March and take the faithful to Heaven. They also expected the end of the world to occur at that time.

Most of the deaths occurred in Kanungu, a small trading centre, about 217 miles southwest of Kampala, the capital of Uganda. While there may still be some sources which continue to assert that the parishioners committed suicide, the consensus opinion is that the leaders murdered the members by luring them inside the church and then setting it on fire. The church's windows had been boarded-up; its doors were nailed shut with the members inside.

There was one initial report, never confirmed, that members had applied gasoline and paraffin to their skin before the explosion and fire. However, it is difficult to see how any observer could have witnessed these preparations if the windows and doors of the church had been nailed shut. It is now almost certain that the tragedy was a mass murder, not a mass suicide. The discovery of additional bodies of members who had been murdered and buried in latrines near the church gives weight to the mass murder theory. The discoveries of many hundreds of murder victims at other locations also point towards mass murder.

The murders seem to have been precipitated by failed prophecy. When the end of the world did not occur on the predicted date, some members of the group demanded their money and possessions back. This, in turn, may have triggered the mass murders.

Interpreting NRM Violence

The earliest approaches to NRM-related violence focused almost entirely on the (explicitly, or by implication, psychopathological) personality of the leader. These early portrayals were often formulated by authors who were not social scientists and who drew heavily on popular stereotypes about sinister, megalomaniacal 'cult leaders' cynically manipulating and brainwashing their members. Though charismatic leadership is clearly a factor in most NRM-related violence, the consensus of contemporary academic specialists is that 'attributing organizational outcomes to the personality of a single individual, even a powerful charismatic leader, usually camouflages much more complex social dynamics' (Bromley 2002, 47). The thrust of subsequent research was to shift attention away from (but not to ignore) the role of the leadership. There have, however, been a handful of more recent studies that have sought to refocus attention on the charismatic leader (e.g. Dawson 2002; Lewis 2005; Walliss 2006).

In the wake of the four major violent events that took place in the nineties, many studies shifted emphasis to these groups' millenarian beliefs. As reflected such titles as *How the Millennium Comes Violently* (Wessinger 2000a), *Millennialism, Persecution and Violence* (Wessinger 2000b) and *Millennium, Messiahs, and Mayhem* (Robbins and Palmer 1997), millennialism was central to these discussions. The near approach of the new millennium in the 1990s seems to have influenced this perspective, and the violence associated with the implosion of the Ugandan group – the MRTCG – in the year 2000 – seemed to confirm the validity of this focus. The obvious problem with this emphasis is that there are many religions with millenarian theologies, but few ever become violent. This has prompted some theorists to put forward typologies that attempt to distinguish harmless millennialism from dangerous millennialism.

Yet another factor considered in attempts to construct a general model of NRM-associated violence is 'totalistic' social organization and ideology. Totalistic groups are high-demand organizations in which participants usually do not have the option of being casual, part-time members. At the level of ideology, religio-ideological totalism often entails an absolute division of humanity into dual categories such as saved/damned, godly/satanic and the like. Totalistic groups are not necessarily – nor even typically – violent, but ideological totalism does feature an impulse to validate an absolute worldview by confronting demonized exemplars of evil as contrast symbols. As discussed in a number of recent and forthcoming studies (e.g. Anthony, Robbins and Barrie-Anthony 2011; Richardson 2011; Robbins 2002), confrontations between totalistic movements and hostile outside forces can escalate out of control and trigger violent outcomes.

Another set of considerations for assessing an NRM's potential for violence are hostile external forces. Although these factors were discussed in earlier studies, it is only relatively recently that analysts have regularly begun to discuss such 'exogenous factors' as a related set of considerations. These external forces are usually identified as: embittered apostates and hostile parents of current members, ACM organizations, sensationalized negative media coverage and interventions by state control agencies (such as child protective services or law enforcement officials). A raid by a law enforcement agency is arguably the single most provocative act by outside forces. (The manner in which law enforcement officials handled the Freemen standoff in Montana [Wessinger 2000a] and the eschatological fervour of the Chen Tao UFO-religion in Texas [Szubin, Jensen and Gregg 2000] have been cited as exemplary models of sensitive police work that defused potentially volatile situations.) However, even the incorporation of such external factors does not necessarily add up to a recipe for disaster.

These two sets of factors – internal characteristics of a religious group (endogenous factors) and external individuals, agencies and organizations (exogenous factors) – regularly play a role in violent events involving alternative religions. These elements are not static. Rather, violence is almost always the end result of a dynamic process of *polarization* that arises from an interaction between internal and external elements (Melton and Bromley 2002, 241–3). This interaction proceeds through a series of stages, and violent outcomes can be averted at any stage. The standard model for this kind of analysis is David G. Bromley's notion of 'Dramatic Denouments' (Bromley 2002). The core structure of Dramatic Denouments is a four-stage processual model of interactive conflict amplification: (1) Latent Tension, (2) Nascent Conflict, (3) Intensified Conflict and (4) Dramatic Denouement. (Marion Goldman's analysis of the Rajneeshpuran conflict [2009, 2011] provides an excellent case study of how a group set on a path to a violent outcome can be pulled back from the edge.)

What we can draw from this research is a model of NRM violence consisting of internal factors and external factors. These factors can be relatively static, or they can interact in such a way that a process of polarization is set in motion that can amplify the conflict until it results in a violent outcome. To oversimplify a highly complex field of study, this 'internal-external-polarization model' (IEP model) represents a key point of reference for current research. Because the core process of the IEP model is the mutual construction of images of opposed groups, researchers who utilize this model tend to draw on contemporary theorizing about social constructionism (also termed social constructivism). The analysis of representations and perceptions, particularly perceptions of 'The Other', is an approach that has been gaining ground across a broad spectrum of social-scientific and cultural studies. An important aspect of this mode of analysis is its focus on understanding what such images reflexively say about the individuals or groups who are constructing representations of others.

Though descriptively useful, the weakness of the IEP model is that one can find other NRMs that appear to exhibit all of the same internal traits, and that have been targeted by the same kinds of hostile external forces, but that have never reacted violently. Thus while researchers generally agree on the combinations of certain factors that are '"necessary" for the eruption of major incidents of cult-related violence, although they are not "sufficient" to predict this violence' (Dawson 2006, 145–6). Even a police raid, which is arguably the single most provocative act by outside forces, does not necessarily result in disasters.

The Island Pond raid in 1984 (King 2008), raids on the Family International (formerly known as the Children of God) in different countries in 1993 (Oliver 1994), and the recent high-profile raid on the Fundamentalist Church of Jesus Christ of Latter Day Saints (Wright and Richardson 2011) in Texas on charges of child abuse contained all of the ingredients – endogenous as well as exogenous – that analysts have put forward as factors contributing to violent outcomes. Yet there were no violent outcomes. Given these disconfirming examples, does it make any sense at all to try and predict NRM violence?

Suicide Cults

At present, the relatively mature state of this body of literature makes it possible to ask different sorts of questions. Specifically, rather than a straightforward comparison of the 'Big Five', what if one focused instead on the three groups that imploded in group suicides – Peoples Temple, Solar Temple and Heaven's Gate? While it is true that both the Peoples Temple and the Solar Temple also engaged in acts of murder, it could be argued that these violent acts were aspects of the suicide event. It is thus possible to distinguish such suicide-related murders from the otherwise comparable violence initiated by the leadership of Aum Shinrikyō and other groups.

As a preliminary move, it should be noted that neither Shōkō Asahara (the leader of Aum Shinrikyō) nor David Koresh (the leader of the Branch Davidians) seriously contemplated suicide. When authorities finally located Asahara in a secret room at Aum's Mount Fuji Center, they also found him with an abundant stash of money that he planned to support himself with into the foreseeable future. And though Koresh seems to have been willing to die a martyr's death, it also appears he was ready to embrace martyrdom only if all other options (or, perhaps more accurately, all other reasonable options within the horizon of his religious ideology) were closed. The fact that during the siege of Mount Carmel Koresh retained a literary attorney to handle his story should be enough to indicate that he envisioned himself living into the post-siege future – not to mention his explicit assertion to FBI negotiators a few days before the final assault that 'I never intended to die in here'.

To now turn our attention to the Peoples Temple, the Solar Temple and Heaven's Gate, what happens when we ruthlessly cut away everything except the bare-bones structure shared by the three 'suicide cults'? Surprisingly, the first trait to drop out is millennialism. Though it is quite possible to argue that Jim Jones was millenarian, in point of fact he had no theology in the proper sense, much less a developed eschatology. Well before the establishment of Jonestown, he had become little more than a secular socialist in religious garb. Even as people lined up to drink a mixture of cyanide and Kool-Aid during the final drama, Jones exhorted his followers with the assertion that 'This is a revolutionary suicide; this is not a self-destructive suicide', rather than consoling them with visions of the afterlife – though, as Jonathan Z. Smith notes (1982, 117), one can also point to portions of the audiotape made during the event that intimate they would be reunited in a post-mortem state.

One could, of course, redefine religion to encompass secular visions, or redefine millennialism to include secular phenomena (as the editors and some of the contributors do in Robbins and Palmer's 1997 book, *Millennium, Messiahs, and Mayhem*). The problem with such approaches is that as soon as one expands millennialism to include non-religious phenomena, then one can legitimately ask, Why stop with survivalism, feminism and radical environmentalism (three groups examined in the Robbins and Palmer collection)? Almost any group of people who look forward to a better tomorrow – including educators and mainstream political parties – could conceivably be viewed as millennialist. At this level of generality, however, millennialism becomes almost meaningless as a category of analysis.

We should also note that millennialism in the primary sense described by Norman Cohn involves a salvation that is 'terrestrial, in the sense that it is to be realized on this earth and not in some other-worldly heaven' (1970, 15). At the time of their dramatic 'exits', however, *not one* of the three suicide groups examined here envisioned returning to a paradisal era that would be established on this planet.

Shifting our attention from the Peoples Temple to Heaven's Gate, we encounter another surprise when we subject the group's dramatic exit to the same kind of analysis: namely, pressing external threats, whether real or imagined, are not essential factors necessary for a group suicide. In all four of the other new religions to be engulfed by violence, hostile outsiders were a factor precipitating each tragedy – though none were quite as dramatic as the military assault on Mount Carmel. The press criticism and government scrutiny directed against the Solar Temple and the Peoples Temple were mild by comparison.

In the case of Heaven's Gate, the group suicide was set in motion by the seemingly innocuous speculation of UFO buffs that a large UFO was approaching earth in the wake of the Hale-Bopp comet. It seems that Applewhite had already decided some years prior that he and his followers would make their exit via a group suicide. Thus he was predisposed to interpret any indication that the space brothers were coming as a sign that it was time to leave. Although Applewhite and Nettles had received hostile media coverage in their early years and even feared assassination – at one point they purchased weapons for fear of being attacked – these were not factors in March 1997 when Applewhite decided they would exit the planet.

To finally shift our attention to the Solar Temple, yet another trait seemingly shared by all of the new religions involved in violence drops out – namely the group's social isolation. It is the social dynamics of the segregated (usually communal) worlds of certain alternative religions that allow extreme actions to be contemplated, whether the internally directed violence of Heaven's Gate or the externally directed violence of Aum Shinrikyō. The Solar Temple, in contrast, was only semi-segregated from the larger society. Although Joseph Di Mambro established his early Pyramid group as a communal organization, the Solar Temple tended to be only partially communal. Thus, for instance, when the Temple was establishing a 'survival farm' in Canada, only a half dozen members actually lived in the group's headquarters. The rest lived outside the house and took their meals there. Yet other members scattered about Quebec travelled to the house once a month for a meeting that took place on the full moon. Perhaps more importantly, many Solar Temple members were wealthy and socially established – belonging to 'the elite of the Francophone west' (Daniels 1999, 147) – people who could have been only partially separated from the larger society without arousing suspicion.

Nevertheless, one could argue that the leader's distance from the voices of all but his closest followers was an essential factor contributing to his radical actions. In fact, Di Mambro tended to stay behind the scenes surrounded by a core of staunch loyalists, even bringing Jouret into the Temple for the purpose of interacting with outsiders. This finally brings us to a core trait of suicide cults, namely a charismatic leader who surrounds himself with absolutely loyal followers and who does not permit any overt disagreement with the group's ideology.

Here the analysis begins to sound rather like a cult stereotype. Focusing on the personality of the leader – usually portrayed, as we have seen, as a warped megalomaniac – is a staple in ACM discussions of NRMs. In contrast, mainstream scholars tend to include an analysis of the leadership as but one factor among others, such as a given group's social dynamics, ideology and other less personal factors. Of course the leadership must interact with the membership in order to have any kind of organization at all. But, in the NRMs we have been discussing, the leader is clearly the epicentre. And the quest for commonalities among suicide groups has boiled down to commonalities among their leaders. So though I am not unmindful of group dynamics, and would never downplay the importance of external factors, for the sake of simplifying this analysis I will focus narrowly on the leadership.

Is there anything that sets Jim Jones, Joseph Di Mambro and Marshall Applewhite apart from David Koresh and Shōkō Asahara?

Some years ago while researching Heaven's Gate for an analysis of the strategies by which Marshall Applewhite legitimated suicide, I came across several sources that mentioned his health was failing (e.g. Perkins and Jackson 1997, 81). Also, Wessinger points out that Applewhite never considered the option of appointing a successor who could lead the group after his passing, which likely made the group suicide option more attractive (2000a, 81). At the time these seemed like minor factors in explaining the Heaven's Gate tragedy.

In the context of the current discussion, however, these become major factors because they are precisely the traits that set the suicide groups apart from the others. In terms of health, Di Mambro was 'suffering from kidney failure and incontinence as well as severe diabetes, and he believed he had cancer' (Wessinger 2000b, 221). And Jones – either because he was sedating a genuine physical problem or because he had become a self-destructive addict – was gradually destroying himself with excessive prescription tranquillizers. Thomas Robbins emphasized the importance of a charismatic leader's health in a personal communication to Hall when the latter was researching and writing *Apocalypse Observed*, though Hall quickly passes over the subject after mentioning Robbins' communication in the latter part of his book (2000, 193). It is easy to understand how Hall, focused as he was on other aspects of NRMs, would have failed to perceive the health of the charismatic leader as a major explanatory factor. In the context of the current discussion, however, the observation that Applewhite, Di Mambro and Jones were in failing health, whereas Koresh and Asahara were not, makes this factor suddenly stand out as important: If the three suicide leaders all perceived themselves as dying, then the notion of bringing the whole group along on their post-mortem journeys might strike them as attractive.

In addition to their physical deaths, all three men knew that their respective groups had not only stopped growing but were also likely to decline precipitously in the future, particularly after they died. Neither Applewhite (as noted) nor Jones (apparently) had given serious thought to grooming a successor. Di Mambro, on the other hand, seems for many years to have thought his daughter Emmanuelle would inherit his mantle. By 12 years of age, however, she was already rebelling against the script her father had imagined her fulfilling, effectively frustrating whatever desire he might have had for a legacy. By the time of the Transit, he had also come to nurse an exaggerated hatred for the 'barbarian, incompetent and aberrant' Jouret, an obvious person to take over should Di Mambro pass from the scene.

To summarize the above discussion into a list of traits, we can say that, based on an analysis of the Peoples Temple, the Solar Temple and Heaven's Gate, the essential characteristics of a suicide group are:

1. Absolute intolerance of dissenting views
2. Members must be totally committed
3. Exaggerated paranoia about external threats
4. Leader isolates himself or herself or the entire group from the non-believing world
5. Leader's health is failing – in a major way, not just a transitory sickness
6. There is no successor and no steps are being taken to provide a successor; or, alternately, succession plans have been frustrated
7. The group is either stagnant or declining, with no realistic hopes for future expansion.

As noted earlier, there are numerous points of overlap with Aum Shinrikyō and the Branch Davidians. However, despite major areas of overlap, both of these groups lack several essential traits. Specifically, David Koresh did not segregate himself from unbelievers and was in good health immediately prior to the ATF raid on Mount Carmel. Koresh had also fathered a number of children he believed would eventually rule the earth – in effect, his successors. Asahara seems to have been in reasonably good health as well, plus he had already indicated to followers that his children would be his spiritual successors (though it should be noted that this successorship was rather vague at the time of the subway attack and only clarified later). Finally, though neither Aum in 1995 and nor the Davidians in 1993 were experiencing rapid growth, they were also not stagnant; both could have reasonably anticipated future growth. In other words, the Davidians lacked traits 4, 5, 6 and 7, whereas Aum lacked 5, 6 and 7.

In contrast to recent theorizing focused on the relational and processual aspects of violence (e.g. Bromley and Melton 2002), the approach of distilling a list of traits may strike some observers as static and regressive. Also, confining the discussion to specific internal factors seems to reproduce the flaws of anti-cult theorizing about cults (Hall 2002, 167), especially when that theorizing focuses on charismatic cult leaders (Melton and Bromley 2002, 46–7). So, to make certain my analysis is not misinterpreted, let me explicitly restate that my goal here was a very narrow one, not intended to constitute anything like a general theory – either of NRM-related violence or, for that matter, of suicide cults. Producing a truly comprehensive account of religious groups that have committed acts of mass suicide would necessarily go beyond the factors discussed above.

17 Opposition to NRMs

George D. Chryssides and Benjamin E. Zeller

Chapter Outline

Christian Opposition to New Religious Movements	164
The Proliferation of Christian Anti-cult Literature	165
The New Wave of NRMs	167
Deprogramming	171
Government-Sponsored and Legal Opposition to NRMs	172
NRMs and the Churches	175
Academic Consideration of the Opposition to NRMs	176

New religions have almost invariably provoked controversy. Early Christianity aroused opposition, first in the form of hostility to Jesus of Nazareth himself, leading to his crucifixion, and subsequently from opponents such as Saul of Tarsus – who ironically became Christianity's most successful proselytizer – and later by various Roman governors and emperors. The story of the rise of Islam is similar, with intense opposition and open warfare by the traditional Arabian religious authorities against the Prophet Muhammad.

New religions become old and established religions, and ironically even when Christianity became a state religion, Christians were not averse to starting own persecution of heretics. Much of the early opposition to NRMs in modern times emerges from such opposition to heresy. Yet as we argue here, the twentieth century witnessed the rise of a new wave of NRMs and with them a new type of opposition not beholden to the idea of heresy. The development of the anti-cult movement (ACM), theories of brainwashing, the practice of deprogramming, government sponsored opposition to NRMs and the relationship of anti-cultism to the academy are all part of the story of opposition to new religious movements.

Christian Opposition to New Religious Movements

Focusing on the modern West, we shall consider primarily Christian and secular opposition to new religious movements. Since Christianity, almost since its inception, has been a heavily doctrinal religion, Christians have tended to target the beliefs of NRMs in an attempt to combat heresy. If acceptance of the gospel in its authentic form is the sole means of salvation, as Christianity traditionally taught, then targeting NRMs may well have been done from the best of motives: it was an attempt to ensure that the proponents of such religions were not at risk of eternal damnation. The early literature attacking NRMs sought to combat such false belief, and was written from the standpoint of traditional Christianity. Likewise, the NRMs that they attacked tended to be predominantly Christian in orientation or derivation. In his popular book *Christian Deviations*, first published in 1954, Horton Davies targets Pentecostalism, Seventh-Day (*sic*) Adventism, Moral Re-armament, the Mormons, Jehovah's Witnesses, British-Israel, Christian Science, Spiritism [Spiritualism] and Theosophy. (The word 'spiritism' designates Spiritualism: numerous Christian opponents of Spiritualism deliberately avoided the term on the grounds that it suggested that the movement was 'spiritual', which they vehemently denied.) Of the groups that Davies targets, only Theosophy is non-Christian. In many cases much of the early opposition to NRMs built on the same themes and criticisms that generations of Protestant Christian leaders had used against Catholicism, which they had identified with despotism, heresy and abuse. Opposition to new religions thus built on an inherited orientation against what Christians understood as heretical and undemocratic movements.

This is not to say that sound doctrine was the only issue in countering NRMs. Nineteenth-century opposition to Mormonism, the most successful and largest of the new religions of that era, generally focused not so much on doctrine as practice. While the Latter-day Saints certainly held a distinctive theology that differed from their (generally Protestant) neighbours, opponents focused primarily on the LDS practice of polygamy and to a lesser extent secret temple ritual as abhorrent practices (Moore 1986, 27–8). Charles Taze Russell's Bible Students (later known as Jehovah's Witnesses) made themselves decidedly unpopular by refusing to participate in the two world wars, and their stance on blood transfusion incurred further public criticism. They could also be provocative, for example in blaring their loudspeaker vans in close proximity to Roman Catholic churches, while worship was taking place. Christian Scientists and New Thought proponents also attracted a reputation for refusing medical treatment in favour of 'mind cure', drawing criticism and opposition on those grounds. Movements led or founded by women were also the targets of scorn and disapproval based on the gender of their leaders; this was especially true among opponents of Spiritualism, Seventh-day Adventism and Christian Science. Race and racism also played a role in opposition to NRMs, especially in the denigration of the 'Black Gods', the new religious movements of the American cities led by urban African Americans such as Father Divine's Peace Mission movement or Sweet Daddy Grace's United House of Prayer for All People.

Overall though, until the mid-twentieth century the primary issue was theology and accusations of heresy. The emphasis on targeting Christian-related groups was partly because these were the main ones in evidence before the rise of the counterculture of the 1960s and 1970s, but also because the so-called Christian deviations presented a double threat. First, they were deviations from the true gospel, but second, by purporting to be Christian they posed the danger of drawing the unwary who might mistake the teachings for the true Christian message. From this perspective a Christian counterfeit was more dangerous than irreligion, since, like counterfeit money, the illusion of possessing the real thing prevents one from knowing that one is truly penniless. As cult critic Jan Groeveld has remarked, 'The most dangerous lie is that which most closely resembles the truth.' For this reason, Christian anti-cultism has generally focused on the Christian NRMs.

The Proliferation of Christian Anti-cult Literature

Initially, countering the 'heresies' was carried out predominantly by literature, often by pamphlets. In the early twentieth century numerous Christian organizations produced short tracts designed to show the errors of the various heretical groups. This approach follows the general pattern of print culture at that time, especially in Britain and the United States, where literacy rates had achieved high enough levels that religious leaders looked to pamphlets, broadsides and books as the best way of reaching religious audiences (Cohen and Boyer 2008). Christian anti-cult groups continue to produce pamphlets today, frequently made available to churches or to pastors, parents or psychologists. Opponents of NRMs also made use of the related genre of tracts, both historically and contemporarily. One of the most popular and commonly seen forms of anti-cult literature in contemporary America are the short tracts produced by Chick Publications and distributed by loosely affiliated networks of Christian fundamentalists and evangelicals, who distribute tracts such as 'Evil Eyes' (on the occult) and 'The Visitors' (on Mormonism) in post offices, transportation centres, car parking lots and sporting events. Chick himself is somewhat controversial, however, with his strong opposition to Catholicism and mainline Protestant groups being taken by some anti-cultists as itself problematic.

Popular journal articles, and sometimes entire books appeared in the early parts of the twentieth century, addressing a variety of movements. One early piece of writing was Lewis B. Radford's *Ancient Heresies in Modern Dress* (1913), which was based on lectures delivered at University of Sydney. Radford compared Seventh-day Adventism, Theosophy and Christian Science with ancient Gnosticism. Interestingly, there is a short appendix on reincarnation and karma. Another comparable work is John Elward Brown's *In the Cult Kingdom: Mormonism, Eddyism, and Russellism* (1916), which focused on the religious errors of Latter-day Saints, Christian Scientists and Russell's Bible Students. Brown, the President of the International Federation of Christian Workers, combined a progressive interest in fostering what he considered true Christian ecumenism and bridging gaps between the proper movements of the Christian Church – such as Methodism and Presbyterianism – and the dangerous 'Isms'. He critiques the three new religions primarily on theological grounds as heretical movements, and his book, like Radford's, is a distillation of a lecture series on the danger of these groups. The famous booklet series *The Fundamentals* (1910–15), which eventually gave name the movement of Christian Fundamentalism, also included volumes targeting Christian Science and Mormonism, though its editors paid far greater attention to the evils of modernism than the recent heresies.

Much wider circulation was achieved by William C. Irvine's anthology entitled *Timely Warnings*, first published in the 1917 and reissued as *Modern Heresies Exposed* in 1919, and *Heresies Exposed* in 1921. The book went through 31 printings by 1960. In addition to the Christian-related groups, its authors targeted agnosticism, humanism, the theory of evolution, and also – perhaps surprisingly to today's readers – Roman Catholicism. Until very recently was not uncommon to find Roman Catholicism defined as a 'heresy' by evangelical Protestant writers, on the grounds that they believed that its teachings were contrary to the Bible. By the late twentieth century the majority of opponents of new religious movements seldom included critiques of Roman Catholicism alongside those of NRMs, partially because Protestants had allied with Catholics in their opposition to new religions and partially because of greater social acceptance of Catholicism. For example, Dutch Reform theologian Anthony A. Hoekema's popular *The Four Major Cults* (1963) considers only Mormonism, Seventh-day Adventism, Christian Science, and the Jehovah's Witnesses, and assumes a pan-Christian form of anti-cultism. Hoekema targets and explicates these groups' 'doctrinal aberrations' from a broad Christian baseline while clearly predicated and rooted in Reformed theology, does not explicitly assume a Reformed or even Protestant reader (Hoekema 1963, 1).

A transitionary book linking the older genre of Christian heresy busting with more recent opposition to NRMs on psychosocial grounds was *The Kingdom of the Cults* by Walter Martin, first published in 1963, augmented in 1985 and recently expanded in 2003 by Ravi Zacharias after the death of its original author. Like the previously mentioned books, *The Kingdom of the Cults* assumes an explicitly evangelical Protestant Christian theology, with chapters critiquing nearly every world religion and readers exhorted to evangelize members of all religions and convert them to evangelical Protestant Christianity. Yet one facet of *The Kingdom of the Cults* differentiating it from the earlier generation of anti-cult literature is its emphasis not just on the heretical nature of NRMs, but their psychological and social dangers. Both types of criticism are found in their coverage of specific new religions, as well as general chapters on the 'psychological structure of cultism' and 'the road to recovery' that assume a reified and monolithic category of 'cults' defined by psychological manipulation and danger to the Christian social order. Despite this, the authors still subsume their criticisms within the rubric of evaluating and rejecting the theology of the new religions and their overall thrust was still to make converts to evangelical Christianity, not to destroy cults for the sake of society or psychology.

Apostate tales serve as another genre of Christian opposition to new religious movements. Such 'great escape' narratives harken back to a similar genre of anti-Catholic literature such as the infamous with their lurid tales of abuse, degeneracy and heresy. Many apostate stories are clearly fictitious, though others reveal apparently true examples of misuse of power, religious scandal and abuse within new religious movements. All apostate narratives emphasize NRMs as illegitimate religions, either heretical in orientation, psychologically manipulative, anti-social or all three. More recent apostate tales have adopted more secular orientations and are written from a more psychological than Christian perspective, but their overt goal of opposing either specific new religious movements or the category as a whole remains. Another subtype of this genre are the explicitly and openly fictional stories, either novels, cinema or television. Many of these stories draw from real-life examples but because they present fictional accounts and are hence not prone to potential libel suits, paint with broad strokes a picture of the danger of new and alternative religions.

The New Wave of NRMs

The 1960s and 1970s witnessed a new wave of NRMs that went beyond the previous generation of mainly Christian-related ones. Some of these were Christian-related, like their predecessors, but others that existed in the West were versions of other faiths. While NRMs originating outside of Christianity had existed in the West since the fin de siècle, through organizations like the

Vedanta Society and Theosophical movements, relatively few of such groups existed as compared to the Christian-derived NRMs. This was due to a variety of factors. Increased global communication made it possible for exponents of these faiths to come to the West, and reciprocally members of the youth culture were able to travel abroad, exploring India and the Far East, where they encountered new gurus. Some high-profile figures, like the Beatles, encountered the Hare Krishna movement and the Maharishi Mahesh Yogi, bringing them into prominence. The increased access to media such as television enabled such encounters to be brought to people's homes. In the United States, 1965 marked the end of the racist quota system that limited immigration and travel visas of non-Europeans. The landmark Immigration and Nationality Act of 1965 allowed not only an increase in the religious diversity of immigrants to the United States but a flood of gurus, teachers, evangelists and swamis who founded new religions or new forms of Asian religions in the West.

The new wave of NRMs had different evangelism tactics from those of their predecessors. Previously, minority groups such as the Jehovah's Witnesses and the Mormons went round to people's doors to evangelize. This tended to result in their having conversations with the householder, and if the householder was persuaded of their truth, then the organization had won over an entire family – much like the early Christian practice of converting households. In the 1960s and 1970s, however, it became increasingly common for a young person to meet members of NRMs as an individual, either by listening to street preaching or as part of self-exploration. The fact that a young individual could be converted to the Unification Church, ISKCON or the Children of God meant that his or her family had now been 'split up', partly because different members now followed different faiths, and partly because the new convert might have physically joined a religious community, rather than continuing to live at home. (Of course, young people leave families for various reasons, such as education, occupation and marriage, but such reasons are conventional and socially acceptable. Joining a new religion is not.) Opposition to NRMs on the grounds that they break up families and threaten social order therefore became one of the main means of critiquing new religious movements in the new era of the 1960s and 1970s.

In addition to all of this, Europe witnessed a marked decline in church attendance from around 1960. As a consequence, fewer people were interested in issues of heresy and orthodoxy, or in promoting the true Christian faith. What tended to disturb them was the lifestyle and practices of the members of those organizations. Across the Atlantic there had been less overt secularization, but the growing ecumenical and interfaith movements in the United States and Canada meant that Protestants, Catholics and Jews had begun to show a more united face when confronting social ills and issues, including NRMs. They increasingly used secular language and secular arguments in keeping

Opposition to NRMs

with their lack of a shared orthodoxy. Evangelical opponents of NRMs such as Walter Martin stood apart both from interfaith ecumenism and secular critiques of new religious movements, and represent an alternative position within the opposition to NRMs during this time period. Thus there emerged altogether three types of commentator on NRMs: evangelical countercultists, official religious commentators and secular anti-cult groups.

In this era the Christian opposition to the new wave of NRMs went beyond the production of pamphlets. Organizations, networks and action committees all formed in the wake of the rise of the new religions of this period. Several of these were overtly Christian organizations. One of the most prominent was the Spiritual Counterfeits Project, founded in 1973 in Berkeley, California. In the same year the Dialog Center International in Denmark was set up. Johannes Aagaard, its founder, believed that cults could not be combated unless one addressed their beliefs, and understood NRMs in the context of the world's major religious traditions. The dialogue that Aagaard recommended was not so much interreligious, but between NRM members and their families. The organization sought to promote education in the field, and offered pastoral support and advice.

Shortly after this in 1981, the Reachout Trust founded by Doug Harris in England took its rise. The Reachout Trust began as a cult-specific organization, targeting Jehovah's Witnesses, but as the organization grew, it acknowledged that it was not only the Jehovah's Witnesses who were in error, but 'cults' more widely. The Trust disseminates literature, and organizes seminars to inform church groups and other bodies were interested. Reachout's stated purpose is to 'share the gospel' with religious organizations who do not share the truths of mainstream Christianity. Of course, it is not merely the 'cults' who do not share the gospel, but the other major world's faiths. Hence Reachout does not merely point out the error of the so-called cults, but also periodically comments on the superiority of the Christian faith to other major traditions, such as Buddhism and Islam.

Other organizations that target cults are fairly firmly secular. Much of their thinking on NRMs can be traced back to psychologist Robert Jay Lifton, an American psychiatrist who studied 'thought reform' among US Air Force combatants during the 1951–3 Korean War. Lifton's theory of 'brainwashing' subsequently found a receptive audience in the anti-cult movement, particularly by Margaret Singer and Steven Hassan. Lifton formulated eight characteristics of 'thought reform': (1) milieu control; (2) mystical manipulation (such as making planned applause seem spontaneous); (3) demand for purity (characterizing the external world as evil); (4) confession; (5) sacred science (presenting the group's ideology as beyond criticism); (6) 'loading the language' – giving new meaning to everyday expressions; (7) 'doctrine over person' (conflicting experiences to be reinterpreted in accordance with the group's ideology); (8)

'dispensing of existence' (rejection of those who do not accept the ideology) (Lifton 1989, 429).

Elements of this list have been used or adapted by various ACM organizations. Margaret Singer, whose *Cults in Our Midst* carries a foreword from Lifton, explicitly states that her 'six conditions' of cult parallel these eight points. Singer's conditions are: (1) leaving the person unaware of the group's agenda; (2) controlling the environment; (3) creating fear and dependency; (4) suppressing the former behaviour; (5) replacing it with new behaviour and attitudes; (6) a closed system of logic (Singer 2003, 64). Lifton distanced himself from Singer's actual model and has not himself supported the deployment of his theory of brainwashing to oppose new religious movements. The ACM's tendency to produce lists of 'marks of the cults' tends to imply that there is a sameness pervading all of these groups, and that the seeker is psychologically controlled by the group and its leader. The fact that an NRM's beliefs and practices are often radically different from those of mainstream religion or conventional secularism can readily cause the public to conclude that the cults must be using some special set of techniques that bypasses the seeker's rational processes: there must be 'brainwashing' or – Hassan's preferred term – 'mind control'. More recently Janja Lalich (2004) has revised the idea of brainwashing under the guise of 'bounded choice', which she defines as reliant on (1) a transcendent belief system; (2) an all-encompassing system of interlocking structural and social controls; (3) a highly charged charismatic relationship between leader(s) and adherents; and (4) a self-sealing system of commitment. Again, Lalich intends her approach of bounded choice to explain unconventional beliefs and practices, including polygamy, violence, terrorism or beliefs in the resurrection of the dead – the last a perhaps unintentional element of irony given that such a belief is quite mainstream within Christianity.

Like Reachout, numerous anti-cult groups began life as individuals or organizations targeting specific NRMs. Thus Steven Hassan, an ex-Unification Church leader, founded Ex-Moon Inc in 1979, but after gaining qualifications in education and counselling psychology, set up the Freedom of Mind Resource Center in 1999. In Britain the organization FAIR (Family Action Information and Rescue) was established in 1972 by Paul Rose, a Member of Parliament who had dealt with parents' complaints about the Unification Church. FAIR sought to disseminate information, to offer advice to anxious parents and friends, and to dissuade seekers from joining 'cults', and to act as a pressure group, seeking to influence politicians. Likewise, the French Union Nationale des Associations de Défence des Familles et de l'Individu Victimes de Sectes (UNADFI, the National Union of Associations for the Defence of Families), founded in 1974 as Association pour la Défense des valeurs Familiales et de l'Individu, originally focused on opposition to the Unification Church. Its founders, Guy and Claire Champollion, formed the group after their son joined the Unification

Church, but soon expanded to counter other groups such as Scientology and the Children of God. The Union is now active throughout the Francophone world. Another example of this pattern of anti-cult movements formed because of an individual's personal experience is the German Aktion für Geistige und Psychische Freiheit (Action for Mental and Psychological Freedom), founded in 1978 by Klaus Karbe. This organization functions as a clearing house of German language materials and resources for those opposed to NRMs, including its own publishing wing.

Additionally, various other anti-cult organizations have arisen. Some are quite small, such as the Cult Information Centre (UK), and it is difficult to understand what niche they might fill. Most of these anti-cult groups engage in networking: in 1994, at the request of UNADFI, the European Federation of Centres of Research and Information on Sectarianism was set up as a European umbrella organization for cult monitoring groups. In 2003 it obtained funding from the French government, and in 2005 gained advisory status to the Council of Europe's Standing Committee of Parliamentary Assembly. The various cult monitoring groups are also linked through the International Cultic Studies Association (ICSA).

ICSA grew out of the American Family Foundation (AFF), which psychiatrist John Clarke established in 1987. It was one of the first US organizations to deal with NRMs in general. The AFF offered access to professionals, in contrast with previous groups that had simply afforded mutual support to concerned friends and relatives. Rather than act as a pressure group, the AFF focused on research and education, producing regular journal entitled *Cultic Studies Review*. In 2004 the AFF became ICSA, and its journal was renamed the *International Journal of Cultic Studies*.

Organized opposition to NRMs is by no means confined to the United States and Europe. In Australia the third Cults Awareness and Information Centre was founded in 1991 by Jan Groenveld. Although deprogramming – discussed below – is on the decline in the United States and Europe, it continues to occur in Japan, where there is also organized opposition to NRMs. In the 1980s the National Network of Lawyers against Spiritual Sale was set up, principally in opposition to the Unification Church. Following the 1995 Aum Shinrikyō sarin gas attack on the Tokyo underground, it developed into the Japan De-Cult Council, becoming the Japan Society for Cults Prevention and Recovery (JSCPR) in 2004.

Deprogramming

Some opponents of NRMs were not content with disseminating information, providing counselling to families, and lobbying politicians. These were the deprogrammers. Possibly the first, but certainly the best-known, was Ted Patrick, sometimes known as 'the father of deprogramming', and whose book *Let Our Children Go!* (1972) is well-known. A black Christian fundamentalist, Patrick was a community relations worker in San Diego and encountered several complaints about the Children of God (COG), who had been evangelizing in the city. Patrick decided to infiltrate the group to get to know them at first hand: they were relatively unknown at the time.

Together with a group of parents who were opposed to their offspring's membership in COG, Patrick helped to found FREECOG ('Free-COG') in 1971, with the aim retrieving their wayward sons and daughters from this NRM. Shortly afterwards in 1974 the Citizens Freedom Foundation (CFF) formed as a broader coalition opposed to cults more widely, on moral, psychological and legal grounds. The CFF published newsletters, lobbied elected officials, and held gatherings of parents, law enforcement officials, psychologists and a new breed of professional 'deprogrammers' dedicated to removing forcibly members from NRMs. Both FREECOG and CFF merged into the Cult Awareness Network (CAN) in 1984, becoming the most widely known anti-cult movement in the United States. CAN continued the work of its predecessor organizations until 1996 when the movement lost a major court case because of its support for forcibly removing individuals from new religions, and effectively disbanded.

While NRM members and eventually the court system in many jurisdictions considered deprogramming a clear violation of civil liberties, from the perspective of the deprogrammers they engaged in the only efficacious form of thought reform possible, since individuals living within NRMs were believed to lack true free will and personal volition. Other well-known deprogrammers include Steven Hassan, formerly a senior member in the Unification Church, and Rick Ross. Deprogramming had its heyday in the 1970s and 1980s, but since then the practice has become less common in most parts of the United States and Europe; being a form of kidnapping, deprogramming is of course illegal, and a number of deprogrammers were convicted and in some cases served prison sentences.

Government-Sponsored and Legal Opposition to NRMs

As a result of anti-cult pressure, a number of government-sponsored reports were published in Europe. Of particular significance is the report produced in France in 1983 by Alain Vivien, Deputy to the National Assembly, entitled 'The Cults in France: Expression of Model Liberty or Carriers of Manipulations?' and in 1984 British MEP member Richard Cottrell served as rapporteur for the report setting out a voluntary code of practice for NRMs, and which gained approval. In 1995 the Parliamentary Commission on Cults in France was set up, and produced a report that listed 173 organizations which the authors believed to be harmful and to be regarded as 'sectes'. This report built on the earlier work of Vivien Alain, and in 1997 the Belgium government approved a similar report listing 189 sects. The French Assembly's report mainly listed organizations that would be regarded by scholars as NRMs, but the Belgian report included some mainstream religions such as the Jain Association and Theravada Buddhism, as well as the Amish, the Quakers and the Young Women's Christian Association (YWCA). In 1996 the *Observatoire interministériel sur les sectes* was set up in France, and was succeeded two years later by MILS (*Mission interministérielle de lutte contre les sectes* – 'Interministerial Mission in the Fight Against Cults'), headed by Alain Vivien to coordinate the government monitoring of 'sectes'. This in turn became MIVILUDES (*Mission interministérielle de vigilance et de lutte contre les dérives sectaires,* – 'Interministerial Mission for Monitoring and Combatting Cultic Deviances').

In 2001 the French government introduced legislation known as the About-Picard Law – so-called after its rapporteurs Nicolas About and Catherine Picard. This legislation enabled sects to be banned if their leaders were found guilty of specified crimes, notably endangering life and mental health, practising medicine illegally or fraud. Some human rights groups believed that the legislation was a serious violation of religious freedom, and in 2002 the Council of Europe passed a resolution stating that the freedom of NRMs should be consistent with democracy, although protecting the public order was permissible. The Council of Europe requested the French government to reconsider its legislation.

The German government took a somewhat more lenient view of NRMs. The Enquete Commission was set up in 1996, consisting of 12 members of the German Bundestag, and 12 NRMs experts. Its report, published in 1998, was entitled 'So-Called Sects and Psychogroups: New Religious and Ideological Communities and Psychogroups in the Federal Republic of Germany'. The term 'Psychogroup' was used in preference to the terms 'cult' and 'sect', which the Commission found problematic, and the term enabled the report's scope to include self-improvement and alternative health services. The Enquete Commission's conclusions were fairly moderate: while agreeing that there were problems relating to 'Psychogroups', the commission did not accept the brainwashing hypothesis, and felt that abuses by NRMs were already covered by existing legislation.

In some European countries religions have been required to register with the state. Normally the right to practise one's religion does not depend on registration, but failure to become registered can affect receipt of state benefits. Registration can be dependent on the length of time the group has been in existence, or the size of its membership. Clearly, both criteria militate against NRMs, since by their very nature they are new and may not yet have attained the membership threshold. In view of such restrictions on NRMs' activities, a number of human rights groups have arisen and championed their cause. Some are government-sponsored, like the European Agency for Fundamental Rights (FRA), while others are campaigning groups, such as the Belgian-based Human Rights Without Frontiers International, chaired by Willy Fautré.

In the United States the most memorable and impacting incident of official government action against an NRM is the 1993 raid on the Branch Davidian community in Waco, Texas, led by David Koresh. In this case, anti-cult activists had convinced government authorities that the Branch Davidians were engaged in a dangerous mix of child abuse and weapons violations. As James Tabor and Eugene Gallagher have argued, this combination of professional anti-cultists from the ACM, law enforcement officials acculturated into a distrust of new religions, and the influence of publicity-driven media led to the violent confrontation that claimed 87 lives over the nearly two-month siege (1997). A similar raid by the government in 1984 on the Twelve Tribes Messianic Community in Island Pond, Vermont had relied on the same mix of professional anti-cultists and child abuse allegations. Though over a hundred children were removed from their parents, the pacifist nature of the Twelve Tribes community and the quick action of a judge overturning the seizure meant that violence was averted and little public fanfare erupted. By contrast the events in Waco were so bloody and extreme that they reinvigorated a national conversation on NRMs that had lain dormant since the deaths of the members of the Peoples Temple in Jonestown, Guyana, in 1978. More recently in 2008, a raid on the polygamist Fundamentalist Latter Day Saint (FLDS) community of the Yearning for Zion Ranch resulted in the removal of over a hundred children. Like the Twelve Tribes raid, dubious accusations of child abuse and activity by professional ACM activists spurred authorities to act.

Government monitoring and action against NRMs are certainly not limited to Europe and the United States. The most notorious of such government sanctioned opposition to NRMs are the raids on The Family (né Children of God) in South America and Australia in the 1980s and 1990s. Acting in collaboration with noted anti-cult activists – some of whom were later accused of planting evidence against the Family – police raided Family homes and arrested hundreds of members. Adults were imprisoned and children sent to detention facilities, sometimes for months at a time. Though judges eventually ordered the members of the NRM to be released, adherents report agonizing tales of abuse by authorities, prison inmates and the justice system (Bainbridge 2002; Chancellor 2000). Russian and Italian authorities have similarly raided Scientology homes and offices, though because the Church of Scientology is far better equipped to legally defend its members, adherents have faced less in the way of active persecution. The Russian government has generally cracked down on what it sees as dangerous cults, often including foreign Protestant groups that Western Europeans or Americans would consider quite benign.

Also well recognized is Chinese governmental opposition to Falun Gong, a new religious movement drawing from multiple religious traditions and claiming to represent as the spiritual heir of Chinese history and culture. Partially because Falun Gong has challenged the moral authority of the Communist Party and Chinese government, opposition and state-sponsored action against Falun Gong have been intense. Though details are murky and contentious, thousands of people have been arrested by Chinese authorities and many of them tortured because of their membership.

The complicating factor in considering government opposition to new religious movements is that at times such opposition seems quite warranted. The most notable example may be that of the self-destructive and dangerous behaviour at the Rajneeshpuram community in Oregon, where in 1984 and 1985 members of the group engaged in an ill-conceived attempt to usurp local control of the local government. According to charges, leaders of this group engaged in voter fraud, arson, wire-tapping and embezzlement. Most disturbingly, the group had planned on poisoning thousands of local residents on Election Day so as to guarantee political victory. Members of the movement apparently had engaged in a sort of test run by depositing salmonella bacteria in the salad bars of local restaurants, sickening over 750 people. Given the presence of such a conspiracy, government opposition seems quite warranted. Yet the Rajneeshpuram case proves instructive: according to sociologist Marion S. Goldberg, who interviewed participants inside and outside of the community, the focus on 'due process' by law enforcement and the internal checks and balances of the Rajneeshpuram community averted more serious bloodshed or injury (2009, 311).

NRMs and the Churches

Other stakeholders who receive less public attention include the Churches, the academic community and human rights groups. Although the evangelical Protestant groups are vociferous, they do not necessarily represent the official views of church bodies. In 1986 several prominent members of the Roman Catholic hierarchy produced a report entitled 'Sects: Of the Pastoral Challenge'. Though not an official Vatican-approved document, this was more widely circulated in unabridged version, published by the Catholic Truth Society, entitled *New Religious Movements: A Challenge to the Church*. This report was compiled by sending a questionnaire to various bishops' conferences, and collating the replies received from the bishops. Although less hostile than much of the evangelical countercult literature, it presented a somewhat negative and stereotypical view of NRMs, identifying College campuses as their 'breeding grounds' describing converts as young, 'footloose', 'vulnerable', and indoctrinated, accusing them of 'love bombing' and 'flirty fishing', and rejecting any form of dialogue. The Roman Catholic Church was even more negative towards the New Age: in 2003 the Vatican issued the document *Jesus Christ, the Bearer of the Water of Life*, in which it stated that the ideas of the New Age were completely at variance with the Church's teachings.

The attitude of the Protestant churches was less negative, although in the United States and United Kingdom various Councils of Churches were quite unsupportive of the Unification Church's attempt to attain membership. In 1986 the World Council of Churches organized a consultation, together with the Lutheran World Federation. While some contributors, such as Johannes Aagaard and Reinhart Hummel presented a very negative view of NRMs, other participants were much more conciliatory, with Kenneth Cracknell maintaining that, 'There are no limits to be set to dialogue' (Brockway and Rajashekar 1986, 157).

Academic Consideration of the Opposition to NRMs

Opposition to NRMs, especially in its more organized form as the anti-cult movement and associations of deprogrammers, has itself become a locus of study for scholars of new religious movements. Anson D. Shupe, David G. Bromley and James T. Richardson have all made extensive study of the ACM, analysing its social functioning and the manner in which the opposition to NRMs relates to social forces and developments. Shupe and Bromley's *The New Vigilantes: Deprogrammers, Anti-Cultists, and the New Religions* argued that the anti-cult movement systematically attempted to exert social control over the new religious movements of the 1970s after these new religions had came into direct conflict with the institutions of church and family (1980). In their analyses, deprogrammers emerged as a service for a new demand of social control. Bromley, Shupe and collaborator Bruce C. Bushing made a similar claim in 'Repression of Religious "Cults"', noting that the ACM targeted religious movements that offered critique of the social structures of family and state, and that the anti-cultists acted to repress such challenges to the social order (1981). Their more recent work continues the same trend (Shupe and Bromley 1994).

Douglas Cowan has also considered the ACM, focusing specifically on Christian opposition to NRMs. Cowan assumes a social constructivist approach and therefore focuses on the sort of social world created and inhabited by anti-cultists. He considers how Christian anti-cultists construct arguments against cults and the religious worldviews under which they operate. Cowan understands anti-cultism as a social movement encompassing ministries, corporations, apologists, deprogrammers, popular writers and social scientists (2003, 4). Another scholar of new religious movements, Roy Wallis, has considered how differing social contexts in the United Kingdom and United States led to different forms of anti-cultism, providing a sociologically and historically rooted study of the opposition to NRMs (1988). Nurit Zaidman-Dvir and Steven Sharot have similarly considered how the social and historical context has shaped opposition to NRMs in France, Germany, United Kingdom, America and Israel. Focusing on ISKCON and comparing it to secular converts to Orthodox Judaism, they argued for a focus on the idea of the 'foreign' in contextualizing how governments and societies respond to new religious movements (Zaidman-Dvir and Sharot 1992).

Another study of the ACM was *NRMs – Challenge and Response*, an anthology edited by Bryan Wilson and Jamie Creswell. Some contributors addressed the ACM phenomenon itself, while others focus on themes such as the status of women, media and mental health. The Institute of Oriental Philosophy European Centre, with whose collaboration the book was published, is affiliated to the Soka Gakkai International, of whom Creswell is an office bearer. No doubt such collaboration between academia and 'the cults' gives momentum to the ACM's view that academics are on the side of NRMs rather than their critics.

In the main the ACM tends to dislike an academic approach to NRMs, largely due to the fact that academics cannot endorse the ACM's somewhat one-sided view that members are victims, that they are brainwashed, that the beliefs of NRMs are absurd and that there are homogeneous 'marks of a cult'. Rather than engage in debate on such issues, the ACM has largely decided to disparage academic study, frequently referring to prominent academics in the field as 'cult apologists'. One former chairman of FAIR described academics as 'an inordinately complacent and self-satisfied lot of mystagogues' (*FAIR News*, October 1984, 16). Though some individuals involved in the opposition to NRMs and affiliating themselves with anti-cult organizations hold academic appointments or possess academic training, very few relationships exist between scholars of NRMs and opponents of NRMs who are also scholars. Scholars opposing new religious movements and those studying these groups generally work from radically different assumptions and have remarkably different worldviews. As a result, few connections exist between these communities, and a strong degree of mistrust exists between anti-cultists and scholars of NRMs. At their worst, opponents of NRMs ignore the research findings of scholars and promote counterfactual positions, while scholars of NRMs at their worst have ignored the true cases of abuse and manipulation within new religious movements. Some recent evidence indicates a thawing of relations, with leading scholars of NRMs attending the conferences and symposiums sponsored by anti-cult organizations, and vice versa.

Seeking as they do to obtain accurate and objective information on NRMs, it is understandable that academics should wish to counter the ACM's approach to the topic by going beyond scholarly publication. In addition to their own academic writing, a number of academics have initiated organizations committed to producing good information and advice. In 1988 Eileen Barker set up INFORM (Information Network Focus on Religious Movements), based in London, and with funding from the Home Office and the support of the Archbishop of Canterbury. In the same year Massimo Introvigne established CESNUR (Center for Studies on New Religions) in Torino, Italy – an international network of academics in the field. Jean François Mayer, a former Swiss academic at the University of Freiburg, set up Institute Religioscope, which disseminates information on religion, particularly although not exclusively on NRMs, and which informs the media on topical matters. In the United States, J. Gordon Melton was the founding director of the Institute of American Religion, and has written prolifically on NRMs, the New Age, the occult, parapsychology and even vampirology.

What has the anti-cult movement achieved? In terms of enabling stakeholders in NRMs to understand the phenomenon, its track record is less than impressive. Its media contacts have ensured that much of the scaremongering about NRMs is disseminated to the public more widely. It has also had some influence on politicians, although political action has not seriously hampered NRMs. On the other hand, there has been a reduction of activity on the part of NRMs, and some of the more worrying abuses of members has declined – for example the use of mobile fundraising teams, concealment of groups' identities and living in communes are now much less common. Additionally, since the 9/11 attacks, government and popular attention has come to focus on radical Islam as a new religious threat, making opposition to cults somewhat less relevant for those inclined towards seeking social control over religious life. However, other factors are at work, such as the virtual disappearance of the 1970s youth counterculture, changes in young people's education and greater emphasis on gaining material rather than spiritual wealth. Additionally, those who joined NRMs in their youth have now grown older, and in many cases are married with families, making their lifestyle less conducive to living in closed religious communities. The ACM has not always kept pace with these changes in NRMs. A recent publication depicts on its cover a family sitting at a table with an empty chair, and avers that cults are growing rapidly, that anyone is vulnerable, that they rob individuals of their freedom and money and that they are disruptive of family life (Chaytor 2012, iii–iv). Memories of the great disasters of Jonestown, Waco, the Solar Temple and Heaven's Gate still persist and appear to be regarded as normative. A recent edition of *FAIR News* commented:

> These examples are just the tip of an iceberg. Therefore it is very sad that FAIR, since the late seventies, has been trying to educate MPs about cult control, with little or no success. (*FAIR News*, Issue 1, 2009, p. 13)

18 Legal Issues

Anthony Bradney

Chapter Outline

NRMs and their Members as Exceptions	181
What Do Courts Know About NRMs? *Re ST (A Minor)*	182
Jehovah's Witness Custody Cases	183
A Right to Die?	185
Being a Mother	186
Conditions Attached in Jehovah's Witness Custody Cases	187
NRMs and Religion in the English Courts	188
Religion and Equality in the Courts	191
Conclusion	192

National and international courts sometimes, although not frequently, deal with cases involving NRMs. In some instances NRMs, like other religions, have their own dispute settlement processes. Such mechanisms may limit the need for members of NRMs to have recourse to national courts. Thus, for example, the Judicial Committee of the Jehovah's Witnesses can function as an arbitration mechanism (Wieczwork, Feirman and Simms III 2000–2001, 84). Nevertheless, despite this, cases involving NRMs in the state courts still occur. The matters in issue in such cases can be of great moment, as in the instance of the prosecution of members of Aum Shinrikyō, following the sarin gas attacks in Japan, becoming 'a matter of public and political debate' (Reader 2004, 191). More usually the cases are of relatively little importance in themselves, being of consequence only to the parties involved.

On some occasions it is clear that the fact that it is an NRM or a member of an NRM that is appearing before a court is, in itself, of no importance at all when the court comes to make a decision. This can be so in two ways. First the court may be unaware that a plaintiff is a member of an NRM or, if it does know that the plaintiff is a member of NRM, this may play no part in the proceedings. Members of NRMs can be the victim of breaches of contract, may steal, may be negligent and so on and so forth. If this happens, court cases may result. However the fact that someone is a member of an NRM is not then necessarily germane to the decision in the case. Second the fact that someone is a member of an NRM can be central to a case without it having any impact on the way in which the court approaches its decision. Thus, for example, in *R v Taylor* ([2001] EWCA Crim 2263) a Rastafarian was charged with possessing a Class B drug, cannabis, with intent to supply, contrary to the Misuse of Drugs Act 1971. In his defence he attempted to invoke Article 8 and Article 9 of the European Declaration on Human Rights, arguing that his rights to family life and freedom of thought and religion were being infringed by the prosecution. In one very important sense the fact that Taylor was a member of an NRM was central to the case, the prosecution accepting that Taylor only intended to supply cannabis for use in a religious service (*R v Taylor* ([2001] EWCA Crim 2263 para 14). However, beyond this, there is no evidence that the fact that Taylor was a Rastafarian played any part in the court's reasoning. No comment about the Rastafarian faith was made by the court and the reasoning that it used in its analysis of Taylor's legal position followed the usual pattern in cases involving the supply of cannabis. This is also so in the case of *R v Andrews* ([2004] EWCA Crim 947), a similar case involving a Rastafarian charged with illegally importing cannabis. Analysis of the legally very different case of *Gallagher v Church of Jesus Christ of Latter-Day Saints* ([2008] 1 Weekly Law Reports 1852) suggests a similar conclusion. In *Gallagher* Mormons had applied for tax relief with respect to a range of buildings including a temple. Whether or not they were entitled to tax relief depended on whether or not the temple could be said to be a 'place of public worship' under the Local Government Finance Act 1988. Here again, as with the two previous cases, although religion is central to the case, it is a temple which is at the heart of the case, the ruling of the court did not turn on any view about the nature of the Mormon faith. Instead the arguments in the House of Lords judgements are about the linguistic meaning to be attributed to the relevant statutory phrase and the importance of a previous ruling on the same point made by the House of Lords, *Henning v Church of Jesus Christ of Latter-Day Saints* ([1962] 1 Weekly Law Reports 1091). The only possible limited exception to this are Lord Scott's very brief remarks about whether or not the state is justified, on policy grounds, in not giving tax advantages to faiths, such as Mormons, when they do not worship in public (*Gallagher v Church of Jesus Christ of Latter-Day Saints* [2008] 1 Weekly Law Reports 1852 at 1867). Whether NRMs or their members should be required to comply with the normal law of the land when it conflicts with their faith in cases like these is, of course, a

Legal Issues

legitimate question. But for the courts to answer this question in the affirmative, as it does in these cases, does not, in itself, involve them in treating NRMs and their members differently from anything else. The courts have long protested that they are 'perfectly neutral in matters of religion' (*Re Carroll* [1931] 1 King's Bench 317 at 336). Not taking countenance of the fact that there are NRMs in these cases can be seen as an example of such neutrality. However, when NRMs or their members are participants in cases before them, do the courts always exhibit this neutrality? In this chapter I will look at whether or not the courts ever treat NRMs and their adherents differently from either other religions and their believers or other entities or individuals who are not religious. Are NRMs and their members sometimes in some way special for the courts; are they ever regarded as being out of the ordinary? There is some reason to think that these questions should be answered in the affirmative.

NRMs and their Members as Exceptions

In *Re B and G* ([1985] Family Law Reports 134) a court was faced with the question of which one of two divorced parents should have custody of their two children, a boy aged 10 and a girl aged 8. Both the children had been living with the father for five years before their mother sought custody of them. Since living with their father was the established status quo the normal practice of the courts would have been to maintain that situation. In such cases the courts were required, under statute, to make a decision that was in the child's best interests. Both the courts and professionals concerned with the welfare of children held strongly to the belief that securing the continuing stability of a child's home outweighed virtually any other factor when determining who should have custody of that child. However, in this instance, the court awarded custody of the children to the mother. The father of the children was a Scientologist. The mother of the children had been a Scientologist but, by the time she sought custody, had left Scientology. In his judgement in the case Latey J. described Scientology as 'immoral and socially obnoxious' and also as being 'corrupt, sinister and dangerous' (*Re B and G* [1985] Family Law Reports 134 at 157). He was particularly concerned that the children might be brought up as Scientologists; a prospect which would, in his words, be 'disastrous' (*Re B and G* [1985] Family Law Reports 134 at 159). In this case Scientology and Scientologists were something that the court felt was so far out of the ordinary as to make it necessary to dispense with the conventional way of deciding cases such as the one before it. It was this factor, and only this factor, that lay at the heart of the decision in the case (*Re B and G* [1985] Family Law Reports 134 at 138).

When deciding how courts treat NRMs too much should not be made of a one decision by one judge even though it should be noted that in *Re B and*

181

G ([1985] Family Law Reports 493) the Court of Appeal subsequently upheld Latey J.'s ruling. Equally the fact that this case involved both Scientology and a Scientologist should not be ignored. Scientology is an NRM, at least in the eyes of many scholars, but Scientology has both its own unique history and sociology which may distinguish it from some, and perhaps most, other NRMs. Even if the courts do take a particular attitude towards Scientology it does not necessarily follow that they will view all NRMs in the same way. Moreover, finally, this is a decision of a court in just one jurisdiction, England and Wales; other courts in other countries may take a different approach. The decision in *Re B and G* poses a question about the relationship between courts and NRMs; analysis of the case cannot, on its own, provide an answer to that question. This chapter will attempt to at least give an indication of how this question should be approached.

No single chapter could ever provide an exhaustive analysis of the attitude of courts to NRMs. Each jurisdiction, each country, has its own particular characteristics. Comparative analysis of various jurisdictions is possible but is fraught with difficulties (Legrand 1995). Its complexity demands a level of detail that a chapter of this length could not supply. Instead this chapter will focus on cases heard in England and Wales in an attempt to illustrate how the questions raised in this chapter can be approached when looking at legal systems in general. However it should be noted that the issues, if not necessarily the particular judicial approaches to these issues, are ones that are common to many jurisdictions.

What Do Courts Know About NRMs? *Re ST (A Minor)*

In *Re ST (A Minor)*, a case decided in 1995, Lord Justice Ward was faced with a very similar problem to that which Latey J. had considered in *Re B and G*.[1] In *Re ST* a grandmother applied for care and control of her grandson, the child at the time of the application being in the care of its mother. The sole reason that the grandmother had for the action was the fact that the mother was a member of The Family and her concerns that arose because of this. The two cases are similar not just with respect to the legal decisions being taken but with regard to the fact that the NRMs involved have both faced considerable hostility in the popular media (Lewis and Melton 1994).

The result in *Re ST* was very different to that in *Re B and* G. Lord Justice Ward, after lengthy consideration of the facts of the case, in the end rejected the grandmother's application, allowing the mother to retain care and control of the child, albeit with a series of conditions attached.[2] A striking feature of *Re ST* which distinguishes it from both *Re B and G* and most other cases of this type is the quantity of expert evidence that was presented. Seven expert witnesses gave evidence. In his judgement Lord Justice Ward notes that there were 10,000 pages of written evidence and that he took 2,000 pages of notes with relation to the oral evidence. While Lord Justice Ward's final judgement is not uncritical of The Family it is much more nuanced than Latey J.'s treatment of Scientology. Is the court's treatment of NRMs therefore a result of the kind of information put before it? Did more detailed evidence about The Family result in a more positive reaction on the part of the court?

In *Re B and G* Latey J. relied on evidence given by Dr John Clark, a psychiatrist, whose work, Latey J. said, was supported by 'large, very large, body of evidence most of it undisputed' (*Re B and G* [1985] Family Law Reports 134 at 156). In fact others have taken a more sceptical approach to Clark's work, questioning its fundamental validity (Richardson 1992). Irrespective of this, what is certain is that Latey J. had access to only a limited amount of expert evidence and does not seem to have considered the work of those academics, such as Wallis, who have taken a more positive view of Scientology (Wallis 1976). Does this suggest that the courts see NRMs or their members as being troubling only when they have not been given full and accurate information about the particular NRM that is before the court; that their distrust is no more than an ordinary fear of the unknown possibly compounded by an unstated acceptance of the sensational reaction to NRMs that is to be found in some parts of the media (Richardson and van Driel 1997)? Such a suggestion is not without merit and receives additional support from consideration of historical changes in the way that Jehovah's Witnesses have been treated when they have been engaged in custody disputes in court.

Jehovah's Witness Custody Cases

The last four decades have seen a number of reported cases in the higher courts involving Jehovah's Witnesses in custody disputes of the kind described above; typically in these cases one parent is a Jehovah's Witness while the other is not. Early cases do show signs of the judicial unease about NRMs that was seen above in *Re B and G*. Thus, for example, in *Buckley v Buckley* ((1973) 3 Family Law 106) a Jehovah's Witness mother of three young daughters lost custody to the non-Jehovah's Witness father because the court thought that, if brought up as Jehovah's Witness children, they would be different from other children around them. In this case, as in *Re B and G*, given the normal approach of the courts to such matters, the facts of the case were such as to lead the NRM parent to have expected that they would retain custody of their children; their membership of an NRM was the deciding factor in them losing custody.

In later Jehovah's Witness cases the courts began to take a rather different approach to that taken in cases such as *Buckley v Buckley*. In *Re T (Custody:*

Religious Upbringing), for example, Scarman LJ argued that 'it was not necessarily wrong or contrary to the welfare of children, that they should be brought up in a narrower sphere of life and subject to a stricter religious discipline than that enjoyed by most other people, nor that they be without parties at Christmas and on birthdays' ((1981) 2 Family Law Reports 239 at 245). Witness parents now regularly get custody of their children (see, for example, *Re H* (1981) 2 Family Law Reports 253 and *M v H* [2008] EWHC 324 (Fam)). Such cases, where custody is awarded to a Witness parent, commonly involve complicated specific orders relating to matters such as what will happen at times like Christmas and birthdays, reflecting the beliefs of Jehovah's Witnesses as regards these matters and the fact that, usually in such cases, the children will be brought up with parents who have two very different belief systems (see, for example, *Re N: A Child: Religion: Jehovah's Witness* (2010) EWHC 3737 at paras 72–103). Nevertheless 'it cannot [now] be said that the beliefs and practices of a parent who is a Jehovah's Witness creates a situation that is so inimical to good family life that ordinary considerations have to give way to it in determining what will best promote the welfare of the relevant child' (*M v H* [2008] EWHC 324 (Fam) para 30). What leads to this significant change in the attitude of the courts towards Jehovah's Witnesses?

The reported custody cases involving Jehovah's Witnesses do not indicate the use of expert evidence of the kind adduced in *Re ST*.[3] This may be because Jehovah's Witnesses do not have the same aura that surrounds NRMs such as The Family or Scientology and such evidence was thus not thought to be necessary. Moreover such controversy as there is in relation to Jehovah's Witnesses rests on matters such as the refusal of blood transfusions or the practice of witnessing which are in fact part of their faith rather than, as in the case of The Family and Scientology, things which either often have little or no foundation in reality or are part of the history of the NRM in question. Expert evidence would not, in any significant way, refute what most judges are likely to think about Jehovah's Witnesses. Instead in Jehovah's Witness cases the courts appear to have relied on evidence produced by social work professionals appointed to enquire into the particular circumstances of the parties in question rather than provide general evidence about the nature of the Witness faith (see, for example, *Re N: A Child: Religion: Jehovah's Witness* (2010) EWHC 3737 at para 7). Upon the face of it familiarity gained over the years seems to have changed the approach of the courts to the Witness faith when custody disputes are being dealt with; constant reconsideration of the circumstances of Jehovah's Witness parents and the implications of those circumstances for the upbringing of any child has meant that that which was abnormal has become normal or, at least, not so far from the normal as to occasion alarm. However, without wishing to deny the very real change in the behaviour of the courts in these cases, consideration of the wider jurisprudence of the courts with regard to Jehovah's

Witnesses suggests that the court's attitude towards the Witness faith, even in the modern era, is rather more complicated than at first it seems.

A Right to Die?

Although Jehovah's Witnesses do not believe in blood transfusions or similar such medical procedures Witness parents are unable to prevent their young children being treated in this way because, if necessary, doctors will apply for a Specific Issue Order from the courts, overriding the need for parental consent to the procedure. Adult Jehovah's Witnesses can, however, refuse such treatment and, normally, this refusal must be accepted by the medical authorities no matter what consequences it has for the life of the patient. The legally difficulty problem arises where, as they get older and acquire a more mature understanding, children acquire a *Gillick* competence to make decisions for themselves, separate from their parent's legal power to make decisions on their behalf.[4] The courts have said that, in principle, minors who are Jehovah's Witnesses who wish to refuse certain kinds of medical treatment can still be adjudged to be *Gillick* competent (*Re W* [1992] Family Court Reports 885 at 903); that is to say, they, like an adult, can choose to refuse medical treatment even when that refusal will result in their death. However, in practice, finding a case where a child, even a child of a putatively *Gillick* competent disposition, has been able to insist in court on their right not to have medical treatment seems to be impossible. Thus, for example, in *Re P (Medical Treatment)* ([2003] EWHC 2327) the court decided that it was 'in the interests of John in the widest possible sense' to allow treatment despite the fact that the child concerned who did not wish to have treatment was aged 16 years and 10 months, only just over a year short of full adult competence in such matters.

In blood transfusion cases involving Jehovah's Witnesses who are minors the views of an NRM are properly understood but are then totally dismissed as being too far outside the norm as to be accepted by the courts. Why the courts take this attitude is not explained in the judgements. It seems unlikely that they simply doubt that those appearing before them are genuine in their beliefs. In *Re P (Medical Treatment)* Mr Justice Johnson notes that in a previous case, involving E, where treatment was ordered against his wishes while he was a child, E went on to refuse medical treatment when he was of adult age and did then die (*Re P (Medical Treatment)* ([2003] EWHC 2327 at para 8). It is not the sincerity of the belief but its legitimacy that seems to be put in question. In taking the attitude that they do, the courts treat the NRM and the believer as being outside the normal order of things in a way that is comparable to what is done in *Re B and G*.

In some ways the court's approach to Witness beliefs may seem understandable and even acceptable. Douglas says of the court's decision in E's case '[s]urely a court could not, in conscience, permit the child to die?' (Douglas 1992, 574). Notwithstanding the example of E noted above it is, of course, highly likely that some Jehovah's Witnesses minors who have asserted their wish not to have blood transfusions, but whose wishes have then been overridden by the courts, have then gone on to lead full adult lives either because they have never subsequently needed blood transfusions again or because they have later left the Witness faith. This, however, is not to the point. It is doubtless the case that some adult Jehovah's Witnesses would have gone on to lead full lives if their wishes as to blood transfusions had been ignored. However, since the Suicide Act 1961, adults have a right to die and in principle *Gillick* competent minors have the same rights as adults; but not, it seems, if they are members of NRMs.

The treatment of NRMs as being out of the ordinary, thus justifying a different legal approach to their cases, is more subtle when the courts are dealing with blood transfusions cases than it is in either the case of *Re B and G* or early Jehovah's Witness custody cases; nevertheless it is still there. Moreover, notwithstanding the broadly positive outcome in *Re ST*, there are important similarities between the courts' attitude to *Gillick* competent children who want to refuse medical treatment and thus probably die and Lord Justice Ward's attitude towards the mother in *Re ST*.

Being a Mother

At a number of points in his judgement in *Re ST* Lord Justice Ward expressed doubts about whether or not the mother in the case, NT, was behaving appropriately. In particular he was concerned about, to use his phrase, NT's 'sense of priorities'. He noted that in concluding her evidence NT asked the court not to denigrate the Family's 'Law of Love', its central tenet of faith. In his judgement Lord Justice Ward said that he was surprised that her closing remarks were not about her desire to retain custody of her child, S. '[S]he fails to put S first. The Family comes first.' What appears to have troubled Lord Justice Ward is both what NT believes and her reasons for believing it. He notes with regard to members of The Family that '[t]he fact is that most of those within The Family remain there because of their faith in what it offers. For most it is blind faith'. Elsewhere in his judgement he writes that in the case of NT '[h]er devotion to Berg [the founder of The Family] is so total that it has drained her intellectual reserves'. Here again, as with the blood transfusion cases above, the court correctly understands the tenets of faith of the NRM in question; for NT, as with other members of The Family, The Family does come first, but Lord Justice Ward cannot see this as being an acceptable view of the world. Additionally the manner in which members of The Family make decisions is regarded as being unacceptable. Thus the fact that NT lacks 'intellectual reserves' and that members of The Family do things simply on grounds of faith is seen as something that ought to be criticized. The Family and NT are, for Lord Justice Ward, out of the normal manner of things, even if he is able to arrive at orders about the behaviour of both NT and The Family at large that allow him to countenance the possibility of NT retaining custody of her child.

Conditions Attached in Jehovah's Witness Custody Cases

While the courts have long followed a practice of awarding custody of children to Witness parents they have equally long followed a practice of attaching conditions to this custody. The conditions usually take the form of non-Witness parents having custody of the child at times such as birthdays and Christmas which Witnesses do not celebrate and the Witness parents not taking their children with them when witnessing. Long ago in the 1981 case, *Wright v Wright*, the Court of Appeal argued that it 'is not a matter for the faith of the Jehovah's witnesses being wrong or right . . . it is a matter of the custodial parent holding one set of views and the non-custodial parent holding a conflicting set of views and the conflict causing damage to the child' (*Wright v Wright* (1981) 2 Family Law Report 276 at 277–8). There are manifest potential problems caused by a child's parents having conflicting religious views, particularly if they are strongly held. However the manner in which the courts seek to solve this problem seems to add weight to the arguments about NRMs being treated as abnormal that have been set out above.

In every reported case the conditions attached to custody arrangements where one parent is a Witness and the other is not are such as to allow a child to live as 'normal' a life as is consistent with a custodial parent being a Witness. Thus, typically, the child is able to have birthdays, experience Christmas and not have to go witnessing because conditions are attached which mean that they spend relevant times with a non-Witness parent or a specific condition is made forbidding participation in witnessing. The child must, of course, realize their Witness parent regards these things as being wrong and some degree of internal conflict within the child must result. Courts never seem to order that the child will not celebrate birthdays or Christmas and must go witnessing as children of two Witness parents will. Witness parents may retain custody of their children but, in this sense, their world and their beliefs are again still treated as being abnormal.

NRMs and Religion in the English Courts

The sections of this chapter above would seem to indicate that the questions posed about the courts' treatment of NRMs can be answered in the affirmative. The cases that have been analysed show that courts do regard NRMs and their members as being out of the normal order of things in at least some instances and this leads them to reach judgements that they would not otherwise have reached. In this next section I will argue that, while this conclusion might once have seemed appropriate, consideration of the courts' approach to the protection of freedom of religion in England and Wales, following the enactment of the Human Rights Act 1998, suggests a rather different conclusion. In fact what the courts find troubling are not NRMs but religion itself.

Until the Human Rights Act 1998 there was no constitutional protection for freedom of religion within England and Wales. Although individual statutes protected believers in particular instances there was no general right to assert that one's freedom of religion had been interfered with before the English courts. Historically the English judiciary have thus had little reason to wrestle with issues related to the protection of religious freedom and the jurisprudence in this area has therefore been relatively sparse compared to many other jurisdictions. The implementation of the 1998 Act changed this by creating a general duty for the court to seek to protect the rights of the individual that had been created by the European Convention on Human Rights, including the Article 9 right protecting freedom of religion and belief. The subsequent passage of the Equality Act 2010, under which religion became a 'protected characteristic' for the purposes of the Act, appeared to further strengthen the position of those religious believers who wished to challenge their treatment before the courts. Superficially there now appears to be substantial legal protection for the position of religions and their believers. A recent Equality and Human Rights Commission report supports such a view, observing that '[t]he overwhelming majority of people in Britain do not experience discrimination because of their religion or beliefs' (Equality and Human Rights Commission 2012, 319). Correct though this conclusion is, it is scarcely surprising given the nature of British society. It has nothing to do with the efficacy of the legal system in general or the role of the courts in particular. In Great Britain, although not in Northern Ireland, as much research has shown, religion plays little part in most people's lives (Bradney 2009, 6–9). Most people in Great Britain cannot experience religious discrimination because their faith, if they have any at all, is so lightly worn as not to influence their behaviour in any discernible manner; there is nothing on which to base any discrimination (Voas and Crockett 2005). However there is still a minority of religious believers in Great Britain whose religion is central to their sense of identity, shaping the way in which they live (Bradney 2009, 20–6). These believers include both members of NRMs and other religions.

Because of the importance that their faith has to them and because of the part it plays in their quotidian lives they can be discriminated against. It is in relation to them, not 'the overwhelming majority of people in Britain', that the value of the Human Rights Act 1998 and the Equality Act 2010 has to be judged.

In practice neither the Human Rights Act 1998 nor the Equality Act 2010 seems to have done much to change the degree of protection that believers can expect from the law. One commentator has asserted that the court's approach to arguments about freedom of religion has been so restrictive that 'litigants will now argue anything *but* Article 9' (Sandberg 2011, 161) (emphasis in original). Another commentator has suggested that as between the various matters that currently receive legal protection such as race, gender, sexuality and so forth there is now a hierarchy of rights with freedom of religion being at the bottom of that hierarchy (Vickers 2010). When the rights of different people have to be balanced against each other it is invariably the rights of religious believers who come last. A detailed answer to the question why the courts have failed to protect religious believers at a time when other groups have been afforded much greater protection than ever before falls outside the scope of this chapter. However some comments by the courts in leading cases in this area, none of which involve NRMs, are instructive when considering the problems about NRMs and their members being discussed in this chapter.

In *Islington Borough Council v Ladele* ([2010] 1 Weekly Law Reports 955) a registrar, who had been appointed to officiate at civil weddings, objected to assisting with civil partnerships following the implementation of the Civil Partnerships Act 2004, their objection being based on their Christian beliefs about the necessarily heterosexual nature of marriage. The court observed 'Ms. Ladele's objection was based on her view of marriage, which was not a core part of her religion . . .' (*Islington Borough Council v Ladele* [2010] 1 Weekly Law Reports 955 at 970). The judgement does not say why the belief was not a core part of Ladele's religion or indeed how one would assesses whether this was so or not. In *Eweida v British Airways Plc* ([2010] EWCA Civ 80), a case involving a Christian who wished to wear a crucifix in a manner which breached British Airways' policy on uniforms, the court said that 'Ms. Eweida herself described it [her desire to wear a crucifix] as personal decision rather than a religious requirement' (*Eweida v British Airways Plc* ([2010] EWCA Civ 80 para 9). What exactly Eweida had said about her beliefs is not to be found in the court's judgement. What the distinction is between a decision to wear a religious symbol because one is a member of that particular religion and a 'religious requirement' is not expanded on. Equally the judgement does not say why this distinction is of consequence. In both these instances the court appears to minimize and even trivialize the litigant's objection. It is difficult to see how either court's description of the place that their beliefs had in the lives of Ladele and Eweida is compatible with their willingness not only to go through lengthy dispute resolution procedures within their places of employment but also, because of these beliefs, to then take their cases to higher courts when they were unsuccessful at their places of work; something which is further underlined by the fact that both cases are now heard by the European Court of Human Rights.

Both *Islington Borough Council v Ladele* and *Eweida v British Airways Plc* raise questions about how the courts perceive the nature of religion and the place that it has in some people's lives. These questions have been raised elsewhere. In *McFarlane v Relate Avon Limited* Lord Carey, a former Archbishop of Canterbury, submitted a witness statement urging the court to recuse itself from hearing the case and asking for the creation of a special panel of judges with a 'proven sensibility and understanding of religious issues' to hear cases involving 'religious rights' (*McFarlane v Relate Avon Limited* [2010] EWCA Civ B1 para 17). While Lord Carey's witness statement refers to 'lack of knowledge about the Christian faith' on the part of the judiciary his concern seems to be not so much the judiciary's alleged lack of empirical knowledge about religion as its lack of empathy with religious sensibilities. In *McFarlane* the court rejected Lord Carey's contentions. There is, nevertheless, a resonance between Lord Carey's concerns and some of the queries about the courts' treatment of NRMs and their members raised above. At this level one might argue that it is because NRMs are religions and because the members of NRMs are religious believers that they sometimes face being treated as being out of the normal order by the courts. Religious belief, or at least fervent religious belief, is something that is troubling for the court. NRMs may be more likely to face difficulties with courts simply because they are more likely to have such believers. Moreover there may be good reason, at least from the court's perspective, why fervent belief is so problematic.

In *Eweida v British Airways Plc* Sedley LJ makes a broader point about religion than just that he made about Eweida's own personal beliefs. Noting that age, disability, gender reassignment, marriage and civil partnership, race, religion or belief, sex and sexual orientation are all matters that were or, at the time of the hearing of the case, would soon be protected by law Sedley LJ goes on to suggest that 'all of these apart from religion or belief are objective characteristics of individuals; religion and belief are matters of choice' (*Eweida v British Airways Plc* [2010] EWCA Civ 80 para 40). On the face of it this remark seems to be either plainly wrong, tendentious or at the very least disputable. Entering into a marriage is, for example, under English law clearly legally a matter of choice. Marriages entered into under duress are voidable, and once voided no longer valid, under section 12(c) and section 16 of the Matrimonial Causes Act 1973. Equally, conversely, some would question whether or not a religious belief is purely a matter of individual choice (Vickers 2011, 138–9). The straightforward opposition that Sedley LJ draws simply is not tenable. However, when looked at from the perspective of the judiciary, the distinction looks more comprehensible. The problem that Sedley LJ seems to be averting to, albeit rather tangentially, is the potential capacity for notions of freedom of religion to subvert all other rights to non-discrimination.

Religion and Equality in the Courts

Religion's capacity to undermine other rights arises in two stages. First it is difficult to assess the existence or validity of a religious belief that is asserted by someone (McColgan 2009, 5–6). It is therefore difficult to challenge such a belief. Second, it is argued that religious beliefs are frequently situated in cultural practices that are historically hostile to modern-day notions of equality in relation to matters such as gender, sexuality or disability (Raday 2002, 669–74). Faced with a claim to a right of religious freedom a court is confronted with the problem that the belief seems subjective in a way that, for example, marriage is not. A person entered into a marriage, at least in Great Britain, because of their own subjective choice but whether or not they are married is something that a court can objectively determine by reference to the relevant legal tests. Religious beliefs vary not just between but within religions. How, then, can a court determine whether or not something is indeed a religious belief? The English courts have been quick to limit the degree to which they are willing to enquire into the quality of a religious belief.

'When the genuineness of a claimant's professed belief is an issue in the proceedings the court will inquire into and decide this issue as a question of fact. This is a limited inquiry. The court is concerned to ensure an assertion of religious belief is made in good faith . . . But, emphatically, it is not for the court to embark on an inquiry into the asserted belief and judge its "validity" by some objective standard such as the source material upon which the claimant founds his belief . . . Freedom of religion protects the subjective beliefs of an individual' (*R (Williamson and others) v Secretary of State for Education and Employment* [2005] 2 Appeal Cases 246 at 258).

However, if the claimed belief, which may only be the subjective belief of this believer before this court, denies other notions of equality how can the courts then avoid religious rights trumping all other rights? Moreover to attempt to rationally or objectively judge the limits to be put round such rights risks raising the challenge that to do so is to ignore the fundamental nature of religion; the religious world is different to the secular world and cannot be judged by its standards. This point is illustrated by Lady Hale's judgement in *Williamson*. In *Williamson* Christian parents and teachers sought to establish a legal right for schools to be able to administer corporal punishment to pupils despite an express statutory prohibition on this being done. Having noted that beliefs about the desirability or otherwise of corporal punishment for children is 'not a scientifically provable fact' Lady Hale then spent much of her judgement discussing both the United Kingdom's international legal obligations with respect to children and various reports which had commented on the use of corporal punishment (*R (Williamson and others) v Secretary of State for Education and Employment* [2005] 2 Appeal Cases 246 at 273 and 274–6). All of this was irrelevant to the parents and teachers who based their arguments and beliefs solely on their understanding of various biblical texts (*R (Williamson and others) v Secretary of State for Education and Employment* [2005] 2 Appeal Cases 246 at 255). If, however, the secular courts simply accept religious arguments such as those of the parents and teachers, are not their judgements then automatically subordinated to the claims of religion? How else could Lady Hale have proceeded? How else can state courts retain a secular, liberal character to their judgements?

Concerns about the nature of religion have led some to question whether accommodation to religious belief is something that is desirable in law (Barry 2001, 44–50; Bedi 2007). Others have argued that protection for religion ought to be 'attenuated' (McCoglan 2009). Courts, however, are faced with the fact that in both national and international legal instruments religion is often protected alongside a list of other matters and that protection, *prima facie*, is given on an equal basis. For the courts of England and Wales this is so with both the Human Rights Act 1998 and the Equality Act 2010. Because of this religion in itself becomes an intransigent problem for the courts.

Conclusion

This chapter has shown that courts do indeed sometimes treat NRMs in a different manner to other entities. Members of NRMs can find that their faith is the determinant factor in the decision that a court makes about them. None of this is necessarily the case; courts can always decide otherwise. In *Jehovah's Witnesses of Moscow v Russia* (2011) (53 *European Human Rights Reports* 4) the European Court of Human Rights rejected an attempt to ban the activities of Jehovah's Witnesses on the grounds, among other things, that they led to an increase in suicides. The court argued that there was no reliable evidence to support such a contention (*Jehovah's Witnesses of Moscow v Russia* [2011], 53 *European Human Rights Reports* 4 paras 109–53). This is exactly the reverse of the decision of the English courts in *Re B and G*, the first case discussed in this chapter. Latey J, the judge in *Re B and G*, could have taken the same approach as the European Court of Human Rights in *Jehovah's Witnesses of Moscow v Russia*. However it would be wrong to conclude that decisions with relation to NRMs and their members are simply the result of the individual reasoning of particular judges at particular times. Instead it is necessary to understand that religion causes structural problems for the judiciary, challenging their normal ways of reasoning. How they answer those challenges varies both according to jurisdictions and according to individual judges but it would be idle to pretend that those challenges do not exist or that they are ever likely to be entirely resolved.

Notes

1. *Re ST (A Minor)* has never been reported in published law reports in the way that other cases referred to in this chapter have been. This is probably because of its length, Lord Justice Ward's judgement being 278 A4 pages long with a 22-page appendix. My analysis is based on a copy of the judgement given to me by The Family.
2. For a more detailed analysis of this case see Bradney 1999 and Bradney 2000.
3. The term 'reported cases' refers to those cases heard in higher courts where judgements have been published. These judgements create legal rules that can be binding in subsequent cases. There is a much larger body of unreported cases in the lower courts. Since lower court judgements are not reported we do not know what use they make of expert witnesses. On sociologists of law as expert witnesses see Wilson 1998 and Hervieu-Lèger 1999.
4. The notion of *Gillick* competence, the right of a child to make decisions for itself, stems from the case of *Gillick v West Norfolk and Wisbech Area Health Authority* ([1986] Appeal Cases 112), 'a landmark in the legal recognition of children as having a distinct right to autonomy' (Douglas 1992, 570).

19 Gender

Megan Goodwin

Chapter Outline	
Why Gender Matters	196
Existing Scholarship	199
Gender Analysis in the Study of New Religions	203
Conclusion	206

As a mode of cultural analysis, the field of gender studies provides critical insights into the beliefs and practices of new religious movements. Several scholars – notably Janet Jacobs, Sarah Pike and Susan Palmer – have emphasized the ways gender norms and expectations shape the theology and praxis of NRMs. However, comparatively few scholars approach the study of new religions through the lens of gender analysis. Those scholars who do engage gender have largely limited their inquiries to the role of women in NRMs.

This is not to dismiss or belittle the active and significant involvement of women in new religions, but rather to insist upon the ubiquity of gender norms. Whether gender-conforming or -transgressive, each of us is shaped and constrained by the cultural assumptions informing our understandings of how 'normal' people inhabit their bodies. Thus a theoretically rigorous approach to gender in new religious movements must attend to masculinity as well as femininity, and account for cis- and transgender as well as intersex and gender-queer presentations. To clarify: transgender here refers to persons whose gender identities are either mutable or ambiguous; cisgendered persons are those whose gender identities match their biological sexes. Genderqueer refers to gender identities that fall outside a masculine/feminine binary. Intersex is a medical term referring persons whose bodies do not neatly conform to a binary classification of biological sex. A thorough analysis of gender's function in the study and practice of new religions must account for both normative as well as non-normative gender presentations.

This chapter demonstrates ways that scholars might use gender analysis to consider the beliefs and practices of new religions. I introduce several basic tenets of gender studies, argue for the significance of gender theory to scholarship on new religions, and survey key contributions to the field of gender and NRMs. While the authors in question demonstrate the importance of gender to the study of NRMs, many elide 'gender' with 'women', failing to interrogate the ways gender also shapes the experiences of male NRM members. These authors moreover occlude the presence and participation of transgender and gender non-conforming persons.

Gender analysis is crucial to the study of new religious movements because NRMs articulate and challenge cultural gender norms in a number of ways. New religions provide space for women to lead religious communities and provide spiritual counsel. Often, NRM theologies expand or challenge traditional understandings of gendered divinity. But new religions can also mirror mainstream cultural attitudes about binary gender, echoing deep-seated cultural attitudes about male/female complementarities or hierarchies. NRM studies may also interrogate religion's role in shaping broader cultural attitudes about gender.

The multivalent significance of gender in the study and practice of new religions highlights a tension between those analyses and customs. Feminist and gender scholars who study NRMS are often invested in using new religions as examples of resistance to or space outside traditional gender roles and expectations (compare Mahmood 2004 on similar tendencies among feminist scholars of Islam). However, the theology of many new religions – as well as many practitioners thereof – have significant investments in a complementary or hierarchical gender binary, based in essential biological differences. Considering gender in the context of either scholarship on or practices of NRMs first requires understanding that gender matters in the study of new religions.

Why Gender Matters

As a position of privilege and oppression, gender influences and constrains our lived experiences. Considerations of gender are therefore crucial to any scholarly analysis of human culture.

First and foremost: all human beings have gender. For the purposes of this essay, 'gender' refers to the cultural organization of 'the knowledge that establishes meanings for bodily differences' (Nicholson 1998, 187). Expectations for how we should act, what we should feel, the ways we ought to think and speak and be, all precede our awareness of our own bodies (Butler 1993, xvii).

Religion plays a significant role in the transmission and interpretation of gendered meanings and symbols; and gendered experience has a significant impact on how individuals or groups might respond to religious beliefs and practices. As Caroline Walker Bynum asserts in *Gender and Religion: On the Complexity of Symbols*, 'there is no such thing as generic *homo religiosus*' (1986, 2). This is to say that there is no neutral religious subject: 'no scholar studying religion, no participant in ritual, is ever neuter' (Bynum 1986, 2). One cannot encounter or experience religion outside gendered meaning-making – indeed, as Bynum insists, 'religious symbols are one of the ways in which such meanings are taught and appropriated' (2006, 7). Consideration of gendered experience is thus crucial to the study of religion in general and new religions in particular.

It is nevertheless important to note that gender – masculinity, femininity or other gendered presentations – does not mean the same thing in all times and places. Though all human beings have gender, not all experience gender in the same way. Gender norms are historically and culturally contingent: thus the visions of a fourteenth-century British anchoress and the poetry of an eighteenth-century African-American freed woman may not be collapsed into a singular unit of 'feminine religious experience'. Our understandings of being man, woman, transgender, intersex or genderqueer, do not issue from an essential gendered reality, but are rather shaped by our own historical and cultural locations (Nicholson 2008, 208). Scholars must therefore be careful to avoid generalizations that presume universal biological criteria for studying gender; contemporary Western scholars must be doubly careful not to impose present-day and/or Euro-American expectations of 'normal' gendered behaviour onto non-Western or historical interlocutors.

Historically, gender has been understood in hierarchical and binary terms. This means we often think of gender as having only two legitimate forms – masculine and feminine – and that historically, cultures have tended to value traits and qualities associated with masculinity more than traits and qualities associated with femininity. (On this point, see Simone de Beauvoir's *The Second Sex* and Luce Irigaray's *This Sex Which Is Not One*, among numerous others.) What is more, we tend to assume that gender follows naturally from biology – that the physical presentation of our bodies dictates who and how we must be. Or, as Freud put it, 'anatomy is destiny' (1995, 394). The scope of this essay precludes an extensive deconstruction of biological essentialism; however, most gender scholars assert gender's social construction. This is to say that the way we think about sex and gender is constructed and constrained by our historical and cultural locations.

That gender is socially constructed is significant for several reasons. First, as I noted above, 'gender' is neither a historical nor cultural constant – it does not and has not meant the same thing at all times or in all places. Second, our understandings of what it is possible for bodies to mean, do, and be is likewise socially constructed. Thus while Western cultures tend to think of gender in binary and hierarchical terms, neither the binary nor the hierarchy is absolute or essential. And, as I shall demonstrate, new religions frequently present both articulations of and challenges to this gendered hierarchical binary.

Gender also functions as a category of privilege and oppression. Gender privilege manifests in a number of ways; two of the most prevalent manifestations are the occlusion of masculinity as an unmarked category and cisgenderedness. Noting masculinity as an unmarked category is to acknowledge that scholars (although scholars are by no means alone in this occlusion) often present men's experiences as generalizable and curiously ungendered – which is to say normative. The cultural prioritization of masculinity over femininity has resulted in the valuation and normalizing of male experience over the experience of women and gender non-conforming persons. (Here again, see Beauvoir and Irigaray.) In the study of new religions, this disparity has led to an oversampling of male experience and the presentation of that experience as the norm (Culpepper 1978; Jacobs 2001). By contrast, women's religious experiences – and the religious experiences of transgender, intersex and genderqueer persons, when they engage these at all – as unusual, curious and remarkable. Thus in the study of new religions, masculinity functions as an unmarked category. This unmarkedness, as Cynthia Eller has noted, is itself a position of privilege: for those who directly experience gender discrimination, thinking about gender is not optional (2003, 125–6).

Cisgender privilege is at once the most common and least remarked form of gender privilege in the study of new religions. Cisgendered persons are those whose gender identities assigned at birth match their biological sexes. The theology and practice of most religions, including new religious movements, assume not only a gender binary but a natural and universal correlation between biological sex and assigned gender identity. Very few NRM scholars have discussed, much less analysed, the participation of transgender, intersex and genderqueer persons. However, as I shall show, new religions can facilitate non-traditional binary gender presentations and create space for religious embodiment among and through genders.

Finally, NRM scholars should be aware that gender is one concern among many in the study of embodied religiosity. While gender is uncontrovertibly significant in the study of new religions, attention to gender should not preclude consideration of other identity categories, including (but not limited to) sexuality, race, class, age and ability (Collins 2000, 18). Failure to take seriously the material complexity of lived religious experience can lead to conflict and impede coalition-building among persons with similar theological and practical commitments.

The field of gender studies offers a number of critical insights into the study of new religions. This field asserts the universality of gender while insisting on the historical and cultural construction of knowledge about bodies. Gender analysis also emphasizes the hierarchical and binary organization of gender, noting that gender functions as a position of both privilege and oppression. Gender scholars moreover observe that while gender represents a significant factor in embodied experience, scholarship of that experience cannot focus solely on gender to the exclusion of race, class, age, ability and other identity categories.

Existing Scholarship

Relatively few scholars have specifically approached the study of new religions from the perspective of gender. Those who have done so focus overwhelmingly on women's experiences and are almost exclusively women themselves. (Stephen Stein's work is a notable exception, though gender is never the primary focus of his treatments of alternative religions. See in particular Stein's (2003) 'Healers and Occultists: Women of Spiritual Means', in *Communities of Dissent: A History of Alternative Religions in America*.) The collected work of Emily Culpepper, Janet Jacobs, Elizabeth Puttick, Susan Jean Palmer, Mary Farrell Bednarowski and Sarah Pike constitutes the greatest part of existent scholarship of gender and new religions. Each of these authors has not only foregrounded gender concerns in her investigations of a specific tradition, but also emphasized the broad pertinence and significance of gender analysis in the study of new religions. Despite similar premises for their investigations, however, these scholars often arrive at broadly disparate interpretations of NRM beliefs and practices.

Thealogian Emily Culpepper was arguably first to call for a gendered analysis of new religious movements. ('Thealogy' refers to the discourse on the nature and meaning of the feminine divine and is related to Goddess worship, the feminist understanding of the divine as singular and female; this is related but not reducible to Neopagan, Heathen, and other new religious traditions that honour specific individual goddesses. On this point, see especially Eller 1995.) Culpepper is perhaps best known for her study of American secondwave feminist spirituality and the emergence of contemporary Goddess worship in the United States. However, her call for a feminist perspective in NRM studies was broader in scope. In 'The Spiritual Movement of Radical Feminist Consciousness', Culpepper notes that many NRMs 'offer only a pseudo-newness for women' (1978, 220). She insists that women's roles in new religions are frequently 'heavily traditional, patriarchal ones', in that NRMs often prioritize heterosexual relationships, reproductive sex and nuclear families – a 'new/old religious reinforcement of . . . conventional oppressive female roles' (1978, 220–1). Even those movements that emphasize individual autonomy and agency do little to challenge the 'patriarchal status quo', Culpepper urges (1978,

221). While the article's primary objective was to argue for the radical feminist potentiality of Goddess worship and religious witchcraft, Culpepper's work in this early piece demonstrates the necessity of a gender studies perspective in scholarly engagement with NRMs.

Though better known for her work on contemporary crypto-Jews and Holocaust studies, sociologist Janet Jacobs has also produced some of the earliest gendered analyses of new religions (1984, 1989). In particular, Jacobs notes that gender is 'a significant determinant' of women's religious experience within NRMs, as many such movements include male-dominated religious hierarchies and 'patterns of socialization [that] encourage women to define their conversion [to a new religion] in terms of love and romantic allusion' (1984, 155–6). Jacobs further notes broad discrepancies in the experiences of men and women NRM members: whereas her women interlocutors detailed 'attachment, rejection, sexual exploitation, and violence', the men she interviewed discussed 'jockeying for positions of power, access to women, and ideological differences with the religious leadership' (2000, 434). Jacobs also speaks frankly about the NRM researchers' broad occlusion of women's experience; seeming indifference towards women's sexual objectification, commodification, and/or coercion (particularly in movements like the Children of God); and assumption that ideologies and practices that sexualized female members were or are normative (2000, 435). Jacobs' uncompromising commitment to disrupting the trivialization, silencing, and erasure of women's experiences within new religions is remarkable, as is her unstinting emphasis on the roles paternalism, abuse, and violence have played under such circumstances (2000, 435; see also Jacobs 2001, 2007, and Jacobs and Davidman 1993). Jacobs is unwavering in her reading of new religions as essentially conservative and potentially exploitative of women; as such, her work stands in stark contrast to that of sociologist of religion Elizabeth Puttick.

Puttick's edited volume, *Women as Teachers and Disciples in Traditional and New Religions* (1993), was among the first collections to foreground gender analysis as an approach to NRM studies. But *Women in New Religions: In Search of Community, Sexuality, and Spiritual Power* (1997) constitutes Puttick's most significant contribution to the study of gender and NRMs. She surveys women members of British Neopaganism, the International Society for Krishna Consciousness, the Human Potential Movement, the Children of God, and in particular, the Rajneesh (now Osho) movement. Puttick, as a scholar and former NRM member, interrogates the liberatory potential for women members of each movement. Puttick argues that new religions facilitate women's 'active, public' participation in 'the creative search for spiritual meaning', and concludes that – while membership in new religions is not always and everywhere an unqualified good for women – the majority of female NRM members are 'relatively "normal" people seeking alternatives to the social, ethical, and spiritual solutions offered by mainstream society' (1997, 232). The utility of Puttick's proposed typology of 'spiritual needs and values' is limited and the author demonstrates a decidedly essentialist conceptualization of 'feminine spirituality' (1997, 232–40, 226, 74). Nevertheless, *Women in New Religions* undoubtedly addresses a lacuna in NRM studies – and whereas earlier scholars of gender and new religions primarily emphasized the danger of NRM membership for women, Puttick convincingly demonstrates the space made by NRMs for women's religious agency and creativity.

Susan Jean Palmer's 1994 *Moon Sisters, Krishna Mothers, Rajneesh Lovers: Women's Roles in New Religions* follows in a similar vein. Palmer's ethnography focuses primarily on a range of female sexual practices and sexual identities in North American NRMs; she surveys ISKCON, the Rajneesh movement, the Unification Church, Applied Metaphysics (IAM), the Messianic Community, the Raelians, and the Harmonious Human Beings in order to illustrate varieties of gendered and sexual practices and moralities among these new religions. Palmer's thesis is reductive: she argues that women convert to 'unconventional religions' in response to the 'rolelessness' that results from 'dramatic upheavals in the structure of society' and posits NRMs as an 'honorable time out' from women's contemporary sexual 'dilemmas' (1994, xiii, xvi). Like Puttick, Palmer relies heavily on a binary and demonstrably essentialized understanding of gender roles and feminine spirituality. Palmer's work is one of the first and few monograph-length engagements with gender in new religious movements (so too Foster 1991). Her consistent emphasis on the importance of gender analysis to the study of NRMs undeniably represents a significant contribution and an important challenge to the field (see also Palmer 2004b). As with Puttick, Palmer's interlocutors are self-possessed (if overwhelmed) religious agents.

American religions scholar Mary Farrell Bednarowski briefly explores gender and new religions through *New Religions and the Theological Imagination in America*'s consideration of LDS theology and Scientology marriage practices, as well as women's roles in LDS and the Unification Church (1989). Her *The Religious Imagination of American Women* deliberates at length on – and indeed originated with – the contributions of feminist Wiccans and Goddess worshippers to the creative and dynamic landscape of American religiosity (1999, 3). Bednarowski makes her most cogent statement on the importance of attention to gender in the study of NRMs in 'Gender in New and Alternative Religions' (2006). She insists that NRM scholars should attend to gender for a number of reasons, among them that new religions often serve as 'arenas of experimentation with gender roles', demonstrate the complexity and multiplicity of gendered religious beliefs and practices, and the historical and cultural contingency of attitudes towards gendered meaning (Bednarowski 2006, 206). Significantly, Bednarowski emphasizes that 'the members of new religions understand themselves as participants in conversations and tensions around [broader cultural conversations regarding] gender' (2006, 206). She addresses gender analysis in NRM scholarship from three angles: the movement's ascription of religious meaning to gendered embodiment; the social ordering of the group with regard to sexuality and fostering spiritual connections between male and female members; and the connection (if any) between gender and leadership (Bednarowski 2006, 207). Bednarowski's work in this essay is also noteworthy for its engagement of gender and race in African-American new religions, a topic often occluded in NRM scholarship (2006, 215–16). She concludes by reiterating the importance of gendered analysis to the study of new religions, urging scholars to consider how analysing NRM membership as a gendered experience helps us better understand a movement's beliefs and practices (2006, 223).

Ethnographer Sarah Pike's work primarily focuses on community and festival culture among contemporary North American Neopagans. Her earlier work demonstrates the ways in which Neopagan communities both resist and replicate broader cultural attitudes about gender (1996). Her 2006 'Men and Women in New Religious Movements: Constructing Alternative Gender Roles' mitigates tensions regarding women's membership in new religions: while Pike acknowledges that NRMs are often abusive or coercive of female members, particularly in groups with charismatic male leadership, she nevertheless insists that NRM scholars must be more nuanced in their consideration of the ways women create meaning in specific movements. Like Jacobs, Pike takes seriously the prevalence of sexist and abusive practices; even so, Pike insists upon crediting women members' own interpretations of their experiences. She presents a four-part typology of gender relations in nineteenth- and twentieth-century NRMs – male dominance, female dominance, partnerships, and merged gender roles – and explores the ways these attitudes towards gender manifest in conceptualizations of the divine, movement leadership and organization, and sexuality, marriage and family. Pike's work is noteworthy both for the credence she lends to her interlocutors' lived experiences and for her consistent attention to the gendered experiences of both men and women in new religions (1996, 2001, 2004).

The work of scholars like Sarah Pike, Mary Farrell Bednarowski, Susan Palmer, Elizabeth Puttick, Janet Jacobs and Emily Culpepper convincingly demonstrates the pertinence of gender analysis to the study of new religious movements. As I have shown, however, these authors interpret the accounts of their interlocutors in multiple and sometimes contradictory ways. Culpepper and Jacobs emphasize what they understand to be essentially patriarchal and often exploitative qualities of new religions, while Puttick, Bednarowski and Palmer foreground the accounts of women NRM members themselves – presenting these women as rational and creative religious agents in their own right. Pike assumes a middle position in this dialogue by frankly acknowledging the persistence of gender inequity in NRMs and by taking seriously the roles women create meaning through innovative religious beliefs and practices.

Much of the scholarship on gender and new religions relies on essentialized notions of 'natural' attributes of femininity and masculinity; nearly all these authors understand gender in strictly binary and cisgendered terms. Nevertheless, the works above comprise a significant and much needed intervention into the study of new religions. Such scholarship should inform scholarly analyses of the ways NRMs articulate and challenge cultural gender norms.

Gender Analysis in the Study of New Religions

I have suggested that gender analysis provides critical insights into the beliefs and practices of new religious movements. This approach to the study of new religions reveals multiple and complex instantiations of gendered assumptions, dogma and behaviours among such movements. Some new religions facilitate women's religious leadership and spiritual authority or provide space for reconsidering the gendered nature of the divine. Some instantiate gender complementarity or reinforce hierarchical gendered social orders that reflect patriarchal norms; others challenge 'traditional' gender roles, identities and performances. New religions' interactions with mainstream religions or professedly secular institutions may also provide opportunities to interrogate broader cultural attitudes about the relationship between religion and gender.

Women in roles of religious leadership or spiritual authority provide one of the richest sources for gender analysis in NRM studies. As Bednarowksi notes, 'women in new religions often have more opportunities for public leadership than is the case in the established religious traditions' (2006, 207). She qualifies, however, that women's religious leadership is less common both among mainstream and new religions and is therefore often controversial (Bednarowski 2006, 207). Mother Ann Lee of the Shakers, Ellen G. White of the Seventh-day Adventists, Mary Baker Eddy of the Church of Christ, Scientist, the Fox sisters and other women mediums in the Spiritualist movement, Starhawk of the feminist Wiccan tradition, and similar women leaders all instantiate both the prevalence of feminine spiritual authority and the conflict that often emerges between new religions and more established traditions or professedly secular mainstream institutions. Of the existent work on women's religious leadership in NRMs, Margot Adler (2006) and Jone Salmonsen's (2002) work on Neopaganisms, Alex Owen (2004) and Molly McGarry's (2008) work on Spiritualism, Elizabeth De Wolfe (2010) and Richard Francis' (2011) treatments of the Shakers, and Laura Vance's (1999) engagement of the Seventh-day Adventists are particularly of note. The history of new religions provides rich fodder for scholars of women's spiritual authority.

New religions also provide space for rethinking the gendered nature (and presumed masculinity) of the divine. (On the significance of God-as-male, see in particular Jantzen 1999.) In 'Gender and New Religions', Pike suggests that 'conceptions of deity' in NRMs approximately correspond to four types of gender roles: a monotheistic male god; a 'complete reversal' of traditional male divinity, that is, a monotheistic goddess; a 'divine pair' such as those found in the Shaker and Unification traditions; or a 'universal force or power' that transcends gender (2006, 213). Pike also observes that some new religions have no concept of deity, as with UFO groups who instead revere ancient alien civilizations (2006, 213). Theologians Mary Daly (1985), Carol Christ and Judith Plaskow (1992) articulate the importance of understanding divinity in female terms, though poet and activist Audre Lorde (1983) challenged the Western imperialism inherent in Daly's Anglicized Goddess. (For more on contemporary Goddess-worship, see Eller 1995 and Wise 2008.) Gardnerian Wicca and feminist theology alike have posited a divinity that includes balanced and equal male and female aspects (Gardner 2004; Ruether 1993). While Pike does not mention them, some new religions work with deities that move between or defy a singular gender identity, revere polytheistic pantheons that include individual gods and goddesses, or understand the practitioner herself as god/dess. Raven Kaldera's 2002 *Hermaphrodeities: The Transgender Spirituality Workbook* offers a practical approach to exploring divine gender ambiguity and fluidity. Jenny Blain's work on contemporary Heathenism (2003) and Adler's ethnography of American Neopaganisms (2006) both demonstrate the prevalence and persistence of polytheisms. Starhawk (1999) and Knight (2007) chronicle the beliefs and practices of contemporary NRM members who understand *themselves* as divine – feminist Neopagans and Five Percenters respectively. In these ways, new religions facilitate challenges to and new understandings of a gendered divine.

New religions also express theological understandings of gender complementarity in doctrine and practice. Shaker communities organized members in a separate but equal system of intentional celibate brother- and sisterhood. Married couples in the Unification Church reflect both the dual nature of the divine and the sacred example of the True Parents. Nation of Islam offshoot the Five-Percent Nation is also known as the Nation of Gods (i.e. male members) and Earths (female members), to reflect the significance of black people as the fathers and mothers of civilization (Knight 2007). As these examples show and as Culpepper in particular has noted, many innovative religions are deeply invested in static and binary understandings of gender.

As Jacobs and Pike have demonstrated, a number of new religious movements affirm male religious leadership and patriarchal authority. Jacobs observes that many women are attracted to the structure and discipline of such movements, but expresses concern that the charismatic figure of leader as divine patriarch often leads to abuse and deprivation (2001, 171–2). Pike moreover remarks that even groups that define themselves as 'aggressively non-hierarchical and decentralized' often replicate broader cultural norms of male dominance or gender dichotomies (1996, 122, 134). Here again, these accounts bear out Culpepper and Jacobs' observations of the persistence – and indeed, the romanticization – of gender essentialism in new religions (Culpepper 1978; Jacobs 2001).

However, new religious movements can also create space for unconventional modes of gender presentation (Wilcox 2006). Neopaganisms in particular have facilitated queer and gender non-conforming religious identities, though certain communities are still coming to terms with including gender non-conforming members. In this context, 'queer' refers to those who are or feel marginalized because of their sexual practices or gender identities. The Reclaiming Witchcraft Tradition and the Dianic Witchcraft Tradition have both recently faced internal conflicts regarding the inclusion of transgender persons. Pike's 'All acts of love and pleasure are my rituals' (2004) and Blain's *Nine Worlds of Seid-Magic: Ecstasy and Neo-shamanism in Northern European Paganism* (2003) both demonstrate the potentialities of Neopaganisms as space for gender play or fluidity (see also Kaldera 2002). Molly McGarry observes that cross-gender channelling in nineteenth-century Spiritualist practice provided complicated modes of gender performance in those communities. American religions scholar Lynne Gerber (2008) has demonstrated the prevalence of 'queerish' masculinities among Christian ex-gay movements; groups like the Radical Faeries have also facilitated alternate modes of masculinity in the context of innovative religiosity (Povinelli 2006). These rich accounts of unconventional or experimental gender presentation further attest to the crucial role gender plays in the beliefs and practices of many new religious movements.

Gender analysis might also help NRM scholars challenge the targeting of new religions as particularly prone to misogyny and/or the sexual exploitation of women and children. Mainstream religions and professedly secular governments often assume that participation in groups with restrictive gender roles or sexual practices must be involuntary or irrational; NRM critics and anti-cult activists – as well as mainstream media and politics – often portray adult male members as sexually predatory and oppressively patriarchal, and female, adolescent, and child NRM members as in need of rescue (Gibson 2010). This is not to excuse exploitation, coercion, or abuse of women or children members of new religions, but rather to insist that the exploitation, coercion, and abuse of women and children is in no way unique to NRMs. Gender analysis both resists the location of misogyny outside or beyond mainstream Western cultures and provides a sharp critique of abuse narratives that fail to prevent or disrupt violence against or coercion of any person (Goodwin 2013).

Conclusion

In this chapter, I have demonstrated the pertinence of gender analysis to the study of new religious movements. I first provided a brief synopsis of key assumptions in the critical study of gender and showed the significance of gender theory to scholarship on new religions. I then surveyed key contributions to the field of gender and NRMs, including the work of Emily Culpepper, Janet Jacobs, Elizabeth Puttick, Susan Palmer, Mary Farrell Bednarowski and Sarah Pike. While each author demonstrates the importance of gender to the study of NRMs, I noted that most elide 'gender' with 'women', rendering masculinity an unmarked category and occluding the presence and participation of transgender and gender non-conforming persons. Finally, I suggested that gender analysis provides critical insights into the beliefs and practices of new religious movements.

New religions create space for members to articulate and challenge broader cultural norms. While scholarly interpretations of members' experiences vary, I have shown that attention to gender provides NRM scholars critical insight into the innovative beliefs and practices of their interlocutors.

20 UFO Religions

Christopher Partridge

Chapter Outline

Occulture and UFOs	208
1947	209
Theosophical UFO Religions	211
UFOism as Physicalist Religion	214
UFO Apocalypticism	216
Concluding Comments	220

Given how incredible fairies seem to most of us, where do fairy beliefs come from in the first place? Human nature seems to abhor a blank space on a map. Where there are no human habitations, no towns, where villages dwindle into farms and farms into woods, mapping stops. Then the imagination rushes to fill the woods with something other than blank darkness: nymphs, satyrs, elves, gnomes, pixies, fairies. Now that we have mapped every inch of our own planet, our remaining blank spaces lie among the stars. Unable, like our forebears to tolerate space uninhabited, we have made with our minds a new legion of bright and shining beings to fill gaps left by our ignorances. Aliens are our fairies, and they behave just like the fairies of our ancestors. In this sense, fairies are not part of a dead-and-gone past. (Purkiss 2000, 3)

The psychological and social forces and the cultural discourses that shape UFO religions are much the same as those that have accompanied humanity throughout history. Imaginations are simply moulded by shifting occultural contexts. The aim of this chapter is to identify the principal religious and cultural contours that have contributed to the development of UFO religions. Hence, although particular UFO religions will be mentioned, this is not intended to be another introduction to individual groups, thinkers and texts, but rather seeks to provide a way of understanding the primary processes, themes and issues underlying the emergence of UFO religion.

Occulture and UFOs

While this is not the place to unpack the theory of occulture as it has developed over the last few years, because some readers may not be familiar with it, something does need to be said (see Partridge 2004a, 2005, 2013). Occulture refers to those social processes by which spiritual, paranormal, esoteric and conspiratorial ideas and meanings are produced, circulated and exchanged. Within occulture, ideas become fungible and related to broader networks of ideas. For example, some years ago two very popular series of books were published: 'Principles of . . .' (published by Thorsons) and 'Elements of . . .' (published by Element). Overall, they constituted a general introduction to a range of beliefs and practices. Although some of the books, such as *Principles of Numerology*, *Principles of Wicca*, *Principles of Tarot*, and *Principles of Your Psychic Potential* could be described as 'spiritual' or 'occult' in the narrower sense of the term, others, such as *Principles of Colonic Irrigation*, discuss subjects that are not inherently spiritual in themselves but have, nevertheless, become occulturally so. In other words, within occulture, the interest in colonic irrigation becomes imbricated with a range of other fungible ideas as part of a broader interest in well-being and the self. Likewise, ideas and practices within established religious traditions are de-traditionalized, in that they are separated from their original contexts and attached to other ideas in the service of the self.

Popular culture is central to the efficacy of occulture, in that it feeds ideas into the occultural pool, develops, mixes, disseminates those ideas, thereby creating new occultural trajectories. Hence, popular occultural ideas such as energies can be, as they were in *Star Wars* or *Star Trek*, given life and related to new ideas, such as extraterrestrial life. Concepts and theories such as the efficacy of spells, the existence of fairies, and alien intelligences have life breathed into them, thereby opening up intriguing avenues of possibility for the occultural imagination. Hence, the theory of occulture argues that *popular occulture*, in various ways, sacralizes the Western mind – introducing it to new forms of the sacred, developing older religious and esoteric ideas, championing the paranormal and often challenging dominant forms of religion.

Over the past 70 years or so, speculation regarding UFOs and extraterrestrial intelligence has become prominent in Western occulture. Books such as particularly Erich von Däniken's *Chariots of the Gods?* (1969) and Whitley Strieber's *Communion* (1987) have appeared on bestseller lists, the former being described at one time as 'the best-selling book of modern times' (Singer and Benassi 1981,

49). This interest, of course, reflects significant and rising levels of UFO belief in the West. Hence, for example, a sociological study of the English town of Kendal found that a quarter of spiritual active people registered a belief in UFOs. 'Nothing surprising about this, one might think. But what is surprising – and surely shows the extent to which ufology has entered the culture – is that around 10 per cent of regular church attendees expressed belief' (Heelas 2003, xiv). Again, a typical example of how occulture operates, creating networks of belief, is provided by the UFO researcher, Andy Roberts, who describes how his own interest in the area began: 'I devoured everything in the local library's adult occult section . . . and found Keel's *Jadoo*, Vallee's *Passport to Magonia*, and all the Shuttlewood books, which were coming out in the late-'60s and early-'70s, along with stuff by Crowley and the occultists. I became completely obsessed with UFOs, ghosts, and many other kinds of strange phenomena' (quoted in Miller 2004, 54). Indeed, Jacques Vallee himself recalls how difficult it was to maintain a focus on science at conferences on UFOs:

> Many years ago I had the privilege of working with J. Allen Hynek, the astronomer who served as scientific consultant to the US Air Force . . . I especially remember a time when we had just finished speaking to a large audience in California. We had been stressing – as we always did – the great need for a genuine sceintific investigation of the unidentified flying object phenomenon. Then it was time for questions, and none of the questions from the audience had to do with science . . . What people wanted to know was, Would the occupants of UFOs help humanity to solve its problems? Did they have a God? Were they responsible for the miracles in the Bible? What kind of philosophy did they bring us? In other words, not only had the audience already jumped to the conclusion that the objects were spacecraft controlled by extraterrestrial beings, but all the questions were concerned with spiritual issues. (Vallee 2007, 193)

This is typical of occulture and provides some insight into the evolution of organized UFO religions.

1947

Central to the shaping of contemporary UFO occulture have been claimed UFO sightings. Indeed, as part of a rationale for their beliefs, many UFO religionists construct what amounts to a sacred history of sightings and contacts. While, as with most sacred histories, this usually stretches back into prehistory, there is one date that is particularly significant for the scholar of UFO occulture, namely 24 June 1947. This is the date when Kenneth Arnold, a businessman from Boise, Idaho, reported a sighting of ten shining discs flying over the Cascade Mountains. According to Arnold, 'they flew like a saucer would if you skipped it across the water.' Misquoted, the sighting was reported as an encounter with 'flying saucers'. While there had been previous modern sightings of, for example, 'balls of fire' accompanying planes during the Second World War ('foo fighters') or cigar- and disc-shaped objects in the sky (such as the wave of Scandinavian 'ghost rocket' sightings in 1946), these tended to be sporadic and vague. Moreover, before 1947 'there is not a single recorded episode involving mass sightings of saucer-like objects' (Bartholomew and Howard 1998, 189). It was Arnold's 'flying saucers' that began the modern waves of sightings. Indeed, it is no coincidence that, within a month, on 2 July 1947, occulture, vibrant with speculation and semiotic promiscuity, received its next sacred moment, the Roswell incident. This time the aliens had crashed, been recovered and officially denied. Conspiracies, a staple of occulture, proliferated. Hence, during 1947 a centre of occultural gravity formed, around which UFO religion began to take shape.

It should be noted that it was particularly significant that media reports provided a consistent vocabulary with which to discuss the phenomenon. Prior to Arnold there had been no handy terms with which to discuss unexplained aerial sightings. Following 1947, the terms 'flying saucer' and then 'UFO' very quickly became two of the most important terms within recent occulture.

UFO religion, of course, has roots that go deep into pre-1947 Western occulture. For example, in the eighteenth century, the Christian esotericist Emanuel Swedenborg, in his *Arcana Coelestia*, outlined the idiosyncrasies of extraterrestrial societies and cultures, such as the Saturnians' unceremonious dumping of their dead by in nearby forests (Hammer 2004a, 388). However, central to his thinking was a conviction that has since become central to UFO religion, namely that, extraterrestrials both resemble humans and represent a utopian projection of humanity's evolutionary goal, being intellectually superior, morally innocent and spiritually advanced. From this point on in the modern period, one can produce a religious history of individuals who claim to have encountered extraterrestrials and even travelled to other planets and experienced advanced civilizations. Even when such fantastic claims were not made, notions of beings from other planets and their advanced civilizations have entertained the minds of thinking people for centuries (Partridge 2003). However, while there are explicit contactee claims prior to 1947, these are not central to the particular belief systems of the individuals and, more particularly, do not involve 'UFOs'. Some might argue, as for example Gordon Melton has done, that there is good evidence for pre-1947 UFO religions, a notable example being Guy Ballard's I AM Religious Activity. Certainly it is true that, in his book *Unveiled Mysteries* (1935) – published under the pseudonym Godfre Ray King – Ballard claimed, not only to have met the enigmatic nineteenth-century alchemist and now ascended master Comte de Saint-Germain on Mount Shasta in California, but also to have been subsequently introduced to 12 Venusians who revealed their planet to be home to a race of technologically and spiritually advanced beings. However, Ballard is clearly developing H. P. Blavatsky's Theosophical doctrine concerning the Venusian 'Lords of the Flame', which were, according to Charles Leadbeater's interpretation of the concept (1912), of the highest rank in the hierarchy of ascended masters (see Stupple 1984, 131). This, according to Melton, is significant: 'Not only did Ballard become the first to actually build a religion on contact with extraterrestrials (as opposed to merely incorporating the extraterrestrial data into another already existing religion), but his emphasis was placed upon frequent contact with the masters from whom he received regular messages to the followers of the world contactee movement' (Melton 1995, 7). But does this qualify it as a 'UFO religion'? While the I AM Religious Activity can be seen as the obvious forerunner to UFO religions such as the Aetherius Society, and to the thought of UFO religionists such as George Adamski (1955), it was not a UFO religion, as we now understand the term. The principal focus was not alien beings and certainly not UFOs (i.e. alien spacecraft), but rather ascended masters, the 'I AM presence'/'Christ self' within us all, karma, reincarnation and so on. Indeed, as David Stupple comments, 'Ballard's meeting with twelve Tall Masters from Venus . . . is only a minor item in his major work, *Unveiled Mysteries*' (1984, 133). In other words, Ballard does what Melton claims he does not, namely incorporates 'the extraterrestrial data into another already existing religion'. He simply develops ideas that already existed within the Theosophical tradition to which he belonged. Hence, while we will see that the idea of ascended masters did undergo explicit ufological reinterpretation after the Arnold sighting, in this pre-1947 period Ballard's thought is more clearly Theosophical than ufological.

The overall point is simply that, while there are claims to 'contact' with beings from other planets prior to the Arnold sighting, they are not the principal focus of such belief systems and UFOs per se are absent. The emergence of religion specifically focused on UFOs is a post-1947 phenomenon. It was, in other words, Arnold's contribution to occulture that provided the necessary organizing principle around which other occultural elements became oriented.

Theosophical UFO Religions

While the I AM Religious Activity was not a UFO religion as such, there are conspicuous continuities between it and much post-1947 UFO religious belief, in that those initially involved in the sacralization of UFOs were steeped in the discourse of the Theosophical Society, formed in 1875 primarily by Helena Blavatsky and Henry Olcott.

Central to Theosophy is its doctrine of 'ascended masters'. As the influential Theosophist Annie Besant comments, 'That the Society was only worthy to live, if it were a witness to and a channel for the masters' teachings, was [Blavatsky's] constant declaration, and she only cared for it as an instrument for carrying out their work in the world' (Besant 1907, 60). Indeed, as far as Blavatsky was concerned, the true founders of the society were two such masters, Koot Hoomi and Morya, whose teachings were channelled through her and other *chelas* (pupils of the masters). The mission of the Theosophical Society was, therefore, to communicate these teachings in order to contribute to the moral and spiritual evolution of the human race.

The ascended masters were living persons who had fully evolved through many reincarnations, had acquired and become the custodians of 'ancient wisdom', and now sought to impart that wisdom to humanity in order to lead it into a new age of peace, spirituality and global community. 'Having themselves solved and mastered the problems of human living, they make a periodical effort to bring more enlightenment to mankind' (Redfern 1960, 31–2). The masters have 'direct insight into the spiritual, psychic and physical workings of our solar system'. Consequently, it was 'on their behalf', insisted T. H. Redfern, that Blavatsky 'gave out teachings giving a corrective lead in the fields of science, religion and ethical standards' (1960, 32). For example, quoting from the channelled *Mahatma Letters*, he makes the following comments:

> '. . . every atmospheric change and disturbance' is 'due to masses between which our atmosphere is compressed! I call this meteoric dust a "mass" for it really is one. High above the earth's surface the air is impregnated and space is *filled* with magnetic . . . dust which does not even belong to our solar system'. The origin of cosmic rays is still debated and the Van Allen belt, which has been described as the Great Barrier Reef in space, was not discovered until 1957. The meteorology of the Mahatma Letters is still not confirmed, but if Mme Blavatsky forged these letters how did she know there was a magnetic mass above the atmosphere. Again, 'Science will *hear* sounds from certain planets before she *sees* them. This is a prophecy.' In 1882 . . . Jodrell Bank wasn't even a dream, radar unthought of, radio-stars unheard of. Radio-planets are still not discovered, but who dare deny the possibility. (Redfern 1960, 33–4)

Regardless of the scientific validity of such passages, the religious point to note is that the masters are beings (a) with a deep concern for the welfare of humanity, (b) who operate as supreme moral and spiritual guides, and (c) whose superior wisdom extends to the spheres of science and technology. While there are some differences between the Theosophical masters/mahatmas of wisdom (who were primarily thought to reside in Tibet) and the early accounts of aliens, in actual fact the similarities between the two are striking. Both are highly spiritually evolved, morally superior, technologically advanced, benevolent sacred beings with a deep salvific concern for a profane race bent on the destruction of the planet. (Particularly during the Cold War and drawing on the popular occulture of the period, it was claimed that the concern of aliens, like that of many humans, was humankind's ability to destroy the planet with nuclear weapons.) Moreover, just as great spiritual founders and leaders of religious history are identified in Theosophy with the ascended masters, so in UFO religions these benevolent beings are similarly understood (Applewhite 2011, 21–2; Rothstein 2007a; Stupple 1981, 134–5; Tumminia 2005, 77–8). Mark-Age, for example, relates the following message from the extraterrestrial master Sananda, who is identified as Jesus: 'I have come many times to the Earth planet as a leader and as a spiritual ruler responsible for that which does happen in this plane or cycle.' This is followed by an editor's note: 'Past incarnations of Sananda include: Khufu, Melchizedek, Moses, Elijah, Zarathustra, Gautama Buddha, Socrates, and Jesus of Nazareth. In addition, he was leader of the Abels [sic] and leader of the Noahs [sic]' (Nada-Yolanda 1995). Indeed, even charismatic founders themselves became identified with key religious figures. Ernest Norman of Unarius, for example, was believed to have been Jesus in a past life and to have confirmed this by displaying stigmata (Tumminia 2005, 193).

The point, however, is that, in early UFO religions, fundamentally the same masters remained, but, following 1947, their location, dress and mode of transport were updated. Hence, aliens cease to simply appear to contactees, as in the case of Ballard, but rather now descend in flying saucers. Again, while Venus, which has been prominent within Western esotericism, tended to retain its privileged position for some years within UFO discourse, as interest in space travel shaped popular occulture, so other planets were identified as inhabited – including unknown ones, such as Clarion, as discussed in Truman Bethurum's *Aboard a Flying Saucer* (1954). Indeed, Venus' popularity as the home planet of advanced civilizations waned somewhat when it was discovered to be shrouded by clouds of sulphuric acid, with an atmosphere constituted almost entirely of carbon dioxide and a surface temperature of 480°C – hardly ideal for comfortable, civilized life. That said, so central was the planet to the doctrines of some Theosophical groups, such as the Aetherius Society, that their cognitive dissonance was assuaged only by continuing to insist that it remains the home of the masters Aetherius, Buddha and Jesus, yet now clarifying that they do not live in its rather bracing physical dimension, but rather reside on a more relaxing 'etheric plane'.

Finally, a religious practice common to both Theosophy and to many UFO religions is mediumship. However, unlike traditional Spiritualism, Theosophical messages were not those of departed loved ones, but teachings of the highly evolved masters of wisdom.[1] It is this notion of advanced beings 'channelling' teachings through sensitive individuals that is wholly adopted by many UFO religions. The beings reside on other planets or occupy spacecraft and, while the process of channelling may be interpreted in much the same way as it is in Theosophy, it is usually described using scientific (often pseudo-scientific) terminology (Denzler 2003). For example, the Aetherius Society describes the channelled messages as 'transmissions' which are 'transmitted by light beams operating upon mental frequencies capable of impressing themselves upon my mind in such a way that translation into the English language was possible. This process of mental reception is called telepathy, which is now regarded by science as an indisputable fact' (King 1957, 5). Indeed, many Aetherius Society publications claim to be transcripts of lectures by Aetherius (who is 'now alive in a physical body upon the planet Venus') channelled through their founder, George King. Again, as with the channelled teachings of the Theosophical Society, entities such as Aetherius and Ashtar – the latter communicating through George Van Tassell to the Ministry of Universal Wisdom (see Helland 2003) – do not communicate the type of personal messages for individuals one would expect in a Spiritualist séance, but rather 'transmit' grand statements of universal import. For example, the following is taken from a fairly typical 'transmission' from Aetherius, through King:

> The New Age will be brought in by a series of catastrophies [sic], which have to come in order to balance Karma in one way or another. *Because you have three adepts on your Earth just now, risking their very salvation for you, the blow has been softened greatly*, but nevertheless, earthquakes, tidal waves, droughts, fierce winds, hurricanes, floods, and so on have, as you know, already started. Strange weather conditions have, just as I prophesized [sic] about this time last year, already started. I also told you only a short time ago what type of conditions you could expect and you have had them exactly as I stated you would. (King 1963, 7)

Most channelled messages from extraterrestrials have similar universal, anthropocentric and spiritual emphases. For the sake of the planet, the human race must progress spiritually. Everything from war to natural disasters is related to the slow progress of human spiritual evolution. Advanced extraterrestrial masters want to help.

UFOism as Physicalist Religion

While much UFO religion contains typically religious themes, including the belief in God, salvation, reincarnation, karma and so on, much of it is fundamentally 'physicalist'. That is to say, while the components of a religious worldview may be there, and while UFO spiritualities clearly do draw from the common pool of occultural ideas, these are often reinterpreted in terms of physical phenomena. Of course, it is important to understand that, while all UFO religion is physicalist to some extent, there are varying degrees ranging from a group such as the Raelian movement which has what might be described as a *strong* physicalist belief system, to the *weak* physicalist beliefs of an organization such as Mark-Age, which is far more supernaturalist in the Theosophical tradition. At the strong end of the spectrum are those forms of religion influenced by science-fictionesque elements within occulture and at the weak end are those far more influenced by the Theosophical elements within occulture. Groups situated at the strong end tend towards atheism and anti-supernaturalism, while those situated at the weak end often claim, for example, that extraterrestrials worship God and live according to divinely instituted cosmic laws.

I use the term 'physicalist religion', rather than 'scientific religion' (which is sometimes used), simply because the understanding of science is always occulturally nuanced and sacralized, often being described as '*spiritual* science' or '*divine* science' (see Andersson 2007; Cross 2007; Denzler 2001, 2003). Hence, the term 'science' in this context is often a misnomer. The concern is not to engage with modern scientific discourse, but rather to interpret paranormal phenomena in terms of 'normal' physical phenomena, to collapse the supernatural into the natural by expanding the sphere of the rational into that of the irrational.

The Aetherius Society provides a good example of this physicalist turn (see Chryssides 2003). While it is a Theosophical group, articulating religious beliefs such as karma, reincarnation, and channelling, it also provides physicalist explanations for these beliefs. For example, channelled messages are described as 'transmissions' from one physical being to another by, it is claimed, the scientifically verifiable process of telepathy. Again, they use technology designed by George King to maximize the effectiveness of prayer, which they understand in terms of energy. Hence, central to their 'Operation Prayer Power' was a distinctive box, sometimes mounted on a tripod, which, it is claimed, is a unique 'prayer battery' that can store up to 700 hours of the psychic energy produced by praying members. This stored psychic energy can then be beamed anywhere in the world in order to disperse violence and hatred and promote love, harmony and spirituality. Prayer is energy which can, in much the same way as electrical energy can, be stored in batteries and used when and where required.

Similarly, very common in UFO religions is the physicalist interpretation of sacred texts and ancient mythologies. For example, developing what became known as 'the ancient astronaut hypothesis', von Däniken's occulturally influential work raises the question as to whether the human race is in fact the result of 'deliberate "breeding" by unknown beings from outer space' (1969, 66). The Genesis account, not only speaks of God creating humanity in his own image (a significant text for many UFO religionists), but also of further visits of the 'sons of God' and of their sexual relations with 'the daughters of men' (Gen. 6.1–4), all of which indicates continuing fertilization experiments. The subsequent flood narrative, he explains, is actually a record of the alien extermination of unsuccessful specimens. Our ancient ancestors, the survivors, were the specimens our alien creators were pleased with. He concludes by making the point that 'today the possibility of breeding an intelligent human race is no longer such an absurd theory' (1969, 66). Since the publication of von Däniken's *Chariots of the Gods?*, a number of very similar theses have appeared in the narratives of UFO religions. Perhaps the most conspicuous example is the Raelian religion's rationale for cloning technology (see Helland 2007; Palmer, 2004a, 27–8). On 13 December 1973, four years after the publication of *Chariots of the Gods?*, the group's founder, Claude Vorilhon, claimed that he had encountered aliens in the volcanic Clermont-Ferrand mountains in France. Although the Raelians' construction of a discourse of revelation understandably denies any occultural influence, nevertheless, Vorilhon's extraterrestrials telepathically provided an interpretation of the Bible very similar to that of von Däniken. Central to their theology is the doctrine that 'the Elohim' mentioned in Genesis were alien beings and that their scientists had produced the first humans by mixing their DNA with that of primates (see Chryssides 2003). This, argues Raël, was the beginning of a history of alien intervention that has consistently involved cloning. Indeed, Raël claims to have met, in 1975, his biological father, 'an Eloha named Yahweh'. 'Yahweh', says Susan Palmer, 'addresses Raël as "*tu*" (in French, the familiar form of *you*), then confesses to having beamed up Raël's mother into his ship, inseminated her, and released her with her memory erased' (Palmer 2003, 264). Interestingly, Yahweh had done exactly the same with Mary, 'chosen for her "virgin DNA"' (Palmer 2003, 264). Hence, Mary's son, Jesus, is Raël's half-brother. However, unlike Raël, he was murdered by an unenlightened society and then resurrected by the Elohim, in the sense that a cell from his dead body was cloned. The new body then underwent an 'Advanced growth process' (AGP) and had the personality from the murdered body transferred to it, the personality being understood in terms of software that can be downloaded into cloned bodily hardware. Consequently, the Raelian movement has become the first organization to construct a religious rationale for cloning (see Palmer 2004a, 177–94). Indeed, these ideas are linked in Raelian thought to a process of physicalist sanctification, referred to as 'elohimization' – becoming Elohim (Palmer 2001).

UFO Apocalypticism

With the above occultural elements in place – UFOs, Theosophical discourse, physicalist hermeneutics – other elements are also added, which may then become dominant and significantly alter the nature of the religion. For example, a recurring discourse within UFO religion relates to the corruption of humanity, the perilous state of the planet, and the need for extraterrestrial redemption – apocalypticism (Wojcik 2003; Zeller 2009). Indeed, even in organizations which cannot be described as 'UFO religions', such as The Nation of Islam, UFO sightings function as harbingers of the apocalypse (Lee 1996, 47, 85–6, 101–2). Moreover, as with other forms of apocalypticism, the confluence of discourses sometimes leads to the construction of an eschatology of violence. Between the contemporary 'last days' and the utopian life to come there is a fracture in history where the forces of evil will be violently overthrown and the principal beliefs of the group vindicated. This, of course, is rooted in a strong sacred-profane dualism and a related combat mythology. In particular, the faithful group is encouraged to understand itself as the *ecclesia contra mundum* (Partridge 2006). While, on the one hand, this leads to an expectation of persecution and ridicule (which serves to verify an eschatology rooted in a sacred-profane dualism), on the other hand, it also cultivates antinomianism, which can lead to a withdrawal from wider society and to the rationalization of violence.

On 26 March 1997, the bodies of 39 people, all dressed in identical black clothes, were found in a mansion in Rancho Santa Fe, an exclusive San Diego suburb. All of them were members of a UFO religion that had, up until this point, remained relatively unknown and peaceful. It was immediately apparent to Rio DiAngelo, the ex-member who discovered the bodies, that they had committed suicide. Why? The answer was to be found in an occulturally eclectic apocalyptic eschatology, which drew on Christian theology, Theosophical ideas, UFOs and science fiction (see Chryssides 2011; Partridge 2006).

Formerly known as Human Individual Metamorphosis and then as Total Overcomers Anonymous, Heaven's Gate was founded by Marshall Herff Applewhite and Bonnie Lu Nettles. Applewhite, the son of a Presbyterian minister, had studied philosophy and had a passing interest in 'rejected knowledge'. Nettles, brought up a Baptist, was a member of the Houston Theosophical Society. Gradually withdrawing from their friends, they became absorbed in occultural speculation: 'visions, dreams and paranormal experiences that included contacts with space beings who urged them to abandon their worldly pursuits' (Balch and Taylor, 215). Eventually, they became convinced that they were the 'two witnesses' mentioned in Revelation 11, who would be killed, resurrected, and ascend from the Earth's surface into a 'cloud' – which they interpreted as physical transportation to a waiting spacecraft.

While occulturally eclectic, it is clear where the principal concepts of their mature eschatology were being drawn from. The garden – central to the 'primeval history' of Genesis – is the paradise that was lost. Likewise, just as Revelation can be interpreted as the story of paradise restored – the return of the Edenic 'garden city' of God – so Heaven's Gate spoke of a paradisiacal 'Next Level'. Moreover, this eschatology was complemented by idiosyncratic, physicalist interpretations of creation and predestination (see Partridge 2003, 21–6). Extraterrestrial creators (Next Level beings)[2] had placed humans in the garden; they elected some for the *gift of life*, in that some were equipped with 'deposits' of the Next Level mind (i.e. souls) to enable them, but not to compel them, to evolve into Next Level beings ('the metaphoric process'); those who respond to the Heaven's Gate gospel progress to the Next Level 'where the Chief resides'; this is 'a level of existence wherein the many members do not experience death or decay' – the 'Kingdom of Heaven' (quoted in Partridge 2006, 55); Next Level beings have appeared around every 2000 years or so for the benefit of evolving souls, offering 'the discipline and "grafting" required . . . [for] transition into membership in My Father's House' (quoted in Partridge 2006, 62); whereas Jesus carried out this mission 2000 years ago (Applewhite 2011, 21–2), 'the Two' are *the last* Next Level shepherds to visit this current earthly garden, which will soon be 'spaded-under'.

Typical of millenarian eschatologies, they were relentlessly pessimistic concerning the current world order. Modern life in all its variety is inherently corrupt. 'We do in all honesty', stated Applewhite, *'hate* this world' (quoted in Balch and Taylor 2003, 233). Consequently, from the outset, much teaching was devoted to training individuals to 'overcome' attachments to 'the world'. As the early name for the group suggests, their aim was to produce 'total overcomers'. Hence, the socialization of members included both strong discouragement from contact with the 'outside' world and disapproval of intimacy within the group that might detract from their transition to the Next Level in these 'last days': 'Don't read newspapers or watch TV; don't call your parents; don't visit old friends; don't pick up hitchhikers . . . Quit using drugs; change your name; shave your beard; get rid of clothing and jewellery that symbolise your old self . . . no sex, no human-level friendships, no socializing on a human level' (quoted in Balch and Taylor 2003, 219).

As one might expect, this eschatological pessimism was amplified as their demonology evolved during the 1990s (see Partridge 2004b). They became convinced that demonic 'space aliens' or 'Luciferians' were committed to reducing the number of those who would finally ascend to the Next Level. And as the group became increasingly apocalyptic, so its teaching became increasingly dualistic, which, in turn, encouraged apocalypticism. Their thought became characterized by semiotic promiscuity and paranoia about sinister forces controlling everything from world governments to shopping transactions (Partridge 2006, 54–8).

The principal shift towards the rationalization of suicide, however, seems to have been the result of cognitive dissonance occasioned by the death of Nettles in 1985. The teaching regarding 'the Demonstration' – what might be understood as a 'technological rapture' – in the 1970s and early 1980s emphasized, in accordance with Revelation 11, *physical* ascension from the Earth's surface to a waiting spacecraft. Nettles' death, however, placed a large question mark against this belief and the revisions required to make sense of it led to the incorporation of suicide into their eschatology (see Peters 2003, 239–60). This was rationalized by a theory which may have been informed by Ruth Montgomery's 'walk-in' theory, which had become popular in new age occulture. Operating with a strong body–spirit dualism, 'walk-in' theory claims that 'a high-minded soul in the spirit realm can exchange places with another soul who wishes to depart the physical plane, by entering as a Walk-in' (Montgomery 1985, 8). Having studied philosophy, Applewhite may also have been influenced by Platonic thought. Hence, understanding the body in terms of 'a suit of clothes' or 'a container', Applewhite argued that the 'container' of flesh could be removed without any harm being done to the individual person, who can then incarnate another container elsewhere. In other words, ascension to a UFO could happen 'spiritually' and invisibly – one need not be, as Nettles had not been, *bodily* transported. Indeed, it is difficult to overestimate the significance of this shift for the rationalization for suicide. The 'flesh' became increasingly objectified, depersonalized, and even demonized as a profane hindrance to spiritual growth.

Applewhite became convinced that Nettles had left him on Earth to bring the mission to a close and had gone ahead in advance. This conviction was confirmed when, on 23 July 1995 the approaching Hale Bopp comet was reported (the expected arrival date being late winter 1997), along with subsequent speculation within new age occulture that a UFO was travelling in its tail. Just as comets have been interpreted in earlier semiotically promiscuous cultures as portentous signs of the end, so Applewhite became convinced that the apocalypse was imminent and that he and his followers were about to experience technological rapture. However, he now claimed that the rapture would *not* include their flesh, their earthly 'containers'. These would have to be left behind, just as Nettles had left hers. Consequently, suicide became interpreted as a spiritual practice, necessary for the removal of profane flesh. Transport to Heaven was simply the evacuation of a container, the soul's liberation from its fleshly prisonhouse. In a carefully phrased article entitled 'Our Position Against Suicide', it is argued that 'the true meaning of "suicide" is *to turn against the Next Level when it is being offered*' (quoted in Partridge 2006, 60). True life, on the other hand, is found in the act of giving oneself to the Next Level: 'the final act of metamorphosis or separation from the human kingdom is the "disconnect" or separation from the human physical container or body in order to be released from the human environment and enter the ... environment of the Next Level ... We will rendezvous in the "clouds" (a giant mothership) for our briefing and journey to the Kingdom of the Literal Heavens' (quoted in Partridge 2006, 60).

While there is a complex of reasons for the turn to violence in new religions, often central to their rationale is the construction of a rigorous dualism. The starker the polarities become, the more extreme the behaviour sanctioned. The more that which is identified as profane – such as the body, humanity, and this world – the more the other is sacralized and idealized – as in the utopian understanding of the Next Level and alien life. When actual or perceived exogenous pressures are introduced the cocktail becomes volatile. In other words, dualism often provides the hermeneutical key: it encourages semiotic promiscuity; it generates conspiracy; it contributes significantly to the leader's messianic elevation; it increases pessimism about the world; it enforces the sense of *ecclesia contra mundum*; it engenders longing for a utopia; it despairs of the possibility of a progressive sanctification of society and insists upon an imminent catastrophic solution; it determines the particular mix of occultural ideas and themes – those of an inclusive, world-affirming nature are abrogated by rigorously exclusivist and world-rejecting discourses.

Concluding Comments

Enthusiastically nurtured within occulture, the post-1947 fascination with flying saucers quickly coalesced into small religious groups as connections were made with other occultural elements, particularly those introduced by Theosophy and by the physicalist discourses within science fiction and, later, the work of writers such as particularly von Däniken. In the teaching that emerged, modern technological jargon was used to articulate Theosophically informed, science-fictionesque myths and techniques. UFOs became linked to a range of disparate subjects from Atlantis, telepathy and Jesus to Plato, reincarnation, and the Nephilim. Indeed, typical of the occultural imagination is its fascination with the discourses of popular culture. As Diana Tumminia says of Unarius, a film or a television show might even 'prompt the creation of a myth'. This would, in turn, 'be verified by a series of testimonies' within the group, drawing from the claimed experiences of past lives. Hence, members of Unarius 'actively watched television episodes of *Star Trek* looking for details about their forgotten lives. Memories of Atlantis, Orion, and Lemuria often surfaced through the viewing of science fiction dramas' (2005, 66). This occultural eclecticism and *bricolage* have led some scholars to suggest that UFO religions can be understood in terms of 'specially late capitalist or postmodern' spirituality (Urban 2011, 119). That said, as noted at the beginning of the chapter, there is much to suggest that UFO religions have evolved according to processes and forces not very different from those that have shaped folklore and religion throughout human history. In the final analysis, sons of God, messiahs, ascended masters and space brothers are close relations.

Notes

1 As Jennifer Porter discusses, some Spiritualists claim to have alien guides (1996, 337–53).
2 It is often noted by UFO groups that Gen. 1.26 appears to refer to a plurality of creators: 'Then God said, "Let *us* make man in *our* image..."'

21 Researching Esoteric Groups

Kennet Granholm

Chapter Outline	
A Matter of Definition	222
What about Secrecy?	225
Be Wary of Ancient Wisdom Narratives	226
Re-evaluating Engrained Terms	228
Researching Esoteric Groups in Practice	230

The title of this chapter might be taken to imply that the study of esoteric groups differs from the study of non-esoteric groups in some fundamental way. This is not the case. Largely, the same research methods as in the study of any other religious or social groupings apply. Much of that which may be researched by use of the approaches and perspectives developed in the study of Western esotericism may also be studied from other perspectives, not engaging with 'esotericism' as a theoretical framework. However, when engaging esotericism as a framework, some new issues are introduced, mainly relating to the reassessment of existing terminology and taken-for-granted perspectives of what esoteric/occult actually implies. Not least of all, the study of esoteric groups involves assuming foci that differ somewhat from that which is common in the study of other religious and social formations. This chapter will delve into these issues, and provide a brief overview of issues of key importance in the study of (particularly contemporary) esotericism.

A Matter of Definition

In any scholarly enquiry it is essential that we know what it is that we are in fact investigating, and matters of definition and demarcation are thus important. This is particularly acute when it comes to the esoteric as we are dealing with phenomena, and a vocabulary, which are historically particularly complex and convoluted. First, 'it' can go under many different names, such as esotericism, the occult, hermeticism, mysticism or even superstition (Hanegraaff 2012, 1). Second, however the esoteric is defined (and whichever term is used), it has always been regarded as something vague and amorphous, and most often defined in reference to what it is not (Hanegraaff 2012, 1). Third, the phenomena included under the label (whichever that label may be) have for a long while been subject to academic, religious, political and other suspicion, and have consequently been largely neglected as subjects worthy of serious academic study (Hanegraaff 2012, 1). Fourth, due to this neglect, research on 'esoteric phenomena' has existed on the fringes of the scholarly establishment (and still more often totally outside scholarly quarters), in disparate fields which have seldom paid much attention to each other, thus compounding the aforementioned problems. In addition, the esoteric is commonly and often problematically associated with 'secret societies', which is a description which simply does not fit most esoteric groups and teachings.

The research on the esoteric that does exist has primarily been conducted by sociologists and historians. Looking at these two traditions of scholarship is thus a good start if we want to unravel the meaning of 'esoteric' (and related terms). In sociology, phenomena that could be labelled esoteric have often been included under the category of 'Cults'. Originating in Ernst Troeltsch's (1911/12) presentation of Mysticism as a form of (Christian) religiosity which eschewed social organization and focused on inner religious experience (see Campbell 1973, 120; Partridge 2004a, 20–1), the Cult was from the 1930s onwards conceived of as 'the organizational response associated with mystical religion' (Campbell 1973, 120), and incorporated into the classic Church-Denomination-Sect-Cult classification of religious organization (see Dawson 2009, 528–9; Partridge 2004a, 25). In contrast to Churches and Sects, Cults are often conceived of as amorphous, loosely structured, eclectic and syncretistic groupings that do not lay exclusivistic claims to religious truth. It is for this reason, with the Cult-category collecting disparate teachings, practices, and groupings which do not fit in other categories, that esoteric phenomena have been studied under the label. However, it was not until the 1970s when sociologists of religion made sustained attempts to delineate *esotericism* in a more strict sense, with Edward Tiryakian defining it as 'those religio-philosophic belief systems' which inform occultism, in turn defined as 'intentional practices, techniques, or procedures which *(a)* draw upon hidden or concealed forces in nature *or* the cosmos that cannot be measured or recognized by the instruments of modern science, and *(b)* which have as their desired or intended consequences empirical results, such as either obtaining knowledge of the empirical course of events or altering them from what they would have been without this intervention' (Tiryakian 1974, 265–6). This theory-practice divide is superfluous, with Tiryakian himself admitting that esoteric knowledge is at its core 'of a participatory sort' (Tiryakian 1974, 266). A major problem in the sociological study of esotericism of the 1970s, which unfortunately partly remains to this day, is the inherent focus on 'deviance'. This is clearly evident in Marcello Truzzi's description of the esoteric/occult as a 'wastebasket, for knowledge claims that are deviant in some way' (Truzzi 1974, 245), comprising of knowledge not accepted in mainstream religion, science or culture. Logically then, the esoteric can only exist as a residual category, ultimately reliant on and subservient to categories and phenomena, beliefs and practices, that are more mainstream and established. Going by this approach, the esoteric, as a category, cannot have any internal consistency.

In stark contrast, historians of esotericism have tended to focus on the consistency of the esoteric, primarily in Renaissance and early modern European culture, from Frances Yates' narrative of a neglected 'hermetic tradition' (Yates 1964) to Antoine Faivre's suggestion of an esoteric 'form of thought' (Faivre 1994). Faivre's historical typology, where the esoteric 'form of thought' is identified by four primary characteristics: the notion of correspondences linking everything in existence; the idea of a living nature animated by divine forces; a focus on imagination and intermediary beings and forces as the primary paths to divine knowledge; and the experience of transmutation where the practitioner purifies and exalts his or her soul or essence so that it reaches the divine (see e.g. Faivre 1994, 10–15), has been particularly influential in the academic study of esotericism. The approach has a number of inherent problems. First, it is based on a limited source material from a specific period, meaning that this material will appear more (or more properly) esoteric than material from later periods. Second, while Faivre never intended his model as an outright typology which could be used to determine if something is esoteric or not, this is in fact how it has often been used. The notion of the esoteric as a more or less self-sustained 'tradition' is also problematic and at times comes close to emic perennialist narratives (see the section 'Be Wary of Ancient Wisdom Narratives' below).

Theoretical and methodological discussion has been active, and at times heated, since the late 1990s, and the main approaches today regard the esoteric not as a *sui generis* 'object', but as a socially, historically, and not least a scholarly constructed category by which a number of varied and disparate phenomena which have been marginalized in European intellectual culture can be studied. The most prominent approaches have been developed by Wouter Hanegraaff and Kocku von Stuckrad. Already in the mid-1990s Hanegraaff adapted Gilles Quispel's notion of three distinct modes of knowledge in Western culture into an ideal typical model which could function as an alternative to Faivre's 'form of thought'-approach (see Hanegraaff 1996, 518–20). In this approach, reason, faith, and gnosis co-exist and intermingle, but have very different rationales (Hanegraaff 2008, 138–40). While reason- and faith-based knowledge can effectively be communicated to others, and the validity of the former can be checked by anyone with the appropriate expertise, gnosis-based knowledge can neither be checked for validity nor communicated by normal means, as it is in essence a form of knowledge which can only be gained by experiencing it personally – often by entering 'altered states of consciousness' (Hanegraaff 2008, 140–1). (On the esoteric and the significance of altered states of consciousness see Hanegraaff 2013.) Somewhat similarly, von Stuckrad's discursive approach presents the esoteric as a structural element in European cultural history, focused on claims to higher or perfect knowledge and ways of gaining this knowledge (von Stuckrad 2005a, 2005b, 2010). These claims are often set in a worldview based on ontological monism, and common ways to achieve perfect knowledge are personal experience and mediation by intermediary beings (e.g. angels, spirits, aliens or even nature itself) (see e.g. von Stuckrad 2005a, 91). Von Stuckrad's approach is very open-ended, and in order to use it effectively in an analytical capacity it needs to be coupled to more focused methodologies. My solution has been to develop an approach where esoteric currents, that is schools of thought and practice, are regarded as discursive complexes, that is specific discourses in specific combinations. These discursive complexes then inform what the higher knowledge sought is, and how it is to be gained (Granholm 2013a).

Finally, Hanegraaff's most recent work (see Hanegraaff 2005, 2007; and particularly 2012) has focused on how historically specific processes, particularly connected to the Reformation and the scientific revolution, have functioned to relegate certain beliefs, practices and topics to the margins. In time, this 'rejected knowledge' has then been lumped together as belonging to the same 'tradition' of unaccepted subject matter (although they had originally been both accepted and disparate). Superficially, this approach appears similar to Truzzi's 'wastebasket'-approach discussed above. However, there are important differences. First, the processes of rejection discussed by Hanegraaff are historically specific rather than general as in Truzzi's approach. Second, Hanegraaff's approach does not contain the judgmental attitude of Truzzi's.

One of the most useful aspects of recent approaches to the esoteric is that they transgress binary opposites which are commonplace in modern popular and scholarly narratives. The esoteric is not relegated to a realm of its own; it is neither exclusively religious nor secular, but can operate both in the realm of religion and science, and thus the study of esotericism can work as a framework which problematizes the apparent essential distinctiveness of the two.

The impetus to the study of the esoteric in a historical phenomenon came from such disparate fields as art history, history of science, and history of religion, and the possibilities for inter-, and trans-, disciplinary work are thus ample.

As we can see, the esoteric has been conceived of in many different ways. None of these conceptions can outright be deemed better or more 'correct' than the others. The complexities in this matter make it necessary for any scholars who wish to explore the esoteric to position themselves in regard to the approaches that exist, taking note of *both* historiographic and sociological scholarship. Some scholars see no major problem with historiographical and typological approaches to the esoteric being kept separate (Hammer 2004b, 448–9). As this makes interdisciplinary research more difficult, I disagree, and follow Hanegraaff in his call for sociologically informed approaches to the esoteric which are compatible with historical ones (Hanegraaff 1998, 41). As the esoteric has been much more consistently characterized in historical studies, it is prudent to start there. Sociological dimensions should, however, be added. This could, for example, entail an examination of what kinds of social organization the esoteric leads to; are there 'esoteric modes of social organization' and what are their repercussions in that case? Another sociological dimension, inherent in the very terms esoteric and occult, is secrecy.

What about Secrecy?

The esoteric is commonly perceived to deal intimately with secrecy. As Faivre expresses it: 'until the present time, both outside and inside observers have often associated the esoteric discourse with the notion of secrecy, to the point of considering them as inseparable' (Faivre 1999, 156). This aspect is a part of many dictionary definitions of the esoteric and the occult, and it is therefore not strange that esoteric groups are often equated with 'secret societies' (for a classic study, see Simmel 1906). Secrecy is in fact an integral part of many sociological definitions to the esoteric. For example, Tiryakian describes esoteric knowledge as 'secret knowledge of the reality of things ... to a relatively small number of persons', and goes on to clarify that '[a]t the heart of esoteric knowledge, is its concealment from public dissemination, from the gaze of the profane or uninitiated' (Tiryakian 1974, 265–6). In contrast, the historiography of esotericism has made a point of *not* projecting secrecy as the core element of its subjects of study. As Faivre writes in the *Dictionary of Gnosis and Western Esotericism*: 'The typological meaning of "esotericism" as referring to secrecy should, however, be clearly distinguished from the historical meaning used in the present reference work and increasingly in general academic parlance' (Faivre 2005, 1056). This does *not*, however, mean that secrecy plays no part in the world of the esoteric, or that when present it is of no scholarly interest. Many esoteric societies, particularly since the nineteenth-century 'occult revival', place great importance on initiatory secrets. At the same time, many of these 'secrets' are not secret in the conventional meaning of being available only to a select few. For example, the 'secret' initiatory rituals of Freemasonry are available for a general public in numerous books (see for example Bogdan 2007). What is of concern in much esoteric discourse is the *'dialectic of the hidden and revealed'* (von Stuckrad 2005b, 10), that is to say secrecy as a rhetoric device. Furthermore, secrecy does usually not relate to texts or information per se, but to revelatory knowledge which can only be accessed by experiencing it firsthand. Thus, the 'secret' rituals of for example Freemasonry only reveal their *true* meaning when the rituals are performed, in their correct setting. This also means that it is the *revelation* of the hidden that is of central importance, not the keeping of secrets.

Thus, while the term 'secret society' can be technically correct in some cases, it is problematic as it introduces a high likelihood of misunderstandings. Also, many teachings, groups and currents that could be labelled esoteric simply do not fit the bill. For example, the stream(s) of contemporary esotericism problematically labelled 'the New Age Movement'[1] often operate in a very open fashion. Even here though, the *revelation* of secrets commonly plays an important role.

Be Wary of Ancient Wisdom Narratives

Notions of tradition are central to many of both the classic and the contemporary currents, movements, and discourses that can be included within the label of esotericism, and sometimes they unfortunately interfere with scholarly accounts. The related but distinct notions *prisca theologia* ('ancient theology') and *philosophia perennis* ('eternal philosophy') were key in Renaissance and early modern esotericism (for a detailed exploration of the concepts and their differences, see Hanegraaff 2012, 7–12), and the perennialist ethos they embody is central to the esoteric even today. However, it was not until the nineteenth century, chiefly in the context of French and British occultism, that the esoteric/occult started to be seen as something of a self-contained and coherent tradition. This is also when the noun 'esotericism' started to be popularized, typically referring to an ageless tradition connected with Hermeticism, alchemy, astrology, magic, etc., but above all with the Kabbalah (Asprem and Granholm 2013, 36–7; Hanegraaff 2012, 153–256). The marginalization of certain subject matter, now labelled as esoteric, also made it appealing to intellectual rebels, both in the late nineteenth century and among the counterculturalists of the late 1960s.

Notions of tradition are so essential to esoteric discourse that they should in fact be included as a core aspect to investigate. Alas, this has not been the case (for a notable exception, see Hammer 2001, 85–200), and the reasons for this are manifold. First, in the history-sociology divide, historians have tended to go for a purely historiographic approach, reporting on notions of tradition but not analysing their construction sufficiently. At the same time sociologists have rarely had sufficient historical know-how to analyse processes of tradition-construction properly. Second, due to the esoteric having been scholarly marginalized, emic notions of ancient wisdom have sometimes been included in seemingly scholarly historiography of esotericism. Unfortunately, claims to tradition are often the result of a *co-production* of tradition by scholars and practitioners (see Asprem and Granholm 2013). The narrative of a separate and oppositional intellectual 'occult tradition' was a standard staple of older scholarly and semi-scholarly research (e.g. Frances Yates' notion of 'the Hermetic tradition', Yates 1964), and it is also a notion where emic and etic historiography often meet. For example, John Holman's *The Return of the Perennial Philosophy* (2008), most likely tries to play in the scholarly field with the subtitle 'The Supreme Wisdom of Western Esotericism'. The idea of a coherent, *sui generis* 'esoteric/occult tradition' also exists among scholars not specialized in the study of esotericism. For example, David Katz's highly problematic *The Occult Tradition* (2005) relays the idea that 'the occult tradition' is something really 'out there', and attempts to trace 'it' through Western history. The result is a vague definition of the occult as 'the readiness to relate the unrelated' and a belief in the supernatural, which only works to confuse matters further.

While most current scholarship on Western esotericism strongly criticizes the idea of a coherent 'esoteric tradition' as being the result of emic historiography (see Hammer 2001; Hanegraaff 2001), it has not altogether disappeared from specialist literature. For example, Nicholas Goodrick-Clarke's much-read introduction to Western esotericism refers to esoteric tradition*s* in the plural, but betrays a far more perennialist position in claiming that the:

> perennial characteristics of *the* esoteric worldview suggest . . . that this is an enduring *tradition* which, though subject to some degree of social legitimacy and cultural coloration, actually reflects an autonomous and essential aspect of the relationship between the mind and the cosmos. (Goodrick-Clarke 2008, 13. Italics added)

The result is that, while (however reluctantly) accepting that sociocultural context may have some *marginal* relevance, 'definitions of "the esoteric" in terms of discourse, social constructions, and legitimacy' are insufficient as they 'lack a hermeneutic interpretation of spirit and spirituality as *an independent ontological reality*' (Goodrick-Clarke 2008, 12. Italics added).

The prominence of ancient wisdom narratives in esoteric discourses, as well as in much popular, scholarly, and semi-scholarly work on the subject, means that one has to be very attentive when engaging literature in the field, and careful not to reproduce problematic aspects of emic historiography. The construction of tradition should be foregrounded as an area of investigation, and proper attention must be paid to scholarly co-construction in this regard.

An interesting aspect of esoteric discourse which has not been sufficiently explored in scholarship thus far is the significance of exoticization in the construction of ancient wisdom narratives. Commonly, we are dealing with a form of 'positive orientalism' where esoteric wisdom is thought to reside 'elsewhere', in the exotic and increasingly far-away as the world shrinks under impact of globalization (see Granholm 2013b). For example, in the Renaissance 'lost wisdom' was brought back to the West from the orient of Greek Orthodox Christianity (on 'Platonic Orientalism', see Burns 2006; Hanegraaff 2012, 12–17), later Egypt became the abode of ancient wisdom, in the late nineteenth century it was time for India to assume the role of the esoteric orient, and since the latter half of the twentieth century it has been increasingly common to gaze into outer space, with esoteric wisdom being conveyed by aliens from increasingly distant stars.

Re-evaluating Engrained Terms

A further problem with researching esoteric groups is that many of the terms and concepts traditionally used in the milieu have gained meanings and connotations which differ greatly from the ones they originally had, and the risks for misunderstanding and misrepresentation are thus considerable. This applies to scholars working on the esoteric, mistakenly operating with the reinterpreted meanings of terms, but also with practitioners deriving their understanding from, and potentially aligning their beliefs and practices to, scholarly reinterpreted notions. This dual-level reinterpretation needs to be carefully considered.

'Magic' is one of the terms which have the greatest potential for being misunderstood. Many attempts have been made to define magic and distinguish it from religion. In the process of recasting the term as a universally applicable one, particularly under the evolutionary paradigm of early anthropology, 'magic' has come to be associated with 'primitive, but misdirected, science' (Frazer 1994, 46–59), a religion-like activity which lacks a community-building aspect (Durkheim 1995, 41–2), or as offering specific compensation for experienced feelings of deprivation (in contrast to the general compensation offered by 'religion' (Stark and Bainbridge 1996, 36–42). Thus, even though originally native only in European intellectual circles, the term nowadays primarily brings associations of 'primitive religion' and European intellectualist magic is interpreted through accounts of non-European 'primitive religion' (for further discussion, see Lehrich 2003, 10; Pasi 2007, 1,134). Further, magic is often considered a static and more or less transhistorical and transcultural phenomenon, when both historical and cultural contexts should (naturally) be considered (Gregorius 2009, 25). An illustrative example of the problems that may ensue when interpreting modern magicians through the lens of misinformed concepts can be had in Gini Graham-Scott's *The Magicians* (1986). Interpreting magic as 'primitive science', Scott can only come to the conclusion that modern Western individuals engaging in magical practice do so in order to achieve a sense of power and control that they lack in their daily lives. Due to the problematic nature and pejorative character of the term some scholars have suggested that it might be best to forgo its use altogether in scholarly contexts (e.g. Hanegraaff 1996, 80). However, the term is used as a self-designate by many in the contemporary esoteric milieu, and for this reason alone it cannot be discarded (see von Stuckrad 2005b,: 62–63n2).

The esoteric is also full of other terms which, while not as common, imply an aura of antiquity – something which itself makes the esoteric attractive to many – and can easily create misunderstandings. Alchemy is such a term. In the history of science it was for a long time common to distinguish between alchemy as 'primitive chemistry' and proper scientific chemistry (see Hanegraaff 2012, 191–207), and this idea is still common among laypeople today. However, this distinction is a construction *ex post facto*, and relates to boundary work during the birth of modern science where certain approaches were deemed unscientific and therefore marginalized. Furthermore, it is common, particularly among people drawn to the esoteric themselves, to cast alchemy as a form of 'spiritual' practice and in this distinguish it from early chemistry. This is commonly, and mistakenly (see Hanegraaff 2012, 290–2), attributed to C. G. Jung. For a scholar studying the esoteric it is important to be aware of such recasting of terms and concepts, and not be blinded by emic (or simply uninformed and biased) interpretations.

Connected to the marginalization of certain beliefs and practices and the ensuing construction of a semi-coherent 'esoteric tradition', alchemy has come to be lumped together with astrology and magic (and at times others, such as Kabbalah) as 'the occult sciences'. However, historically these practices and systems were originally not as closely related as their post hoc collation might suggest. In fact, the practices often existed in very different social contexts: astrology played an important part in politics (e.g. to calculate the correct dates for the coronation of kings and popes), alchemy in science and medicine (e.g. Paracelsus' medical theories and practices), and magic in religious practice (von Stuckrad 2010, 115, 143–6). Noting these historical separations, and the processes by which 'the occult sciences' came to be lumped together, is important in order to properly analyse modern esoteric discourse as well.

There are also modern terms which may interfere in the proper analysis of esoteric groups and practices. While other terms could be mentioned, the category of 'Shamanism' is one of the most crucial ones to deconstruct. This term, conceived of as a 'universal and archaic technique of ecstasy', and often as the 'original form of religion', was popularized due to the influence of Mircea Eliade (Eliade 1989), who himself drew on the work of Finnish Folklorists engaged in national-romantic pursuits (see Asprem and Granholm 2013, 38–43; Znamenski 2007, 28). Eliade was strongly influenced by the Traditionalist current of modern esotericism, and his creation of Shamanism as a universal religiosity is in itself a form of the notion of *philosophia perennis* (Wasserstrom 1999, 38, 40; Asprem and Granholm 2013, 42. For Traditionalism, see Sedgwick 2004). Shamanism has in turn influenced a creation upon a creation in the form of Neoshamanism. Due to the marginalization of the esoteric, it can be easy not to notice when it influences scholarship.

Researching Esoteric Groups in Practice

By current definitions, demarcations, and descriptions, the study of esoteric groups does not imply looking at a particular 'genre' of religiosity. Rather, it implies a particular focus, looking at phenomena in specific ways. This might involve a focus on how claims to higher knowledge are articulated, which methods are used to access it and how this in turn affects community building and social relations. It might also involve analysis of the social processes involved in the marginalization of certain phenomena (i.e. the very construction of the category of the esoteric), and, particularly in contemporary times, how the marginalized status of certain phenomena is used as a 'marketing device' on the religious market place. Not least, 'the esoteric' could be used as a scholarly tool to shed light on the interplay between the secular and the religious, and highlight phenomena that do not fully fit either bill. This means that Neopagan groups, for example, can be studied without much explicit focus on the esoteric, as has been common, but they can also be approached by the perspectives and approaches offered by scholarship on the esoteric.

Still, while researching esoteric groups does not in any substantial way differ from researching 'non-esoteric' groups, and the same research methods and approaches used for studying other religious and social communities commonly apply, the potential for misunderstanding and misrepresentation due to ingrained and ultimately false notions regarding the nature of esotericism requires the reiteration of some basic points concerning research methodology. Thus, it is of utmost importance to do the necessary background research and familiarize oneself with the history of the terms and practices used instead of relying on 'common sense interpretations'. For example, Scott's *The Magicians* (1986) is made nearly unusable by the numerous errors in regard to almost every aspect of philosophy, practice and administrative structures of the groups she examines. On the other side of the coin, Tanya Luhrman's *Persuasion of the Witch's Craft* (1989), while far superior to Scott's study and rightfully considered a classic, has a tendency to make uncritical use of insider perspectives instead of relying on more unbiased sources.

There is one area, though, where the study of the esoteric differs more or less greatly from the study of most other religious and social groups. This is when looking at initiatory societies. In contrast to the field of religion in general, the esoteric milieu since the eighteenth century, and increasingly so in the twentieth, has involved social groupings in which information and material are divulged to the members in a gradual, formalized and ritualized way. This may potentially introduce problems for the researcher interested in such groups. How is one to gain access to such material? In my own research on the magic order Dragon Rouge (for the most recent accounts, see Granholm 2012; forthcoming). I joined the order and went through the same initiatory steps as any other members, and in that order gained access to the order's material. Consequently I also gained a deep ethnographic insight into the practice of Dragon Rouge which would not have been possible by simply accessing the order's material. Going this route, however, does raise ethical questions that need to be carefully considered. For example, should one identify oneself as a researcher and clarify one's intentions with the research? In current ethnographic practice, doing covert research is deemed to be (more or less) unacceptable, and the view that it does often yield poorer results is common (see e.g. Richardson 1991, 64–70). Furthermore, in participatory research the researcher will gain access to material, information, and experiences that those researched may not want to see published. For example, the researcher might witness conflicts among members that those involved would rather keep private. It is difficult to give a definite answer as to a proper code of conduct in instances such as this. Ultimately it is up to the researcher's sense of integrity and his or her respect for those researched. In my own research, particularly as I have befriended some of the people researched, I have resolved the issue by strictly clarifying when I am in fact doing research and when I am talking to informants as a private individual. Certainly, this might have disqualified some interesting information as valid field data, but it has also secured my possibility to remain in the field and do longitudinal research. In contrast to my own experiences, I have by way of anecdote heard of colleagues who could only gain access to the material of esoteric groups by *not* being members. This is due to them not engaging in the initiatory processes of the groups in question, and thus not having these processes sabotaged by accessing higher degree materials before their due time. In any case, the researcher needs to carefully negotiate his or her entry into the field or access to material, and be prepared to change research methodologies and foci depending on what kind of access is possible. There may also be instances where access is simply impossible by conventional means, or where sufficient access would be too time-consuming or expensive to be feasible. With the opportunities afforded by the internet it is often possible to access material which would previously have been inaccessible. It is then up to each researcher's moral judgement of what is acceptable use and what is not. An example would be the leaked OT-level material of the Church of Scientology. Reaching these levels would be difficult in a normal research situation, and the discussion of the material connected to those levels unacceptable by edict of the group in question if reaching so far. Is it then acceptable to use the documents which were leaked on the internet some years ago? In any case, the authenticity and representability of any documents which are obtained by unofficial means need to be meticulously established.

Finally, I want to highlight one of the major benefits of the perspectives offered by the study of the esoteric and their applicability for research on religious groupings today; the potential to problematize and historically deconstruct the taken-for-granted separateness of religion and science. This affords unique opportunities to investigate religious and social change in the contemporary West, particularly in a time when many sociological core assumptions are put to question. This also relates to contemporary processes where the previously marginalized is becoming mass-popularization in the contemporary West (see Partridge 2004a, 2005, 2013), largely under the influence of modern communication technologies and entertainment media. If secularism, an ideology and discourse presenting non-religious interpretative models as superior to religious ones, have been hegemonic since early modernity, then we can today see the emergence of discourses which erode this hegemony and are prepared to provide new and expanded societal and cultural roles for religion. These discourses may be termed post-secular, as they engage with and are dependent on the previous hegemony of secularism (for this understanding of 'post-secular' and its relation to the understandings of Jürgen Habermas and others, see Granholm 2013c; Moberg, Granholm and Nynäs 2012, 3–8), and the individualistic ethos of much esotericism appears to resonate with the sensibilities of a 'post-secular age'.

Note

1 It should be noted that 'New Age' is a highly problematic concept. No scholarly consensus as to what exactly should be included under the label exists, and the result is that 'New Age' remains an amorphous category into which more or less anything can be incorporated. For this reason, the issue of whether 'New Age' in its totality falls within esotericism is also complex (for the connection between esotericism and 'New Age', see Hanegraaff 1996). For myself I have resolved the issue by using a stricter definition of 'New Age Movement', principally consisting of what Hanegraaff describes as 'New Age in a strict sense' (1996, 98–103), and regard the movement as an

esoteric current which had its heyday from the 1970s to the early 1990s (i.e. the movement was more or less past its prime when scholars started writing about it, although its impact on later forms of esotericism was considerable and remnants remain and surface quite strongly from time to time). In the perspective of esoteric currents as discursive complexes, discussed shortly above, the New Age Movement operates with discourses concerning the coming of an enlightened new age for humanity, and *new thought*-discourses concerning the power of the human mind to create its reality along with discourses on the *human potential* for extraordinary, even supernatural, feats. If these components are not present, particularly the notion of the coming of a glorious new age, the label 'New Age' simply does not fit. For a more detailed discussion of my take on 'New Age' and of the discursive approach advocated here, see Granholm 2013a.

22 African New Religious Movements

Afe Adogame

Chapter Outline	
Terminology	236
The Historiography of ANRMs	237
Africa as Object	239
Africa as Subject	243
Islam-related ANRMs	244
Indigenous ANRMs	246
The Afrikania Mission or Sankofa	247
Mungiki	248
ANRMs in the Diaspora	249
Conclusion	250

The African continent covering about 30 million square area kilometres, comprising at least 50 countries with over 800 million people, is characterized by complex historical, cultural, religious, social, and linguistic affinities and diversities. The innumerable ethnic, social groupings have cultures, each different from the other, but which together represent the mosaic of cultural diversity of Africa. Religious vitality and revitalization are very pronounced in sub-Saharan Africa. African religions comprise the indigenous religions of various African societies that share common affinities in their religious ideas, rituals and worldviews. The emergence and expansion of Islam, Christianity, eastern and Western-related spiritualities saw the introduction of new religious ideas and practices into indigenous religions. The encounter transformed indigenous religious thought and practice but did not supplant it; indigenous religions preserved some beliefs and rituals but also adjusted to the new sociocultural milieu. Owing to social changes, aspects of indigenous beliefs and rituals were abandoned, transformed or reinvented with the impingement of European, Arab and Asian religious cultures. The change also led to the revivification of other aspects of the indigenous religions and cultures. In many cases, Islam and Christianity became domesticated on the African soil. The contact produced new religious movements, with some appropriating indigenous symbols and giving them a new twist.

The sustained mutual influence of and interaction between the various indigenous and exogenous religions that characterize the religious landscape of Africa have produced new religious constellations that continue to attract scholars, policy makers, media and public attention. The interface of religious cultures of sub-Saharan Africa with globalization needs to be located against the backdrop of the interlocking relationship and mutual enhancement of the various old and new religions rather than in any unilateral perspective. Some new movements have appropriated symbols and employed religious imagery from one or the other religious tradition, giving them a novel interpretation and producing a new kind of religious creativity.

Terminology

From a historical-descriptive point of view, African new religious movements (ANRMs) refer to the various religious initiatives that have emerged both within and outside Africa, especially since the dawn of the twentieth century. The groups in this category are mainly African-led and Africans largely dominate their membership. ANRMs cut across Christianity, Islam, indigenous religions, and include spiritual science movements impacting on African religious landscapes. These religious formations are hardly considered as new in terms of any novelty of their ideologies, the originality of beliefs, practices, polity and ethos. Rather, they are groups whose emergence is historically unprecedented in the specific local contexts where they have emerged. For instance, within Christianity, ANRMs include newer forms of Christianity succeeding mainline Christianity, and which have reshaped, and revitalized contemporary Christianity. Christian ANRMs include the so-called African Initiated Churches (AICs), and the African Pentecostal/Charismatic movements. Many other ANRMs have emerged from Islam and the indigenous African religions. The acronym fits because they are movements that usually fall outside the gamut of mainstream religiosity in their specific local contexts. Thus, new religious movements (NRMs) refer to non-mainstream religions within the African context, although some have experienced vertical-horizontal growths, increasing institutionalization, and take on public roles that enhance their visibility and social relevance.

ANRMs remain useful as a typology when our defining criteria focus on it as a recent phenomenon and based also on its positioning as a non-mainstream religion. My appropriation of NRMs to envelope new indigenous religious creativities in Africa marks a departure from popular definitions as cults and sects, although it may not necessarily eliminate all the definitional characteristics employed by anti-cultists, pro-cultists, countercultists. While my definition may cover a wide spectrum of religious movements across Christianity, Islam, indigenous religious, spiritual science movements, I would not necessarily locate them under the same terminological corpus with 'cults' and 'sects' as some Western scholars have done (cf. Braden (1951), Larson (1982), Martin (1985), Mackenzie and Morrison (1992)).

The Historiography of ANRMs

The historiography of ANRMs spans the colonial era, particularly from the early twentieth century to the contemporary period. The period in which virtually all African societies were subjugated under colonialism coincided with when the indigenous religions (re-)encountered Christianity, Islam and eastern and Western-related spiritualities in a much more dynamic way. While some new religious movements were indigenous and home spun, others grew out of external stimuli and influence from outside Africa. Although Islam and Christianity were introduced to various parts of Africa much earlier, it was from the colonial historical phase that there emerged a renewed religious encounter, interaction and competition. The *raison d' étre*, motivations and modus operandi of ANRMs are diverse as the movements themselves. While it is difficult to generalize on *why* these new religions are emerging, any attempt to understand this development must take cognizance of *how* and *where* they are emerging in different historical epochs. A multiplicity of factors is adduced by scholars to explain the emergence and mobility of ANRMs. Certain factors may be more prominent than others depending on the specific context, remote and immediate circumstances surrounding their emergence and expansion.

Religious fervour, charismatic vision, religious expansion and innovation, cultural renaissance, economic empowerment, personality clashes, land dispute, social and religious protest combined with the desire for religious and political self-determination, have inspired a variety of NRMs throughout Africa. Thus, an understanding of the complex identities of NRMs in Africa is central to any definition and description of their growth locally and globally. ANRMs have been defined from a variety of perspectives. The collective identities of NRMs also derive from each group's self-identity.

Historians pay attention to biographies of leaders who reshaped the religious landscape. Phenomenologists of religion look into the interior of the phenomenon, and search for its specific features and inner spirituality. This has produced conclusions that some of the NRMs, like the AICs movement, have used an indigenous religious stamp in shaping a new version of Christianity. Missiologists and theologians express concern about the potentials of tapping into unwholesome spirits in these movements, and regard the movements as syncretistic, routes back to tradition, heathenism, neo-traditional or post-Christianity.

Social science approaches of ANRMs explain them as products of social change and seek to investigate how indigenous structures respond to external change agents. To account for their emergence and spread in Africa, some works of a sociological and historical nature concentrate on the role of deprivation and anomie as causes of growth (Clarke 2006; Daneel 1971, 1988; Oosthuizen 1989, 1992; Robbins 1988; Sundkler 1961; Welbourn 1961). Akin to a Marxist analysis of religion, ANRMs were largely described as an urban phenomenon, the religion of the poor, the masses, the disenfranchised and displaced persons. Cargo cults are portrayed as irrational quests for wealth or manifest cases of neurosis and crisis. Some scholars regard the new religions that emerged during the colonial era in Africa as manifestations of social or religious protest – by-products of the struggle for political self-determination and the establishment of independent nation states (cf. Hinchliff 1972). ANRMs are mirrored as covert protest movements against colonialism. Ethiopian, Zionist, Aladura, Spirit, prophetic and Kimbanguist movements which emerged and proliferated in various regions of sub-Saharan Africa in the wake of European colonialism were interpreted as one response of Africans to the loss of cultural, economic and political control. Some arose in reaction to European Christianity and played a significant role in postcolonial struggle for independence.

The political factor in terms of social or religious protest hardly does justice to the complex phenomenon. The resilience of the AICs in post-independent Africa makes this explanation tenuous. Similar movements continue to emerge that can rarely be linked to any forms of social or religious protest. This welter of social science perspectives often undercut dimensions of new religious cultures. The narrow emphasis on the *why* of conversion and recruitment undermines *how* ANRMs negotiate or transform the cultures into which they are introduced. Any causative explanation must take into consideration the internal religious dynamic and characteristics of a specific NRM and its articulation within external social processes. The rich, local varieties, manifestations, expressions and experiences of ANRMs shed light on considering them as a global phenomenon.

The attempt to provide causal explanations of and to typologize ANRMs proves daunting owing to their complex histories, cultural backgrounds, and wide permutations in their spiritualities and polities. In the early years of several NRMs in Africa, typologies and terminologies were employed, quite often loosely and derogatorily, to characterize the complex genre. Most of the labels employed as a descriptive idiom for ANRMs have been abandoned owing to the burden of monocausal explanations of origins or the overemphasis of one characteristic feature to the detriment of their internal dynamics.

Two main phases can be identified in the evolution of ANRMs historiography. The first era (prior to the 1950s) was mainly defined and dominated by Western (European) scholarship. The second phase (from the 1950s and 1960s onwards) witnessed the emergence of African scholars and their integration in the academic enterprise on ANRMs. Platvoet's (1996) historical exploration of the study of the religions of Africa as a shift from two overlapping phases 'Africa as object' to 'Africa as subject' is illuminating in comprehending the evolution of ANRMs scholarship. The earlier refers to an epoch when ANRMs were studied virtually exclusively by scholars, and other observers, from outside Africa; and the latter, when the religions of Africa had begun to be studied also, and increasingly mainly, by African scholars. Although the second phase is still largely dominated by Western scholars, African scholars have further enriched the field, bringing rich insights and fresh perspectives.

Africa as Object

One of the earliest ANRMs that has attracted the robust scholarly gaze and interpretation of several Western scholars is what became known as the African Initiated (or Independent) Churches. Amateur ethnographers, colonial and academic anthropologists, liberal Christian missionaries, historians, political scientists, sociologists, psychologists, missiologists, theologians and others took their fair share in presenting and representing ANRMs in the colonial years and the immediate post-independent period in the 1950s and 1960s. The indigenous religious creativity crystallizing in the acronym, AICs represent one profound development in the transmission and transformation of African Christianities. AICs started to emerge from the 1920s and 1930s under similar but also remarkably distinct historical, religious, cultural, socio-economic and political circumstances particularly in the western, southern, central and eastern fringes of the continent. The AICs have received considerable scholarly attention since the 1940s. Available literature reveals the dominance of theological, missiological, sociological perspectives. While the earliest historical developments, theologies and hierarchical structures of these churches have been largely documented; their growth process in contemporary time has been left largely under-investigated.

The acronym 'AICs' is used variously by scholars to refer to 'African Initiated Churches', 'African Indigenous Churches', 'African Independent Churches' and 'African Instituted Churches'. There is no consensus as to which phrase is most appropriate. This classification in its narrow sense refers to the indigenous churches that emerged and succeeded the mission churches in different parts of Africa especially from the dawn of the twentieth century. The explanations offered by scholars for their emergence vary from religious to cultural, political to economic and social to psychological factors. Examples of pioneering work carried out by scholars in this field include Bengt Sundkler (1948), Christian Baeta (1962), Victor Hayward (1963), Harold W. Turner (1967), John Peel (1968), David Barrett (1968) and Gerard Oosthuizen (1967).

Bengt Sundkler was one of the pioneer scholars who engaged systematic exploration of what later partly became popularized as AICs. His pivotal study ended in a monograph, *Bantu Prophets in South Africa*, published in 1948. He conducted research in rural KwaZulu during the mid-1940s. Sundkler took a terminological leap over a decade later by opting for Bantu Independent Churches as against the official appellation of Native Separatist Churches. The labels Native, Separatist and his own appropriation of Bantu were considered offensive baggage, and thus attracted a critical uppercut in the very tensile racial, political atmosphere that characterized apartheid South Africa.

With the limitations of 'Bantu' as more of a linguistic rather than a racial category, 'African' appeared as a more-embracing replacement that took cognizance not only of the partly racial sense but also of religious manifestations elsewhere within the continent. The categorization of these indigenous religious initiatives as independent, separatist, syncretistic, protest, nativistic, tribal, Neopagan, spiritist, sectarian, nationalist, Hebraic, cultic, messianic, post-Christian, at different levels of their histories reveals the ideological, political, religious orientations and climate which pervade scholarship as well as the public sphere at the time. Although most of the labels are now obsolete, some contemporary scholars still continue to appropriate these loaded terms or their variations. In spite of the criticisms, 'African Independent Churches' has received a more popular acclamation as a working definition, as a provisional terminology that was perceived to be far less-nuanced.

Some of the early AIC typologies are provided by Sundkler (1948; Oosthuizen (1968); Barrett (1968); and Turner (1979). One of the less-polemical categories adopted to aggregate a large genre of independent churches in South Africa was Zionist-type churches (Sundkler 1976). AICs in South Africa have received significant scholarly attention and the existing literature is quite extensive. These include: Oosthuizen (1967, 1992); West (1975); Daneel (1987); Oosthuizen and Hexham (1992); and Kiernan (1990). Sundkler popularized his broad distinction between two types of South African Independent churches, which he described as Ethiopian and Zionist (1948, 53). In Zimbabwe, Marthinus Daneel made the same distinction between the 'Spirit-type' and 'Ethiopian-type' churches. 'Zionist' or 'Spirit-type' corresponds to the term 'prophet-healing', and distinguishes 'prophetic movements which emphasize the inspiration and revelation of the Holy Spirit, from the non-prophetic church groups' (Daneel 1971, 285). In West Africa, Christian Baeta dealt extensively with this phenomenon to be later popularized in Ghana as 'Spirit' or 'Spiritist' churches (Baeta 1962). Harold Turner (1967) and John Peel (1968) popularized AICs with their seminal works on the Aladura phenomenon in western Nigeria. The scenario in pre-independent Kenya was not any different as Welbourn and Ogot studied AICs in western Kenya (Welbourn 1961, Welbourn and Ogot 1966). An earlier significant work that dealt on the AICs in Kenya was that of Jomo Kenyatta (1962 [1938]).

David Barrett's *Schism and Renewal in Africa: An Analysis of Six Thousand Contemporary Religious Movements* (1968) was based on three years' research in Africa to compile data on these movements and to elaborate the theory of independency. He applied a rudimentary cross-cultural methodology to show that these movements of renewal and independency emerge spontaneously from a well-defined background of social and religious tension, whose strength is assessed for any particular ethnic group on a scale of 18 variable factors, account for the presence or absence of independency in that ethnic group. He covers 'the widespread phenomenon in which large numbers of former adherents of mission churches have seceded in order to assert their right to freedom from a larger ecclesiastical control, and in which others have founded new movements and organizations independent of direct or indirect control from the Western world' (Crane 1969, 359). Barrett's research methods were heavily criticized for generalizations in his broad study of the one single phenomenon of independency among so many African ethnic groups, instead of an in-depth study of one single society. In spite of the criticisms, Barrett highlighted series of parallels in movements of independency from one part of Africa to another. The book also demonstrates how the dynamic nature of African religious creativity produced a phenomenon in some respects unique in the history of religious movements. The whole movement is shown in the conclusion to represent one of the most remarkable achievements of the African genius for religion.

It was perhaps Harold W. Turner who popularized and gave AICs a distinctive identity marker as ANRMs by launching it into global academic discourse. Turner researched in Nigeria and wrote an ethnographic description of a significant new religious movement, The Church of the Lord Aladura (Turner 1967). From this previous intensive study, Turner employed phenomenological, sometimes theological perspectives, and developed a comparative framework for studying what he called PRINERMS (New Religious Movements in Primal Societies). According to Turner, the African religious landscape was so varied and distinctive that the particular movements found there had to be designated by different names. But more importantly, Turner points out that the impact of Western culture and missionary domination have changed African traditions, offering new forms of religion in what he called 'Modern African Religious Movements'.

In an attempt to bring definitional clarity to the expanding phenomenon, Turner adduced a provisional definition of African Independent Churches in the late 1960s as 'churches founded in Africa, by Africans and for Africans'. While this definition may appear to hold water especially when located within the specific milieu within which Turner first wrote, contemporary demographic profiles and the expanding geographies of these churches now render his definitional gaze suspect and short-sighted. Turner's suggestion that AICs were intended to be primarily for Africans or that those movements have all African membership are hardly tenable. Even the appropriateness of 'Independent' was revisited by several scholars.

The resilience and dynamism that characterized these churches in post-independent Africa, coupled with their rapid proliferation and splinter formations, reified the politics and inherent polemics that galvanize such a terminological construct. This opened the floodgate to alternative terminologies such as 'African [Initiated, Indigenous, Instituted, International] Churches'. The revolving abbreviation, 'AIC', in all of them may lend credence to the fact that the designations do not necessarily suggest varied connotations beyond their semantic variations.

Besides providing an extensive history and phenomenology of the Church of the Lord Aladura, Turner devoted much of his research life contributing and sometimes championing theoretical, typological and methodological debates about ANRMs (1967, 1977, 1979). The subject that attracted his research interest since the late 1950s, and in fact throughout his academic career, led to his personal collection of primary and secondary data on these movements while teaching in universities in West Africa in the 1960s. His rich collection on 'New Religious Movements in Primal Societies' was first housed at the University of Aberdeen until 1981, when it moved to the Central Library of Selly Oak Colleges. On his retirement, he donated his unique, extensive documentation to the Selly Oak Colleges Library, where he set up the Study Centre for New Religious Movements in Primal Societies, with himself as its first Director until retirement in 1986. During this time he continued to add new materials to the collection. The Harold Turner Collection became an internationally renowned centre with approximately 27,000 items. It is a unique and specialized collection, comprising documents from journals, books, unpublished papers, newspapers, original material from the movements themselves, and dissertations.

The Centre metamorphosed under different names as: The Study Centre for New Religious Movements in Primal Societies, 1981–4; The Centre for New Religious Movements, 1984–91; INTERACT Research Centre, 1991–5; The Centre for the Study of New Religious Movements, 1996–9; and finally Research Unit for New Religions and Churches, the name change necessitated by the transfer to the University of Birmingham in August 1999. By the 1990s, NRMs in primal societies had come to be recognized alongside the so-called world religions – Hinduism, Buddhism, Islam, Judaism and Christianity. Turner's phenomenological perspective brought to light the diversity of ANRMs in contemporary world.

Africa as Subject

The legacies and foundational works of earlier scholars on ANRMs were enlivened by a sustained interest of a new generation of African and Western scholars. Omoyajowo's *Cherubim and Seraphim: The History of an African Independent Church* (1982); Friday Mbon's *Brotherhood of the Cross and Star: A New Religious Movement in Nigeria* (1992); and Afe Adogame's *Celestial Church of Christ: The Politics of Cultural Identity in a West African Prophetic-Charismatic Movement* (1999) were some of the notable monographs emanating from West Africa. Other works on NRMs in Nigeria included Rosalind Hackett's (ed.) *New Religious Movements in Nigeria* (1987); Jacob Olupona's *New Religious Movements in Contemporary Nigeria* (1989, 1991). Some significant works that dealt on the AICs in Kenya include Cynthia Hoehler-Fatton's *Women of Fire and Spirit: Faith and Gender in Roho Religion in Western Kenya* (1996) and Francis Githieya's *The Freedom of the Spirit: African Indigenous Churches in Kenya* (1997).

While we have focused above solely on ANRMs with Christian extraction, there are numerous Christian-related ANRMs such as the diverse African-led Pentecostal/Charismatic movements that have further diversified the religious landscape of Africa and the African diaspora (for an overview, see Adogame 2010). The most recent development within African Christianity is the emergence and proliferation of Pentecostal/Charismatic Churches, especially from the 1950s and 1960s onwards. There have been two waves of Pentecostal movements, the indigenous Pentecostal groups such as the Redeemed Christian Church of God, the Deeper Life Bible Church, Winners Chapel; and those such as the Four Square Gospel Church, the Full Gospel Businessmen Fellowship International, Campus Crusade for Christ, Youth with a Mission, and Christ for all Nations, which exist as branches or missions of Pentecostal organizations outside Africa.

At the same time, the genre is even more diverse with new religious collectivities related to and emanating from Islam and the indigenous religions alike. It would appear that the literature on Christian-related NRMs is fairly more extensive than that on Islam, indigenous religious and eastern esoteric and western-related spiritual science movements in Africa. This only suggests that the former are more extensively studied and written about than the latter. On the whole, Africa remains and represents one of the most dynamic religious/

spiritual laboratories of the world. In the following paragraphs I shall draw briefly on examples of new religious developments within Islam and the indigenous religions in Africa and the African diaspora.

Islam-related ANRMs

Islam penetrated sub-Saharan Africa in the eleventh century, long before the advent of European Christianity in the fifteenth century. It spread through North Africa by conquest, but the situation differed considerably in sub-Saharan Africa where it took on the insignia of trade and commerce. Islam pursued a conversion policy that became successful in several sub-Saharan countries over the centuries. Its spread to sub-Saharan Africa revealed its commercial and sometimes military outlook. Until about 1450, Islam provided the major external contact between sub-Saharan Africa and the world. The Islamization process also served to link sub-Saharan Africa more closely internally through trade, religion and politics (Brenner 1993; Trimingham 1968).

The emergence of Islamic civilization coincides largely with the spread of Sufi philosophy in Islam. New religious, economic, and political patterns developed in relation to the Islamic surge, but great diversity remained. Thus, there is now a considerable variety of Islamic-related NRMs in Africa. The dynamics of contemporary Muslim communities could be expressed as 'African Islam' and 'Islam in Africa' (Rosander and Westerlund 1997). The former refers to Muslim beliefs and practices that Africans have contextualized over the years, often under the guidance of Sufis, and the latter refers to the ideology of religious reform, usually articulated in the Islamist call for greater implementation of the *sharia*.

Islamic influence upon Africa is largely confined to the Sunnis and their Sufi traditions, groups that have interacted with African cultures to produce varied Islam-related NRMs. The spread of Sufism has been considered a definitive factor in the spread of Islam, and in the creation of integrally Islamic cultures, especially in Africa.

Sufism is popular in such African countries as Morocco and Senegal, where it is seen as a mystical expression of Islam (Babou 2007). Sufism is traditional in Morocco but has seen a growing revival with the renewal of Sufism around contemporary spiritual teachers such as Sidi Hamza al Qadiri al Boutshishi. Mbacke (2005) suggests that one reason Sufism has taken hold in Senegal is because it can accommodate local beliefs and customs, which tend towards the mystical.

Islamic Sufi Orders (Brotherhoods) such as the Qadiriyya, Tijaniyya, Ahmadiyya, Muridiyya and Yan Izala emerged in sub-Saharan Africa, thus creating several Muslim identities. The Qadiriyya and Tijaniyya movements are most prominent in West Africa with the latter spreading across Nigeria, Senegal,

Mali, Guinea, Chad, Cameroon and Ivory Coast (Levtzion 1994). In Eastern and Central Africa, their expansion was much more recent (Trimingham 1980, 78). Muridiyya (Muridism) is claimed by its members as the first Brotherhood in sub-Saharan Africa founded by a Wolof (Senegal) Sufi, Sheikh Ahmadu Bamba, who was a former member of the Qadiriyya Brotherhood. Political Islam has also gained firm roots among Muslim communities and has become intricately connected to global discourses and networks. The Islamic reformist movement, Al-Muwahhiddun (Wahhabism), also known as Salafis, has spread across African countries such as Ivory Coast, Mali and Guinea. A few Islamic-influenced spirit-possession movements which appealed to women and marginal groups include the Zar in Ethiopia and Sudan in the nineteenth century, the Kitombo of the Kamba in Kenya in the 1890s, the Maouka of the Songhay in Niger in the 1920s, the Lebu in Senegal and the Bori movement among the West African Hausas in the twentieth century.

Turner (1993) chronicles NRMs in 'Islamic West Africa' focusing on NRMs such as the Láye Fraternity of Seydina Limamu in Cape Verde and Senegal; the Mourides of Amadou Bamba – the Muridiyya Brotherhood in Senegal and whose influence extended to Mauritania, Ivory Coast and Zaire; the Hamallism or Reformed Tijaniyya Islamic movement founded by Shaykh Sidi Muhammed in Mali. The diversity and complexity of Islamic movements in Nigeria are partly exemplified by the Sufi Orders. Two major movements involved in the Islamization process in Nigeria were the Qadiriyya and Tijaniyya. The former is much older and has spread widely in northern Nigeria since the nineteenth century. The Qadiriyya emphasizes intellectual pursuits more than the Tijaniyya (which was introduced in the same century).

Other Islamic organizations oppose these brotherhoods on the basis of doctrine. Thus Yoruba Muslims have formed various societies whose task is to provide Muslims with a modern education that does not conflict with Islamic values. The Ahmadiyya Brotherhood considers itself as followers of a contemporary interpretation of Sunni Islam. They are very influential in Nigeria, Benin, Sierra Leone, Liberia and Ghana which serve as its West African headquarters. It has spread to Eastern African countries of Tanzania and Kenya with Nairobi serving as its East African headquarters. In Nigeria, the Ahmadiyya Muslim movement has made significant impact in the southwest, where it is very popular. In 1923 a group broke away and formed the Ansar-ud-Deen Society. Both movements have enhanced the development of secular education, particularly in Southwest Nigeria. The Ansar-ud-Deen was probably the most popular of these Muslim educational organizations. By 1960 it already ran numerous primary and secondary schools and training colleges.

The Izala (*Jamaatu Izalat al-Bida*) emerged in 1978, enjoining its members to reject innovation and instead to work for the preservation of the Sunna. The leading representative of Izala until his death in 1992 was Abubakar Gumi, whose most important concern was to try to unite Muslims politically. However, between 1978 and 1985, many northern Nigerian towns and cities were shaken by the armed insurrections led by Mohammed Marwa Maitatsine and his Yan Tatsine movement.

Maitatsine had a long history of fomenting Islamic unrest in northern Nigeria. The source of his inspiration was the belief, especially in Sufi Islam, that a *mujaddid* (reformer) will arise each century to purify and revitalize Islam. Maitatsine's brand of Islam seemed largely to combine traditional Muslim conceptions with local indigenous elements.

Islam has also witnessed the emergence of NRMs like the Nasru-Lahil-Fatih Society of Nigeria (NASFAT), founded in Lagos in 1995 by Alhaji Abdul-Latif Olasupo to cater to the spiritual and practical needs of young, educated, and upwardly mobile Muslims, and to grapple with contemporary developments while sustaining Islamic goals. NASFAT, like other Islamic societies such as Ansarud-Din, Ansarul-Islam, Anwarul-Islam, Ahmadiyyah movement, Islahud-Din, Istijabah Group of Muslims, and the Qareeb Society, now has branches in various parts of Nigeria and abroad. One of the most recent NRMs in Nigeria that has attracted local and global attention is the group popularly referred to as Boko Haram. The Boko Haram uprising since July 2009 was significant in that it not only set a precedent, but also reinforced the attempts by Islamic conservative elements at imposing a variant of Islamic religious ideology on a secular state (Adesoji 2010).

Sufism, but also Dawah movements have attracted scholarly attention owing to their impact on several African societies. Adbulkader Tayob's *Islamic Resurgence in South Africa* (1995) draws attention to the proliferation of the Muslim youth movement, Sufi Orders and Dawah movements in South Africa. Knut Vikor's (2000) survey of the Sufi Orders in many parts of the continent demonstrates the vast networks they have established from the seventeenth century. Muhammed Haron (2005) has shown how, during the last three decades of the twentieth century, the Jama'at al-Tabligh and Dawah movements such as the International Propagation Islamic Centre in Durban established by Ahmad Deedat, Africa Muslim Agency and other Islamic Dawah Movements of South Africa have dominated Dawah activities in the region. His works shed light on the activities of contemporary Sufi Tariqahs (Orders or Brotherhoods) such as the Chistiyyah, Murabitun, Qadriyyah, Alawiyyah, Naqshbandi. This suggests that Islamic-related NRMs are widespread in Africa.

Indigenous ANRMs

Modernizing social change has resulted in the decline of some indigenous practices and modes of thought even as it has brought about a revitalization and modification of others. Any claim that Christianity and Islam have totally outweighed indigenous religion is suspect. The indigenous religious worldview, or aspects of it, still largely pervade, consciously or unconsciously, in the outlook of many Africans regardless of new religious convictions. The pertinence of indigenous religions for many is evident in the resilient belief in supernatural forces, the reality of ancestors and the growing popularity of pantheon of divinities. Kingship rituals, secret societies, masquerades, divination, healing, and oracle systems, and the prevalent belief in the reality of witchcraft and sorcery avenues through which indigenous religions manifest resilience in the face of a complex, multi-religious and rapidly changing society.

The historical and cultural significance of indigenous African religious traditions is partly discerned in their plurality and multivocality both in Africa and the African diaspora. In various parts of Africa, the indigenous religions have encountered other religious forms and responded to social change leading to revitalization of indigenous religions and in some contexts synthesis, reinvention and change. Their dynamism is exemplified by their tendency towards growth and innovation, a development that has given birth to what is now described as neo-traditional or neo-indigenous religious movements. A few examples will suffice here.

West Africa has witnessed the resurgence of neo-indigenous NRMs in the last several decades. A case in point is Ijo Orunmila, a movement founded in the 1930s and seeking to re-establish links with their traditional religious heritage. In 1963 the Arousa Cult (Edo National Church), which developed from Bini indigenous religion, fused with another neo-traditional movement, the National Church of Nigeria, to form Godianism. As we mentioned above, the Bori, a neo-traditional religious movement prominent among Hausa women, draws partly on Islamic beliefs and practices. I shall now focus briefly on two recent neo-traditional religious movements: the Afrikania Mission or Sankofa from Ghana; and the Mungiki from Kenya.

The Afrikania Mission or Sankofa

The Afrikania Mission, also known as the Afrikan Renaissance Mission or Sankofa Faith, marks one striking example of this tendency towards indigenous religious revival. Founded in Ghana in 1982 by Rev. Dr Osofo-Okomfo Kwabena Damuah, a Ghanaian theologian and former ordained priest of the Roman Catholic Church of Ghana, Afrikania took a reformist stance towards the traditional religion (Azasu 1999; Damuah 1998; Gyanfosu 1995). Afrikania has set itself 'the task of redefining, reforming and renaming the Religion of Afrika'. Quite unequivocally, the group discountenances any claim of Afrikania as a new concept and asserts that it is the rebirth, revival and reorganization of the 'Afrikan' traditional religion. Such a religious innovation, with its teaching and modus operandi, was meant as a critique of Christianity and other religious forms considered as external to African sensibilities, but which were also inherently intolerant.

Afrikania indicts slavery and colonization for the loss of African traditional spirituality and criticizes government, foreign diplomatic missions, and non-governmental organizations for corrupting and demonizing traditional values and imposing foreign religious beliefs. Nevertheless, the Catholic background of its founder seem to leave significant Christian imprints in Afrikania's belief and ritual systems, thus producing a religious synthesis. The attempt to re-brand or reposition indigenous African religious traditions has also resulted in the tendency to universalize, canonize and institutionalize it.

Mungiki

The emergence of the Mungiki was linked to the late 1980s when Ibrahim Wairunge (a secondary school leaver) with six other young people co-founded the new religious movement in 1987 (Kagwanga 2003; Wamue 2001). Mungiki's ideology was particularly attractive to Kenyan youths, students, but also the poor, the unemployed within the society. Beyond Mungiki's self-description as a religious movement, public perception varies in considering the group as a political movement. One account suggests that the initial Mungiki members were followers of The Tent of the Living God, another new religious movement founded by Ngonya wa Gakonya in Kenya. Raised as a Christian, in later life he began to question the Christian faith as professed by his parents.

Wa Gakonya was intensely involved in sensitizing people about African religious beliefs through public campaigns. He was banned by the Kenyan government in 1990, arrested and imprisoned. The Tent of the Living God eventually disintegrated, with some members forming a 'splinter movement', the Mungiki. Mungiki and the Tent of the Living God share a similarity in that they emerged owing to a feeling of alienation from the dominant religions in Kenya (Christianity and Islam), and an attempt to seek religious 'truth' in African religious heritage (Wamue 2001). Mungiki's religious and ideological roots are also traceable to Mau Mau as a result of the distinctive nature of their political engagement and resistance (Kagwanja 2003; Kenyatta 1965). A strong desire for the resurgence of indigenous religions and cultures becomes a striking commonality between Mungiki and Mau Mau.

The Mungiki aimed to 'redeem the Gikuyu (Kenyans) from Western culture; to unite the Gikuyu people, and consequently other Kenyans to fight against both "mental" and "political" oppression' (Wamue 2001, 460). This political, religious and cultural liberation was pitched against both colonial and contemporary governments in Kenya. The Mungiki movement locates the enormous crisis and ills of the Kenyan society at the behest of the political apparatus, but also due to the erosion of indigenous values. They demonstrate with optimism that a return to indigenous culture and religion will result in the restoration of indigenous values. To facilitate the restoration of indigenous values, *Kirira*, the teaching of African indigenous values must occur, that will lead to *guthera*, a cleansing ritual where foreign cultures and faiths are denounced through traditional rites (Wamue 2001, 460–1). Mungiki vehemently rejected Christianity and Islam until September 2000 when 13 leaders publicly announced their conversion to Islam, claiming that this would aid their fight against corruption, bad governance, poverty, immorality and diseases in Kenya.

Mungiki members remained critical of successive Kenyan governments despite alleged connections made between their activities and the ruling elite/Kenyan government. The popular understanding of Mungiki's involvement in the electoral violence of the 1997 general elections in Kenya heightens public negative image about them (Kagwanja 2003, 37; Wamue 2001, 466). Their activities mostly considered as subversive by Kenyan security agencies attracted reprehension leading to their eventual proscription in 2002.

Not all neo-traditional movements in Africa have political overtones. There are examples of new religious creativities that are less controversial, whose activities are less prone to conflict and public criticisms. With growing revitalization and internationalization of indigenous religions, many sub-Saharan Africans are beginning to appreciate their 'indigenous' religions. Indigenous peoples have experienced something of a religious revival and have become concerned with the preservation of their cultural and religious heritage. Communal rituals, ceremonies and festivals in commemoration of specific local divinities are becoming internationalized. The annual Osun-Oshogbo festival for the Yoruba Osun divinity in Nigeria has become an international event that attracts devotees and tourists from all parts of the world.

ANRMs in the Diaspora

Most African migrants to Europe, America and elsewhere carried aspects of their religion with them. ANRMs have burgeoned in these contexts owing greatly to increasing transnational migration, improved transportation systems and new forms of global communications networks. In the face of contemporary religious, political and sociocultural realities, ANRMs are increasingly engaged in charting local–global religious networks to further their self-insertion and self-assertion in the host religious landscape.

The African diaspora influences cultures in Brazil, Cuba, and Haiti, partly leading to the development of African-derived religions such as Santería,

Candomblé, Vodou and Yoruba-Orisa traditions across the Americas. In 1981, an Act of Parliament in Trinidad and Tobago raised the Yoruba religion to the status of an official religion. In contemporary Cuba, orisa veneration exists as part of a larger continuum of religious change in the Americas in which religious practices, now known as Santería but also referred to as Lukumi and *regla de ocha*, have transformed the shape of orisa veneration outside of West Africa. These religious forms are proliferating in the diasporic context with their practitioners and clientele widening ethnically and racially. The proliferation of groups of orisa practitioners outside of West Africa continues to attract millions of adherents of Yoruba and Santería religious practices (Clarke 2004, 5). Ifa priests and devotees now include Yoruba, Africans, African Americans and non-Africans alike. 'African-derived religions have entered a new phase with the growing presence of western adepts. These have become part of an evolving tradition' (Bellegarde-Smith 2005, 5). Santería practitioners – some claiming Hispanic roots, others claiming Afro-Cuban national identities, and still others claiming American or African heritage – are active participants in the production of Yoruba-based practices in America (Clarke 2004, 17). The growth of neo-indigenous African religions in the United States and Europe has been characterized by the proliferation of virtual-based religiosity in which most Orisa and Ifa priests exist, operate and communicate through their internet websites with old and new clientele as well as with the wider public.

African Islam was spread to the diaspora through migration. Within the context of the African diaspora, Muslims from parts of Africa brought their religion to North America. Two of such religious groups that emerged to challenge segregation in America and colonialism in Africa were the Moorish Science Temple (Timothy Drew) and the Nation of Islam (Wallace Fard, later known as Farrad Mohammed). Contemporary migration has brought many African Muslims to Europe and North America where they have joined other Muslim immigrants in furthering religious diversification of the host societies. For instance, Somalis, Sudanese and Senegalese Muslims have migrated to Europe and North America particularly in the 1980s and 1990s. Muridism, an integral part of the Sufi Order, has spread around the multi-sited migration network and evolved (Salzbrunn 2004, 489).

Conclusion

With the proliferation of ANRMs in Africa and the African diaspora, Africa has become fully part of a global cosmos in religious terms. The character of ANRMs in conditions of globality will continue to be determined and shaped by how and to what extent they negotiate continuity, identity and change. A consideration of religious development in Africa must be seen in terms of its relation and links with the global context, but also in how and to what extent it interrogates and negotiates wider external influences and global forces. In addition, the ways in which ANRMs are contributing to the enrichment and pluralization of old and new geo-cultural and religious spaces become significant. Africa and its diaspora provide both old and new spaces for the contestation, reinvention and shaping of ANRM's ethos, polity, rituals and worldviews.

23 Vernacular/Lived Religion

Marion Bowman

Chapter Outline

Religion as it Is Lived	253
Vernacular Religion	255
Vernacular Religion, NRMs and Narrative	257
Vernacular Religion, NRMs and Material Culture	259
Case Study in Vernacular New Religiosity:	
The Goddess in – and beyond – Glastonbury	260
Fieldwork and the Study of NRMs	267
Conclusion	268

This chapter explores the relationship between vernacular religion and NRMs, and what vernacular religion as both a category of analysis and field of practice can bring to the study of NRMs. The term vernacular religion describes both *what* is studied and *how* it is researched. An 'interdisciplinary approach to the study of the religious lives of individuals with special attention to the process of religious belief, the verbal, behavioral, and material expressions of religious belief, and the ultimate object of religious belief', the emphasis of vernacular religion is on the need to study religion 'as it is lived: as human beings encounter, understand, interpret, and practice it' (Primiano 1995, 44).

Religion as it Is Lived

The term religion has been defined, contested and negotiated in a number of ways, but there has been growing academic recognition of the need to challenge the supposed homogeneity of any so-called religious tradition. While we conventionally talk about Christianity as if it is self-evidently one thing, it would probably be more helpful and more correct to talk about 'Christianities'. Similarly, to talk about Catholicism, Orthodoxy, Protestantism obscures the considerable variety to be found within such denominations according to time, place, sociopolitical and cultural contexts. Such terms are used as helpful labels, but we should not be fooled into thinking that they represent neat packages of uniform ideas, beliefs and practices that constitute 'pure' or 'real' religion. Religion is not monolithic. What is nominally the 'same' religious tradition turns out differently in different times, cultures and contexts. This is as true for NRMs as it is for other forms of religiosity.

Increasingly within religious studies and the sociology of religion, there has been a trend to pay more attention to what is variously referred to as practical, popular, lived or everyday religion (Ammerman 2007; McGuire 2008; Reader and Tanabe 1998), which attempts to examine and understand the day to day practice, rather than purely the theory, of religion. Reader and Tanabe, for example, writing in the context of contemporary Japanese religion, state

> We treat religion as a matter not only of doctrine and belief but of participation, custom, ritual, action, practice, and belonging. It is as much a matter of social and cultural influences and behavioral patterns located in day to day concerns and the ordinary processes of life – as concerned with ameliorating problems in the present, in producing explanations of why things have gone wrong, and in proposing mechanisms that offer the hope of improvement – as it is with ultimate concerns, theological explanations of the nature of the universe, or the destination of the soul. Rather than reject the term 'religion' defined in narrow theological terms, we employ the word with expansive meanings drawn from a broad spectrum ranging from theological abstractions to mundane practicalities. (1998, 5–6)

Similarly, the focus of vernacular religion is on what people believe, and how this is expressed in everyday life, rather than on some idealized notion of what they should be doing or believing, based on the formal pronouncements of institutionalized forms of religiosity. In this approach, cultural tradition, informal transmission, social mores, local conditions and personal experience must all be given weight as they are constitutive of individuals' perception, performance and experience of religion. This was demonstrated vividly for me some years ago in Newfoundland (Bowman 2000) when a Wiccan woman showed me a maypole erected inside a barn, climate and confidentiality being factors affecting Beltane celebrations there. Similarly, there are inevitably cultural, climactic, political, culinary and other local variations within ISKCON as lived in India, in the United States and in Europe, although it may be regarded as 'the same' NRM. The 'bidirectional influences of environments upon individuals and of individuals upon environments in the process of believing' (Primiano 1995, 44) are variables that have significant qualitative effects in relation to NRMs.

Vernacular Religion

The concept of vernacular religion is 'a theoretical hybrid of several fields studying religion: folklore and folklife; religious studies; religious history; ethnographic disciplines including anthropology, sociology, oral history, and ethnomusicology,' in the words of Leonard Norman Primiano, who has brought the concept to the fore (2012, 383). Primiano claims that vernacular religion's conceptual value lies in the fact that it 'highlights the power of the individual and communities of individuals to create and re-create their own religion' (Primiano 2012, 383): 'It shifts the way one studies religion with the people becoming the focus of study and not "religion" or "belief" as abstractions' (Primiano 2012, 384). The attention to religion as it is lived, and its complex interrelationship with institutional forms of religion, have long been the focus of attention of ethnological/ anthropological/ folkloristic studies in relation to religion: all approaches that rely heavily on fieldwork. This is because many of the activities and experiences which individuals draw upon as proof or confirmation of their worldviews and lifestyles occur outside formally religious settings.

Folklorist Don Yoder succinctly describes folk religion as 'the totality of all those views and practices of religion that exist among the people apart from and alongside the strictly theological and liturgical forms of the official religion' (1974, 14), recognizing the huge and frequently under-studied area of religious life that should be taken into account to provide a rounded picture of religion as it is lived. In an attempt to bring this neglected area more to the fore in religious studies, some years ago I suggested that to obtain a realistic view of religion as it is lived, it should be viewed in terms of three interacting components: official religion (meaning what is accepted orthodoxy at any given time, although this is subject to change), folk religion (meaning that which is generally accepted and transmitted belief and practice, regardless of the institutional view) and individual religion (the product of the received tradition – folk *and* official – plus personal beliefs, interpretations and experiences) (Bowman 2004 [1992]). My point was that different components interact to produce what, for each person, constitutes religion; that these are not 'neat' compartments; that folk religion is not a tidy and easily recognizable category separate from (and possibly inferior to) official religion; and that folk and individual religion are not the result of people getting 'pure' religion wrong.

```
Official Religion  ←——————————→  Folk Religion
             ↘         ↙
          Individual Religion
```

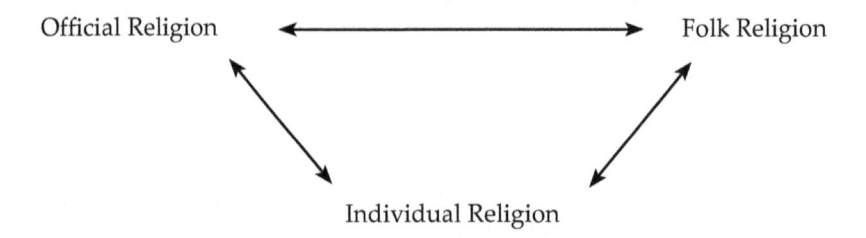

However, folk religion is a contested category within both the study of religions and folklore. Yoder (1974) shows how the term 'folk religion' has been used both by religious professionals and by scholars to make judgements about 'lived religion' in relation to or in contradistinction to 'proper' or official religion. The semantic loading of the term differs, depending on national and historical context. Some European countries have produced rich literatures that discuss the specific meanings attached to the category and the contextual historical, social and intellectual factors that gave rise to these meanings. In the United States, United Kingdom and some other parts of Europe, however, 'vernacular religion' has become the term and concept increasingly used by scholars working at the interstices of folklore/ethnology and religious studies. Primiano rejects any two-tiered model of 'folk' and 'official' religion as it 'residualizes the religious lives of believers and at the same time reifies the authenticity of religious institutions as the exemplar of human religiosity' (1995, 39). Claiming that 'Religious belief takes as many forms in a tradition as there are individual believers' (Primiano 1995, 51), he asserts that no one, including members of institutional hierarchies, 'lives an "officially" religious life in a pure unadulterated form' (Primiano 1995, 46). Thus he calls for scholars to stop perpetuating 'the value judgement that people's ideas and practices, because they do not represent the refined statements of a religious institution, are indeed unofficial and fringe' (Primiano 1995, 46). Whereas, as Yoder shows, there have been many debates over and conceptualizations of folk religion, Primiano problematizes the category of official religion.

Primiano claims that 'One of the hallmarks of the study of religion by folklorists has been their attempt to do justice to belief and lived experience' (Primiano 1995, 41). Building on the tradition of taking a broad and 'realistic' view of religious belief and practice, and employing largely fieldwork-based, qualitative methodology, folklorists and ethnologists have studied a variety of 'folklore genres' (see Bowman and Valk 2012) in relation to how people live their religion. These include festival and custom, such as calendar customs (events that happen on a fixed point each year) and rites of passage; tradition (described by

folklorist Henry Glassie as 'the creation of the future out of the past' (1995, 395));
music, song, dance, drama and both formal and informal ritual performances;
herbalism and healing; 'foodways' including dietary restrictions and fasting,
feasting, festive and regional food; material culture; and, very significantly, narrative. In the context of this chapter, I shall concentrate on the articulation of
worldviews and expressions of belief revealed and articulated in narratives and
material culture in relation to NRMs.

Vernacular Religion, NRMs and Narrative

Contrary to popular usage, and following the example of Ninian Smart, religious studies scholars frequently employ 'myth' as a neutral term to describe
a 'significant story', making no judgement as to the story's truth or falsehood.
'Significant stories' of divine, other than human or human figures and events
have been recognized as a vital element in the foundation of religions, and the
same is true of NRMs. However, the story-telling process itself is an ongoing,
constantly evolving feature of religion, and folklorists/ethnologists studying religion have paid particular attention to narrative in various forms, such
as legend (aetiological, local, historical) and Personal Experience Narratives
(PENs), a key component of vernacular religion. Of particular interest in relation to NRMs, is the 'belief story', characterized by folklorist Gillian Bennett
(1989, 291), as that class of informal stories which illustrate current community beliefs; which tell not only of personal experiences but also of those that
have happened to other people; and which are used to explore and validate the
belief traditions of a given community by showing how experience matches
expectations. Fieldwork-based study of the relationship between belief, practice and narrative produces material that is invaluable not only in the study of
religion in traditional contexts (e.g. Honko 1964) but also in relation to NRMs,
whose foundation myths may be relatively recent and evolving, and less formal
aspects of contemporary spirituality, providing insights into the worldview of
groups and individuals for whom there may be no 'official' spokesperson or
recognized 'canon' of literature. From fieldwork, I have found the dissemination of PENs and belief stories to be powerful confirmatory forces in contexts as
varied as vernacular Catholicism, among devotees of Sathya Sai Baba, and the
'alternative' scene at Glastonbury.

Adherents of the Church of Jesus Christ of the Latter-day Saints (LDS),
popularly known as Mormons, for example, have a distinctive foundation
myth, a canon of writings and highly 'institutionalized' religiosity. However,
lived Mormonism has been well studied for a number of decades in the United
States, with the Brigham Young University Folklore Archives established in
1985, pioneered by LDS adherent and folklorist William A. Wilson. Material

has been gathered here that is valued for what it tells not only about Mormon beliefs and practices, but the ways in which these are alluded to (sometimes humorously), acted out, narrated and confirmed in everyday life, in different locations and in varied social, political, economic or popular culture contexts. A popular narrative with numerous variants in Mormon circles (in different American states and in different countries), for example, involves a loaf of bread baked by a Mormon woman who places it on a tea towel, napkin, embroidered or patterned cloth then puts it on the windowsill to cool. The bread and cloth mysteriously disappear, although there is a variant in which the bread is given to a hungry stranger. Some time later, when the woman's husband/son returns from his distant missionary work, the woman discovers the cloth in his luggage and asks how he acquired it, to be told that one day in the mission field when he had no food, a stranger gave him bread wrapped in the cloth. This motif is familiar in a number of religious traditions, and is indicative of the extent to which people of faith anticipate, perpetuate and accept the possibility of the miraculous in everyday life. The 'Vanishing Hitchhiker' contemporary legend usually involves a driver giving a lift to a hitchhiker, who disappears when they reach the supposed destination, only to be told by the people at the house that the description of the hitchhiker matches a family member who died or disappeared on that date some years before (see Brunvand 1981). There is also a Mormon variant on the 'Vanishing Hitchhiker' studied by Wilson (1975), involving the three Nephites. In the Book of Mormon, the three Nephites appear as disciples of Jesus granted continued earthly existence until the Second Coming, who 'can show themselves unto whatsoever man it seemeth them good' (3 Nephi 28.30, quoted in Brunvand 1981, 35); numerous stories of them appearing to Mormons in difficult circumstances or times have circulated in Mormon cultural tradition. Wilson studied 50 versions of the stories from the Brigham Young University Folklore Archives, in which a hitchhiker dispenses advice to the Mormon driver(s), often about the importance of getting in a store of enough food for a year (officially sanctioned LDS policy from 1936), then disappears to be recognized retrospectively as one of the Nephites. Wilson concluded that such stories were significant in relation (and reaction) to events such as the Korean War and the Cold War, which some were identifying as indicative of the onset of the final apocalypse, during which the food stocks would be needed. The narratives were thus useful indicators of both creative Mormon interaction with and adaptation of popular culture and church teaching.

In the case of Sai Baba devotion, there are numerous belief stories telling of people (often named individuals) in car crashes who, while the car is hurtling over a cliff or whatever, suddenly realize that Sai Baba is in the car with them, telling them that all will be well. The circulation of such stories formally, informally and on the internet confirms for believers the extent to which Sai Baba remains active, and 'proves' his efficacy. In relation to *vibuthi* or the 'holy ash' said to be manifested by Sai Baba, I have been told a PEN of a photograph of him in a believer's home that manifested *vibhuti*, thereby strengthening that woman's devotion, but also sacralizing her home and giving rise to various individual material culture practices involving the ash, such as using the ash for healing purposes. Retelling her PEN and getting it into circulation among her fellow believers validated her belief and that of the hearers. In fieldwork, if a person is asked about religion one common response is to direct the questioner to an authority figure; asking whether the person has ever heard any stories about unusual occurrences about a significant place/person/event/object often leads to belief stories and PENs. As I have commented elsewhere (Bowman 2003–4, 140), scholars

> need to appreciate the value of exploring the significant stories *beyond* the authorised version. We need to know what stories are significant, and for whom. We need to know if a myth is 'live', and how is it being used to inform, construct, support or modify belief in a variety of contexts. If we truly want to engage with 'religion as it is lived: as humans encounter, understand, interpret and practice it' (Primiano 1995, 44), we need to take stories seriously.

Vernacular Religion, NRMs and Material Culture

An important element in the approach of vernacular religion to the study of NRMs is material culture, which can refer to any aspect of the material world, constructed or natural, and it encompasses an enormous range of experiential interaction with the physical world. As David Morgan puts it:

> If culture is the full range of thoughts, feelings, objects, words, and practices that human beings use to construct and maintain the life-worlds in which they exist, material culture is any aspect of that world-making activity that happens in material form. That means things, but it also includes the feelings, values, fears, and obsessions that inform one's understanding and use of things. (Morgan 2008, 228)

This engagement with 'things' is seen in myriad way, such as the use of food as a vehicle for marking special times of the year or ritual events, ensuring 'in group' socialization, or expressing beliefs about either the interconnectedness of species or mastery over other living creatures. Pictures or statues which feature in narratives as actants, or simply give rise to considerable emotion, are indicative of the feelings involved and aroused in relationship to material culture. Clothing can be the marker of special occasions (ceremonial as opposed to everyday dress), of rank, of received aesthetics (the adoption of clothing from a particular location or historical period) or moral appropriateness in relation to gender (e.g. reflecting ideas of modesty) or can be used as hidden but potent reminder of identity (such as Mormon temple garments).

While anthropologists and ethnographers have paid considerable attention to religious material culture, there has been a tendency to underplay its importance in some spheres of religious studies, under the influence of a rather Western, Protestant, intellectual, text-based (and text-biased), belief-based (and belief-biased) approach to the study of religion, suspicious or dismissive of visual and material expressions of religion and some embodied practices of religion from communal ritual to individual devotional practices. However, as Engelke comments, 'The move to materiality allows us to reconsider (and resuscitate) the very concept of *religion* itself . . . Approaching "religion" as "material religion" allows us to consider the material as part and parcel of our interests and of the religious worlds of the people we study' (Engelke 2011, 209). Any study of NRMs which does not include or acknowledge the role of material culture will potentially neglect important aspects of lived religion.

Case Study in Vernacular New Religiosity: The Goddess in – and beyond – Glastonbury

While much is globalized in the contemporary context of NRMs, relationships with local landscape and specific cultural contexts and aesthetics remain significant. Such considerations are exemplified in the following example of a new religious movement, the Glastonbury Goddess movement, and its translocation to Hungary. The case study exemplifies the way in which individuals can discover and create personal spiritual experiences without recourse to traditional and supposedly authoritative sources such as sacred texts or a religious hierarchy. Having said this, however, the Glastonbury Goddess movement itself claims to discover an alternative, lost tradition, and in gaining momentum assumes fresh institutionalized forms. I consider the Glastonbury case here as an example of how the concept of vernacular religion helps elucidate the study of an NRM.

I have conducted a long-term study of religion in Glastonbury, the small town in the southwest of England that is regarded as sacred by a range of people on account of its Christian / Druidic / Celtic / Arthurian / Avalonian / Pagan / Goddess / Earth Energy / interplanetary significance – and many additional reasons (see Bowman 1993, 2005, 2008). One of the most striking features of the past two decades has been the development, flourishing and institutionalization of the Goddess movement in Glastonbury, and the way in which what might be termed the 'Glastonbury Goddess package' has taken root in different parts of Europe, including Hungary (see Bowman 2007 and 2009). By exploring how this has occurred, key concepts of vernacular religion and its use in the study of NRMs emerge. In particular, Glastonbury presents a means of organizing and expressing personal religious experience, enabling religious creativity to combine with wider movements such as feminism, lost traditions that its supporters attempt to re-create, and elements of the local material culture found in Glastonbury's geography.

There has been a variety of influences on the Glastonbury Goddess movement. It can be seen as part of the broader, Western revival of interest in Goddess spirituality, the growth of feminist ideas and the contemporary fascination with pre-Christian, indigenous religiosity. Influenced by the 'survivalism' of early folklore studies, the 'archeo-mythology' of Marija Gimbutas and similar ideas, many in the Goddess movement look back to a golden age of matriarchy, characterized by Eller in the following terms: 'there was no war, people lived in harmony with nature, women and men lived in harmony with one another, children were loved and nurtured, there was food and shelter for all, and everyone was playful, spontaneous, creative, and sexually free under the loving gaze of the goddess' (Eller 1995, 161). Devotion to the Virgin Mary and more particularly to St Bridget in Glastonbury is seen by many involved in the Goddess movement simply as Christian continuities (or subversions) of Goddess worship: 'Where we find St Bridget we know that the goddess Bridie was once honoured' (Jones 2000, 16). (Bride, Bridie, Brigit and Bridget are all regarded as synonymous, and the names are used interchangeably.) Some of its roots may be traced back to late nineteenth- and early twentieth-century Glastonbury, when John Arthur Goodchild was convinced that there had been a female community of Goddess worshippers in Glastonbury, for example, and Alice Buckton had written the sacred drama 'The return of St Bride' (see Benham 1993; Cutting 2004). Marion Bradley's novel *Mists of Avalon* (1982) created and sustains great interest in a female, Goddess-based interpretation of Arthurian legend in Glastonbury.

Although the seeker can draw eclectically on these various sources, the Glastonbury Goddess movement goes beyond personal religious creativity and is presented as very much rooted in Glastonbury's prehistoric and mythical past, and in its landscape. Many people consider that Glastonbury was a significant, ancient, sacred site of Goddess worship, and is now above all a centre of Goddess spirituality, where the Goddess can be 'restored' in her own right. One of the most influential actors in the Glastonbury Goddess movement has been Kathy Jones, author, creator of sacred dramas, and highly creative and charismatic co-founder of the Glastonbury Goddess Conference in 1996. Jones regards The Lady of Avalon as the fundamental Goddess around whom Glastonbury Goddess devotion is centred, and the landscape of Glastonbury as the outer world counterpart of the inner world of Avalon. Jones and others involved in Goddess spirituality there see the Goddess in a variety of figures and features in the landscape of Glastonbury – in one such figure the Tor (a distinctively shaped hill) is considered the left breast of the Goddess, while the red waters of the chalybeate Chalice Well are interpreted as her menstrual flow. Jones also envisages Glastonbury as falling within the landscape outline of a huge swan, 'the swan being one of Bride's totem creatures' (Jones 2000, 14–15).

Here we see religious creativity becoming ritualized, with a sacred calendar emerging, which also draws on other indigenous religious traditions. Although rituals are framed around the eight fold or so-called Celtic calendar, the Glastonbury 'wheel of the year' is also influenced by Native American tradition, typical of the integrative nature and global awareness of contemporary spirituality. It is referred to as Britannia's wheel or Bridget Anna's wheel, the British Isles being thought of as originally Bridget's Isles. There are eight quarters connected with eight Goddesses, animals, colours, and objects, all intimately connected to the landscape of Avalon/ Glastonbury. New moons and full moons are also observed. Rather than the more common threefold 'maiden, mother, crone' form, the Glastonbury Goddess is envisaged as fourfold: maiden (whose colours are green and white); lover (red); mother (yellow and gold); crone (black and purple). It is interesting to speculate upon the extent to which this rich ritual year marking has been influenced by the existing context of Roman Catholicism and High Anglicanism in Glastonbury, for vernacular NRMs can interact with their context by adapting as well as rejecting the status quo.

Although the earlier part of my discussion suggested that vernacular religion exists apart from theological and liturgical expressions, it can acquire aspects of institutionalization, and perhaps paradoxically assume its own liturgical forms of expression, extending beyond Britain. The annual Glastonbury Goddess Conference, founded in 1996, has not only been important in the consolidation and celebration of Goddess spirituality in the town itself, it has become influential in Europe, the United States, the Antipodes and elsewhere. Always held to include the date 1 August (Lammas or Lugnasad), the five-day annual conference has created and 'restored' a number of traditions: vernacular Irish Catholic traditions such as making 'Bridie Crosses' and baking Lammas bread have been 'reclaimed' to honour the Goddess. The conference has become an important institution and inspiration for a great variety of Goddess-loving women and men, a forum for creativity in relation to Goddess-related music and material culture, ritual and myth. Usually (although not always) each year in rotation a different aspect of the Goddess has been celebrated and an image of her created and decorated for the conference; this determines the predominant colour for the event. Now in its second decade, the organizers strive to maintain some consistent elements, but also to remain innovative, ludic, and dynamic, drawing together material culture, myth and ritual, and taking Glastonbury spirituality beyond a local phenomenon to a wider global expression.

One of the most striking features of the Glastonbury Goddess Conference and one that reveals the way in which individuals live within personally meaningful vernacular religious worlds is the Goddess Procession. There has always been an important element of reclaiming Glastonbury for the Goddess in the procession, and it is the most public aspect of the Goddess Conference, usually held on Sunday, the last day of the conference. In earlier years a large effigy of the Goddess constructed at the conference was pulled through the streets in a cart, though lighter willow statues are now used. The visual impact of the processions is heightened by the use of colourful banners portraying 'sacred images of the divine feminine from the many cultures of the world' produced by American-based artist Lydia Ruyle; these banners are constantly taken 'to sacred sites to empower, teach and share their stories around the globe' (Ruyle 2005). The banners reflect the eclecticism, global aspirations and historical understanding of the Goddess movement; ancient and contemporary female figures from a variety of religious traditions and cultures are portrayed, as they are 'all the goddess'. The procession route has varied over the years, but generally it has started from the Town Hall (beside the entrance to Glastonbury Abbey), gone up the High Street, passing the Anglican, Methodist and United Reformed churches, stopped for ritual celebration at Chalice Well (and sometimes the White Spring), and culminated in ritual, dancing and a ceremonial Fruit Feast on top of the Tor. In this respect it has become, in effect, a mirror image of the Roman Catholic Pilgrimage procession which traditionally set out from the foot of the Tor, came down the High Streets and culminated in a Mass in the Abbey grounds.

One of the most significant conferences, one that drew together many of the themes of vernacular religion, took place in 2004, when the focus was 'Celebrating Bridie and the Maiden Goddess', and a greater area than ever was processed and proclaimed for the Goddess (see Bowman 2007 for greater detail). For the first time, the procession was staged on Thursday rather than Sunday, and was much longer than ever, with the image of Bridie being taken during the course of the afternoon and evening to four 'sacred sites' within Glastonbury (Chalice Hill, the Tor, Chalice Well, and Bushey Coombe). At Chalice Hill there was an Earth Ceremony, during which Bride's healing was to be transmitted, and which encapsulated ideas of local and global, interconnectedness and a particular vision/version of the Earth:

> As we face outwards to all the directions we will sing our Earth Chant and send clearing and healing energy outwards from Avalon through the meridians and energy lines of the Earth, which is Her sacred body, to the

whole of the land which is Brigit's Isles, and connecting to the land of Europe and to all the continents.

On Friday the entire day was devoted to 'Honouring Bridie', and on that afternoon the image of Bridie was taken out again, the route this time taking the procession past the Catholic Church, and up and over Wearyall Hill. The destination of this procession was Bride's Mound, site of a chapel once dedicated to St Bridget. It was felt that Bride truly had come home to Glastonbury and that Glastonbury had been 'restored' to Bride.

The institutionalization of Goddess spirituality itself both facilitates personal spiritual experience, and also enables wider transnational migration. Through the Goddess Conference, many have either discovered the Goddess, or have been stimulated or sustained in their devotion. While for some years the Goddess community in Glastonbury used to create temporary shrines on special days of the eight-fold calendar, the establishment of Britain's first officially registered Goddess Temple in 2002 provided a year-round focus for celebration and pilgrimage. Furthermore, a training programme for Priestesses and Priests of Avalon has been developed, producing confident, creative and experienced ritual celebrants schooled in 'the Glastonbury tradition'. An ever-increasing range of books, CDs and artwork has been created and/or promoted in connection with Conference and the Temple. A former church hall has also been acquired to provide activity space beyond the Temple. We have, in effect, seen in Glastonbury the institutionalization of the Goddess movement. At a time when 'de-institutionalization' is a trend in relation to some traditional religious groups, new forms of institutionalization are emerging in relation to NRMs. Drawing on and reinterpreting some long-established legends, developing new myths about the Goddess in Glastonbury, relating belief stories and PENs of personal encounters with or perceptions of the Lady of Avalon (whether through dreams, ritually induced trance states or simply being in the Glastonbury landscape), there is now a body of constantly evolving, powerfully confirmatory narratives which are spread in oral communication, in print and through numerous websites and other forms of social media. Glastonbury Goddess spirituality has developed distinctive material culture, particular aesthetics in costuming and art, and related rituals, music and sacred drama.

Transnational migration is a hallmark of many NRMs, and although the Glastonbury Goddess movement remains very much rooted in the landscape of Avalon, it is now being replicated, or to be more accurate, re-negotiated, re-envisaged and re-narrated beyond Glastonbury. This proceeds not in a formal or normative manner, but in the vernacular. Hungary has experienced the growth of 'alternative' events, publications and shops; (neo)Shamanism; interest in yoga, meditation and assorted forms of healing; and the contestation of pilgrimage sites such as Csíksomlyó as various groups and individuals

Vernacular/Lived Religion

seek to 'reclaim' or re-narrate sacred places. As elsewhere in Europe, early studies in Hungarian folklore and comparative religion were much exercised by survivals and reconstructions (Barna 2004, 128–30) and these have 'trickled down' to be used later by 'reclaimers' or 'revivers' interested in restoring native, pre-Christian spirituality. However, a Goddess conference, a Goddess Temple and a Goddess priestess and priest training programme with a direct Glastonbury connection were established through the experience, inspiration and enterprise of one woman, Kriszta Veres. Veres had studied English at university and was fascinated by Arthurian myth; she read and loved *Mists of Avalon*, but as she says, 'didn't think there could be such a place now.' Already involved in Budapest's burgeoning alternative scene, she found out through the internet about the Glastonbury Goddess Conference and attended in 2004, the year of Bridget. Inspired by her Glastonbury experience, she started to train as a Priestess of Avalon, and in 2006 organized her first Goddess Conference in Hungary. Personnel from Glastonbury, including Kathy Jones and Brian Charles, came over to facilitate the event. The conference convinced Veres of the need for a temple, which was opened on the autumn equinox of 2006. Banners of Goddesses created for the first conference were used to decorate the Temple. There is a shrine to the elements in each corner of the Temple, dressed in different colours according to the season. A Carpathian Basin wheel of the year was developed, with associated Goddesses, animals, objects and so on. Brian Charles decided to stay on in Hungary, and with him Veres began a priestess and priest training programme. Just as the Glastonbury conference is timed to include August, Lammas, the Hungarian conference included the midsummer solstice on 21 June. The mission of the conferences was to reconnect with and revive the Hungarian Goddess tradition; as the poster for the 2008 conference put it, 'Come and join us, here in the very centre of Europe, where our distant ancestors lived, loved and died, to reclaim the continent for the Goddess who lives in us all and who is the very land itself!' (Conference poster, 2008).

In keeping with the fluidity of vernacular religion, the programme for the 2008 conference reveals both continuity and change, as features of the Glastonbury conference were replicated but re-negotiated in their new physical, cultural and (pre)historical environment:

> Brigit, Bride, Brighdie, Bridie, Saint Brigit ... Her name once meant Goddess. Once She was the Great Goddess, Maiden, Lover, Mother, Crone and Lady of the four elements. She still is the healing Goddess whose presence we feel in the healing springs and in the fire of our hearts. In Hungary, the name of the very first Roman settlement in Pannonia, established on the land of the Celtic Azalus tribe, Brigetio, bears witness to the honour that was paid to Brigit in those days [. . .]

265

Brigit rules over the healing springs and wells, and She has certainly blessed Budapest with a lot of them! This afternoon we will ritually offer ourselves to the healing waters of Széchenyi Spa – the biggest spa in Europe – which is watched over by Brigit's swan – to be cleansed, refreshed and renewed. (Conference programme, 2008).

The conference also involved a procession, with Lydia Ruyle's Banners, ending up with a celebration in the park, with a shared lunch and gift exchange (also a feature of the Glastonbury conference). The 'Glastonbury Goddess package' of conference, temple, priestess/priest training programme, locally adapted wheel of the year, ritual and material culture, developed over a long period in Glastonbury and essentially embedded in the landscape of Avalon, was transplanted into Hungary. Veres drew on her experiences in Glastonbury to make conceptual connections between Glastonbury and Hungary in a number of ways, her 'discovery' of Bridget in Hungary via Brigetio being one example. She saw a topographical correspondence between Wearyall Hill, the Tor and Chalice Well and the two hills and the 'red' spring at Csíksomlyó. After an experience at sunrise when the mist at Csíksomlyó had hidden the town, Veres speculated on Csíksomlyó as a place where one can 'access Avalon'. Physical connections with Glastonbury were maintained also, as until 2009 she was undertaking priestess training in Glastonbury, as well as attending the Goddess conference there, and bringing her trainees over to Britain.

These Avalonian influences have converged with and added to a number of pre-existing speculations, trends and actors in contemporary Hungarian spirituality. There is the image and inspiration of an ancient, conflict free, Goddess infused past, as indicated in the poster for the 2007 conference: 'The Carpathian Basin was the heart of Old Europe, where the culture of our peaceful, Goddess-loving Neolithic ancestors flourished.' Veres and others began to reinterpret and re-narrate a number of figures in Hungarian vernacular religion and folklore in relation to the Goddess, such as Gladwoman. Building on prior speculations concerning the cult of Babba Maria at Csíksomlyó, in the Budapest Goddess Temple there are two icons of Our Lady of Csíksomlyó; as she tends to appear dressed in red, she is associated with the Goddess as Lover. Veres mentioned that taking a group to bathe at the Cross Bath in Bath (site of Britain's only hot springs, and connected with a Romano-Celtic cultic site dedicated to Sul/Sulis Minerva) had made her realize how much Hungarians take their springs for granted, and made her wonder whether there had been a goddess associated with every spring. When I met Veres and Charles after the Beltane 2007 training weekend, they mentioned that they had gone with the trainee priestesses and priests to the Museum of Ethnography in Budapest to look for hidden goddesses, and to impress upon the trainees the importance in Hungarian traditional culture of festivals, and of dressing ceremonially and elaborately for special occasions. Indeed, such activity is more familiar in Hungary than it is in the United Kingdom. In traditionally Protestant Britain, religious processions involving ceremonially robed figures, statues and banners have been exceptional rather than commonplace, unlike the situation in Catholic areas of Hungary.

Elements of the Glastonbury Goddess movement, a highly localized, landscape-rooted form of contemporary spirituality developed in a much mythologized, contested site of pilgrimage in England, have transplanted (thanks to the internet) to a new context with quite different topography, history, mythology and cultural traditions to draw upon in the creation of new forms of ancient religion for the twenty-first century. Primiano contends that 'Vernacular religion is a way of communicating, thinking, behaving within, and conforming to, particular cultural circumstances' (1995, 42), elements observable in both Glastonbury and Hungary. In both cases, the Goddess is being restored, or perhaps more accurately 're-storied', as a new relationship with the past and the land is being negotiated in local but globalized arenas. We also see the significant impact of individuals – Jones and Veres – stressing the importance of 'bidirectional influences of environments upon individuals and of individuals upon environments in the process of believing' (1995, 44). Those witnessing a procession in honour of Bridget in Glastonbury in 2004 could not have known that within a couple of years its impact would be felt in the heart of Europe, in the busy streets of Budapest. People witnessing a small and possibly puzzling procession of people with colourful banners in Budapest would have no reason to connect to that with a little town in Somerset, England. The study of religion, including NRMs,

> necessitates a complete process of contextualisation; a dedicated, and by necessity intensive method of detail and nuance gathering; structure and relevant text appreciation; and the elevation of people's own voices and aesthetic and classificatory systems, especially over the edifice of the theoretical creations of powerful scholars. (Primiano 2012, 384)

Fieldwork and the Study of NRMs

It will have become obvious by now that fieldwork is important, if not inevitable, in the vernacular religious approach. NRMs will differ as to how controlling or accommodating they are in relation to qualitative research (particularly longitudinal qualitative research of the type I have conducted in Glastonbury) whether through participant observation, informal inclusion or formal interviews. As with all fieldwork-based research, there is an element of serendipity; while some data can be obtained through formal interviews, or conversations that have been initiated for a stated purpose, other material comes informally or fortuitously, such as through overheard conversations in cafes and casual comments in the public domain. There is value in just 'being there', to appreciate how rhetoric feeds into reality in terms of lived religion, how material culture is used and regarded in everyday life, how belief stories are circulated formally and informally. (In relation to gender matters, for example, I have often asked students conducting fieldwork in a particular context to listen to what is said, but to observe who does the washing up!)

There is a willingness among many in Glastonbury to cooperate in research, for example, seeing academic interest as a form of recognition (if not validation) of their beliefs and praxis, and the academic as a potential advocate. Many leaders and participants in NRMs see themselves as in the business of both research and teaching, although the distinction between teaching religion and teaching *about* religion may be one that is not obvious or meaningful. While wishing to remain on good terms with partners in research-based dialogue, one should nevertheless be aware that some people will be talking to you on the assumption that you will eventually become 'one of them', and that is an issue that should be anticipated and honestly addressed. One aspect of conducting qualitative longitudinal research that traditionally has been anticipated, indeed frowned upon, is the 'danger' of the academic 'going native'. Of course, there are numerous assumptions underlying that attitude: that the academic was not native at the start, that 'going native' necessarily compromises the soundness of the data and analysis and so on. There are also counterarguments, and examples of scholarship where 'going native' (temporarily or permanently) might be said to bring greater understanding and depth of analysis. However, in the field of contemporary religion and NRMs, particularly over a long period in one place or with one group, an equally pressing issue is that of our influence *in* and *on* the field of study through our presence, our questions and our writings. Many of those involved in NRMs and developing forms of contemporary spirituality are highly informed and educated, and technologically skilled, so the work of the scholar will not remain hidden from those researched. The questions we ask, the vocabulary we use, the way we frame dialogue may well have an impact on the very phenomena we are there to study. However, as Barz and Coooley contend, 'If globalization theories have taught us anything, it is that we already are social actors within just about any cultural phenomena that we might wish to study. Another way to look at this is that we are all already in the field. We are all fieldworkers' (2008, 24).

Conclusion

In arguing for the value of vernacular religion as both a category of analysis and field of practice in relation to NRMs, I am signalling that the study of NRMs can and should be more richly nuanced than some previous scholarship of more established religious traditions has been. There can be no reason to observe and report on only the small proportion of a movement's 'life-world' comprised by its 'official' sources, its hierarchically approved personnel or its public or ritual manifestations, when the study of material culture, narrative and 'the totality of all those views and practices of religion that exist among the people apart from and alongside the strictly theological and liturgical forms of the official religion' (Yoder 1974, 14) can reveal so much more. Primiano claims that vernacular religion as an approach 'challenges religious studies to incorporate the interdisciplinary strengths of folklore/folklife in the study of the religious individual and the significance of religion as it is lived in the contemporary context' (1995, 52). There is a strong imperative for fieldwork and participant-observation in this approach. Primiano argues that vernacular religion is 'conceptually valuable' because

> The study of vernacular religion, like the study of folklore, appreciates religion as an historic, as well as contemporary, process and marks religion in everyday life as a construction of mental, verbal, and material expressions. Vernacular religious theory understands religion as the continuous art of individual interpretation and negotiation of any number of influential sources. (2012, 384)

Claiming that 'Religious belief takes as many forms in a tradition as there are individual believers' (1995, 51), Primiano points out that many factors that can influence the individual in the formation of his or her conception and practice of religion, which coalesce to produce 'a unified organic system of belief' (copying a term from Yoder 1974, 13); he feels scholars should 'emphasize the integrated ideas and practices of all individuals' (1995, 47). In the study of NRMs, it might be helpful for scholars to break with past assumptions, to stop acting as though people engaged in living out religion keep getting it wrong, while 'official religion' gets it right, for no one, including members of institutional hierarchies, 'lives an "officially" religious life in a pure unadulterated form' (Primiano 1995, 46). If we accept that 'All religion is both subtly and vibrantly marked by continuous interpretation even after it has been reified in expressive or structured forms' (Primiano 2012, 384), the study of NRMs can be enriched by *anticipating* heterogeneity, individual creativity and 'non-conformity'. Focusing on any NRM 'as it is lived: as human beings encounter, understand, interpret, and practice it' (Primiano 1995, 44), the stories told within it, the myriad material cultural expressions of it can only lead to an ever deeper understanding of the phenomena presented by it.

Part III

New Directions in the Study of New Religious Movements

24 Globalization
Liselotte Frisk

Chapter Outline

Universalism and Particularism	274
Transnational Cultures	275
Homogenization and Hybridity	276
Conclusion	278

Globalization has been a popular theme during the last two decades, discussed in media as well as in several academic disciplines. The term is used by scholars since the 1980s (Beyer 2007, 444). The process of globalization is firmly linked to communication, which today is world-wide and increasingly dense. Peoples, cultures, societies and civilizations that previously were more or less isolated from one another are now in regular contact (Beyer 1994, 2). Many new religions – both today and historically – are products of cultural communication and cultural migration. Thus, increasing global communication is one of the factors important for new religions, not only to form but also to spread. New religions today have the possibility to spread to other parts of the globe with increasing speed, using new communication technologies as media and the internet.

Globalization theories introduce a global level of analysis to supplement local, national and regional levels (Beyer 1994, 2; Martikainen 2004, 42). The term could refer to both compression of the world and consciousness of the world as a whole, as well as to the sense of belonging to a global community (Steger 2009, 10–13). There are different opinions as to the time span for which it is relevant to use the term. Some writers limit the historical scope of globalization to 1990s onwards, while others argue that globalization represents continuation and extention of complex processes that began with the emerging of modernity and the capitalist world system several centuries ago, or that it has unfolded for millennia (Steger 2009, 17–36). Globalization is, however, uneven and neglects and even excludes some areas of the world (Ritzer 2011, 164).

Most globalization theoreticians divide the globalization discussion into several different dimensions. Manfred B. Steger, for example, distinguishes between economical, political, cultural and ecological dimensions of globalization (2009). Arjun Appadurai differs between five dimensions of global flows: ethnoscapes, mediascapes, technoscapes, finanscapes and ideoscapes (Appadurai 1997, 296). Religion is just a small part of the immense area of the globalization debate. And within the area of religion and globalization, this essay will focus on only new religions and globalization.

Globalization could thus be discussed in innumerable different ways. I have chosen some themes to discuss, which are both common in the general globalization discussion and of great importance for new religions. These themes will form three different parts of this essay: Universalism and particularism; Transnational cultures; and Homogenization and hybridity.

Universalism and Particularism

Some theoreticians of globalization, as Roland Robertson and Peter Beyer, stress *relativization* as a key process of globalization (Robertson 1998, 29; see also Berger 1990, 151–3, for a discussion of pluralism, relativization and secularization). In a global society, all particular cultures, including religions that form part of these cultures, are relativized (Beyer 1994, 9), and individuals form their religious identity in the knowledge that their religion is only one among several possibilities (Beyer 1994, 30). The process of relativization gives rise to the dual and simultaneous process of search for, on the one hand, particularistic identities, and on the other hand, universalistic identities (Beyer 1994, 30; Robertson 1998, 100), a process which could also be expressed religiously. Globalization is thus producing universalism and cosmopolitanism, but also, as a reaction, the assertion of particularistic identities, as opposition to the conception of the world as a series of culturally equal, relativized, entities or ways of life (Robertson 1998, 102). An example of this resistance or particularism is religious fundamentalism, reacting to the cultural complexity of a globalized world as disturbing and dangerous, taking refuge in renewed and purified traditions (Giddens 2002, 4–5). Particularistic groups, however, often in different ways absorb globally transmitted cultural values – most of them do, for example, use the media technology characteristic of globalization (Rajagopal 2001; Smith 2000).

Robertson emphasizes the interpenetration of universalism and particularism. He illustrates with Japan. Robertson argues that Japan has a very long and successful history of selective incorporation and syncretization of ideas from other cultures in such a way as to particularize the universal, and return the product of that process to the world as a uniquely Japanese contribution to the universal (Robertson 1998, 102).

New religions are sometimes quite universalistic in their identity, including and promoting global values, as for example Bahá'í, Soka Gakkai and Unification Church. Global values could be, for example, the belief that different religions are just different expressions of the same faith, or the importance of the unification of the world and humanity (Beckford 2008, 25; Hexham and Poewe 1997, 52; MacEoin 2005, 296; Warburg 2005, 8). However, there are also particularistic orientations, as for example Neopagan groups, reacting to globalization and aspiring to revive a particular tradition. Often there is, however, a mixture of universalism and particularism. Examples would be Jehovah's Witnesses or ISKCON, claiming a unique and exclusive truth, but offering their message for everyone.

Transnational Cultures

One outcome of increasing communication or globalization is the growth of cultures without a clear anchorage in any one territory, transnational cultures or deterritorialized cultures. In a globalized world, culture is no longer as tied as it once was to the constraints of local geography (Ritzer 2011, 165). Many new religions could be seen as examples of such transnational cultures. Members are residents of many different countries, but have a feeling of commonness, and of sharing a history and a destiny with other members world-wide. Margit Warburg calls these new religions 'transnational imagined communities' (Warburg 2008, 49–50). Examples of such new religions which function as transnational communities, are for example The Family International, or Bahá'í. In recent years, the internet has become an important medium for the transnational communities to keep in contact with other members of the same group.

The social anthropologist Ulf Hannerz notes that cosmopolitans may be somewhat footloose: They are as ready to move on as they are to stay in order to immerse themselves temporarily within other cultures and religions (Hannerz 1997, 240–1). According to Hannerz, a global culture is a transnational network of cosmopolitan people who self-consciously cultivate 'an intellectual and aesthetic stance of openness toward divergent cultural experiences' (Hannerz 1997, 239). My own observation is, however, that several of the new religions, although existing as transnational groups in different cultures, rather try to keep to their own culture than immensing themselves with the geographical culture where they happen to be. Children growing up in these communities, however, often master several languages and have lived in several countries during their upbringing, and thus have a weaker sense of belonging to a specific geographic and national space. In some new religions it is common to send their teenagers to other communities around the world before adulthood, as in The Family International. In the Unification Church, there is the possibility for teenagers to attend a boarding school in Korea (Frisk 2007a).

Historically, there have been transnational religions with universal aspirations, like Buddhism, Christianity, and Islam, religions contradicting political boundaries (Beyer 1994, 50). Common to these has been the aspiration to include everyone, not excluding people because of, for example, nationality or ethnic origin. Hexham and Poewe observe that the new religionist practice often includes people for whom the co-existence of ideas from diverse cultures, traditions and practices is an inner experience (Hexham and Poewe 1997, 46–7). This is a common practice in the new age spiritualities, but also some new religions selectively and consciously combine aspects of many traditions to create a new culture, a process only possible under strongly globalized conditions. One example is the Rajneesh (Osho neo-sannyas) movement (Hexham and Poewe 1997, 41–3).

Homogenization and Hybridity

It is highly relevant to adopt a power perspective to globalization, as globalization affects different parts of the world in uneven ways. Doreen Massey discusses power relations between 'centre' and 'periphery' regarding different areas (like economy, politics, media) and different places. While there are increasing mixtures of cultures in all parts of the world, the directions of this mixing are unequal (Massey 1995, 70). Culture flows comparatively easily across the globe, but not all cultures, or parts of cultures, flow as easily or at the same rate (Ritzer 2011, 154). There are barriers to global fluidity like region of the world, social class, gender and ethnicity, all related to power (Ritzer 2011, 7–16). Although not all cultural flows run in the same direction, many observers point out that it is clear there are broad systematic lines and directions: from 'West' to 'rest' (Giddens 2002, 15; Massey 1995, 71). Modernization in the West has directly resulted in the spread of certain vital institutions of Western modernization to the rest of the globe, as the modern capitalist economy and scientific rationality in the form of modern technology. Some, like Anthony Giddens, emphasize democracy as a Western contribution to the rest of the world (Giddens 2002, 5; Steger 2009, 75).

Ulf Hannerz remarks that transnational cultures are, in different ways, extensions or transformations of the cultures of Western Europe and North America, and are organized so as to make people from Western Europe and North America feel as much at home as possible (by, for example, using their own languages) (Hannerz 1997, 244). Several of the new religions – as for example ISKCON, The Family International, The Unification movement – have also spread from or via the United States to the rest of the world. Some writers interpret Western practitioners of non-Western religions as a continuation of imperialism, a theft also of religious elements. This has been evident concerning native religions (see for example Rothstein 2005) and Buddhism (Plank 2011).

Peter Beyer argues, that although key globalizing structures originated in the West, globalization is not just another word for Western expansion. Globalization is more than the spread of one historically existing culture at the expense of all others. It is the creation of a new global culture, one that increasingly becomes the broader social context of all particular cultures in the world, including those of the West. The spread of the global social reality therefore occurs quite as much at the cost of the latter as of non-Western cultures. All cultures change dramatically in the process (Beyer 1994, 8–9). Hexham and Poewe argue that it is characteristic for a global culture, travelling the world, to take on a local colour. It has both a global, or metacultural, and a local, or situationally distinct, dimension (Hexham and Poewe 1997, 41). George Ritzer writes about cultural hybridization, the production of new and unique hybrid cultures that is not reducible to either local or global culture. The integration of global processes with various local realities produces new and distinctive hybrid forms that indicate continued global heterogenization rather than homogenization. This is sometimes called glocalization, defined as the interpenetration of the global and the local, resulting in unique outcomes in different geographic areas. The world would thus become more pluralistic (Ritzer 2011, 159; Robertson 1998, 173–4). One example, given by J. Gordon Melton, is reiki healing. In the process of spreading globally, different traditions developed in the interplay between the global and the local, in contact with other traditions in different parts of the world (Melton 2001, 73–93). Yoga is another example of this kind of development, as different kinds of yoga, some originating in the West, are spreading rapidly – also back to India in new packages (Frisk and Åkerbäck 2013, forthcoming). There is often a tension between keeping the tradition 'pure', and between adapting to local culture. Thus, ISKCON has, for example, in Western countries developed a more equal gender practice than in the original culture (Frisk 2007a).

Conclusion

New religions are often a product of globalization (increasing communication, migration and syncretism), and express a mixture of universalistic and particularistic identities, both, however, responses to globalization. Some are examples of transnational or deterritorialized cultures, an effect of a globalized world. Many of them reflect Western cultural flows; however, the integration of global and local processes also produces new forms indicating increased heterogenization.

25 Science

Benjamin E. Zeller

One of the more bizarre cases of the intersection between new religious movements (NRMs) and science occurred in July 2009, when a month after the death of pop star Michael Jackson, the Raelian-associated human cloning project Clonaid released a public statement that neither confirmed nor denied that it had cloned the late King of Pop. 'Clonaid prides itself on never releasing the identity of the numerous individuals who have been cloned in the past six years', project director and Raelian Brigitte Boissellier said. In other words, the Raelians might have cloned Jackson, or they might not have. But never one to waste an opportunity, Boissellier's press release advertised both the project's cloning technology and their 'Stemaid' service, which they claim utilizes cloned stem cells to reverse human aging (Clonaid 2009).

Beyond the oddity of the late King of Pop requesting help from a new religious movement's (NRM) outreach project – which given Michael Jackson's life is vaguely believable, one supposes – what makes this case so interesting is that there is absolutely no evidence that Clonaid ever actually successfully cloned a human being. Scientists note that even putting aside ethical questions the science behind cloning has not advanced far enough to try on humans (American Medical Association 2001). Most outside observers believe that Clonaid's claim to have successfully cloned 'Baby Eve' in 2002 was a fraud and publicity stunt. In any case, neither Clonaid nor the Raelian movement with which it is affiliated has ever produced any empirical evidence, scientific studies or verifiable materials supporting their claims.

Yet cloning is at the heart of not only Clonaid but also the theology and worldview of the Raelian movement, founded in 1974 by Raël, né Claude Vorilhon (1946–), a French race car driver who claimed contact with extraterrestrials. Categorized by NRM scholars as a 'UFO religion', the Raelians believe that their founder not only communicated with the extraterrestrial piloting a flying saucer, but actually visited an extraterrestrial planet. During these contacts, it was revealed to Raël that the Bible records the interaction between humans and extraterrestrials erroneously perceived as divine figures. The extraterrestrials not only created and nurtured human life on Earth, but intend to return once we are ready. As part of the millennial vision that they promise, the extraterrestrials indicated to Raël that humans can achieve immortality through a form of cloning. Clonaid's efforts to clone human beings – and their press release following the death of Michael Jackson – are part of this religious worldview. For Raelians, cloning is not just a technology; it is a religious belief and act. (For more on the Raelians, see Palmer [2004a].)

The International Raelian Movement, as they are formally called, is not alone in combining elements of science, technology and religion within an NRM. While most evident among other UFO religions such as Heaven's Gate and Unarius, new religious movements across the spectrum invoke, utilize, comment on, draw from and otherwise engage with science. From the NRMs of the nineteenth century and fin de siècle, such as Theosophy and Christian Science, to New Age movements, Neopagan groups, Esoteric movements, and groups that are offshoots of major world religions, nearly all new religious movements engage with science in some ways. In other words, science has been important to NRMs since at least the rise of the centrality of science and technology in the wake of the late Industrial Revolution.

The study of new religious movements and science raises several central themes. Most notably, it points to the cultural power of science and the centrality of science in contemporary and near-contemporary society. Second, the ways that NRMs invoke science indicate a broad cultural view of legitimacy that science and technology possess. Third, the study of science and NRMs shows that science functions not only as a means of studying the natural world (as a scientist might define it), but as a symbol of modernity itself. Responses to science are therefore also responses to modernity. Finally, it indicates the fundamentally unstable definitions of science at play in contemporary culture, the many ways that the idea of 'science' is constructed, and tensions within society regarding the nature of science.

Before considering these themes, it is helpful to think about the ways in which NRMs have engaged science. As historians and sociologists of science have noted, the nature of 'science' and its offspring 'technology' has changed over time (Golinski 1998; Harding 1998; Kuhn 1962). Therefore one must consider how NRMs relate to science within their historical and cultural context. Though one could certainly look earlier, among the first wave of new religious movements to extensively engage with science were those active at the end of the nineteenth century and the beginning of the twentieth. Theosophy, Christian Science, the Unity School of Christianity, and many other New Thought groups made extensive forays into the consideration of the connections between religion and science (Rapport 2011). Many of these groups came to see themselves as operating in a scientific manner, most notably Christian Science and parallel groups like Jewish Science. Others invoked science and saw themselves as new religions for modern scientific times. The Unity School, Theosophy, and some New Thought groups fell within this category. All such groups extolled science and sought to harness the legitimacy of science, as well as position themselves as new religions in harmony with contemporary scientific developments.

It is in fact impossible to understand those nineteenth-century and fin de siècle NRMs apart from the rise of science and technology during that era. Scientists had only recently come to understand the nature of such mysterious forces as electricity and magnetism, and technologists had begun to create products that blurred the line between miraculous and everyday. The telegraph, telephone, and radio in particular all conjured almost religious awe among early witnesses. Science had only recently separated itself from natural philosophy and theology, and these NRMs represented the vanguard of responses to such a change.

Among NRMs of the later twentieth century, science had changed yet again. The revolutions instigated by Einstein, Heisenberg, Bohr, and other scientists working on relativity and quantum mechanics annihilated the sense of order and objectivity that had dominated science since Newton. Simultaneously, science and technology had come to dominate Western society as never before. Microwave ovens, antibiotics, television, space travel, and nuclear weapons had ushered in a brave new world that conjured images both utopian and dystopian. New religious movements responded to this as well. Some, such as Raelianism, Heaven's Gate, and Scientology, envisioned themselves as scientific new religions that internalized the essence of science within themselves. New Age movements tend to follow this tract as well, claiming to fuse religious and scientific knowledge and techniques. Other groups rebelled against this new scientific world, either shying away from science or explicitly rejecting it, as the Twelve Tribes and other 'modern primitivist' groups do, or redefined what science means, as ISKCON and some Asian-looking groups do (Zeller 2010). Asian-oriented groups such as ISKCON or Transcendental Meditation (TM) offer alternative forms of 'Vedic science' that they envision as superior to the Western scientific tradition. Both such groups claim 'scientific truth' to support their claims, and sometimes blend Indian and Western scientific approaches in attempts to support their positions. Both, for example, claim that (Western) scientific research supports the efficacy of their specific forms of meditation, yet they simultaneously challenge the validity of such Western science! (Lowe 2011).

To return to the central themes that emerge from the study of new religious movements and science, the most obvious conclusion from even this brief foray is that science and technology have achieved massive cultural power and centrality in contemporary and near-contemporary society. While a few other-worldly or apocalyptic-oriented NRMs paid little attention to science, most embraced ideas or positions of science or technology. Those that rejected science in its conventional form, such as TM and ISKCON, offered alternative visions of science. Even groups highly suspicious of science, such as New Age movements rejecting modern medicine, offer alternatives that they envision as 'scientific'. The vast level of attention that these movements paid to science itself testifies the power and position of science in today's culture.

Additionally, the manner by which NRMs invoke science indicates a broad sense of cultural legitimacy that science and technology possess. Often movements attempt to harness this power directly. Turn-of-the-century Theosophists, mid-century members of Unarius (officially named the 'Unarius Academy of Science') and today's new age adherents all claim to 'be scientific' in their religious pursuits (Frøystad 2011). As James R. Lewis has indicated, these claims often root their practices and beliefs in the legitimacy and authority of science and technology. 'Any religion that claimed its approach was in some way scientific drew on the prestige and perceived legitimacy of natural science', explained Lewis (2003, 93). The prevalence of science within the rhetoric of NRMs bears out Lewis' observation.

One discovers in studying how NRMs engage science that 'science' is a very fluid thing, that it often serves as a rhetorical tool to discuss modernity itself. When a movement takes a negative view of science and technology, as the Twelve Tribes or some new age groups do, they are rejecting aspects of modernity that they see emblemized in science, such as increased mobility, gender egalitarianism or cultural relativism. Often such groups embrace science or technology in other forms, such as 'green technology' or 'alternative medicine', that they envision as less threatening or more conducive to their religious orientation.

Scientists tend to define science either methodologically (based on empiricism or naturalism) or as fields of study predicated on such a methodology. Yet new religious movements treat 'science' in ways that scientists would never imagine. The UFO group Heaven's Gate considered the uploading and downloading of human souls to be a 'science'. The Hare Krishnas said the same thing about psychic travel to extraterrestrial worlds. Further back in time, Theosophists and Spiritualists considered contact with ghosts and spirits to be forms of science. All such groups define 'science' in very different ways. Yet this is equally true in popular culture within the non-religious sphere. Climate change deniers, anti-vaccine activists, and Christian Creationists all possess alternative visions of what 'science' means, none of which accord with how a scientist would define it. NRMs show that there are many ways in which the idea of 'science' is constructed, and reveals tensions within societies regarding the nature of science.

The fluidity of the nature of science and the many ways that NRMs have responded to science and its offspring technology indicate that there are many fruitful avenues for future research in this field. Many new religious movements are what I call 'science central NRMs', since they place the idea of science at the centre of their worldviews, practices or beliefs. Scientology, Raelianism and Transcendental Meditation are clearly within this stratum of movements.

Scholars are already engaged in good work on these groups, and new research promises to explore how science functions within these NRMs and what this reveals about the groups, broader society, and the nature of science and religion.

But there are many other groups that I call 'science secondary NRMs'. These movements do not envision science or technology as central to their religious worldviews, practices or beliefs. It is harder to find 'science' within these groups, since they do not tend to publish tracts or books about science or issue press releases invoking science. However, the place of science and technology is still just as relevant to the study of these groups. Here, science functions as one of several cultural products within a religious world. Just as scholars have studied food, art, and clothing within new religious movements wherein food, art, and clothing are not the central aims of the groups – consider the Shakers or Hare Krishnas, for example – so too can researchers look to what these groups say about science and how science and technology function within these movements. Much less research exists on these groups, primarily because science is less visible here. Yet it is a very fruitful avenue for future research. All people today live in a world shaped by science and technology, and all groups have been similarly shaped. The next arena for scholars of NRMs to consider when it comes to science is how groups that do not consider themselves particularly interested in science or technology nevertheless function within the contemporary scientific, technological world.

26 The Role of the Internet

Jean-François Mayer

Several new religious movements (NRMs) have been prompt in seeing the potential of the internet (Brasher 2001, 70). Furthermore, the newer a movement is, the more it tends to incorporate contemporary trends. NRMs generally do not have a dense territorial network of centres, places of worship and local groups: the internet allows them to connect people across space and time zones. It also allows even small groups or individuals with little access to classical media such as television, radio or newspapers to make their voices heard. Finally, since most NRMs are eager to share their faith and attract new believers, the internet opens unprecedented possibilities for missionary activity. However, it has also brought challenges to NRMs, both in relation to the outside world and the way in which they function (Barker 2005; Mayer 2000).

In the public debate, the use of the internet by NRMs was highlighted in 1997 by the suicide of 39 members of Heaven's Gate in California. Not only had the group been involved in the business of web design and attempted to recruit new members over the internet, but it announced its 'departure' online and left a website behind. There was also talk of 'online predators' and innocent surfers being 'sucked in' by dubious groups (Cowan 2011).

Observations did not confirm such concerns: 'while the Internet makes it cheaper for NRMs to disseminate their beliefs . . . it is unlikely that it has intrinsically changed the capacity of NRMs to recruit new members' (Dawson et al. 2004, 164). This observation remains valid, although the internet can serve as an entry point, and 'certain [of its] interactive aspects . . . can function as human-to-human communication in lieu of face-to-face situations' (Arthur 2008, 419).

The internet has made it possible for any entity, religious or not, to access a potentially much larger audience. But it also means competing for attention with a huge variety of other groups and dealing with the fact that web surfers, far from resembling a captive audience, are eager to jump to another site, with other messages just a click away. Initial contacts with a religious message can take place over the internet, in the same way that people discover a movement through a pamphlet handed out in the street or a book, with the added advantage of anonymity if desired. Nevertheless, social interaction seems to remain a key to most conversions.

The internet makes it easy to access both positive and negative information: typing the names of groups in a search engine often reveals hostile comments by critics or disaffected members. An early article on NRMs' use of the internet remarked that the main concern of Jehovah's Witnesses about the new technology was the fear of 'apostasy', since members surfing the Web would come into contact with material critical of the movement (Chryssides 1996). More recently, it has been stated that the internet 'with its free traffic of information' seems to play an important role in increasing the number of Mormons leaving the faith: 'The Internet is filled with thousands of pages of anti-Mormon polemic' (Sunstone 2012).

Controversies, even internal ones, tend to be reported online: this creates a pressure towards transparency, not only for NRMs. The internet thus threatens groups that insist on keeping some teachings or material secret. For many years the Church of Scientology has fought adversaries who make the movement's confidential (and copyrighted) material public, but the development of the internet has made this a losing battle: once material has been posted online and recopied, it effectively remains in the public domain, whatever court decisions may be.

A number of movements had opponents before the advent of the Web, but most critics had limited ways to share their views. However, the internet has empowered even individual opponents to reach a global audience:

> Prior to the advent of the Internet, there were never more than a few hundred countercult apologists, with certainly fewer than 50 publishing commercially and consistently.... With the ready availability of Internet access, countercult evangelism on the . . . Web has become increasingly popular, and hundreds of countercult Web sites have appeared in recent years. (Cowan 2006, 145)

Similarly, a study of French online controversies around the Jehovah's Witnesses indicates the existence of a number of independent activists who are critical of the organization for whom the internet is the main channel (Couchouron-Gurung 2007, 141–3). And regarding the Bahá'í community, Momen (2007, 205) points out that the internet has played a crucial role in allowing networks of former members to 'reach others who might join their cause' and creating 'an effective platform of opposition to [this] community'.

On the other hand, the internet is attractive for movements eager to challenge misperceptions: it allows them to present their views (Arthur 2008). More dramatically, in cases of persecution, such as that experienced by Falun Gong in China, the internet helps believers not only to present their case online (although this also led to an intensification of cybercontrol in China), but also to coordinate their efforts via the internet and make their grievances known (Thornton 2003). While 'the centre of Falun Gong's religious life is outside of virtual space', the movement's main website also serves as a central point for new orientations and instructions (Šindelář 2009, 116–17).

The internet thus includes sometimes contradictory aspects. Centralized groups can use it to convey teachings directly from the centre to their followers. But what characterizes it is primarily its horizontality: the internet marks 'the death of the centre' and its replacement with a 'networked system' (Ryan 2010, 7). In his study of the use of the internet among Japanese Buddhists, Fukamizu (2007) remarks that 'by increasing the number of information sources, the Internet promotes horizontal interaction and undermines the one-way, top-down information flow of doctrine'. 'As Steve Jobs observed in 1996, the Web is "an incredible democratizer"' (Ryan 2010, 179).

It is no surprise that some movements felt hesitant about using a tool that imposed its own logic on them. Jehovah's Witnesses tended to discourage individual members from using the Web for propagating their faith (although some did and continue to do so) and the group developed websites that do not engage in or facilitate interactive online exchange. A more recent and successful religious movement, Kofuku no Kagaku (founded in 1986 in Japan), known in the West as 'Happy Science', was reluctant to use the Web until 2004; today, it has a number of quite professional and attractive websites, although meant for advertising and informing rather than interacting. There has been a change of strategy over the years, but 'consistent with the image choices made by the group over the past decade' (Baffelli 2010, 272).

A small number of movements maintain a 'no-go area' policy towards the internet for their members (while themselves sometimes having a showcase website online, such as the Exclusive Brethren), but most are aware that they can at best advise discretion. Other movements may encourage the faithful to go online, as the Mormons have done for several years; however, members had already eagerly embraced the new technology not just for personal use, but also to defend (or discuss) their faith (Gold 2000).

The internet has not meant the same for all movements. It has been beneficial to alternative beliefs without any central structure and based on networking, thus replicating the logic of the internet itself. The best example is the multifaceted Neopagan movement. Neopagans primarily meet in small, local groups (or are solitary practitioners), but through websites and forums there has been a 'Pagan explosion'. The internet thus allows networking with people holding similar interests and for building religious knowledge:

> Unlike many religions, becoming a Witch is less a process of conversion to a particular set of beliefs . . . than it is a process of learning about and participating in the practices that make one a Witch.. . . The Internet serves as one important source in this ongoing process. (Berger et al. 2004, 176)

This process goes beyond a recourse to useful tools: many modern Pagans have a positive attitude towards technology, contradicting assumptions regarding the impact of technology is resulting in 'disenchantment of the world' (Aupers 2009): 'Many Wiccans openly affirm the relationship between magic and the computer culture' (Drury 2002, 98).

The internet has also allowed the creation of some groups. In the United States, this was the case with the House of Netjer, which claims to offer (neo-Egyptian) Kemetic Orthodoxy: 'While some people meet together in Chicago or in regional groups, most people learn about Kemetic Orthodoxy, meet other believers, convert, and worship online' (Krogh et al. 2004a, 168). In the second half of the 2000s I monitored a Kemetic forum in France for some time. Very few French people are interested in worshipping the gods and goddesses of Ancient Egypt, and people with such inclinations would most likely have remained alone in their quest: the internet allowed them to contact like-minded people and, after some time, to organize offline meetings among them. Here we are dealing mostly with people who already felt a fascination for the Egyptian gods and goddesses: the internet thus opened a virtual space for training and connecting, offering 'a blend of online and offline relationships' (Krogh et al. 2004b, 218).

One of the early questions that interested researchers dealt with opportunities for new types of religious activities and rituals. Helland (2000) introduced the distinction between *religion online* (i.e. the presentation of religious information and material on websites, in the same way it could be found in print or in other forms, following a traditional vertical structure) and *online religion* (i.e. the creation of an online space for religious activities based on non-hierarchical interaction and possibly leading to new types of communities). Should we in the future therefore expect entirely new developments, new types of rituals or practices, or even religious groups that exist only online?

Some initial descriptions of online Neopagan rituals suggested a potential in that direction. 'In terms of religion whose traditional roots are more fluid . . . cyberspace does present interesting opportunities for online religion – especially those movements, like Neopaganism, whose ritual space is imaginatively constructed' (Cowan et al. 2004, 134). But it soon became clear that 'successful online rituals are notoriously difficult to find' (Cowan 2005, 121), a situation that has not changed much. There are some exceptions, very much on the fringe, such as cybershamans, who develop solitary practices such as attempting to enter altered states of consciousness by watching fractal videos on the desktop for extended periods, until they feel immersed in this environment, 'tripping the whole night *in* cyberspace, freed from almost all the Earth-based feelings' (Martínková 2008, 48). For most people who use the internet for religious purposes, however, it does not open new types of spiritual experiences, but represents an extension of offline experiences.

While there are scholarly resources on the 3D virtual world Second Life, there has been little research related to NRMs in this space, although several of them are present. The general decline of interest in Second Life may explain this lack of interest. Nonetheless, we ought to remain aware of the potential of virtual worlds for the future. In a report on his visits in Mormon 'areas' of Second Life, a Mormon scholar remarks: 'I was surprised that, on several occasions, I felt a true sense of the numinous when particular monuments or artifacts led me through a narrative that I found both real and immersive' (Scott 2011, 99).

Regarding religious groups existing only online, those that have been created thus far have been rather evanescent and have not attracted much following. Online activities tend rather to supplement existing, offline religious involvements: 'the Internet does not reduce overall social involvement, as many early pundits of online community feared.. . . online religious activities represent simply one part of an individual's overall religious involvement' (Campbell 2011, 241). However, the internet offers opportunities for online participation to small, dispersed groups with weak geographical concentrations, for example by connecting online with the place where a ritual is conducted (Krogh et al. 2004b, 214).

Communities of interest are given an additional boost by the flourishing of social media, as illustrated by the Facebook phenomenon. There is little research on NRMs and social media, however. Movements are using Facebook not only for connecting the faithful, but also for missionary purposes. The official Mormon Facebook page is clearly meant for people interested to learn more about the faith. Interviewed by *The Times*, Elder Erich Kopischke, head of the church's European operation, stated that 'Door-knocking was really the old way of communicating things', suggesting that social networking is becoming more effective in comparison and would become still more efficient over time (Gledhill 2012). If such an assessment is correct, it might be one of the next stages in the story of NRMs online. But ten years ago none could have predicted the success of Facebook. Nobody – not even founders of new religions – can foresee what the future holds for the development of the internet.

27 Invented Religions
Carole M. Cusack

The majority of new religious movements (NRMs) consciously emulate the models established by older religions with regard to their origin and development, through a range of recognized strategies. Leaders deliberately link new teachings to an existing tradition, arguing that it is not really 'new' but a contemporary statement of ancient wisdom; they also stress the authority of new scriptures through elaborate claims of divine inspiration, including channelling, translation and the recording of mystical experiences (Lewis 2003). Rituals are often modelled on familiar religious practices. Examples include: Joseph Smith, who founded the Church of Jesus Christ of Latter-day Saints in 1830, claiming to have translated the Book of Mormon from gold plates in 'Reformed Egyptian'; Sun Myung Moon, the founder of the Unification Church, presenting his teachings as 'spiritual communications' received from Moses, Jesus, Muhammad and Buddha; and L. Ron Hubbard, founder of the Church of Scientology (CoS), framing the practices of 'auditing' and 'touch assists' around confession and the laying on of hands in the Christian tradition (Lewis and Hammer 2007, 1–17). Once a religion is established as authentic, aspects of its development may be framed as innovative without affecting its status as a 'real' religion or spiritual tradition. This is particularly the case for 'world religions' (Judaism, Christianity, Islam, Hinduism and Buddhism), which have their origins in the distant past and have undergone great changes over time. For example, groups that initiate change in the Christian tradition may be classified as orthodox, schismatic, or heretical, yet their existence does not compromise Christianity as a religion.

The first noteworthy characteristic of 'invented religions' is that they explicitly reject these means of establishing spiritual or historical respectability, and openly announce their fictional status (Cusack 2010, 1). This extends to the rejection of continuity with existing historical traditions, in the sense, for example, that early Wiccans and Pagans claimed unbroken transmission from pre-Christian European Paganism. The second noteworthy feature is that invented religions view fictions, the ludic, and play as legitimate sources of ultimate meaning; in no sense inferior materials upon which to base a religion than factual accounts, attested experiences or historical events. For this reason Markus A. Davidsen has argued that they are more properly called 'fiction-based religions' (Davidsen 2012, 185). A third noteworthy feature of invented religions is that, due to their antinomian tendency to engage in mockery and humour, they are often classified as 'parody religions' (Chidester 2005). This designator is applied to Discordianism and the Church of the SubGenius (COSG), both of which play with conspiracy theories, send-ups of ecclesiastical hierarchies, nonsensical doctrines and amusing rituals, and both of which have members who affirm that they are religious, members who affirm that they are not religious, and members who hold both positions simultaneously.

A third descriptor has been proposed by Adam Possamai, in addition to 'invented', and 'fiction-based'. He argues that as such phenomena are largely based on popular culture and mediated by the internet, they are 'hyper-real religions', based on Jean Baudrillard's notion that the hyper-real is the displacement of the real by simulacra (Possamai 2005). All three designations are useful, as they draw attention to specific features of movements such as Discordianism, the Church of All Worlds (CAW), COSG, Jediism, and Matrixism. It can be argued that 'fiction-based' is especially applicable to Jediism, Matrixism and CAW, as they are all based on a particular literary or filmic text, although the engagement with their foundational text that these groups manifest is more creative and engaged than the passive term, 'fiction-based', would suggest. Further, Discordianism and the COSG did not select existing fictions; the founders of these two religions wrote the fictional narrative on which the religion was based, and extrapolated a worldview, doctrines, and ritual practices from it. The term 'hyper-real' may be applied to Jediism and Matrixism, both of which are based on popular films and function largely as online phenomena, although there are 'meat world' (physical world, not on the internet) Jedi organizations, such as the Temple of the Jedi Order in the United States and the International Church of Jediism in the United Kingdom (Cusack 2010, 127–8).

The earliest invented religion of significance is Discordianism, founded by teenage students Kerry Thornley (1938–98) and Greg Hill (1941–2000) in East Whittier, California in 1957, and dedicated to Eris, the Goddess of discord. Discordianism began as a parody, a joke and a deliberate mockery of religion. Thornley and Hill took the religious names Omar Khayyam Ravenhurst (Lord Omar) and Malaclypse the Younger (Mal-2), and created an ecclesiastical organization, the Discordian Society, in which every member is a pope. The religion had two factions, the Paratheo-Anametamystikhood of Eris Esoteric (POEE), and the Erisian Liberation Front (ELF). In 1965 Hill wrote the first version of the classic subcultural scripture, *Principia Discordia*, known as the Magnum Opiate of Malaclypse the Younger, and subtitled *How I Found Goddess and What I Did to Her When I Found Her* (Malaclypse the Younger 1994). This was an anarchic 'zine, illustrated by sketches, reproductions of 'found' documents, multiple typefaces, and a non-linear, surreal structure (Cusack 2010, 28). First published in 1969, it has been freely available ever since due to the Discordian policy of 'kopyleft'. It is appropriate that the principal means of evangelism within Discordianism was the incorporation of much of the *Principia Discordia* into the best-selling science fiction trilogy *Illuminatus!* (1975), authored by Robert Shea and the champion of alternative and suppressed knowledge(s) and fringe religionist Robert Anton Wilson (Robertson 2012, 421, 429). Due to its popularity among college subcultures, including computer 'geeks' and comic-book fans, Discordianism made a seamless transition to the internet, and became (in a sense) the 'parent' tradition to other eclectic religious and esoteric systems, including the Church of the SubGenius (founded 1979 by Philo Drummond and Ivan Stang) and Chaos Magic, a movement heralded by the publication of Peter Carroll's *Liber Null* in 1978. Phil Hine has testified to the power of fiction in modern magical practice when he argued that Chaos Magic 'borrowed freely from Science Fiction ... Chaos magic is an approach that enables the individual to use anything that s/he thinks is suitable as a temporary belief or symbol system ... What matters is the results you get, not the "authenticity" of the system you use' (Hine 1992–7, 10).

A second model of invented religion is exemplified in the Church of All Worlds (CAW), which was founded in 1962 by college students Lance Christie (1944–2010) and Tim Zell (1942–) at Westminster College, Fulton, Missouri. This religion is based on Robert A. Heinlein's science fiction novel *Stranger in a Strange Land* (1961), in which Valentine Michael Smith, raised on Mars, brings a message of sexual liberation and religious pluralism to humanity. In the early years of CAW's existence, rites and doctrines were based on Heinlein's novel, but in 1968 Tim Zell registered CAW as a religion in California, and began incorporating elements of modern Paganism into its practice, in part due to his friendship with Frederick McLaren Adams (1928–2008), founder of Feraferia (Cusack 2010, 62–3). Tim Zell had a powerful vision in 1970 which changed the course of CAW's theology, with the focus shifting from the polytheistic Goddess of revived Paganism to the notion that the Earth itself was the Goddess, Gaia, a conscious entity incorporating all living being in which humans function as planetary consciousness (Zell-Ravenheart 2009, 90–5). From that time on, Lance Christie devoted himself to environmental activism, and Tim Zell (as Otter G'Zell, later Oberon Zell-Ravenheart, now Oberon Zell) and his second wife Morning Glory Zell (b. Diana Moore, 1948), explored spiritual travel to ancient Pagan sites such as Eleusis, and devoted themselves to the modern revival of mythological beings such as unicorns, the pursuit of a sustainable, rural and communal lifestyle, and the practice of polyamory, which is the philosophy and lifestyle of responsible non-monogamy (Vale and Sulak 2001, 130–6). In the twenty-first century, CAW remains loyal to its fiction-based origins, has become a major voice in modern environmental Paganism, and leads the way as an invented religion that documents its history and records its cultural activities, both on websites and through a programme of intensive print publication (including promotion of the CAW magical education system, the Grey School of Wizardry, and the Pagan art business Mythic Images).

Over time scholarship has identified further members of the family of invented religions, including the Tribunal of the Sidhe, a group that used J. R. R. Tolkien's *Lord of the Rings* trilogy as scripture (Davidsen 2012, 191–2), Jediism, based on George Lucas' *Star Wars* film trilogy, and Matrixism, based on Larry and Andy Wachowski's *The Matrix* film trilogy (Cusack 2010, 113–40). Fictional texts are also used in the broader Pagan and magical community (which is itself a spiritual and religious network with a fictional genealogy). Tolkienian Elven rituals and Chaos workings invoking Teletubbies are, while not mainstream, certainly present among eclectic Pagans and magical practitioners. The study of invented religions is still an emergent field, but it has the potential to affect the discipline of religious studies profoundly through its challenge to the normative definitions employed therein. As early as 1981 Lonnie D. Kliever hazarded the view that all 'religious belief systems' and 'life-worlds' were fictional (Kliever 1981, 658). This important contention has only recently attracted the attention it deserves, having been enthusiastically taken up by both cognitive scientific and social constructionist theorists of religion. Invented religions fit newer models of religion that emphasize story, play, creativity, and the importance of meaning-making, both individual and collective. Whether the stories are fictions or 'actually happened' is, ultimately, unimportant. Mikael Rothstein has noted that the ways that 'human beings think and act during the formation of new religious thoughts and ways in general' have certain commonalities. He concludes that '[a]ll religions are negotiated cultural phenomena which only have me into existence because human beings have created them in a variety of cognitive and social transactions' (Rothstein 2007b, 315). This statement perfectly encapsulates the origins of invented religions, and points to the urgent necessity of recognizing them, not as 'parody' nor as 'fake' religions, but simply as religions (Cusack 2010, 149).

28 Race and Ethnicity

Marie W. Dallam

Chapter Outline	
Race and Religion	296
Ethnicity and Religion	297
Gesturing towards the Future	299

As academic fields, the studies of race and ethnicity have noteworthy parallels to the study of NRMs. For example, scholars engaged in these areas often have to struggle against misconceptions as their first working step. This is because race, ethnicity, and NRMs are all things that the general public thinks they implicitly understand, aided in part by the approximate usage of terminology that occurs in both popular culture and the media. Additionally, the studies of race and ethnicity and NRMs are interdisciplinary fields in which scholars typically 'agree to disagree' for the sake of coming together around a common, sometimes fraught, topic. Thus, just as with NRMs, scholars should appreciate that the studies of race and ethnicity are complex and deeply layered and should not be casually added to our work as ideological asides.

The precise meanings of the terms *race* and *ethnicity*, as well as appropriate ways to employ the concepts in other types of research, are not without contest. Increasingly the study of race and the study of ethnicity are moving in different academic directions, and while the tendency has been to lump them together as one subject we should not assume this is always the best approach. In most situations, it will behoove the attentive scholar to consider them as distinct areas of inquiry. As the practical implications of race and ethnicity often vary from place to place, it is also crucial to understand how the histories of race and ethnicity have unfolded within the particular context under investigation.

Race and Religion

For many centuries, the primary idea of *race* was that a shared ancestry led to commonalities in both physical and cultural traits. Though over time scientists offered several possible taxonomies, the most popular asserted that all humans had their origins in one of three races: Negroid, Caucasoid or Mongoloid. This system of human categorization was proven genetically false through scientific advancements in the latter half of the twentieth century, and increased cultural awareness worldwide demonstrated that 'characteristics' previously attributed to one race or another were unstable, shifting in time and place. In other words, scientists recognized that ideas about race are socially constructed and not genetically programmed. Nonetheless, the imprint of these ideas has been difficult to shed, and so *race* remains an operative concept. *Race* is now commonly employed as a category of people whose physical features resemble each other (most especially skin colour, hair type and facial features), and therefore the people are thought to be part of a single social group. Race can be an important marker in places where there has been a history of racial prejudice, especially because today there may be measures in place to prevent ongoing discrimination. For example, while a fourth-generation Black Briton may have very little in common – both genetically and culturally – with a recent Haitian immigrant to the United Kingdom, they are both considered to be of the same race, 'Black', and in turn may benefit from certain anti-discrimination protections. Hence, race may only be a social construct, but it can also have political importance, so while not a biological category race is very much an operative classification ('Race', 2003; Fluehr-Lobban 2006; Hill Collins et al. 2010).

The social experience of race can be a primary motivating factor in NRM affiliation, especially when an NRM builds ideas about race into its theology. For example, since at least the early twentieth century many African Americans have deliberately disaffiliated from Christianity, considering it a religion that has historically privileged white people at the expense of other races. In new varieties of Islam such as the Moorish Science Temple of America, and in new Judaisms such as the Church of God and Saints of Christ, African Americans have found religions that celebrate African history, promote Black nationalism and offer unlimited access for participation. Similarly, some white people have joined groups within the Christian Identity Movement because the ideology explicitly links the Caucasian race with a heightened spiritual value. Still other NRMs, such as the Peoples Temple and Father Divine's Peace Mission Movement, embraced a theology of radical racial equality and attracted people dedicated to that vision. Thus, while many people in the world are moving towards a social order in which racial categories have little significance because they only speak to superficial difference, it remains true that some NRMs have strong racial components that should not be ignored as part of thorough scholarship.

Because race is a social construct, there is no precise, predictable, or inherent relationship between race and religion. Ethnicity, however, is a different matter, and scholars have been careful to distinguish patterns in the ways that ethnicity and religion have historically functioned together. It is also worth noting that scholarship on 'ethnicity and religion' is far more plentiful and varied than that on 'race and religion'.

Ethnicity and Religion

At the core of *ethnicity* is the concept of nationality and, in turn, a particular culture that is associated with that nationality; however, ethnicity and nationality should not simply be equated. In most cases, multiple ethnic groups are found within a given nation, and a particular ethnic identity may be even stronger than any affinity to the country itself. Ethnicity generally refers to a host of shared cultural traits such as language, worldview, artistic forms, customs, and beliefs about origins and history, and religion is frequently but not always a part of this list. No one attempts to make the argument that ethnicity is somehow biologically based; ethnicity is clearly the result of a dialectical relationship between people and their cultural circumstances. However, there is a range of arguments about how ethnic groups first begin, what is at their core and what causes them to change (for examples see Hoddie 2006; Ibrahim 2011; Kivisto 2007).

In contrast to ideas associated with race, perceptions about ethnicity are relatively stable and thus identifiable. This is not to say that ethnicities do not change; history has proven that among those who emigrate, ethnic ties typically weaken as people assimilate and transform in a variety of ways. Some would argue that people become less ethnically identified over time, yet we also recognize the emergence of new ethnicities, such as the unique hybrid identities Nuyorican and BrAsian (New York/Puerto Rican and British/Asian, respectively). As there are thousands of possible ethnicities that can be identified worldwide, ethnicity is clearly a much more finely tuned set of characteristics delimiting a group of people than those characteristics associated with giant categories of race.

There is no single way that religion and ethnicity correspond, but there are several common patterns (Abramson 1980; for arguments challenging these patterns, see Hammond et al. 1993). For example, one possibility is that a particular religion is the essential foundation of an ethnicity such that the culture is built upon the religion. The religion ultimately becomes nearly inseparable from the ethnicity yet is nonetheless identifiable as a set of beliefs and practices. This is often called an 'ethno-religious' identity (also 'religio-ethnic'), and a clear present-day example of it is Jews. Very few NRMs will exhibit this kind of correlation because it takes a significant amount of time to develop, during which time the religion at the core usually becomes widely accepted. Thus an ethno-religious identity is found among only a few historic NRMs that have remained somewhat marginalized, such as the Amish and the Fundamentalist Latter Day Saints (FLDS).

Another pattern is based on a historic connection between a place and a religion. Over time, people from the geographic region are likely to be part of a specific religion simply because it has been the most dominant faith there; hence one thinks of Greeks as Eastern Orthodox and the Khmer as Buddhist, but we know that there will be exceptions to this rule. Because this relationship between ethnicity and religion is essentially flimsy, some scholars argue that the religious aspect is particularly subject to erosion when people migrate to places that do not have the same dominant religion. In contrast, however, others have found that this circumstance can cause the opposite result, because at times immigrants become more involved with a familiar religion abroad in order to find social community. In such cases, religion becomes a realm of ethnic reinforcement. There is an extensive range of scholarship on these issues that comes out of interdisciplinary fields as well from the social sciences (for examples see Spickard 2005; Stone et al. 2003; Warner et al. 1998). The relevance of this kind of relationship on NRMs can be quite varied, depending on the particular circumstances. Some examples can be seen with eastern-derived faiths that became known as NRMs in the Western world, and which experienced significant demographic shifts as immigration patterns changed (see discussions in Clarke 2000; Nye 2001).

A third possible and very common pattern, which can overlap with either of the first two, is when one religion is shared by people of various ethnicities. We see this, for example, with Catholicism, which is shared among a range of ethnic peoples from places as widespread as Mexico, Italy and Ireland. Any of these could be further broken down into more specific divisions; rather than 'Italian Catholics', for example, Italians themselves might recognize ethnic divides such as Sicilian Catholics and Calabrian Catholics, et cetera. The influences of different ethnic subcultures on the religion can create unexpected variants in belief or practice, not only around the world but also from one localized region to the next. For practitioners that may mean that coming together causes strain; for scholars the challenge is to understand the unifying threads as well as the sources of tension. This type of correlation between ethnicity and religion is relatively straightforward and most scholars of mainstream religion have been careful to include it as an aspect of research. Scholarship on NRMs has been slower to consider the impact of ethnic divisions, but this is at least partly because there are fewer instances of it. Some examples can be seen in groups such as Twelve Tribes and ISKCON, both of which demonstrate multiple ethnicities striving to unite through a religion that has traditionally had an ethnic component. As globalization increasingly affects NRMs that were once quite localized, causing them to expand in unexpected places, this pattern will surely emerge as a more fruitful area of examination.

The final pattern of relationship with ethnicity and religion is when the two are utterly inseparable and always have been, such that we cannot begin to imagine the ethnic identity standing alone without the religious aspect; the religion is woven into the culture in such a way that it is not readily isolable. Examples of this include subgroups of Native Americans, and Australian Aboriginese. This kind of correlation may not be applicable to the study of NRMs for obvious reasons, however it can be partially relevant in rare instances when a significant number of any such ethnic group converts to an NRM. This is the case, for example, with the many Zulu people who joined the amaNazaretha in South Africa. While some scholars would consider this an example of syncretism, such a lens tends to diminish the significance of ethnicity in the new formulation.

Gesturing towards the Future

In addition to new directions discussed above, an increasingly important area of inquiry is diasporic New Religions. Although diasporic NRMs – such as Seicho-No-Ie, a Japanese NRM that has flourished in Brazil – are atypical, when they present themselves it compels scholars to examine a particularly unique combination of questions regarding culture, ethnicity, assimilation and power. Relevant theoretical literature will largely be found within the scholarship that examines immigrants and religion, so researchers will have much to sort through when seeking appropriate frameworks (see Johnson 2007; Knott et al. 2010; Kokot et al. 2004).

Finally, one last trend gaining strength in both race and ethnicity studies is the recognition of the vast array of ethnicities that exist among people who have often been lumped together as one racial category, and the re-examination of assumptions that were previously made on that basis. Surely such assumptions have been operative in NRM studies just as they have in other areas, and scholars would be well advised to keep that in mind as they pursue new research. Earlier histories of NRMs that were racially homogenous but ethnically diverse may be worth revisiting and revising based on new awareness about ethnic identities and inter-ethnic relationships.

29 Children and Generational Issues

E. Burke Rochford, Jr.

Chapter Outline

Children in New Religious Movements	302
Second-generation Adults	303
The Second Generation, Religious Culture and Change in NRMs	305
Conclusion	306

New religious movements are prone to change and children and family life represent one significant force in their transformation (Rochford 2007a). As Barker (1995a, 170) notes, NRMs face both 'the challenge *of* and the challenge *from* children'. For in socializing and educating those born into the faith, NRMs must devote resources that could otherwise be invested in missionary work, or in other activities critical to realizing movement goals and purposes. Moreover, as Richard Niebuhr (1929, 19–20) noted long ago, the socialization of children plays a decisive role in the development of sectarian religious communities for as 'generation succeeds generation, the isolation of the community from the world becomes more difficult'." However, accommodation is by no means certain as effective socialization limits the potential for defection and reduced strictness as children grow into adulthood (Stark 1996, 143–4).

Today, second- and third-generation members represent the majority membership of many of the more prominent 1960s NRMs given their general inability to capture the imagination of a new generation of converts (Barker 2004, 98; Hardman 2004, 386). As this suggests, both the present and future of these NRMs rest on the fate of the children born and raised within. Yet the literature on children and generational issues in NRMs is limited and much of what we know centres on the issue of child abuse. There are two reasons for this. First, the focus on child abuse represents a continuation of the politics surrounding NRMs (Jenkins 2000). Like allegations of 'brainwashing' before it, claims and counterclaims surrounding child abuse are part of what Bromley (2001) refers to as the 'political imbroglio' that surrounds NRMs. Second, highly publicized incidents of violence during the 1990s involving a small number of new religions grabbed the attention of both NRM scholars and publishers who saw a market for research reporting on 'cults and violence'. Because many children in NRMs were growing into adolescence and adulthood in the late 1980s and 1990s, the interest in collective violence effectively eclipsed research that might otherwise have been conducted on children and generational issues.

This essay briefly considers research on the childhood experiences of the second generation, how second-generation adults identify with the NRM they grew up in as well as with mainstream society, and, lastly, how children and family life have shaped the development of NRMs.

Children in New Religious Movements

Like utopian communities throughout history, many contemporary NRMs have developed alternatives to the conventional nuclear family, a fact that has made them all the more controversial (Beckford 1985, 187; Wilson 1990, 63). Growing out of the 1960s counterculture, many denounced the nuclear family as destructive. Rajneesh, for example, condemned the modern family 'as the root cause of all our neurosis' and childbearing and childrearing were discouraged (Puttick 1999, 90–1). In place of the nuclear family, communal living and collective forms of childrearing have prevailed among many NRMs. The 'ideal' family thus became the collectivity as a whole, rather than the biological family. Parents typically were discouraged from becoming overly involved in the lives of their children as other adults assumed primary responsibility for socializing children. During their formative years, both ISKCON and The Sullivan Institute/Fourth Wall community, for example, sent their children to boarding schools when children were as young as 5 and 6 years of age (Rochford 2007b, 60; Siskind 2001, 424). In ISKCON's case, the movement's boarding schools (*gurukula*) freed parents to work full-time distributing religious literature and preaching in public locations (Rochford 1985, 171–89, 2007b, 82). Most children in The Family/Children of God also lived apart from their parents or otherwise spent considerable time away from them before the age of 16 (Chancellor 2000, 217). For the most part children in The Family were home schooled a practice that allowed parents to continue full-time missionary work (Bainbridge 2002, 150). Today, however, a significant and growing number of children in The Family are attending state/public schools (Amsterdam 2006) as are children in

ISKCON (Rochford 2007b, 66) and Sahaja Yoga in the United Kingdom (Coney 1999, 115). (For a discussion of schooling in a number of different religious groups and movements, see Palmer and Hardman 1999.)

Allegations of child abuse have been widely associated with children growing up in NRMs. Such claims, in whole or in part, have been used to legitimate intervention by the state in a number of NRMs including the Northeast Kingdom Community in Island Pond, Vermont (Palmer 1999), the Branch Davidians in Waco, Texas (Tabor and Gallagher 1995), and in numerous raids carried out by authorities across the globe against The Family (Bainbridge 2002, 7–19; Chancellor 2000; Richardson 1999). Similar claims of abuse and accompanying raids have also been directed at fundamentalist Mormon groups (Homer 2006). In addition, abuse allegations have played a role in child custody cases where a parent, or grandparent, has sought custody of one or more children living with a parent actively involved in an NRM (Bradney 1999; Chancellor 2000, 133–7; Hardman 2004, 397–9; Homer 1999; Richardson 2006, 74–5; Siskind 1999, 62–6).

While it is true that child abuse did occur in a limited number of NRMs such as ISKCON (Rochford 2007b, 74–96) and The Family (Chancellor 2000), the widespread moral panic surrounding NRMs and child abuse has been driven principally by anti-cult propaganda and a media hungry for sensational (if often false) reports of child abuse within unconventional minority religions. For as Richardson (1999) argues, allegations of child abuse have served as the 'ultimate weapon' against NRMs, especially in light of the fact that the 'brainwashing' narrative of cult involvement has been largely rejected by the courts in the United States and elsewhere. Despite the attention given to child abuse, there has been little systematic research in cases where abuse has occurred (but see Chancellor 2000; Rochford 2007b, 74–96; Siskind 1999). What we do know, however, suggests that many of the factors involved mirror those found in the Catholic Church sexual abuse scandal and in cases of child physical abuse by conservative Protestant parents (Ellison and Sherkat 1993; Greven 1990; Jenkins 1996; Krebs 1998).

Second-generation Adults

As might be expected, there is considerable diversity among second-generation adults with respect to their level of involvement and identification with the NRM they grew up in. Some have grown into full-time membership while significant numbers have moved to the periphery becoming congregational members or movement sympathizers. Defection too has been commonplace especially among the first wave of children who grew up during the formative years of their movement's development (Bainbridge 2002, 158; Chancellor

2000, 242; Puttick 1999, 103; Rochford 2007b, 95). In still other cases, such as The Family, young adults who failed to meet the level of strictness required of full-time members were forced to choose between upping their commitment and involvement, or leaving the communal fold which several hundred chose to do (Melton 1997, 61). In general, it appears that the 1960s NRMs have retained far fewer of their children into adulthood than have older sectarian groups such as the Amish (Kraybill 2000, 186) and the Hutterites (Janzen and Stanton 2010, 240–1) who hold on to 85 to 90 per cent of their children.

Whether young people remain as members into adulthood depends upon their experiences growing up and the extent to which they were given useful and significant things to do on behalf of their faith. The latter functions to promote commitment and loyalty to the group and its mission (Stark 1996, 144). However, NRMs have dealt differently with their youths and young adults and dissimilar outcomes have resulted. After significant numbers of young people began leaving The Family in the 1980s and early 1990s, the leadership instituted a number of reforms meant to give young people greater opportunities and responsibility. These included: allowing second-generation youths to become voting members, to contribute to movement decision-making, and to serve in positions of leadership, first at the local home level and subsequently at the national and international levels, for example, in Asia and South America (Melton 1997, 60). Many second-generation members also took the lead in opening new preaching fields in Eastern Europe and Africa (Chancellor 2000, 242). As these changes reveal, retaining the youth became an organizational priority for the Family.

ISKCON, by contrast, proved far less responsive to its second-generation members. Although a few second-generation adults did take on responsible positions within the movement during the 1980s and 1990s (e.g. as temple presidents), the renunciate leadership steadfastly resisted shifting organizational priorities away from missionary work, even when recruitment and book distribution slowed dramatically. Disinterest in children and family life both contributed to the child abuse that occurred within ISKCON's schools and led large numbers of second-generation adults to defect or to otherwise limit their dealings with the organization (Rochford 2007b, 204–5).

Because large numbers of second-generation youths and adults from a variety of NRMs transitioned into the outside society, they faced the task of remaking their social identities. For some this meant rejecting their past life in order to forge a more conventional self-identity. It appears that many more, however, chose to combine elements of their past and present lives crafting 'hybrid' (Pike 2011, 45) or 'adhesive' (Yang 1999, 17–18) identities. Evidence of such dual identities can be seen in the comments of a young man who spent his childhood in ISKCON but who as an adult lives and works apart from the movement: 'Now that I'm not so frightened to be different and am as comfortable living in American culture as I used to be in ISKCON culture, these differences are almost what define me. This tension between American culture and ISKCON culture and this almost-dance I do on the edges of both are in many ways who I am. I don't really want to become all American, but neither do I want to be a full-time devotee' (Deadwyler 2001, 20). As he states further, for himself and his peers, the contexts and circumstances they face dictate which portion of their identity emerges; 'One day we will be running around and swimming in our shorts and bikinis, boys and girls freely mixing. Listening to rock and roll or hip-hop, and then the next day we'll be at the Sunday programme [at an ISKCON temple] in *dhotis* and *saris* singing and dancing in the *kirtana*' (2001, 17).

The Second Generation, Religious Culture and Change in NRMs

Because of their radical quality, new religions face the daunting task of constructing oppositional religious cultures that support their unconventional beliefs and lifestyles. These cultures provide the institutional structures, practices, and symbols that integrate followers internally while, at the same time, segregating them from the corrosive effects of the secular culture. Yet each of the major new religions of the 1960s struggled in its effort to develop broad-based religious cultures in support of children and families. Without fully formed domestic cultures, The Family, the Unification Church and ISKCON each experienced significant numbers of families leaving the communal fold to establish independent lives (Barker 1995b; Chancellor 2000; Introvigne 2000; Mickler 2006; Rochford 2007b). As they did, the communal structures of each group gave way to congregationalism, growing accommodation to the dominant culture, and a reduction in strictness among both first- and second-generation members alike. These changes led to a reworking of membership categories to make them more inclusive (Amsterdam 2006; Barker 1995b, 174–5; Rochford 2000, 2007b). The Family presently recognizes five distinct membership categories that range from full-time disciples ('Family Discipleship') to marginally committed 'General Members' (Amsterdam 2006; Zerby and Kelly 2009). By the mid-1990s, the Unification Church had a large congregation of less committed and involved 'Home Church' members with few full-time members (Barker 1995b; Introvigne 2000, 47). A similar pattern of member diversity is also apparent in ISKCON where the topic of who is a legitimate member of the organization has become a topic of some discussion (see e.g. Kripamoya Das 2012; Urmila Dasi 2012).

As communalism gave way to a more inclusive congregational structure, NRMs have undergone a number of noteworthy changes that include: adults taking jobs in the outside employment market, children attending secular schools, sharp reductions in proselytizing and rates of recruitment, declining levels of member commitment, marriages with non-members, the privatization of religious practice at the expense of collective forms of worship, and challenges to the authority of the leadership (Amsterdam 2006; Barker 1995a; Chancellor 2000; Introvigne 2000; Mickler 2006, 168; Rochford 1995, 2000, 2002, 2007b). Not surprisingly perceptions of the outside society also changed as images of a 'corrupt' and 'evil' system became difficult to sustain when the everyday lives of substantial numbers of first- and second-generation members included conventional forms of involvement (Chancellor 2000; Rochford 2000, 2007b). Moreover, organizational priorities changed as well. Setting aside their world-rejecting stance, The Family (Chancellor 2000), ISKCON (Rochford 1985, 271–2) and the Unification Church (Introvigne 2000a, 47) all embraced charitable and humanitarian work on behalf of society's poor and needy, often in cooperation with people of other faiths. In giving up their struggle to change society and to model a viable alternative to it, these NRMs transformed into established religious organizations where children and family life had increasing significance (Chancellor 2000; Rochford 2007b).

Conclusion

There is a great need for more research on children and generational issues within NRMs. While researchers uniformly acknowledge the importance of those born within for the long-term stability of an NRM, the fact remains that we have little in the way of detailed studies of the socialization process and how children construct their religious and organizational identities (but see Berger 1999; Kermani 2011; Rochford 2007b, 2011). Recent scholarship on children and religion highlights the ways that children actively and creatively construct their religious worlds, often in complex but pragmatic ways (Ridgely 2011). Given the importance of new generations to the fate of religious movements, we also need studies of how the views and lifestyles of each generation shape the careers of NRMs. For example, many of the young adults who grew up in The Family hold far more conservative views about sexuality than their parents' generation, a fact that has helped reshape the sexual ethos of the movement (Chancellor 2000, 230–2). Finally, to date, there has been no research on the third generation, yet many NRMs now have a substantial and growing number of young people who are the grandchildren of the converts who led the way during the 1960s and 1970s. One can only wonder whether this generation will continue the march towards greater societal accommodation or whether it will stir the winds of revival and attempt to reclaim the more radical values and goals that defined the early days of contemporary NRMs. For as Marcus Hansen hypothesized in his celebrated essay, 'The Problem of the Third Generation Immigrant' 'what the son wishes to forget the grandson wishes to remember' (1990, 195).

30 Healing

Holly Folk

Subjective and social perceptions of physical and psychic well-being are among the main sites where a worldview is expressed. Beliefs about and practices directed to healing are features of most religions. They are especially prominent themes in new religious movements, whose sectarian outlook predisposes them to reject mainstream cultural forms, including orthodox medicine. Some of the best-known groups to emerge over the past 100 years have had distinct health ideas at their core: Adventist Christians, for their sanitariums like the one at Battle Creek, Michigan; Jehovah's Witnesses, for their rejection of blood transfusions; Christian Scientists, for spiritual healing; the Church of Scientology, for elaborate detoxification programmes and the rejection of psychiatry.

Quite frequently, healing is foundational for NRMs. Max Weber noted miraculous cures were associated with prophetic charisma, and attributed to figures like Jesus, George Fox and Joseph Smith. In many contemporary NRMs, followers also have believed their leaders to be in possession of healing powers, as is the case with 'Rav' Philip Berg of the Kabbalah Centre. Both the Indian guru Sathya Sai Baba and the Reverend Jim Jones staged elaborate healing performances. The symbolic potential of the human body leads many religious groups to form doctrines about physical wellness. Some, like the Hare Krishnas, have elevated vegetarianism as a healthier and morally higher form of eating, showing that techniques for health such as diet, exercise, and body cleanliness can serve as both inclusive and exclusive boundary mechanisms for group identity. Unificationists would blow on food offered by outsiders to purify it, but the Order of the Solar Temple used health clubs and public lectures as recruiting tools. Health practices refract group dynamics in many ways. Bodily mortifications like fasting and abstaining from alcohol can serve as 'control mechanisms' of collective discipline. Followers of Sri Chinmoy became well known for their endurance events, including weeks-long sessions of marathon running. Furthermore, the spiritual goals of new religious movements can be expressed in terms of healing and recovery. In Westernized Buddhism meditation is frequently understood to have psychologically therapeutic benefits, and the goal of many New Age therapies is physical or emotional regeneration. Moreover, some NRMs extend a healing trope onto greater entities, such as the environment. For practitioners of woman-centred spiritualities, society must recover from the injuries of patriarchy. Groups as diverse as Neopagan nature religions and Aum Shinrikyō have interpreted their actions as the 'healing' of a 'sick' world.

Alternative medicine often has been compared to religious nonconformity (see Marc Galanter 1989). The epithet 'healing cults' has been flung at many systems, even while unorthodox practitioners have called themselves 'medical sectarians' for more than 200 years. Clearly, social protest runs through both religious and health alternatives, and these concerns converge in many illuminating case studies. The political dimensions of Mesmerism on both sides of the Atlantic are explored by Robert Darnton (France) and Robert C. Fuller (United States); while the social historian Logie S. Barrow has shown ties between the labour movement and anti-vaccination campaigns in the United Kingdom. Also, cultural dissent is an organizing theme in Ann Braude's study of American Spiritualism. It merits mention that while not the primary focus, her work addresses how the dead came to be seen as healing entities. Populist ideology strongly characterized American nineteenth-century 'health reform'. 'Irregular' systems are of special importance, for many of their practices stand as forerunners to contemporary alternative medicine. Among others, researchers should consult the work of Stephen Nissenbaum, Ronald Numbers, Norman Gevitz and John S. Haller. They document how different unorthodox systems, such as vegetarianism and water cure, shared a common therapeutic logic based on eighteenth-century medical vitalism.

The conversation about religion and healing is robust in the area of the American Metaphysical Movement, where there is an ample historical record. Physical healing is an optimal site for the actualization of Harmonial philosophies like Christian Science and New Thought. Because human consciousness is seen as a microcosmic expression of the divine, these traditions claim it is possible to affect the material world through thought and regard Mental Healing as a demonstration of spiritual prowess. (The most comprehensive treatment is by Catherine L. Albanese. Also see Charles S. Braden, J. Stillson Judah, Donald Meyer, Gail Thain Parker and Beryl Satter.) Rennie B. Schoepflin's study of Christian Science is very interesting for its framing of the late nineteenth century as a moment for the 'radical spiritualization' of irregular medicine, which raises provocative questions about the boundary between religious and medical healing models in this family of traditions.

There also is an abundance of scholarly and popular literature on healing in contemporary alternative spiritualities, such as the New Age Movement, Paganism, Wicca and Nature Religions. The theme of healing is well brought out in works by Meredith B. McGuire and Deborah L. Kantor, Pamela E. Klassen, Sarah M. Pike, Catherine M. Roach and many others. Even so, the field reflects an imbalance: its connections to the alternative spirituality preferred by liberal countercultural movements have been well documented, but alternative medicine also is popular in many conservative social movements and subcultures. There is a great need for studies of American reactionary social movements like Christian Identity and the Patriot Movement, which reject the corporate medicine of 'Big Pharma' and include 'Health Liberty' in their visions for national redemption.

Beyond its consideration in Metaphysical and 'New Age' spiritualities, healing is seldom broken out and given primary importance in academic studies of new religions. For example, Theosophy deserves far more attention than it has received for its treatment of healing, which is complex. Theosophists have held that the 'Laws of Health' are part of the gift of wisdom to humanity, but in contrast to New Thought, they have not usually made physical and psychological wellness reflections of spiritual advancement. Yet some Theosophists acknowledge a deity of healing, 'Lady Master Meta'; others have posited that spiritual healing is actually an accomplishment of the advanced human mind. The medical backgrounds of Elliot Coues and Alexis Carrel led them to develop combinative reinterpretations of the biological sciences. Perhaps most significant, Theosophical and other esoteric ideas have influenced many twentieth-century health alternatives, including the later theories of the founders of osteopathy (A. T. Still) and chiropractic (D. D. Palmer).

As the case of Theosophy shows, the topic of healing in new religions is relatively unexplored, and the state of the subfield makes healing a potentially fruitful area for new research. Researchers advancing such inquiries would do well to consider how scholarship has evolved to see understandings of maladies as culturally informed. Presenting even some of the relevant insights from history of medicine or cultural anthropology goes beyond the scope of this essay, but it is broadly recognized that the vocabulary of healing is polysemous. 'Maladies' can be physical, psychic, spiritual or social. 'Treatments' operate on several different levels of well-being, and 'recovery' can be from corporeal illness or psychological, spiritual or even communal distress. The cultural contextualization of healing and its expansive meanings have been well explored by scholars in religious studies, most recently by Thomas J. Csordas, Linda L. Barnes and Susan S. Sered, and Candy Gunther Brown. The theoretical approach known as 'Lived Religion' stands out for its focus on healing (see works by Robert A. Orsi, as well as Pamela E. Klassen and Meredith B. McGuire). In fact, Robert Orsi has proposed that healing is the *primary* focus of religious activity.

Vitalism – the belief that the human body is animated by a vital force – has proved a persistent theory in alternative medicine, and practically ubiquitous in new religions. Vitalist beliefs stand behind Western holism, where they are captured in the phrase, 'Body, Mind and Spirit'. Yet they are common around the world, and are fertile sites for inquiry. Vitalist theories take near infinite expressions, and they justify heterogeneous practices such as crystal healing, aura cleansing and energy therapies (see Edith L. B. Turner). In Qigong, of which

Falun Gong is the best-known form, exercises and bodily practices like walking and shouting are used to access 'qi' energy. Practitioners believe Qigong has many curative properties, including the curing of cancer (see David A. Palmer). Vitalist ideas also are prominent in systems that use the physical laying on of hands. Catherine Albanese and Candy Gunther Brown have pointed out the metaphysical dimensions of chiropractic, but there is a great need for additional studies on touch-based therapies.

Reiki is arguably the best-known vitalist practice with a strong spiritual valance. Originating in Japan and popularized first in Hawaii by a Japanese-American woman named Hawayo Hiromi Takata, Reiki uses 'attunement' to access 'life force energy'. It also includes beliefs and practices related to reincarnation and getting in touch with previous incarnations. Because the system is understood as a religious path on which healers serve as spiritual guides, it has triggered accusations of being a dangerous cult. This has been documented by European scholars, including Massimo Introvigne; J. Gordon Melton was among the first to write about Reiki in English (in Rothstein 2001).

New religions vibrate with broader cultural reactions to social change. For more than 200 years, beliefs about science and new technologies have been incorporated into popular spiritualities. On both sides of the Atlantic, the nineteenth-century Spiritualists understood the 'spiritual telegraph' as a conduit for healing energies. More recently, beings from outer space have been understood as a source of therapeutic power. Partridge's *UFO Religions* carries a lively discussion about healing across several essays. The theme is also well addressed by Diana G. Tumminia, who finds an influence from the New Age Recovery Movement in the subculture devoted to healing from the trauma of alien abduction.

The rapid social changes associated with globalization have greatly affected religious life in many nations, generating many promising avenues for religion and NRMs. For example, responses to the AIDS crisis reflect the interplay between globalization, religion and healing. This is examined by Leslie Butt and Richard Eves, and Felicitas Becker and Wenzel Giessler. In developing regions, and especially Africa, the epidemic has stood as a factor in the development of millenarian movements. Emmanuel K. Twesigye notes that a cure was a promised benefit of the initiation rituals of the Movement for the Restoration of the Ten Commandments of God.

Japan arguably has the greatest number of officially recognized 'new religions'. As in American Metaphysical movements, Japanese NRMs regard physical healing as sign of spiritual progress and salvation. Physical and spiritual healing thus are major goals in most *shinskūkyō* and *shin-shinshūkyō*, though they have different therapeutic substrates. In Kurozumi-kyo followers look to the sun goddess, Amaterasu for the curing of disease. In contrast, Nichiren promised healing through the Daimoku. 'Divine Light', often called 'Jyorei' (or

Johrei), is used for spiritual purification in many sects, including Shumei and the Church of World Messianity. With ties to the ideas of New Thought teacher Ernest Holmes, Seicho-No-Ie maintains the 'unreality' of illness. Japanese scholars have long been aware of the role of healing in the *shinshūkyō*, but relatively little of their work is available in English. Books by Helen Hardacre and Clark B. Offner and Henry van Straelen, though older, are still regarded as standard in the field. More recently, the work of Susumu Shimazono has become available in translation.

Of religious changes brought about by globalization, the most important development is the explosion of Pentecostalism – which, though one of the largest Protestant sub-traditions, falls under the purview of new religious movements for many reasons, including tension with host societies, decentralized leadership and ecstatic worship. Because it is promised as one of the Gifts of the Holy Spirit, healing is critical in Charismatic and Pentecostal Christianity, among the fastest-growing religious traditions worldwide. The best recent studies are by Candy Gunther Brown, whose work is especially useful for its interdisciplinary theoretical insights.

Pentecostalism's biggest competitor in the Global South, Catholic renewal movements also carry healing as a prominent spiritual goal. Catholics have long associated the Virgin Mary with healing, and though best known through the instances at Fatima, Portugal and Lourdes, France, appearances of the Virgin Mary have occurred worldwide and seem to be increasing in number. Kristy Nabhan-Warren has done groundbreaking work on Marian Apparitions, and she specifically addresses the messages about healing revealed to Estela Ruiz, the Pheonix, Arizona-based founder of Mary Ministries.

Encounters with universalizing religions often result in the folding of traditional practices into local interpretations of an incoming religion. In Zionist Christianities, healing rituals carry patterns from both Pentecostalism and African shamanism. Healing beliefs and behaviours in NRMs with Roman Catholic origins also tend to be syncretistic, as is seen in East African movements like Lakwena. Emmanuel K. Twesigye is the best authority on MRCTG. Matthew Schoffeleers, Tabona Shōkō, and Isabel Mukonyora also have written insightfully on healing in African Christianities.

The migrations of Asian religions to Western countries illustrate yet another pattern of cultural exchange. Buddhism and Hinduism have been reinterpreted to fit a 'progressive' lifestyle. Similarly, traditional Indian Yoga and Ayurvedic medicine have been adapted and aligned with alternative medicine and spirituality. Good books by Gregory P. Fields and Lola Williamson opened the discussion on Asian health directives, but their massive popularity invites more scholarship, on yoga in particular.

Demographic shifts have moved animist, polytheist and shamanic traditions into new social settings. In their new host societies, the treatment of traditional religions often has been similar to that of new religions, in that both are perceived as strange, dangerous 'cults'. This bears especially on spirit possession rituals in which healing rituals figure strongly, illustrated in Anne Fadiman's acclaimed book on the clash between Hmong animists and the American health care system. Exemplary studies exist on Vodou and Candomblé (such as those by Karen McCarthy Brown and Emma Cohen) and on African-American folk healing (see Yvonne Patricia Chireau and Stephanie Y. Mitchem). Much more good scholarship on polytheist religions is currently coming out, but there is a great deal left to explore. For example, scholars have noted that while healing practices often remain restricted to members of a subculture, client-based practices have started to extend their reach into new populations. Santaria, Candomblé and Vodou are transcending ethnic boundaries and becoming increasingly popular with participants in New Age spirituality. This follows several decades of 'reverse migration' of Europeans and Americans travelling to the Philippines and Brazil for 'psychic surgery', which combines shamanic healing, popularized conceptions of Western medicine and considerable stagecraft. Long a favourite of sceptics and debunkers, there is a great need for serious studies on this practice and other types of 'healing tourism'.

Physical suffering, in the form of injury, sickness and death, represents one of the primary forms through which human beings experience theodicy, a central concern for religion. The global presentation of healing beliefs and behaviours makes a strong argument for reconfiguring the categories used to evaluate data in religious studies. Invoking the theoretical model proposed by Ninian Smart, it may be worth thinking of the 'therapeutic' as an additional dimension of religion. Yet it is also possible that the conditions associated with modern life have made healing a dominant cultural form. The prominence of healing may represent a particular specific moment, in which recovery and repair are attractive tropes for spiritual work. The future prospects for NRMs are unknown, but they are sure to contribute to this theoretical question.

31 Travel and New Religious Movements

Alex Norman

Chapter Outline	
Travel in NRM Histories	314
Travel as Part of NRM Formation	315
Tourism and Exposure to NRMs	316
Travel Within NRMs	317
Travel as NRM	317
Conclusions	318

Travel, be it for leisure, work, exile, or under duress, is of great interest to scholars of religious phenomena, and particularly new religious movements (NRMs) from the mid-nineteenth century onwards. Indeed, the emergence of many NRMs, throughout history, can be traced to cultural flows enabled by the mobility of human beings. While travel has been a constant in human societies, the advent of steam powered travel, followed by the internal combustion engine, and then air travel enabled the exposure of millions of people around the world to the societies, cultures and religious ideas of others often quite distinct from their own. The inevitable reflexive social critique that comes with exposure to the worldviews and lifestyles of others has subsequently given rise to a multitude of religious iterations and innovations. Travel, however, can also be part of the history and formation of many NRMs, such as when leaders travel to a new place to distribute the teachings, or when the group itself is forced to move homes. Indeed, in many instances the designation 'new religious movement', meaning 'new to the people around it', relies upon some kind of travel to have taken place, be it of people or ideas. NRMs themselves can also become touristic attractions, or part of the social milieu of a place that attracts tourists. The subject of travel, including tourism, pilgrimage, trade, and a variety of other forms of human mobility, thus provides a useful inroad to NRMs and the social dynamics of their 'newness'.

Travel in NRM Histories

Travel events feature strongly in the histories of many NRMs, leading to their formation or to defining the group, or to both. The Church of Jesus Christ of Latter-day Saints offers a useful example of how travel events come to feature not only in the history of religious groups, but also in the narratival themes they develop. The 'structural motif' (Givens 2009, 15) of the biblical Exodus within the Book of Mormon, with its heavy connotations of travel, was used by early leaders to encourage the migrations of the early Church. Indeed, Jan Shipps argues that Exodus was crucial for the development of religious meaning for believers, and 'key to the pioneer experience' (1985, 122). It is worth remembering that not just individuals but whole cities of Mormons were expelled or forcibly driven from their homes by government officials (Reps 1979), travelling ever further west across the American continent before finally settling in Utah and surrounds.

The troubled histories of other NRMs also present instances where travel was part of a key moment. For Afro-Caribbean religious movements, such as Candomblé, the very fact of their existence, in addition to their characteristics, is a result of a travel experience in the form of the slave trade (Prandi 2000). Evidencing the paradigm in new religions studies of 'old religion made new', Candomblé refers to the practices of Orixás and Vodou brought from West Africa by slaves, but that have since become mixed with other local spiritual entities (Sansi-Roca 2005). Similar to Candomblé, exile and diaspora form crucial parts of the academic examination of NRMs such as the Bahá'í Faith. Bahá'u'lláh's exodus from Tehran to Baghdad to Constantinople, and then to Akka (modern Acre) in Israel has formed a central part of the group's narrative of social renewal and regeneration (Warburg 2006). Lastly, the final, soteriological actions of members of the group Heaven's Gate included a journey. The 1997 suicide, initiated after the discovery of the comet Hale-Bopp along with reports of an alien spacecraft hidden behind it, was understood by group members as a rendezvous. The 39 suiciding group members recorded farewell messages to their families, dressed themselves identically (including patches that read 'Heaven's Gate Away Team'), while 'beside each bed was a small luggage case, suggesting an intended journey' (Chryssides 2011, 1). The symbolism clearly indicates this was to be travel to 'the next level' as they called it; a movement towards a new life, not an end.

Travel as Part of NRM Formation

While in the above examples a negative travel event features as an historic moment for each group, in many cases the travel is construed more positively. Some significant NRM leaders portrayed their religious innovation or reiteration as one brought about by a travel act. Indeed, H. P. Blavatsky (1831–91), G. I. Gurdjieff (c. 1866–1949) and L. Ron Hubbard (1911–86) each constructed their claim to authenticity and truth based on claims of travel adventures. Blavatsky, co-founder of the Theosophical Society, circulated stories of her travels as part of her promotion of 'the East' as the home of the perennial religion. She claimed to have travelled for ten years from the age of seventeen, journeying to Western Europe, Egypt, South America, and most importantly spending two years in India, and seven years in Tibet studying with the 'Himalayan Masters' (Washington 1993). Like Blavatsky, Gurdjieff alleged he spent his formative years travelling through the Middle East and Central Asia absorbing the mystical wisdom of forgotten masters over a period of 20 years (Moore 1991). In his book, *Meetings With Remarkable Men,* Gurdjieff related that he was convinced that in ancient traditions there lived on '"a certain something" which people formerly knew' (2002, 87). Like Blavatsky, however, Gurdjieff's tales 'read more like an adventure story than biographical fact', as Petsche (2013, 165) notes.

Similar to Blavatsky and Gurdjieff, L. Ron Hubbard, founder of Scientology, claimed to have travelled extensively while a young man. He claimed that his extensive travels resulted in the insights into the mysteries of the human mind that became the basis of Scientology teachings. Claiming to have travelled widely in Asia, including being accepted into lamaseries, Hubbard's travel experiences are promoted in support of his authority as an explorer of the human condition (Christensen 2005). In all cases, the travel narratives of each of these leaders, while being of dubious veracity, are nonetheless crucial in the overall scheme of what came to be their respective religious movements. Their travel experiences not only underpinned their authority as visionary leaders, but also exposed them to a variety of ideas they later uniquely combined.

Other leaders brought about religious innovation through travel following changes in migration laws or government policy which enabled travel for the leader in some capacity that again either exposed them to new ideas or to a new audience. In the case of A. C. Bhaktivedanta, what became the International Society for Krishna Consciousness grew after his migration from India to New York; a movement only possible with the then recent rescinding of a number of immigration restriction acts. Bhaktivedanta's immediate success in the United States showed not only that there was increasing interest in religious ideas alternative to hegemonic Christianity, but that 'otherness' and foreignness were not impediments to religious success. Another notable example of travel as a result of government policy changes concerns American Buddhism. Jack

Kornfield was a volunteer for the Peace Corps and returned from his duties in Thailand a Buddhist monk (Kornfield 1993). He has since become a leader in the American/Western Buddhist tradition, founding the Spirit Rock Meditation Center and publishing numerous books.

Tourism and Exposure to NRMs

The example of Kornfield evinces what is so compelling about travel and tourism studies as a field in which to examine NRMs. Travel enables, even allows through various social norms, exposure to new religious ideas for the individual. To add to the currency of this more firmly within religious studies, 'seeking' has distinct connotations of travel. The seeker searches for religious content with which to construct meaning and make sense of their lives. This often involves acts of travel, and it is interesting to note a parallel to Campbell's 'seeker thesis' (1972) in tourism studies, with Erik Cohen's phenomenology of tourist experiences (1979). Cohen's typology signals the search for a 'centre' away from one's inherited home as one of five observable types of tourist phenomena. It is thus no surprise to find that numerous formative encounters with NRMs can be found to involve travel. The liminoid nature of travel, even with its sometimes mundane status in the developed world, often results in a relative openness to new ideas on the part of the traveller. It is thus that we are able to observe tourists attending yoga courses, taking meditation classes or making pilgrimages without the ostensibly necessary prerequisites of belief or belonging (Norman 2011). Travel, it is now quite apparent, offers the individual a time-space for religious experimentation. Indeed, in the context of travel it is possible to conceive of all religions as 'new' as travellers appraise them with liminal eyes.

The spread of interest in eastern religious forms in the late nineteenth century, for example, spurred an important uptake of those ideas in the West. However, with immigration restrictions in place the availability of 'authentic' teachers from Asia was limited. Travel to places like India in search of teachers thus became a recognizable phenomenon in the West, and leaders such as Satya Sai Baba and Ramana Maharishi gained followers from foreign lands without ever leaving the country. Travelling to find oneself became common with the advent of the jet age, and now travellers can be found all over the world, exploring not only new cultures and places, but new religions too. Tourist locations, particularly backpacker gathering points, are often littered with flyers advertising NRMs and their activities. At home it may be different, but while travelling, attending a lecture from an NRM leader may be completely acceptable to a wide range of individuals. Thus traveller hubs sometimes also become NRM hubs, as teachers go to gather new students, and travellers go to experience novel ideas.

To this extent, NRMs and their cultural products can also become tourist attractions. The new religious milieu has been a context in which acts of travel have been critical for providing cultural impetus for the formation of sites that become travel destinations. Glastonbury is one such example with a number of studies indicating the town operates as a general tourist drawcard as well as a pilgrimage site for Christians and new age practitioners (Bowman 2008). The gaze of tourists is there drawn to the 'New Age' aesthetic, providing a unique branding for the town that dovetails well with its other religious attractions. Similarly, New Orleans' Jackson Square has, for some decades, featured a variety of new age and occult practitioners offering their services to tourists and locals alike (Sheehan 2012). The gaze of tourists is again drawn in part because of the carnivalesque character of new religious aesthetics. The city of Sedona, in Arizona, attracts significant numbers of tourist interested in new age and alternative religious practices (Coats 2008). There are, in fact, as yet uncounted numbers of new religious tourism sites that future research will hopefully shed light on.

Travel Within NRMs

In addition to the touristic draw of new religious sites, NRMs also create their own traditions of travel. Established or formalized pilgrimages can be found in a number of NRMs, the most prominent of which are those Mormon journeys such as pilgrimages to Hill Cumorah. Added to this within the Church are other traditions of travel associated with mission and proselytism. Numerous new age pilgrimages have also developed in the last 40 years, with particular emphasis being placed on Goddess traditions (Rountree 2006). At Auroville international tourists have continued to visit, though as Sharpley and Sundaram (2005) note, most appear to be there intentionally, rather than happening upon it. Such phenomena demand the attention for their ability to develop a sense of *communitas* within pilgrim cohorts, and for the way they indicate orthodoxy within the NRM. Also included within the field of NRMs and travel, we should not forget, is the phenomenon of teachers travelling the world to deliver their teachings. One such example, termed the 'satsang network', includes the circulation of numerous teachers to locations around the world with notable regularity (Frisk 2002).

Travel as NRM

When scholars began unpicking the cultural and social forces responsible for generating mass tourism, especially following the Second World War, a number quickly noted its coincidence with secularization and with the emergence of alternatives to religious experience. Dean MacCannell, for instance, argued that the modern typically lived a life devoid of authenticity, in part thanks to the degredation of such socio-structural elements as religions. Moderns were, therefore, 'condemned to look elsewhere, everywhere, for . . . authenticity, to . . . catch a glimpse of it reflected in the simplicity, poverty, chastity, or purity of others' (MacCannell 1999, 41). In the light of a range of theories that attempt to explain putatively 'non-religious' phenomena as 'religious' (e.g. Birrell 1981; McFarlane 1989), we must address the question of travel itself being a 'new' form of religious practice. A notable example can be found in the mid-twentieth century when Jack Kerouac wrote *On The Road* (1957), a classic of the 'Beat Generation', in which the principal ideas revolve around the search for meaning and identity which Kerouac characterized as best found while travelling. Scholars have also found that tourists operate religiously, even where the context is not religious, such as was found by Narayanan and Macbeth's (2009) study of 4WD tours of the Australian desert. The question of travel and the habitual practice of travel itself as religious must therefore be treated by scholars of NRMs to assist in unravelling the complex of processes, social, cultural, political, economic, that we scholars have called 'religion'.

Conclusions

At this stage, scholarship that specifically examines NRMs and travel is uncommon, despite the clear connections. As a subject within the field of NRM studies, travel offers a number of interesting access points to new religious phenomena. In many locations tourists encounter a range of NRMs they might otherwise not be exposed to in their everyday lives. Studying tourism and NRMs can thus yield significant insights as to how new forms of religiosity and spirituality are enacted and disseminated by looking at what tourists do with them on holiday. In addition, many NRMs operate with travel as a core part of their practice, whether we call it pilgrimage or something else. The investigation of travel behaviours and events in relation to religious movements, here new ones, must not make the mistake of relegating the religious to what can all too easily be decried as 'frivolous', as tourists so often have been. Travel can lead to remarkable and unexpected outcomes for individual social actors and religious movements which, often thrown by the journey into new contexts, become themselves 'new'.

Part IV
Resources: A–Z

This section offers brief comment on additional topics that are not covered substantially in the preceding essays.

Anti-Cult Movement

The anti-cult movement (ACM) refers to the social movement that began in the wake of the rise of the NRMs in the mid-twentieth century that opposed the new religions on social, religious, moral and familial grounds. The ACM is a diffuse social movement with multiple overlapping organizations, groups, governmental taskforces, associations and church bodies. It includes clergy, mental health workers, academics, former members of NRMs and family members of the adherents of new religions.

Groups and individuals that are parts of the ACM oppose new religious movements on various grounds, but most commonly they accuse the new religions of psychological coercion and abuse of members. Religiously affiliated elements of the ACM oppose NRMs in theological grounds, and some individuals and groups are concerned primarily with a single NRM rather than the category as a whole. The ACM also displays a wide variety of methods of opposing new religions, ranging from producing literature to active involvement in deprogramming and persecution of new religious groups.

The anti-cult movement is part of a historical trajectory of groups and individuals opposing new religions, and it has taken different forms across the world in differing contexts. For more on the ACM, **see Chapter 17**.

Charisma

The concept of charisma has shaped the study of new religious movements. Popularized by the German sociologist Max Weber, charisma as he uses it is 'a certain quality of an individual personality by virtue of which he is set apart from ordinary men and treated as endowed with supernatural, superhuman, or at least specifically exceptional powers or qualities' (Weber and Parsons 1947, 358–9). Marked by distinction and specialness, the bearer of charisma possesses the ability to speak with authority and to legitimate his or her beliefs through appeal to the supernatural or superhuman.

Rather than inborn, most scholars of NRMs treat charisma as a property developed and inculcated by individuals, and one that exists within the context of the relationships between charismatic leader and his or her followers. Charisma is produced, and charisma can dwindle. Charisma can also continue on after the death of the charismatic leader in the form of routinized or institutionalized charisma.

For more on charisma, see Chapter 13, 'Charisma and Charismatic Authority in New Religious Movements'.

Communalism

Communalism refers to the practices of groups that live in intentional communities under some form of socialized or utopian sharing of recourses, which might include food, housing or labour. Communalist groups may be separatist, in which case they tend to create remote communes, or they may engage broader society from the context of communalist communities embedded within more populous regions. Members of communalist movements may create communities within single homes, clusters of buildings or even entire towns or regions. Communalist new religious movements demonstrate a wide diversity of theologies, practices and geographies (Zellner and Petrowsky 1998).

Not all new religious movements are communal, but a disproportionate number do exhibit communalist practices at some point in their histories. Many of the most notable NRMs of the counterculture, such as the Children of God (COG) and Hare Krishnas featured communalism, as did many of the older generation of NRMs such as the Branch Davidians and Church Universal and Triumphant. Looking even further into history, new religions of the radical reformation such as the Hutterites and Amish, and nineteenth-century NRMs such as the Oneida community and Mormons also embraced communalism.

Groups have different reasons to practise communalism, ranging from theological rationales, to cultural patterns, to convenience. Many Christian NRMs seek to emulate the early Church (*primitivism*), which the Christian scriptures describe as holding a common purse. New Christian religions such as COG, Catholic Workers or the Twelve Tribes explicitly invoke such logic in creating communalist movements. Similarly, some new religions drawing from the Buddhist and Hindu traditions have adopted the model of the monastery or ashram as a model for creating communalist communities. The NRMs of the Anglo-American counterculture especially reflected the broader culture out of which they emerged, and many featured a communalist ethos that paralleled the wider hippie subculture (Miller 1999). Finally, some movements embrace communalism for purely pragmatic reasons and then move beyond such practices when communalism no longer serves a useful purpose. The early Latter-day Saints lived communally in their new Zion founded on the banks of the Great Salt Lake, but adopted non-communalist patterns as the movement matured and the settlement achieved greater stability.

Communalism is often tied to the concept of utopianism and with it the ideal of progressive millennialism. This constellation of ideas each reinforce the others as groups seek to create ideal communities in keeping with their specific goals, theologies and practices. That being said, communalist movements are inherently unstable and the maintenance of communalism entails social controls and carefully management. The history of NRMs is replete with examples of failed communalist movements (Bainbridge 1985).

Cult

The term 'cult' derives from the Latin *cultus*, meaning worship, and previously referred to the focus of collective participation in religious rites. The term is now not necessarily confined to religion, but can be used to designate widespread but loosely organized participation in or enthusiasm about a topic: science fiction fandom is one such example. In religion the term sometimes denotes loosely organized devotion, as for example to Marian shrines or various devotional forms of Greco-Roman antiquity.

The term 'cult' has a history stemming from the sociologist Max Weber, who distinguished between Church and sect. This distinction was further developed by Ernst Troeltsch, who added the 'mystical', to designate more individual or personal religious experience. Howard Becker preferred the term 'cult', under which he placed Spiritualism, Theosophy, Christian Science and 'pseudo-Hinduisms'. This last category has tended to define the more common present-day use of 'cult' to designate groups that are not offshoots of a culture's dominant religion. Offshoots can generally be labelled as 'sects', while eastern-derived groups merited the label 'cults'.

In his *Perspectives on New Religious Movements*, John A. Saliba distinguishes three different ways in which the term 'cult' has been defined: theological, psychological and sociological. Theological definitions are generally favoured by the Christian countercult movement, who define organizations as 'cults' on the grounds that they deviate from the truth of the Christian gospel. Psychological definitions are more prevalent among anti-cultists, who emphasize their effects on the minds of their converts: mind control, deception, and forms of psychological damage that these organizations are believed to inflict. Sociological definitions are those, following the tradition of Weber, which attempt to place the group in the context of its wider social and religious climate, without making judgements about the organization's truth or falsity, or about psychological benefits or harm.

William Sims Bainbridge and Rodney Stark make a further distinction between 'audience cults', 'client cults' and 'cult movements', each of which offer 'compensators' – rewards for the time, money or effort expended on them – like other religions. The audience cult lacks formal organization, and its ideas are propagated through books, magazines and other social media such as television. No participation is involved, although a book may recommend practices to be performed personally by the reader. The client cult offers services, usually for a fee, such as psychic readings, meditation sessions or past-life regression. A cult movement is a fully fledged organization, but it differs from a sect in that it is not a splinter group of a wider religion. The audience cult can develop into a client cult, as happened when the Church of Scientology was established as a means of offering services such as auditing, which were described in L. Ron Hubbard's *Dianetics*. Equally, a client cult can offer its services to a wider public, with open meetings and participation. Bainbridge (1997) has stated subsequently that he would prefer to have avoided the term 'cult'.

Other uses of the word 'cult' include the expression 'doomsday cult', sometimes used by sociologists to refer to millenarian or apocalyptic NRMs. The anti-cult movement frequently uses the term 'destructive cult'. Sometimes this label is contrasted with 'benign cult', thus implying that not all of the so-called cults are necessarily harmful. At other times the word 'destructive' is simply applied to all NRMs.

Apart from those sociologists who continue to follow Bainbridge and Stark's use of 'cult', most scholars of religion now regard the term as pejorative, and replace it with NRM. The anti-cult movement largely rejects this substitution, regarding the term 'NRM' as a euphemism which conceals the harmful nature of these organizations.

Disengagement

Despite the fears of parents and friends that NRM members are 'lost to the cults', disengagement, meaning the uncompelled departure of a member, is a fairly common phenomenon. In her study of the Unification Church, Eileen Barker discovered that the average length of a convert's membership was a mere two years and that therefore a vast majority of members of the Unification Church at the time of study would later disengage themselves from the movement.

Research tends to be somewhat lacking on disengagement, no doubt because it can be difficult to identify and locate ex-members of NRMs, while it is much easier to find those who are inside them. The most visible ex-members are those who subsequently join or even found anti-cult organizations and publicize their passage into and out of the NRM. James Beckford speculates that, in describing their experiences, they frequently devise scenarios to account for their conversion and life in the movement, which are 'negotiated' with other stakeholders, such as family members, the media and anti-cult groups. If Beckford is correct, this helps to fuel brainwashing hypotheses, by which they exonerate themselves from responsibility in becoming involved. By contrast, the vast majority of former members who disengage and do not publicize their former religious affiliations are invisible to social scientific scrutiny.

Disengagement can proceed due to a variety of factors. These include a loss of faith on the part of a convert, disillusionment about an NRM's purpose or leadership or simply a desire to move on to a different style of living. Occasionally there are break-away movements that take members always from the main organization. Another relatively uncommon reason for leaving is expulsion – known as 'disfellowshipping' in organizations such as the Christadelphians and Jehovah's Witnesses. Probably the most common explanations for leaving an NRM are fairly mundane. One former member told the author that she simply did not like being out late at night to attend meetings; another stated that she thought the Scientology course was 'quite good' and served its purpose, but that she did not feel any need to pursue Scientology further. Another left a Japanese Buddhist organization because he came to think that it was 'culturally inappropriate' – he was probably embarrassed about being seen in public wearing monks' robes.

At times friends and relatives may initiate forcible abduction – known as 'deprogramming' – in which abductors are hired, usually for a substantial fee, to trap the member and remove him or her from the organization. The member is then placed in isolation and subjected to intense verbal or physical harassment, in order to reverse the presumed 'brainwashing' to which he or she has been subjected by the NRM. The degree of success in deprogrammings is contested. In some cases it seems likely that the member was intent on leaving in any case, while in other cases members have been known to feign cooperation with deprogrammers, and subsequently find their way back into the organization. Failed deprogrammings inevitably make relationships worse between members and their families.

While it is true that disengagement can prove difficult, the same can also be said about leaving mainstream and religious organizations. It can be embarrassing to tell other members of one's decision to quit, and – particularly if one has been living in a community – leaving the organization probably means abandoning one's friends and social stability. If one's commitment to the NRM has been full-time, that is the additional problem of finding a job and accounting for one's period of time in the organization when submitting a job application. Additionally, those who have had full-time commitment have found problems in how to spend time which was previously taken up by religious and administrative duties within the group. Sometimes this phenomenon has been known as 'floating': the erstwhile member may have successfully disengaged, but has not yet found anything to replace the commitment. In some cases ex-members become 'serial converts' to NRMs, seeking new groups with which to affiliate as they seek religious satisfaction in their lives.

Ethics

In the strict sense, the field of ethics is a subfield of philosophy wherein one creates distinctions between right and wrong and explores the meaning of those two concepts. Ethicists generally focus on specific issues – for example bioethics, environmental ethics or sexual ethics – and explore these issues from specific ethical frameworks, often but not exclusively religious in nature. Outside of the academy ethics has the same meaning but often becomes conflated with morality, which deals more with behaviours and the way that individuals live within their ethical frameworks.

Understood in this way one finds copious examples of new religious movements developing new and alternative ethical systems, modifying existing ones and contesting the ethics received by tradition. Critics often charge NRMs with violating the ethical norms of their host societies, while those within new religions similarly critique the ethics of non-members. Ethics often becomes a locus for conflict between NRMs and other groups, as well as a means for members to develop meaningful ways of relating to the world around them.

New religions offer a variety of ethical codes, but generally these codes diverge even from the traditions out of which the NRMs emerged. To take just one set of examples, both the Children of God and the Unification Church emerged from the broad Christian tradition, yet both have radically different sexual ethics from each other and from older and more socially respected Christian groups. During its formative years the adherents of the Children of God upheld sexual ethics predicated on models of free and open sexuality, and even the pragmatic deployment of sexuality for recruitment purposes. The Unification Church's sexual ethics contrasted with this, with members upholding ethical codes curtailing sexuality not only within the bounds of marriage but also under a rubric that envisioned sexuality as needing to be sharply controlled.

Several NRMs became notorious for upholding ethical codes that permitted members to engage in practices considered unethical outside of the new religions. Such antinomianism generally derived from theologies that were either sharply dualistic in tone (members of the NRMs vs the outside world), apocalyptic in orientation, or envisioned the world as illusionary and therefore ethics as irrelevant. Examples include condoning the use of drugs or other intoxicants, deceptive or manipulative forms of recruitment and fundraising, the fostering of abusive relationships within unequal power dynamics and even the use of violence. The most notorious examples involve acts on grand scales such as the Aum Shinrikyō attack on the Tokyo subway or the Jonestown murder/suicides. In both those cases, adherents believed that a higher ethical calling permitted and even necessitated acts of violence.

While most members of most new religions did not accept such ethical abnormalities, critics have tended to assume that all such practices characterize all new religions. In fact, most NRMs possess ethical systems that vary from other religions but do not encourage or condone behaviours far outside social norms.

Food and Eating

Everybody eats, and nearly every religious movement offers religious teachings about food and eating. New religious movements are no different. With a few exceptions, scholars have paid remarkably little attention to the intersection of food and NRMs. Yet new religions' engagements with food have often been central to the emergence and growth of those groups, and often have served as central practices both in daily life and ritual actions. On a sociological level, food and eating serve to attract new converts, solidify socialization, mark boundaries between insiders and outsiders. From a theological perspective, food (or abstaining from food) often functions as a means of worship, remembrance, demonstration of commitment, and daily devotion.

Perhaps the most obvious places to look to consider the relationship between NRMs and food are those groups wherein food serves central ideological and practical roles. Father Divine's International Peace Mission Movement and the International Society for Krishna Consciousness (ISKCON, or the Hare Krishnas) offer two examples of such, predicated on extremely different religious foundations and emerging at very different times and cultural contexts. One of the foremost of the 'Black Messiahs' of the twentieth-century United States, Father Divine (1879–1965) founded his International Peace Mission

Movement as a means of establishing a millennial communal movement focusing on racial harmony and economic uplift. Though several communal practices characterized the movement, they were most famous for their banquets, the 'Holy Communion Banquet Services'. The banquets served as zeniths of food culture within the movement, which also supported farms, grocery stores, food charities and restaurants. The meals themselves emphasized plenty in an atmosphere characterized by the reverse, especially during the Great Depression. Foods included numerous cuts of meat, fowl, fishes, vegetables, salads, fruits, cheeses, breads and desserts. They were equal or superior to banquets found in the fanciest hotels and clubs of the upper-class elites. On a sociological level, while outsiders were also invited to the banquet services as means of proselytizing, generally the banquets functioned to create and foster social bonds among members. On a liturgical level, the banquets served as holy communion, a chance to revel in the presence of the divine, enjoy the bounty of the Earth as provided by God, and as a means of offering thanks and graciousness (Primiano, 2014).

The International Society for Krishna Consciousness offers a similar window into the intersection of NRMs and food. Like Father Divine's movement, ISKCON treated food as a means of proselytizing, social bonding and worship. During the late 1960s the group's founder Prabhupada gave away Indian food as a means of attracting converts, and found that the combination of exoticism, nutrition and sensuality of his Indian feasts served a valuable role in evangelism. As the movement grew so did the feasts, with free Indian feasts becoming staples of ISKCON. The movement used these feasts to introduce converts to spiritual vegetarianism, a central practice in their devotional tradition, as well as the actual means of worship wherein devotees present food offerings to the God Krishna. Like the International Peace Mission Movement, communal eating and the joyous nature of the feasts served to heighten social bonds within the movement as well (Zeller 2012).

Food and eating have served a variety of roles in NRMs. For example, vegetarianism functioned as an important practice in both the Adventist tradition and its offshoots. Responses to the African-American culinary 'soul food' tradition in the Nation of Islam – which rejected the tradition – and Daddy Grace's United House of Prayer for all People – which embraced it – reveal the interconnectedness of ethnicity, food and religion. Though these groups utilize food and eating in a variety of ways, in all cases it functions as an important role in defining and delineating membership and religious practice.

Fundamentalism

In a broad sense the word 'fundamentalism' is applied to extreme forms of religion, particularly those involved in violence, and to groups that are believed to take an excessively literal approach to their scriptures or fundamental doctrines. The term has therefore been used in connection with a variety of religions – especially Islam, but also to certain Hindus, Sikhs and sometimes Buddhists. In recent times the term has been extended to apply to the 'new atheism' of popular writers like Richard Dawkins and Christopher Hitchens.

The term is most appropriate and has a more precise meaning when applied to Christianity, where the fundamentalist movement was a reaction against 'modernism', as expressed in Darwin's theory of evolution, and the rise of higher criticism of the Bible, which questioned its origins and historicity. In 1895 the Bible Conference of Conservative Protestants in Niagara, New York, met and defined five principles which they regarded as the 'fundamentals' of the faith. These were: the inerrancy of the Bible: the Virgin Birth of Christ; Christ's substitutionary atonement; Christ's bodily resurrection; and the authenticity of Christ's miracles. The American Bible League was founded in 1902, and promoted the principles of fundamentalism by a series of 12 books, written by R. A. Torrey and A. C. Dixon. These were circulated between 1901 and 1915, and offered without charge to clergy and ordinands. Published under the name *The Fundamentals*, this series gave name to the inchoate movement.

The five principles assumed slightly different forms: for example, one variant inserted 'the deity of Christ' as the second principle, added 'the bodily return of Christ' after 'the physical resurrection', and dispensed with 'miracles' (although of course this did not imply their rejection). The fundamentalists who inserted 'the bodily return of Christ' tended to emphasize millenarianism and apocalypticism, predicting the 'Rapture', in which Jesus would return to take his true followers up to heaven, leaving the rest of humankind to undergo the great tribulation. These ideas found recent popular expression in Tim LaHaye and Jerry B. Jenkins' series of novels *Left Behind*.

A number of Christian NRMs are committed to the principles of fundamentalism, for example the International Churches of Christ, the Jesus Fellowship Church and the Family International. This does not preclude innovative interpretations of the Bible, however, as is evidenced by the Family's interpretation of sexual morality. In some cases it is inappropriate to describe New Christian groups as fundamentalist, since their inception anticipates the rise of fundamentalism – for example the Christadelphians, and the Watch Tower Society. Although fundamentalism is particularly associated with biblical literalism, some New Christian organizations accept the inerrancy of scripture, but do not espouse some of the other principles. For example, while the Way International claims to base their teachings exclusively on scripture, they do not affirm Christ's deity.

One important problem involved in accepting biblical inerrancy is the question of how to regard the Old Testament. Some Christian organizations, particularly those in the Adventist tradition, accepted the Jewish dietary laws and celebrated the traditional Jewish festivals. By contrast, the Jehovah's Witnesses adopted the view that the New Testament had supremacy, and that the commandments of the Jewish Law are only binding if they are reaffirmed in Christian scriptures.

Some New Christian NRMs reject biblical inerrancy. Some claim a new revelation, and sometimes adding their own scriptures to the Bible. The Unification Church interprets Christian scripture through the revelations attributed to Sun Myung Moon, regarding many statements in the Bible as symbolic, and Raël, the founder of Raelian movement, regards Christian scriptures as a garbled distortion of accounts of extraterrestrial visitations to the Earth.

God

Unsurprisingly, the adherents of most of the world's new religious movements believe in the divine, whether they conceive of it as God, Goddess, Gods or some less anthropomorphic form. Since most NRMs form within the context of a particular religious system, they often track the perspectives on the divine found within that religious system. New religions emergent from Christian religious origins tend towards incarnational monotheism, those deriving from Hindu sources represent more polytheistic, pantheistic or monistic theologies, and NRMs coming from Jewish and Muslim points of origin tend towards monotheism. Yet new religious movements feature high degrees of syncretism, and as such they do not always perfectly represent a single source tradition. The Rajneesh (Osho) movement, for example, draws from both Rajneesh's Hindu birth tradition as well as Buddhist theological sources in its representation of the divine. In some cases new religions lack any clear origin point whatever, or emerge from popular rather than religious culture. Such new religions feature an array of perspectives on the divine. Jediists conceive of the divine in keeping with the representation of the Force in George Lucas' *Star Wars* mythology, for example.

While new religions feature a host of theological models, most are united in terms of offering visions of the divine that are easy to understand, relatable to everyday lives and intended to offer direct religious value to believers. Some scholars have argued that much of the attraction to NRMs radiates from such clear, vivid, and accessible religious beliefs, which appeal to those overwhelmed by the choices of the modern world, put off by what they consider the apparent blasé teachings of their birth traditions, or seeking unmediated religious fulfilment and divine contract. New religions as diverse as the Hare Krishna movement, Peoples Temple, Heaven's Gate, the Unification Church and Nation of Islam each offered direct experience of the divine. Some featured ecstatic worship, whereas others proclaimed that God had incarnated on Earth as living founders, yet all agreed that members could directly experience the divine in their religious lives.

Many new religious movements of the past half-century have emphasized binary models of God, usually predicated on a model of gender or sex complementarity. The nineteenth-century Mormons offered one earlier example, but more recent groups such as the Branch Davidians, Kabbalah Centre, Hare Krishnas, and many Neopagan movements uphold a theology of the divine as a paired God and Goddess, sometimes personified using the Hebrew word for the feminine divine spirit, the Shekinah. Numerous NRMs have also embraced matriarchal models of the divine, featuring beliefs in Goddess rather than God. Such positions are common among Neopagan proponents and movements. The matriarchal and binary models of theology as well as the revival of polytheism in the West all indicate the manner in which inherited patriarchal models of the Godhead – found in most of the world's religions – have not satisfied all religious individuals in the contemporary world.

Guru/Disciple

The Sanskrit term 'guru' originates in the religious milieu of India. Within that context the guru has a very specific meaning as a spiritual teacher. Different subtraditions within Hinduism and Buddhism understand the guru differently, ranging from envisioning the guru as a spiritual guide to seeing the guru as a manifestation of the divine. The term has carried these various perspectives as it made its way into English and the study of new religious movements.

Scholars discuss gurus in NRMs in two ways: first as religious teachers representing – or claiming to represent – new religions derived from the Indian context. Maharishi Mahesh Yogi, A. C. Bhaktivedanta Prabhupada, Rajneesh and Gurumayi all represent this type of guru as the founders and central religious teachers of Transcendental Meditation, ISKCON, the Osho movement, and Siddha Yoga (Siddha Yoga Dham Association, or SYDA). Journalists and the public, and sometimes scholars, also use the term guru to refer to other religious teachers outside the Indian religious tradition or even outside of religious movements altogether. New Age teacher Eckhart Tolle, the physician Deepak Chopra and even television star Oprah have all been called gurus. The study of gurus outside of religions derived from the Indian context is an act of comparison akin to studying other cross-cultural religious phenomena and carries the same advantages and disadvantages as other forms of comparative studies.

A guru generally embodies divine sanction and divine presence and claims a form of intrinsic religious authority apart from an institution or social movement. To follow Weber, gurus function akin to the prophet or charismatic leader and unlike leaders within institutionalized religions wherein the authority has been routinized within an office. The disciple, or śiṣya to use the Sanskrit term, associates the teacher's high degree of religious authority with spiritual potency that enables their spiritual development and religious pursuits. Within religions derived from the Indian context, especially Hinduism and some Buddhist forms such as Tibetan and Zen Buddhism as well as many NRMs, disciples fully invest themselves in their relationship with the guru and grant the guru complete spiritual authority over themselves. In some NRMs the guru often retains worldly authority as well, determining who disciples will marry, where they will live and what jobs they may take.

Given the high degree of the guru's spiritual and temporal authority, it is not surprising that some gurus take advantage of their positions and some disciples feel taken advantage of. A string of guru controversies in the 1970s, 1980s and 1990s revealed the mismatch between the ideal of guru and its functioning within the Indian context and the cultural contexts of NRMs in the modern West. Critics have criticised gurus on the grounds that such unassailable sources of religious authority pose risks for psychological manipulation and have targeted NRMs as psychologically dangerous since many are led by gurus or guru-like figures. One strain of scholarship regarding the guru controversies indicates that Western disciples do not have the cultural heritage or preparedness for relating to gurus, and that gurus in the West find themselves living in an unfettered new social context.

Institutionalization

Institutionalization refers to the process by which the lived religious practices, beliefs, norms and moods become formalized and routinized within the formal structure of a new religious movement. Like many sociological concepts useful to the study of new religious movements, the idea of institutionalization emerged from the work of sociologist Max Weber, who focused on the institutionalization and routinization of the charismatic power of a religious founder. Weber's *Veralltäglichung*, literally 'to become everyday-like', involves the transformation of a new religion or sectarian group from being predicated on the words and deeds of a founder to one embedded in social structures and organizations. Institutionalization is therefore a crucial concept to understand how a NRM develops and maintains itself beyond its initial kernel of founder(s) and members.

Numerous studies have considered how NRMs institutionalize. Much of this scholarship has focused on the routinization of charisma, a central Weberian concept. To take one well-known example, that of the Hare Krishna movement, Bryant and Ekstrand's recent anthology and E. Burke Rochford's monograph on the post-charismatic fate of ISKCON indicate the complexities of the process of routinization of charisma and the manner in which competing and conflicting groups and individuals sought to transform the founder's charisma into an institutionalized form (Bryant and Ekstrand 2004; Rochford 2007). Similar research exists on other new religions with charismatic founders, ranging from studies of historical NRMs such as Adventism to more recent ones such as SYDA Yoga (Bowen 2008; Brooks 1997; Miller 1991).

Yet the routinization of charisma is only part of the process of institutionalization. As a new religious movement evolves generally its religious beliefs and practices become institutionalized into sacred scriptures, hymnals, epistles, worship manuals or other written forms. Canonization therefore functions as one way in which NRMs institutionalize, and while most obvious among those new religions that are no longer new – Christianity, Islam, Bahá'í, etc. – this process is nearly universal. The creation of the 'MO Letters' within the Children of God, Falun Gong's eponymous text, or the written prophecies of various twentieth-century Marian visionaries all function analogously as ways in which beliefs, practices and religious norms became institutionalized through canonization.

As inhabitants of a neoliberal age, the members of NRMs also institutionalize their movements through multinational legal structures. Particularly well-known in this regard, the founders of the Unification Church created a byzantine structure of corporations, NGOs and thinktanks as it institutionalized. Most new religions now exist legally in multiple institutionalized forms, often with boards of oversight or directorship and various forms of legal or institutional authority overlapping with – and at times conflicting with – religious authorities within the movements.

Legitimation

New religions seldom claim or achieve legitimacy during their first generations. Even the major world religions were not accepted as legitimate during their formative periods, with Christianity, Islam, and Buddhism all being criticized by outsiders as erroneous, dangerous and inappropriate. Yet such older religions did achieve legitimacy, and this slow process is part of the natural life cycle of most religious movements. What is noteworthy is how striated and localized the process is. Several nineteenth-century NRMs still seek legitimation in some corners, whereas the same NRMs are considered completely legitimate in others. The Latter-day Saints (Mormons), Seventh-day Adventists, Bahá'í, and Jewish Reform movements all emerged during that time, and while in many social circles and geographic locations all of these groups are recognized as completely normal, legitimate, acceptable religions, in other social and physical locations they are fiercely contested by members of their larger faith traditions and outsiders. This is even more the case with NRMs emerging in the twentieth and twenty-first centuries.

The process of legitimation does not occur the same way for all NRMs, but in nearly every case the founders, leaders and members of the new religious movements explicitly engage in the pursuit of legitimation. They follow multiple means. James R. Lewis has identified several of such legitimation approaches, which he labels as 'strategies' to gain legitimacy. Lewis builds on the approach of Weber, who identifies legitimation as predicated on appeals to charisma, legal-rationality or tradition. For Weber, legitimation based on charisma signifies that a movement and leader appeal to a special spiritual status of the movement's leader or founder. Rationalistic legitimation appeals to logical or interpretive approaches, often textual in nature. Finally, traditionalistic legitimacy derives from claims to follow in the line of older legitimate groups, individuals or texts (Weber 1958). Lewis subdivides Weber's typology into multiple legitimation strategies within Weber's overall schema, for example noting that 'charismatic' legitimation might exist in distinct forms as the performing of spiritual powers, demonstrating superior wisdom, proven leadership or direct revelation (Lewis 2003, 13–14).

Numerous other legitimating strategies exist outside of Weber's typology (and Lewis' updated subdivision of it). Some new religious movements seek legitimacy by seeking to show their charitable or social value, and others seek to join ecumenical or interfaith umbrella organizations so as to demonstrate their similarity to other religions. The specific means by which groups may seek legitimacy are theoretically as diverse as groups themselves. Still other groups might disdain broader social claims of legitimacy and willfully remain on the cultural sidelines.

Yet these myriad approaches of seeking legitimacy all reveal that the quest for legitimacy is part of a broader negotiation of authority and power. In some nation states, the line between legitimate and illegitimate religion means the difference between legal and illegal standing. In others, tax advantages are awarded to legitimate religions. And in most societies, membership in illegitimate religions immediately marks one as suspect, which may have a variety of negative ramifications.

Scholars of NRMs have recognized multiple gatekeepers of legitimacy. James A. Beckford's and Sean McCloud's research on media in the United Kingdom and United States respectively indicate that media publishers and journalists play an important role in constructing public views of religious legitimacy (Beckford 1999; McCloud 2004). Courts, government agencies, non-governmental organizations, and the legal apparatus also play a role, though this varies by country (Lucas and Robbins 2004). Finally, psychologists, social workers, academics and other social scientists help construct the nature of legitimacy. In some cases, such social scientists take different perspectives of the nature of legitimacy and which groups merit that label. Scholars of NRMs themselves have sometimes been drawn into this conflict, with the first generation of scholars sometimes being attacked as 'cult apologists' for being perceived as being too willing to recognize some NRMs as legitimate religions.

Liberation/salvation

These terms refer to the final state of deliverance and ultimate spiritual goal afforded by all the major religious traditions. The term 'salvation' is more commonly used by Jews and Christians, and occasionally by Muslims. *Moksha* (liberation) is the Hindu term for the final goal, while *nirvana* is more commonly used by Buddhists, and less commonly by Hindus. Liberation/salvation is deliverance from an endemic human condition.

Hindu thought diagnoses humankind's fundamental malady as *maya* (ignorance or illusion), which ties all living beings to the constant round of birth and rebirth (*samsara*). The Hindu tradition characteristically had two schools of thought: *advaita vedanta* (non-dualism), and *dvaita vedanta* (dualism). The former school teaches the ultimate oneness of the soul (*atman*) and the divine (*brahman*), and diagnoses the human condition as a failure to perceive that they are one. The latter entails a duality between the self and God which is not bridged, even in the ultimate state of *moksha*, and thus the ultimate goal is a paradisiacal state, in which the devotee continues his or her devotion to the supreme God. In a modified form as 'qualified non-dualism', *dvaita vedanta* is embraced by organizations such as ISKCON, which emphasize the path of devotion (*bhakti*) as the means of liberation. Other spiritual paths are *raja yoga* (acquiring spiritual knowledge), *jnana yoga* (meditation) and *karma yoga* (performance of good deeds).

Buddhism entails the elimination of selfish attachment (*tanha*) and false view, which bind living beings to *samsara*: nirvana is characteristically defined as seeing things as they really are. The religion has acquired the reputation for being a religion of self-effort, and Buddhists groups in the West have tended to emphasize meditation as the means of escaping from *samsara*. However, particularly in Mahayana Buddhism, spiritual help is available through *bodhisattvas* – beings who have attained enlightenment, but who have renounced full entry into nirvana in order to help living beings. New religions predicated on Pure

Land Buddhism envision a two-step process of liberation wherein adherents in this world can seek rebirth in another so as to achieve salvation.

The Jewish concept of liberation is less clear-cut. Traditionally Jews have looked towards corporate salvation in the form of the coming messiah who will create a this-worldly paradise. This includes the righteous dead who will experience resurrection, though rabbinic authorities have never unanimously proclaimed any specific Jewish teachings on the nature of judgement and individual salvation. The Kabbalistic tradition from which many Jewish NRMs derive tends to offer more mystic visions of individual liberation involving direct access to the numinous divine.

In Christianity the condition requiring escape is sin. Like Judaism, Christians look to a messiah who would bring redemption. Christians of course believe that Jesus Christ fulfilled this role, and brought salvation through his vicarious suffering on the cross. Particularly in the Protestant tradition the notion of divine grace has received emphasis, with good works being the outcome rather than the means of salvation. Traditional Christianity has taught that there are two eternal destinies – heaven and hell – but a number of non-traditional forms of Christianity, as well as some present-day mainstream Christians, have questioned whether eternal punishment is consistent with a benevolent God. Accordingly, groups like Unitarians and Universalists have affirmed that all humankind will ultimately be saved. Others have embraced a doctrine of 'conditional immortality' – the notion that everlasting life after death is not automatic, but is dependent on one's present spiritual life. Jehovah's Witnesses, although disliking the term 'immortality', teach that there are three different afterlife states: eternal life in heaven with Christ, everlasting existence in paradisical Earth, or oblivion.

The word 'salvation' is only used once in the Qur'an, but Islam maintains its traditional teaching that there will be a day of judgement, which will be followed by eternal destinies in either heaven or hell. Salvation depends on one's belief in one God, accompanied by good deeds.

Meditation

Meditation is practised in all the major world religions, although it has taken different forms. The type of meditation used in NRMs tends to relate to the major religion with which they are associated. Many NRMs in the Hindu and Buddhist traditions laid great emphasis on meditation, but it is also found elsewhere. For example the Kabbalah, derived from Judaism, involves meditative exercises, and Islam has a tradition of *dhikr (suti)*. Christianity also has its meditative tradition, which is more contemplative, frequently focusing on biblical texts. Meditation is practised individually and in groups.

In the Hindu tradition, many meditative practices derive from the Yoga Sutras of Patanjali (c. 150 BCE), and have found their way into *raja yoga* (classical or 'royal' yoga) and Transcendental Meditation (TM). *Raja yoga* involves controlling the mind, in contrast with *hatha yoga*, the latter being a set of physical and breathing exercises that do not offer any particular religious advantage. *raja yoga* is named 'royal' yoga, being said to be 'king among yoga', affording the possibility of *moksha* (spiritual enlightenment). Meditation can also exist within the *bhakti* tradition of devotion, wherein one meditates upon one's devotional focus.

Buddhists typically hold that their meditative practices can be traced back to the Buddha himself, and that Gautama the Buddha gained enlightenment through meditation. Buddhist meditation is particularly emphasized by Western practitioners, who have probably exaggerated its role in its indigenous forms. Buddhist meditation is divided into two types – *samatha* and *vipassana*. The former aims at calming the mind, and involves practices like the 'mindfulness of breathing', while the latter is designed to create awareness of the nature of reality. The school of Buddhism laying the greatest emphasis on meditation is Zen, whose founder Bodhidharma (5th/6th c. CE) was a profound meditator.

Some forms of meditation involve the use of a mantra – a sacred sound without cognitive meaning, but believed to have special potency. Most commonly associated with the use of mantras is TM, in which the teacher provides the student with a personalized mantra to fit his or her personality. The most common mantra in the Hindu tradition is OM, but this is not used in TM. Also renowned for its use of mantra is the Hare Krishna organization, where the mantra 'Hare Krishna, Hare Krishna, Krishna Krishna, Hare Hare' is regularly chanted, and is regarded as having great spiritual potency. Mantra chanting is also found within Buddhism: use of the mantra 'Om mani padme hum' is characteristically found within Tibetan organizations. In the Nichiren tradition, the Soka Gakkai regard the mantra *'nam myoho renge kyo'* – derived from the title of their scripture, the Lotus Sutra – as offering pragmatic as well as spiritual benefits. Some Christian NRMs make use of mantra meditation as well, drawing upon the medieval Christian monastic tradition. Many such groups make use of prayer beads as part of this practice.

Other types of meditation, especially within the Buddhist tradition, involve 'visualization': this entails using an image of a buddha or *bodhisattva*, which the meditator seeks to recall internally and thus appropriate the spiritual qualities associated with the celestial being. 'Creative visualization' proved popular within the New Age Movement, where meditative techniques from various traditions could be brought together, or simply devised creatively by the meditation teacher. Other NRMs make use of physical activity as a meditative focus. The Sufi derived new religion of 'Sufi Sam' focused on dance as a form of meditation. New religions drawing from Native American or indigenous African religious sources also utilize dance.

Meditation has been used for a variety of purposes: obtaining pragmatic benefits, improving personal efficiency by increasing concentration and reducing stress and making spiritual progress towards the ultimate goal of enlightenment or liberation, however it is conceived.

Messianism

Although Jewish scripture expressed firm belief in a coming golden age, Messianism did not take its rise until the first or second centuries BCE. The Hebrew word *masiach* means 'anointed', and was applied to kings and priests. It is rendered in Greek as *christos* – 'Christ'. The Jewish expectation was for a coming saviour figure, who would conquer the Romans and usher in a new utopian kingdom. Christians have seen Jesus of Nazareth as that predicted Messiah, despite the fact that he was crucified without social or political achievement. Christians developed messianic belief, claiming that Jesus was divine, in contrast with the Jewish belief that the Messiah is a human figure. They also spiritualized his victory, promising a heavenly rather than an earthly rule. For most traditional Christians the Messiah is also equated with the 'Son of Man', who is expected to return on the clouds of heaven.

Messianism is variously interpreted by Jews, not all of whom continue to believe in a coming saviour figure, but prefer to look forward to some kind of new political system. Recent Jewish movements, such as Liberal and Reform Judaism continue to acknowledge that messianic expectations are as yet unfulfilled. A few Jewish NRMs have declared that the Messiah has come, for example the Lubavich movement. Messianic Jews hold, in common with Christians, that Jesus was the Messiah, but continue to practise Jewish law and ritual.

Most Christian NRMs accept traditional views of Jesus' messiahship. However, Jesus is reported as warning against false messiahs (e.g. Mt. 24.5), and messianic claimants have arisen throughout the centuries. Several NRMs have had a leader who has claimed messianic status, although there are different understandings of what this means. David Koresh, for example, claimed to be the 'sinful Messiah' – a kind of anti-type of Jesus; Jim Jones, of the Peoples Temple, once claimed to be the reincarnated Christ; and Ernest Norman (founder of Urantia) and, later, Russian NRM leader Sergei Tropp (aka Vissarion) each proclaimed himself as a returned Jesus. Raël (né Claude Vorhilhon), founder leader of the Raelians, has claimed messianic status, being allegedly the offspring of the extraterrestrial leader Yahweh and his human mother, who was called Mary. There are also female messianic claimants, such as Maria Devi Christos (born Marina Tsvigun) of the Great White Brotherhood. Occasionally the messianic role is not explicitly accepted by its occupant: the Rastafari pointed to Emperor Haile Selassie as the Messiah figure, although initially he was unaware of this attribution.

The expectation of a new messiah was prevalent among Korean new religions that arose in the mid-twentieth century. Best known is the Unification Church, which taught that Jesus was unable fully to complete his mission, and hence a new Messiah – the Lord of the Second Advent – was needed. *Divine Principle* explains the UC's belief that this new Messiah must be born in Korea in the early part of the twentieth century, and Unificationists teach that their leader Sun Myung Moon fulfilled this function. A number of UC splinter groups have rejected this interpretation, placing their own leader in this role, for example Cleopas Kundiona in the Zimbabwean group, and more recently Jung Myung Seok in Korea.

It is difficult to disentangle messianism from belief in a superhuman leader, an apocalyptic figure, or a figure who has a comparable role in some other religious tradition, and at times these ideas merge. Messianic belief recurs in Islam in the concept of the Mahdi. The Ahmadiyya regard their founder Mirza Ghulam Ahmad (1825–1908) as fulfilling this role. Benjamin Creme, the leader of Christ Maitreya, claims sightings of the unknown Mahdi, who will shortly reveal himself to humanity. Shōkō Ashara, leader of Aum Shinrikyō, has sometimes been referred to as the Messiah, despite being in the Buddhist rather than Christian tradition.

Other religious groups endow their leader with supernatural, although not necessarily messianic status. Father Divine (George Baker) is regarded as God, although the term Messiah is not applied to him, and new age teacher David Icke proclaimed himself as the Son of God and channel of the Christ spirit.

As can be seen, messianism is by no means a unified concept. It takes different forms in different NRMs, and lacks clear boundaries.

Millennialism

Millennialism is the belief in the imminent end of the current era of existence. The term is generally synonymous with eschatology (beliefs about the end of time) and apocalypticism (literally, beliefs about revealed secrets, but colloquially meaning beliefs about the end of the world). The term derives from the Christian Book of Revelation, which describes Christ's thousand-year reign, or Millennium, as a central moment in the transition from the current epoch to a new one (Rev. 20.1–10). Scholars use the term both within and beyond the Christian theological context to describe a range of beliefs centred on the end of the current epoch.

There are numerous varieties of millennialism. In the classic Christian theological context, theologians distinguish between pre millennialism, which envisions a series of upheavals before Christ's advent, and postmillennialism, which looks to a gradual process of social uplift culminating in the second coming of Christ. Catherine Wessinger has reformulated and extended this distinction in her theorization of catastrophic millennialism and progressive millennialism, which offers value in understanding millennialism outside the Christian context. Millennialism has been a key feature in many but not all new religious movements.

For more on millennialism, see Chapter 15, 'Millennialism'.

Modernity / Postmodernity

While identical terms exist in art history, literary studies, and other disciplines, in the fields of religious studies and sociology of religion modernity can be defined as the era characterized by a confluence of factors including industrialization, urbanization, nationalism, the rise of capitalism and economic liberalism, and scientific developments. As scholars use the term, modernity has led to increases in individualism, naturalism, and the atomization of belief and believers, and decreases in communalism, supernaturalism and social cohesion. Following in the vein of Max Weber, Marcel Gauchet refers to modernity as a disenchantment that has stripped religion of much of its vitality and led to the growth of alternative institutions such as the nation state and corporation (Gauchet 1997). The concept is therefore linked to that of secularization.

Scholars of NRMs have generally argued that new religions responded to the emergence of modernity by rejecting its various components or repercussions and embracing premodernity in some form. Such scholars often see the late twentieth century as the full flowering of modernity and the complete unfolding of its destabilizing repercussion. Charles Y. Glock championed such a view as early as 1976 when he positioned the new religions of the Anglo-American counterculture as a reaction to modernity and the failings of the older religious-social-political systems of Liberalism and Orthodoxy. James Davidson Hunter offered a more complete extension of this position, arguing that NRMs serve as responses to the growth of modernity, and all are structurally (though not necessarily theoretically) opposed to modernity. In keeping with the German sociological tradition, Hunter understands modernism as characterized structurally by the breakdown of traditional institutions, heightened division between private and public sphere, and growth of pluralism (Hunter 1981).

Recently scholars have considered NRMs as not merely reactions to modernity but forces acting within the forces of postmodernity. Like modernity, scholars use the term postmodernity in different ways. Within the study of NRMs, postmodernity refers to the destabilized, creative, media-driven, syncretistic practices present in a globalized world. James Beckford (1992, 19) identifies four features of postmodernism: (1) the rejection of positivism and rationalism; (2) a tendency to combine symbols from different sources; (3) spontaneity and playfulness; (4) the rejection of overarching meta-narratives. One can find evidence of such features in a range of NRMs, many of which reject the normal canons of biblical and historical scholarship – as evidenced by the rise of UFO-religions, for example, which combine a questioning of scientific explanations with novel interpretations of the Bible (Chryssides 2011; Partridge 2003; Zeller 2010). The New Age is a further manifestation of a counterculture, which rejects orthodox science and medicine, and is typically eclectic in the way in which it draws from a variety of religious sources. Cusack's approach of envisioning 'invented religions' also fits within this paradigm.

Mysticism

Ever since Ernest Troeltsch created a tripartite typology of Christian groups as churches, sects or mystical movements – a division that his friend and colleague Max Weber later drew upon in his own work – the idea of mysticism has become linked to the study of new religious movements. Troeltsch and Weber both looked to mysticism as formative in how religious innovators created new movements, and Troeltsch saw mysticism both as a force with mass appeal as well as an influence within sectarian groups (1931). The first wave of twentieth-century scholarship on NRMs also relied on the concept of mysticism in explaining the rise of new religions and the popular interest in new religiosity. Robert N. Bellah, Charles Y. Glock, Robert Wuthnow and their colleagues studying the NRMs of the 1960s and 1970s counterculture argued that mysticism underlay a 'new religious consciousness' and 'consciousness reformation' that was reshaping contemporary religion (Bellah and Glock 1976; Wuthnow 1976). More recent scholarship has indicated a continued interest in the sort of radically individualistic inward spirituality that characterizes mysticism, especially in the United States where such a mentality has had continued appeal (Albanese 2007).

Many founders and adherents of NRMs predicate their religious practices on the notion of mysticism. Founders such as Ellen G. White (Adventism), Sun Myung Moon (Unification Church), Park Chung-bin (Won Buddhism) and Swami Muktananda (SYDA Yoga) all claimed profound mystical experiences including visions and direct access to the numinous that led them to become religious teachers and form the movements that they later led. While few of the adherents of those movements seek or experience the same sort of mysticism as their founders, they nevertheless are heirs to the mystical tradition in NRMs.

Other NRMs actively promote the idea of individual mysticism and encourage followers to seek mystical experiences. Neo-shamanic groups, especially those that uphold the use of hallucinogenic substances such as peyote and ayahuasca, place mysticism at the heart of religious practice. While not all new religions focusing on meditation necessarily uphold mysticism as a goal, some of those influenced by Tantric or Zen teachings do encourage followers to seek mystical experiences through meditative practices. Groups descendent from the Western mystical traditions such as neo-Hasidic Judaism or the Christian monastic tradition similarly look to mysticism as a key to religious practice.

Mysticism and mystic new religions often lead to social quietude and even separatism, since practitioners can sometimes stress the other-worldly nature of inward contemplation over and against worldly concerns. New religions following in such a vein run a risk of numerical decline or stagnation. However mystics can also develop strong antinomian tendencies, as is evidenced by the 'crazy guru' tradition in the Zen and Vajrayana traditions of Buddhism. Such mystical new religions – as well as those calling for drug use to invoke mystical experiences – face social disapproval and possible persecution for their violations of normative social mores.

Peace

Although media attention, as well as NRMs scholarship, has tended to focus on the violent activities of NRMs, a significant number of NRMs have the stated aim of peace. Peace has been a traditional concern in the major world religions: Jesus Christ is described as the 'Prince of Peace', the word 'Islam' is derived from the Arabic *salaam*, meaning peace. *Ahimsa* (non-violence) is a key principle of the Jains, and in the Hindu tradition it is one of the bases of Patanjali's system of *raja yoga*. Although Buddhists are not inherently pacifist, the Pali canon emphasizes non-violence. Despite holding peace as an ideal, most major religions allow that war may be justifiable in certain circumstances. Christianity developed the doctrine of the just war, and the Islamic concept of *jihad* permits armed combat in defence of the faith.

In Japan, in the wake of Hiroshima, numerous Japanese NRMs arose with the explicit goal of world peace. The most visible of these in the West have been Soka Gakkai, Risso-Kosei-kai and Nipponzon Myohoji, the last of which has made itself visible by constructing peace pagodas worldwide, while other Japanese groups have erected small pillars bearing the inscription 'May peace prevail on Earth'. A number of ecumenical and interfaith groups focus on peace, such as the Peace Pledge Union, Religions for Peace Global Interfaith Network, the Women of Faith Network and Christian CND.

The Vietnam War in the 1960s prompted a desire for peace in the youth counterculture, resulting in a number of movements stressing love and peace: the Children of God (now The Family International) is one such example. Only a small number of religious groups have been totally opposed to war and violence. Examples include the Quakers, the Amish, and the Jehovah's Witnesses, as well as Mahatma Gandhi's *satyagraha* movement. The Raelian movement is also committed to non-violence, although it has never lived through circumstances that have tested its principles.

Numerous religious groups hold that the key to world peace is not the refusal of military service but rather the practice of their faith. Thus, ISKCON contends that chanting the Hare Krishna mantra is efficacious in solving the world's problems, and Soka Gakkai Buddhists make similar claims about their mantra *nam myoho renge kyo*. The Bahá'í faith seeks ultimately to establish a world government, and hence the key to world peace would be universal acceptance of their teachings and practices. Although Bahá'í encourage members to assume non-combative roles during war time, loyalty to one's government takes precedence where such alternatives to military service are not permitted.

While organizations like the Quakers have been willing to take up non-combative roles in wartime, Jehovah's Witnesses have gone further and refuse to engage in any activity that helps a war effort, even refusing alternative civil duties. This is despite the fact that they do not regard themselves as strictly pacifist. Basing their beliefs on the Bible, they acknowledge that God instructed the ancient Israelites to go into battle. However, they argue that modern wars carry no divine authorization, and that the wars in the Bible had a purpose of promoting the establishment of God's kingdom.

The concept of peace is not limited to the absence of war. Much New Age spirituality expresses concern for the environment: one noted example is James Lovelock's 'Gaia hypothesis', which views the Earth as a unified interdependent living entity, thus necessitating a concern with ecology. Recent interest in Native American spirituality and in Paganism entails an interest in maintaining peaceful harmony with the Earth and living beings within it. Associated with respect for living beings is vegetarianism, which has been particularly championed in some Western forms of Buddhism, and in ISKCON.

Peace is frequently a concept that serves to define the ultimate goal of religion. The term *samadhi*, used in the Hindu and Buddhist traditions, refers to the final cessation of activity in the realms of birth and rebirth, when final liberation (*moksha* or *nirvana*) is attained.

Politics

Since NRMs inevitably arise within political systems, they must decide how to position themselves with regard to the State. Stances vary from opposition to cooperation and accommodation. By their very nature, NRMs are not bound up with state government, since this is the function of a country's dominant religion.

Some NRMs have been closely bound up with politics to the extent that they have been accused of being political organizations rather than religions. The Unification Church has been noted for its vehement stance against communism: its satellite organization CAUSA ('Confederation of the Associations for the Unification of the Societies of the Americas') aims to provide anti-communist education. The Soka Gakkai has close links with the Japanese political party New Komeito, the vast majority of whose members also belong to the Soka Gakkai, and the two organizations share senior office bearers. In 1992, the Transcendental Meditation organization set up the Natural Law Party, contesting elections in various countries. Occasionally, NRMs have acted as pressure groups for political change: in Britain the Church of Scientology campaigned – unsuccessfully – for a Bill of Rights.

Opposition may be initiated either by governments or by NRMs. Particularly in Islamic countries, communist and formerly communist regimes, the presence of NRMs is generally unwelcome, and perceived as a threat to the prevailing religion or to the State. At times NRMs have had teachings and practices that have brought them into conflict: notable examples include the Jehovah's Witnesses during the war years, when they were prepared to be subjected to arrest and imprisonment for their refusal to take part in armed conflict. Islamic regimes, particularly Iran, have been particularly intolerant of the Bahá'í, on account of their recognition of Bahá'u'lláh as a prophet succeeding Muhammad.

In most countries governments have sought to restrict NRMs' activities. Some have required registration of religious organizations, and many NRMs have found it difficult to satisfy the requirements relating to age or membership numbers. In the United States, Canada, Europe and Australasia there is no explicit discriminatory legislation against NRMs. However, authorities can make use of existing laws to prosecute NRMs for certain activities: one such example is the Church of Scientology, which has been prosecuted in Belgium, France, Italy and Spain variously for fraud, illegal practice of medicine and violation of employment laws.

Generally NRMs have a presumption in favour of compliance with the law of the land, and New Christian groups frequently refer to Paul's injunction that one should obey civil authorities (Rom. 13.1). In some instances they have given up illicit practice in order to achieve compliance, for example the abandonment of polygamy in 1890 by the Church of Jesus Christ of Latter-day Saints.

The members of some NRMs perceive themselves as belonging to a spiritual realm that transcends the physical world, viewing membership of civil society is only a temporary necessity. The practice of living in communes or ashrams provides a visible way of living apart from civil society. Some organizations attempt separation from the world by adopting a monastic lifestyle, as is practised by some Buddhist groups, and some ISKCON devotees. The Jehovah's Witnesses are particularly renowned for their belief that the present political regimes will soon be replaced by Jehovah's new theocratic system of government. They hold that, after the Battle of Armageddon, Christ will be victorious over all present-day systems of government, which they believe are controlled by Satan. Some UFO-religions, like the Raelians, look forward to the arrival of super-intelligent extraterrestrials, who will help to establish a system of government known as 'geniocracy' – a system in which only the most intelligent citizens will be eligible for political office.

Prayer

Members of nearly every NRM engage in some form of prayer, whether it is liturgical prayer, petitionary prayer, or meditative prayer, or the use of a mantra. This is hardly surprising, since prayer functions as one of the most important forms of practice within the majority of the world's religions. New religions developing out of existing religious groups often assume the same sort of prayer practices as do their predecessor religions, but even radically new or syncretistic NRMs involve prayer. Only the new 'religious' movements that are avowedly secular or non-religious in orientation, such as Church of the Flying Spaghetti Monster or the popular culture religion of Matrixism, lack prayer practices, though of course whether such groups merit designation within the schema of NRM is itself contested.

Scholars have developed several typologies for studying prayer, with theologian Friedrich Heiler's basic approach most influential. Heiler differentiated ritual and ceremonial forms of prayer, which are often petitionary in nature, from mystical or meditative prayers, though as a theologian he denigrated the former and upheld the latter. A more complex typology derives from Sam Gill's succinct summation in the *Encyclopedia of Religion*, where he designed prayer as fitting within the categories of petition, invocation, thanksgiving, dedication, supplication, intercession, confession, penitence and benediction.

Extending these typologies and approaches to the study of NRMs one finds a remarkable diversity in the way in which adherents of new religions pray. To take a few well-known examples, devotees of Krishna who belong to the Hare Krishna movement engage in meditative and ritual prayer utilizing Sanskrit mantras as well as celebratory prayers in Bengali. By contrast members of The

Family pray privately using either improvisational vernacular petitionary prayer – often silent – or communally in the form of glossolalia. In both the cases of ISKCON and The Family one must understand their prayer practices as part of broader religious-cultural systems, Bengali Hindu devotionalism or American Evangelical Pentecostalism respectively.

One commonality of most types of prayer in NRMs is that they are accessible, direct and central in the lives of adherents. Individuals tend to join new religious movements because they seek higher demand, more involved, and livelier religious practices and communities than they experienced in lives prior to joining. Often such converts come from secularized or religiously liberal backgrounds and embrace new religious lives centring on intensive religious practices such as frequent or demanding prayer. While these generalizations do not hold for all NRMs or their adherents, the overall pattern means that members of new religions often engage in far longer, more arduous and more frequent prayers than adherents of older more conventional religions.

Predicament

Religions typically identify some overarching undesirable state in which humanity is situated, and which from men and women need to escape. In the main, NRMs' teachings about the human predicament are derived from the parent tradition from which they developed.

Christianity claims that sin lies at the root of the world's problems, while the Hindu tradition posits *maya* (illusion) as the state to be overcome, and Buddhism teaches that the fundamental ill is *dukkha* (unsatisfactoriness – often inappropriately translated as 'suffering'). The seriousness of such fundamental problems is such that they cannot readily be righted by simply improving one's behaviour, or by sociopolitical action.

As well as identifying a serious predicament, religions typically posit a superior alternative and, most importantly, offer a spiritual path by which it can be achieved. The action that is needed to rectify the human predicament is frequently contested within mainstream traditions. Christianity has been divided on the question of whether faith or works enable the follower to attain salvation, and Hindu spirituality has recommended a variety of paths: *jnana* (insight), *bhakti* (devotion), and *karma* (deeds), while Western Buddhists groups reflect the practices of the specific traditions from which they come.

In some cases, it may be less easy to perceive a serious predicament from which escape is sought. Pagans, Wiccans and Druids are such examples, although arguably their members – particularly those who live in an urban environment – find themselves alienated from nature, or from a lost tradition that has existed before the advent of Christianity, and may perceive impending environmental disaster as a predicament to which a solution must be sought. Various Jewish NRMs envision a broken world as in need of healing (*tikkun olam*) and similarly look to this-worldly predicaments.

As Eileen Barker has pointed out, NRMs tend to be composed of first-generation converts; hence members often tend to display a greater awareness of humanity's predicament and the need to follow a rigorous path affording a solution. Some NRMs display a consciousness of greater urgency, particularly those that expect an imminent end of the world. This urgency is often manifested in intensified spiritual practice, for example by adopting a celibate or ascetic lifestyle, or by close spiritual supervision (called 'discipling' or 'shepherding' in the International Churches of Christ), or the persistent house-to-house evangelizing of the Jehovah's Witnesses. On rare occasions, more radical solutions for escaping one's predicament are required, as in Heaven's Gate, where death was regarded as the means of transition from a doomed earth to an extraterrestrial world. Conversely, other NRMs offer 'short cuts', such as the mantra chanting of ISKCON devotees or the Soka Gakkai.

A few NRMs do not appear to highlight a serious predicament. Particularly in the somewhat world-affirming New Age Movement, one's predicament might be seen to be less serious than those identified by major religious traditions, and may consist of loss of inner peace, physical illness or inability to realize one's true self. Occasionally, religion itself is regarded as the predicament: Bhagwan Shree Rajneesh (aka Osho) advocated enjoyment of life, rather than escape from any earthly predicament, but regarded religion itself as repressive and even dangerous, particularly when it appears to require blind and unquestioning allegiance to its leaders. Older movements such as the Latter-day Saints and the Jehovah's Witnesses teach that an original ideal Church became corrupt, and has contributed to the predicament in which humanity finds itself.

In sum, most religions – old and new – look towards a new transformed state of existence that surpasses the present one. However, there is inevitable divergence of belief as to what this might be, and what the precise nature of the human predicament is.

Schism

Schism refers to the splintering of a religious institution or body into multiple strands, and is a term derived from the study of Christian history. It its historical sense, it refers to the divide between Eastern and Western Christendom and later divisions within the Western Church. When used to refer to contemporary movements, schism can refer to any religious splinter. New religious movements often form from schism, and many NRMs experience schisms themselves. Importantly, few groups refer to themselves as schisms or as schismatics. The result of a schism is almost always two or more groups claiming to possess the true mantle and authority of the original movement.

Weber and Troeltsch's original theorizations of the formation of NRMs, variants of the Church-sect model, predicated the emergence of new religions on the process of schism. Specifically, schisms form when doctrinal innovators split from the stable, often established, churches or denominations, resulting in new cults and sects, to use their language. Sociologist and theologian H. Richard Niebuhr further developed this particular concept of schism, focusing on social rather than doctrinal sources, but offering the same basic argument that schism serves as the primary means of the creation of new religious groups.

James R. Lewis and Sarah M. Lewis have categorized schism into five types: those resulting from underlying social or demographic factors, such as race or class; personal conflicts or ambitions; disagreements over doctrine or matters related to religious practice; the death of a charismatic founder and the ensuing power vacuum or power struggle; and alternative claims of religious authority, such as revelation or mediumship (Lewis and Lewis 2009, 3). Such a typology is clearly comprised of ideal types, and actual schisms would fall within multiple categories.

In addition to serving in the creation of NRMs, schisms occur within new religions as well. Particularly after the death of a charismatic founder, schisms occur as different individuals claim leadership. Failed predictions, apostasy of a founder or leader, social conflict, and a variety of other challenges can all lead to schisms within an NRM. The best-known and researched historical examples concern nineteenth-century new religions such as the Latter-day Saints and the Adventists, though numerous other examples exist in more recent decades (Miller 1991). New religious movements that promote more individualistic worldviews include practices involving revelation, prophecy, channelling, or other forms of direct access to the divine, and those that are anti-institutional in tone all create spaces for schisms.

Scripture

Most NRMs have their scriptures or authoritative writings. Not all NRMs are comfortable with the term 'scripture', however – a term which does not have a totally clear definition. It may connote sacred writings that are regarded as infallible, or as direct supernatural revelation, or formally defined canonical writings. Not all 'religions of the book' necessarily regard their writings as inerrant or as having divine rather than human authorship, although all those who belong to a book religion regard them as in some sense authoritative.

A work may come to qualify as scripture in a number of ways, presumed inerrancy or revealed status being two. A set of writings may be formally pronounced to be scripture; they may be the subject of intense study and reflection; they may be used as the basis for establishing true doctrine; or they may be employed within a ritual context. In the Jewish and Christian traditions, all these criteria are satisfied, while in the case of NRMs the distinctive writings may fall into some of these categories, but not others.

In some instances it is not clear whether a piece of writing bears scriptural authority, whether it is regarded as a piece of spiritual or theological writing. For example, Sun Myung Moon's *Divine Principle* is the focus for intensive study, yet only the Christian Bible is used at worship. Hare Krishna members use only Vedic materials in worship, yet read founder Prabhupada's commentaries with something approaching scriptural intent.

Where an NRM is associated with a major world faith it typically adopts the scriptures of the parent tradition. A few NRMs have added their own sacred texts, like the Book of Mormon, and channellers have produced texts like *The Urantia Book* and *A Course in Miracles*. Some 'invented religions' have devised their own texts, for example *Principia Discordia* by Gregory Hill (aka Malaclypse the Younger).

Sacred texts have a number of functions. They serve as a record of new revelations given to a founder leader, and they give greater permanence to the teachings following the founder-leader's death. They can recount and authenticate key events that the tradition proclaims, for example the Mormon history of the lost tribes. The alleged discovery of *The Life of St Issa* by Nicolas Notovich in the late nineteenth century gave credence to the tradition that Jesus lived in India – a theory that gained momentum through Helena Blavatsky, and the Church Universal and Triumphant, among others. (Scholars agree, of course, that the 'discovery' was a hoax.)

Scriptures function ritually, for example in the Soka Gakkai's ritually chanting of parts of the Lotus Sutra as part of their *gongyo* ceremony, and a Christian Science service consists predominantly of reading the works of Mary Baker Eddy. At a Church of Scientology service only L. Ron Hubbard's writings are read, without any addition, alteration or comment. In 1996 the Church of Scientology declared that all of Hubbard's writings on Dianetics and Scientology were scriptures.

Occasionally an NRM will deprecate a set of scriptures for its own ends. Raël's writings acknowledge a residual truth in the Christian Bible, viewing it as a distorted account of extraterrestrial visitations. Rajneesh/Osho was scathing of authoritative religious writings, claiming that his followers should follow no one, although paradoxically – in common with the Zen tradition – he had regard for the Heart Sutra, which he expounded in some detail.

Christians have tended to view unfavourably the addition of new scriptures, sometimes citing the words of John the Revelator: 'If anyone adds anything to [this book], God will add to him the plagues described in this book' (Rev. 22.18).

Secularization

Secularization generally refers to two different concepts: the decline of the power, position, or authority of religion; and a thesis that such a decline is endemic to contemporary Western modernity. Scholars of NRMs have often invoked the idea of secularization to explain the connection of new religions to the broader religious environment. Yet the particular way in which NRMs reflect secularization and what such a process entails are highly contentious matters.

While few people disagree that religious institutions have lost much of the power they held in the premodern era, precisely why and how this has occurred and whether such a process is an intrinsic fact of modernization are at the heart of this debate. One school of thought proffered by sociologists of religion with interests in NRMs argues that Western society has not only become more secular, but that this process is irreversible and inherent to modern life. Bryan Wilson and Roy Wallis have each argued that NRMs reflect small and generally irrelevant social movements that react to secularization by embracing premodern forms of religion, and reflect discontent with the broader social processes of secularization (Wallis 1984; Wilson 1990). Steve Bruce offers perhaps the most succinct restatement of this approach, envisioning NRMs in the secular West as dying gasps of the old premodern order (2002).

In opposition to the approach of Wilson, Wallis, and Bruce, a group of sociologists operating under the rubric of the 'rational choice model' have offered an alternative vision of secularization as a cyclical process of formation of new high-demand sects and cults that desecularize society in response to waning secularized religious movements. Borrowing from the cult-sect typology of Weber and Troeltsch, sociologists under the lead of Rodney Stark, William Sims Bainbridge and Laurence Iannaccone have argued that as the more mainstream denominations and churches decline in power and influence, a variety of new 'firms' appear on the religious marketplace. These firms – new religious movements, revivals of older traditions and schismatic groups – offer more nimble responses to the religious market and succeed to the detriment of the older churches. Secularization is therefore a self-limiting process since it entails new groups such as NRMs that emerge and re-sacralize society. Stark et al. have pointed to groups such as the Methodists, Baptists, Latter-day Saints and Pentecostals as examples (Stark and Bainbridge 1985; Stark and Finke 2000).

The debate between the proponents of secularization theory and the rational choice school has become acrimonious and in some cases personal (Bruce and

Wallis 1985; Stark 1999). Yet a few scholars have attempted to resolve the debate in alternative ways. Phillip Hammond has proposed a redefinition of secularization in light of the emergence of NRMs and other recent religious developments, casting it in a more limited manner (1985). More recently, scholars have crafted the model of post-secularism wherein they reject the secularization model's contention that religion will fade away and disappear, but accept the overall thrust of secularization as a process entailing the loss of religion's social authority (Nynäs et al. 2012).

Spirituality

Although widely used popularly, it is generally agreed by scholars that the term has no clear meaning. Historically, the word relates to 'spirit' (*pneuma*), which indicates that the spiritual person or teaching is inspired by God's Holy Spirit. In the Christian tradition, the word applied to those who were more deeply engaged in spiritual practice, and in living their faith. The term came to be particularly associated with religious experience, especially with regard to the mystic, who claimed to seek, or to have attained union with God. Spirituality is not to be conflated with spiritualism, the latter being a form of religion that incorporates alleged contact with the dead.

The emphasis on religious experience gained momentum through the work of Friedrich Schleiermacher, who influenced William James, famed for his *The Varieties of Religious Experience*. At roughly the same time the Theosophical Society took its rise, questing for secret teachings that formed the core of various world religions. In turn, spirituality came to be associated with mystical or esoteric religious experience, including the religious life of eastern traditions, such as Hinduism and Buddhism.

The post-traditional use of the term 'spirituality' tends to differentiate the 'spiritual' from the religious, frequently encapsulated in the assertion (some would say cliché) that one is 'spiritual but not religious' and conveying a sense of non-institutional or non-dogmatic religion. Such a claim is frequently made within the New Age Movement, whose adherents wish to distinguish themselves from the practices of organized religion, particularly traditional Christianity. Their form of religious life acknowledges that there exists something more than the physical world, which may be designated as God, spirit, or source of being, and they typically seek to find some meaning and purpose of existence beyond the present life, and the aim of inner peace. Such spiritual questing involves personal development and transformation, often involving spiritual practices such as meditation and visualization. Frequently 'spiritual seekers' do not confine their quest to one particular organization, but take an eclectic approach to this search for meaning. The search may involve innovative spiritual groups, or the seeker may explore several traditional forms of religion. Mysticism, monism and holism are particularly associated with spirituality, being ways of recognizing one's oneness either with the sacred, or with the rest of the universe.

Syncretism

The concept of syncretism encompasses several practices and qualities present within new religious movements, including the intentional combination of beliefs and practices drawn from different religious traditions, the presence of religious survivals from earlier groups, unintentional mimicking influenced by social or cultural factors, and blendings as the result of experiences or histories of members. At its heart, the term implies multiplicity and combinativeness. Because in some quarters the term implies the pollution of imagined 'pure' traditions, some scholars prefer concepts such as contact or combinativeness to that of syncretism (Albanese 1997). Others prefer creolization, a term that properly referred only to blendings of African cultures with New World ones, but has been expanded more broadly (Stewart and Shaw 1994). Still other scholars have embraced the idea of syncretism, indicating that it reveals the complexity and ingenuity of human thought and religion-making (Leopold and Jensen 2004). Regardless of nomenclature, the process of syncretism and the resulting movements have clear relevance for the study of new religious movements.

Scholars have forefronted the idea of syncretism especially when studying religion in colonial contexts and the new religions that form in such geographic and social locations. Often individuals and groups living under colonial or immediately postcolonial circumstances engage in extensive acts of religious syncretism so as to combine indigenous religious practices and beliefs with those imposed or imported by colonial powers. These explicit blendings of religious traditions are by their nature syncretistic. Scholars have particularly noted syncretism within the new religions created by African-Caribbean peoples, for example Vodou, Santería and Candomblé, all of which emerged when enslaved Africans combined aspects of West African Yoruba religion with colonial Catholicism. Researchers have also considered syncretism in the recent Indian context in terms of the combinations of Islam, Hindu devotional and intellectual movements, and Christianity. Colonial and postcolonial Africa and Korea have also been areas of research where the idea of syncretism has proved useful (Chung 2001; Greenfield and Droogers 2001).

The value of syncretism lies in its utility in explaining why some new religious movements seem to blend so many apparently disparate elements within a single religious system. Though reasons for each syncretism must be rooted within their particular social-religious context, syncretistic religions all share the same qualities of fluidity, flexibility and creativity. Rather than envision combinatory new religions as inauthentic since they draw from multiple traditions, positioning them as syncretistic allows researchers to forefront the manner in which individuals creatively responded to social forces through the religious resources available to them.

Third Millennium Religion

After the 1970s, there appeared to be a decline in the inception of new religions, as well as less strident proselytizing, and less community living. These phenomena are probably attributable to a variety of factors. The youth counterculture of the 1960s and 1970s broke up, and a change in socio-economic climate was encouraged by the Thatcher and Reagan governments, which extolled economic prosperity. More young people now embark on higher education, and fewer students take 'gap' years, no doubt affecting NRM recruitment. The passing of the year 2000 without any obvious supernatural event caused some millennial interest to shift to the year 2012, supposedly the year in which the Mayan prophecy would be fulfilled, yet this fizzled as well.

New religions taking their rise after the year 2000 tended to be of two different varieties. The first arose from the schisms from existing religions. Many derive from within the Anglican Church, where some members objected to the ordination of women, the large-scale abandonment of the Book of Common Prayer, and increasingly liberal attitudes on moral issues such as homosexuality. The Continuing Anglican Movement includes organizations such as the Church of England (Continuing) in England, and several similar organizations in the United States. Some Buddhist and Hindu NRMs continue to emerge based on particular teachings of gurus within those traditions, and of course various new pagan and New Age groups develop when teachers within those traditions break away from existing structures.

The second variety of third millennium NRM is cyber-religion. Cyber-religion is defined as a spiritual organization that operates substantially on the internet, rather than as a conventional bodily community. Such organizations include 'invented religions', such as Jediism. However, there are other online religions that are forms of mainstream religion. For example, the Church of Fools was set up in 2004 (renamed St Pixels in 2009) as a way of enabling Christians to worship online, without being present at a conventional church. Its services included hymns, prayers, Bible reading and a sermon. Various religious faiths have experimented with online devotion, and online 'pilgrimage', encouraging activities such as cyber-puja in Hinduism, and cyber-Hajj in Islam. Cyber-religion poses the questions of how valid such quasi-religious activities really are (e.g. can one really make a pilgrimage without physical inconvenience?), and which religious activities are and are not possible in cyber-space. Within Christianity, at least one attempt has been made to make the Eucharist available online: the Open Episcopal Church provides ready-consecrated bread and wine to be consumed during its online services, although many Christians would question whether such a sacrament can be valid.

Generally, most NRMs have now taken to exploiting the opportunities afforded by the internet for disseminating first-hand information about themselves. Equally, this has been matched by the online activities of anti-cult detractors.

Part V

Resources

Chronology

1744 Emanuel Swedenborg receives his first vision.

1776 Adam Weishaupt founds the Illuminati.

1787 (Swedenborgian) Church of the New Jerusalem is founded.

1830 Latter-day Saint movement founded by Joseph Smith in Palmyra, New York.

Publication of the Book of Mormon.

1831 William Miller begins to preach about the world's imminent end.

1834 Ralph Waldo Emerson and others found the Transcendentalist Club.

1844 Murder of Mormon leader Joseph Smith.

22 October: The 'Great Disappointment' William Miller's expectation of Christ's return is unfulfilled.

The Declaration of the Báb (announcing the coming of 'him whom God shall manifest'), an important figure with the Bahá'í movement.

1848 The Fox sisters hear 'rappings' in their New York State home.

Followers of John Thomas name themselves the Christadelphians.

1848–58 Madame Blavatsky's 'veiled time'.

1852 Beginning of Bahá'u'lláh's mission (traditional dating).

1861 Seventh-day Adventists founded by Ellen G. White.

1863 Bahá'u'lláh declares his mission.

1875 Helen P. Blavatsky and Henry Steel Olcott establish the Theosophical Society.

Science and Health with Key to the Scriptures by Mary Baker Eddy is published.

Anglo-Israel Association is founded in London.

1877 Helena P. Blavatsky publishes *Isis Unveiled*.

1879 Mary Baker Eddy founds the Church of Christ, Scientist.

First edition of *Zion's Watch Tower* is published.

1881 Zion's Watch Tower Tract Society is founded.

Chronology

The Unity School of Christianity is founded by Charles and Myrtle Fillmore.

1888 Order of the Golden Dawn is founded.

H. P. Blavatsky's *The Secret Doctrine* is published.

1893 World's Parliament of Religions, Chicago.

National Spiritualist Association of Churches is set up in Chicago.

1894 Ibrahim Kheirella brings Bahá'í movement to North America.

1895 Bible Conference of Conservative Protestants at Niagara define 'five points of fundamentalism'.

Ordo Templi Orientis (OTO) is founded.

1897 Ramakrishna Mission in India founded by Vivekananda.

1899 Vivekananda's tour of the United States and Europe commences.

1901 Spiritualists' National Union is established.

1904 Ancient Mystical Order of the Rosy Cross is established.

1906 Azusa Street Revival in Los Angeles, forerunner of Pentecostalism.

1907 Rosicrucian Fellowship and Societas Rosicruciana founded.

1908 Krishnamurti 'discovered' by Theosophists Annie Besant and Charles Leadbeater.

1910 Sufism introduced to North America by Pir Hazrat Inayat Khan.

Sufi Order of the West founded in England.

1911 Order of the Star of the East founded.

1912 Aleister Crowley joins the Ordo Templi Orientis.

1913 The Anthroposophical Society is established by Rudolf Steiner.

1914 Rastafari leader Marcus Garvey establishes the United Negro Improvement Association in Jamaica.

International New Thought Alliance founded.

Aurobindo creates his first ashram.

Vipassana 'rediscovered' by Ven Ledi Sayadaw.

1916 Death of Charles Taze Russell.

1917 *The Finished Mystery*, attributed posthumously to Charles Taze Russell is published.

Joseph Franklin ('Judge') Rutherford is appointed as Russell's successor.

1919 British Israel World Federation founded.

1919 Rudolf Steiner sets up the first Waldorf School.

1920 Joseph Franklin Rutherford publishes *Millions Now Living Will Never Die!*

1921 Cao Dai is founded by Ngo Van Chieue.

Margaret Murray publishes *The Witch-Cult in Western Europe*.

First Century Christian Fellowship (later Moral Re-Armament) founded by Frank Buchman.

1922 The Institute for the Harmonious Development of Man is established in France by George Ivanovitch Gurdjieff.

Christian Mystic Lodge of the Theosophical Society established by Dion Fortune in Glastonbury.

Swami Yogananda arrives in North America.

1923 The Arcane School is founded by Alice Bailey.

1926 The Ramakrishna Vedanta Society of Boston is established.

1927 Institute of Religious Science and School of Philosophy founded by Ernest Holmes.

1928 Opus Dei is established.

1929 Krishnamurti breaks from the Theosophical Society.

Publication of *Magick in Theory and Practice* by Aleister Crowley.

1930 Haile Selassie coronated as Emperor of Ethiopia.

Soka Gakkai is founded in Japan.

The Church of the Lord (Aladura) is founded by Josiah Olunowa Oshitelu.

1931 The name 'Jehovah's Witnesses' is adopted by J. F. Rutherford's Bible Students at Columbus, Ohio.

Meher Baba visits North America.

1932 Emissaries of Divine Light founded by Lloyd Meeker.

1933 Herbert W. Armstrong established the Radio Church of God.

1934 I AM movement founded by Guy Ballard.

The Plain Truth is first published.

1935 Sun Myung Moon receives his inaugural vision of Jesus in Korea.

1938 Brahma Kumaris founded.

Frank Buchman initiates his 'moral re-armament' (MRA) programme.

Risshō Kōsei-kai founded.

1940 Satya Sai Baba declares himself the returned Sai Baba of Shirdi.

1942 Vesper Chimes (subsequently known as The Way International) founded by Victor Paul Weirwille.

1946 Yogananda's *Autobiography of a Yogi* is published.

1948 Beginning of Latter-Rain movement within Pentecostalism.

1950 L. Ron Hubbard's *Dianetics* is first published.

Chronology

1954 Sun Myung Moon sets up the Holy Spirit Association for the Unification of World Christianity in Korea.

Church of Scientology is founded.

Publication of *Witchcraft Today* by Gerald Gardner.

Unarius (UFO-religion) is founded.

1956 The Mother, née Mirra Alfassa, declares herself an avatar, following Aurobindo.

Leon Festinger publishes *When Prophecy Fails*.

1957 Transcendental Meditation is introduced to the West.

1958 Summit Lighthouse founded by Mark L. Prophet.

Inaugural Rastafarian Universal Convention.

1959 Chinese invasion of Tibet.

Muhammad Subuh visits the United States, and G. I. Gurdjieff becomes a follower.

Maharishi Mahesh Yogi visits the United States.

1961 Jehovah's Witnesses' New World Translation of the Bible is completed.

1962 Pope John XXIII convenes the Second Vatican Council, which continues until 1965

    Catholic Neocatechumenate movement founded

    Focolare movement receive papal approval.

    Eileen and Peter Caddy set up the Findhorn community.

1963 Jane Roberts begins channelling 'Seth'.

Universal House of Justice founded by Bahá'í in Haifa, Israel.

1964 Sri Chinmoy visits the United States.

Death of Gerald Gardner. Alexander Sanders assumes the title 'king of the witches'.

1965 Swami Prabhupada arrives in New York; founds International Society for Krishna Consciousness (ISKCON).

Eckankar founded by Paul Twitchell.

Assassination of Malcolm X.

1966 The Church of Satan founded by Anton LaVey.

Integral Yoga Institute founded by Swami Satchidananda in the United States.

Association of Unity Churches founded.

John Lofland publishes *Doomsday Cult*.

1966 Emperor Haile Selassie visits Jamaica.

The Urantia Book is published.

The Aetherius Society (UFO-religion) is founded by George King.

1967 The Children of God (later known as The Family) takes its rise in California.

Commencement of the California 'Jesus movement'.

Indra Devi visits California, lectures on Satya Sai Baba.

Friends of the Western Buddhist Order, later known as Triratna, founded by the Ven. Maha Sthavira Sangharakshita (Dennis Lingwood).

Narayanananda Universal Yoga Trust founded.

H. Neill McFarland publishes *The Rush Hour of the Gods.*

First papers on NRMs presented at Society for the Scientific Study of Religion (SSSR) under auspices of Church/sect typology.

1968 Beatles meet Maharishi Mahesh Yogi in India.

Children of God founded by David Berg (Moses David).

Yogi Bhajan visits the United States and Canada.

Herbert Armstrong's organization adopts the name Worldwide Church of God.

Troy Perry establishes Metropolitan Community Churches.

Anton LaVey publishes *The Satanic Bible.*

Erich von Däniken publishes *Chariots of the Gods.*

George Harrison releases his song 'My Sweet Lord'.

The Mother establishes experimental city of Auroville.

1969 The Charles Manson murders.

3HO (Healthy Happy Holy) founded by Yogi Bhajan.

Church of Armageddon founded by Paul Erdmann (Love Israel).

Acharya Vimalananda visits the United States, brings Ananda Marga tradition.

J. Gordon Melton founds the Institute for the Study of American Religions (ISAR).

1970 Free Daist Communion founded by Franklin Jones.

Muktananda (Siddha Yoga Dham) arrives in the United States.

Rajneesh initiates first disciples as sannyasins.

Sri Mataji begins teaching Sahaja Yoga.

Sun Bear begins teaching beyond Native Americans.

Gurudev Amrit Desai founds yoga community at Summit Station, Pennsylvania.

1971 Himalayan Institute founded by Swami Rama.

The Farm founded in central Tennessee, the United States.

Arica Institute founded by Oscar Ichazo.

Inaugural Erhard Seminars Training (est) seminar held in San Francisco.

Guru Maharaj Ji visits the United States.

Neopagan feminist Zsuzsanna Budapest establishes a coven in the Dianic tradition.

First Glastonbury Festival.

1972 Sun Myung Moon takes up residence in the United States.

Franklin Jones founds Shree Hridayam Satsang (Company of the Heart) ashram.

FREECOG founded, first major American anti-cult movement group.

1973 Raël's inaugural encounter with the Elohim.

First ISKCON temple is built in San Francisco.

Spiritual Counterfeits Project is established in California.

Dialog Center founded in Denmark.

1974 Citizens' Freedom Foundation founded.

Jach Pursel begins channelling Lazaris.

1974 Rajneesh (Osho) establishes communities in Bombay and Poona.

Naropa Institute founded by Chogyam Trungpa in Boulder, Colorado.

1975 The Temple of Set is founded by Michael Aquino.

A Course in Miracles by Helen Schucman is published.

Covenant of the Goddess founded in California.

1976 FAIR (Family Action Information and Rescue) is established by Paul Rose in Britain.

Tony Alamo establishes community in Arkansas.

Kundalini Research Institute founded in California.

1977 ISKCON leader Prabhupada dies.

Oberto Airaudi establishes Damanhur in Valchiusella Valley, North Italy.

Brahma Kumaris establishes its first centre in the United States.

Geshe Kelsang Gyatso arrives in England.

JZ Knight first channels Ramtha.

New Religious Movements Center founded at Graduate Theological Union, in Berkeley, California, under Jacob Needleman's directorship.

Unification Church invites scholars to attend theological conferences and begins sponsoring their attendance.

1978 Jonestown suicides (919 die).

JZ Knight's inaugural channelling session.

Temple of Love founded by Yahweh ben Yahweh.

1979 Boston Church of Christ founded.

American Family Foundation founded.

Starkhawk publishes *The Spiral Dance*.

James Lovelock publishes *Gaia: A New Look*.

1980 Unification Church sponsors conference on NRMs, 'The Social Impact of New Religious Movements' attended by many leading scholars in the field.

1981 David Koresh arrives at the Mount Carmel Center, Waco.

Rajneesh takes up residence in the United States.

Ryuho Okawa (founder of Happy Science) attains 'Great Enlightenment'.

Unification Church loses its libel case against the British *Daily Mail*.

American Academy of Religion (AAR) hosts first paper session on NRMs.

1982 The AIDS epidemic begins.

1983 Alain Vivien presents his report 'The Cults in France: Expression of Model Liberty or Carriers of Manipulations?' to France's National Assembly.

1984 Citizens' Freedom Foundation becomes Cult Awareness Network (CAN).

Sun Myung Moon imprisoned for tax evasion until 1985.

AAR establishes 'New Religious Movements Group' as programme unit to sponsor annual paper sessions.

1985 Social implosion and legal problems at Rajneeshpuram commune, USA.

Nityananda becomes a private meditation teacher in California.

1986 L. Ron Hubbard dies.

Vatican report *Sects: The Pastoral Challenge* is published by the Catholic Truth Society.

Margaret Adler publishes *Drawing Down the Moon*.

1987 Aum Shinrikyō founded in Japan by Shōkō Asahara.

1988 INFORM founded in Britain.

CESNUR founded in Torino, Italy.

1989 Demolition of the Berlin Wall.

Chronology

Levi H. Dowling publishes *The Aquarian Gospel of Jesus the Christ*.

Ulf Ekman (Word of Life Church) publishes *Financial Freedom*.

1990 Osho (aka Rajneesh) dies.

1991 Kelsang Gyatso's followers form New Kadampa Tradition (NKT).

Schism divides Soka Gakkai and Nichiren Shoshu.

1992 Falun Gong is established by Master Li Hongzhi.

Schism between Nichiren Shoshu and Soka Gakkai: Taiseki-ji Temple priests in Japan excommunicate Daisaku Ikeda.

1993 Siege of Cult Davidians at Waco, Texas (93 die).

1994 Solar Temple deaths (53 die).

FECRIS (Secta Fédération Européenne des Centres de Recherche et d'Information sur le Sectarismerianism) established in France.

Moses David dies.

1995 Sarin gas attack on Tokyo underground by Aum Shinrikyō members.

Margaret Singer publishes *Cults in Our Midst*.

1996 Cult Awareness Network (CAN) is declared bankrupt, and purchased by the Church of Scientology.

The Plain Truth ceases publication.

1997 Heaven's Gate suicides – 39 die, including leader and co-founder Marshall Herff Applewhite.

Unification Church adopts the name Family Federation for World Peace and Unification (FFWPU)

Nova Religio: The Journal of Alternative and Emergent Religion is founded by Phillip Lucas and members of the steering committee of the AAR's NRM programme unit.

1999 Falun Gong is banned by the Chinese government.

2000 Mass deaths in the Movement for the Restoration of the Ten Commandments of God, in Uganda.

Aum Shrinrikyō is renamed Aleph.

2001 (11 September) '9/11' – Al Queda attack on the World Trade Center, New York.

2002 The Raelian movement announces the birth of the world's first cloned human.

2002–3 Kip McKean resigns from the International Churches of Christ, establishes a rival International Christian Church.

2003 The Vatican issues *Jesus Christ, the Bearer of the Water of Life*.

2004 Milton G. Henschel (fifth Watch Tower president) dies.

Yogi Bhajan (Healthy, Happy, Holy) dies.

The American Family Foundation adopts the name International Cultic Studies Association.

2005 Bobby Henderson writes his open satirical letter 'The Flying Spaghetti Monster'.

2006 Publication of *The Gospel of the Flying Spaghetti Monster*.

2007 Sri Chinmoy dies.

Jean-François Mayer sets up Religioscope.

The American Academy of Religion's annual conference includes a panel on The Flying Spaghetti Monster.

2007–8 For six months Members of True Russian Orthodox Church holed up in a cave near Nikolskoye, Russia, expecting end-of-world.

2008 Maharishi Mahesh Yogi (founder-leader of Transcendental Meditation) dies.

Sun Myung Moon appoints his youngest son Hyung Jin as president of the Family Federation for World Peace and Unification (FFWPU).

2009 Elizabeth Clare Prophet (co-founder of Summit Lighthouse / Church Universal and Triumphant) dies.

2010 Friends of the Western Buddhist Order is renamed the Triratna Buddhist Community.

International Association for the Study of New Religions founded, publishing the *IJSNR*.

2011 Satya Sai Baba dies.

2012 Date of the 'Mayan Prophecy'. At the winter solstice, the Mayan calendar returns to 'zero point'.

Sun Myung Moon dies.

Academic Resources for the Study of New Religious Movements

Associations and Centres

CESNUR

www.cesnur.org
The Italian Center for Studies on New Religious Movements operated by Massimo Introvigne.

INFORM

www.inform.ac
The Information Network on Religious Movements (UK).

ESSWE

www.esswe.org
The European Society for the Study of Western Esotericism sponsors an international conference and publishes *Aries: Journal for the Study of Western Esotericism.*

FINYAR

www.finyar.se
FINYAR is the Nordic association for the study of NRMs. Its operating language is Swedish.

Journals

Nova Religio: The Journal of Alternative and Emergent Religions
Nova Religio is the major journal for the field of the study of NRMs.
   www.novareligio.org

Pomegranate: The International Journal of Pagan Studies
The major American journal on the study of contemporary Paganism.
   www.equinoxpub.com/journals/index.php/POM

International Journal for the Study of New Religions
The ISSNR publishes its own journal, *the International Journal for the Study of New Religions.*
   www.equinoxpub.com/journals/index.php/IJSNR

Websites

These websites give access to useful information about NRMs and their critics. Some of the following provide general independent information on NRMs; others belong to specific NRMs, and some come from critics. The editors have omitted the websites operated by the associations, centres and journals listed above. The vast majority of NRMs now host their own websites, and these can easily be accessed by means of search engines. It would be pointless to list many of these. The following have been selected for the range of standpoints they provide, and the quantity of hyperlinks and other information they provide. All URLs are correct at time of printing.

Websites Sponsored by Scholars or Academic Organizations

Networking Religious Movements
www.networkingreligiousmovements.org
   A website that 'maps' NRMs and other groups through time and space. It aims to be a 'hub of research'.

Religioscope
www.religion.info
   Operated by Jean-François Mayer of the Religioscope Institute in Fribourg, Switzerland, and available in both English and French, this website focuses on providing information and analysis on contemporary religious developments.

Religious Worlds
www.religiousworlds.com

By Gene T. Thursby (formerly University of Florida), offering extensive hyperlinks offering good information on world religions, new religions and journals.

World Religions and Spirituality Project (Virginia Commonwealth University)
www.has.vcu.edu/wrs

Project co-ordinated by David Bromley, including extensive peer-reviewed material on NRMs. Some of the material is adapted from the now-defunct 'Religious Movements' website that the late Jeffrey Hadden created and hosted at the University of Virginia.

Websites Sponsored by Proponents of Religious Freedom or Pluralism

Adherents.com
www.adherents.com

A clearing house of statistics on religious organizations. There are over 44,000 in all, together with citation of sources.

Beliefnet
www.beliefnet.com

Focuses primarily on the major world religions, but features relatively straightforward sections on some NRMs.

CIA World Factbook
www.cia.gov/library/publications/the-world-factbook

The US Central Intelligence Agency operates a website that notes religious developments throughout the world, with special attention to issues of religious freedom.

Ontario Consultants on Religious Tolerance
www.religioustolerance.org

Quick, fairly reliable information on minority religious organizations.

Patheos
www.patheos.com

A commercial website focusing on religious pluralism, its 'library' section features peer reviewed essays on several major NRMs such as Scientology, ISKCON and Paganism.

Academic Resources for the Study of New Religious Movements

Websites Sponsored by Cult Awareness or ACM Organizations

Apologetics Index
www.apologeticsindex.org
   A Christian organization, providing an extensive index of organizations, it contains links on religious movements, cults, sects, world religions and related issues.

Cult Awareness and Information Library, Australia
www.caic.org.au

Cult Awareness Network (CAN)
www.cultawarenessnetwork.org
   CAN is now owned by the Church of Scientology.

FAIR (Family Action Information and Resource)
www.fair-news.org

Freedom of Mind Institute (Steven Hassan)
www.freedomofmind.com

Info-Cult
www.infocult.org
   A Canadian ACM website.

International Cultic Studies Association (ICSA)
www.icsahome.com

Rick Ross
www.rickross.com
   Highly critical of 'cults', but has a large number of useful hyperlinks.

Spiritual Counterfeits Project
www.scp-inc.org

Watchman Fellowship
www.watchman.org
   This site has a special interest in the Jehovah's Witnesses.

Websites on Specific NRMs

Alternative Considerations of Jonestown and Peoples Temple
jonestown.sdsu.edu
   Extensive information about Jim Jones' Peoples Temple, by Rebecca Moore and Fielding M. McGehee III (San Diego State University).

Church of Scientology
www.scientology.org
   Official Scientology website, providing hyperlinks to other Scientology/Dianetics projects.

Heaven's Gate
www.heavensgate.com
   Marshall Herff Applewhite's site continues to be maintained after the 1997 mass suicide.

ISKCON / Hare Krishna Movement
iskcon.org
   The official website of ISKCON and Hare Krishna movement.
www.krishna.org
   A rival site operated by adherents of Krishna Consciousness who are not part of ISKCON proper.

Jehovah's Witnesses
www.jw.org/en
   Official website with access to Watch Tower publications and New World Translation of the Bible.

Pagan Federation
www.paganfed.org
   A UK pan-Pagan site.

The Family International (TFI)
www.thefamilyinternational.org
   TFI is formerly known as the Children of God.

Unification Church (Family Federation for World Peace and Unification)
www.familyfed.org
   Introduction to the organization and its history.

www.tparents.org
 Gives access to literature, including many of Sun Myung Moon's sermons and talks.

Encyclopedias and Sourcebooks

Bromley, D. and Hadden, J. (eds) (1993). *Handbook of Sects and Cults in America*. Greenwich, CT: JAI Press.
Chryssides, G. D. (ed.) (2012). *Historical Dictionary of New Religious Movements*. 2nd ed. Lanham: Scarecrow Press.
Cusack, C. M. and Norman, A. (eds) (2012). *Handbook of New Religions and Cultural Production*. Leiden: Brill.
Gallagher, E. W. and Ashcraft, W. M. (eds) (2006). *Introduction to New and Alternative Religions in America*. 5 vols. Westport, CT: Greenwood Press.
Hammer, O. and Rothstein, M. (eds) (2013). *Handbook of the Theosophical Current*. Leiden: Brill.
Kemp, D. and Lewis J. R. (eds) (2007). *Handbook of New Age*. Leiden: Brill.
Landes, R. (ed.) (2000). *Encyclopedia of Millennialism and Millennial Movements*. New York: Routledge.
Lewis, J. R. (ed.) (2004). *Oxford Handbook of New Religious Movements*. Oxford: Oxford University Press.
— (2012). *Cults: A Reference and Guide*. 3rd ed. Sheffield: Equinox.
Melton, J. G. (ed.) (1990). *New Age Encyclopedia*. Detroit: Gale Research.
— (2009). *Melton's Encyclopedia of American Religions*. Detroit: Gale Cengage Learning.
Partridge, C. H. (ed.) (2004). *New Religions: A Guide: New Religious Movements, Sects and Alternative Spiritualities*. Oxford: Oxford University Press.
Pizza, M. and Lewis, J. R. (eds) (2009). *Handbook of Contemporary Paganism*. Leiden: Brill.
Possamai, A. (ed.) (2012). *Handbook of Hyper-Real Religions*. Leiden: Brill.
Wessinger, C. (ed.) (2011). *The Oxford Handbook of Millennialism*. Oxford: Oxford University Press.

Primary Source Collections and Readers

Chryssides, G. D. and Wilkins, M. Z. (eds) (2006). *A Reader in New Religious Movements*. London: Bloomsbury.
Daniels, T. (ed.) (1999). *A Doomsday Reader: Prophets, Predictors, and Hucksters of Salvation*. New York: New York University Press.
Daschke, D. and Ashcraft, W. M. (eds) (2005). *New Religious Movements: A Documentary Reader*. New York: New York University Press.
Dawson, L. L. (ed.) (2003). *Cults and New Religious Movements: A Reader*. Malden, MA: Blackwell.
Harvey, G. and Clifton, C. S. (eds) (2004). *The Paganism Reader*. London: Routledge.
Stone, J. R. (ed.) (2000). *Expecting Armageddon: Essential Readings in Failed Prophecy*. New York: Routledge.
Wessinger, C. (ed.) (2000). *Millennialism, Persecution and Violence: Historical Cases*. Syracuse: Syracuse University Press.

Bibliography

(1) General and Reference Works

Bainbridge, W. S. (1997). *The Sociology of Religious Movements.* London: Routledge.
Chryssides, G. D. (1999). *Exploring New Religions.* London: Cassell.
— (2012). *Historical Dictionary of New Religious Movements.* Lanham, MD: Scarecrow Press.
Clarke, P. (2006). *New Religions in Global Perspective.* London: Routledge.
Cowan, D. E. and Bromley, D. G. (2008). *Cults and New Religions: A Brief History.* Oxford: Blackwell.
Dawson, L. (ed.) (2003). *Cults and New Religious Movements: A Reader.* Oxford: Blackwell.
Hammer, O. and Rothstein, M. (2012). *The Cambridge Companion to New Religious Movements.* Cambridge: Cambridge University Press.
Lewis, J. R. (2012). *Cults: A Reference and Guide.* 3rd ed. Sheffield, UK: Equinox.
Lewis, J. R. and Petersen, J. A. (eds) (2005). *Controversial New Religions.* Oxford: Oxford University Press.
Melton, J. G. (2009). *Melton's Encyclopedia of American Religions.* 5th ed. Detroit, MI and London: Gale Cengage Learning.
Miller, T. (ed.) (1995). *America's Alternative Religions.* Albany: State University of New York Press.
Neusner, J. (ed.) (2009). *World Religions in America.* 4th ed. Louisville, KY: Westminster John Knox Press.
Oliver, P. (2012). *New Religious Movements: A Guide for the Perplexed.* London: Bloomsbury.
Partridge, C. (2004). *Encyclopedia of New Religions: New Religious Movements, Sects and Alternative Spiritualities.* Oxford: Lion Hudson.
Rawlinson, A. (1997). *The Book of Enlightened Masters: Western Teachers in Eastern Traditions.* Chicago: Open Court.
Scotland, N. (2005). *A Pocket Guide to Sects and New Religions.* Oxford: Lion Hudson.
Zeller, B. E. (2010). *Prophets and Protons: New Religious Movements and Science in Late Twentieth-Century America.* New York: New York University Press.

(2) Themes in NRMs

Arweck, E. (2006). *Researching New Religious Movements: Responses and Redefinitions.* London: Routledge.
Geertz, A. W. and Warburg, M. (eds) (2008). *New Religions and Globalization.* Aarhus: Aarhus University Press.

Bibliography

Lewis, J. R. (2003). *Legitimating New Religions*. New Brunswick, NJ: Rutgers University Press.
Lewis, J. R. and Hammer, O. (2007). *The Invention of Sacred Tradition*. Cambridge: Cambridge University Press.
Wessinger, C. (2000). *How the Millennium Comes Violently*. New York: Seven Bridges Press.
Wilson, B. and Cresswell, J. (1999). *New Religious Movements: Challenge and Response*. London: Routledge.

(3) Specific NRMs

Bainbridge, W. S. (2002). *The End-Time Family: Children of God*. Albany: State University of New York Press.
Chryssides, G. D. (1991). *The Advent of Sun Myung Moon: The Origins, Beliefs and Practices of the Unification Church*. London: Macmillan.
— (2008). *Historical Dictionary of Jehovah's Witnesses*. Lanham, MD: Scarecrow Press.
Chryssides, G. D. (ed.) (2011). *Heaven's Gate: Postmodernity and Popular Culture in a Suicide Group*. Farnham, UK: Ashgate.
Cusack, C. (2010). *Invented Religions: Imagination, Fiction and Faith*. Farnham, UK: Ashgate.
Lewis, J. R. (2009a). *The Order of the Solar Temple: The Temple of Death*. Farnham, UK: Ashgate.
— (2009b). *Scientology*. Oxford: Oxford University Press.
Newport, K. G. C. (2006). *The Branch Davidians of Waco: The History and Beliefs of an Apocalyptic Sect*. Oxford: Oxford University Press.
Palmer, S. (2004). *Aliens Adored: Raël's UFO Religion*. New Brunswick, NJ: Rutgers University Press.
Partridge, C. (ed.) (2003). *UFO Religions*. London: Routledge.
Rochford, E. B., Jr. (1991). *Hare Krishna in America*. New Brunswick, NJ: Rutgers University Press.

(4) New Age

Kemp, D. and Lewis, J. R. (2007). *Handbook of the New Age*. Leiden: Brill.
Possamai, A. (2006). *In Search of New Age Spiritualities*. Aldershot: Ashgate.
Sutcliffe, S. (2002). *Children of the New Age*. London: Routledge.
Sutcliffe, S. and Bowman, M. (eds) (2000). *Beyond New Age: Exploring Alternative Spirituality*. Edinburgh: Edinburgh University Press.

(5) Counter-cult and Cult Monitoring

Cowan, D. E. (2003). *Bearing False Witness?: An Introduction to the Christian Countercult*. Westport, CT: Praeger.
Shupe, A. D., Jr. and Bromley, D. G. (1980). *The New Vigilantes: Deprogrammers, Anti-Cultists, and the New Religions*. Thousand Oaks, CA: Sage.

(6) Journals

Alternative Spirituality and Religion Review, ISSN: 1946–0538 (electronic).
Culture and Cosmos, ISSN: 1368–6534.
Diskus Vol. 10, ISSN: 0967–8948. Available at http://basr.ac.uk/diskus/diskus10/chryssides.htm
Fieldwork in Religion, ISSN: 1743–0615.
International Journal for the Study of New Religions, ISSN: 2041–9511.
Journal of Alternative Spiritualities and New Age Studies, ISSN: 1750–3191.
Journal of the American Academy of Religion, ISSN: 0002–7189.
The Journal of Beliefs and Values, ISSN: 1361–7672.
Journal of Contemporary Religion, ISSN: 1353–7903 (formerly *Religion Today*, ISSN: 0267–1700).
Journal for the Scientific Study of Religion, ISSN: 0021–8294.
Marburg Journal of Religious Studies, ISBN: 1612–2941.
Numen, ISSN: 0029–5973.
Religion, ISSN: 0048–721X.
Sociology of Religion, ISSN: 1069–4404.

Works Cited

Abramson, H. (1980). 'Religion', *Harvard Encyclopedia of American Ethnic Groups*. Cambridge, MA: Belknap Press: 869–75.
Adamski, G. (1955). *Inside the Flying Saucers*. New York: Warner.
Adesoji, A. (2010). 'The Boko Haram Uprising and Islamic Revivalism in Nigeria', *Africa Spectrum*, 45(2): 95–108.
Adler, M. (1979/2006). *Drawing Down the Moon: Witches, Druids, Goddess-Worshippers and Other Pagans in America Today*. Boston: Beacon.
Adogame, A. (1999). *Celestial Church of Christ: The Politics of Cultural Identity in a West African Prophetic-Charismatic Movement*. Frankfurt a/M: Peter Lang.
— (2002). 'Traversing Local-Global Religious Terrain: African New Religious Movements in Europe', *Zeitschrift für Religionswissenschaft*, 10: 33–49.
— (2003). 'Betwixt Identity and Security: African New Religious Movements and the Politics of Religious Networking in Europe', *Nova Religio*, 7(2): 24–41.
— (2005). 'African Christian Communities in Diaspora', in Kalu (2005): 494–514.
— (2007). 'Religion in Sub-Saharan Africa', in P. Beyer and L. Beaman (eds) *Religion, Globalization and Culture*. Leiden: Brill: 533–54.
— (2008). 'Globalization and African New Religious Movements in Europe', in O. Kalu and A. Low (eds) *Interpreting Contemporary Christianity: Global Processes and Local Identities*. Grand Rapids, MI: Eerdmans: 296–316.
— (2010). 'Pentecostal and Charismatic Movements in a Global Perspective', in B. S. Turner (ed.) *The New Blackwell Companion to the Sociology of Religion*. Chichester, UK: Wiley-Blackwell: 498–518.
Adogame, A. and Jafta, L. (2005). 'Zionists, Aladura and Roho: African Instituted Churches', in Kalu (2005): 309–29.
Al-Rasheed, M. and Shterin, M. (eds) (2009). *Dying for Faith: Religiously Motivated Violence in the Contemporary World*. London: I. B. Tauris.

Bibliography

Albanese, C. L. (1977). *Corresponding Motion: Transcendental Religion and the New America.* Philadelphia: Temple University Press.
— (1990). *Nature Religion in America: From Algonkian Indians to the New Age.* Chicago: University of Chicago Press.
— (1997). 'Exchanging Selves, Exchanging Souls: Contact, Combination, and American Religious History', in T. A. Tweed (ed.) *Retelling American Religious History.* Berkeley: University of California Press: 200–26.
— (2007/2008). *A Republic of Mind and Spirit: A Cultural History of American Metaphysical Religion.* New Haven, CT: Yale University Press.
Alternative Considerations of Jonestown and Peoples Temple. Available at http://jonestown.sdsu.edu (accessed 9 October 2013).
American Medical Association (2012). *Human Cloning* 2001. Available at http://ama-assn.org/ama/pub/physician-resources/medical-science/genetics-molecular-medicine/related-policy-topics/stem-cell-research/human-cloning.page (accessed 7 June 2012).
Ammerman, N. (2007). *Everyday Religion: Observing Modern Religious Lives.* Oxford: Oxford University Press.
Amsterdam, P. (2004). 'The Family – Restructuring and Renewal: An Overview of Organizational Changes – 1994–2006'. Paper presented at the CESNUR International Conference, Waco, Texas. Available at http://cesnur.org/2004/waco_cp.htm (accessed 9 October 2013).
Anderson, D. M. and Johnson, D. H. (eds) (1995). *Revealing Prophets: Prophecy in East African History.* Athens: Ohio University Press.
Andersson, P. (2007). 'Ancient Alien Brothers, Ancient Terrestrial Remains: Archeology or Religion?', in Tumminia (2007): 264–74.
Anonymous (2004). 'Beneath the Surface', *the jonestown report*, vol. 6. Available at http://jonestown.sdsu.edu/AboutJonestown/JonestownReport/Volume6/reflanon1.htm (accessed 9 October 2013).
Anthony, D. (1990). 'Religious Movements and Brainwashing Litigation: Evaluating Key Testimony', in T. Robbins and D. Anthony (eds) *In Gods We Trust.* New Brunswick, NJ: Transaction: 295–344.
— (1999). 'Pseudoscience and Minority Religions: An Evaluation of the Brainwashing Theories of Jean-Marie Abgrall', *Social Justice Research*, 12: 421–56.
Anthony, D. and Robbins, T. (1992). 'Law, Social Science, and the Brainwashing Exception to the First Amendment', *Behavioral Sciences and the Law*, 10: 5–27.
Anthony, D., Robbins, T. and Barrie-Anthony, S. (2011). 'Reciprocal Totalism: The Toxic Interdependence of Anticult and Cult Violence', in Lewis (2011): 63–92.
Appadurai, A. (1997). 'Disjuncture and Difference in the Global Cultural Economy', in Featherstone (1997): 295–310.
Applewhite, M. H. (2011). ''88 Update – The UFO Two and their Crew', in Chryssides (2011): 1–16.
Arthur, S. (2008). 'Proselytization or Information? Wicca and Internet Use', in Hackett (2008): 409–30.
Arweck, E. (2002). 'The Insider/Outsider Problem in the Study of New Religious Movements', in Arweck and Stringer (2002): 115–32.
— (2006). *Researching New Religious Movements: Responses and Redefinition.* London: Routledge.
Arweck, E. and Stringer, M. D. (2002). *Theorizing Faith: The Insider/Outsider Problem in the Study of Ritual.* Birmingham, UK: University of Birmingham Press.
Asprem, E. and Granholm, K. (eds) (2013). *Contemporary Esotericism.* Sheffield, UK: Equinox.
Asprem, E. and Granholm, K. (2013). 'Constructing Esotericisms: Sociological, Historical and Critical Approaches to the Invention of Tradition', in Asprem and Granholm (2013): 25–48.

Aston, J. and Walliss, J. (eds) (2013). *Small Screen Revelations: Apocalypse in Contemporary Television*. Sheffield: Sheffield Phoenix Press.

Aune, D. E. (1983). *Prophecy in Early Christianity and the Mediterranean World*. Grand Rapids, MI: Eerdmans.

Aupers, S. (2009). '"The Force is Great": Enchantment and Magic in Silicon Valley', *Masaryk University Journal of Law and Technology*, 3(1): 153–73. Available at http://mujlt.law.muni.cz/storage/1267474036_sb_09-aupers.pdf (accessed 9 October 2013).

Azasu, K. (1999). *African Traditional Religion: Afrikania. A Brief Exposition*. Accra: Afrikania Renaissance Books.

Babou, C. A. (2007). 'Sufism and Religious Brotherhoods in Senegal', *The International Journal of African Historical Studies*, 40(1): 184–6.

Baëta, C. G. (1962). *Prophetism in Ghana: A Study of Some 'Spiritual' Churches*. London: SCM Press.

Baffelli, E. (2005). *Vendere la Felicità: Media, Marketing e Nuove Religioni Giapponesi. Il caso del Kōfuku no Kagaku*. PhD Dissertation. Ca' Foscari University of Venice.

— (2007). 'Mass Media and Religion in Japan: Mediating the Leader's Image', *Westminster Paper in Communication and Culture*, 4(1): 83–99.

— (2010). 'Japanese New Religions and the Internet: A Case Study', *Australian Religion Studies Review*, 23(3): 255–76.

— (2011). 'Charismatic Blogger? Authority and New Religions on the Web 2.0', in Baffelli, Reader and Staemmler (2011): 118–35.

Baffelli, E. and Reader, I. (2012). 'Editors' Introduction: Impact and Ramification: The Aftermath of the Aum Affair in the Japanese Religious Context', *Japanese Journal of Religious Studies*, 39(1): 1–28.

Baffelli, E. and Reader, I. (eds) (2012). *Aftermath: The Impact and Ramifications of the Aum Affair* (Special Issue), *Japanese Journal of Religious Studies*, 39(1): 7–15.

Baffelli, E., Reader, I. and Staemmler, B. (eds) (2011). *Japanese Religions on the Internet: Innovation, Representation, and Authority*. London: Routledge.

Bainbridge, W. S. (1984). 'Religious Insanity in America: The Official Nineteenth Century Theory', *Sociological Analysis*, 45: 223–40.

— (1985). 'Utopian Communities: Theoretical Issues', in Hammond (1985): 21–35.

— (1997). *The Sociology of Religious Movements*. London: Routledge.

— (2002). *The Endtime Family: Children of God*. Albany: State University of New York Press.

Bainbridge, W. S. and Stark, R. (1980). 'Client and Audience Cults in America', *Sociological Analysis*, 41(3) (Autumn): 199–214.

Baird, L. (2004). 'Notes on Jonestown Carpet, 2004', *the jonestown report*, vol. 6.

Baird, R. D. (1971). *Category Formation and the History of Religions*. The Hague: Mouton.

Bakhtin, M. M. (1981). *The Dialogic Imagination*, ed. M. Holquist, trans. C. Emerson and M. Holquist. Austin: University of Texas Press.

Balch, R. (1988a). 'The Evolution of a New Age Cult: From Total Overcomers to Death at Heaven's Gate', in Zellner and Petrowsky (1998): 1–25.

— (1988b). 'Money and Power in Utopia: An Economic History of the Love Family', in J. Richardson (ed.) *Money and Power in the New Religions*. Lewiston, NY: Edwin Mellen: 185–220.

Balch, R. W. and Taylor, D. (1977). 'Seekers and Saucers: The Role of the Cultic Milieu in Joining a UFO Cult', *American Behavioral Scientist*, 20(6) (July/August): 839–60. Reprinted in G. D. Chryssides (ed.) *Heaven's Gate: Postmodernity and Popular Culture in a Suicide Group*. Farnham, UK: Ashgate, 2011: 37–52.

— (2003). 'Heaven's Gate: Implications for the Study of Commitment to New Religions', in Lewis (ed.) (2003): 211–38.

Balch, R. W., Farnsworth, G. and Wilkins, S. (1983). 'When the Bombs Drop: Reactions to Disconfirmed Prophecy in a Millennial Sect', *Sociological Perspectives*, 26(2) (April): 137–58.
Barcan, R. (2011). *Complementary and Alternative Medicine: Bodies, Therapies, Senses.* Oxford: Berg.
Barker, E. (1984). *The Making of a Moonie: Choice or Brainwashing?* Oxford: Blackwell.
— (1989). *New Religious Movements: A Practical Introduction.* London: Her Majesty's Stationery Office.
— (1995a). 'Plus ça change . . .', *Social Compass*, 42(2): 165–80.
— (1995b). 'The Unification Church', in Miller (1995): 223–9.
— (1995c). 'The Scientific Study of Religion? You Must Be Joking!', *Journal for the Scientific Study of Religion*, 34: 287–310. Reprinted in L. L. Dawson (ed.) (2003). *Cults and New Religious Movements: A Reader.* Oxford: Blackwell: 7–25.
— (2004). 'Perspective: What Are We Studying? A Sociological Case for Keeping the "Nova"', *Nova Religio*, 8(1): 88–102.
— (2005). 'Crossing the Boundary: New Challenges to Religious Authority and Control as a Consequence of Access to the Internet', in M. T. Højsgaard and M. Warburg (eds) *Religion and Cyberspace.* London: Routledge: 67–85.
Barkun, M. (1974). *Disaster and the Millennium.* New Haven, CT: Yale University Press.
— (1997). *Religion and the Racist Right: The Origins of the Christian Identity Movement.* 2nd ed. Chapel Hill: University of North Carolina Press.
Barna, G. (2004). 'The Ethnological Research of Religion in Hungary', in G. Barna (ed.) *Ethnology of Religion.* Budapest: Akademiai Kiado: 127–58.
Barnes, L. L. and Starr, S. S. (2004). *Religion and Healing in America.* Oxford: Oxford University Press.
Barrett, D. B. (1968). *Schism and Renewal in Africa. An Analysis of Six Thousand Contemporary Religious Movements.* Oxford: Oxford University Press.
Barrett, D. B. (ed.) (1971). *African Initiatives in Religion.* Nairobi: East African Publishers.
Barrett, J. (2010). 'Religion in New Places: Rhetoric of the Holy in the Online Virtual Environment of Second Life', *Changing Societies – Values, Religions and Education – Working Papers in Teacher Education*, 7: 19–23.
Barrow, L. (1986). *Independent Spirits: Spiritualism and English Plebians, 1850–1910.* London: Routledge.
Barry, B. (2001). *Culture and Equality: An Egalitarian Critique of Multiculturalism.* Cambridge: Polity Press.
Bartholomew, R. E. and Howard, G. S. (1998). *UFOs and Alien Contact: Two Centuries of Mystery.* Amherst, NY: Prometheus Books.
Barton, J. (2007). *Oracles of God: Perceptions of Ancient Prophecy in Israel after the Exile.* Rev. ed. Oxford: Oxford University Press.
Barz, G. and Cooley, T. J. (eds) (2008). *Shadows in the Field: New Perspectives for Fieldwork in Ethnomusicology.* 2nd ed. Oxford: Oxford University Press.
Becker, F. and Geissler, W. (2009). *AIDs and Religious Practice in Africa.* Leiden: Brill.
Becker, H. (1960). 'Notes on the Concept of Commitment', *American Journal of Sociology*, 66: 32–40.
Beckford, J. A. (1978a). 'Accounting for Conversion', *British Journal of Sociology*, 29: 249–62.
— (1978b). 'Through the Looking-glass and Out the Other Side: Withdrawal from the Rev. Moon's Unification Church', *Archives de Sciences Sociales des Religions*, 45(1): 95–116.
— (1985). *Cult Controversies: The Societal Response to New Religious Movements.* London: Tavistock.
— (1992). *Religion and Advanced Industrial Society.* London: Routledge.

— (1999). 'The Mass Media and New Religious Movements', in Wilson and Cresswell (1999): 103–20.
— (2008). 'Religious Interaction in a Global Context', in Geertz and Warburg (2008): 23–42.
Bedi, S. (2007). 'Debate: What is so Special About Religion? The Dilemma of the Religious Exemption', *The Journal of Political Philosophy*, 15(2): 235–49.
Bednarowski, M. F. (1989). *New Religions and the Theological Imagination in America*. Bloomington: Indiana University Press.
— (1999). *The Religious Imagination of American Women*. Bloomington: Indiana University Press.
— (2006). 'Gender in New and Alternative Religions', in Gallagher and Ashcraft (2006), vol. 1: 206–23.
Bell, C. (1992). *Ritual Theory/Ritual Practice*. Oxford: Oxford University Press.
— (1997). *Ritual: Perspectives and Dimensions*. Oxford: Oxford University Press.
Bellah, R. N. and Glock, C. Y. (eds) (1976). *The New Religious Consciousness*. Berkeley: University of California Press.
Bellefountaine, M. (2005). '*The Peoples Temple*: The Audience as Participants', *the jonestown report*, vol. 7.
Bellegarde-Smith, P. (ed.) (2005). *Fragments of Bone: Neo-African Religions in a New World*. Chicago: University of Chicago Press.
Bender, C. (2007). 'American Reincarnations: What the Many Lives of Past Lives Tells us About Contemporary Spiritual Practice', *Journal of the American Academy of Religion*, 75(3): 589–614.
Benham, P. (1993). *The Avalonians*. Glastonbury: Gothic Image Publications.
Bennett, G. (1989). '"Belief Stories": The Forgotten Genre', *Western Folklore*, 48(4): 289–311.
Berger, H. (1999). 'Witches: The Next Generation', in Palmer and Hardman (1999): 11–28.
Berger, H. A. and Ezzy, D. (2004). 'The Internet as Virtual Spiritual Community: Teen Witches in the United States and Australia', in Dawson and Cowan (2004): 175–88.
— (2006). *Teenage Witches: A Transnational Study*. New Brunswick, NJ: Rutgers University Press.
Berger, H. A., Leach, E. A. and Shaffer, L. S. (2004). *Voices from the Pagan Census: A National Survey of Witches and Neo-Pagans in the United States*. Columbia, SC: University of South Carolina Press.
Berger, P. L. (1967/1990). *The Sacred Canopy: Elements of a Sociological Theory of Religion*. Garden City, NY: Doubleday.
— (1992). *A Far Glory: The Quest for Faith in an Age of Credulity*. New York: Anchor Books.
Bernegger, B. (1987). *Ōmoto-kyō – die Lehre vom Grossen Ursprung: Historische, Religionsphilosophische und Kunstgeschichtliche Aspekte*. Phil. Dissertation. Zürich: Offset Kaeser.
Berner, U. (2000). 'Reflections upon the Concept of "New Religious Movement"', *Method and Theory in the Study of Religion*, 12(1/2): 267–76.
Berthon, J.-P. (1985). *Omoto: Espérance Millénariste d'une Nouvelle Religion Japonaise*. Paris: Atelier Alpha Bleue.
Besant, A. (1907). *H. P. Blavatsky and the Masters of Wisdom*. London: Theosophical Publishing House.
Bethurum, T. (1954). *Aboard a Flying Saucer*. Los Angeles: DeVorss & Co.
Beyer, P. (1994). *Religion and Globalization*. Thousand Oaks, CA: Sage.
— (2007). 'Religion and Globalization', in G. Ritzer (ed.) *The Blackwell Companion to Globalization*. Oxford: Blackwell: 444–60.

Bibliography

Bird, F. and Reimer, W. (1982). 'Participation Rates in New Religious Movements', *Journal for the Scientific Study of Religion*, 21: 1–14.
Birrell, S. (1981). 'Sport as Ritual: Interpretations from Durkheim to Goffman', *Social Forces*, 60(2): 354–76.
Blackwood, S. (2009). *We Agreed to Meet Just Here*. New Issues, Kalamazoo.
Blain, J. (2001/2003). *Nine Worlds of Seid Magic: Ecstasy and Neo-Shamanism in North-European Paganism*. East Sussex: Psychology Press.
Blain, J., Ezzy, D. and Harvey, G. (eds) (2004). *Researching Paganisms*. Lanham, MD: AltaMira.
Bogdan, H. (2007). *Western Esotericism and Rituals of Initiation*. Albany: State University of New York Press.
Bonino, S. (2010). *Il Caso Aum Shinrikyo: Società, Religione e Terrorismo nel Giappone Contemporaneo*. Chieti: Edizioni Solfanelli.
Bornstein, K. (1994). *Gender Outlaw: On Men, Women and the Rest of Us*. East Sussex: Psychology Press.
Bowman, M. (1993). 'Drawn to Glastonbury', in I. Reader and T. Walter (eds) *Pilgrimage in Popular Culture*. London: Macmillan: 29–62.
— (2003–4). 'Taking Stories Seriously: Vernacular Religion, Contemporary Spirituality and the Myth of Jesus in Glastonbury', *Temenos*, 39–40(1): 125–42.
— (2004). 'Phenomenology, Fieldwork and Folk Religion' (reprinted with newly written Afterword) in S. Sutcliffe (ed.) *Religion: Empirical Studies*. Aldershot: Ashgate: 3–18. Originally appeared as *Phenomenology, Fieldwork and Folk Religion*, British Association for the Study of Religions, Occasional Paper, No. 6, 1992.
— (2005). 'Ancient Avalon, New Jerusalem, Heart Chakra of Planet Earth: Localisation and Globalisation in Glastonbury', *Numen*, 52(2): 157–90.
— (2007). 'Arthur and Bridget in Avalon: Celtic Myth, Vernacular Religion and Contemporary Spirituality in Glastonbury', *Fabula, Journal of Folktale Studies*, 48(1/2): 1–17.
— (2008). 'Going with the Flow: Contemporary Pilgrimage in Glastonbury', in P. J. Margy (ed.) *Shrines and Pilgrimage in the Modern World: New Itineraries into the Sacred*. Amsterdam: Amsterdam University Press: 241–80.
— (2009). 'From Glastonbury to Hungary: Contemporary Integrative Spirituality and Vernacular Religion in Context', in G. Vargyas (ed.) *Passageways: From Hungarian Ethnography to European Ethnology and Sociocultural Anthropology*. Budapest: University of Pécs – L'Harmattan Publishing House: 195–221.
Bowman, M. and Valk, Ü. (2012). 'Vernacular Religion, Generic Expressions and the Dynamics of Belief: Introduction', in Bowman and Valk (2012): 1–19.
Bowman, M. and Valk, Ü. (eds) (2012). *Vernacular Religion in Everyday Life: Expressions of Belief*. Sheffield, UK: Equinox.
Boyer, P. (1992). *When Time Shall Be No More: Prophecy Belief in Modern American Culture*. Cambridge, MA: Harvard University Press.
Braden, C. S. (1951). *These Also Believe*. London: Macmillan.
— (1963). *Spirits in Rebellion: The Rise and Development of New Thought*. Dallas: Southern Methodist University Press.
Bradley, M. Z. (1986). *Mists of Avalon*. London: Sphere Books.
Bradney, A. (1999). 'Children of a Newer God: NRMs and Custody Cases', in Palmer and Hardman (1999): 210–23.
— (2000). 'Faced by Faith', in P. Oliver, S. D. Scott and V. Tadros (eds) *Faith in Law*. Oxford: Hart Publishing: 89–105.
— (2009). *Law and Faith in a Sceptical Age*. London: Routledge.
Brandou, A. (2007). 'Artist Depicts Jonestown Lessons in Children's Animals', *the jonestown report*, vol. 9.

Brasher, B. E. (2001). *Give me that Online Religion*. San Francisco: Jossey-Bass.
Brasher, B. E. and Quinby, L. (eds) (2006). *Gender and Apocalyptic Desire*. Sheffield, UK: Equinox.
Braude, A. (2001). *Radical Spirits: Spiritualism and Women's Rights in Nineteenth-Century America*. 2nd ed. Bloomington: Indiana University Press.
Brenner, L. (ed.) (1993). *Muslim Identity and Social Change in Sub-Saharan Africa*. London: Hurst.
British Broadcasting Company (2012). 'Sweden Recognises New File-sharing Religion Kopimism', Available at http://bbc.co.uk/news/technology-16424659 (accessed 25 July 2012).
Brockway, A. R. and Rajashekar, J. P. (1987). *New Religious Movements and the Churches*. Geneva: WCC Publications.
Bromley, D. G. (1998). *The Politics of Religious Apostasy: The Role of Apostates in the Transformation of Religious Movements*. Westport, CT: Praeger.
— (2001). 'A Tale of Two Theories: Brainwashing and Conversion as Competing Political Narratives', in Zablocki and Robbins (2001): 318–48.
— (2002). 'Dramatic Denouements', in Bromley and Melton (2002): 11–41.
— (2004). 'Violence and New Religious Movements', in Lewis (2004): 143–62.
— (2007a). 'Methodological Issues in the Study of New Religious Movements', in Bromley (2007b): 65–89.
Bromley, D. G. (ed.) (2006). *Teaching New Religious Movements*. Oxford: Oxford University Press.
— (2007b). *Teaching New Religious Movements – AAR Teaching Religious Studies Series*. Oxford: Oxford University Press.
Bromley, D. G. and Bobbitt, R. (2011). 'Visions of the Virgin Mary: The Organizational Development of Marian Apparition Movements', *Nova Religio*, 14: 5–41.
Bromley, D. G. and Hadden, J. K. (eds) (1993). *The Handbook on Cults and Sects in America*. Vol. 3. Greenwich, CT: Jai Press.
Bromley, D. G. and Melton, J. G. (2012). 'Reconceptualizing Types of Religious Organization: Dominant, Sectarian, Alternative, and Emergent Tradition Groups', *Nova Religio*, 15: 4–28.
Bromley, D. G. and Melton, J. G. (eds) (2002). *Cults, Religion and Violence*. Cambridge: Cambridge University Press.
Bromley, D. G. and Richardson, J. T. (eds) (1983). *The Brainwashing/deprogramming Controversy: Sociological, Psychological, and Historical Perspectives*. Lewiston, NY: Edwin Mellen.
Bromley, D. G. and Shupe, A. D., Jr. (1979). *Moonies in America: Cult, Church, and Crusade*. Thousand Oaks, CA: Sage.
Bromley, D. G., Shupe, A. D., Jr. and Busching, B. C. (1981). 'Repression of Religious "Cults"', in L. Kriesberg (ed.) *Research in Social Movements, Conflicts, and Change*. Greenwich, CT: Jai Press: 25–45.
Brooks, D. R. (ed.) (1997). *Meditation Revolution: A History and Theology of the Siddha Yoga Lineage*. South Fallsburg, NY: Agama Press.
Brooks, M. (1983). *Heavenly Deception*. London: Chatto & Windus.
Brown, C. G. (2012). *Testing Prayer: Science and Healing*. Cambridge, MA: Harvard University Press.
Brown, K. M. (1991/2001). *Mama Lola: A Vodou Priestess in Brooklyn*. Berkeley: University of California Press.
Brown, W. and Caetano, C. (1992). 'Conversion, Cognition, and Neuropsychology', in Malony and Southard (1992): 147–58.
Bruce, S. (2002). *God Is Dead: Secularization in the West*. Oxford: Blackwell.

Bruce, S. and Wallis, R. (1985). 'Homage to Ozymandias: A Rejoinder to Bainbridge and Stark', *Sociological Analysis*, 46(1): 73–75.
Brunvand, J. H. (1981). *The Vanishing Hitchhiker: American Urban Legends and Their Meanings*. New York and London: W. W. Norton.
Bryant, E. and Ekstrand, M. (eds) (2004). *The Hare Krishna Movement: The Postcharismatic Fate of a Religious Transplant*. New York: Columbia University Press.
Burns, D. (2006). 'The Chaldean Oracles of Zoroaster, Hekate's Couch, and Platonic Orientalism in Psellos and Plethon', *Aries*, 6(2): 158–79.
Butler, J. (1990). *Gender Trouble: Feminism and the Subversion of Identity*. London: Routledge.
— (1993). *Bodies That Matter: On the Discursive Limits of 'Sex.'* London: Routledge.
Butt, L. and Eves, R. (2008). *Making Sense of AIDs: Culture, Sexuality, and Power in Melanesia*. Honolulu: University of Hawaii Press.
Bynum, C. W. (1986). *Gender and Religion: On the Complexity of Symbols*. Boston: Beacon.
Campbell, C. (1972). 'The Cult, the Cultic Milieu and Secularization', in M. Hill (ed.) *A Sociological Yearbook of Religion in Britain* 5: 119–36.
Campbell, H. (2011a). 'Internet and Religion', in M. Consalvo and C. Ess (eds) *The Handbook of Internet Studies*. Chichester, UK: Wiley-Blackwell: 232–50.
— (2011b). 'Understanding the Relationship between Religion Online and Offline in a Networked Society', *Journal of the American Academy of Religion*, 80(1): 64–93.
Camping, H. (2010). *We Are Almost There!* Rev. ed. Oakland, CA: Family Stations.
Carrette, J. and King, R. (2005). *Selling Spirituality: The Silent Takeover of Religion*. London: Routledge.
Carroll, R. P. (1979). *When Prophecy Failed: Reactions and Responses to Failures in the Old Testament Prophetic Traditions*. London: SCM Press.
Carter, L. (1998). 'Carriers of Tales: On Assessing Credibility of Apostate and Other Outsider Accounts of Religious Practices', in Bromley (1998): 221–37.
Chancellor, J. (2000). *Life in the Family: An Oral History of the Children of God*. Syracuse: Syracuse University Press.
Chaytor, A. (2012). *Cults: Who is Vulnerable?* Middlesborough, UK: Quoin Publishing.
Chidester, D. (1988). *Salvation and Suicide: An Interpretation of Jim Jones, the Peoples Temple, and Jonestown*. Bloomington: Indiana University Press. (Retitled *Salvation and Suicide: Jim Jones, the Peoples Temple, and Jonestown* [2003]).
— (2003). *Salvation and Suicide: Jim Jones, the Peoples Temple, and Jonestown*. Bloomington: Indiana University Press.
— (2005). *Authentic Fakes: Religion and American Popular Culture*. Berkeley: University of California Press.
Chireau, Y. P. (2006). *Black Magic: Religion and the African American Conjuring Tradition*. Berkeley: University of California Press.
Christ, C. P. (1987). *Laughter of Aphrodite: Reflections on a Journey to the Goddess*. San Francisco: Harper & Row.
Christ, C. and Plaskow, J. (eds) (1992). *Womanspirit Rising: A Feminist Reader in Religion*. San Francisco: HarperCollins.
Christensen, D. R. (2005). 'Inventing L. Ron Hubbard: On the Construction and Maintenance of the Hagiographic Mythology of Scientology's Founder', in Lewis and Petersen (2005): 227–58.
Chryssides, G. D. (1991). *The Advent of Sun Myung Moon: The Origins, Beliefs and Practices of the Unification Church*. London: Macmillan.
— (1996). 'New Religions and the Internet', *Diskus*, 4(2). Available at http://basr.ac.uk/diskus/diskus1–6/CHRYSSI4_2.txt (accessed 9 October 2013).
— (2001). 'Unrecognized Charisma? A Study and Comparison of Four Charismatic Leaders: Charles Taze Russell, Joseph Smith, L Ron Hubbard, Swami Prabhupada'.

Paper presented at the International CESNUR/INFORM Conference, London, 19–22 April. Available at http://cesnur.org/2001/london2001/chryssides.htm (accessed 18 August 2012).
— (2007). 'Defining the New Age', in Kemp and Lewis (2007): 5–24.
— (2008). *Historical Dictionary of Jehovah's Witnesses*. Lanham, MD: Scarecrow Press.
Chryssides, G. D. (ed.) (2003). 'Scientific Creationism: A Study of the Raëlian Church', in Partridge (2003): 45–61.
— (2011). *Heaven's Gate: Postmodernity and Popular Culture in a Suicide Group*. Farnham, UK: Ashgate.
Chung, D. (2001). *Syncretism: The Religious Context of Christian Beginnings in Korea*, ed. Kang-nam Oh. Albany: State University of New York Press.
Clanton, D. W., Jr. (2012). *The End Will Be Graphic: Apocalyptic in Comic Books and Graphic Novels*. Sheffield: Sheffield Phoenix Press.
Clark, J. (1979). 'Cults', *Journal of the American Medical Association*, 242: 279–81.
Clarke, K. M. (2004). *Mapping Yoruba Networks: Power and Agency in the Making of Transnational Communities*. Durham: Duke University Press.
Clarke, P. (1987). 'The Maitstsine Movement in Northern Nigeria in Historical and Current Perspective', in Hackett (1987): 93–115.
— (2006). *New Religions in Global Perspective: A Study of Religious Change in the Modern World*. London: Routledge.
Clarke, P. (ed.) (2000). *Japanese New Religions in Global Perspective*. Richmond, UK: Curzon Press.
Clarke, P. and Somers, J. (eds) (1994). *Japanese New Religions in the West*. Sandgate, Kent: Japan Library and Curzon Press.
Clifton, C. S. (2006). *Her Hidden Children: The Rise of Wicca and Paganism in America*. Lanham, MD: AltaMira.
Clonaid (2012). *Commending Michael Jackson's 'Pioneer Vision of Cloning', Clonaid Reaffirms Its Privacy Policy* 2009. Available at http://clonaid.com/page.php?18 (accessed 2 June 2012).
Coats, C. (2008). 'Is the Womb Barren? A Located Study of Spiritual Tourism in Sedona, Arizona, and Its Possible Effects on Eco-consciousness', *Journal for the Study of Religion, Nature and Culture*, 2(4): 483–507.
Cohen, C. L. and Boyer, P. S. (eds) (2008). *Religion and Culture of Print in Modern America*. Madison: University of Wisconsin Press.
Cohen, E. (1979). 'A Phenomenology of Tourist Experiences', *Sociology*, 13(2): 179–201.
— (2010). *The Mind Possessed: The Cognition of Spirit Possession in an Afro-Brazilian Religious Tradition*. Oxford: Oxford University Press.
Cohen, S. (1972). *Folk Devils and Moral Panics: The Creation of the Mods and Rockers*. Oxford: Blackwell.
Cohn, N. (1970). *The Pursuit of the Millennium*. Rev. ed. Oxford: Oxford University Press.
Collins, P. H. (2000). *Black Feminist Thought: Knowledge, Consciousness, and the Politics of Empowerment*. Rev. 10th anniversary 2nd ed. London: Routledge.
Coney, J. (1999). 'Growing Up as Mother's Children: Socializing a Second Generation in Sahaja Yoga', in Palmer and Hardman (1999): 108–23.
Conway, F. and Siegelman, J. (1979). *Snapping: America's Epidemic of Sudden Personality Change*. New York: Dell.
Cook, D. (2005). *Understanding Jihad*. Berkeley: University of California Press.
Couchouron-Gurung, C. (2007). 'Les Témoins de Jéhovah sur Internet: l'utilisation du web dans la mobilisation des acteurs d'une controverse', *Archives de Sciences Sociales des Religions*, 139: 139–56.
Cowan, D. E. (2003a). *Bearing False Witness?: An Introduction to the Christian Countercult*. Westport, CT: Praeger.

— (2003b). 'Confronting the Failed Failure: Y2K and Evangelical Eschatology in Light of the Passed Millennium', *Nova Religio,* 7(2) November: 71–85.
— (2005). *Cyberhenge: Modern Pagans on the Internet.* London: Routledge.
— (2006). 'Evangelical Christian Countercult Movement', in Gallagher and Ashcraft: (eds) (2006), vol. 5: 143–64.
— (2011). '"A Sometimes Mysterious Place": Heaven's Gate and the Manufactured Crisis of the Internet', in Chryssides (2011): 139–54.
Cowan, D. E. and Bromley, D. G. (2007*). Cults and New Religions: A Brief History.* Oxford: Blackwell.
Cowan, D. E. and Hadden, J. K. (2004a). 'God Guns, and Grist for the Media's Mill: Constructing the Narratives of New Religious Movements and Violence', *Nova Religio:* 8(2): 64–82.
— (2004b). 'Virtually Religious: New Religious Movements and the World Wide Web', in Lewis (2004): 119–40.
Cross, A. (2007). 'A Confederacy of Fact and Faith: Science and the Sacred in UFO Research', in Tumminia (2007): 249–63.
Csordas, T. J. (2002). *Body/Meaning/Healing.* New York: Palgrave.
Culpepper, E. (1978). 'The Spiritual Movement of Radical Feminist Consciousness', in Needleman and Baker (1978): 220–34.
Cusack, C. M. (2010). *Invented Religions.* Farnham, UK: Ashgate.
Cusack, C. M. and Norman, A. (eds) (2012). *Handbook of New Religions and Cultural Production.* Leiden: Brill.
Cutting, T. (2004). *Beneath the Silent Tor: The Life and Work of Alice Buckton.* Glastonbury, UK: Appleseed Press.
D'Aguiar, F. (1998). *Bill of Rights.* London: Chatto & Windus.
Daily Mail. 'Paradise Postponed: World Will Now End on October 21 Says Preacher Who Was Surprised We All Survived Saturday' (2011), *Daily Mail* [online edition], 24 May.
Daly, M. (1985). *Beyond God the Father: Toward a Philosophy of Women's Liberation.* Boston: Beacon.
Damuah, O. K. (1998). *The Introduction to Afrikania.* Accra: Afrikania Mission.
Daneel, M. L. (1971/1974). *Old and New in Southern Shona Independent Churches. Vol I&II.* The Hague: Mouton.
— (1987). *Quest for Belonging. Introduction to a Study of African Independent Churches.* Gweru, Zimbabwe: Mambo Press.
Danfulani, U. H. D. (1999). 'Factors Contributing to the Survival of The Bori Cult in Northern Nigeria', *Numen,* 46: 412–47.
Däniken, E. von (1969). *Chariots of the Gods? Unsolved Mysteries of the Past,* trans. M. Heron. London: Souvenir Press.
Darnton, R. (1968). *Mesmerism and the End of the Enlightenment in France.* Cambridge, MA: Harvard University Press.
Davidsen, M. A. (2012). 'The Spiritual Milieu Based on J. R. R. Tolkien's Literary Mythology', in A. Possamai (ed.) *Handbook of Hyper-real Religions.* Leiden: Brill: 185–204.
Davies, D. J. (2000). *The Mormon Culture of Salvation: Force, Grace and Glory.* Aldershot: Ashgate.
— (2010). *Joseph Smith, Jesus, and Satanic Opposition: Atonement, Evil and the Mormon Vision.* Aldershot: Ashgate.
Davis, W. (1980). *Dojo: Magic and Exorcism in Modern Japan.* Stanford, CA: Stanford University Press.
Davy, B. J. (2005). 'Being at Home in Nature: A Levinasian Approach to Pagan Environmental Ethics', *The Pomegranate,* 7(2): 157–72.

Dawson, L. L. (1992). 'Self-affirmation, Freedom, and Rationality', *Journal for the Scientific Study of Religion*, 29: 141–63.
— (1999). 'When Prophecy Fails and Faith Persists: A Theoretical Overview', *Nova Religio*, 3(1) (October): 62–82.
— (2002). 'Crises of Charismatic Legitimacy and Violent Behavior in New Religious Movements', in Bromley and Melton: 80–101.
— (2006). *Comprehending Cults: The Sociology of New Religious Movements*. Oxford: Oxford University Press.
— (2011). 'Church-Sect-Cult: Constructing Typologies of Religious Groups', in P. B. Clarke (ed.) *The Oxford Handbook of the Sociology of Religion*. Oxford: Oxford University Press: 525–44.
Dawson, L. L. and Cowan, D. E. (eds) (2004). *Religion Online: Finding Faith on the Internet*. London: Routledge.
Dawson, L. L. and Hennebry, J. (2004). 'New Religions and the Internet: Recruiting in a New Public Space', in Dawson and Cowan (eds) (2004): 151–73.
De Beauvoir, S. (2012). *The Second Sex*. London: Vintage.
De Wolfe, E. (2010). *Domestic Broils: Shakers, Marriage, and the Narratives of Mary and Joseph Dyer*. Amherst: University of Massachusetts Press.
Deadwyler, G. (2001). 'Fifteen Years Later: A Critique of Gurukula', *ISKCON Communications Journal*, 9(1): 13–22.
Dein, S. (2001), 'What Really Happens When Prophecy Fails: The Case of Lubavitch', *Sociology of Religion*, 62(3): 383–401.
— (2010). 'A Messiah from the Dead: Cultural Performance in Lubavitcher Messianism', *Social Compass*, 57(4): 537–54.
Dein, S. and Dawson, L. L. (2008). 'The "Scandal" of the Lubavitch Rebbe: Messianism as a Response to Failed Prophecy', *Journal of Contemporary Religion*, 23 (May): 163–80.
Delgado, R. (1977). 'Religious Totalism: Gentle and Ungentle Persuasion Under the First Amendment', *University of Southern California Law Review*, 51: 1–99.
Denzler, B. (2001). *The Lure of the Edge: Scientific Passions, Religious Beliefs, and the Pursuit of UFOs*. Berkeley: University of California Press.
— (2003). 'Attitudes towards Religion and Science in the UFO Movement in the United States', in Partridge (2003): 301–13.
Dillon, J. and Richardson, J. T. (1994). 'The "Cult" Concept: A Politics of Representation Analysis', *SYZYGY: Journal of Alternative Religion and Culture*, 3: 185–97.
Dorman, B. (2003). 'Waves of Fear: A New Religion Stirs Controversy in Japan', *Virginia Review of Asian Studies*. Available at http://virginiareviewofasianstudies.com/wp-content/uploads/2012/06/Dorman.pdf (accessed 9 October 2013).
— (2005a). 'Pana Wave: The New Aum Shinrikyō or Another Moral Panic?', *Nova Religio*, 8(3): 83–103.
— (2005b). 'Mixed Blessings: Reactions of Two Japanese NRMs to Postwar Media Portrayals', *Nova Religio*, 9(2): 7–32.
— (2011). 'Caught in the Net: Celebrity Representation and Japanese Religion from Historical and Contemporary Perspectives', in Baffelli, Reader and Staemmler (2011): 136–49.
— (2012). *Celebrity Gods: New Religions, Media, and Authority in Occupied Japan*. Honolulu: University of Hawaii Press.
Douglas, G. (1992). 'The Retreat from *Gillick*', *Modern Law Review*, 55(4): 569–76.
Doyle, C. with Wessinger, C. and Wittmer, M. D. (2012). *A Journey to Waco: Autobiography of a Branch Davidian*. Lanham, MD: Rowman & Littlefield.
Drury, N. (2002). 'Magic and Cyberspace: Fusing Technology and Magical Consciousness in the Modern World', *Esoterica*, 4: 96–100. Available at http://esoteric.msu.edu/VolumeIV/MagicCyber.htm (accessed 9 October 2013).

Bibliography

Duffy, J. C. (2012). 'Review: Saints Under Siege: The Texas State Raid on the Fundamentalist', *Journal of the American Academy of Religion*, 80(2): 551–4.
Durkheim, E. (1912/1995). *The Elementary Forms of Religious Life*. New York, NY: Free Press.
Earhart, H. B. (1989). *Gedatsu-kai and Religion in Contemporary Japan*. Bloomington: Indiana University Press.
Edelman, B. and Richardson, J. T. (2005). 'Imposed Limitations on Freedom of Religion in China and the Margin of Appreciation Doctrine: A Legal Analysis of the Crackdown on the Falun Gong and Other "Evil Cults"', *Journal of Church and State*, 47: 243–67.
Ehrhardt, G. (2009). 'Rethinking the Komeito Voter', *Japanese Journal of Political Science*, 10(1): 1–20.
Eliade, M. (1951/1989). *Shamanism: Archaic Techniques of Ecstasy*. London: Arkana.
Eller, C. (1995). *Living in the Lap of the Goddess: The Feminist Spirituality Movement in America*. Boston: Beacon.
— (2003). *Am I a Woman? A Skeptic's Guide to Gender*. Boston: Beacon.
Ellison, C. and Sherkat, D. (1993). 'Conservative Protestantism and Support for Corporal Punishment', *American Sociological Review*, 58: 131–44.
Ellwood, R. S., Jr. (1973). *Religious and Spiritual Groups in Modern America*. Englewood Cliffs, NJ: Prentice-Hall.
— (1979). *Alternative Altars: Unconventional and Eastern Spirituality in America*. Chicago: University of Chicago Press.
Engelke, M. (2011). 'Material Religion', in R. A. Orsi (ed.) *The Cambridge Companion to Religious Studies*. Cambridge: Cambridge University Press: 209–29.
Equality and Human Rights Commission (2012). *Human Rights Review 2012: How Fair is Britain? An Assessment of How Well Public Authorities Protect Human Rights*. London: Equality and Human Rights Commission.
Fadiman, A. (1997). *The Spirit Catches You and You Fall Down: A Hmong Child, Her American Doctors, and the Collision of Two Cultures*. New York: Farrar, Straus and Giroux.
Faivre, A. (1994). *Access to Western Esotericism*. Albany: State University of New York Press.
— (1999). 'The Notions of Concealment and Secrecy in Modern Esoteric Currents since the Renaissance (A Methodological Approach)', in E. R. Wolfson (ed.) *Rending the Veil: Concealment and Secrecy in the History of Religions*. New York: Seven Bridges Press: 155–76.
— (2005). 'Secrecy III: Modernity', in W. J. Hanegraaff, with A. Faivre, R. van den Broek and J. P. Brach (eds) *Dictionary of Gnosis and Western Esotericism*. Leiden: Brill: 1056–61.
Family Radio (2011). 'What Happened on May 21?', *eBible Fellowship*. Available at http://ebiblefellowship.com/archives/2011/06/14/what-happened-on-may-21/ (accessed 14 June).
Featherstone, M. (ed.) (1997). *Global Culture: Nationalism, Globalization and Modernity*. Thousand Oaks, CA: Sage.
Ferret, R. B. (2008). *Charisma and Routinisation in a Millennialist Community*. Lewiston, NY: Edwin Mellen.
Festinger, L. (1957). *A Theory of Cognitive Dissonance*. Stanford, CA: Stanford University Press.
Festinger, L., Riecken, H. W. and Schachter, S. (1956/2008). *When Prophecy Fails*. London: Pinter & Martin.
Fields, G. P. (2001). *Religious Therapeutics: Body and Health in Yoga, Ayurveda, and Tantra*. Albany: State University of New York Press.
Finke, R. and Stark, R. (1992). *The Churching of America, 1776–1990: Winners and Losers in Our Religious Economy*. New Brunswick, NJ: Rutgers University Press.
Fischman, M. (2010). *Stumbling Into Infinity*. New York: Morgan James.

Fluehr-Lobban, C. (2006). *Race and Racism: An Introduction.* Lanham, MD: AltaMira.
Forsthoefel, T. A. and Humes, C. A. (eds) (2005). *Gurus in America.* Albany: State University of New York Press.
Fort, J. (1985). 'What is Brainwashing and Who Says So?', in B. Kilbourne (ed.) *Scientific Research and New Religions.* San Francisco: American Association for the Advancement of Science: 57–63.
Foster, L. (1991). *Women, Family, and Utopia: Communal Experiments of the Shakers, the Oneida Community, and the Mormons.* Syracuse: Syracuse University Press.
Francis, R. (2011). *Ann the Word: The Story of Ann Lee, Female Messiah, Mother of the Shakers, The Woman Clothed with the Sun.* New York: Arcade.
Frankl, V. (2006). *Man's Search for Meaning.* Boston: Beacon.
Frazer, J. G. (1890/1994). *The Golden Bough: A Study in Magic and Religion.* Oxford: Oxford University Press.
Freud, S. (1995). 'On the Universal Tendency to Debasement in the Sphere of Love', in P. Gay (ed.) *The Freud Reader.* New York and London: W. W. Norton: 394–9.
Frisk, L. (2002). 'The Satsang Network: A Growing Post-Osho Phenomenon', *Nova Religio*, 6(1): 64–85.
— (2007a). *De nya religiösa rörelserna – vart tog de vägen?* Nora: Nya Doxa.
— (2007b). 'Quantitative Studies of New Age: A Summary and Discussion', in Kemp and Lewis (2007): 103–21.
Frisk, L. and Åkerbäck, P. (2013). *Den mediterande dalahästen.* Nora: Nya Doxa.
Frøystad, K. (2011). 'Roping Outsiders In', *Nova Religio*, 14(4): 77–98.
Fukamizu, K. (2007). 'Internet Use among Religious Followers: Religious Postmodernism in Japanese Buddhism', *Journal of Computer-Mediated Communication*, 12(3), article 11. Available at http://jcmc.indiana.edu/vol12/issue3/fukamizu.html (accessed 9 October 2013).
Fuller, R. C. (1982). *Mesmerism and the American Cure of Souls.* Philadelphia: University of Pennsylvania Press.
— (1989). *Alternative Medicine and American Religious Life.* Oxford: Oxford University Press.
Gager, J. G. (1975). *Kingdom and Community: The Social World of Early Christianity.* Englewood Cliffs, NJ: Prentice-Hall.
Galanter, M. (1978). 'The "Relief Effect": A Sociobiological Model for Neurotic Distress and Large-group Therapy', *American Journal of Psychiatry*, 135: 588–91.
— (1980). 'Psychological Induction into the Large Group: Findings from a Modern Religious Sect', *American Journal of Psychiatry*, 137: 1574–9.
— (1989). *Cults: Faith, Healing, and Coercion.* Oxford: Oxford University Press.
— (1999). *Cults: Faith, Healing, and Coercion.* 2nd ed. Oxford: Oxford University Press.
Galanter, M. and Diamond, L. C. (1981). '"Relief" of Psychiatric Symptoms in Evangelical Religious Sects', *British Journal of Hospital Medicine*, 26: 495–8.
Gallagher, E. V. and Ashcraft, W. M. (2006). *Introduction to New and Alternative Religions in America.* 5 vols. Westport, CT: Greenwood Press.
Gardner, G. (2004). *Witchcraft Today.* New York: Citadel.
Gelfgren, S. (2010). 'Virtual Churches: Transforming Religious Values and Practices', *Changing Societies – Values, Religions and Education – Working Papers in Teacher Education*, 7: 43–50.
Gerber, L. (2008). 'The Opposite of Gay: Nature, Creation, and Queerish Ex-gay Experiments', *Nova Religio*, 11(4) (May): 8–30.
Gerth, H. H. and Mills, C. W. (1958). *From Max Weber: Essays in Sociology.* Oxford: Oxford University Press.
Gevitz, N. (1982). *The D.O.S: Osteopathic Medicine in America.* Baltimore: Johns Hopkins University Press.

Gevitz, N. (ed.) (1988). *Other Healers: Unorthodox Medicine in America*. Baltimore: Johns Hopkins University Press.
Gibson, M. (2010). '"However Satisfied a Man Might Be:" Sexual Abuse in Fundamentalist Latter-day Saints Communities', *The Journal of American Culture*, 33: 280–93.
Giddens, A. (2002). *Runaway World: How Globalisation is Reshaping Our Lives*. London: Profile Books.
Gilhus, I. S. (2012). 'Angels in Norway: Religious Border-crossers and Border-markers', in Bowman and Valk (2012): 230–45.
Gill, S. D. (2005). 'Prayer', *Encyclopedia of Religion*, ed. L. Jones. 2nd ed. Vol. 11. Detroit: Macmillan Reference USA.
Gillespie, C. (2011). *Jonestown: A Vexation*. Detroit: Lotus Press.
Gilmore, L. (2010). *Theater in a Crowded Fire*. Berkeley: University of California Press.
Ginsburg, G. and Richardson, J. T. (1998). 'Brainwashing Evidence in Light of *Daubert*', in H. Reece (ed.) *Law and Science*. Oxford: Oxford University Press: 265–88.
Githieya, F. K. (1997). *The Freedom of the Spirit: African Indigenous Churches in Kenya*. Atlanta: Scholars Press.
Givens, T. L. (2009). *The Book of Mormon: A Very Short Introduction*. Oxford: Oxford University Press.
Glassie, H. H. (1995). 'Tradition', *Journal of American Folklore*, 108(1): 395–412.
— (1999). *Material Culture*. Bloomington: Indiana University Press.
Gledhill, R. (2012). 'Mormons Knock on Heaven's Door, Online'. *The Australian*, 2 July. Available at http://theaustralian.com.au/news/world/mormons-knock-on-heavens-door-online/story-e6frg6so-1226414152159 (accessed 9 October 2013).
Glock, C. Y. (1976). 'Consciousness among Contemporary Youth: An Interpretation', in Bellah and Glock (1976): 353–66.
Glock, C. Y. and Bellah, R. N. (1976). *The New Religious Consciousness*. Berkeley: University of California Press.
Goffman, E. (1959). *Presentation of Self in Everyday Life*. Garden City, NY: Doubleday.
Gold, L. (2000). *Mormons on the Internet, 2000–2001*. Roseville, CA: Prima.
Goldman, M. S. (1995). 'Continuity in Collapse: Departures from Shiloh', *Journal for the Scientific Study of Religion*, 34(3): 342–53.
— (2009). 'Averting Apocalypse at Rajneeshpuram', *Sociology of Religion*, 70(3): 311–27.
— (2011). 'Cultural Capital, Social Networks, and Collective Violence at Rajneeshpuram', in Lewis (2011): 307–23.
Golinski, J. (1998). *Making Natural Knowledge: Constructivism and the History of Science*. Cambridge: Cambridge University Press.
Goode, E. and Ben-Yehuda, N. (1994). *Moral Panics*. Oxford: Blackwell.
Goodrick-Clarke, N. (1993). *The Occult Roots of Nazism: Secret Aryan Cults and Their Influence on Nazi Ideology*. New York: New York University Press.
— (2008). *The Western Esoteric Traditions: A Historical Introduction*. Oxford: Oxford University Press.
Goodwin, M. (2009). 'Queer, Not Gay: Limits of Acceptable Sexual Transgressions in NRM Discourse', *ARC, The Journal of the Faculty of Religious Studies, McGill University*, 36: 75–95.
— (2013). *Good Fences: American Sexual Exceptionalism and Minority Religions*. PhD Dissertation. University of North Carolina at Chapel Hill.
— (forthcoming). 'A Woman's Part? Vikings, Unmanliness, and Seið Magic', in R. Styers and M. E. Bever, *Magic and the Modern*.
Gordon, D. (1987). 'Getting Close by Staying Distant: Fieldwork with Proselytizing Groups', *Qualitative Sociology*, 10(3): 267–87; cited in Waterhouse (2002): 65.
Granholm, K. (2012). 'Dragon Rouge: Left-Hand Path Magic with a Neopagan Flavour', *Aries*, 12(1): 131–56.

— (2013a). 'Esoteric Currents as Discursive Complexes', *Religion*, forthcoming.
— (2013b). 'Locating the West: Problematizing the *Western* in Western Esotericism and Occultism', in H. Bogdan and G. Djurdjevic (eds) *Occultism in Global Perspective*. Sheffield, UK: Equinox, forthcoming.
— (2013c). 'The Secular, the Post-Secular, and the Esoteric in the Public Sphere', in Asprem and Granholm (2013): 309–29.
— (forthcoming). *Dark Enlightenment: The Historical, Sociological, and Discursive Contexts of Contemporary Esoteric Magic*. Manuscript.
Greenfield, S. M. and Droogers, A. (eds) (2001). *Reinventing Religions: Syncretism and Transformation in Africa and the Americas*. Lanham, MD: Rowman & Littlefield.
Gregg, S. E. and Scholefield, L. (forthcoming). *Engaging with Living Religion*. London: Routledge.
Gregorius, F. (2009). *Modern Asatro: Att konstruera etnisk och kulturell identitet*. Lund: Lunds universitet.
Greil, A. and Rudy, D. (1984). 'What Have We Learned from Process Models of Conversion?' *Sociological Focus*, 17: 305–23.
Greven, P. (1990). *Spare the Child: The Religious Roots of Punishment and the Psychological Impact of Physical Abuse*. New York: Knopf.
Gribben, C. and Sweetnam, M. S. (eds) (2011). *Left Behind and the Evangelical Imagination*. Sheffield: Sheffield Phoenix Press.
Grimes, R. L. (1990). *Ritual Criticism: Case Studies in Its Practice, Essays on Its Theory*. Columbia, SC: University of South Carolina Press.
— (1995). *Beginnings in Ritual Studies*. Columbia, SC: University of South Carolina Press.
— (2000). *Deeply Into the Bone: Re-inventing Rites of Passage*. Berkeley: University of California Press.
— (2006). *Rite Out of Place: Ritual, Media, and the Arts*. Oxford: Oxford University Press.
Grünschloß, A. (2003). 'UFO Faith and Ufological Discourses in Germany', in Partridge (2003): 179–93.
Guachet, M. (1985/1997). *The Disenchantment of the World: A Political History of Religion*, trans. Oscar Burge. English ed. Princeton, NJ: Princeton University Press.
Gurdjieff, G. I. (2002). *Meetings With Remarkable Men*. New York: Penguin.
Guthrie, S. (1988). *A Japanese New Religion: Rissho Kosei-Kai in a Mountain Hamlet* (Michigan Monograph Series in Japanese Studies 1). Ann Arbor: Center for Japanese Studies, University of Michigan.
Gutierrez, C. and Schwartz, H. (eds) (2006). *The End That Does: Art, Science, and Accomplishment*. Sheffield, UK: Equinox.
Gyanfosu, S. (1995). *The Development of Christian-related Independent Religious Movements in Ghana, with Special Reference to the Afrikania Movement*. Unpublished PhD Thesis. University of Leeds.
Hackett, R. I. J. (2004). 'Prophets, "False Prophets", and the African State: Current Issues of Religious Freedom and Conflict', in Lucas and Robbins (2004): 151–78.
Hackett, R. I. J. (ed.) (1987). *New Religious Movements in Nigeria*. Lewiston, NY: Edwin Mellen.
— (2008). *Proselytization Revisited. Rights Talk, Free Markets and Culture Wars*. Sheffield, UK: Equinox.
Hall, J. R. (1987). *Gone from the Promised Land: Jonestown and American Cultural History*. New Brunswick, NJ: Transaction.
— (1995). 'Public Narratives and the Apocalyptic Sect: From Jonestown to Mt. Carmel', in Wright (1995): 205–35.
— (2002). 'Mass Suicide and the Branch Davidians', in Bromley and Melton (2002): 149–69.
— (2009). *Apocalypse: From Antiquity to the Empire of Modernity*. Cambridge: Polity Press.

Bibliography

Hall, J. R. and Schuyler, P. (2000). 'The Mystical Apocalypse of the Solar Temple', in Hall, Schuyler and Trinh (eds) (2000): 111–48.

Hall, J. R., Schuyler, P. D. and Trinh, S. (2000). *Apocalypse Observed: Religious Movements and Violence in North America, Europe, and Japan*. London: Routledge.

Hall, S. (1997). 'The Work of Representation', in S. Hall (ed.) *Representation: Cultural Representations and Signifying Practices*. Thousand Oaks, CA: Sage: 13–64.

— (2000). 'Encoding Decoding', in S. During (ed.) *The Cultural Studies Reader*. London: Routledge: 507–17.

Haller, J. S. (1994). *Medical Protestants: The Eclectics in American Medicine, 1825–1939*. Urbana: University of Illinois Press.

— (1997). *Kindly Medicine: Physio-Medicalism in America, 1836–1911*. Kent, OH: Kent State University Press.

Hamburg, P. and Hoffman, D. (1989). 'Psychotherapy of Cult Members', in M. Galanter (ed.) *Cults and New Religious Movements: A Report of the American Psychiatric Association*. Washington, DC: American Psychiatric Association: 3–19.

Hamilton, M. (2000). 'An Analysis of the Festival for Mind-Body-Spirit, London', in Sutcliffe and Bowman (2000): 188–200.

Hammer, O. (2001). *Claiming Knowledge: Strategies of Epistemology from Theosophy to the New Age*. Leiden: Brill.

— (2004a). *Claiming Knowledge: Strategies of Epistemology from Theosophy to New Age*. Leiden: Brill.

— (2004b). 'Esotericism in New Religious Movements', in Lewis (2004): 445–65.

Hammond, P. E. (ed.) (1985). *The Sacred in a Secular Age: Towards Revision in the Scientific Study of Religion*. Berkeley: University of California Press.

Hammond, P. E. and Warner, K. (1993), 'Religion and Ethnicity in Late-twentieth Century America', *Annals*, 527 (May): 55–66.

Hanegraaff, W. J. (1996). *New Age Religion and Western Culture: Esotericism in the Mirror of Secular Thought*. Leiden: Brill.

— (1998). 'On the Construction of "Esoteric Traditions"', in A. Faivre and W. J. Hanegraaff (eds) *Western Esotericism and the Science of Religion*. Leuven: Peeters: 11–61.

— (2001). 'Beyond the Yates Paradigm: The Study of Western Esotericism between Counterculture and New Complexity', *Aries*, 1(1): 5–37.

— (2005). 'Forbidden Knowledge: Anti-Esoteric Polemics and Academic Research', *Aries*, 5(2): 225–54.

— (2007). 'The Trouble with Images: Anti-Image Polemics and Western Esotericism', in O. Hammer and K. von Stuckrad (eds) *Polemical Encounters: Esotericism and Its Others*. Leiden: Brill: 107–36.

— (2008). 'Reason, Faith, and Gnosis: Potentials and Problematics of a Typological Construct', in P. Meusburger, M. Welker and E. Wunder (eds) *Clashes of Knowledge: Orthodoxies and Heterodoxies in Science and Religion*. Dordrecht: Springer Science & Business Media: 133–44.

— (2012). *Esotericism and the Academy: Rejected Knowledge in Western Culture*. Cambridge: Cambridge University Press.

— (2013). 'Entheogenic Esotericism', in Asprem and Granholm (2013): 392–409.

Hannerz, U. (1997). 'Cosmopolitans and Locals in World Culture', in Featherstone (1997): 237–51.

Hansen, M. L. (1937/1990). 'The Problem of the Third Generation'. Reprinted in P. Kivisto and D. Blanck (eds) *American Immigrants and Their Generations: Studies and Commentaries on the Hansen Thesis After Fifty Years*. Urbana: University of Illinois Press: 191–203.

Hardacre, H. (1984). *Lay Buddhism in Contemporary Japan: Reiyūkai Kyōdan*. Princeton, NJ: Princeton University Press.

— (1986/1988). *Kurozumikyō and the New Religions of Japan*. Princeton, NJ: Princeton University Press.
Harding, S. G. (1998). *Is Science Multicultural?: Postcolonialisms, Feminisms, and Epistemologies*. Bloomington: Indiana University Press.
Hardman, C. (2004). 'Children in New Religious Movements', in Lewis (2004): 386–417.
Hardyck, J. A. and Braden, M. (1962). 'Prophecy Fails Again: A Report of a Failure to Replicate', *Journal of Abnormal and Social Psychology*, 65(2): 136–41.
Haron, M. (2005). 'Sufi Tariqahs and Dawah Movements: Competing for Spiritual Spaces in Contemporary South(ern) Africa', *Journal of the Institute of the Muslim Minority Affairs*, 25(2): 273–97.
Harris, W. (1996). *Jonestown*. London: Faber and Faber.
— (2002). 'Theatre of the Arts', in H. Maes-Jelinek and B. Ledent (eds) *Theatre of the Arts: Wilson Harris and the Caribbean*. New York: Rodopi: 1–10.
Harvey, G. (2006). *Listening People, Speaking Earth: Contemporary Paganism*. 2nd rev. ed. London: Hurst.
— (2012). 'Ritual in New Religions', in Hammer and Rothstein (2012): 97–112.
Harvey, G. and Clifton, C. S. (eds) (2004). *The Paganism Reader*. London: Routledge.
Hassan, S. (1988). *Combatting Cult Mind Control: Protection, Rescue and Recovery from Destructive Cults*. Wellingborough, England: Aquarian Press.
Hatcher, C. (1989). 'After Jonestown: Survivors of Peoples Temple', in Moore and McGehee III (1989b): 127–46.
Hayward, V. E. W. (ed.) (1963). *African Independent Church Movements*. London: Edinburgh House Press.
Healy, J. P. (2010). *Yearning to Belong: Discovering a New Religious Movement*. Farnham, UK: Ashgate.
Heelas. P. (1996). *The New Age Movement*. Oxford: Blackwell.
— (2003). 'Foreword', in Partridge (2003): xiv–xv.
— (2008). *Spiritualities of Life: New Age Romanticism and Consumptive Capitalism*. Oxford: Blackwell.
Heiler, F. (1932). *Prayer: A Study in the History and Psychology of Religion*, ed. and trans. Samuel McComb. London: Oxford University Press.
Heirich, M. (1977). 'Change of Heart: A Test of Some Widely Held Theories about Religious Conversion', *American Journal of Sociology*, 83: 653–80.
Helland, C. (2000). 'Online-religion/religion-online and Virtual Communitas', in J. K. Hadden and D. E. Cowan (eds) *Religion on the Internet: Research, Prospect and Promises*. New York: Elsevier Science: 205–23.
— (2003). 'From Extraterrestrials to Ultraterrestrials: The Evolution of the Concept of Ashtar', in Partridge (2003): 162–78.
— (2007). 'The Raëlian Creation Myth and the Art of Cloning: Reality of Rhetoric?', in Tumminia (2007): 275–90.
Hervieu-Lège, D. (1999). 'The Sociologist of Religion in Court: Neither Witness nor Expert?' *Swiss Journal of Sociology*, 25(3): 421–6.
Heschel, A. J. (1969). *The Prophets*. 2 vols. San Francisco: Harper & Row.
Hess, D. (1993). *Science in the New Age: The Paranormal, Its Defenders and Debunkers, and American Culture*. Madison: University of Wisconsin Press.
Hexham, I. and Poewe, K. (1997). *New Religions as Global Cultures: Making the Human Sacred*. Oxford: Westview Press.
Hicks, D. (2010). 'The Material-Cultural Turn: Event and Effect', in D. Hicks and M. C. Beaudry (eds) *The Oxford Handbook of Material Culture Studies*. Oxford: Oxford University Press: 25–98.
Hill Collins, P. and Solomos, J. (2010), *The Sage Handbook of Race and Ethnic Studies*. Thousand Oaks, CA: Sage.

Himes, J. V. (ed.) (1842). *Views of the Prophecies and Prophetic Chronology, Selected from the Manuscripts of William Miller, with a Memoir of His Life*. Vol. 1. Boston: Moses A. Dow.
Hinchliff, P. (1972). 'African Separatists: Heresy, Schism or Protest Movement?', in D. Baker (ed.) *Schism, Heresy and Protest*. Vol. 9. Cambridge: Cambridge University Press: 391–404.
Hine, P. (1992–7). *Oven-Ready Chaos*. Available at http://philhine.org.uk/writings/ pdfs/orchaos.pdf (accessed 21 February 2011).
Hoddie, M. (2006). *Ethnic Realignments: A Comparative Study of Government Influences on Identity*. Lanham, MD: Lexington Books.
Hoehler-Fatton, C. (1996). *Women of Fire and Spirit: Faith and Gender in Roho Religion in Western Kenya*. Oxford: Oxford University Press.
Höhe, S. (2011). *Religion, Staat und Politik in Japan: Geschichte und Zeitgeschichtliche Bedeutung von Sōka Gakkai, Kōmeitō und Neuer Kōmeitō*. München: Iudicium Verlag.
Holman, J. (2008). *The Return of the Perennial Philosophy: The Supreme Wisdom of Western Esotericism*. London: Watkins.
Homer, M. W. (1999). 'The Precarious Balance between Freedom of Religion and the Best Interests of the Child', in Palmer and Hardman (1999): 87–209.
— (2006). 'Children in New Religious Movements: The Mormon Experience', in Gallagher and Ashcraft (2006), vol. 1: 224–42.
Honko, L. (1964). 'Memorates and the Study of Folk Beliefs', *Journal of the Folklore Institute*, 1: 5–19.
Hoover, S. (1998). *Religion in the News: Faith and Journalism in American Public Discourse*. Thousand Oaks, CA: Sage.
Howard, R. G. (ed.) (2011). *Network Apocalypse: Visions of the End in an Age of Internet Media*. Sheffield: Sheffield Phoenix Press.
Hubbard, L. R. (1950). *Dianetics: The Modern Science of Mental Health*. New York: Hermitage House.
Humphrey, C. and Laidlaw, J. (1994). *The Archetypal Actions of Ritual: A Theory of Ritual Illustrated by the Jain Rite of Worship*. Oxford: Clarendon Press.
Hunter, E. (1951). *Brainwashing in Red China*. New York: Vanguard Press.
Hunter, J. D. (1981). 'The New Religions: Demodernization and the Protest against Modernity', in B. Wilson (ed.) *The Social Impact of New Religious Movements*. New York: Rose of Sharon Press: 1–19.
Hüsken, U. (ed.) (2007). *When Rituals Go Wrong: Mistakes, Failure, and the Dynamics of Ritual*. Leiden: Brill.
Hutton, R. (1991). *The Pagan Religions of the Ancient British Isles*. Chichester, UK: Wiley-Blackwell.
Ibrahim, V. (2011). 'Ethnicity', in S. M. Caliendo and C. D. McIlwain (eds) *The Routledge Companion to Race and Ethnicity*. London: Routledge: 12–20.
Iida, T., Nakano, T. and Yamanaka, H. (eds) (1997). *Shūkyō to Nashonarizumu*. Kyoto: Sekai Shisōsha.
Inoue, N. (1992). *Shinshūkyō no Kaidoku*. Tokyo: Chikuma Shobō.
Inoue, S. (1995). *Shinshūkyō Būmu to Josei*. Tokyo: Shinhyōron.
Inoue, N., Kōmoto, M., Tsushima, M., Nakamaki, H. and Nishiyama, S. (eds) (1990). *Shinshūkyo Jiten*. Tokyo: Kōbundō.
Introvigne, M. (2000). *The Unification Church*. Salt Lake City: Signature Books.
— (2001). 'After the New Age: Is There a Next Age?', in Rothstein (2001): 58–69.
Irigaray, L. (1985). *This Sex Which is Not One*. Ithaca, NY: Cornell University Press.
Ishii, K. and Shimazono, S. (eds) (1996). *Shōhi Sareru Shūkyō*. Tokyo: Shunjūsha.
Jacobs, J. (1984). 'The Economy of Love in Religious Commitment: The Deconversion of Women from Nontraditional Religious Movements', *Journal for the Scientific Study of Religion*, 23(2): 155–71.

— (1989). *Divine Disenchantment: Deconverting from New Religions*. Bloomington: Indiana University Press.
— (2000). 'Hidden Truths and Cultures of Secrecy: Reflection on Gender and Ethnicity in the Study of Religion', *Sociology of Religion*, 61(4): 433–41.
— (2001). 'Gender and Power in New Religious Movements: A Feminist Discourse on the Scientific Study of Religion', in D. Juschka (ed.) *Feminism in the Study of Religion: A Reader*. London: Bloomsbury: 168–79.
— (2007). 'Abuse in New Religious Movements: Challenges for the Sociology of Religion', in Bromley (2007): 231–44.
Jacobs, J. L. (1989). *Divine Disenchantment: Deconverting from New Religions*. Bloomington and Indianapolis: Indiana University Press.
Jacobs, J. L. and Davidman, L. (1993). 'Feminist Perspectives on New Religious Movements', in Bromley and Hadden (1993): 173–90.
Jantzen, G. (1999). *Becoming Divine: Toward a Feminist Philosophy of Religion*. Bloomington: Indiana University Press.
Janzen, R. and Stanton, M. (2010). *The Hutterites in North America*. Baltimore: Johns Hopkins University Press.
Jenkins, P. (1992). *Intimate Enemies: Moral Panics in Contemporary Great Britain*. Hawthorne, NY: Aldine de Gruyter.
— (1996). *Pedophiles and Priests*. Oxford: Oxford University Press.
— (2000). *Mystics and Messiahs: Cults and New Religions in American History*. Oxford: Oxford University Press.
Johnson, B. (2011). 'Revisiting *when Prophecy Fails*', in Tumminia and Swatos (eds) (2011): 9–19.
Johnson, P. (2007). *Diaspora Conversions: Black Carib Religion and the Recovery of Africa*. Berkeley: University of California Press.
Jones, C. and Baker, G. (1994). 'Television and Metaphysics at Waco', in J. R. Lewis (ed.) *From the Ashes: Making Sense of Waco*. Lanham, MD: Rowman & Littlefield: 149–56.
Jones, J. W. (2008). *The Blood That Cries Out from the Earth: The Psychology of Terrorism*. Oxford: Oxford University Press.
Jones, K. (2000). *In the Nature of Avalon: Goddess Pilgrimages in Glastonbury's Sacred Landscape*. Glastonbury: Ariadne Publications.
Judah, J. S. (1967). *The History and Philosophy of the Metaphysical Movements in America*. Philadelphia: Westminster Press.
Jules-Rosette, B. (ed.) (1979). *The New Religions of Africa*. Norwood, NJ: Ablex.
Kagwanja, P. M. (2003). 'Facing Mount Kenya or Facing Mecca? The Mungiki, Ethnic Violence and the Politics of the Moi Succession in Kenya, 1987–2002', *African Affairs*, 102: 25–49.
Kaldera, R. (2002). *Hermaphrodeities: The Transgender Spirituality Workbook*. Bloomington: Xlibris.
— (2006). *Dark Moon Rising: Pagan BDSM and the Ordeal Path*. Raleigh: Lulu.
Kalu, O. (2005) (ed.). *African Christianity: An African Story*. Pretoria: University of Pretoria.
Kaplan, J. (1997). *Radical Religion in America: Millenarian Movements from the Far Right to the Children of Noah*. Syracuse: Syracuse University Press.
Kaplan, J. (ed.) (2002). *Millennial Violence: Past, Present and Future*. London: Frank Cass Publishers.
Katz, D. S. (2005). *The Occult Tradition: From the Renaissance to the Present Day*. London: Jonathan Cape.
Katz, J. (1972). 'Deviance, Charisma, and Rule-defined Behavior', *Social Problems*, 20: 186–202.
— (1975). 'Essences as Moral Identities: Verifiability and Responsibility in Imputations of Deviance and Charisma', *American Journal of Sociology*, 80(6): 1369–90.

Kawabata, A. and Tamura, T. (2007). 'Online-religion in Japan: Websites and Religious Counseling from a Comparative Cross-cultural Perspective', *Journal of Computer-Mediated Communication*, 12(3), article 12. Available at http://jcmc.indiana.edu/vol12/issue3/kawabata.html (accessed 9 October 2013).
Kenyatta, J. (1938/1962). *Facing Mount Kenya*. London: Vintage.
Kermani, Z. (2011). 'Playing with Fire (and Water, Earth, and Air)', in Ridgely (2011): 108–20.
Kienle, P. and Staemmler, B. (2003). 'Self-representation of Two New Religions on the Japanese Internet: Jehovah's Witnesses and Seichō no Ie', in N. Gottlieb and M. McLelland (eds) *Japanese Cybercultures*. London: Routledge: 222–34.
Kiernan, J. P. (1990). *The Production and Management of Therapeutic Power in Zionist Churches within a Zulu City*. Lewiston, NY: Edwin Mellen.
Kilbourne, B. (1986). 'Equity or Exploitation: The Case of the Unification Church', *Review of Religious Research*, 28: 143–50.
Kilbourne, B. and Richardson, J. T. (1984). 'Psychotherapy and the New Religions', *American Psychologist*, 39: 237–51.
— (1989a). 'Paradigm Conflict, Types of Conversion, and Conversion Theories', *Sociological Analysis*, 50: 1–21.
— (1989b). 'A Social Psychological Analysis of Healing', *Journal of Integrative and Eclectic Psychology*, 7: 20–43.
Kinane, K. and Ryan, M. A. (eds) (2009). *End of Days: Essays on the Apocalypse from Antiquity to Modernity*. Jefferson, NC: McFarland & Company.
King, G. (1957). *The Practices of Aetherius*. London: Aetherius Society.
— (1963). *Become a Builder of the New Age!* London: Aetherius Society.
King, G. R. (1935). *Unveiled Mysteries*. Chicago: Saint-Germain Press.
King, T. (2008). *The Island Pond Raid, The Inside Story: Factual Account of the Infamous Island Pond Raid*. Bloomington: AuthorHouse Publishing.
Kisala, R. J. (1999). *Prophets of Peace: Pacificism and Cultural Identity in Japan's New Religions*. Honolulu: University of Hawaii Press.
— (2005). 'Soka Gakkai: Searching for the Mainstream', in Lewis and Petersen (2005): 139–52.
Kisala, R. J. and Mullins, M. R. (2001). *Religion and Social Crisis in Japan: Understanding Japanese Society through the Aum Affair*. New York: Palgrave.
Kivisto, P. (2007). 'Rethinking the Relationship between Ethnicity and Religion', in J. Beckford and N. J. Demerath (eds) *The Sage Handbook of the Sociology of Religion*. Thousand Oaks, CA: Sage: 490–510.
Klassen, P. E. (2011). *Spirits of Protestantism: Medicine, Healing, and Liberal Christianity*. Berkeley: University of California Press.
Klein, A. (2011). 'Wenn Religionsgemeinschaften zur politischen Reformation ansetzen: Der Fall der japanischen "Kōfuku no Kagaku"', *Asien: The German Journal on Contemporary Asia*, 119: 9–25.
Kliever, L. D. (1981). 'Fictive Religion: Rhetoric and Play', *Journal of the American Academy of Religion*, 49(4): 657–69.
— (1999). 'Meeting God in Garland: A Model of Religious Tolerance', *Nova Religio*, 3: 45–53.
Klippenstein, J. (2005). 'Imagine No Religion: On Defining "New Age"', *Studies in Religion*, 34(3–4): 391–403.
Knight, M. M. (2007). *The Five Percenters: Islam, Hip-hop, and the Gods of New York*. London: Oneworld.
Knott, K. and McLoughlin, S. (eds) (2010). *Diasporas: Concepts, Identities, Intersections*. London: Zed Books.
Koenig, H. G., King, D. and Benner Carson, V. (2012). *Handbook of Religion and Health*. 2nd ed. Oxford: Oxford University Press.

Kohl, L. J. (2010). *Jonestown Survivor: An Insider's Look*. New York: iUniverse.
Kohut, H. (1971). *The Analysis of the Self*. New York: International Universities Press.
Kokot, W., Tololyan, K. and Alfonso, C. (eds) (2004). *Diaspora, Identity and Religion: New Directions in Theory and Research*. London: Routledge.
Köpping, K. P. (1974). *Religiöse Bewegungen im modernen Japan als Problem des Kulturwandels*. Köln: Wienand Verlag.
Kornfield, J. (1993). *A Path with Heart: A Guide Through the Perils and Promises of Spiritual Life*. New York: Bantam Books.
Kozawa, H. (1997). *Shinshūkyō no Fūdo*. Tokyo: Iwanami Shoten.
Kraybill, D. B. (2001). *The Riddle of Amish Culture*. Baltimore: Johns Hopkins University Press.
Krebs, T. (1998). 'Church Structures that Facilitate Pedophilia among Roman Catholic Clergy', in A. Shupe (ed.) *Wolves Within the Fold*. New Brunswick, NJ: Rutgers University Press: 15–32.
Kripamoya Das. (2012). 'Who is a Member of ISKCON? The Types of Membership'. ISKCON News. Available at http://news.iskcon.com/node/4450 (accessed 16 June 2012).
Krogh, M. C. and Pillifant, B. A. (2004a). 'Kemetic Orthodoxy: Ancient Egyptian Religion on the Internet – a Research Note', *Sociology of Religion*, 65(2): 167–75.
— (2004b). 'The House of Netjer: A New Religious Community Online', in Dawson and Cowan (2004): 205–19.
Kuhn, T. S. (1962). *The Structure of Scientific Revolutions*. Chicago: University of Chicago Press.
Lalich, J. (2004). *Bounded Choice: True Believers and Charismatic Cults*. Berkeley: University of California Press.
Lambrev, G. (2009). *Dogstar and Poems from Other Planets*. Berkeley: Beatitude Press.
Landes, R. (2011). *Heaven on Earth: The Varieties of Millennial Experience*. Oxford: Oxford University Press.
Landes, R. (ed.) (2000). *Encyclopedia of Millennialism and Millennial Movements*. London: Routledge.
Langone, M. (ed.) (1993). *Recovery from Cults: Help for Victims of Psychological and Spiritual Abuse*. New York and London: W. W. Norton.
Lanternari, V. (1963). *The Religions of the Oppressed: A Study of Messianic Cults*, trans. Lisa Sergio. New York: Knopf.
Larson, B. (1982). *Larson's New Book of Cults*. Wheaton, IL: Tyndale House.
Lassander, M. T. (2009). 'Modern Paganism as a Legitimating Framework for Post-Materialist Values', *Pomegranate*, 11(1): 74–96.
Lau, K. (2000). *New Age Capitalism: Making Money East of Eden*. Philadelphia: University of Pennsylvania Press.
Laube, J. (1978). *Oyagami: Die Heutige Gottesvorstellung der Tenrikyō* (Studien zur Japanologie 14). Wiesbaden: Harrassowitz Verlag.
Leadbeater, C. (1912). *A Textbook of Theosophy*. London: Theosophical Publishing House.
Lee, M. F. (1996). *The Nation of Islam: An American Millenarian Movement*. Syracuse: Syracuse University Press.
Legrand, P. (1995). 'Comparative Legal Studies and Commitment to Theory', *Modern Law Review*, 58(2): 262–73.
Lehrich, C. I. (2003). *The Language of Demons and Angels: Cornelius Agrippa's Occult Philosophy*. Leiden: Brill.
Leopold, A. M. and Jensen, J. S. (eds) (2004). *Syncretism in Religion: A Reader*. London: Routledge.
Levi, K. (ed.) (1982). *Violence and Religious Commitment: Implications of Jim Jones's People's Temple Movement*. University Park, PA: Pennsylvania State University Press.

Levtzion, N. (1994). 'Eighteenth Century Renewal and Reform in Islam: The Role of Sufi Turuq in West Africa', in *Islam in West Africa: Religion: Society and Politics to 1800*. Aldershot: Variorum: 1–18.
Lewis, I. M. (1989). *Ecstatic Religion: A Study of Shamanism and Spirit Possession*. 2nd ed. London: Routledge.
Lewis, J. R. (2003). *Legitimating New Religions*. New Brunswick, NJ: Rutgers University Press.
— (2005). 'The Solar Temple "Transits": Beyond the Millennialist Hypothesis', in Lewis and Petersen (2005): 95–317.
— (2006). *The Order of the Solar Temple*. Farnham, UK: Ashgate.
— (2011). *Violence and New Religious Movements*. Oxford: Oxford University Press.
— (2012). *Cults: A Reference and Guide*. 3rd ed. Sheffield, UK: Equinox.
Lewis, J. R. (ed.) (1995). *The Gods Have Landed: New Religions from Other Worlds*. Albany: State University of New York Press.
— (2003). *Encyclopedic Sourcebook of UFO Religions*. Amherst, NY: Prometheus Books.
— (2004). *The Oxford Handbook of New Religious Movements*. Oxford: Oxford University Press.
— (2011). *Violence and New Religious Movements*. Oxford: Oxford University Press.
Lewis, J. R. and Lewis, S. M. (2009). *Sacred Schisms: How Religions Divide*. Cambridge: Cambridge University Press.
Lewis, J. R. and Melton, J. G. (eds) (1994). *Sex, Slander and Salvation: Investigating the Family/Children of God*. Stanford: Center for Academic Publishing.
Lewis, J. R. and Petersen, J. A. (eds) (2005). *Controversial New Religions*. Oxford: Oxford University Press.
Lifton, R. J. (1961/1985/1989). *Thought Reform and the Psychology of Totalism: A Study of 'Brainwashing' in China*. Chapel Hill: University of North Carolina Press.
— (1999). *Destroying the World to Save It: Aum Shinrikyo, Apocalyptic Violence, and the New Global Terrorism*. New York: Henry Holt and Company.
Lindblom, J. (1962). *Prophecy in Ancient Israel*. Oxford: Blackwell.
Lins, U. (1976). *Die Ōmoto-Bewegung und der Radikale Nationalismus in Japan*. München: R. Oldenbourg Verlag.
Linton, R. (1943). 'Nativist Movements', *American Anthropologist*, 45(2): 230–40.
Lofland, J. (1966). *Doomsday Cult: A Study of Conversion, Proselytization, and Maintenance of Faith*. Englewood Cliffs, NJ: Prentice-Hall.
— (1979). 'Becoming a World-saver Revisited', in Richardson (1978/1979): 10–23.
Lofland, J. and Skonovd, N. (1981). 'Conversion Motifs', *Journal for the Scientific Study of Religion*, 20: 373–85.
Lofland, J. and Stark, R. (1965). 'Becoming a World-Saver: A Theory of Conversion to a Deviant Perspective', *American Sociological Review*, 30(6): 862–75.
Lorde, A. (1983). 'An Open Letter to Mary Daly', in C. Moraga and G. Anzaldua (eds) *This Bridge Called My Back: Writings by Radical Women of Color*. New York: Kitchen Table: 95–6.
Lowe, S. (2011). 'Transcendental Meditation, Vedic Science and Science', *Nova Religio*, 14(4): 54–76.
Lucas, P. C. (1995). *The Odyssey of a New Religion: The Holy Order of MANS from New Age to Orthodoxy*. Bloomington: Indiana University Press.
Lucas, P. C. and Robbins, T. (eds) (2004). *New Religious Movements in the 21st Century: Legal, Political, and Social Challenges in Global Perspective*. London: Routledge.
Ludwar-Ene, G. (ed.) (1991). *New Religious Movements and Society in Nigeria*. Bayreuth: Bayreuth African Studies.
Luhrmann, T. M. (1989a). *Persuasions of the Witch's Craft: Ritual Magic in Contemporary England*. Cambridge, MA: Harvard University Press.

Bibliography

— (1989b). *Persuasions of the Witch's Craft; Ritual Magic in Contemporary England*. Oxford: Blackwell.
Maaga, M. M. (1998). *Hearing the Voices of Jonestown: Putting a Human Face on an American Tragedy*. Syracuse: Syracuse University Press.
MacCannell, D. (1999). *The Tourist: A New Theory of the Leisure Class*. Berkeley: University of California Press.
MacEoin, D. (2005). 'Bahá'ism: Some Uncertainties About Its Role as a Globalizing Religion', in Warburg, Hvithamar and Warmind (2005): 287–306.
Machalek, R. and Snow, D. (1993). 'Conversion to New Religious Movements', in *Religion and the Social Order* 3, 53–74.
MacKenzie, U. and Morrison, B. (1982). *New Religious Movements in Britain Today: A Resource Paper from CYFA*. London: Church Youth Fellowships Association.
Macpherson, J. (2008). *Women and Reiki: Energetic/Holistic Healing in Practice*. Sheffield, UK: Equinox.
Magliocco, S. (2004). *Witching Culture: Folklore and Neo-Paganism in America*. Philadelphia: University of Pennsylvania Press.
Mahmood, S. (2004). *Politics of Piety: The Islamic Revival and the Feminist Subject*. Princeton, NJ: Princeton University Press.
Malaclypse the Younger (1994). *Principia Discordia: How I Found Goddess and What I Did to Her When I Found Her*. Austin, TX: Steve Jackson Games.
Malony, N. and Southard, S. (1992). *Handbook of Religious Conversion*. Birmingham, AL: Religious Education Press.
Mapel, T. (2007). 'The Adjustment Process of Ex-Buddhist Monks to Life after the Monastery', *Journal of Religion and Health*, 46(1): 19–34.
Marshall, J. S. (1981). *The Komeito in Japanese Politics*. Ann Arbor: UMI.
Martikainen, T. (2004). *Immigrant Religions in Local Society: Historical and Contemporary Perspectives in the City of Turku*. Åbo: Åbo akademis Förlag.
Martin, W. (1985). *The Kingdom of the Cults*. Minneapolis, MN: Bethany House.
Martin, W. and Zacharias, R. (2003). *The Kingdom of the Cults*. Rev. ed. Bloomington, MN: Bethany House.
Martínková, L. (2008). 'Computer Mediated Religious Life of Technoshamans and Cybershamans: Is there Any Virtuality?' *Heidelberg Journal of Religions on the Internet*, 3(1): 43–60. Available at http://archiv.ub.uni-heidelberg.de/volltextserver/volltexte/2008/8289/pdf/libuse.pdf (accessed 9 October 2013).
Marty, M. (2012). 'Switching Denominations, Shopping for Religion'. Available at http://christianpost.com/news/switching-denominations-shopping-for-religion-31445/ (accessed 22 September 2012).
Marty, M. and Greenspahn, F. (1988). *Pushing the Faith: Proselytism and Civility in a Pluralistic World*. New York: Crossroad Publishing.
Massey, D. (1995). 'The Conceptualization of Place', in D. Massey and P. Jess (eds) *A Place in the World: Places, Cultures and Globalization*. Oxford: Open University Press: 45–85.
Matthew, S. (1991). 'Ritual Healing and Political Acquiescence in African Independent Churches', *Africa: Journal of the International African Institute*, 61(1): 1–25.
Mayer, J. F. (2000). 'Religious Movements and the Internet: The New Frontier of Cult Controversies', *Religion and the Social Order* 8: 249–76.
Mbacke, K. (2005). *Sufism and Religious Brotherhoods in Senegal*, trans. from the French by Eric Ross and ed. John Hunwick. Princeton, NJ: Markus Wiener.
Mbon, F. (1992). *Brotherhood of the Cross and Star: A New Religious Movement in Nigeria*. Frankfurt a/M: Peter Lang.
McCloud, S. (2004). *Making the American Religious Fringe: Exotics, Subversives, and Journalists, 1955–1993*. Chapel Hill: University of North Carolina Press.

McColgan, A. (2009). 'Class Wars? Religion and (In)equality in the Workplace', *Industrial Law Journal*, 38(1): 1–19.
McCutcheon, R. T. (ed.) (1999). *The Insider/Outsider Problem in the Study of Religion*. London: Cassell.
McFarland, N. (1967). *The Rush Hour of the Gods: A Study of New Religious Movements in Japan*. London: Macmillan.
McFarlane, S. (1989). 'Bodily Awareness in the Wing Chun System', *Religion*, 19(3): 241–53.
McGarry, M. (2008). *Ghosts of Futures Past: Spiritualism and the Cultural Politics of Nineteenth-Century America*. Berkeley: University of California Press.
McGuire, M. B. (2008). *Lived Religion: Faith and Practice in Everyday Life*. Oxford: Oxford University Press.
McGuire, M. B. and Kantor, D. (1988). *Ritual Healing in Suburban America*. New Brunswick, NJ: Rutgers University Press.
McLaughlin, L. (2003). 'Faith and Practice: Bringing Religion, Music and Beethoven to Life in Soka Gakkai', *Social Science of Japan Journal*, 6(2): 161–79.
— (2009). *Sōka Gakkai in Japan*. PhD Dissertation. Princeton University. UMI: ProQuest Dissertations & Theses.
McQuail, D. (2000). *McQuail's Mass Communication Theory*. Thousand Oaks, CA: Sage.
McVeigh, B. (1991). *Gratitude, Obedience and Humility of Heart: The Cultural Construction of Belief in a Japanese New Religion*. PhD Thesis: Princeton University.
— (1997). *Spirits Selves and Subjectivity in a Japanese New Religion*. Lewiston, NY: Edwin Mellen.
Melton, J. G. (1978). *Encyclopedia of American Religions*. Wilmington, NC: Consortium Books.
— (1985). 'Spiritualization and Reaffirmation: What Really Happens when Prophecy Fails', *American Studies*, 26(2) (Fall): 17–29.
— (1991). 'Introduction: When Prophets Die: The Succession Crisis in New Religions', in Miller (1991): 1–12.
— (1995). 'The Contactees: A Survey', in Lewis (1995): 1–14.
— (1997). *The Children of God*. Salt Lake City: Signature Books.
— (1999). 'Brainwashing and the Cults: The Rise and Fall of a Theory'. CESNUR: Center for Studies of New Religions. Available at http://cesnur.org/testi/melton.htm (accessed 6 February 2013).
— (2001). 'Reiki: The International Spread of New Age Healing Movement', in Rothstein (2001): 73–93.
— (2006). 'Critiquing Cults: An Historical Perspective', in Gallagher and Ashcraft (2006), vol. 1: 126–42.
— (2007). 'Perspective: New New Religions: Revisiting a Concept', *Nova Religio*, 10(4): 103–12.
— (n.d.). 'Scientology: Rites and Ceremonies'. Available at http://patheos.com/Library/Scientology/Ritual-Worship-Devotion-Symbolism/Rites-and-Ceremonies.html (accessed 14 January 2013).
Melton, J. G. and Bromley, D. G. (2009). 'Violence and New Religions: An Assessment of Problems, Progress, and Prospects in Understanding the NRM-Violence Connection', in Al-Rasheed and Shterin (2009): 27–41.
Métraux, D. (1988). *The History and Theology of Soka Gakkai: A Japanese New Religion*. Lewiston, NY: Edwin Mellen.
— (1992). 'The Dispute between the Sōka Gakkai and the Nichiren Shōshū Priesthood: A Lay Revolution Against a Conservative Clergy', *Japanese Journal of Religious Studies*, 19: 325–36.

— (2001). *The International Expansion of a Modern Buddhist Movement: The Soka Gakkai in Southeast Asia and Australia*. Lanham, New York and London: University Press of America.

Meyer, B. et al. (2010). 'The Origin and Mission of Material Religion', *Religion*, 40(3): 207–11.

Meyer, B., Morgan, D., Paine, C. and Plate, S. B. (1980). *The Positive Thinkers: Religion as Pop Psychology from Mary Baker Eddy to Oral Roberts*. New York: Pantheon Books.

Micheals, A., et al. (eds) (2010). *Ritual Dynamics and the Science of Ritual*. Vols 1–3. Wiesbaden: Harrassowitz Verlag.

Mickler, M. L. (2006). 'The Unification Church/Movement in the United States', in Gallagher and Ashcraft (2006), vol. 4: 158–84.

Miller, S. (2004). 'An Interview with Andy Roberts: Tough on Ufology, Tough on the Causes of Ufology', *UFO Review*, 4: 52–75.

Miller, T. (1999). *The 60's Communes: Hippies and Beyond*. Syracuse: Syracuse University Press.

Miller, T. (ed.) (1991). *When Prophets Die: The Postcharismatic Fate of New Religious Movements*. Albany: State University of New York Press.

Miller, W. (1840). *Evidence from Scripture and History of the Second Coming of Christ about the Year 1843; Exhibited in a Course of Lectures*. Boston: B. B. Mussey.

Mills, C. W. (1967). *Power, Politics and People. The Collected Essays of C. Wright Mills*, ed. I. L. Horowitz. Oxford: Oxford University Press.

Mitchell, R. C. and Turner, H. W. (1966). *A Bibliography of Modern African Religious Movements*. Evanston, IL: Northwestern University Press.

Mitchem, S. Y. (2007). *African American Folk Healing*. New York: New York University Press.

Moberg, M., Granholm, K. and Nynäs, P. (2012). 'Trajectories of Post-Secular Complexity: An Introduction', in Nynäs, Lassander and Utriainen (2012): 1–25.

Momen, M. (2007). 'Marginality and Apostasy in the Bahá'í Community', *Religion*, 37(1): 187–209.

Montgomery, R. (1985). *Aliens among Us*. New York: Fawcett Crest.

Moore, J. (1991). *Gurdjieff: The Anatomy of a Myth: A Biography*. Brisbane: Element Books.

Moore, R. (1985). *A Sympathetic History of Jonestown: The Moore Family Involvement in Peoples Temple*. Lewiston, NY: Edwin Mellen.

— (1986). *The Jonestown Letters: Correspondence of the Moore Family 1970–1985*. Lewiston, NY: Edwin Mellen.

— (1988). *In Defense of Peoples Temple*. Lewiston, NY: Edwin Mellen.

— (2000). 'Is the Canon on Jonestown Closed?', *Nova Religio*, 4(1): 7–27.

— (2009a). 'Jonestown in Literature: Caribbean Reflections on a Tragedy', *Literature & Theology*, 23(1): 69–83.

— (2009b). *Understanding Jonestown and Peoples Temple*. Westport, CT: Praeger.

— (2011a). 'Narratives of Persecution, Suffering, and Martyrdom: Violence in the Peoples Temple and Jonestown', in Lewis (2011): 95–112.

— (2011b). 'The Stigmatized Deaths in Jonestown: Finding a Locus for Grief', *Death Studies*, 35: 42–58.

Moore, R. and McGehee, F., III (eds) (1989a). *New Religious Movements, Mass Suicide, and Peoples Temple: Scholarly Perspectives on a Tragedy*. Lewiston, NY: Edwin Mellen.

— (eds) (1989b). *The Need for a Second Look at Jonestown*. Lewiston, NY: Edwin Mellen.

Moore, R., Pinn, A. B. and Sawyer, M. R. (eds) (2004). *Peoples Temple and Black Religion in America*. Bloomington: Indiana University Press.

Moore, R. L. (1986). *Religious Outsiders and the Making of Americans*. Oxford: Oxford University Press.

Morgan, D. (2008). 'The Materiality of Cultural Construction', *Material Religion*, 4(2): 228–9.
Morgan, L. (ed.) (2012). *Philosophical Explorations of New and Alternative Religious Movements*. Farnham, UK: Ashgate.
Muffler, J., Langrod, J., Richardson, J. and Ruiz, P. (1997). 'Religion', in *Substance Abuse: A Comprehensive Test Book*. 3rd ed. Baltimore: Williams and Wilkin: 492–99.
Mukonyora, I. (2007). *Wandering a Gendered Wilderness: Suffering & Healing in an African Initiated Church*. Frankfurt a/M: Peter Lang.
Mulholland, P. (2011). 'Marian Apparitions, the New Age and the FÁS Prophet', in O. Cosgrove, L. Cox, C. Kuling and P. Mulholland (eds) *Ireland's New Religious Movements*. Newcastle-upon-Tyne: Cambridge Scholars: 176–98.
Murakami, S. (1980). *Shinshūkyō: Sono Kōdō to Shisō*. Tokyo: Hyōronsha.
Murphy, C. M. (2003). *John the Baptist: Prophet of Purity for a New Age*. Collegeville, MN: Liturgical Press.
Myers, J. E. (2007). *Kabbalah and the Spiritual Quest: The Kabbalah Centre in America*. Westport, CT: Praeger.
Nabhan-Warren, K. (2005). *The Virgin of El Barrio: Marian Apparitions, Catholic Evangelizing, and Mexican American Activism*. New York: New York University Press.
Nada-Yolanda (1995). *Reappearance of Christ Consciousness on Earth*. Pioneer: Mark-Age. Available at http://thenewearth.org/reappear.rtf (accessed 18 August 2012).
Narayanan, Y. and Macbeth, J. (2009). 'Deep in the Desert: Merging the Desert and the Spiritual through 4WD Tourism', *Tourism Geographies*, 11(3): 369–89.
Neal, L. (2011). 'They're Freaks: The Cult Stereotype in Fictional Television Shows, 1958–2008', *Nova Religio*, 14(3): 81–107.
Needleman, J. and Baker, G. (eds) (1978). *Understanding the New Religions*. New York: Seabury.
Newport, K. G. C. (2006). *The Branch Davidians of Waco: The History and Beliefs of an Apocalyptic Sect*. Oxford: Oxford University Press.
Newport, K. G. C. and Gribben, C. (eds) (2006). *Expecting the End: Millennialism in Social and Historical Contexts*. Waco, TX: Baylor University Press.
Newport, K. G. C. and Searle, J. (eds) (2012). *Beyond the End: The Future of Millennial Studies*. Sheffield: Sheffield Phoenix Press.
Nicholson, L. (1998). 'Interpreting "Gender"', in N. Zack, L. Shrage and C. Sartwell (eds) *Race, Class, Gender, and Sexuality: The Big Questions*. Chichester, UK: Wiley-Blackwell.
Niebuhr. H. R. (1929). *The Social Sources of Denominationalism*. New York: Meridian.
Nishiyama, S. and Ōmura, E. (1988). *Gendaijin no Shūkyō*. Tokyo: Yūhikaku.
Nissenbaum, S. (1980). *Sex, Diet, and Debility in Jacksonian America: Sylevester Graham and Health Reform*. Westport, CT: Greenwood Press.
Nordquist, T. (1978). *Ananda Cooperative Village: A Study in the Attitudes of New Age Religious Beliefs, Values, and Community*. Uppsala University: Religionshistoriska Institutionen Monograph Series.
Norman, A. (2011). *Spiritual Tourism: Travel and Religious Practice in Western Society*. London: Bloomsbury.
Numata, K. (1988). *Gendai Nihon no Shinshūkyō: Jōhō Shakai ni okeru Kamigami no Saisei*. Tokyo: Sōgensha.
Numbers, R. L. (2008). *Prophetess of Health: Ellen G. White and the Origins of Seventh-day Adventist Health Reform*. 3rd ed. Grand Rapids, MI: Eerdmans.
Numbers, R. L., Risse, G. B. and Leavitt, J. W. (eds) (1977). *Medicine Without Doctors: Home Health Care in American History*. New York: Science History Publications.
Nye, M. (2001). *Multiculturalism and Minority Religions in Britain*. Richmond, UK: Curzon Press.

Nynäs, P., Lassander, M. and Utriainen, T. (eds) (2012). *Post-Secular Society.* New Brunswick, NJ: Transaction.

O'Leary, S. D. (1994). *Arguing the Apocalypse: A Theory of Millennial Rhetoric.* Oxford: Oxford University Press.

O'Leary, S. D. and McGhee, G. S. (eds) (2005). *War in Heaven/Heaven on Earth: Theories of the Apocalyptic.* Sheffield, UK: Equinox.

O'Shea, T. B. (2011). *Jonestown Lullaby: Poems and Pictures.* New York: iUniverse.

Offner, C. B. and van Straelen, H. (1963). *Modern Japanese Religion – with Special Emphasis upon their Doctrines of Healing.* Leiden: Brill.

Okuyama, M. (ed.) (2002). *Shohyō Tokushū: Shimazono Susumu 'Posutomodan no Shinshūkyō' o Yomu* (Special Issue), *Nanzan Shūkyō Bunka Kenkyūsho Kenkyūsho-hō,* 12: 26–53.

Oleson, T. and Richardson, J. T. (2007). 'The Confluence of Research Traditions on Terrorism and Religion: A Social Psychological Examination', *Psicologia Politica,* 34: 39–55.

Oliver, M., Jr. (1994). 'Today's Jackboots: The Inquisition Revisited', in Lewis and Melton (1994): 137–51.

Olupona, J. (1989). 'New Religious Movements in Contemporary Nigeria', *Journal of Religious Thought,* 46: 53–68.

— (1991). 'New Religious Movements and the Social Order in Nigeria', in Ludwar-Ene (1991): 31–52.

Omoyajowo, J. A. (1982). *Cherubim and Seraphim. The History of an African Independent Church.* New York and Lagos: NOK Publishers.

Oosthuizen, G. C. (1968). *Post-Christianity in Africa: A Theological and Anthropological Study.* London: Hurst.

— (1992). *The Healer-Prophet in Afro-Christian Churches.* Leiden: Brill.

Oosthuizen, G. C. and Hexham, I. (eds) (1992). *Empirical Studies of African Independent/Indigenous Churches.* Lewiston, NY: Edwin Mellen.

Orsi, R. A. (2006). *Between Heaven and Earth: The Religious Worlds People Make and the Scholars Who Study Them.* Princeton, NJ: Princeton University Press.

Owen, A. (2004). *The Darkened Room: Women, Power, and Spiritualism in Late Victorian England.* Chicago: University of Chicago Press.

Ownby, D. (2010). *Falun Gong and the Future of China.* Oxford: Oxford University Press.

Palmer, D. A. (2007). *Qigong Fever: Body, Science, and Utopia in China.* New York: Columbia University Press.

Palmer, S. J. (1994/1996). *Moon Sisters, Krishna Mothers, Rajneesh Lovers: Women's Roles in the New Religions.* Syracuse: Syracuse University Press.

— (1999). 'Frontiers and Families: The Children of Island Pond', in Palmer and Hardman (1999): 153–71.

— (2001). 'The Raël Deal', *Religion in the News* 4.2 (Summer). Available at http://trincoll.edu/depts/csrpl/rinvol4no2/rael.htm (accessed 18 August 2012).

— (2003). 'The Raëlian Apocalypse', in Lewis (2003): 261–80.

— (2004a). *Aliens Adored: Raël's UFO Religion.* New Brunswick, NJ: Rutgers University Press.

— (2004b). 'Women in New Religious Movements', in Lewis (2004): 375–85.

— (2010). *The Nuwaubian Nation: Black Spirituality and State Control.* Farnham, UK: Ashgate.

Palmer, S. J. and Finn, N. (1992). 'Coping with Apocalypse in Canada: Experiences of Endtime in la mission de l'esprit saint and the Institute of Applied Metaphysics', *Sociological Analysis,* 53(4), Winter: 397–415.

Palmer, S. J. and Hardman, C. (eds) (1999). *Children in New Religions.* New York: Rutgers University Press.

Paloutzian, R., Richardson, J. T. and Rambo, L. (1999). 'Religious Conversion and Personality Change', *Journal of Personality*, 67: 1047–80.
Parker, G. T. (1973). *Mind Cure in New England: From the Civil War to World War One*. Hanover, New Hampshire: University Press of New England.
Parsons, T. (1957/2002). 'Malinowski and the Theory of Social Systems', in R. Firth (ed.) *Man and Culture: An Evaluation of the Work of Bronislaw Malinowski*. London: Routledge: 53–70.
Partridge, C. (2004a). *The Re-Enchantment of the West: Alternative Spiritualities, Sacralization, Popular Culture and Occulture*. Vol. 1. London: T&T Clark.
— (2004b). 'Alien Demonology: The Christian Roots of the Malevolent Extraterrestrial in UFO Religions and Abduction Spiritualities', *Religion*, 34: 163–89.
— (2005). *The Re-Enchantment of the West: Alternative Spiritualities, Sacralization, Popular Culture and Occulture*. Vol. 2. London: T&T Clark.
— (2006). 'The Eschatology of Heaven's Gate', in Newport and Gribbin (2006): 49–66.
— (2012). *Anthems of Apocalypse: Popular Music and Apocalyptic Thought*. Sheffield: Sheffield Phoenix Press.
— (2013). 'Occulture is Ordinary', in Asprem and Granholm (2013): 113–33.
Partridge, C. (ed.) (2003). *UFO Religions*. London: Routledge.
Pasi, M. (2007). 'Magic', in K. von Stuckrad (ed.) *The Brill Dictionary of Religion*. Leiden: Brill: 1134–9.
Pearson, J. (2007). *Wicca and the Christian Heritage: Ritual Sex and Magic*. London: Routledge.
Peel, J. D. Y. (1968). *Aladura: A Religious Movement among the Yoruba*. Oxford: Oxford University Press.
Peters, T. (2003). 'UFOs, Heaven's Gate, and the Theology of Suicide', in Lewis (2003): 239–60.
Petsche, J. (2013). 'Reflexivity and Objectivity in the Study of a Modern Esoteric Teacher: In the Footsteps of G. I. Gurdjieff', in A. Norman (ed.) *Journeys and Destinations: Studies in Travel, Identity, and Meaning*. Newcastle-upon-Tyne: Cambridge Scholars: 159–76.
Phan, K. P. (2011). 'Harold Camping Breaks Silence, Predicts October 21 Doomsday', *The Christian Post* [online edition], 23 May.
Pike, S. M. (1996). 'Forging Magical Selves: Gendered Bodies and Ritual Fires at Neo-pagan Festivals', in J. Lewis (ed.) *Magical Religion and Modern Witchcraft*. Albany: State University of New York Press: 121–40.
— (2001). *Earthly Bodies, Magical Selves: Contemporary Pagans and the Search for Community*. Berkeley: University of California Press.
— (2004). *New Age and Neopagan Religions in America*. New York: Columbia University Press.
— (2006). 'Men and Women in New Religious Movements: Constructing Alternative Gender Roles', in Bromley (2006): 211–30.
— (2011). 'Religion and Youth in American Culture', in Ridgely (2011): 33–49.
Plank, K. (2011). *Insikt och närvaro: Akademiska kontemplationer kring buddism, meditation och mindfulness*. Göteborg: Makadam.
Poewe, K. (2006). *New Religions and the Nazis*. London: Routledge.
Pokorny, L. and Winter, F. (eds) (forthcoming). *Handbook of East Asian New Religious Movements* (Brill Handbooks of Contemporary Religion). Leiden: Brill.
Pontifical Council for Culture, and Pontifical Council for Interreligious Dialogue (2003). *Jesus Christ, The Bearer of the Water of Life: A Christian Reflectionon the 'New Age'*. Available at http://vatican.va/roman_curia/pontifical_councils/interelg/documents/rc_pc_interelg_doc_20030203_new-age_En.html (accessed 4 April 2013).
Porter, J. (1996). 'Spiritualists, Aliens and UFOs: Extraterrestrials as Spirit Guides', *Journal of Contemporary Religion*, 11: 337–53.

Possamai, A. (2005). *Religion and Popular Culture: A Hyper-Real Testament*. Frankfurt a/M: Peter Lang.
— (2006). *In Search of New Age Spiritualities*. Aldershot: Ashgate.
Povinelli, E. (2006). *The Empire of Love: Toward a Theory of Intimacy, Genealogy, and Carnality*. Durham: Duke University Press.
Prandi, R. (2000). 'African Gods in Contemporary Brazil: A Sociological Introduction to Candomblé Today', *International Sociology*, 15(4): 641–63.
Primiano, L. (1995). 'Vernacular Religion and the Search for Method in Religious Folklife', *Western Folklore*, 54(1): 37–56.
— (2012). 'Afterword – Manifestations of the Religious Vernacular: Ambiguity, Power and Creativity', in Bowman and Valk (2012): 382–94.
— (2014). '"And As We Dine, We Sing and Praise God": Father and Mother Divine's Theologies of Food', in Zeller, Dallam, Neilson and Rubel (2014): 42–67.
Prohl, I. (2006). *Religiöse Innovationen: Die Shintō-Organisation World Mate in Japan*. Berlin: Reimer.
Prus, R. C. (1976). 'Religious Recruitment and the Management of Dissonance: A Sociological Perspective', *Sociological Inquiry*, 46(2): 127–34.
Purkiss, D. (2000). *Troublesome Things: A History of Fairies and Fairy Stories*. New York: Penguin.
Puttick, E. (1997). *Women in New Religions: In Search of Community, Sexuality, and Spiritual Power*. New York: St. Martin's Press.
— (1999). 'Osho Ko Hsuam School: Educating the "New Child"', in Palmer and Hardman (1999): 88–107.
Puttick, E. and Clark, P. (eds) (1993). *Women as Teachers and Disciples in Traditional and New Religions*. Lewiston, NY: Edwin Mellen.
Raday, F. (2003). 'Culture, Religion and Gender', *International Journal of Constitutional Law*, 1(4): 663–715.
Radford, L. B. (1913). *Ancient Heresies in Modern Dress*. Melbourne and London: George Robertson.
Rahn, P. (2002). 'The Chemistry of a Conflict: The Chinese Government and the Falun Gong', *Terrorism and Political Conflict*, 14(4) (Winter): 41–65.
Rajagopal, A. (2001). *Politics after Television: Hindu Nationalism and the Reshaping of the Public in India*. Cambridge: Cambridge University Press.
Rambo, L. (1993). *Understanding Religious Conversion*. New Haven, CT: Yale University Press.
Ranger, T. O. (1986). 'Religious Movements and Politics in Sub-Saharan Africa', *African Studies Review*, 29(2): 1–69.
Rappaport, R. (1999). *Ritual and Religion in the Making of Humanity*. Cambridge: Cambridge University Press.
Rapport, J. (2011). 'Corresponding to the Rational World', *Nova Religio*, 14(4): 11–29.
Reader, I. (1996). *A Poisonous Cocktail? Aum Shinrikyō's Path to Violence*. Kopenhagen: NIAS Special Report.
— (2000). *Religious Violence in Contemporary Japan: The Case of Aum Shinrikyō*. Richmond, UK: Curzon Press.
— (2004). 'Consensus Shattered: Japanese Paradigm Shift and Moral Panic in the Post-Aum Era', in Lucas and Robbins (2004): 191–201.
Reader, I. and Tanabe, G. J. (1998). *Practically Religious: Worldly Benefits and the Common Religion of Japan*. Honolulu: University of Hawaii Press.
Redfern, T. H. (1960). *The Work and Worth of Mme Blavatsky*. London: Theosophical Publishing House.
Redles, D. (2005). *Hitler's Millennial Reich: Apocalyptic Belief and the Search for Salvation*. New York: New York University Press.

Repp, M. (1997). *Aum Shinrikyō: Ein Kapitel Krimineller Religionsgeschichte*. Marburg: Diagonal-Verlag.
— (2005). 'Aum Shinrikyo and the Aum Incident: A Critical Introduction', in Lewis and Petersen (2005): 153–94.
— (2011a). '"When Science Fiction Becomes Science Fact": The Role of Science, Science Fiction and Technology in Aum Shinrikyo', in J. R. Lewis and O. Hammer (eds) *Handbook of Religion and the Authority of Science* (Brill Handbooks on Contemporary Religion 3). Leiden: Brill: 185–204.
— (2011b). 'Religion and Violence in Japan: The Case of Aum Shinrikyo', in Lewis (2011): 147–71.
Reps, J. W. (1979). *Cities of the American West: A History of Frontier Urban Planning*. Princeton, NJ: Princeton University Press.
Rhodes, J. M. (1980). *The Hitler Movement: A Modern Millenarian Revolution*. Stanford, CA: Hoover Institution Press.
Rice, D. (1990). *Shattered Vows: Exodus from the Priesthood*. Belfast: Blackstaff Press.
Richardson, J. T. (1980). 'Conversion Careers', *Society*, 17: 47–50.
— (1985a). 'The Active vs. Passive Convert: Paradigm Conflict in Conversion/recruitment Research', *Journal for the Scientific Study of Religion*, 24: 163–79.
— (1985b). 'Psychological and Psychiatric Studies of New Religions', in L. Brown (ed.) *Advances in the Psychology of Religion*. New York: Pergamon Press: 209–23.
— (1991a). 'Cult/brainwashing Cases and Freedom of Religion', *Journal of Church and State*, 33: 55–74.
— (1991b). 'Experiencing Research on New Religions and Cults: Practical and Ethical Considerations', in W. B. Shaffir and R. A. Stebbins (eds) *Experiencing Fieldwork: An Inside View on Qualitative Research*. Thousand Oaks, CA: Sage: 62–71.
— (1992a). 'Conversion Processes in the New Religions', in Malony and Southard (1992): 78–89.
— (1992b). 'Mental Health of Cult Consumers: Legal and Scientific Controversy', in J. Schumaker (ed.) *Religion and Mental Health*. Oxford: Oxford University Press: 233–44.
— (1993a). 'Definitions of Cult: From Socio-technical to Popular-negative', *Review of Religious Research*, 34: 348–56.
— (1993b). 'Religiosity as Deviance: Negative Religious Bias in the Use and Misuse of the DSM-III', *Deviant Behavior*, 14: 1–21.
— (1993c). 'A Social Psychological Critique of "Brainwashing" Claims about Recruitment to New Religions', in Bromley and Hadden (1993): 75–98.
— (1995a). 'Clinical and Personality Assessment of Participants in New Religions', *International Journal of Psychology of Religion*, 5: 145–70.
— (1995b). 'Manufacturing Consent about Koresh: A Structural Analysis of the Role of Media in the Waco Tragedy', in Wright (1995): 153–76.
— (1996a). '"Brainwashing" Claims and Minority Religions Outside the United States: Cultural Diffusion of a Questionable Concept in the Legal Arena', *Brigham Young University Law Review*, 1996: 873–904.
— (1996b). 'Sociology and the New Religions: "Brainwashing," the Courts, and Religious Freedom', in P. Jenkins and J. S. Kroll-Smith (eds) *Witnessing for Sociology: Sociologists in Court*. Westport, CT: Praeger: 115–34.
— (1998). 'The Accidental Expert', *Nova Religio*, 2: 31–43.
— (1999). 'Social Control of New Religions: From "Brainwashing" Claims to Child Sex Abuse Accusations', in Palmer and Hardman (1999): 172–86.
— (2001). 'Minority Religions in the Context of Violent: A Conflict/Interactionist Perspective', *Terrorism and Political Violence*, 13(1) (Spring): 103–33.
— (2006). 'New Religious Movements and the Law', in Gallagher and Ashcraft (2006), vol. 1: 65–83.

— (2011). 'Minority Religions and the Context of Violence: A Conflict/Interactionist Perspective', in Lewis (2011): 31–62.
Richardson, J. T. (ed.) (1978/1979). *Conversion Careers: In and Out of the New Religions*. Thousand Oaks, CA: Sage.
Richardson, J. T. and Davis, R. (1983). 'Experiential Fundamentalism: Revisions of Orthodoxy in the Jesus Movement', *Journal of the American Academy of Religion*, 51(3): 397–425.
Richardson, J. T. and Introvigne, M. (2001). '"Brainwashing" Theories in European Parliamentary and Administrative Reports on "Cults" and "Sects"', *Journal for the Scientific Study of Religion*, 40(2) (June): 143–68.
Richardson, J. T. and Kilbourne, B. (1983). 'Classical and Contemporary Applications of Brainwashing Models: A Comparison and Critique', in Bromley and Richardson (1983): 29–45.
Richardson, J. T. and Stewart, M. W. (1979). 'Conversion Process Models and the Jesus Movement', *American Behavioral Scientist*, 20: 819–38.
— (2004). 'Medicalization and Regulation of Deviant Religion: An Application of Conrad and Schneider's Model', in J. T. Richardson (ed.) *Regulating Religion: Case Studies from Around the Globe*. New York: Kluwer: 507–34.
Richardson, J. T. and van Driel, B. (1997). 'Journalists' Attitudes towards New Religious Movements', *Review of Religious Research*, 39(2): 116–36.
Richardson, J. T., Stewart, M. and Simmonds, R. (1979). *Organized Miracles: A Study of a Contemporary, Youth, Communal, Fundamentalist Organization*. New Brunswick, NJ: Transaction.
Richardson, J. T., van der Lans, J. and Derks, F. (1986). 'Leaving and Labeling: Voluntary and Coerced Disaffiliation from Religious Social Movements', in L. Krisberg (ed.) *Research in Social Movements, Conflicts, and Change*. Greenwich, CT: Jai Press: 97–126.
Ridgely, S. B. (2011). *The Study of Children in Religions: A Methods Handbook*. New York: New York University Press.
RIRC (Religious Information Research Center), *Kyōdan Dētabēsu*, Available at http://rirc.or.jp/xoops/modules/xwords/search.php (accessed 9 October, 2013).
Ritzer, G. (2011). *Globalization: The Essentials*. Chichester, UK: Wiley-Blackwell.
Roach, C. M. (2003). *Mother/Nature: Popular Culture and Environmental Ethics*. Bloomington: Indiana University Press.
Robbins, T. (1988). *Cults, Converts and Charisma*. Thousand Oaks, CA: Sage.
— (2002). 'Sources of Volatility in Religious Movements', in Bromley and Melton (2002): 57–79.
Robbins, T. and Anthony, D. (1978). 'New Religious Movements and the Social System: Integration, Disintegration and Transformation', *The Annual Review of the Social Sciences of Religion*, 2: 1–27.
— (1980). 'The Limits of "Coercive Persuasion" as an Explanation for Conversion to Authoritarian Sects', *Political Psychology*, 2(22) (Summer): 22–37.
— (1982). 'Deprogramming, Brainwashing and the Medicalization of Deviant Religious Groups', *Social Problems*, 29: 283–97.
— (1995). 'Sects and Violence: Factors Enhancing the Volatility of Marginal Religious Movements', in Wright (1995): 236–59.
Robbins, T. and Palmer, S. J. (eds) (1997). *Millennium, Messiahs, and Mayhem: Contemporary Apocalyptic Movements*. London: Routledge.
Robbins, T., Anthony, D. and Curtis, T. (1973). 'The Limits of Symbolic Realism: Problems of Empathetic Field Observation in a Sectarian Context', *Journal for the Scientific Study of Religion*, 12(3): 259–71; cited in Waterhouse (2002): 65.
— (1975). 'Youth Culture Religious Movements: Evaluating the Integrative Hypothesis', *Sociological Quarterly*, 16: 48–64.

Robertson, D. G. (2012). 'Making the Donkey Visible: Discordianism in the Works of Robert Anton Wilson', in Cusack and Norman (2012): 421–42.
Robertson, R. (1998). *Globalization: Social Theory and Global Culture*. Thousand Oaks, CA: Sage.
Rochford, E. B., Jr. (1980). 'Recruitment Strategies, Ideology, and Organization in the Hare Krshna Movement', *Social Problems*, 29: 399–410.
— (1985). *Hare Krishna in America*. New Brunswick, NJ: Rutgers University Press.
— (1995). 'Family Structure, Commitment and Involvement in the Hare Krishna Movement', *Sociology of Religion*, 56(2): 153–75.
— (2000). 'Demons, Karmies, and Non-devotees: Culture, Group Boundaries, and the Development of Hare Krishna in North America and Europe', *Social Compass*, 47(2): 169–86.
— (2002). 'Family, Religious Authority and Change in the Hare Krishna Movement'. Presented at the meetings of the Center for Studies on New Religious Movements, Salt Lake City (June).
— (2007a). 'The Sociology of New Religious Movements', in A. J. Blasi (ed.) *American Sociology of Religion*. Leiden: Brill: 253–90.
— (2007b). *Hare Krishna Transformed*. New York: New York University Press.
— (2011). 'Boundary and Identity Work among Hare Krishna Children', in Ridgely (2011): 95–107.
Roof, W. C. and Hadaway, K. (1979). 'Denominational Switching in the Seventies: Going beyond Stark and Glock Wade Clark Roof and Kirk Hadaway', *Journal for the Scientific Study of Religion*, 18(4) (December): 363–77.
Rosander, E. E. and Westerlund, D. (eds) (1997). *African Islam and Islam in Africa: Encounters between Sufis and Islamists*. London: Hurst.
Rosenfeld, J. E. (1999). *The Land Broken into Two Halves: Land and Renewal among the Maori of New Zealand*. University Park, PA: Pennsylvania State University Press.
— (2001). 'The Use of the Military at Waco: The Danforth Report in Context', *Nova Religio*, 5(1) (October): 171–85.
Ross, A. (1991). 'New Age – a Kinder, Gentler Science?', in A. Ross (ed.) *Strange Weather: Culture, Science and Technology in the Age of Limits*. London: Verso: 15–74.
Rothstein, M. (2005). 'The Spiritualization of Land and People', *FINYAR*, 2: 94–113.
— (2007a). 'Hagiography and Text in the Aetherius Society: Aspects of the Social Construction of a Religious Leader', in Tumminia (2007): 3–24.
— (2007b). 'Hawaii in New Age Imaginations: A Case of Religious Invention', in Kemp and Lewis (2007): 315–40.
Rothstein, M. (ed.) (2001). *New Age Religion and Globalization*. Aarhus: Aarhus University Press.
Rountree, K. (2006). 'Journeys to the Goddess: Pilgrimage and Tourism in the New Age', in W. H. Swatos (ed.) *On the Road to Being There: Studies in Pilgrimage and Tourism in Late Modernity*. Leiden: Brill: 33–60.
— (2010). *Crafting Contemporary Pagan Identities in a Catholic Society*. Farnham, UK: Ashgate.
Ruah-Midbar, M. and Klin-Oron, A. (2010). 'Jew Age: Jewish Praxis in Israeli New Age Discourses', *Journal of Alternative Spiritualities and New Age Studies*, 5: 33–63.
Rudert, A. (2010). 'Research on Contemporary Indian Gurus: What's New about New Age Gurus?' *Religion Compass*, 4(10): 629–42.
Ruether, R. R. (1993). *Sexism and God Talk: Toward a Feminist Theology*. Boston: Beacon.
Rupp, I. D. (1844). *He Pasa Ekklesia: An Original History of the Religious Denominations at the Present Existing in the United States, etc.* Philadelphia: J. Y. Humphreys.
Ryan, J. (2010). *A History of the Internet and the Digital Future*. London: Reaktion Books.
Sakurai, Y. (2009). *Rei to Kane: Supirichuaru Bijinesu no Kōzō*. Tokyo: Shinchōsha.

Saliba, J. A. (1995). *Perspectives on New Religious Movements*. London: Geoffrey Chapman.
Salmonsen, J. (2002). *Enchanted Feminism: The Reclaiming Witches of San Francisco*. London: Routledge.
Sanada, T. and Norbeck, E. (1975). 'Prophecy Continues to Fail: A Japanese Sect', *Journal of Cross-Cultural Psychology*, 6 (September): 331–45.
Sandberg, R. (2011). 'The Right to Discriminate', *Ecclesiastical Law Journal*, 13(2): 157–81.
Sansi-Roca, R. (2005). 'The Hidden Life of Stones: Historicity, Materiality and the Value of Candomblé Objects in Bahia', *Journal of Material Culture*, 10(2): 139–56.
Satter, B. (1999). *Each Mind a Kingdom: American Women, Sexual Purity, and the New Thought Movement, 1875–1920*. Berkeley: University of California Press.
Sawyer, J. F. H. (1993). *Prophecy and the Biblical Prophets*. Oxford: Oxford University Press.
Schein, E., Schneier, J. and Becker, C. (1961). *Coercive Persuasion*. New York and London: W. W. Norton.
Schoepflin, R. B. (2002). *Christian Science on Trial: Religious Healing in America*. Baltimore: Johns Hopkins University Press.
Schrimpf, M. (forthcoming). *Self-Cultivation and Guidance to Living in Japanese New Religions: A Discourse Analytical Approach* (working title).
Schwartz, L. L. and Kaslow, F. W. (2001). 'The Cult Phenomenon: A Turn of the Century Update', *American Journal of Family Therapy*, 29(1): 13–22.
Scott, D. W. (2011). 'The Discursive Construct of Virtual Angels, Temples, and Religious Worship: Mormon Theology and Culture in Second Life', *Dialogue: A Journal of Mormon Thought*, 44(1): 85–104.
Scott, G. G. (1986/2007). *The Magicians: An Investigation of a Group Practicing Black Magic*. Lincoln, NE: Asja Press.
Sebald, H. (1984). 'New-Age Romanticism: The Quest for an Alternative Lifestyle as a Force of Social Change', *Humboldt Journal of Social Relations*, 11(2): 106–27.
Sedgwick, M. (2004). *Against the Modern World: Traditionalism and the Secret Intellectual History of the Twentieth Century*. Oxford: Oxford University Press.
Seret, I. (2011). 'A Director Under the Influence of History', *the jonestown report*, vol. 13.
Shaffir, W. (1995). 'When Prophecy Is Not Validated: Explaining the Unexpected in a Messianic Campaign', *The Jewish Journal of Sociology*, 37 (December): 119–36.
Sharpley, R. and Sundaram, P. (2005). 'Tourism: A Sacred Journey? The Case of Ashram Tourism, India', *International Journal of Tourism Research*, 7(3): 161–71.
Sheehan, R. (2012). 'Tourism and Occultism in New Orleans's Jackson Square: Contentious and Cooperative Publics', *Tourism Geographies*, 14(1): 73–97.
Shein, E. (1959). 'Brainwashing and Totalitarianization in Modern Society', *World Politics*, 2: 430–41.
Shepherd, G. and Shepherd, G. (2011). 'Learning the Wrong Lessons: A Comparison of FLDS, Family International, and Branch Davidian Child-Protection Interventions', in C. K. Jacobson and L. Burton (eds) *Modern Polygamy in the United States: Historical, Cultural, and Legal Issues*. Oxford: Oxford University Press: 238–58.
Shepherd, G. and Shepherd, G. (eds) (2010). *Talking with the Children of God: Prophecy and Transformation in a Radical Religious Group*. Urbana: University of Illinois Press.
Shimada, H. (2007). *Nihon no Jū Dai-shinshūkyō*. Tokyo: Gentōsha.
— (2008). *Shinshūkyō Bijinesu*. Tokyo: Kōdansha.
Shimazono, S. (1992). *Shinshinshūkyō to Shūkyō Būmu*. Tokyo: Iwanami Shoten.
— (1997). *Gendai Shūkyō no Kanōsei: Ōmu Shinrikyō to Bōryoku*. Tokyo: Iwanami Shoten.
— (2001). *Posutomodan no Shinshūkyō: Gendai Nihon no Seishin Jōkyō no Teiryū*. Tokyo: Tōkyōdō Shuppan.

Bibliography

— (2004). *From Salvation to Spirituality: Popular Religious Movements in Modern Japan*. Melbourne: TransPacific Press.
Shimazono, S. (ed.) (1992). *Sukui to Toku: Shinshūkyō Shinkōsha no Seikatsu to Shisō*. Tokyo: Kōbundō.
Shipps, J. (1985). *Mormonism: The Story of a New Religious Tradition*. Urbana: University of Illinois Press.
Shōkō, T. (2007). *Karanga Indigenous Religion in Zimbabwe: Health and Well-Being*. Aldershot: Ashgate.
Shuck, G. W. (2005). *Marks of the Beast: The 'Left Behind' Novels and the Struggle for Evangelical Identity*. New York: New York University Press.
Shūkyō Shakaigaku Kenkyūkai (ed.) (1987). *Kyōso to sono Shūhen*. Tokyo: Yūzankaku.
Shupe, A. D., Jr. and Bromley, D. G. (1980). *The New Vigilantes: Deprogrammers, Anti-Cultists, and the New Religions*. Thousand Oaks, CA: Sage.
— (1982). 'Shaping the Public Response to Jonestown: People's Temple and the Anticult Movement', in Levi (1982): 105–32.
— (1994). *Anti-Cult Movements in Cross-Cultural Perspective*. Religious Information Systems. New York: Garland.
Shupe, A. D., Jr. and Hadden, J. (1995). 'Cops, News Copy and Public Opinion: Legitimacy and the Social Construction of Evil in Waco', in Wright (1995): 177–202.
Simmel, G. (1906). 'The Sociology of Secrecy and of Secret Societies', *The American Journal of Sociology*, 11(4): 441–498.
Šindelář, P. (2009). 'Whose Message Will Win the Souls? The Future Development of Religious Life in Cyberspace and Its "Chinese Characteristic"', *Masaryk University Journal of Law and Technology*, 3(1): 111–24. Available at http://mujlt.law.muni.cz/storage/1267475009_sb_07-sindelar.pdf (accessed 9 October 2013).
Singer, B. and Benassi, V. A. (1981). 'Occult Beliefs', *American Scientist*, 69: 49–55.
Singer, M. T. (1979). 'Coming out of the Cults', *Psychology Today*, 12: 72–82.
— (1995). *Cults in Our Midst: The Hidden Menace in Our Every-day Lives*. San Francisco: Jossey-Bass.
Siskind, A. (1999). 'In Whose Interest? Separating Children from Mothers in the Sullivan Institute/Fourth Wall Community', in Palmer and Hardman (1999): 51–68.
— (2001). 'Child-rearing Issues in Totalist Groups', in Zablocki and Robbins (2001): 415–51.
Sitler, R. K. (2006). 'The 2012 Phenomenon: New Age Appropriation of an Ancient Mayan Calendar', *Nova Religio*, 9(3): 24–38.
— (2012). 'The 2012 Phenomenon Comes of Age', *Nova Religio*, 16(1): 61–87.
Skolnick, J. (1969). *The Politics of Protest*. New York: Ballentine Books.
Skonovd, N. (1983). 'Leaving the Cultic Religious Milieu', in Bromley and Richardson (1983): 91–105.
Smith, C. (2000). *Christian America? What Evangelicals Really Want*. Berkeley: University of California Press.
Smith, J. Z. (1982). 'The Devil in Mr. Jones', in Smith (1988): 102–20.
— (1988). *Imagining Religion: From Babylon to Jonestown*. Chicago: University of Chicago Press.
Snow, D. and Phillips, C. (1980). 'The Lofland-Stark Model: A Critical Assessment', *Social Problems*, 27: 430–47.
Snow, D., Zurcher, L. and Ekland-Olson, S. (1980). 'Social Networks and Social Movements: A Microstructural Approach to Differential Recruitment', *American Sociological Review*, 45: 787–801.
Solomon, T. (1983). 'Programming and Deprogramming the "Moonies:" Social Psychology Applied', in Bromley and Richardson (1983): 163–82.

Spickard, P. (ed.) (2005). *Race and Nation: Ethnic Systems in the Modern World*. London: Routledge.
Srinivas, S. (2008). *In the Presence of Sai Baba: Body, City, and Memory in a Global Religious Movement*. Leiden: Brill.
St. John, G. (ed.) (2008). *Victor Tuner and Contemporary Cultural Performance*. New York: Berghahn Books.
Staemmler, B. (2009). *Chinkon Kishin: Mediated Spirit Possession in Japanese New Religions*. (Bunka-Wenhua Tuebingen East Asian Studies 7). Hamburg: LIT Verlag.
Staemmler, B. and Dehn, U. (eds) (2011). *Establishing the Revolutionary: An Introduction to New Religions in Japan*. (Bunka-Wenhua Tuebingen East Asian Studies 20). Hamburg: LIT Verlag.
Stalker, N. (2008). *Prophet Motive: Deguchi Onisaburō, Ōomoto, and the Rise of New Religions in Imperial Japan*. Honolulu: University of Hawaii Press.
Starhawk (1999). *The Spiral Dance: A Rebirth of the Ancient Religion of the Goddess*. San Francisco: HarperCollins.
Stark, R. (1965). 'Psychopathology and Religious Commitment', *Review of Religious Research*, 12: 165–76.
— (1984). 'The Rise of a New World Faith', *Review of Religious Research*, 26: 18–27.
— (1987). 'How New Religions Succeed: A Theoretical Model', in D. G. Bromley and P. Hammond (eds) *The Future of New Religions*. Macon, GA: Mercer University Press: 11–29.
— (1996). 'Why Religious Movements Succeed or Fail: A Revised General Model', *Journal of Contemporary Religion*, 11(2): 133–46.
— (1999). 'Secularization, R.I.P.', *Sociology of Religion*, 60(3): 249–73.
Stark, R. and Bainbridge, W. S. (1979). 'Of Churches, Sects, and Cults: Preliminary Concepts for a Theory of Religious Movements', *Journal for the Scientific Study of Religion*, 18(2): 117–33.
— (1980). 'Networks of Faith: Interpersonal Bonds and Recruitment to Cults and Sects', *American Journal of Sociology*, 85: 1376–95.
— (1985). *The Future of Religion: Secularization, Revival, and Cult Formation*. Berkeley: University of California Press.
— (1987/1996). *A Theory of Religion*. New Brunswick, NJ: Rutgers University Press.
Stark, R. and Finke, R. (2000). *Acts of Faith: Explaining the Human Side of Religion*. Berkeley: University of California Press.
Stark, R., Bainbridge, W. S. and Kent, L. (1981). 'Cult Membership in the Roaring Twenties: Assessing Local Receptivity', *Sociological Analysis*, 41(2): 137–62.
Stark, R., Finke, R. and Iannaccone, L. E. (1995). 'Pluralism and Piety: England and Wales, 1851', *Journal for the Scientific Study of Religion*, 34(4): 431–44.
Steger, M. B. (2009). *Globalization: A Very Short Introduction*. Oxford: Oxford University Press.
Stein, S. (2003). *Communities of Dissent: A History of Alternative Religions in America*. Oxford: Oxford University Press.
Stephenson, D. (2005). *Dear People: Remembering Jonestown*. San Francisco: California Historical Society Press and Heydey Books.
Stewart, C. and Shaw, R. (eds) (1994). *Syncretism/Anti-Syncretism: The Politics of Religious Synthesis*. London: Routledge.
Stone, J. and Dennis, R. (eds) (2003). *Race and Ethnicity: Comparative and Theoretical Approaches*. Oxford: Blackwell.
Stone, J. R. (2011). 'The Festinger Theory on Failed Prophecy and Dissonance: A Survey and Critique', in Tumminia and Swatos (2011): 41–68.
Stone, J. R. (ed.) (2000). *Expecting Armageddon: Essential Readings in Failed Prophecy*. London: Routledge.

Stoner, C. and Parke, J. A. (1977). *All God's Children: The Cult Experience – Salvation or Slavery?* New York: Penguin.

Stout, D. and Scott, D. (2003). 'Mormons and Media Literacy: Exploring the Dynamics of Religious Media Education', in J. Mitchell and S. Marriage (eds) *Mediating Religion*. London: T&T Clark: 143–57.

Straus, R. (1976). 'Changing Oneself: Seekers and the Creative Transformation of Life Experience', in J. Lofland (ed.) *Doing Social Life*. New York, NY: John Wiley & Sons: 252–72.

— (1979). 'Religious Conversion and as a Personal and Collective Accomplishment', *Sociological Analysis*, 40: 158–65.

Streiker, L. D. (1984). *Mind-bending: Brainwashing, Cults, and Deprogramming in the '80s*. Garden City, NY: Doubleday.

Strieber, W. (1987). *Communion: A True Story of Encounters with the Unknown*. London: Century.

Strmiska, M. F. (2005). *Modern Paganism in World Cultures*. Santa Barbara: ABC-CLIO.

Strozier, C. B. (1994). *Apocalypse: The Psychology of Fundamentalism in America*. Boston: Beacon.

Strozier, C. B. and Flynn, M. (eds) (1997). *The Year 2000: Essays on the End*. New York: New York University Press.

Strozier, C. B., Terman, D. M., Jones, J. W. and Boyd, K. A. (eds) (2010). *The Fundamentalist Mindset*. Oxford: Oxford University Press.

Stupple, D. (1984). 'Mahatmas and Space Brothers: The Ideologies of Alleged Contact with Mahatmas and Space Brothers: The Ideologies of Alleged Contact with Extraterrestrials', *Journal of American Culture*, 7: 131–9.

Sundkler, B. G. M. (1948). *Bantu Prophets in South Africa*. Oxford: Oxford University Press.

— (1976). *Zulu Zion and Some Swazi Zionists*. Oxford: Oxford University Press.

Sunstone (2012). 'Where do Questioning Mormons Go?', *Sunstone: Mormon Experience, Scholarship, Issues and Art*, 167 (June): 63.

Sutcliffe, S. (2003a). *Children of the New Age: A History of Spiritual Practices*. London: Routledge.

— (2003b). 'Category Formation and the History of "New Age"', *Culture and Religion*, 4(1): 5–29.

Sutcliffe, S. and. Gilhus, I. S (eds) (2013). *New Age Spirituality: Rethinking Religion*. Sheffield, UK: Equinox.

Szubin, A., Jensen III, C. J. and Gregg, R. (2000). 'Interacting with "Cults": A Policing Model', *The FBI Law Enforcement Bulletin*, 69: 16–24.

Tabor, J. D. and Gallagher, E. V. (1995/1997). *Why Waco?* Berkeley: University of California Press.

Takagi, H. (1958). *Shinkō Shūkyō: Taishū o Miryō suru Mono*. [Tokyo?]: Mirion Bukkusu.

Talmon, Y. (1966). 'Millenarian Movements', *Archieves Européènes de Sociologie*, 7: 159–200.

Tamura, D. and Tamura, T. (2011). 'Reflexive Self-identification of Internet Users and the Authority of Sōka Gakkai: Analysis of Discourse in a Japanese BBS', in Baffelli, Reader and Staemmler (2011): 173–95.

Tayob, A. (1995). *Islamic Resurgence in South Africa. The Muslim Youth Movement*. Cape Town: University of Cape Town Press.

Thomsen, H. (1963). *The New Religions of Japan*. Tokyo: Charles E. Tuttle.

Thornton, P. M. (2003). 'The New Cybersects: Resistance and Repression in the Reform Era', in E. J. Perry and M. Selden (eds) *Chinese Society: Change, Conflict and Resistance*. London: Routledge: 251–75.

Thrash, C. (H.) as told to Towne, M. K. (1995). *The Onliest One Alive: Surviving Jonestown, Guyana*. Indianapolis: Marian K. Towne.

Tiryakian, E. A. (1974). 'Towards the Sociology of Esoteric Culture', in Tiryakian (1974): 257–80.
Tiryakian, E. A. (ed.) (1974). *On the Margins of the Visible: Sociology, the Esoteric, and the Occult*. New York, NY: John Wiley & Sons.
Trimingham, J. S. (1968). *The Influence of Islam upon Africa*. London: Longmans.
Troeltsch, E. (1931). *The Social Teachings of the Christian Churches and Groups*, trans. Olive Wyon. London: Allen and Unwin.
— (1931/1992). *The Social Teaching of the Christian Churches*. 2 vols. Louisville, KY: Westminster John Knox Press.
Trompf, G. (1990). *Cargo Cults and Millenarian Movements in Melanesia: Transoceanic Comparisons of New Religious Movements*. Berlin: Mouton de Gruyter.
Truzzi, M. (1974). 'Definition and Dimensions of the Occult: Towards a Sociological Perspective', in Tiryakian (1974): 243–55.
Tumminia, D. G. (1998). 'How Prophecy Never Fails: Interpretive Reason in a Flying-saucer Group', *Sociology of Religion*, 59(2) (Summer): 157–70.
— (2005). *When Prophecy Never Fails: Myth and Reality in a Flying Saucer Group*. Oxford: Oxford University Press.
Tumminia, D. G. (ed.) (2007). *Alien Worlds: Social and Religious Dimensions of Extraterrestrial Contact*. Syracuse: Syracuse University Press.
Tumminia, D. G. and Swatos, W. H., Jr. (eds) (2011). *How Prophecy Lives*. Leiden: Brill.
Turner, E. L. B. (2005). *Among the Healers: Stories of Spiritual and Ritual Healing Around the World*. Westport, CT: Praeger.
Turner, H. W. (1967a). 'A Typology for African Religious Movements', *Journal of Religion in Africa*, 1(1): 1–34.
— (1967b). *History of an Independent Church: The Church of the Lord Aladura*. 2 vols. Oxford: Oxford University Press.
— (1977). *Bibliography of New Religious Movements in Primal Societies. Black Africa*. Boston: G.K. Hall.
— (1979). *Religious Innovation in Africa: Collected Essays on New Religious Movements*. Boston: G. K. Hall.
— (1993). 'New Religious Movements in Islamic West Africa', *Islam and Christian-Muslim Relations*, 4(1): 3–35.
Turner, H. W. and Mitchell, R. C. (1967). *A Comprehensive Bibliography of Modern African Religious Movements*. Evanston, IL: Northwestern University Press.
Turner, V. (1969). *The Ritual Process: Structure and Anti-Structure*. Ithaca, NY: Cornell University Press.
— (1974). *Dramas, Fields and Metaphors: Symbolic Action in Human Society*. Ithaca, NY: Cornell University Press.
— (1982). *From Ritual to Theatre: The Human Seriousness of Play*. New York: PAJ Publications.
Turner, V. and Turner, E. (1978). *Image and Pilgrimage in Christian Culture*. New York: Columbia University Press.
Twesigye, E. K. (2010). *Religion, Politics and Cults in East Africa*. Frankfurt a/M: Peter Lang.
Tylor, E. B. (1903). *Primitive Culture: Researches into the Development of Mythology, Philosophy, Religion, Language, Art, and Custom*. London: John Murray.
Unsigned. 'Race' (2003), in G. Bolaffi, R. Bracalenti, P. Braham and S. Gindro (eds) *Dictionary of Race, Ethnicity and Culture*. Thousand Oaks, CA: Sage: 239–45.
Urban, H. B. (2011). 'The Devil at Heaven's Gate: Rethinking the Study of Religion in the Age of Cyberspace', in Chryssides (2011): 105–38.
Urmila Dasi. (2012). 'What is ISKCON? Who is a Member of ISKCON?' ISKCON News. Available at http://new.iskcon.com/node/4161(accessed 14 June 2012).

Bibliography

Vale, V. and Sulak, J. (2001). *Modern Pagans: An Investigation of Contemporary Pagan Practices*. San Francisco: RE/Search Publications.
Vallee, J. (2007). 'Consciousness, Culture and UFOs', in Tumminia (2007): 193–209.
Van Gennep, A. (1960). *The Rites of Passage*, trans. Monika B. Vizedom and Gabrielle L. Caffee. Chicago: University of Chicago Press.
Vance, L. (1999). *Seventh-day Adventism in Crisis: Gender and Sectarian Change in an Emerging Religion*. Urbana: University of Illinois Press.
— (2008). 'Converging on the Heterosexual Dyad: Changing Mormon and Adventist Sexual Norms and Implications for Gay and Lesbian Adherents', *Nova Religio*, 11: 56–76.
Verter, B. (2003). 'Spiritual Capital: Theorizing Religion with Bourdieu against Bourdieu', *Sociological Theory*, 21(2): 150–74.
Vickers, L. (2010). 'Religious Discrimination in the Workplace: An Emerging Hierarchy?' *Ecclesiastical Law Journal*, 12(2): 280–303.
— (2011). 'Promoting Equality or Fostering Resentment? The Public Sector Equality Duty and Religion or Belief', *Legal Studies*, 30(1): 135–58.
Vikor, K. (2000). 'Sufi Brotherhoods in Africa', in N. Levtzion and R. L. Powels (eds) *The History of Islam in Africa*. Athens: Ohio University Press: 441–76.
Voas, D. and Crockett, A. (2005). 'Religion in Britain: Neither Believing nor Belonging', *Sociology*, 39(1): 11–28.
Voegelin, E. (2000). *The Collected Works of Eric Voegelin, vol. 5, Modernity without Restraint: The Political Religions; The New Science of Politics; and Science, Politics, and Gnosticism*. Columbia, MO: University of Missouri Press.
von Stuckrad, K. (2005a). 'Western Esotericism: Towards an Integrative Model of Interpretation', *Religion*, 35(2): 78–97.
— (2005b). *Western Esotericism: A Brief History of Secret Knowledge*. Sheffield, UK: Equinox.
— (2010). *Locations of Knowledge in Medieval and Early Modern Europe: Esoteric Discourse and Western Identities*. Leiden: Brill.
Wagner-Wilson, L. (2009). *Slavery of Faith*. New York: iUniverse.
Wallace, A. F. C. (1956). 'Revitalization Movements', *American Anthropologist*, 58(2) (April): 264–81.
— (2004). *Apocalyptic Trajectories: Millenarianism and Violence in the Contemporary World*. Frankfurt a/M: Peter Lang.
— (2006). 'Charisma, Volatility and Violence: Assessing the Role of Crises of Charismatic Authority in Precipitating Incidents of Millenarian Violence', in T. Ahlbäck (ed.) *Exercising Religion: The Role of Religions in Concord and Conflict*. Åbo, Finland: The Donner Institute for Research in Religious and Cultural History: 77–94.
Wallis, R. (1974). 'Ideology, Authority, and the Development of Cultic Movements', *Social Research*, 41(2): 299–327.
— (1976). *The Road to Total Freedom: A Sociological Analysis of Scientology*. London: Heinemann.
— (1984). *The Elementary Forms of the New Religious Life*. London: Routledge.
— (1988). 'Paradoxes of Freedom and Regulation: The Case of New Religious Movements in Britain and America', *Sociological Analysis*, 48(4): 355–71.
Walliss, J. (2004). *Apocalyptic Trajectories: Millennialism and Violence in the Contemporary World*. Frankfurt a/M: Peter Lang.
Walliss, J. and Quinby, L. (2010). *Reel Revelations: Apocalypse and Film*. Sheffield: Sheffield Phoenix Press.
Walls, A. F. and Shenk, W. F. (eds) (1990). *Exploring New Religious Movements*. Elkhart: Mission Focus.
Wamue, G. N. (2001). 'Revisiting our Indigenous Shrines through Mungiki', in *African Affairs*, 100: 453–67.

Warburg, M. (2005). 'Introduction', in Warburg, Hvithamar and Warmind (2005): 7–14.— (2006). *Citizens of the World: A History and Sociology of the Bahá'is from a Globalisation Perspective.* Leiden: Brill.
— (2008). 'Religion and Globalisation, or Globalisation and Religion', in Geertz and Warburg (2008): 43–59.
Warburg, M., Hvithamar, A. and Warmind, M. (eds) (2005). *Bahá'i and Globalisation.* Aarhus: Aarhus University Press.
Warner, M. (2004). 'Memoirs of a Pentecostal Boyhood', in S. Bruhm (ed.) *Curiouser: On The Queerness of Children.* Minneapolis: University of Minnesota Press.
Warner, S. R. and Wittner, J. G. (eds) (1998). *Gatherings in Diaspora: Religious Communities and the New Immigration.* Philadelphia: Temple University Press.
Washington, P. (1993). *Madame Blavatsky's Baboon: Theosophy and the Emergence of the Western Guru.* London: Secker & Warburg.
Wasserstrom, S. M. (1999). *Religion after Religion: Gershom Scholem, Mircea Eliade, and Henry Corbin at Eranos.* Princeton, NJ: Princeton University Press.
Watanabe, M. (2007). *Gendai Nihon Shinshūkyō-ron: Nyūshin Katei to Jikō Keisei no Shiten kara.* Tokyo: Ochanomizu Shobō.
Waterhouse, H. (2002). 'Insider/Outsider Perspectives on Ritual in Sōka Gakkai International–UK', in Arweck and Stringer (2002): 57–75.
Weber, M. (1958). 'The Three Types of Legitimate Rule', *Berkeley Publications in Society and Institutions*, 4(1): 1–11, trans. Hans Gerth.
— (1963). *The Sociology of Religion.* Boston: Beacon.
— (1964). *The Theory of Social and Economic Organization*, trans. A. M. Henderson and T. Parsons. New York: Free Press.
Weber, M. and Parsons, T. (ed. and trans.) (1947). *The Theory of Social and Economic Organization.* New York: Free Press.
Webster, J. B. (1964). *The African Churches among the Yoruba 1888–1922.* Oxford: Oxford University Press.
Weiser, N. (1974). 'The Effects of Prophetic Disconfirmation of the Committed', *Review of Religious Research*, 16(1) (Fall): 19–30.
Welbourn, F. B. (1961). *East African Rebels: A Study of Some Independent Churches.* London: SCM Press.
Welbourn, F. B. and Ogot, B. A. (1966). *A Place to Feel at Home: A Study of Independent Churches in Western Kenya.* Oxford: Oxford University Press.
Welch, C. (2007). 'Complicating Spiritual Appropriation: North American Indian Agency in Western Alternative Spiritual Practice', *Journal of New Age & Alternative Spiritualities*, 3: 97–117.
Wessinger, C. (1997). 'Millennialism with and without the Mayhem', in Robbins and Palmer (1997): 47–59.
— (1999). 'Religious Studies Scholars, FBI Agents, and the Montana Freemen Standoff', *Nova Religio*, 3: 36–44.
— (2000a). *How the Millennium Comes Violently: From Jonestown to Heaven's Gate.* New York: Seven Bridges Press.
— (2006). 'New Religious Movements and Violence', in Gallagher and Ashcraft (2006), vol. 1: 165–205.
Wessinger, C. (ed.) (2000). *Millennialism, Persecution and Violence: Historical Cases.* Syracuse: Syracuse University Press.
— (2011). *The Oxford Handbook of Millennialism.* Oxford: Oxford University Press.
West, M. (1975). *Bishops and Prophets in a Black City. African Independent Churches in Soweto, Johannesburg.* Cape Town: David Philip.
Westermann, C. (1967). *Basic Forms of Prophetic Speech*, trans. H. C. White. Philadelphia: Westminster Press.

Whitehead, H. (1987). *Renunciation and Reformulation: A Study of Conversion in an American Sect*. Ithaca, NY: Cornell University Press.

Wieczorek, D., Feirman, S. and Sims III, J. (2000–1). 'Arbitration Train Runs Out of Track', *Franchise Law Journal*, 20: 84–97.

Wieczorek, I. (2002). *Neue Religiöse Bewegungen in Japan: Eine Empirische Studie zum Gesellschaftspolitischen Engagement in der Japanischen Bevölkerung*. Hamburg: Institut für Asienkunde.

Wilcox, M. (2006). 'Same-sex Eroticism and Gender Fluidity in New and Alternative Religions', in Gallagher and Ashcraft (2006), vol. 1: 243–65.

William H. C. (1969). Book Review: Barrett, D. B., *Schism and Renewal in Africa. An Analysis of Six Thousand Contemporary Religious Movements*. Oxford: Oxford University Press, 1968. In *The Journal of Modern African Studies*, 7(2): 359–61.

Williamson, L. (2010). *Transcendent in America: Hindu-Inspired Meditation Movements as New Religion*. New York: New York University Press.

Wilson, B. R. (1990). *The Social Dimensions of Sectarianism: Sects and New Religious Movements in Contemporary Society*. Oxford: Clarendon Press.

— (1998). 'The Sociologist of Religion as Expert Witness', *Swiss Journal of Sociology*, 24(1): 17–27.

Wilson, R. R. (1980). *Prophecy and Society in Ancient Israel*. Philadelphia: Fortress Press.

Wilson, W. A. (1975). 'The Vanishing Hitchhiker among the Mormons', *Indiana Folklore*, 8(1): 80–97.

Wöhr, U. (1989). *Frauen und Neue Religionen: Die Religionsgründerinnen Nakayama Miki und Deguchi Nao*. (Beiträge zur Japanologie 27). Wien: Institut für Japanologie.

Wojcik, D. (1997). *The End of the World as We Know It: Faith, Fatalism, and Apocalypse in America*. New York: New York University Press.

— (2003). 'Apocalyptic and Millenarian Aspects of American UFOism', in Partridge (2003): 274–300.

Wood, M. (2007). *Possession, Power and the New Age: Ambiguities of Authority in Neoliberal Societies*. Aldershot: Ashgate.

Worsley, P. (1968). *The Trumpet Shall Sound: A Study of 'Cargo Cults' in Melanesia*. New York: Schocken.

Wright S. A. (1987). *Leaving Cults: The Dynamics of Defection*. Washington, DC: The Society for the Scientific Study of Religion.

— (2007). *Patriots, Politics, and the Oklahoma City Bombing*. Cambridge: Cambridge University Press.

— (2009). 'Reframing Religious Violence After 9/11: Analysis of the ACM Campaign to Exploit the Threat of Terrorism', *Nova Religio*, 12(4): 5–27.

Wright, S. A. (ed.) (1995). *Armageddon at Waco: Critical Perspectives on the Branch Davidian Conflict*. Chicago: University of Chicago Press.

Wright, S. A. and Richardson, J. T. (2011). *Saints Under Siege: The Texas State Raid on the Fundamentalist Latter Day Saints*. Albany: State University of New York Press.

Wuthnow, R. (1976). *The Consciousness Reformation*. Berkeley: University of California Press.

Yang, F. (1999). *Chinese Christians in America*. University Park, PA: Pennsylvania State University Press.

Yates, F. A. (1964/2002). *Giordano Bruno and the Hermetic Tradition*. London: Routledge.

Yoder, D. (1974). 'Toward a Definition of Folk Religion', *Western Folklore*, 33(1): 2–15.

York, M. (1995). *The Emerging Network: A Sociology of the New Age and Neo-Pagan Movements*. Lanham, MD: Rowman & Littlefield.

Zablocki, B. and Robbins, T. (eds) (2001). *Misunderstanding Cults*. Toronto: University of Toronto Press.

Zaidman-Dvir, N. and Sharot, S. (1992). 'The Response of Israeli Society to New Religious Movements: ISKCON and Teshuvah', *Journal for the Scientific Study of Religion*, 31(3): 279–95.

Zell-Ravenheart, O. (2009). 'TheaGenesis: The Birth of the Goddess', in O. Zell-Ravenheart (ed.) *Green Egg Omelette: An Anthology of Art and Articles from the Legendary Pagan Journal*. Franklin Lakes, NJ: New Page Books: 90–5.

Zeller, B. E. (2006). 'Scaling Heaven's Gate: Individualism and Salvation in a New Religious Movement', *Nova Religio*, 10: 75–102.

— (2009). 'Apocalyptic Thought in UFO-based Religions', in Kinane and Ryan (2009): 328–48.

— (2010). *Prophets and Protons: New Religious Movements and Science in Late-Twentieth Century America*. New York: New York University Press.

— (2011a). 'New Religious Movements and Science', *Nova Religio*, 14: 4–10.

— (2011b). 'Science and Social Identity Marker', *Nova Religio*, 14: 30–53.

— (2012a). 'Food Practices, Culture, and Social Dynamics in the Hare Krishna Movement', in Cusack and Norman (2012): 681–702.

— (2012b). 'Heaven's Gate, Science Fiction Religions, and Popular American Culture', in A. Possamia (ed.) *Handbook on Hyper-Real Religions*. Leiden: Brill.

Zeller, B. E., Dallam, M. W., Neilson, R. L. and Rubel, N. L. (eds) (2014). *Religion, Food, and Eating in North America*. New York: Columbia University Press.

Zellner, W. W. and Petrowsky, M. (eds) (1998). *Sects, Cults, and Spiritual Communities: A Sociological Analysis*. Westport, CT: Praeger.

Zerby, K. [Maria] and Kelly, S. [Peter Amsterdam] (2009). 'The Future of The Family International: Establishing a Culture of Innovation and Progress'. Presented at the Conference of the Center for Studies on New Religious Movements (CESNUR), Salt Lake City, Utah (June).

Znamenski, A. A. (2007). *The Beauty of the Primitive: Shamanism and the Western Imagination*. Oxford: Oxford University Press.

Zygmunt, J. F. (1970). 'Prophetic Failure and Chiliastic Identity: The Case of Jehovah's Witnesses', *American Journal of Sociology*, 75, 926–48.

— (1972). 'When Prophecies Fail: A Theoretical Perspective on the Comparative Evidence', *American Behavioral Scientist*, 16(2) (November–December): 245–68.

Index

Aagaard, Johannes 9, 11, 169, 176
About-Picard Law 173
abuse 59, 60, 152, 164, 167, 174, 177, 200, 205, 302, 303, 319
Adejobi, Adeleke 9
Adler, Margot 37, 203, 204, 361
Adventism 2, 14, 19, 20, 59, 151, 164, 166, 203, 307, 326, 328, 331, 332, 339, 346, 355 *see also* Seventh-day Adventism
Aetherius Society 211, 213–15, 359
Africa 121, 131, 137, 235–51, 299, 304, 310, 314, 350
African Independent/Initiated Churches 9, 236, 238, 239, 240, 241, 242, 243
Afrikania Mission 247
agnosticism 26, 166
AIDS 310
Al Qaeda 19
Aladura movement 9, 238, 241, 357 *see also* Church of the Lord Aladura
Albanese, Catherine 308, 310, 339, 350
alchemy 226, 229
alcohol 78, 97, 307
American Academy of Religion 12, 38, 87, 147, 361, 363
American Family Foundation 8, 171, 361, 363
Amish 173, 298, 304, 320, 341
Ammachi 105, 109
amulets 36, 39
angels 43, 49, 130, 138, 224
animism 39, 40, 311, 312
Anthony, Dick 7, 75, 97–100, 146
anthropology 2, 15, 27, 29, 33, 35, 37, 37, 50, 67, 121, 126, 228, 239, 255, 260, 309

anti-cult movement 4, 7, 10, 19, 30, 31, 56, 59, 62, 63, 73, 75, 76, 92, 99, 141, 150, 162, 163–78, 205, 303, 319, 322, 323, 352, 360
apocalypticism 20, 58, 127, 135–43, 145–8, 150, 152–3, 154, 216–20, 258, 281, 322, 325, 327, 337
apostasy 6, 27, 32, 74, 157, 167, 286, 346
Appadurai, Arjun 274
apparitionists 105, 112 *see also* Marian apparitions
Applewhite, Marshall Herff 5, 20, 113, 154, 159–61, 213, 217–19, 362, 368
Applied Metaphysics (IAM) 201
archaeology 33, 49
Areopagus 9
Arnold, Kenneth 209–11
art 34, 74, 83, 84, 87, 88, 108, 264, 283
Arweck, Elisabeth 26, 30, 31
Asahara, Shoko 55, 130, 142, 153, 154, 158, 161, 162, 337, 361
ascended masters 113, 130, 138, 152, 211, 212, 213, 220
asceticism 53
astrology 226, 229
ATF 8, 62, 141, 143, 149, 152, 162
Athanasius 1
atheism 215, 327
Atkins, Gaius Glenn 2
attrition 92
Augustine 1
Aum Shinrikyō 4, 19, 54–6, 130, 142, 143, 145, 146, 151, 153, 154, 158, 160, 162, 171, 179, 308, 325, 337, 361, 362
authenticity 9, 21, 47, 49, 68, 69, 164, 232, 256, 291, 293, 315, 316, 318, 327

415

Index

authority 16, 83, 95, 103, 104, 105, 110–14, 116, 122, 132, 135, 143, 175, 203, 204, 259, 282, 291, 306, 311, 315, 320, 330, 331, 332, 346–9

Bach, Marcus 2
Bahá'í 19, 33, 275, 286, 314, 331, 332, 341, 342, 355, 356, 358
Bainbridge, W. S. 13, 16, 17, 91, 130, 174, 228, 302, 303, 321, 322, 348
Baird, Laura 84
Bakhtin, Mikhail 74, 82–6
Balch, Robert W. 5, 6, 26, 27, 30, 114, 127, 217, 218
Ballard, Guy 129, 210, 211, 213, 357
Barker, Eileen xvii, 7, 8, 10, 12, 14, 25, 26, 27, 58, 93, 96, 178, 285, 301, 305, 306, 323, 345
Barkun, Michael 119, 120, 123, 137, 146
Barrett, David 28, 240, 241
Baudrillard, Jean 292
Beauvoir, Simone de 198
Becker, Howard 4, 5, 92, 98, 310, 321
Beckford, James 7, 32, 89, 91, 92, 93, 96, 275, 302, 323, 332, 333, 339
Bednarowski, Mary Farrell 199, 201, 202, 203, 206
Bell, Catherine 69
Bellah, Robert N. 11, 339
Bennett, Gillian 257
Berg, Moses David 108, 111–13, 186, 359
Berg, Philip 307
Berger, Peter 17, 30, 38, 103
Besant, Annie 212, 356
Beverley, James A. 9
Beyer, Peter 273–4, 276–7
Bible 2, 9, 110, 120, 131, 132, 138, 141, 147, 164, 166, 209, 216, 243, 279, 327, 328, 339, 341, 347, 351, 356, 357, 358, 359, 368
Bible Students *see* Jehovah's Witnesses
biblical inerrancy 328
biblical studies 2, 4, 126, 132
Black Messiahs 14, 325
Blavatsky, Helena Petrovna 2, 129, 130, 138, 211, 212, 315, 347, 355, 356
blood transfusions 185, 186, 307
bodhisattvas 333, 335
Boisselier, Brigitte 115, 279
Book of Genesis 215–17
Book of Mormon 21, 258, 291, 314, 347, 355

Book of Revelation 110, 119, 134, 135, 154, 217, 218, 337
Boyer, Paul 138, 165
Braden, Marcia 126
Braden, Charles S. 308
brainwashing 4, 6, 7, 8, 10, 27, 32, 63, 73–4, 75, 80, 89–101, 141, 156, 163, 169, 170, 173, 177, 302, 303, 323
Branch Davidians 19, 20, 59, 62, 75, 76, 108, 110, 111, 114, 133, 141–4, 146, 150–2, 158, 162, 174, 303, 320, 329
Brandou, Andrew 83, 84
Brigham Young University 11, 48, 257, 258
British-Israel 164
Bromley, David G. 16, 25, 67, 75, 76, 89, 99, 103, 107, 110, 134, 143, 149, 150, 156, 157, 162, 176, 302, 366
Brown, Candy Gunther 309, 311
Brown, John Elward 166
Brown, Karen McCarthy 31, 312
Brownsville Revival 115
Bruce, Steve 17, 176, 348
Buddhism 3, 5, 29, 30, 53, 54, 79, 140, 153, 169, 173, 243, 276, 277, 287, 291, 298, 307, 311, 315, 316, 323, 327–31, 333–5, 337, 339, 340, 341, 344, 349, 351, 359, 363
Butler, Judith 57, 196
Bynum, Caroline Walker 197

Calvary Chapel 111, 112
Campbell, C. 44, 222, 316
Campbell, H. 28, 289
Camping, Harold 111, 114, 119, 120, 131
Canada 18, 152, 153, 160, 168, 342, 359
Candomblé 250, 312, 314, 350
capitalism 44, 137, 338
Carey, George 190
cargo cults 9, 137, 238
Catholic Truth Society 12, 175, 361
celibacy 57, 58, 113, 204, 345
Centre for New Religious Movements 9, 10, 242
CESNUR xvii, 10, 178, 361, 365
Champollion, Claire 170
Champollion, Guy 170
channelling 105, 106, 110, 112, 121, 123, 129, 155, 205, 212–15, 291, 337, 346, 347, 358, 360, 361
Chaos Magic 293

charisma 19, 103–17, 122, 123, 131, 142, 143, 152, 236, 243, 307, 311, 320, 331, 332
charismatic leadership 59, 103–16, 123, 131, 156, 160, 161, 320, 330
Charles, Brian 265, 266
chatrooms 28
Chen Tao 142, 157
Chick Publications 165
Chidester, David 58, 75, 150, 292
children 6, 59, 73, 74, 79, 83, 84, 115, 137, 138, 144, 151–3, 157, 158, 162, 174, 181–7, 191–3, 205, 261, 301–6
  child abuse 152, 158, 174, 302, 303, 304
Children of God *see* The Family International
China 98, 100, 101, 139, 144, 145, 286
Christ, Carol 38, 204
Christadelphians 323, 327, 355
Christian Countercult Movement 8
Christian Identity 20, 137, 243, 296, 309
Christian Science 2, 164, 165, 166, 280, 308, 321, 347
Christianity 1, 3, 5, 8, 9, 11, 12, 19, 38, 44, 47, 49, 53, 54, 134, 138, 147, 163, 164, 167, 169, 170, 228, 235, 236, 237, 238, 243, 244, 247, 248, 249, 254, 276, 280, 291, 296, 311, 315, 327, 331, 334, 340, 344, 349, 350, 352, 356, 358
Chryssides, George D. 26, 105, 147
Church of All Worlds 292–4
Church of Satan 11, 111, 114, 358
Church of the Lord Aladura 9, 241, 242
Church of the SubGenius 292–3
Church Universal and Triumphant 130, 320, 347, 358, 363
cisgender 195, 198, 203
Citizens Freedom Foundation 8, 172
civil partnership 190
Clark, Elmer T. 2
Clarke, John 8, 171, 183
Clarke, Peter 10, 298
Clifton, Chas 38
Clonaid 115, 279–80
clothing 34, 110, 218, 260, 283
cognitive contamination 30
cognitive dissonance 26, 123, 127, 213, 218
Cohn, Norman 120, 135–7, 140, 159
Cold War xviii, 213, 258
colonialism 44, 85, 137, 237–9, 248, 250, 350
communalism 305, 320, 321, 338

communism 98, 99, 139, 144, 145, 175, 342
Community of Christ 48
Confucianism 53
conversion 6, 9, 11, 13, 19, 26, 75, 89–101, 107, 110, 112, 113, 125, 167, 175, 177, 200, 238, 244, 249, 285, 287, 299, 301, 306, 322–6, 344, 345
Cottrell, Richard 10, 172
Council of Europe 173
countercult movement 3, 4, 9, 10, 12, 31, 175, 286, 322
counterculture 3, 25, 42, 45, 59, 68, 73, 106, 107, 111, 165, 178, 302, 308, 320–1, 338, 339, 341, 351
covert research 5, 26–8, 30
Cowan, Douglas 62, 67, 146, 148, 176, 285, 286, 288
Cracknell, Kenneth 176
Creswell, Jamie 177
Culpepper, Emily 198–200, 202, 204–6
cult apologists 8, 177, 333
Cult Awareness Network 8, 172, 361, 362, 367
Cult Information Centre 171
cultic milieu 44
Cultic Studies Review 8, 171
cults 2–5, 7–10, 15, 16, 20, 29, 32, 54, 56, 57, 62–5, 73–9, 82, 86–8, 90, 97, 99, 127, 137, 141–5, 149, 150, 151, 153, 156, 158–60, 162, 165–7, 169–78, 222, 237, 238, 266, 302, 303, 308, 310, 312, 321–3, 333, 346, 348, 361, 362, 367, 368
  client and audience cults 16, 322
  cult apologists xix, 8, 176, 177, 286, 333
  cult/sect typology 5, 15–16, 321–2
  destructive cults 32, 322
  doomsday cult 322, 358
  marks of 7, 170, 177
custody 181, 183, 184, 186, 187, 303
cyber-religion 20, 351

D'Aguiar, Fred 85
Daly, Mary 204
Däniken, Erich von 208, 215, 216, 220, 359
Darby, J. N. 138
Davidsen, Marcus A. 294
Davies, Douglas 19, 48, 50
Davies, Horton 164
Davis, Andrew Jackson 130
Dawah movements 246
Dawson, Lorne 57, 59, 91, 96, 127, 156, 158, 222, 285

Index

decoding 64, 65
deconversion 89, 90, 92, 96, 98
demographics 39, 64, 242, 298, 346
denominations 12, 222, 254, 346, 348
depression 77, 78
deprogramming 144, 163, 171, 172, 176, 319, 323
deviance 5, 57, 59, 63, 64, 223
Di Mambro, Joseph 152–3, 160–1
Dialog Center International 9, 169
dialogue 31, 82–7, 123, 169, 176, 202, 268
Dianetics 32, 115, 129, 322, 347, 357, 368
Disciples of Christ 151
disconfirmation 124–8, 158
Discordianis 292–3
disengagement 6, 32, 322–4
Dispensationalism 138, 146, 148
dissonance 124, 125, 126, 127, 128, 129
divination 121, 122, 131, 247
Divine Light Mission 3, 11, 114
Divine Principle 11, 337, 347
Dorman, Benjamin 55, 56, 142
Dragon Rouge 231
dreams 121, 130, 217, 264
drugs 78, 97, 114, 180, 218, 325, 340
Druids 39, 344
Durkheim, Emile 29, 44, 228

ecology 38, 41, 45, 152, 274
ecumenism 11, 166, 169
Eddy, Mary Baker 130, 203, 347, 355
education 3, 4, 64, 168, 169, 170, 171, 178, 245, 294, 342, 351
Eliade, Mircea 29, 230
Eller, Cynthia 198–9, 204, 261
Ellwood, Robert S. 15, 129, 136, 140
emic/etic issues 26, 31, 68, 223, 227, 228, 229
empathy 30–1, 190
endtimes 110–11, 119–21, 124, 148, 152, 153, 155, 337, 345
Enlightenment 39, 361
Enquete Commission 173
environmentalism 159
equality 191, 296
Equality Act 188, 189, 192
Erhard, Werner 108, 110, 360
eschatology, 131, 157, 159, 217, 218, 337
esotericism 15, 37, 38, 39, 42, 67, 152, 208, 213, 221–33, 243, 280, 293, 309, 349
est 108, 110, 360

ethics 25–7, 30, 39, 50, 51, 54, 123, 200, 212, 231, 324, 325
ethnicity 39, 139, 235, 241, 276, 295–9, 312, 326
ethnography 26, 28, 29, 31, 35, 69, 121, 201, 204, 231, 239, 241, 255, 260
Europe 2, 3, 8, 18, 39, 42, 100, 106, 138, 153, 168, 171–4, 249, 250, 254, 256, 261, 262, 264, 265, 266, 267, 277, 304, 315, 342, 356, 357
European Court of Human Rights 190, 192
evangelicalism 3, 4, 8, 9, 165–7, 169, 175
evolution 17, 69, 100, 166, 209, 212, 214, 239, 327
Eweida, Nadia 189–90
Exclusive Brethren 287
ex-members xviii, 27, 31, 32, 63, 74, 77–81, 87, 99, 150, 217, 286, 319, 323, 324
exoticism 2, 228, 326
extraterrestrials 129, 130, 135, 138, 139, 208–16, 279, 282, 328, 336, 343, 345, 347

Facebook 289
Faivre, Antoine 36, 223, 224, 225
Falun Gong 100, 144, 145, 150, 175, 286, 310, 331, 362
Family Action Information and Rescue 8, 170, 177, 178, 360, 367
Family International, The 3, 14, 20, 58, 59, 73, 87, 101, 107, 108, 110, 112, 113, 130, 158, 168, 171, 172, 174, 182–4, 186, 187, 193, 200, 275–7, 302–6, 320, 324, 327, 331, 341, 344, 359, 368
Family Law Reports 181–4, 187
fasting 257, 307
Father Divine 14, 130, 151, 165, 296, 325, 326, 337
Fautré, Willy 174
FBI 8, 75, 141, 144, 146, 149, 152, 158
feminism 37, 38, 50, 159, 196, 198–201, 204, 260, 261
Festinger, Leon 5, 26, 28, 30, 121–9, 358
fieldwork 25–8, 70, 255, 256, 257, 259, 267, 268, 269
film 39, 61, 64, 65, 69, 83, 98, 147, 220, 292, 294
Findhorn 36, 358
Fishman, Robert 7, 99
flirty fishing 58, 101, 176
folklore 37, 220, 255–7, 261, 265, 266, 269
Fondakowski, Leigh 81

418

Food 35, 93, 152, 257, 258, 259, 261, 283, 307, 320, 325, 326
former members *see* ex-members
Fowler, Nancy 112
France 10, 100, 101, 152, 172–3, 177, 216, 288, 308, 311, 342, 357, 361, 362
FREECOG 172, 360
freedom of religion 53, 100, 188, 189, 191
Freemasonry 226
Freud, Sigmund 103, 197
Frisbee, Lonnie 111
fundamentalism 2, 48, 145, 165, 166, 274, 327, 356
Fundamentalist Church of Jesus Christ of Latter-day Saints 48, 58, 59, 158, 174, 298
fundraising 4, 96, 178, 325

Gaia 293, 341, 361
Galanter, Marc 7, 78, 93, 97, 145, 308
Gallagher, Eugene V. 141, 146, 174, 303
Gardner, Gerald 39, 204, 358
Geertz, A. W. 27
gender 37–9, 50, 57, 58, 59, 82, 165, 189, 190, 191, 195–206, 260, 268, 276, 277, 282, 329
genderqueer 197, 198
Gennep, Arnold van 68
Gerber, Lynne 205
Ghost Dance 130, 137
Giddens, Anthony 276
Gillespie, Carmen 85–6
Gillick competence 185–6
Glassie, Henry 33, 257
Glastonbury 36, 257, 260–8, 317, 357, 360
globalization 17, 37, 228, 236, 268, 273–8, 299, 310, 311, 339
Glock, Charles 10, 11, 338, 339
gnosis 224
Goddess 38, 39, 199, 200, 201, 204, 260–7, 292, 293, 317, 328, 329, 360
Goffman, E. 27
Goldberg, Marion S. 175
Goodrick-Clarke, Nicholas 140, 227
Gordon, David 30
Graduate Theological Union 10, 361
Graham-Scott, Gini 229
Great White Brotherhood 336
Grimes, Ronald 68–9
Gurdjieff, G. I. 315, 357, 358
Guru Maharaji 3, 114

gurus 5, 65, 73, 74, 98, 114, 116, 120, 142, 168, 307, 329, 330, 340, 351

Hadden, Jeffrey 62, 65, 366
hagiography 110–11
Hale, Lady 191–2
Hall, John 141, 142, 148, 150, 161, 162
Hall, Stuart 62–5, 75, 76, 106
Hammond, Philip 297, 349
Hanegraaff, Wouter 38, 41, 42, 222–9, 232
Hannerz, Ulf 275, 277
Hansen, Marcus 306
Happy Science 287
Hardyck, Jane 126
Hare Krishnas *see* ISKCON
Harmonious Human Beings 201
Harris, Doug 169
Harris, Wilson 85
Hassan, Steven 7, 169, 170, 172, 367
Hatcher, Chris 77–8, 87
healing 36, 41, 97, 111, 121, 122, 240, 247, 257, 259, 263–6, 277, 307–12, 345
Healthy-Happy-Holy (3HO) 11, 150, 359
Healy, J. P. 27
Heathenry 39, 199
Heaven's Gate 5, 6, 14, 19, 20, 27, 30, 62, 113, 130, 142, 143, 149, 151, 154, 158–62, 178, 217, 218, 280–2, 285, 314, 329, 345, 362, 368
heresy 1, 4, 35, 50, 163–8, 291
Hermeticism 226–7
heteroglossia 82, 83, 86, 87
heteronormativity 57–9
heterosexuality 57, 58, 189, 199
Hexham, Irving 9, 240, 275, 276, 277
Hinduism 3, 15, 67, 107, 243, 291, 311, 321, 327, 328, 329, 330, 333, 334, 335, 340, 341, 344, 349, 350, 351
Hoekema, Anthony A. 2, 166
Holman, John 227
Holy Order of MANS 136
Holy Spirit 109, 241, 311, 349, 358
homosexuality 50, 57, 59, 351
Hoof, Mary Ann van 109
Hoover, Stuart 62
Howell, Vernon *see* Koresh, David
Hubbard, L. Ron 62, 111, 115, 291, 315, 322, 347, 357, 361
Human Potential movement 11, 200
human predicament 344–5
human rights 173–5, 180, 188–90, 192
humanism 166

419

Index

Humphrey, Caroline 69
Hungary 260, 261, 264–7
Hunter, Edward 98
Hunter, James Davison 18, 338
Hutterites 304, 320
Hutton, Ronald 38
Hynek, I. Allen 209

I AM 129, 210–11, 357
ideology 7, 82, 156, 158, 160, 169, 170, 232, 244, 246, 248, 296, 308
India 2, 109, 114, 115, 168, 228, 254, 277, 315, 316, 329, 347, 356, 359
indigenous religions 38, 235–7, 243, 244–9
INFORM 10, 178, 361, 365
initiation 15, 30, 226, 231, 310
insider/outsider issues 29–32, 50
insiders 26, 32, 37, 325
inspiration 115, 122, 129, 131, 241, 246, 262, 265, 266, 291
Institute for the Study of American Religions 11
Institute of American Religion 178
institutionalization 3, 12, 19, 53, 58, 59, 108, 112, 237, 254, 257, 260, 262, 264, 320, 330, 331
Integral Yoga 115, 358
interfaith movement 11, 168, 169, 332, 340
International Churches of Christ 327, 345, 362
International Cultic Studies Association 8, 171, 363, 367
International Journal of Cultic Studies 8, 171
International Society for Krishna Consciousness *see* ISKCON
internet 19, 20, 27, 50, 56, 63, 80, 87, 147, 148, 154, 232, 250, 258, 265, 267, 273, 275, 285–9, 292, 293, 351, 352
intersex 195, 197, 198
interviewing 7, 26, 27, 29, 81, 130, 267
Introvigne, Massimo 10, 42, 100, 178, 305, 306, 310, 365
Irigaray, Luce 197, 198
Irvine, William c. 2, 166
ISKCON 3, 11, 12, 14, 31, 32, 35, 73, 93, 107, 115, 116, 168, 177, 200, 201, 254, 275, 277, 281, 282, 283, 298, 302–7, 315, 320, 325, 326, 329, 331, 333, 335, 341, 343, 344, 345, 347, 358, 360, 367, 368
Islam 19, 48, 134, 137, 140, 163, 169, 178, 196, 235–7, 243–50, 276, 291, 296, 327, 331, 334, 337, 340, 342, 350, 351
Islamism 137, 244
Island Pond 158, 174, 303
isolation 160, 301, 323

Jackson, Michael 279–80
Jacobs, Janet 195, 198–200, 202, 204–6
Jainism 69, 173, 340
James, William 349
Japan 4, 14, 53–6, 106, 138, 140, 142, 145, 153, 171, 179, 254, 274, 275, 287, 299, 310, 323, 340, 342, 357, 361, 362
Jediism 13, 14, 28, 292, 294, 351
Jehovah's Witnesses 2, 5, 14, 20, 21, 30, 63, 91, 140, 147, 164, 166, 168, 169, 179, 183–6, 192, 275, 286, 287, 307, 323, 328, 334, 341–3, 345, 357, 358, 368
Jenkins, Jerry 138, 327
Jesus 2, 3, 11, 20, 36, 47, 48, 59, 78, 93, 97, 101, 108, 109, 111, 124, 132, 135, 138, 146, 158, 163, 176, 180, 213, 216, 218, 220, 257, 258, 291, 307, 314, 327, 334, 336, 337, 340, 342, 347, 357, 359
Jesus Freaks 108
Jesus Movement 93, 97, 101
Jesus People 3, 78
Jewish Identity 11
Jihadism 137, 140, 145, 148, 150
Jones, James W. 138, 140, 145–6
Jones, Jim 6, 74–8, 80, 83, 86, 87, 113, 141, 151, 159, 161, 307, 336
Jones, Kathy 261–2, 265, 267
Jonestown xvii, 6, 73–88, 133, 140–3, 149, 151, 159, 174, 178, 325, 361, 368
Jouret, Luc 152, 160, 161
Judah, J. Stillson 10, 11, 308
Judaism 1, 6, 11, 21, 63, 132, 134, 139–40, 145, 147, 168, 177, 200, 243, 280, 291, 297, 328, 332–4, 336, 340, 345, 347
Judgement Day 119, 120
Jung, Carl 138, 229, 337

Kabbalah 226, 229, 307, 329, 334
Karbe, Klaus 171
karma 2, 166, 211, 214, 215, 333, 344
Katz, David 105, 112, 227
Kelly, Galen 8
Kemetic Orthodoxy 288

420

Kenya 241, 243, 245, 247–9
Khan, Hazrat Inayat 2, 356
Kilbourne, Brock 95–8
King, George 214–15, 359
Kisser Cynthia 8
Kliever, Lonnie D. 294
Knight, J. Z. 105, 108–10, 112, 204, 360, 361
Kōfuku no Kagaku 287
Kohl, Laura 81
Kohut, Heinz 31
Kopimism 28
Korea 3, 5, 6, 9, 98, 106, 169, 258, 276, 337, 350, 357, 358
Korean War 6, 106, 169, 258
Koresh, David 58, 108, 110, 111, 113, 141, 143, 144, 151, 152, 158, 161, 162, 174, 336, 361
Kornfield, Jack 316
Krishna 35, 109, 326
Krishnamurti 2, 356, 357

Ladele, Lillian 189
LaHaye, Tim 138, 327
Laidlaw, James 69
Lalich, Janja 170
Landes, Richard 137, 139, 146–8
Langone, Michael D. 8, 78, 96
Lanternari, Vittorio 137
Latey, J. 181–3, 192
Latter-day Saints xvii, xviii, 2, 5, 14, 19, 21, 47–52, 59, 64, 110, 158, 164–6, 168, 180, 257, 258, 286, 287, 291, 314, 320, 321, 329, 332, 342, 345, 346, 348
LaVey, Anton 111, 114, 358, 359
Leadbeater, Charles 211, 356
Lee, Mother Ann 130, 203
Left Behind 138, 146, 147, 327
legal issues 7, 17, 49, 53, 90, 99, 100, 101, 104, 145, 172, 179–93, 331, 332, 333, 361
legitimacy 21, 110, 116, 143, 185, 227, 280, 281, 282, 331, 332, 333
legitimation 107, 331, 332
Levi-Strauss, Claude 27
Lewis, James R. 8, 121, 139, 144, 149, 150, 156, 182, 282, 291, 332, 346
Lewis, Sarah M. 346
liberation 219, 248, 293, 333, 334, 336, 341
Lifton, Robert Jay 6–8, 145, 169, 170
liminality 68

Lindsey, Hal 138
Linton, Robert 137
literacy 64, 165
living in 5, 29
Lofland, John 5, 11, 13, 26, 30, 91, 93–6, 101, 358
love bombing 95, 176
Love Israel 112, 359
Lovelock, James 341, 361
Lucas, Philip Charles 136
Luhrmann, Tanya 37, 231
Lutheran World Federation 8, 12, 176

McCloud, Sean 59, 63, 332, 333
McFarland, H. Neill 4, 54, 359
McGarry, Molly 203, 205
McGehee, Fielding 78, 79, 368
McPherson, Aimee Semple 130
McVeigh, Brian 55
McVeigh, Timothy 137
magic 37–9, 92, 98, 121–3, 131, 137, 226, 228, 229, 231, 288, 293, 294
Maharishi Mahesh Yogi 168, 329, 358, 359, 363
mainstream religion 5, 6, 8, 21, 25, 48, 58, 59, 61, 63, 64, 135, 142, 149, 154, 159, 160, 169, 170, 173, 196, 201, 203, 205, 223, 236, 237, 294, 298, 302, 307, 324, 334, 344, 348, 351
Malinowski, Bronislaw 27
Marian apparitions 112, 136, 143, 311, 311, 331
Mark-Age, 213, 215
marriage 31, 58, 60, 113, 168, 189, 190, 191, 201, 202, 325
Martin, Dorothy 5
Martin, Walter 3, 5, 167, 169
Marx, Karl 103
Marxism 139, 148, 238
Mary, the Virgin 49, 109, 113, 155, 216, 261, 311, 327
Masada 6
Massey, Doreen 276
material culture 18, 33–6, 39, 257, 259, 260, 261, 262, 263, 264, 266, 268, 269
Matrixism 292, 294, 343
Mayan calendar 120, 148, 363
Mayan prophecy 120, 351
Mayer, Jean-François xvii, 12, 178, 285, 363, 366
media 5, 18, 19, 20, 29, 31, 55, 56, 59, 61–5, 69, 74, 97, 99, 100, 119, 120, 129, 141,

Index

145, 148, 150, 151, 157, 160, 168, 174, 177, 178, 182, 183, 205, 210, 232, 236, 264, 273, 274, 276, 285, 289, 295, 303, 322, 323, 332, 339, 340
medical treatment 164, 185, 186
meditation 67, 264, 281, 307, 316, 322, 333, 334, 335, 340, 349, 361
Melton, Gordon xvii, 8, 11, 14, 15, 16, 37, 67, 76, 116, 128, 134, 143, 149, 150, 157, 162, 178, 182, 210, 211, 277, 304, 310, 359
membership 4, 7, 17, 30, 53, 64, 92, 106, 107, 108, 111, 116, 128, 160, 172, 173, 175, 176, 183, 200, 201, 202, 218, 236, 242, 301, 303, 305, 323, 326, 332, 342, 343
Mesmerism 308
Messianic Community 201
messianism 111, 113, 123, 128, 132, 135, 220, 240, 336, 337
metaphysical 308–10
Methodism 166
methodology 4, 15, 19, 25, 26, 27, 28, 35, 42, 43, 51, 61, 223, 224, 231, 242
Metropolitan Community Church 109, 115
migration 42, 48, 68, 249, 250, 264, 273, 278, 298, 312, 315
millennialism 20, 41, 42, 49, 76, 121, 124, 128, 133–48, 156, 159, 218, 279, 310, 321, 322, 337, 338, 351
Miller, William 120, 128, 131n. 1, 355
mind control 170, 322
Mind, Body, Spirit Festivals 36
missiology 9, 239
missions 2, 3, 9, 109, 113, 123, 131, 212, 218, 219, 239–41, 243, 248, 258, 265, 289, 301, 302, 304, 317, 337, 355
modernity 18, 43, 44, 107, 232, 274, 280, 282, 338, 348
monotheism 53, 328
Montana Freemen 76, 142, 157
Moon, Sun Myung 3, 37, 58, 106, 109, 110, 113, 115, 130, 170, 201, 291, 328, 337, 339, 347, 357, 358, 360, 361, 363, 369
Moonies *see* Unification Church
Moore, Rebecca 6, 73, 75, 79, 82, 85, 141, 164, 293, 315, 368
Moral Re-armament 164
Mormons *see* Latter-day Saints
Movement for the Restoration of the Ten Commandments of God 19, 143, 155, 310, 362

Muhammad 163, 291, 342, 358
Mungiki 247–9
murder 6, 48, 74, 141, 149, 150, 151, 155, 158, 216, 325
mysticism 7, 142, 169, 222, 244, 291, 315, 321, 334, 339, 340, 343, 349, 350
myth 103, 110, 220, 257, 259, 262, 263, 265
mythology 110, 215, 217, 261, 267, 328

Nation of Islam 14, 130, 204, 217, 250, 326, 329
nationalism 53, 56, 296, 338
Native Americans 136, 262, 336, 341
nativist 136, 137, 139, 147
Nature Religions Scholars Network 38
Nazism 136, 139, 140, 145, 147, 148
Needleman, Jacob 10, 75, 361
neopaganism 15, 37, 199–205, 230, 240, 275, 280, 287, 288, 308, 329, 360
Nettles, Bonnie L. 5, 113, 154, 160, 217–19
New Age 33, 36, 38, 41–5, 55, 120, 129, 148, 152, 154, 176, 178, 212, 214, 219, 226, 232, 233, 276, 280, 281, 282, 310–17, 329, 335, 337, 339, 345, 349, 351
New Thought 164, 280, 308, 309, 311, 356
Newport, Kenneth G. C. 143, 144, 147, 148, 150
Niebuhr, Richard 301, 346
Nigeria 9, 10, 241, 243, 244, 245, 246, 247, 249
Nipponzon Myohoji 340
Nordquist, Ted 96
Norman, Ernest 130, 213, 336
North America 10, 11, 37, 42, 53, 85, 124, 137, 201, 202, 250, 277, 356, 357
Nostradamus 153
nuclear family 302
Nuwaubian Nation 27

Oahspe 129
occult 42, 75, 152, 154, 165, 178, 208, 209, 221, 222, 223, 225, 226, 227, 229, 317
occulture 207–20
Olcott, Henry Steel 2, 211, 355
Oneida community 38, 320
Oosthuizen, Gerard 238, 240
orientalism 228
Orthodoxy 21, 177, 228, 254, 288, 298, 338, 363
O'Shea, Teri Buford 81–2
Osho 59, 111–15, 200, 201, 276, 302, 328, 329, 345, 347, 359–62

422

Index

Otto, Rudolf 29
Outsider 19, 26, 29, 84, 85
outsiders 31, 32, 37, 47, 48, 61, 74, 75, 76, 94, 119, 125, 134, 159, 160, 307, 325, 326, 331, 332

Paganism 35, 37, 40, 42, 67, 205, 260, 287, 288, 291, 293, 294, 308, 341, 344, 365, 367, 368
Palmer, Susan 9, 26, 27, 96, 127, 135, 139, 142, 156, 159, 195, 199, 201, 202, 206, 216, 280, 303, 309, 310
paranormal 78, 107, 208, 215, 217
parapsychology 178
participant observation 26–31, 145, 267, 269
Partridge, Christopher 38, 139, 147, 207, 208, 210, 217, 218, 219, 222, 232, 310, 339
patriarchal 27, 49, 58, 59, 199, 202, 203, 204, 205, 329
Patrick, Ted 8, 172
Peace Mission 14, 151, 165, 296, 325, 326
Pentecostalism 126, 151, 164, 236, 243, 311, 344, 356, 357
Peoples Temple 6, 74–87, 113, 141, 143, 151, 158, 159, 162, 174, 296, 329, 336, 368 *see also* Jonestown
Perry, Troy 109, 115, 359
philosophy 29, 98, 209, 217, 219, 226, 230, 244, 281, 293, 324
Pike, Sarah 195, 199, 202, 204, 205, 206, 304, 308
pilgrimage 36, 264, 267, 314, 316, 317, 318, 351, 352
Plaskow, Judith 204
pluralism 53, 274, 293, 338, 367
politics 13, 25, 36, 53, 56, 59, 74, 91, 94, 100, 123, 131, 134, 138, 142, 152, 159, 175, 178, 179, 205, 222, 229, 237–40, 242, 244, 248, 249, 254, 258, 274, 276, 296, 302, 308, 318, 336, 338, 342, 343
polygamy 48, 59, 164, 170, 174, 342
popular culture 39, 147, 220, 258, 282, 292, 295, 343
Possamai, Adam 292
postcolonialism 238, 350
postmodernism/postmodernity 220, 338–9
Prabhupada, A. C. Bhakhtivedanta 12, 31, 116, 315, 326, 329, 347, 358, 360
prayer 30, 215, 343

prediction 119–22, 124–8, 153, 346
Presbyterianism 166, 217
Primiano, Leonard Norman 253, 255, 256, 259, 267, 269, 326
prophecy 5, 6, 47, 105, 109, 111, 114, 116, 119–32, 138, 141, 153, 155, 212, 238, 240, 241, 307, 330, 331, 342, 346, 351
  failed prophecy 5, 121, 122, 126–9
Prophet, Elizabeth Clare 130, 363
Prophet, Mark 130, 358
proselytizing 119, 125, 126, 129, 163, 305, 326, 351
Protestantism 3–5, 21, 35, 39, 48, 107, 138, 164, 166, 167, 174, 175, 176, 254, 260, 267, 303, 311, 334
Prus, R. C. 127, 128
psychiatry 7, 8, 78, 87, 94, 97, 134, 145, 307
psychic surgery 312
psychology 7, 26, 67, 74, 77, 78, 87, 98, 123, 126, 134, 145, 165, 167, 170, 172, 239, 333
psychopathology 91, 93, 96, 156
psychotherapy 44, 97
publishing 8, 12, 79, 171, 286, 316, 363
Puttick, Elizabeth 199, 200, 201, 202, 206, 302, 304

Qigong 309, 310
Quakers 173, 341
queer 195, 205
questionnaires 27
Quimby, Phineas 130
Quran 138

race 82, 151, 189, 190, 198, 199, 202, 211–16, 240, 279, 295–9, 326, 346
racism 4, 141, 165
Radford, Lewis B. 2, 166
radio 3, 19, 61, 62, 212, 281, 285
Raël 108, 109, 110, 115, 130, 216, 279, 328, 336, 347, 360
Raelianism 13, 81, 108–10, 115, 139, 201, 215–16, 279, 282, 328, 336, 341, 343, 362
Rajneesh *see* Osho
Rajneeshpuram 115, 150, 157, 175, 361
Ramtha *see* Knight, J. Z.
Rappaport, Roy 69
Rapture 138, 219, 327
Rastafari 180, 337, 356, 358
rationalism 37, 339
Reachout Trust 169
Reader, Ian 55, 56, 142, 143, 146, 179, 254

423

Index

recruitment 19, 89, 92–8, 100, 101, 106, 107, 109, 111, 238, 304, 305, 324, 325, 351
Redles, David 136, 140
reflexivity 31, 49
Reformation 138, 224
registration of religious groups 173, 342
reiki 43, 277, 310
reincarnation 2, 43, 62, 166, 211, 214, 215, 220, 310
religious studies 2, 13, 36, 37, 39, 43, 55, 142, 145, 254–7, 260, 269, 294, 309, 312, 316, 338
Renaissance 223, 226, 228, 247
reproductive issues 58, 199
revelation 21, 47, 49, 87, 108, 109, 110, 113, 122, 131, 216, 226, 241, 328, 332, 346, 347
Richardson, James T. 7, 59, 62, 63, 75, 89, 90–101, 133, 144, 145, 156, 158, 176, 183, 231, 303
Risso-Kosei-kai 340
rites of passage 67, 68, 256
ritual 18, 19, 26, 30, 31, 33, 38, 39, 48, 50, 67–70, 74–5, 103, 121, 127, 136, 164, 197, 205, 226, 235–6, 247–9, 251, 254, 257, 259, 260, 262–4, 266, 269, 288, 289, 292, 294, 310–12, 325, 336, 343, 347
Ritzer, George 274, 275, 276, 277
Robbins, Anthony 7, 156
Roberts, Andy 209
Robertson, Roland 274–5, 277, 293
Rochford, E. Burke 91, 93, 331
Roden, Ben 143
Roden, Lois 111, 114, 143, 151
Roman Catholicism 11, 12, 21, 49, 79, 83, 107, 109, 138, 140, 143, 155, 164, 166–8, 175, 176, 247, 248, 254, 262, 263, 264, 267, 298, 303, 311, 321, 350, 358, 361
Rose, Paul 170
Rosenberg, John Paul *see* Erhard, Wertner
Ross, Rick 8, 172, 368
Rothstein, Mikael 43, 139, 213, 277, 294, 310
Rountree, K. 35, 317
routinization 330–1
Russell, Charles Taze 3, 147, 164, 166, 356
Rutherford, Joseph Franklin 147, 356, 357
Ruyle, Lydia 263, 266
Ryan, Leo 140, 141, 151

Sahaja Yoga 303, 359
Sai Baba 105, 107, 112, 257, 258, 259, 307, 316, 357, 359, 363
Saliba, John A. 139, 321
salvation 50, 53, 58, 106, 120, 133–7, 139, 159, 164, 214, 310, 333, 334, 344
Sananda 5, 6, 26, 124, 213
Santeria 249, 250, 312, 350
Satan 114, 138, 343
Saul of Tarsus 90, 92, 163
Saunders, Alex 39
Saunders, Maxine 39
Scarman, Lord Justice 184
schism 115, 241, 345, 346, 351, 362
Schleiermacher, Friedrich 349
science 7, 13, 17, 43, 103, 104, 120, 169, 209, 212, 214, 215, 217, 220, 223–5, 228, 229, 232, 236, 237, 238, 243, 279–83, 293, 310, 321, 339
Scientology 5, 7, 8, 14, 26, 27, 29, 62, 65, 67, 87, 96, 99, 111, 115, 171, 174, 181, 182, 183, 184, 201, 232, 281, 282, 286, 291, 307, 315, 322, 323, 342, 347, 358, 362, 367, 368
Scofield, Cyrus 138
Scott, David 64
scriptures 21, 138, 291, 292, 294, 321, 327, 328, 331, 335, 336, 346, 347
second generation 115, 116, 302–6
Second Life 28, 289
Second World War 4, 14, 106, 140, 210, 317
secrecy 50, 225, 226, 286
sects 2, 4, 5, 7, 9, 12, 15, 16, 90, 149, 150, 173, 175, 222, 237, 311, 321, 339, 346, 348, 361, 367
secularism 170, 232, 349
secularization 3, 17, 18, 38, 168, 274, 318, 338, 348, 349
Seicho-No-Ie 299, 311
Seret, Isaiah 86
Seventh-day Adventism 2, 59, 130, 151, 164–6, 203
sex 113 *see also* celibacy, children, cisgender, flirty fishing, gender, homosexuality
  for recruitment 101n 2, 234
sexism 141
sexual abstinence 113, 218
sexual freedom 261, 324, 338–9
sexuality 57–60, 154, 189, 191, 198, 202, 306, 324, 325

424

Shakers 14, 19, 58, 130, 203, 204, 283
shamanism 9, 121, 205, 230, 264, 311, 312, 340
Shapiro, Eli 8
Sharot, Steven 177
Shepherd, Gary 59, 130
Shepherd, Gordon 59, 130
Shepherd's Rod 151
Shimazono, Susumu 53, 54, 55, 56, 311
Shinnyo-en 4, 55
shinshinshūkyō 14
shinshūkyō 4, 53
Shinshūkyō Jiten 53, 54, 55
Shinto 53, 54
Shugendo 53
Shupe, Anson 65, 75, 99, 110, 176
Singer, Margaret 7, 8, 96, 98, 99, 100, 169, 170, 208, 362
Skolnick, Jerome 91
Smart, Ninian 257, 312
Smith, Chuck 111
Smith, Jonathan Z. 58, 75, 159
Smith, Joseph 47–9, 130, 291, 307, 355
snake handling 91
social networks 62, 91, 94, 101
social sciences 103, 104, 119–21, 123, 126, 130, 132, 156, 176, 333
socialization 200, 218, 301, 302, 306, 325
sociology 4, 5, 7, 10, 13, 15–19, 25, 37, 87, 98, 120, 121, 123, 134, 143, 145, 182, 193, 222, 227, 239, 254, 255, 280, 322, 338, 348
Soka Gakkai 3, 4, 29, 30, 55, 56, 142, 177, 275, 335, 340, 341, 342, 345, 347, 357, 362
Solar Temple xvii, 19, 76, 113, 142, 143, 149–53, 158, 159, 160, 162, 178, 307, 362
Spiritual Counterfeits Project 169, 360, 368
Spiritualism 2, 15, 164, 165, 203, 213, 220, 282, 308, 310, 321, 349, 356
spirituality 3, 36, 41, 44, 154, 199, 201, 212, 215, 220, 227, 238, 248, 257, 261–8, 308, 311, 312, 318, 339, 341, 344, 349, 350
Sri Chinmoy 307, 358, 363
Starhawk 203, 204
Stark, Rodney 11, 13, 16, 17, 26, 48, 91, 93, 94, 95, 109, 130, 228, 301, 304, 322, 348, 349
Stein, Stephen 199
Stephenson, Denice 75
Stone, Jacqueline 140
Stone, Jon R. 124, 127, 128, 129, 131, 135

Stonehenge 33
Stout, Daniel 64
Strang, James 48
Straus, Roger 91, 96
Strieber, Whitley 208
Strozier, Charles B. 136, 138, 140, 145, 147
Stuckrad, Kocku von 224, 226
Sufism 2, 244–6, 250, 335, 356
suicide 5, 6, 20, 27, 65, 74, 78, 87, 113, 143, 150, 151, 154, 155, 158, 159, 160, 161, 162, 186, 217, 218, 219, 285, 314, 368
Summit Lighthouse *see* Church Universal and Triumphant
Sundkler, Bengt 238, 240
supernatural 13, 16, 29, 41, 104, 122, 129, 135, 215, 227, 233, 247, 320, 337, 346, 351
survivalism 151, 152, 159
survivors 32, 74, 76, 77, 78, 79, 80, 81, 82, 85, 87, 88, 216
Sutcliffe, Steven J. 5, 36, 41–4
Swedenborg, Emanuel 130, 210, 355
Sweeney, John 62
Sweet Daddy Grace 165, 326
Synanon 11
syncretism 9, 222, 238, 240, 278, 299, 311, 328, 339, 343, 350–1

Tabor, James D. 141, 174, 303
Tarot 36, 208
Taylor, David 5, 6, 26, 27, 30, 217, 218
technology 17, 43, 138, 154, 212, 215, 216, 218–20, 274, 276, 279–83, 286, 287, 288
telepathy 214–16, 220
Teletubbies 294
television 3, 19, 39, 61, 62, 65, 68, 69, 98, 147, 167, 168, 218, 220, 281, 285, 322, 329
terminology 15, 17, 19, 25, 42, 48, 63, 64, 76, 100, 131, 138, 140, 146, 148, 154, 170, 214, 221, 236, 239, 240, 242, 295
terrorism 19, 76, 100, 138, 140, 146, 148, 154, 170
Tertullian 1
thealogy 199, 204
theology 1, 2, 4, 11, 48, 49, 58, 75, 126, 141, 154, 159, 164, 165, 166, 167, 195, 196, 198, 201, 204, 216, 217, 226, 238, 239, 279, 281, 293, 296, 329, 338
Theosophy 2, 15, 129, 138, 139, 164, 166, 168, 211–17, 220, 280, 282, 309, 315, 321, 355–7

Index

third generation 306
Third Millennium religion 351
Third Reich 136, 139
Thomas, Paul Brian 139
thought reform 7, 169
Thrash, H. 81
Tibet 212, 315, 358
Tiryakian, Edward 222–3, 225
Torrey, R. A. 2, 327
tourism 312, 314, 316–18
Transcendental Meditation 3, 67, 115, 281, 282, 329, 335, 342, 358, 363
transformative 41, 107, 108, 109, 116, 122
transgender 195–8, 205
transmutation 127, 223
travel 2, 3, 42, 130, 151, 168, 213, 281, 282, 293, 313–18
Troeltsch, Ernst 4, 15, 16, 222, 321, 339, 346, 348
Trompf, Gary 137
True Word 126
Truzzi, Marcello 223–4
Tumminia, Diana 124, 127, 139, 213, 220, 310
Turner, Edith L. B. 309
Turner, Harold W. 5, 9, 12, 13, 240–3, 245
Turner, Victor 68
Twelve Tribes 110, 112, 174, 281, 282, 298, 321
Twesigye, Emmanuel K. 310, 311
Tylor, E. B. 34
typologies 4, 15, 16, 36, 68, 76, 156, 201, 202, 223, 237–40, 316, 332, 339, 343, 346, 348, 359

UFOs 5–6, 14, 26, 65, 108, 124, 125, 129, 138, 139, 148, 154, 157, 159, 204, 207–20
Unarius 130, 139, 213, 220, 280, 282
Unification Church 3, 5, 7, 9, 11, 14, 26, 30–1, 58–9, 64–5, 73, 78, 92, 93, 96–7, 106–7, 113, 115, 130, 168, 170–2, 176, 201, 204, 275–6, 291, 305–6, 323–4, 328, 329, 331, 337, 339, 342, 361, 362, 368
United Kingdom 1, 3, 8, 18, 39, 176, 177, 192, 256, 267, 292, 296, 303, 308, 332
United States 2, 3, 10, 11, 18, 26, 38, 47, 79, 85, 106, 112, 113, 114, 115, 138, 153, 165, 168, 171, 172, 174, 176, 178, 199, 250, 254, 256, 257, 262, 277, 288, 292, 303, 308, 315, 325, 332, 339, 342, 351, 356, 358, 359, 360, 361
Urantia 336, 347, 359
utopianism 20, 74, 210, 217, 219–20, 281, 302, 320, 321, 336

Vallee, Jacques 209
Vatican 175, 176, 358, 361, 362
vegetarianism 307, 308, 326, 341
Veres, Kriszta 265–7
vernacular religion 253–69
Vietnam War 3, 106, 341
violence 19, 20, 21, 59, 75, 76, 133–7, 138, 140, 141, 142, 143, 144, 145, 146, 148, 149–62, 170, 174, 200, 205, 215, 217, 219, 249, 302, 325, 327, 340, 341
vitalism 309–10
Vivekananda 2, 356
Vivien, Alain 10, 172, 173, 361
Vodou 31, 250, 312, 314, 350
Vorilhon, Claude, *see* Raël

Waco 8, 19, 59, 62–4, 75, 141, 143, 144, 150, 174, 178, 303, 361, 362
Wallace, Anthony F. C. 137
Wallis, Roy 9, 16, 26, 176, 183, 348, 349
Walliss, John 143, 147, 150, 156
Ward, Lord Justice 182, 183, 186, 187, 193
Watch Tower 3, 327, 355, 363, 368
Waterhouse, Helen 29, 30
Way International 115, 327, 357
Weber, Max 4, 15–17, 25, 103, 104, 115, 117, 122, 123, 130, 131, 307, 320, 321, 322, 330–2, 338, 339, 346, 348
Weiser, Neil 127, 128
Wessinger, Catherine 20, 76, 120, 121, 133–7, 139–46, 148, 150, 156, 157, 161, 338
West, L. Jolyon 8
White, Ellen G. 130, 203, 339, 355
Whitehead, H. 25, 27
Wicca 39, 201, 203, 254, 288, 291, 344
Wilson, Anton 293
Wilson, Bryan 177, 348
Wilson, Lesley Wagner 81
Wilson, William A. 257–8
witches 39, 231, 287, 357 *see also* Wicca
Wojcik, Daniel 125, 136, 139, 217
World Council of Churches 12, 176
world religions 1, 43, 48, 167, 291
World Trade Center 19, 79, 362

Worsley, Peter 137
Wright, Stuart A. 137, 141, 143, 144

Yates, Frances 223, 227
Yoder, Don 255, 256, 269
yoga 153, 264, 277, 311, 316, 329, 331, 333, 335, 339, 340, 360

Zacharias, Ravi 167
Zaidman-Dvir, Nurit 177
Zeller, Benjamin E. 35, 139, 163, 217, 279, 281, 326, 339
Zen 3, 330, 335, 340, 347
Zionist churches 238, 240, 311
Zygmunt, Joseph 127–8